MW00837553

The Complete Rust Programming Reference Guide

Design, develop, and deploy effective software systems using the advanced constructs of Rust

Rahul Sharma
Vesa Kaihlavirta
Claus Matzinger

BIRMINGHAM - MUMBAI

The Complete Rust Programming Reference Guide

First published: May 2019

Production reference: 1200519

Published by Packt Publishing Ltd.
Livery Place
35 Livery Street
Birmingham
B3 2PB, UK.

ISBN 978-1-83882-810-3

www.packtpub.com

mapt.io

Mapt is an online digital library that gives you full access to over 5,000 books and videos, as well as industry leading tools to help you plan your personal development and advance your career. For more information, please visit our website.

Why subscribe?

- Spend less time learning and more time coding with practical eBooks and Videos from over 4,000 industry professionals

- Improve your learning with Skill Plans built especially for you

- Get a free eBook or video every month

- Mapt is fully searchable

- Copy and paste, print, and bookmark content

Packt.com

Did you know that Packt offers eBook versions of every book published, with PDF and ePub files available? You can upgrade to the eBook version at www.packt.com and as a print book customer, you are entitled to a discount on the eBook copy. Get in touch with us at customercare@packtpub.com for more details.

At www.packt.com, you can also read a collection of free technical articles, sign up for a range of free newsletters, and receive exclusive discounts and offers on Packt books and eBooks.

Contributors

About the authors

Rahul Sharma is passionately curious about teaching programming. He has been writing software for the last two years. He got started with Rust with his work on Servo, a browser engine by Mozilla Research as part of his GSoC project. At present, he works at AtherEnergy, where he is building resilient cloud infrastructure for smart scooters. His interests include systems programming, distributed systems, compilers and type theory. He is also an occasional contributor to the Rust language and does mentoring of interns on the Servo project by Mozilla.

Vesa Kaihlavirta has been programming since he was five, beginning with C64 Basic. His main professional goal in life is to increase awareness of programming languages and software quality in all industries that use software. He's an Arch Linux Developer Fellow, and has been working in the telecom and financial industry for a decade. Vesa lives in Jyvaskyla, central Finland.

Claus Matzinger is a software engineer with a very diverse background. After working in a small company maintaining code for embedded devices, he joined a large corporation to work on legacy Smalltalk applications. This led to a great interest in programming languages early on, and Claus became the CTO for a health games start-up based on Scala technology. Since then, Claus' roles have shifted toward customer-facing roles in the IoT database technology start-up crate.io and, most recently, Microsoft. There, he hosts a podcast, writes code together with customers, and blogs about the solutions arising from these engagements. For more than 5 years, Claus has implemented software to help customers innovate, achieve, and maintain success.

Packt is searching for authors like you

If you're interested in becoming an author for Packt, please visit authors.packtpub.com and apply today. We have worked with thousands of developers and tech professionals, just like you, to help them share their insight with the global tech community. You can make a general application, apply for a specific hot topic that we are recruiting an author for, or submit your own idea.

Table of Contents

Preface

Rust is a powerful language with a rare combination of safety, speed, and zero-cost abstractions. This Learning Path is filled with clear and simple explanations of its features along with real-world examples, demonstrating how you can build robust, scalable, and reliable programs.

You'll get started with an introduction to Rust data structures, algorithms, and essential language constructs. Next, you will understand how to store data using linked lists, arrays, stacks, and queues. You'll also learn to implement sorting and searching algorithms, such as Brute Force algorithms, Greedy algorithms, Dynamic Programming, and Backtracking. As you progress, you'll pick up on using Rust for systems programming, network programming, and the web. You'll then move on to discover a variety of techniques, right from writing memory-safe code, to building idiomatic Rust libraries, and even advanced macros.

By the end of this Learning Path, you'll be able to implement Rust for enterprise projects, writing better tests and documentation, designing for performance, and creating idiomatic Rust code.

This Learning Path includes content from the following Packt products:

- Mastering Rust - Second Edition by Rahul Sharma and Vesa Kaihlavirta
- Hands-On Data Structures and Algorithms with Rust by Claus Matzinger

Who this book is for

If you are already familiar with an imperative language and now want to progress from being a beginner to an intermediate-level Rust programmer, this Learning Path is for you. Developers who are already familiar with Rust and want to delve deeper into the essential data structures and algorithms in Rust will also find this Learning Path useful.

What this book covers

Chapter 1, *Getting Started with Rust*, gives a brief history on Rust and the motivation behind its design, and covers basic language syntax. The chapter ends with an exercise covering all the language features.

Chapter 2, *Managing Projects with Cargo*, shows how Rust organizes large projects with its dedicated package manager. This serves as the basis for further chapters. It also covers editor integration with the Visual Studio Code editor.

Chapter 3, *Tests, Documentation, and Benchmarks*, explores the built-in testing harness, writing unit tests, integration tests, and how to write documentation in Rust. We also cover the benchmarking facilities of Rust code. Later, as a final exercise, we build a complete crate with documentation and tests.

Chapter 4, *Types, Generics, and Traits*, explores Rust's expressive type system and goes on to explain various ways of using the type system by building a complex number library.

Chapter 5, *Memory Management and Safety*, starts with the motivation for memory management and the various pitfalls in conventional low-level programming languages related to memory. It then moves toward explaining Rust's unique compile-time memory management ideas. We also explain various smart pointer types in Rust.

Chapter 6, *Error Handling*, starts with the motivation for error handling and explores different models of error handling in other languages. The chapter then examine Rust's error-handling strategy and types, before exploring handling errors in non-recoverable situations. The chapter ends with a library implementing custom error types.

Chapter 7, *Advanced Concepts*, explores some of the concepts already introduced in previous chapters, in more detail. It provides details on the underlying model of some of the type system abstractions provided by Rust.

Chapter 8, *Concurrency*, explores Rust's concurrency models and APIs in the standard libraries and teaches you how to build highly concurrent programs with no data races.

Chapter 9, *Metaprogramming with Macros*, examines how you can write code to generate code using the powerful and advanced macro construct of Rust, and outlines the language's declarative and procedural macros by building both types of macros.

Chapter 10, *Unsafe Rust and Foreign Function Interfaces*, explores the unsafe mode of Rust and the APIs on offer for interoperating Rust with other languages. The examples includes both calling into Rust from other languages, such as Python, Node.js, and C, as well as covering how Rust can be called from other languages.

Chapter 11, *Logging*, explains why logging is an important practice in software development, answering why we need logging frameworks, and exploring the crates on offer in the Rust ecosystem that can be used to help integrate logging into the application.

Chapter 12, *Network Programming in Rust Sync*, gives a brief introduction to network programming. After going through the basics, the chapter covers building a Redis server that can talk to the official Redis client. Lastly, the chapter explains how to use the standard library networking primitives and the Tokio and futures crates.

Chapter 13, *Building Web Applications with Rust*, starts by exploring the HTTP protocol and builds a simple URL shortener server using the hyper crate, followed by building a URL shortener client using the reqwest crate. In the end, we explore actix-web, a highperformance Async web application framework to build a bookmarks API server.

Chapter 14, *Lists, Lists, and More Lists*, covers the first data structures: lists. Using several examples, this chapter goes into variations of sequential data structures and their implementations.

Chapter 15, *Robust Trees*, continues our journey through popular data structures: trees are next on the list. In several detailed examples, we explore the inner workings of these efficient designs and how they improve application performance considerably.

Chapter 16, *Exploring Maps and Sets*, explores the most popular key-value stores: maps. In this chapter, techniques surrounding hash maps; hashing; and their close relative, the set; are described in detail.

Chapter 17, *Collections in Rust,* attempts to connect to the Rust programmer's daily life, going into the details of the Rust std::collections library, which contains the various data structures provided by the Rust standard library.

Chapter 18, *Algorithm Evaluation*, teaches you how to evaluate and compare algorithms.

Chapter 19, *Ordering Things*, will look at sorting values, an important task in programming—this chapter uncovers how that can be done quickly and safely.

Chapter 20, *Finding Stuff*, moves onto searching, which is especially important if there is no fundamental data structure to support it. In these cases, we use algorithms to be able to quickly find what we are looking for.

Chapter 21, *Random and Combinatorial*, is where we will see that, outside of sorting and searching, there are many problems that can be tackled algorithmically. This chapter is all about those: random number generation, backtracking, and improving computational complexities.

Chapter 22, *Algorithms of the Standard Library*, explores how the Rust standard library does things when it comes to everyday algorithmic tasks such as sorting and searching.

To get the most out of this book

To really grasp the content of this book, it is recommended that you write out the example code and try fiddling with code to get familiar with the Rust's error messages, so they can guide you toward writing correct programs. You can either use Linux or Windows OS.

Here are a few recommendations for text editors and other tools:

- Microsoft's Visual Studio Code (https://code.visualstudio.com/), arguably one of the best Rust code editors
- Rust support for Visual Studio Code via a plugin (https://github.com/rust-lang/rls-vscode)
- Rust Language Server (RLS), found at https://github.com/rust-lang/rls-vscode, installed via rustup (https://rustup.rs/)
- Debugging support using the LLDB frontend plugin (https://github.com/vadimcn/vscode-lldb) for Visual Studio Code.

Download the example code files

You can download the example code files for this book from your account at www.packt.com. If you purchased this book elsewhere, you can visit www.packt.com/support and register to have the files emailed directly to you.

You can download the code files by following these steps:

1. Log in or register at www.packt.com.
2. Select the **SUPPORT** tab.
3. Click on **Code Downloads & Errata**.
4. Enter the name of the book in the **Search** box and follow the onscreen instructions.

Once the file is downloaded, please make sure that you unzip or extract the folder using the latest version of:

- WinRAR/7-Zip for Windows
- Zipeg/iZip/UnRarX for Mac
- 7-Zip/PeaZip for Linux

The code bundle for the book is also hosted on GitHub at https://github.com/ PacktPublishing/The-Complete-Rust-Programming-Reference-Guide. In case there's an update to the code, it will be updated on the existing GitHub repository.

We also have other code bundles from our rich catalog of books and videos available at https://github.com/PacktPublishing/. Check them out!

Conventions used

There are a number of text conventions used throughout this book.

CodeInText: Indicates code words in text, database table names, folder names, filenames, file extensions, pathnames, dummy URLs, user input, and Twitter handles. Here is an example: "However, it makes the whole thing safe—thanks to RefCells checking borrowing rules at runtime."

A block of code is set as follows:

```
struct Node {
value: i32,
next: Option<Node>
}
```

Bold: Indicates a new term, an important word, or words that you see onscreen. For example, words in menus or dialog boxes appear in the text like this. Here is an example: "Select **System info** from the **Administration** panel"

Warnings or important notes appear like this.

 Tips and tricks appear like this.

Get in touch

Feedback from our readers is always welcome.

General feedback: If you have questions about any aspect of this book, mention the book title in the subject of your message and email us at customercare@packtpub.com.

Errata: Although we have taken every care to ensure the accuracy of our content, mistakes do happen. If you have found a mistake in this book, we would be grateful if you would report this to us. Please visit www.packt.com/submit-errata, selecting your book, clicking on the Errata Submission Form link, and entering the details.

Piracy: If you come across any illegal copies of our works in any form on the Internet, we would be grateful if you would provide us with the location address or website name. Please contact us at copyright@packt.com with a link to the material.

If you are interested in becoming an author: If there is a topic that you have expertise in and you are interested in either writing or contributing to a book, please visit authors.packtpub.com.

Reviews

Please leave a review. Once you have read and used this book, why not leave a review on the site that you purchased it from? Potential readers can then see and use your unbiased opinion to make purchase decisions, we at Packt can understand what you think about our products, and our authors can see your feedback on their book. Thank you!

For more information about Packt, please visit packt.com.

Getting Started with Rust

Learning a new language is like building a house – the foundation needs to be strong. With a language that changes the way you think and reason about your code, there's always more effort involved in the beginning, and it's important to be aware of that. The end result, however, is that you get to shift your thinking with these new-found concepts and tools.

This chapter will give you a whirlwind tour on the design philosophy of Rust, an overview of its syntax and the type system. We assume that you have a basic knowledge of mainstream languages such as C, C++, or Python, and the ideas that surround object-oriented programming. Each section will contain example code, along with an explanation of it. There will be ample code examples and output from the compiler, that will help you become familiar with the language. We'll also delve into a brief history of the language and how it continues to evolve.

Getting familiar with a new language requires perseverance, patience, and practice. I highly recommend to all readers that you manually write and don't copy/paste the code examples listed here. The best part of writing and fiddling with Rust code is the precise and helpful error messages you get from the compiler, which the Rust community often likes to call error-driven development. We'll see these errors frequently throughout this book to understand how the compiler thinks of our code.

In this chapter, we will cover the following topics:

- What is Rust and why should you care?
- Installing the Rust compiler and the toolchain
- A brief tour of the language and its syntax
- A final exercise, where we'll put what we've learned together

What is Rust and why should you care?

" Rust is technology from the past came to save the future from itself. "

- Graydon Hoare

Rust is a fast, concurrent, safe, and empowering programming language originally started and developed by *Graydon Hoare* in 2006. It's now an open source language that's developed mainly by a team from Mozilla with collaboration from lots of open source folks. The first stable version, 1.0, was released in May 2015. The project began with the hope of mitigating memory safety issues that came up in **gecko** with the use of C++. Gecko is the browser engine that's used in Mozilla's Firefox browser. C++ is not an easy language to tame and has concurrency abstractions that can be easily misused. With gecko using C++, a couple of attempts were made (in 2009 and 2011) to parallelize its **cascading style sheets** (**CSS**) parsing code to leverage modern parallel CPUs. They failed, as the concurrent C++ code was too hard to maintain and reason about. With a large number of developers collaborating on the mammoth code base that gecko has, writing concurrent code with C++ is not a joyride. In the hope of incrementally removing the painful parts of C++, Rust was born and, with it, Servo, a new research project of creating a browser engine from scratch was initiated. The Servo project provides feedback to the language team by using the bleeding edge language features that, in turn, influences the evolution of the language. Around November 2017, parts of the Servo project, particularly the **stylo** project (a parallel CSS parser in Rust) started shipping to the latest Firefox release (Project Quantum), which is a great feat in such a short amount of time. Servo's end goal is to incrementally replace components in gecko with its components.

Rust is inspired by a multitude of languages, the notable ones being Cyclone (a safe dialect of C language) for its ideas on region-based memory management techniques; C++ for its RAII principle, and Haskell for its type system, error handling types, and typeclasses.

 RAII stands for **Resource Acquisition Is Initialization**, a paradigm suggesting that resources must be acquired during the initialization of an object and must be released when their destructors are called or when they are deallocated.

The language has a very minimal runtime, does not need garbage collection, and prefers stack allocation by default over heap allocation (an overhead) for any value that's declared in a program. We'll explain all of this in Chapter 5, *Memory Management and Safety*. The Rust compiler, **rustc**, was originally written in Ocaml (a functional language) and became a self-hosting one in 2011 after being written in itself.

Self-hosting is when a compiler is built by compiling its own source code. This process is known as bootstrapping a compiler. Compiler its own source code acts as a really good test case for the compiler.

Rust is openly developed on GitHub at https://github.com/rust-lang/rust and continues to evolve at a fast pace. New features are added to the language through a community-driven **Request For Comments (RFC)** process where anybody can propose new language features. These are then described in detail in an RFC document. A consensus is then sought after for the RFC and if agreed upon, the implementation phase begins for the feature. The implemented feature then gets reviewed by the community, where it is eventually merged to the master branch after undergoing several tests by users in nightly releases. Getting feedback from the community is crucial for the language's evolution. Every six weeks, a new stable version of the compiler is released. Along with fast moving incremental updates, Rust also has this notion of editions, which is proposed to provide a consolidated update to the language. This includes tooling, documentation, its ecosystem, and to phase in any breaking changes. So far, there have been two editions: *Rust 2015*, which had a focus on stability, and *Rust 2018*, which is the current edition at the time of writing this book and focuses on productivity.

While being a general purpose multi-paradigm language, it is aiming for systems programming domain where C and C++ have been predominant. This means that you can write operating systems, game engines, and many performance critical applications with it. At the same time, it is also expressive enough that you can build high-performance web applications, network services, type-safe database **Object Relational Mapper (ORM)** libraries, and can also run on the web by compiling down to WebAssembly. Rust has also gained a fair share of interest in building safety-critical, real-time applications for embedded platforms such as the Arm's Cortex-M based microcontrollers, a domain mostly dominated by C at present. This gamut of applicability in various domains – which Rust exhibits quite well – is something that very rare to find in a single programming language. Moreover, established companies Cloudflare, Dropbox, Chuckfish, npm, and many more are already using it in production for their high-stakes projects.

Rust is characterized as a statically and strongly typed language. The static property means that the compiler has information about all of the variables and their types at compile time and does most of its checks at compile time, leaving very minimal type checking at runtime. Its strong nature means that it does not allow things such as auto-conversion between types, and that a variable pointing to an integer cannot be changed to point to a string later in code. For example, in weakly typed languages such as JavaScript, you can easily do something like `two = "2"; two = 2 + two;`. JavaScript weakens the type of 2 to be a string at runtime, thus storing 22 as a string in `two`, something totally contrary to your intent and meaningless. In Rust, the same code, that is, `let mut two = "2"; two = 2 + two;`, would get caught at compile time, throwing the following error: `cannot add `&str` to `{integer}``. This property enables safe refactoring of code and catches most bugs at compile time rather than causing issues at runtime.

Programs written in Rust are very expressive as well as performant, in the sense that you can have most of the features of high-level functional style languages such as higher-order functions and lazy iterators, yet it compiles down to efficient code like a C/C++ program. The defining principles that underline many of its design decisions are compile-time memory safety, fearless concurrency, and zero cost abstractions. Let's elaborate on these ideas.

Compile time memory safety: The Rust compiler can track variables owning a resource in your program at compile time and does all of this without a garbage collector.

 Resources can be memory address, a variable holding a value, shared memory reference, file handles, network sockets, or database connection handles.

This means that you can't have infamous problems with pointers use after free, double free, or dangling pointers at runtime. Reference types in Rust (types with `&` before them) are implicitly associated with a lifetime tag (`'foo`) and sometimes annotated explicitly by the programmer. Through lifetimes, the compiler can track places in code where a reference is safe to use, reporting an error at compile time if it's illegal. To achieve this, Rust runs a borrow/reference checking algorithm by using these lifetime tags on references to ensure that you can never access a memory address that has been freed. It also does this so that you cannot free any pointer while it is being used by some other variable. We will go into the details of this in `Chapter 5`, *Memory management and Safety*.

Zero-cost abstractions: Programming is all about managing complexity, which is facilitated by good abstractions. Let's go through a fine example of abstraction in both Rust and Kotlin (a language targeting **Java virtual machines** (**JVM**) that lets us write high-level code and is easy to read and reason about. We'll compare Kotlin's streams and Rust's iterators in manipulating a list of numbers and contrast the zero cost abstraction principle that Rust provides. The abstraction here is to be able to use methods that take other methods as arguments to filter numbers based on a condition without using manual loops. Kotlin is used here for its visual similarity with Rust. The code is fairly simple to understand and we aim to give a high-level explanation. We'll be glossing over the details in code as the whole point of this example is to understand the zero cost property.

First, let's look at the code in Kotlin (the following code can be run online: `https://try.kotlinlang.org`):

```
1. import java.util.stream.Collectors
2.
3. fun main(args: Array<String>) {
5.     // Create a stream of numbers
6.     val numbers = listOf(1, 2, 3, 4, 5, 6, 7, 8, 9, 10).stream()
7.     val evens = numbers.filter { it -> it % 2 == 0 }
8.     val evenSquares = evens.map { it -> it * it }
9.     val result = evenSquares.collect(Collectors.toList())
10.    println(result)        // prints [4,16,36,64,100]
11.
12.    println(evens)
13.    println(evenSquares)
14. }
```

We create a stream of numbers (line 6) and call a chain of methods (`filter` and `map`) to transform the elements to collect only squares of even numbers. These methods can take a closure or a function (that is, `it -> it * it` at line 8) to transform each element in the collection. In functional style languages, when we call these methods on the stream/iterator, for every such call, the language creates an intermediate object to keep any state or metadata in regard to the operation being performed. As a result, `evens` and `evenSquares` will be two different intermediate objects that are allocated on the JVM heap. Allocating things on the heap incurs a memory overhead. That's the extra cost of abstraction we have to pay in Kotlin !

When we print the value of evens and evenSquares, we indeed get different objects, as show here:

```
java.util.stream.ReferencePipeline$Head@51521cc1
```

```
java.util.stream.ReferencePipeline$3@1b4fb997
```

The hex value after the @ is the object's hash code on the JVM. Since the hash codes are different, they are different objects.

In Rust, we do the same thing (the following code can be run online: https://gist. github.com/rust-play/e0572da05d999cfb6eb802d003b33ffa):

```
1. fn main() {
2.     let numbers = vec![1, 2, 3, 4, 5, 6, 7, 8, 9, 10].into_iter();
3.     let evens = numbers.filter(|x| *x % 2 == 0);
4.     let even_squares = evens.clone().map(|x| x * x);
5.     let result = even_squares.clone().collect::<Vec<_>>();
6.     println!("{:?}", result);      // prints [4,16,36,64,100]
7.     println!("{:?}\n{:?}", evens, even_squares);
8. }
```

Glossing over the details, on line 2 we call vec![] to create a list of numbers on the heap, followed by calling into_iter() to make it a iterator/stream of numbers. The into_iter() method creates a wrapper Iterator type, IntoIter([1,2,3,4,5,6,7,8,9,10]), out of a collection (here, Vec <i32> is a list of signed 32 bit integers). This iterator type references the original list of numbers. We then perform filter and map transformations (lines 3 and 4), just like we did in Kotlin. Lines 7 and 8 print the type of evens and even_squares, as follows (some details have been omitted for brevity):

evens:	Filter { iter: IntoIter(<numbers>) }
even_squares:	Map { iter: Filter { iter: IntoIter(<numbers>) }}

The intermediate objects, Filter and Map, are wrapper types (not allocated on the heap) on the base iterator structure, which itself is a wrapper that holds a reference to the original list of numbers at line 2. The wrapper structures on lines 4 and 5 that get created on calling filter and map, respectively, do not have any pointer indirection in between and impose no heap allocation overhead, as was the case with Kotlin. All of this boils down to efficient assembly code, which would be equivalent to the manually written version using loops.

Fearless concurrency: When we said Rust is concurrent-safe, we meant that the language has **Application Programming Interface (API)** and abstractions that make it really easy to write correct and safe concurrent code. Contrasting this with C++, the possibility of making mistakes in concurrent code is quite high. When synchronizing data access to multiple threads in C++, you are responsible for calling `mutex.lock()` every time you enter the critical section, and `mutex.unlock()` when you exit this section:

```
// C++

mutex.lock();                        // Mutex locked, good to go
  // Do super critical stuff
mutex.unlock();                      // We're done
```

 Critical section: This is a group of instructions/statements that need to be executed atomically. Here, atomically means no other thread can interrupt the currently executing thread in the critical section, and no intermediate value is perceived by any thread during execution of code in the critical section.

In a large code base with many developers collaborating on the code, you might forget to call `mutex.lock()` before accessing the shared object from multiple threads, which can lead to data races. Others cases, you might forget to unlock the `mutex` and starve the other threads that want access to the data.

Rust has a different take on this. Here, you wrap your data in a `Mutex` type to ensuring synchronized mutable access to data from multiple threads:

```
// Rust

use std::sync::Mutex;

fn main() {
    let value = Mutex::new(23);
    *value.lock().unwrap() += 1;    // modify
}                                    // unlocks here automatically
```

In the preceding code, we were able to modify the data after calling `lock()` on `value`. Rust uses the notion of protecting the shared data itself and not code. The interaction with `Mutex` and the protected data is not independent, as is the case with C++. You cannot access the inner data without calling `lock` on the `Mutex` type. What about releasing the `lock`? Well, calling `lock()` returns something called `MutexGuard`, which automatically releases the lock when the variable goes out of scope. It's one of the many safe concurrency abstractions Rust provides. We'll go into detail on them in Chapter 8, *Concurrency*. Another novel idea is the notion of marker traits, which validate and ensure synchronized and safe access to data in concurrent code at compile time. Traits are described in detail in Chapter 4, *Types, Generics, and Traits*. Types are annotated with marker traits called `Send` and `Sync` to indicate whether they are safe to send to threads or safe to share between threads, respectively. When a program sends a value to a thread, the compiler checks whether the value implements the required marker trait and forbids the usage of the value if it isn't the case. In this way, Rust allows you to write concurrent code without fear, where the compiler catches mistakes in multi-threaded code at compile time. Writing concurrent code is already hard. With C/C++, it gets even harder and more arcane. CPUs aren't getting more clock rates; instead, we have more cores being added. As a result, concurrent programming is the way forward. Rust makes it a breeze to write concurrent code and lowers the bar for many people to get into writing safe, concurrent code.

Rust also employs C++'s RAII idiom for resource initialization. This technique basically ties a resource's lifetime to objects' lifetimes, whereas the deallocation of heap allocated types is performed through the `drop` method, which is provided by the `drop` trait. This is automatically called when the variable goes out of scope. It also replaces the concept of null pointers with `Result` and `Option` types, which we'll go into detail in Chapter 6, *Error Handling*. This means that Rust doesn't allow null/undefined values in code, except when interacting with other languages through foreign function interfaces and when using unsafe code. The language also puts emphasis on composition over inheritance and has a trait system, which is implemented by data types and is similar to **Haskell** typeclasses, also known as Java interfaces on steroids. Traits in Rust are the backbone to many of its features, as we'll see in upcoming chapters.

Last but not least, Rust's community is quite active and friendly, and the language has comprehensive documentation, which can be found at `https://doc.rust-lang.org`. For the third year in a row (2016, 2017, and 2018), Stack Overflow's Developer Survey highlights Rust as the most-loved programming language, so it can be said that the overall programming community is very interested in it. To summarize, you should care about Rust if you aim to write high performing software with less bugs while enjoying many modern language features and an awesome community!

Installing the Rust compiler and toolchain

The Rust toolchain has two major components: the compiler, **rustc**, and the package manager, **cargo**, which helps manage Rust projects. The toolchain comes in three release channels:

- **Nightly**: The daily successful build from the master development branch. This contains all the latest features, many of which are unstable.
- **Beta**: This is released every six weeks. A new beta branch is taken from nightly. It contains only features that are flagged as stable.
- **Stable**: This is released every six weeks. The previous beta branch becomes the new stable release.

Developers are encouraged to use the stable release channel. However, the nightly version enables bleeding edge features, and some libraries and programs require it. You can change to the nightly toolchain easily with rustup. We'll see how we can do that in a moment.

Using rustup.rs

Rustup is a tool to that installs the Rust compiler on all supported platforms. To make it easier for developers on different platforms to download and use the language, the Rust team developed rustup. It's a command-line tool written in Rust that provides an easy way to install pre-built binaries of the compiler and binary builds of the standard library for cross compiling needs. It can also install other components, such as the Rust source code, documentation, **Rust formatting tool** (**rustfmt**), **Rust Language Server** (**RLS** for IDEs), and other developer tools, and it runs on all platforms, including Windows.

From their official page at https://rustup.rs, the recommended way to install the toolchain is to run the following command:

```
curl https://sh.rustup.rs -sSf | sh
```

By default, the installer installs the stable version of the Rust compiler, its package manager, Cargo, and the language's standard library documentation so that it can be viewed offline. These are installed by default under the ~/.cargo directory. Rustup also updates your PATH environment variable to point to this directory.

The following is a screenshot of running the preceding command on Ubuntu 16.04:

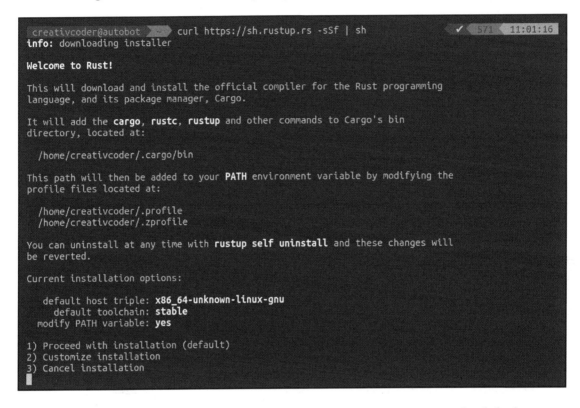

If you need to make any changes to your installation, choose **2**. However, the defaults are fine for us, so we'll go ahead and choose **1**. Here's the output after the installation:

```
info: syncing channel updates for 'stable-x86_64-unknown-linux-gnu'
info: latest update on 2019-01-16, rust version 1.32.0 (9fda7c223 2019-01-16)
info: downloading component 'rustc'
 72.1 MiB /   72.1 MiB (100 %)   5.8 MiB/s ETA:   0 s
info: downloading component 'rust-std'
 56.1 MiB /   56.1 MiB (100 %)   5.4 MiB/s ETA:   0 s
info: downloading component 'cargo'
info: downloading component 'rust-docs'
  8.8 MiB /    8.8 MiB (100 %)   6.0 MiB/s ETA:   0 s
info: installing component 'rustc'
info: installing component 'rust-std'
info: installing component 'cargo'
info: installing component 'rust-docs'
info: default toolchain set to 'stable'

  stable installed - rustc 1.32.0 (9fda7c223 2019-01-16)


Rust is installed now. Great!

To get started you need Cargo's bin directory ($HOME/.cargo/bin) in your PATH
environment variable. Next time you log in this will be done automatically.

To configure your current shell run source $HOME/.cargo/env
→  ~
```

Rustup also has other capabilities, such as updating the toolchain to the latest version, which can be done by running `rustup update`. It can also update itself via `rustup self update`. It also provides directory-specific toolchain configuration. The default toolchain is set globally to whatever toolchain gets installed, which in most cases is the stable toolchain. You can view the default one by invoking `rustup show`. If you want to use the latest nightly toolchain for one of your projects, you can tell rustup to switch to nightly for that particular directory by running `rustup override set nightly`. If, for some reason, someone wants to use an older version of the toolchain or downgrade (say, the nightly build on 2016-06-03), rustup can also download that if we were to run `rustup install nightly-2016-06-03`, followed by setting the same using the `override` sub-command. More information on rustup can be found at `https://github.com/rust-lang-nursery/rustup.rs`.

Note: All of the code examples and projects in this book are based on compiler version `rustc 1.32.0 (9fda7c223 2019-01-16)`.

Now, you should have everything you need to compile and run programs written in Rust. Let's get Rusty!

A tour of the language

For the fundamental language features, Rust does not stray far from what you are used to in other languages. At a high level, a Rust program is organized into modules, with the root module containing a `main()` function. For executables, the root module is usually a `main.rs` file and for libraries, a `lib.rs` file. Within a module, you can define functions, import libraries, define types, create constants, write tests and macros, or even create nested modules. We'll see all of them, but let's start with the basics. Here's a simple Rust program that greets you:

```
// greet.rs

1. use std::env;
2.
3. fn main() {
4.     let name = env::args().skip(1).next();
5.     match name {
6.         Some(n) => println!("Hi there ! {}", n),
7.         None => panic!("Didn't receive any name ?")
8.     }
9. }
```

Let's compile and run this program. Write it to a file called `greet.rs` and run `rustc` with the file name, and pass your name as the argument. I passed the name `Ferris`, Rust's unofficial mascot, and got the following output on my machine:

```
→ book rustc greet.rs
→ book ./greet Ferris
Hi there ! Ferris
→ book █
```

Awesome! It greets `Ferris`. Let's get a cursory view of this program, line by line.

On line 1, we import a module called `env` from the `std` crate (libraries are called **crates**). `std` is the standard library for Rust. On line 3, we have our usual function `main`. Then, on line 4, we call the function `args()` from the `env` module, which returns an iterator (sequence) of arguments that has been passed to our program. Since the first argument contains our program name, we want to skip it, so we call `skip` and pass in a number, which is how many elements (1) we want to skip. As iterators are lazy and do not pre-compute things in Rust, we have to explicitly ask it to give the next element, so we call `next()`, which returns an enum type called `Option`. This can be either a `Some(value)` value or a `None` value because a user might forget to provide an argument.

On line 5, we use Rust's awesome `match` expression on the variable `name` and check whether it's a `Some(n)` or a `None` value. `match` is like the `if else` construct, but more powerful. On line 6, when it's a `Some(n)`, we call `println!()`, passing in our inner string variable `n` (this gets auto-declared when using match expressions), which then greets our user. The `println!` call is not a function, but a *macro* (they all end with a !). Finally, on line 7, if it's a `None` variant of the enum, we just `panic!()` (another macro), which aborts the program, making it leave an error message.

The `println!` macro, as we saw, accepts a string, which can contain placeholders for items using the `"{}"` syntax. These strings are called **format strings**, while the `"{}"` in the string are called **format specifiers**. For printing simple types such as primitives, we can use the `"{}"` format specifier, whereas for other types, we use the `"{:?}"` format specifier. There are more details to this, though. When `println!` encounters a format specifier, that is, `"{}"`, and a corresponding substitution value, it calls a method on that value, which returns a string representation of it. This method is part of a trait. For the `"{}"` specifier, it calls a method from the `Display` trait, whereas for `"{:?}"`, it calls a method from the `Debug` trait. The latter is mostly used for debugging, while the former is for displaying a human readable output of data types. It is somewhat similar to the `toString()` method in Java. When developing, you usually need to print your data types for debugging. The cases where these methods are not available on a type when using the `"{:?}"` specifier, we then need to add a `#[derive(Debug)]` **attribute** over the type to get those methods. We'll explain attributes in detail in subsequent chapters, but expect to see this in future code examples. We'll also revisit the `println!` macro in `Chapter 9`, *Metaprogramming with Macros*.

Running **rustc** manually is not how you will do this for real programs, but it will do for these small programs in this chapter. In subsequent chapters, we will be using Rust's package manager to build and run our programs. Apart from running the compiler locally, another tool that can be used to run the code examples is the official online compiler called **Rust playground**, which can be found at `http://play.rust-lang.org`. Following is the screenshot from my machine:

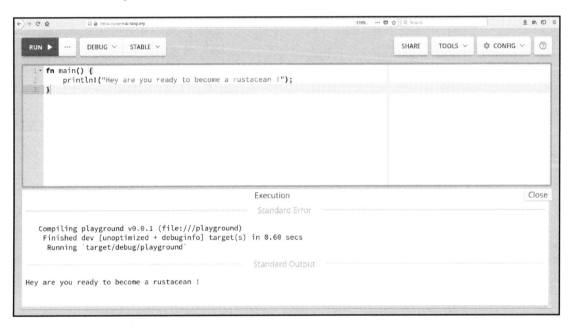

The Rust playground also supports external libraries to be imported and to be used when trying out sample programs.

With the previous example, we got a high-level overview of a basic Rust program, but did not dive into all of the details and the syntax. In the following section, we will explain the language features separately and their syntax. The explanations that follow are here to give you enough context so that you can quickly get up and running in regard to writing Rust programs without going through all of the use cases exhaustively. To make it brief, each section also contains references to chapters that explain these concepts in more detail. Also, the Rust documentation page at `https://doc.rust-lang.org/std/index.html` will help you get into the details and is very readable with its built-in search feature. You are encouraged to proactively search for any of the constructs that are explained in the following sections. This will help you gain more context about the concepts you're learning about.

All of the code examples in this chapter can be found in this book's GitHub repository (`PacktPublishing/The-Complete-Rust-Programming-Reference-Guide`).

 Some of the code files are deliberately presented to not compile so that you can fix them yourselves with the help of the compiler.

With that said, let's start with the fundamental primitive types in Rust.

Primitive types

Rust has the following built-in primitive types:

- `bool`: These are the usual booleans and can be either `true` or `false`.
- `char`: Characters, such as e.
- Integer types: These are characterized by the bit width. Rust supports integers that are up to 128 bits wide:

signed	unsigned
i8	u8
i16	u16
i32	u32
i64	u64
i128	u128

- `isize`: The pointer-sized signed integer type. Equivalent to `i32` on 32-bit CPU and `i64` on 64-bit CPU.
- `usize`: The pointer-sized unsigned integer type. Equivalent to `i32` on 32-bit CPU and `i64` on 64-bit CPU.
- `f32`: The 32-bit floating point type. Implements the IEEE 754 standard for floating point representation.
- `f64`: The 64-bit floating point type.
- `[T; N]`: A fixed-size array, for the element type, `T`, and the non-negative compile-time constant size N.

- `[T]`: A dynamically-sized view into a contiguous sequence, for any type `T`.
- `str`: String slices, mainly used as a reference, that is, `&str`.
- `(T, U, ..)`: A finite sequence, (T, U, ..) where T and U can be different types.
- `fn(i32) -> i32`: A function that takes an `i32` and returns an `i32`. Functions also have a type.

Declaring variables and immutability

Variables allow us to store a value and easily refer to it later in code. In Rust, we use the `let` keyword to declare variables. We already had a glimpse of it in the `greet.rs` example in the previous section. In mainstream imperative languages such as C or Python, initializing a variable does not stop you from reassigning it to some other value. Rust deviates from the mainstream here by making variables immutable by default, that is, you cannot assign the variable to some other value after you have initialized it. If you need a variable to point to something else (of the same type) later, you need to put the `mut` keyword before it. Rust asks you to be explicit about your intent as much as possible. Consider the following code:

```
// variables.rs

fn main() {
    let target = "world";
    let mut greeting = "Hello";
    println!("{}, {}", greeting, target);
    greeting = "How are you doing";
    target = "mate";
    println!("{}, {}", greeting, target);
}
```

We declared two variables, `target` and `greeting`. `target` is an immutable binding, while `greeting` has a `mut` before it, which makes it a mutable binding. If we run this program, though, we get the following error:

```
→  Chapter01 git:(master) ✗ rustc variables.rs
error[E0384]: cannot assign twice to immutable variable `target`
 --> variables.rs:8:5
  |
4 |     let target = "world";
  |         ------ first assignment to `target`
...
8 |     target = "mate";
  |     ^^^^^^^^^^^^^^^^ cannot assign twice to immutable variable

error: aborting due to previous error

For more information about this error, try `rustc --explain E0384`
```

As you can see from the preceding error message, Rust does not let you assign to `target` again. To make this program compile, we'll need to add `mut` before `target` in the `let` statement and compile and run it again. The following is the output when you run the program:

```
$ rustc variables.rs
$ ./variables
Hello, world
How are you doing, mate
```

`let` does much more than assign variables. It is a pattern-matching statement in Rust. In `Chapter 7`, *Advanced Concepts*, we'll take a closer look at `let`. Next, we'll look at functions.

Functions

Functions abstract a bunch of instructions into named entities, which can be invoked later by other code and help manage complexity. We already used a function in our `greet.rs` program, that is, the `main` function. Let's look at how we can define another one:

```
// functions.rs

fn add(a: u64, b: u64) -> u64 {
    a + b
}

fn main() {
    let a: u64 = 17;
    let b = 3;
    let result = add(a, b);
    println!("Result {}", result);
}
```

In the preceding code, we created a new function named `add`. The `fn` keyword is used to create functions followed by its name, `add`, its parameters inside parentheses a and b, and the function body inside { } braces. The parameters have their type on the right, after the colon `:`. Return types in functions are specified using a `->`, followed by the type, `u64`, which can be omitted if the function has nothing to return. Functions also have types. The type of our `add` function is denoted as `fn(u64, u64) -> u64`. They can also be stored in variables and passed to other functions.

If you look at the body of add, we don't need a return keyword to return a + b as in other languages. The last expression is returned automatically. However, we do have the return keyword available for early returns. Functions are basically expressions that return a value, which is a () (Unit) type by default, akin to the *void* return type in C/C++. They can also be declared within other functions. The use case for that is when you have a functionality within a function (say, foo) that is hard to reason as a sequence of statements. In this case, one can extract those lines in a local function, bar, which is then defined within the parent function, foo.

In main, we declared two variables, a and b, using the let keyword. As is the case with b, we can even omit specifying the type as Rust is able to infer types of variables in most cases by examining your code. This is also the case with the result, which is a u64 value. This feature helps prevent type signature clutter and improves the readability of code, especially when your types are nested inside several other types that have long names.

 Rust's type inference is based on the Hindly Milner type system. It's a set of rules and algorithms that enable type inference in a programming language. It's an efficient type inference method that performs in linear time, making it practical to type check large programs.

We can also have functions that modify their arguments. Consider the following code:

```
// function_mut.rs

fn increase_by(mut val: u32, how_much: u32) {
    val += how_much;
    println!("You made {} points", val);
}

fn main() {
    let score = 2048;
    increase_by(score, 30);
}
```

We declare a score variable with 2048 as the value, and call the increase_by function, passing score and the value 30 as the second argument. In the increase_by function, we have specified the first parameter as mut val, indicating that the parameter should be taken as mutable, which allows the variable to be mutated from inside the function. Our increase_by function modifies the val binding and prints the value. Following is the output when running the program:

```
$ rustc function_mut.rs
$ ./function_mut
You made 2078 points
```

Next, let's look at closures.

Closures

Rust also has support for closures. Closures are like functions but have more information of the environment or scope in which they are declared. While functions have names associated with them, closures are defined without a name, but they can be assigned to a variable. Another advantage of Rust's type inference is that, in most cases, you can specify parameters for a closure without their type. Here's the the simplest possible closure: `let my_closure = || ();`. We just defined a no-parameter closure that does nothing. We can call this by invoking `my_closure()`, just like functions. The two vertical bars `||` hold the parameters for the closure (if any), such as `|a, b|`. Specifying the types of parameters (`|a: u32|`) is sometimes required when Rust cannot figure out the proper types. Like functions, closures can also be stored in variables and invoked later or passed to other functions. The body of the closure, however, can either have a single line expression or a pair of braces for multi-line expressions. A more involved closure would be as follows:

```
// closures.rs

fn main() {
    let doubler = |x| x * 2;
    let value = 5;
    let twice = doubler(value);
    println!("{} doubled is {}", value, twice);

    let big_closure = |b, c| {
        let z = b + c;
        z * twice
    };

    let some_number = big_closure(1, 2);
    println!("Result from closure: {}", some_number);
}
```

In the preceding code, we have defined two closures: `doubler` and `big_closure`. `doubler` doubles a value given to it; in this case, it is passed `value` from the parent scope or environment, that is, the function `main`. Similarly, in `big_closure`, we use the variable `twice` from its environment. This closure has multi-line expressions within braces and needs to end with a semi-colon to allow us to assign it to the `big_closure` variable. Later, we call `big_closure`, passing in `1, 2`, and print `some_number`.

The major use case for closures are as parameters to higher-order functions. A higher-order function is a function that takes another function or closure as its argument. For example, the `thread::spawn` function from the standard library takes in a closure where you can write code you want to run in another thread. Another example where closures provide a convenient abstraction is when you have a function that operates on collection such as `Vec` and you want to filter the items based on some condition. Rust's `Iterator` trait has a method called `filter`, which takes in a closure as an argument. This closure is defined by the user and it returns either `true` or `false`, depending on how the user wants to filter the items in the collection. We'll get more in-depth with closures in `Chapter 7`, *Advanced Concepts*.

Strings

Strings are one of the most frequently used data types in any programming language. In Rust, they are usually found in two forms: the `&str` type (pronounced *stir*) and the `String` type. Rust strings are guaranteed to be valid UTF-8 encoded byte sequences. They are not null terminated as in C strings and can contain null bytes in-between them. The following program shows the two types in action:

```
// strings.rs

fn main() {
    let question = "How are you ?";            // a &str type
    let person: String = "Bob".to_string();
    let namaste = String::from("नमस्ते");          // unicodes yay!

    println!("{}! {} {}", namaste, question, person);
}
```

In the preceding code, `person` and `namaste` are of type `String`, while `question` is of type `&str`. There are multiple ways you can create `String` types. Strings are allocated on the heap, while `&str` types are usually pointers to an existing string, which could either be on stack, the heap, or a string in the data segment of the compiled object code. The `&` is an operator that is used to create a pointer to any type. After initializing the strings in the preceding code, we then use the `println!` macro to print them together using format strings. That's the very basics of strings. Strings are covered in detail in `Chapter 7`, *Advanced Concepts*.

Conditionals and decision making

Conditionals are also similar to how they're found in other languages. They follow the C-like if {} else {} structure:

```
// if_else.rs

fn main() {
    let rust_is_awesome = true;
    if rust_is_awesome {
        println!("Indeed");
    } else {
        println!("Well, you should try Rust !");
    }
}
```

In Rust, the if construct is not a statement, but an expression. In general programming parlance, *statements* do not return any value, but an *expression* does. This distinction means that if else conditionals in Rust always return a value. The value may be an empty () unit type, or it may be an actual value. Whatever remains in the last line inside the braces becomes the return value of the if else expression. It is important to note that both if and else branches should have the same return type. Also, we don't need parentheses around the if condition expression, as you can see in the preceding code. We can even assign the value of if else blocks to a variable:

```
// if_assign.rs

fn main() {
    let result = if 1 == 2 {
        "Wait, what ?"
    } else {
        "Rust makes sense"
    };

    println!("You know what ? {}.", result);
}
```

When assigning values that have been returned from an `if else` expression, we need to end them with a semicolon. For example, `if { ...` is an expression, while `let` is a statement that expects us to have a semicolon at the end. In the case of assignment, if we were to remove the `else {}` block from the preceding code, the compiler would throw an error, like so:

```
→ Chapter01 git:(master) X rustc if_assign.rs
error[E0317]: if may be missing an else clause
 --> if_assign.rs:4:18
  |
4 |         let result = if 1 == 2 {
  |  _____^
5 | |             "Wait, what ?"
6 | |         };
  | |_____^ expected (), found &str
  |
  = note: expected type `()`
             found type `&str`

error: aborting due to previous error

For more information about this error, try `rustc --explain E0317`.
```

Without the `else` block, if the `if` condition evaluates to `false`, then the result will be `()`, and there would be two possible values for the `result` variable, that is, `()` and `&str`. Rust does not allow multiple types to be stored in one variable. So, in this case, we need both the `if {}` and `else {}` blocks returning the same types. Also, adding a semicolon in the conditional branches changes the meaning of the code. By adding a semicolon after the strings in the `if` block in the following code, the compiler would interpret it as you wanting to throw the value away:

```
// if_else_no_value.rs

fn main() {
    let result = if 1 == 2 {
        "Nothing makes sense";
    } else {
        "Sanity reigns";
    };

    println!("Result of computation: {:?}", result);
}
```

In this case, the result will be an empty `()`, which is why we had to change the `println!` expression slightly (the `{:?}`); this type cannot be printed out in the regular way. Now, for the more complex multi-valued decision making; Rust has another powerful construct called `match` expressions, which we'll look at next.

Match expressions

Rust's `match` expressions are quite a joy to use. It's basically C's `switch` statement on steroids and allows you to make decisions, depending on what value the variable has and whether it has advanced filtering capabilities. Here's a program that uses match expressions:

```
// match_expression.rs

fn req_status() -> u32 {
    200
}

fn main() {
    let status = req_status();
    match status {
        200 => println!("Success"),
        404 => println!("Not Found"),
        other => {
            println!("Request failed with code: {}", other);
            // get response from cache
        }
    }
}
```

In the preceding code, we have a `req_status`, function that returns a dummy HTTP request status code of `200`, which we call in `main` and assign to `status`. We then match on this value using the `match` keyword, followed by the variable we want to check the value of (`status`), followed by a pair of braces. Within braces, we write expressions – these are called **match arms**. These arms represent the possible values that the variable being matched can take. Each match arm is written by writing the possible value of the variable, followed by a `=>`, and then the expression on the right. To the right, you can either have a single line expression or a multi-line expression within `{}` braces. When written in a single line expression, they need to be delimited with a comma. Also, every match arm must return the same type. In this case, each match arm returns a Unit type `()`.

Another nice feature or you can call guarantee of match expressions is that we have to match exhaustively against all possible cases of the value we are matching against. In our case, this would be listing all the numbers up until the maximum value of i32. However, practically, this is not possible, so Rust allows us to either ignore the rest of the possibilities by using a catch all variable (here, this is other) or an _ (underscore) if we want to ignore the value. Match expressions are a primary way to make decisions around values when you have more than one possible value and they are very concise to write. Like if else expressions, the return value of a match expression can also be assigned to a variable in a let statement when it's delimited with a semicolon, with all match arms returning the same types.

Loops

Repeating things in Rust can be done using three constructs, namely loop, while, and for. In all of them, we have the usual continue and break keywords, which allow you to skip and break out of a loop, respectively. Here's an example of using loop, which is equivalent to C's while(true):

```
// loops.rs

fn main() {
    let mut x = 1024;
    loop {
        if x < 0 {
            break;
        }
        println!("{} more runs to go", x);
        x -= 1;
    }
}
```

loop represents an infinite loop. In the preceding code, we simply decrement the value x until it hits the if condition x < 0, where we break out of the loop. An extra feature of using loop in Rust is being able to tag the loop block with a name. This can be used in cases where you have two or more nested loops and want to break out from any one of them and not just the loop immediately enclosing the break statement. The following is an example of using loop labels to break out of the loop:

```
// loop_labels.rs

fn silly_sub(a: i32, b: i32) -> i32 {
    let mut result = 0;
    'increment: loop {
```

```
            if result == a {
                let mut dec = b;
                'decrement: loop {
                    if dec == 0 {
                        // breaks directly out of 'increment loop
                        break 'increment;
                    } else {
                        result -= 1;
                        dec -= 1;
                    }
                }
            } else {
                result += 1;
            }
        }
        result
    }

    fn main() {
        let a = 10;
        let b = 4;
        let result = silly_sub(a, b);
        println!("{} minus {} is {}", a, b, result);
    }
```

In the preceding code, we are doing a very inefficient subtraction just to demonstrate the usage of labels with nested loops. In the inner `'decrement` label, when `dec` equals 0, we can pass a label to break (here, this is `'increment`) and break out of the outer `'increment` loop instead.

Now, let's take a look at `while` loops. Nothing fancy here:

```
    // while.rs

    fn main() {
        let mut x = 1000;
        while x > 0 {
            println!("{} more runs to go", x);
            x -= 1;
        }
    }
```

Rust also has a `for` keyword and is similar to for loops used in other languages, but they are quite different in their implementation. Rust's `for` is basically a syntax sugar for a more powerful repetition construct known as *iterators*. We'll discuss them in more detail in `Chapter 7`, *Advanced Concepts*. To put it simply, for loops in Rust only work on types that can be converted into iterators. One such type is the `Range` type. The `Range` type can refer to a range of numbers, such as `(0..10)`. They can be used in `for` loops like so:

```
// for_loops.rs

fn main() {
    // does not include 10
    print!("Normal ranges: ");
    for i in 0..10 {
        print!("{},", i);
    }

    println!();        // just a newline
    print!("Inclusive ranges: ");
    // counts till 10
    for i in 0..=10 {
        print!("{},", i);
    }
}
```

Apart from the normal range syntax, that is, `0..10`, which does not include `10`, Rust also has inclusive range syntax `0..=10`, which iterates all the way until `10`, as can be seen in the second `for` loop. Now, let's move on to user-defined data types.

User-defined types

As the name says, user-defined types are types that are defined by you. These can be composed of several types. They may either be a wrapper over a primitive type or a composition of several user defined types. They come in three forms: structures, enumerations, and unions, or more commonly known as **structs**, **enums**, and **unions**. They allow you to easily express you data. The naming convention for user-defined types follows the CamelCase style. Structs and enums are more powerful than C's structs and enums, while unions in Rust are very close to C and are there mainly to interact with C code bases. We'll cover structs and enums in this section, while unions are covered in `Chapter 7`, *Advanced Concepts*.

Structs

In Rust, there are three forms of structs that we can declare. The simplest of them is the **unit struct**, which is written with the `struct` keyword, followed by its name and a semicolon at the end. The following code example defines a unit struct:

```
// unit_struct.rs

struct Dummy;

fn main() {
    let value = Dummy;
}
```

We have defined a unit struct called `Dummy` in the preceding code. In `main`, we can initialize this type using only its name. `value` now contains an instance of `Dummy` and is a zero sized value. Unit structs do not take any size at runtime as they have no data associated with them. There are very few use cases for unit structs. They can be used to model entities with no data or state associated with them. Another use case is to use them to represent error types, where the struct itself is sufficient to understand the error without needing a description of it. Another use case is to represent states in a state machine implementation. Next, let's look at the second form of structs.

The second form of struct is the **tuple struct**, which has associated data. Here, the individual fields are not named, but are referred to by their position in the definition. Let's say you are writing a color conversion/calculation library for use in your graphics application and want to represent *RGB* color values in code. We can represent our `Color` type and the related items like so:

```
// tuple_struct.rs

struct Color(u8, u8, u8);

fn main() {
    let white = Color(255, 255, 255);
    // You can pull them out by index
    let red = white.0;
    let green = white.1;
    let blue = white.2;

    println!("Red value: {}", red);
    println!("Green value: {}", green);
    println!("Blue value: {}\n", blue);

    let orange = Color(255, 165, 0);
```

```
        // You can also destructure the fields directly
        let Color(r, g, b) = orange;
        println!("R: {}, G: {}, B: {} (orange)", r, g, b);

        // Can also ignore fields while destructuring
        let Color(r, _, b) = orange;
}
```

In the preceding code, `Color(u8, u8, u8)` is a tuple struct that was created and stored in `white`. We then access the individual color components in `white` using the `white.0` syntax. Fields within the tuple struct can be accessed by the `variable.<index>` syntax, where the `index` refers to the position of the field in the struct, which starts with 0. Another way to access the individual fields of a struct is by destructuring the struct using the `let` statement. In the second part, we created a color `orange`. Following that, we wrote the `let` statement with `Color(r, g, b)` on the left-hand side and to the right we put our `orange`. This results in three fields in `orange` getting stored within the `r`, `g`, and `b` variables. The types of `r`, `g`, and `b` are also inferred automatically for us.

The tuple struct is an ideal choice when you need to model data that has less than four or five attributes. Anything more than that hinders readability and reasoning. For a data type that has more than three fields cases, it's recommended to use a C-like struct, which is the third form and the most commonly used one. Consider the following code:

```
// structs.rs

struct Player {
    name: String,
    iq: u8,
    friends: u8,
    score: u16
}

fn bump_player_score(mut player: Player, score: u16) {
    player.score += 120;
    println!("Updated player stats:");
    println!("Name: {}", player.name);
    println!("IQ: {}", player.iq);
    println!("Friends: {}", player.friends);
    println!("Score: {}", player.score);
}

fn main() {
    let name = "Alice".to_string();
    let player = Player { name,
                          iq: 171,
                          friends: 134,
```

```
                    score: 1129 };

    bump_player_score(player, 120);
}
```

In the preceding code, structs are created in the same way as tuple structs, that is, by writing the `struct` keyword followed by the name of the struct. However, they start with braces and their field declarations are named. Within braces, we can write fields as `field:` `type` comma-separated pairs. Creating an instance of a struct is also simple; we write `Player`, followed by a pair of braces, which contains comma-separated field initializations. When initializing a field from a variable that has the same name as the field name, we can use the **field init shorthand** feature, which is the case with the `name` field in the preceding code. We can then access the fields from the created instance easily by using the `struct.field_name` syntax. In the preceding code, we also have a function called `bump_player_score`, which takes the struct `Player` as a parameter. Function arguments are immutable by default, so when we want to modify the score of the player, we need to change the parameter to `mut player` in our function, which allows us to modify any of its fields. Having a `mut` on the struct implies mutability for all of its fields.

The advantage of using a struct rather than a tuple struct is that we can initialize the fields in any order. It also allows us to provide meaningful names to the fields. As a side note, the size of a struct is simply the sum of its individual field members, along with any data alignment padding, if required. They don't have any extra metadata size overhead associated with them. Next, let's look at enumerations, also known as enums.

Enums

When you need to model something that can be of different kinds, enums are the way to go. They are created using the `enum` keyword, followed by the name of the enum, followed by a pair of braces. Within braces, we can write all the possibilities of the type, which are called **variants**. These variants can be defined with or without data contained in them, and the data contained can be any primitive type, structs, tuple structs, or even an enum. However, in the recursive case, where you have an enum, `Foo`, and also a variant which holds `Foo`, the variant needs to be behind a pointer (`Box`, `Rc`, and so on) type to avoid having recursively infinite type definitions. Because enums can also be created on the stack, they need to have a predetermined size, and infinite type definitions makes it impossible to determine the size at compile time. Now, let's take a look at how to create one:

```
// enums.rs

enum Direction {
    N,
```

```
        E,
        S,
        W
    }

    enum PlayerAction {
        Move {
            direction: Direction,
            speed: u8
        },
        Wait,
        Attack(Direction)
    }

    fn main() {
        let simulated_player_action = PlayerAction::Move {
            direction: Direction::N,
            speed: 2,
        };
        match simulated_player_action {
            PlayerAction::Wait => println!("Player wants to wait"),
            PlayerAction::Move { direction, speed } => {
              println!("Player wants to move in direction {:?} with speed {}",
                    direction, speed)
            }
            PlayerAction::Attack(direction) => {
                println!("Player wants to attack direction {:?}", direction)
            }
        };
    }
```

The preceding code defines two enum types: `Direction` and `PlayerAction`. We then create an instance of them by choosing any variant, such as `Direction::N` or `PlayerAction::Wait` using the double colon `::` in between. Note that we can't have something like an uninitialized enum, and it needs to be one of the variants. Given an enum value, to see what variant an enum instance has, we use pattern matching by using *match* expressions. When we match on enums, we can directly destructure the contents of the variants by putting variables in place of fields such as `direction` in `PlayerAction::Attack(direction)`, which in turn means that we can use them inside our match arms.

As you can see in our preceding `Direction` enum, we have a `#[derive(Debug)]` annotation. This is an attribute and it allows `Direction` instances to be printed using the `{:?}` format string in `println!()`. This is done by generating methods from a trait called `Debug`. The compiler tells us whether the `Debug` trait is missing and gives suggestions about how to fix it, and so we need the attribute there:

```
→ Chapter01 git:(master) X rustc enums.rs
error[E0277]: `Direction` doesn't implement `std::fmt::Debug`
 --> enums.rs:29:17
    |
29 |             direction, speed)
    |             ^^^^^^^^^ `Direction` cannot be formatted using `{:?}`
    |
    = help: the trait `std::fmt::Debug` is not implemented for `Direction`
    = note: add `#[derive(Debug)]` or manually implement `std::fmt::Debug`
    = note: required by `std::fmt::Debug::fmt`

error[E0277]: `Direction` doesn't implement `std::fmt::Debug`
 --> enums.rs:32:63
    |
32 |         println!("Player wants to attack direction {:?}", direction)
    |                                                           ^^^^^^^^^ `Direction` cannot be formatted using `{:?}`
    |
    = help: the trait `std::fmt::Debug` is not implemented for `Direction`
    = note: add `#[derive(Debug)]` or manually implement `std::fmt::Debug`
    = note: required by `std::fmt::Debug::fmt`

error: aborting due to 2 previous errors

For more information about this error, try `rustc --explain E0277`.
```

From a functional programmer's perspective, structs and enums are also known as **Algebraic Data Types (ADTs)** because the possible range of values they can represent can be expressed using the rules of algebra. For instance, an enum is called a **sum type** because the range of values that it can hold is basically the sum of the range of values of its variants, while a struct is called a **product type** because its range of possible values is the cartesian product of their individual fields' range of values. We'll sometime refer to them as ADTs when talking about them in general.

Functions and methods on types

Types without behavior can be limiting, and it's often the case that we want to have functions or methods on types so that we can return new instances of them rather than constructing them manually or so that we have the ability to the manipulate fields of a user-defined type. We can do this via **impl blocks**, which is read as providing implementations for a type. We can provide implementations for all user-defined types or any wrapper type. First, let's take a look at how to write implementations for a struct.

Impl blocks on structs

We can add behavior to our previously defined `Player` struct with two functionalities: a constructor-like function that takes a name and sets default values for the remaining fields in `Person`, and getter and setter methods for the friend count of `Person`:

```
// struct_methods.rs

struct Player {
    name: String,
    iq: u8,
    friends: u8
}

impl Player {
    fn with_name(name: &str) -> Player {
        Player {
            name: name.to_string(),
            iq: 100,
            friends: 100
        }
    }

    fn get_friends(&self) -> u8 {
        self.friends
    }

    fn set_friends(&mut self, count: u8) {
        self.friends = count;
    }
}

fn main() {
    let mut player = Player::with_name("Dave");
    player.set_friends(23);
    println!("{}'s friends count: {}", player.name, player.get_friends());
    // another way to call instance methods.
    let _ = Player::get_friends(&player);
}
```

We use the `impl` keyword, followed by the type we are implementing the methods for, followed by braces. Within braces, we can write two kinds of methods:

- **Associated methods**: Methods without a `self` type as their first parameter. The `with_name` method is called an associated method because it does not have `self` as the first parameter. It is similar to a static method in object-oriented languages. These methods are available on the type themselves and do not need an instance of the type to invoke them. Associated methods are invoked by prefixing the method name with the struct name and double colons, like so:

  ```
  Player::with_name("Dave");
  ```

- **Instance methods**: Functions that take a `self` value as its first argument. The `self` symbol here is similar to *self* in Python and points to the instance on which the method is implemented (here, this is `Player`). Therefore, the `get_friends()` method can only be called on already created instances of the struct:

  ```
  let player = Player::with_name("Dave");
  player.get_friends();
  ```

If we were to call `get_friends` with the associated method syntax, that is, `Player::get_friends()`, the compiler gives the following error:

```
→  Chapter01 git:(master) ✗ rustc struct_methods.rs
error[E0061]: this function takes 1 parameter but 0 parameters were supplied
  --> struct_methods.rs:32:13
   |
18 |        fn get_friends(&self) -> u8 {
   |        --------------------------------- defined here
...
32 |        let _ = Player::get_friends();
   |                ^^^^^^^^^^^^^^^^^^^^^ expected 1 parameter

error: aborting due to previous error

For more information about this error, try `rustc --explain E0061`.
```

The error is misleading here, but it indicates that instance methods are basically associated methods with `self` as the first parameter and that `instance.foo()` is a syntax sugar. This means that we can call it like this, too: `Player::get_friends(&player);`. In this invocation, we pass the method an instance of `Player`, that is, `&self` is `&player`.

There are three variants of instance methods that we can implement on types:

- `self` as the first parameter. In this case, calling this method won't allow you to use the type later.
- `&self` as the first parameter. This method only provides read access to the instance of a type.
- `&mut self` as the first parameter. This method provides mutable access to the instance of a type.

Our `set_friends` method is a `&mut self` method, which allows us to mutate the fields of `player`. We need the `&` operator before `self`, meaning that `self` is borrowed for the duration of the method, which is exactly what we want here. Without the ampersand, the caller would move the ownership to the method, which means that the value would get de-allocated after `get_friends` returns and we would not get to use our `Player` instance anymore. Don't worry if the terms move and borrowing does not make sense as we explain all of this in Chapter 5, *Memory Management and Safety*.

Now, onto implementations for enums.

Impl blocks for enums

We can also provide implementations for enums. For example, consider a payments library built in Rust, which exposes a single API called `pay`:

```
// enum_methods.rs

enum PaymentMode {
    Debit,
    Credit,
    Paypal
}

// Bunch of dummy payment handlers

fn pay_by_credit(amt: u64) {
    println!("Processing credit payment of {}", amt);
}
fn pay_by_debit(amt: u64) {
```

```
        println!("Processing debit payment of {}", amt);
}
fn paypal_redirect(amt: u64) {
    println!("Redirecting to paypal for amount: {}", amt);
}

impl PaymentMode {
    fn pay(&self, amount: u64) {
        match self {
            PaymentMode::Debit => pay_by_debit(amount),
            PaymentMode::Credit => pay_by_credit(amount),
            PaymentMode::Paypal => paypal_redirect(amount)
        }
    }
}

fn get_saved_payment_mode() -> PaymentMode {
    PaymentMode::Debit
}

fn main() {
    let payment_mode = get_saved_payment_mode();
    payment_mode.pay(512);
}
```

The preceding code has a method called get_saved_payment_mode(), which returns a user's saved payment mode. This can either be a *Credit Card*, *Debit Card*, or *Paypal*. This is best modeled as an enum, where different payment methods can be added as its variants. The library then provides us with a single pay() method to which we can conveniently provide an amount to pay. This method determines which variant of the enum it is and dispatches methods accordingly to the correct payment service provider, without the library consumer worrying about checking which payment method to use.

Enums are also widely used for modeling state machines, and when combined with match statements, they make state transition code very concise to write. They are also used to model custom error types. When enum variants don't have any data associated with them, they can be used like C enums, where the variants implicitly have integer values starting with 0, but can also be manually tagged with integer (isize) values. This is useful when interacting with foreign C libraries.

Modules, imports, and use statements

Languages often provide a way to split large code bases into multiple files to manage complexity. Java follows the convention of a single public class per `.java` file, while C++ provides us with header files and include statements. Rust is no different and provides us with **modules**. Modules are a way to namespace or organize code in a Rust program. To allow flexibility in organizing our code, there are multiple ways to create modules. Modules are a complex topic to understand and to make it brief for this section, we'll highlight only the important aspects about using them. Modules are covered in detail in Chapter 2, *Managing Projects with Cargo*. The following are the key takeaways about modules in Rust:

- Every Rust program needs to have a root module. In executables, it is usually the `main.rs` file, and for libraries, it is `lib.rs`.
- Modules can be declared within other modules or can be organized as files and directories.
- To let the compiler know about our module, we need to declare it using the `mod` keyword, as in `mod my_module;`, in our root module.
- To use any of the items within the module, we need to use the `use` keyword, along with the name of the module. This is known as bringing the item into scope.
- Items defined within modules are private by default, and you need to use the `pub` keyword to expose them to their consumers.

That was modules in brief. Some of the advanced aspects of modules are also covered in Chapter 7, *Advanced Concepts*. Next, let's look at the commonly used collection types that are available in the standard library.

Collections

It's often the case that your program has to process more than one instance of data. For that, we have collection types. Depending on what you want and where your data resides in memory, Rust provides many kinds of built-in types to store a collection of data. First, we have *arrays* and *tuples*. Then, we have dynamic collection types in the standard library, of which we'll cover the most commonly used ones, that is, *vectors* (list of items) and *maps* (key/value items). Then, we also have references to collection types, called *slices*, which are basically a view into a contiguous piece of data owned by some other variable. Let's start with arrays first.

Arrays

Arrays have a fixed length that can store items of the same type. They are denoted by `[T, N]`, where `T` is any type and `N` is the number of elements in array. The size of the array cannot be a variable, but has to be a literal `usize` value:

```
// arrays.rs

fn main() {
    let numbers: [u8; 10] = [1, 2, 3, 4, 5, 7, 8, 9, 10, 11];
    let floats = [0.1f64, 0.2, 0.3];

    println!("Number: {}", numbers[5]);
    println!("Float: {}", floats[2]);
}
```

In the preceding code, we declared an array, `numbers`, which contains `10` elements for which we specified the type on the left. In the second array, `floats`, we specified the type as a suffix to the first item of the array, that is, `0.1f64`. This is another way to specify types. Next, let's look at tuples.

Tuples

Tuples differ from arrays in the way that elements of an array have to be of the same type, while items in a tuple can be a mix of types. They are heterogeneous collections and are useful for storing distinct types together. They can also be used when returning multiple values from a function. Consider the following code that uses tuples:

```
// tuples.rs

fn main() {
    let num_and_str: (u8, &str) = (40, "Have a good day!");
    println!("{:?}", num_and_str);
    let (num, string) = num_and_str;
    println!("From tuple: Number: {}, String: {}", num, string);
}
```

In the preceding code, `num_and_str` is a tuple of two items, `(u8, &str)`. We can also extract values from an already declared tuple into individual variables. After printing the tuple, we destructure it on the next line into the `num` and `string` variables, and their types are inferred automatically. That's pretty neat.

Vectors

Vectors are like arrays, except that their content or length doesn't need to be known in advance and can grow on demand. They are allocated on the heap. They can be created by either calling the `Vec::new` constructor or by using the `vec![]` macro:

```
// vec.rs

fn main() {
    let mut numbers_vec: Vec<u8> = Vec::new();
    numbers_vec.push(1);
    numbers_vec.push(2);

    let mut vec_with_macro = vec![1];
    vec_with_macro.push(2);
    let _ = vec_with_macro.pop();    // value ignored with `_`

    let message = if numbers_vec == vec_with_macro {
        "They are equal"
    } else {
        "Nah! They look different to me"
    };

    println!("{} {:?} {:?}", message, numbers_vec, vec_with_macro);
}
```

In the preceding code, we created two vectors, `numbers_vec` and `vec_with_macro`, in different ways. We can push elements to our vector using `push()` method and can remove elements using `pop()`. There are more methods for you to explore if you go to their documentation page: `https://doc.rust-lang.org/std/vec/struct.Vec.html`. Vectors can also be iterated using the `for` loop syntax as they also implement the `Iterator` trait.

Hashmaps

Rust also provides us with maps, which can be used to store key-value data. They come from the `std::collections` module and are named `HashMap`. They are created with the `HashMap::new` constructor function:

```
// hashmaps.rs

use std::collections::HashMap;

fn main() {
    let mut fruits = HashMap::new();
    fruits.insert("apple", 3);
```

```
fruits.insert("mango", 6);
fruits.insert("orange", 2);
fruits.insert("avocado", 7);
for (k, v) in &fruits {
    println!("I got {} {}", v, k);
}

fruits.remove("orange");
let old_avocado = fruits["avocado"];
fruits.insert("avocado", old_avocado + 5);
println!("\nI now have {} avocados", fruits["avocado"]);
}
```

In the preceding code, we created a new `HashMap` called `fruits`. We then insert some fruits into our `fruits` map, along with their count, using the `insert` method. Following that, we iterate over the key value pairs using `for` loop, where in we take a reference to our fruit map by `&fruits`, because we only want read access to the key and value. By default, the value will be consumed by the `for` loop. The `for` loop in this case returns a two field tuple (`(k ,v)`). There are also seperate methods `keys()` and `values()` available to iterate over just keys and values, respectively. The hashing algorithm used for hashing the keys of the `HashMap` type is based on the *Robin hood* open addressing scheme, but can be replaced with a custom hasher depending on the use case and performance. That's about it.

Next, let's look at slices.

Slices

Slices are a generic way to get a view into a collection type. Most use cases are to get a read only access to a certain range of items in a collection type. A slice is basically a pointer or a reference that points to a continuous range in an existing collection type that's owned by some other variable. Under the hood, slices are fat pointers to existing data somewhere in the stack or the heap. By fat pointer, it means that they also have information on how many elements they are pointing to, along with the pointer to the data.

Slices are denoted by &[T], where T is any type. They are quite similar to arrays in terms of usage:

```
// slices.rs

fn main() {
    let mut numbers: [u8; 4] = [1, 2, 3, 4];
    {
        let all: &[u8] = &numbers[..];
        println!("All of them: {:?}", all);
    }

    {
        let first_two: &mut [u8] = &mut numbers[0..2];
        first_two[0] = 100;
        first_two[1] = 99;
    }

    println!("Look ma! I can modify through slices: {:?}", numbers);
}
```

In the preceding code, we have an array of numbers, which is a stack allocated value. We then take a slice into the array numbers using the &numbers[..] syntax and store in all, which has the type &[u8]. The [..] at the end means that we want to take a full slice of the collection. We need the & here as we can't have slices as bare values – only behind a pointer. This is because slices are **unsized types**. We'll cover them in detail in Chapter 7, *Advanced Concepts*. We can also provide ranges ([0..2]) to get a slice from anywhere in-between or all of them. Slices can also be mutably acquired. first_two is a mutable slice through which we can modify the original numbers array.

To the astute observer, you can see that we have used extra pair of braces in the preceding code when taking slices. They are there to isolate code that takes mutable reference of the slice from the immutable reference. Without them, the code won't compile. These concepts will be made clearer to you in Chapter 5, *Memory Management and Safety*.

 Note: The &str type also comes under the category of a slice type (a [u8]). The only distinction from other byte slices is that they are guaranteed to be UTF-8. Slices can also be taken on Vecs or Strings.

Next, let's look at iterators.

Iterators

An iterator is a construct that provides an efficient way to act on elements of collection types. They are not a new concept, though. In many imperative languages, they are implemented as *objects* that are constructed from collection types such as lists or maps. For instance, Python's `iter(some_list)` or C++'s `vector.begin()` are ways to construct iterators from an existing collection. The main motivation for iterators to exist in the first place is that they provide a higher level abstraction of walking through items of a collection instead of using manual `for` loops, which are very much prone to off by one errors. Another advantage is that iterators do not read the whole collection in memory and are lazy. By lazy, we mean that the iterator only evaluates or accesses an element in a collection when needed. Iterators can also be chained with multiple transformation operations, such as filtering elements based on a condition, and do not evaluate the transformations until you need them. To access these items when you need them, iterators provide a `next()` method, which tries to read the next item from the collection. This occurs when the iterator evaluates the chain of computation.

In Rust, an iterator is any type that implements the `Iterator` trait. This type can then be used in a `for` loop to walk over its items. They are implemented for most standard library collection types such as `Vector`, `HashMap`, `BTreeMap`, and many more and one can also implement it for their own types.

 Note: It only makes sense to implement the `Iterator` trait if the type has a collection, such as semantics. For instance, it doesn't make sense to implement the iterator trait for a `()` unit type.

Iterators are frequently used whenever we are dealing with collection types in Rust. In fact, Rust's `for` loop is desugared into a normal match expression with `next` calls on the object being iterated over. Also, we can convert most collection types into an iterator by calling `iter()` or `into_iter()` on them. That's enough information on iterators – now, we can tackle the following exercise. We'll go deep into iterators and implement one ourselves in `Chapter 7`, *Advanced Concepts*.

Exercise – fixing the word counter

Armed with the basics, it's time to put our knowledge to use! Here, we have a program that counts instances of words in a text file, which is passed to it as an argument. It's almost complete, but has a few bugs that the compiler catches and a couple of subtle ones. Here's our incomplete program:

```rust
// word_counter.rs

use std::env;
use std::fs::File;
use std::io::prelude::BufRead;
use std::io::BufReader;

#[derive(Debug)]
struct WordCounter(HashMap<String, u64>);

impl WordCounter {
    fn new() -> WordCounter {
        WordCounter(HashMap::new());
    }

    fn increment(word: &str) {
        let key = word.to_string();
        let count = self.0.entry(key).or_insert(0);
        *count += 1;
    }

    fn display(self) {
        for (key, value) in self.0.iter() {
            println!("{}: {}", key, value);
        }
    }
}

fn main() {
    let arguments: Vec<String> = env::args().collect();
    let filename = arguments[1];
    println!("Processing file: {}", filename);
    let file = File::open(filenam).expect("Could not open file");
    let reader = BufReader::new(file);
    let mut word_counter = WordCounter::new();

    for line in reader.lines() {
        let line = line.expect("Could not read line");
        let words = line.split(" ");
        for word in words {
```

```
        if word == "" {
            continue
        } else {
            word_counter.increment(word);
        }
    }
}
word_counter.display();
}
```

Go ahead and type the program into a file; try to compile and fix all the bugs with the help of the compiler. Try to fix one bug at a time and get feedback from the compiler by recompiling the code. The point of this exercise, in addition to covering the topics of this chapter, is to make you more comfortable with the error messages from the compiler, which is an important mental exercise in getting to know more about the compiler and how it analyzes your code. You might also be surprised to see how the compiler is quite smart in helping you removing errors from the code.

Summary

We covered so many topics in this chapter. We got to know a bit about the history of Rust and the motivations behind the language. We had a brief walkthrough on its design principles and the basic features of the language. We also got a glimpse of how Rust provides rich abstractions through its type system. We learned how to install the language toolchain, and how to use `rustc` to build and run trivial example programs.

In the next chapter, we'll take a look at the standard way of building Rust applications and libraries using its dedicated package manager, and also set up our Rust development environment with a code editor, which will provide the foundation for all the subsequent exercises and projects in this book.

Managing Projects with Cargo 2

Now that we are familiar with the language and how to write basic programs, we'll level up towards writing practical projects in Rust. For trivial programs that can be contained in a single file, compiling and building them manually is no big deal. In the real world, however, programs are split into multiple files for managing complexity and also have dependencies on other libraries. Compiling all of the source files manually and linking them together becomes a complicated process. For large-scale projects, the manual way is not a scalable solution as there could be hundreds of files and their dependencies. Fortunately, there are tools that automate building of large-scale software projects—package managers. This chapter explores how Rust manages large projects with its dedicated package manager and what features it provides to the developer to enhance their development experience. We will cover the following topics:

- Package managers
- Modules
- The Cargo package manager and crates (libraries) as units of compilation
- Creating and building projects
- Running tests
- Cargo subcommands and installing third-party binaries
- Editor integrations and setup in Visual Studio code

As a final exercise, we'll create imgtool, a trivial command-line tool that can rotate images from the command line using a library, and use Cargo to build and run our program. We have a lot to cover, so let's dive in!

Package managers

"The key to efficient development is to make interesting new mistakes."

– Tom Love

A real-world software code base is often organized into multiple files and will have many dependencies, and that calls for a dedicated tool for managing them. Package managers are a class of command-line tools that help manage projects of a large size with multiple dependencies. If you come from a Node.js background, you must be familiar with npm/yarn or if you are from Go language, the go tool. They do all the heavy lifting of analyzing the project, downloading the correct versions of dependencies, checking for version conflicts, compiling and linking source files, and much more.

The problem with low-level languages like C/C++ is that they do not ship with a dedicated package manager by default. The C/C++ community have been using the GNU make tool for a long time, which is a language-agnostic build system and has arcane syntax, that puts off many developers. The problem with make is that it does not know what header files are included in your C/C++ sources, so they have to be manually given this information. It has no built-in support for downloading external dependencies, nor does it know about the platform you are running on. Fortunately, this is not the case with Rust as it ships with a dedicated package manager which has more context on the project being managed. What follows is a tour of Cargo, Rust's package manager, which makes it easy to build and maintain Rust projects. But first, we need to dig into Rust's module system a bit more.

Modules

Before we explore more about Cargo, we need to be familiar with how Rust organizes our code. We had a brief glimpse at modules in the previous chapter. Here, we will cover them in detail. Every Rust program starts with a root module. If you are creating a library, your root module is the lib.rs file. If you are creating an executable, the root module is any file with a main function, usually main.rs. When your code gets large, Rust lets you split it into modules. To provide flexibility in organizing a project, there are multiple ways to create modules.

Nested modules

The simplest way to create a module is by using the mod {} block within an existing module. Consider the following code:

```
// mod_within.rs

mod food {
    struct Cake;
    struct Smoothie;
    struct Pizza;
}

fn main() {
    let eatable = Cake;
}
```

We created an inner module named food. To create a module within an existing one, we use the mod keyword, followed by the name of the module, food, followed by a pair of braces. Within braces, we can declare any kind of item or even a nested module. Within our food module, we declared three structs: Cake, Smoothie, and Pizza. In main, we then create a Cake instance from the food module using the path syntax food::Cake. Let's compile this program:

```
→   Chapter02 git:(master) X rustc mod_within.rs
error[E0425]: cannot find value `Cake` in this scope
   --> mod_within.rs:10:19
    |
10  |        let eatable = Cake;
    |                      ^^^^ not found in this scope
help: possible candidate is found in another module, you can import it into scope
    |
3   | use food::Cake;
    |

error: aborting due to previous error

For more information about this error, try `rustc --explain E0425`.
```

Strange! The compiler does not see any Cake type being defined. Let's do what the compiler says and add use food::Cake:

```
// mod_within.rs

mod food {
    struct Cake;
    struct Smoothie;
    struct Pizza;
}
```

```
use food::Cake;

fn main() {
    let eatable = Cake;
}
```

We added use food::Cake;. To use any item from a module, we have to add a use declaration. Let's try again:

```
→  Chapter02 git:(master) ✗ rustc mod_within.rs
error[E0603]: struct `Cake` is private
  --> mod_within.rs:9:11
   |
9  |   use food::Cake;
   |             ^^^^

error: aborting due to previous error

For more information about this error, try `rustc --explain E0603`.
```

We get another error saying that Cake is private. This brings us to an important aspect about modules, providing privacy. Items within a module are private by default. To use any item from a module, we need to bring the item into scope. This is a two-step process. First, we need to make the item itself public by prefixing our item declaration with the pub keyword. Second, to use the item, we need to add a use statement, as we did previously with use food::Cake.

What comes after the use keyword is the item path in the module. The path to any item within a module is specified using the path syntax, which uses two double colons (::) between item names. The path syntax usually starts with the module name for importing items, though it is also used for importing individual fields of some types, such as enums.

Let's make our Cake public:

```
// mod_within.rs

mod food {
    pub struct Cake;
    struct Smoothie;
    struct Pizza;
}

use food::Cake;

fn main() {
    let eatable = Cake;
}
```

We added pub before our Cake struct and used it in the root module via use food::Cake. With those changes, our code compiles. It's not apparently clear now as to why one would need to create nested modules like so, but we'll get to see how they are used when we write tests in Chapter 3, *Tests, Documentation, and Benchmarks*.

File as a module

Modules can also be created as files. For instance, for a main.rs file in a directory named foo, we can create a module bar as a file in the same directory as foo/bar.rs. Then in main.rs, we need to tell the compiler of this module, that is, declare the module with mod foo;. This is an extra step when using file-based modules. To demonstrate using a file as a module, we have created a directory named modules_demo, which has the following structure:

```
+ modules_demo
 └── foo.rs
 └── main.rs
```

Our foo.rs contains a struct Bar, with its impl block:

```
// modules_demo/foo.rs

pub struct Bar;

impl Bar {
    pub fn init() {
        println!("Bar type initialized");
    }
}
```

We want to use this module in main.rs. Our main.rs, has the following code:

```
// modules_demo/main.rs

mod foo;

use crate::foo::Bar;

fn main() {
    let _bar = Bar::init();
}
```

We declare our module, foo, using mod foo;. We then use the Bar struct from the module by writing use crate::foo::Bar. Notice the crate prefix in use crate::foo::Bar; here. There are three ways to use an item from a module depending on the prefix you use:

Absolute imports:

- crate: An absolute import prefix that refers to the the current crate's root. In the preceding code, this would be the root module, that is, main.rs file. Anything after the crate keyword is resolved from the root module.

Relative imports:

- self: A relative import prefix that refers to an item relative from the current module. This is used when any code wants to refer to its containing module, for example, use self::foo::Bar;. This is mostly used when re-exporting items from a child module to be available from the parent module.
- super: A relative import prefix that can use and import an item from the parent module. A child module such as the tests module would use this to import items from the parent module. For example, if a module bar wants to access an item Foo from its parent module foo, it would import it as use super::foo::Foo; in module bar.

The third way to create modules, is to organize them as directories.

Directory as module

We can also create a directory that represents a module. This approach allows us to have submodules within modules as a file and directory hierarchy. Let's assume that we have a directory, my_program, that has a module named foo as a file foo.rs. It contains a type called Bar along with foo's functionality. Over time, the Bar APIs have grown in number and we wish to separate them as a submodule. We can model this use case with directory-based modules.

To demonstrate creating modules as directories, we have created a program in a directory named my_program. It has an entry point in main.rs and a directory named foo. This directory now contains a submodule within it named bar.rs.

Following is the structure of the directory my_program:

```
+ my_program
  └── foo/
       └── bar.rs
  └── foo.rs
  └── main.rs
```

To let Rust know about bar, we also need to create a sibling file named foo.rs alongside the directory foo/. The foo.rs file will contain mod declarations for any submodules created (here bar.rs) within the directory foo/.

Our bar.rs has the following content:

```rust
// my_program/foo/bar.rs

pub struct Bar;

impl Bar {
    pub fn hello() {
        println!("Hello from Bar !");
    }
}
```

We have a unit struct Bar having an associated method hello. We want to use this API in main.rs.

Note: In the older Rust 2015 edition, submodules don't need a sibling foo.rs alongside the foo directory, and instead use a mod.rs file within foo to convey to the compiler that the directory is a module. Both of these approaches are supported in Rust 2018 edition.

Next, our foo.rs has the following code:

```rust
// my_program/foo.rs

mod bar;
pub use self::bar::Bar;

pub fn do_foo() {
    println!("Hi from foo!");
}
```

We added a declaration of the module bar. Following that, we re-exported the item Bar from the module bar. This requires that Bar is defined as pub. The pub use part is how we re-export an item from a child module to be available from the parent module. Here, we used the self keyword to reference the module itself. Re-exports are mainly a convenience step when writing use statements, which helps remove the clutter when importing an item that is hidden away in nested submodules.

self is a keyword for relative imports. While it's encouraged to use absolute imports using crate, it is much cleaner to use self when re-exporting items from submodules in the parent module.

Finally main.rs uses both modules as:

```
// my_program/main.rs

mod foo;

use foo::Bar;

fn main() {
    foo::do_foo();
    Bar::hello();
}
```

Our main.rs declares foo and then imports the struct Bar. We then invoke the method do_foo from foo and also invoke hello on Bar.

There's more to modules than meets the eye and thus we cover some of the details about them in Chapter 7, *Advanced Concepts*. With modules explored, let's continue with Cargo.

Cargo and crates

When projects get large, a usual practice is to refactor code into smaller, more manageable units as modules or libraries. You also need tools to render documentation for your project, how it should be built, and what libraries it depends on. Furthermore, to support the language ecosystem where developers can share their libraries with the community, an online registry of some sort is often the norm these days.

Cargo is the tool that empowers you to do all these things, and `https://crates.io` is the centralized place for hosting libraries. A library written in Rust is called a crate, and crates.io hosts them for developers to use. Usually, a crate can come from three sources: a local directory, an online Git repository like GitHub, or a hosted crate registry like crates.io. Cargo supports crates from all of these sources.

Let's see Cargo in action. If you ran rustup, as described in the previous chapter, you will already have cargo installed, along with rustc. To see what commands are available to us, we can run cargo without any parameters:

```
→  ~ cargo
Rust's package manager

USAGE:
    cargo [OPTIONS] [SUBCOMMAND]

OPTIONS:
    -V, --version           Print version info and exit
        --list              List installed commands
        --explain <CODE>    Run `rustc --explain CODE`
    -v, --verbose           Use verbose output (-vv very verbose/build.rs output)
    -q, --quiet             No output printed to stdout
        --color <WHEN>      Coloring: auto, always, never
        --frozen            Require Cargo.lock and cache are up to date
        --locked            Require Cargo.lock is up to date
    -Z <FLAG>...            Unstable (nightly-only) flags to Cargo, see 'cargo -Z help' for details
    -h, --help              Prints help information

Some common cargo commands are (see all commands with --list):
    build       Compile the current project
    check       Analyze the current project and report errors, but don't build object files
    clean       Remove the target directory
    doc         Build this project's and its dependencies' documentation
    new         Create a new cargo project
    init        Create a new cargo project in an existing directory
    run         Build and execute src/main.rs
    test        Run the tests
    bench       Run the benchmarks
    update      Update dependencies listed in Cargo.lock
    search      Search registry for crates
    publish     Package and upload this project to the registry
    install     Install a Rust binary
    uninstall   Uninstall a Rust binary
```

It shows a list of common commands that we can use, along with some flags. Let's use the the new subcommand to create a new Cargo project.

Creating a new Cargo project

The cargo new <name> command creates a new project name as a directory. We can get more context on any subcommand by adding a help flag between cargo and the subcommand. We can view documentation for the new subcommand by running cargo help new, as shown in the following screenshot:

```
→  ~ cargo help new
cargo-new
Create a new cargo package at <path>

USAGE:
    cargo new [OPTIONS] <path>

OPTIONS:
        --registry <REGISTRY>    Registry to use
        --vcs <VCS>              Initialize a new repository for the given version control system (git, hg, pijul, or
                                 fossil) or do not initialize any version control at all (none), overriding a global
                                 configuration. [possible values: git, hg, pijul, fossil, none]
        --bin                    Use a binary (application) template [default]
        --lib                    Use a library template
        --edition <YEAR>         Edition to set for the crate generated [possible values: 2015, 2018]
        --name <NAME>            Set the resulting package name, defaults to the directory name
    -v, --verbose                Use verbose output (-vv very verbose/build.rs output)
    -q, --quiet                  No output printed to stdout
        --color <WHEN>           Coloring: auto, always, never
        --frozen                 Require Cargo.lock and cache are up to date
        --locked                 Require Cargo.lock is up to date
    -Z <FLAG>...                 Unstable (nightly-only) flags to Cargo, see 'cargo -Z help' for details
    -h, --help                   Prints help information

ARGS:
    <path>
```

By default, cargo new creates a binary project; the --lib parameter has to be used when creating a library project. Let's try it out by typing cargo new imgtool and taking a look at the directory structure it creates:

```
→  ~ cargo new imgtool
      Created binary (application) `imgtool` package
→  ~ tree imgtool
imgtool
├── Cargo.toml
└── src
    └── main.rs

1 directory, 2 files
→  ~ cat imgtool/src/main.rs

        File: imgtool/src/main.rs

   1    fn main() {
   2        println!("Hello, world!");
   3    }
```

Cargo has created some starter files, Cargo.toml and src/main.rs, with the function main printing Hello World!. For binary crates (executables), Cargo creates a src/main.rs file and for library crates it creates, src/lib.rs under the src/ directory.

Cargo also initializes a Git repository for new projects with the usual defaults, like preventing the target directory from being checked in with a .gitignore file, and checking in the Cargo.lock file for binary crates and ignoring it in library crates. The default Version Control System (VCS) that's used is Git, which can be changed by passing the --vcs flag to Cargo (--vcs hg for mercurial). Cargo as of now supports Git, hg (mercurial), pijul (a version control system written in Rust), and fossil. If we want to modify this default behavior, we can pass --vcs none to instruct Cargo to not configure any vcs when creating our project.

Let's take a look at Cargo.toml for the project imgtool that we created. This file defines your project's metadata and dependencies. It's also known as the project's manifest file:

```
[package]
name = "imgtool"
version = "0.1.0"
authors = ["creativcoders@gmail.com"]
edition = "2018"

[dependencies]
```

This is the minimal Cargo.toml manifest file needed for a new project. It uses the TOML configuration language, which stands for Tom's Obvious Minimal Language. It is a file format that was created by Tom Preston-Werner. It is reminiscent of standard .INI files, but adds several data types to it, which makes it an ideal modern format for configuration files and simpler than YAML or JSON. We'll keep this file minimal for now and add things to it later.

Cargo and dependencies

For projects that depend on other libraries, the package manager has to find all of the direct dependencies in the project and also any indirect dependencies, and then compile and link them to the project. Package managers are not just a tool for facilitating dependency resolution; they should also ensure predictable and reproducible builds of a project. Before we cover building and running our project, let's discuss how Cargo manages dependencies and ensures repeatable builds.

A Rust project managed with Cargo has two files through which it does all its magic: Cargo.toml (introduced before) is the file where you, as the developer, write dependencies and their needed versions with SemVer syntax (like 1.3.*), and a lock file called Cargo.lock, which gets generated by Cargo upon building the project and that contains absolute versions (like 1.3.15) of all the immediate dependencies and any indirect dependencies. This lock file is what ensures repeatable builds in binary crates. Cargo minimizes the work it has to do by referring to this lock file for any further changes to the project. As such, it is advised that binary crates include the .lock file in their repository, while library crates can be stateless and don't need to include it.

Dependencies can be updated using the cargo update command. This updates all of your dependencies. For updating a single dependency, we can use cargo update -p <crate-name>. If you update the version of a single crate, Cargo makes sure to only update parts that are related to that crate in the Cargo.lock file and leaves other versions untouched.

Cargo follows the semantic versioning system (SemVer), where your library version is specified in the format of major.minor.patch. These can be described as follows:

- Major: Is only increased when new breaking changes (including bug fixes) are made to a project.
- Minor: Is only increased when new features are added in backward compatible ways.
- Patch: Is only increased when bug fixes are made in backward compatible ways and no features are added.

For example, you might want to include the serialization library, serde, in your project. At the time of writing this book, the latest version of serde is 1.0.85 , and you probably only care about the major version number. Therefore, you write serde = "1" as the dependency (this translates to 1.x.x in SemVer format) in your Cargo.toml and Cargo will figure it out for you and fix it to 1.0.85 in the lock file. The next time you update Cargo.lock with the cargo update command, this version might get upgraded to whichever is the latest version in the 1.x.x match. If you don't care that much and just want the latest released version of a crate, you can use * as the version, but it's not a recommended practice because it affects the reproducibility of your builds as you might pull in a major version that has breaking changes. Publishing a crate with * as the dependency version is also prohibited.

With that in mind, let's take a look at the cargo build command, which is used to compile, link, and build our project. This command does the following for your project:

- Runs cargo update for you if you don't yet have a Cargo.lock file and puts the exact versions in the lock file from Cargo.toml
- Downloads all of your dependencies that have been resolved in Cargo.lock
- Builds all of those dependencies
- Builds your project and links it with the dependencies

By default, cargo build creates a debug build of your project under the target/debug/ directory. A --release flag can be passed to create an optimized build for production code at the target/release/ directory. The debug build offers faster build time, shortening the feedback loop, while production builds are a bit slower as the compiler runs more optimization passes over your source code. During development, you need to have a shorter feedback time of fix-compile-check. For that, one can use the cargo check command, which results in even shorter compile times. It basically skips the code generation part of the compiler and only runs the source code through the frontend phase, that is, parsing and semantic analysis in the compiler. Another command is cargo run, which performs double duty. It runs cargo build, followed by running your program in the target/debug/ directory. For building/running a release version, you can use cargo run --release . On running Cargo run in our imgtool/ directory, we get the following output:

```
→  imgtool git:(master) ✗ cargo run
   Compiling imgtool v0.1.0 (/home/creativcoder/imgtool)
    Finished dev [unoptimized + debuginfo] target(s) in 0.37s
     Running `target/debug/imgtool`
Hello, world!
```

Running tests with Cargo

Cargo also supports running tests and benchmarks. In-depth testing and benchmarking is covered in `Chapter 3`, *Tests, Documentation, and Benchmarks*. In this section, we will go over a brief introduction on how to run tests using Cargo. We'll write tests for a library crate. To work our way through this section, let's create a crate by running cargo new myexponent --lib:

```
→  Chapter02 git:(master) ✗ cargo new myexponent --lib
    Created library `myexponent` package
→  Chapter02 git:(master) ✗ cd myexponent
→  myexponent git:(master) ✗ tree

├── Cargo.toml
└── src
    └── lib.rs

1 directory, 2 files
→  myexponent git:(master) ✗ cat src/lib.rs

      File: src/lib.rs

   1    #[cfg(test)]
   2    mod tests {
   3        #[test]
   4        fn it_works() {
   5            assert_eq!(2 + 2, 4);
   6        }
   7    }
```

A library crate is similar to a binary crate. The difference is that instead of `src/main.rs` and a main function inside as an entry point, we have `src/lib.rs` with a trivial test function, it_works, which is marked with a `#[test]` annotation. We can run the it_works test function right away using cargo test and see it pass:

```
→  myexponent git:(master) ✗ cargo test
   Compiling myexponent v0.1.0 (/home/creativcoder/book/Mastering-RUST-Second-Edition
    Finished dev [unoptimized + debuginfo] target(s) in 0.45s
     Running target/debug/deps/myexponent-79952b1e9d49f293

running 1 test
test tests::it_works ... ok

test result: ok. 1 passed; 0 failed; 0 ignored; 0 measured; 0 filtered out

   Doc-tests myexponent

running 0 tests

test result: ok. 0 passed; 0 failed; 0 ignored; 0 measured; 0 filtered out
```

Now, let's try a bit of **Test Driven Development (TDD)** with Cargo. We will extend this library by adding a pow function ,with which the users of our library can calculate the exponent for a given number. We'll write a test for this function that initially fails and then fill in the implementation until it works. Here's the new `src/lib.rs`, featuring the pow function without any implementation:

```
// myexponent/src/lib.rs

fn pow(base: i64, exponent: usize) > i64 {
    unimplemented!();
}

#[cfg(test)]
mod tests {
    use super::pow;
    #[test]
    fn minus_two_raised_three_is_minus_eight() {
        assert_eq!(pow(-2, 3), -8);
    }
}
```

Don't worry about the details right now. We have created a single pow function that takes in a base as i64 and a positive exponent as usize, and returns a number that's been raised to the exponent. Under mod tests {, we have a test function called minus_two_raised_three_is_minus_eight that does a single assertion. The assert_eq! macro checks for the equality of the two values that were passed to it. If the left argument is equal to the right argument, the assertion passes; otherwise, it throws an error and the compiler reports the failed test. If we run cargo test, the unit tests obviously fails for pow invocation because we have an unimplemented!() macro invocation there:

```
running 1 test
test tests::minus_two_raised_three_is_minus_eight ... FAILED

failures:

---- tests::minus_two_raised_three_is_minus_eight stdout ----
thread 'tests::minus_two_raised_three_is_minus_eight' panicked at 'not yet implemented', src/lib.rs:3:5
note: Run with `RUST_BACKTRACE=1` for a backtrace.

failures:
    tests::minus_two_raised_three_is_minus_eight

test result: FAILED. 0 passed; 1 failed; 0 ignored; 0 measured; 0 filtered out
```

In brief, unimplemented!() is just a convenient macro to mark unfinished code or code that you wish to implement later, but want the compiler to compile it anyway without giving a type error. Internally, this calls panic! with a message, "not yet implemented". It can be used in cases where you are implementing multiple methods of a trait. For instance, you start implementing one method, but you haven't planned on the implementation for other methods. When compiled, you would get compile errors for the other unimplemented methods if you just placed the function with an empty body. For these methods, we can place an unimplemented!() macro call inside them, just to make the type checker happy and compile for us, and offload the errors at runtime. We will look at more convenient macros like this in Chapter 9, *Metaprogramming with Macros*.

Now, let's fix this problem by implementing a quick and dirty version of the pow function and try again:

```
// myexponent/src/lib.rs

pub fn pow(base: i64, exponent: usize) -> i64 {
    let mut res = 1;
    if exponent == 0 {
        return 1;
    }
    for _ in 0..exponent {
        res *= base as i64;
    }
    res
}
```

Running Cargo test gives the following output:

```
→  myexponent git:(master) ✗ cargo test
    Finished dev [unoptimized + debuginfo] target(s) in 0.01s
     Running target/debug/deps/myexponent-79952b1e9d49f293

running 1 test
test tests::minus_two_raised_three_is_minus_eight ... ok

test result: ok. 1 passed; 0 failed; 0 ignored; 0 measured; 0 filtered out
```

This time, the test passes. Well, that's the basics. We'll do more testing in Chapter 3, *Tests, Documentation, and Benchmarks*.

Running examples with Cargo

To enable users to quickly get started with your crate, it's a good practice to communicate to users how to use your crate with code examples. Cargo standardize this practice, meaning that you can add an examples/ directory within your project root that can contain one or more .rs files, with a main function showing example usage of your crate.

The code under the examples/ directory can be run by using cargo run --examples <file_name>, where the filename is given without the .rs extension. To demonstrate this, we've added an example/ directory for our myexponent crate containing a file named basic.rs:

```rust
// myexponent/examples/basic.rs

use myexponent::pow;

fn main() {
    println!("8 raised to 2 is {}", pow(8, 2));
}
```

Under the examples/ directory, we imported our pow function from our myexponent crate. The following is the output upon running cargo run --example basic:

```
→  myexponent git:(master) X cargo run --example basic
   Compiling myexponent v0.1.0 (/home/creativcoder/book/Mastering-RUST-Second-Edition/Chapter02/myexponent)
    Finished dev [unoptimized + debuginfo] target(s) in 0.38s
     Running `target/debug/examples/basic`
8 raised to 2 is 64
```

Cargo workspace

Over the course of time, your project has gotten quite large. Now, you are thinking about whether you could split the common parts of your code as separate crates to help manage complexity. Well, a Cargo workspace allows you to do just that. The concept of workspaces is that they allow you to have crates locally in a directory that can share the same Cargo.lock file and a common target or output directory. To demonstrate this, we'll create a new project that incorporates Cargo workspaces. The workspace is nothing but a directory with a Cargo.toml file in it. It doesn't have any [package] section, but has a [workspace] section in it. Let's create a new directory called workspace_demo and add the Cargo.toml file like so:

```
mkdir workspace_demo
cd workspace_demo && touch Cargo.toml
```

We then add the workspace section to our Cargo.toml file:

```
# worspace_demo/Cargo.toml

[workspace]
members = ["my_crate", "app"]
```

Within [workspace], the members key is a list of crates within the workspace directory. Now, within the workspace_demo directory, we'll create two crates: my_crate, a library crate and app, a binary crate that uses my_crate.

To keep things simple, my_crate has a public API that simply prints a greeting message:

```
// workspace_demo/my_crate/lib.rs

pub fn greet() {
    println!("Hi from my_crate");
}
```

Now, from our app crate, we have the main function, which calls the greet function of my_crate:

```
// workspace_demo/app/main.rs

fn main() {
    my_crate::greet();
}
```

However, we need to let Cargo know about our my_crate dependency. As my_crate is a local crate, we need to specify it as a path dependency in the Cargo.toml file of app, like so:

```
# workspace_demo/app/Cargo.toml

[package]
name = "app"
version = "0.1.0"
authors = ["creativcoder"]
edition = "2018"

[dependencies]
my_crate = { path = "../my_crate" }
```

Now, when we run cargo build, the binary gets generated in the workspace_demo directory's target directory. Accordingly, we can add multiple local crates within the workspace_demo directory. Now, if we want to add a third-party dependency from crates.io, we need to add it in all of the crates where we need it. However, during cargo build, Cargo makes sure to only have a single version for that dependency in the Cargo.lock file. This ensures that third-party dependencies do not get rebuilt and duplicated.

Extending Cargo and tools

Cargo can also be extended to incorporate external tools for enhancing the development experience. It is designed to be as extensible as possible. Developers can create command-line tools and Cargo can invoke them via simple cargo binary-name syntax. In this section, we'll take a look at some of these tools.

Subcommands and Cargo installation

Custom commands for Cargo fall under the subcommand category. These tools are usually binaries from crates.io, GitHub, or a local project directory, and can be installed by using cargo install <binary crate name> or just cargo install when within a local Cargo project. One such example is the cargo-watch tool.

cargo-watch

Cargo-watch helps you shorten your fix, compile, run cycle by automatically building your project in the background whenever you make changes to your code. By default, this just runs Rust's type checker (the cargo check command) and does not undergo the code generation phase (which takes time) and shortens the compile time. A custom command can also be provided instead of cargo check using the -x flag.

We can install cargo-watch by running cargo install cargo-watch, and then within any Cargo project we can run it by invoking cargo watch. Now, whenever we make changes to our project, cargo-watch will run cargo check in the background and recompile the project for us. In the following code, we made a typo and corrected it, and cargo-watch recompiled the project for us:

```
    Checking myexponent v0.1.0 (/home/creativcoder/book/Mastering-RUST-Second-Edition/Chapter02/myexponent)
    Finished dev [unoptimized + debuginfo] target(s) in 0.11s
[Finished running]
[Running cargo check]
    Checking myexponent v0.1.0 (/home/creativcoder/book/Mastering-RUST-Second-Edition/Chapter02/myexponent)
error[E0412]: cannot find type `i6` in this scope
 --> src/lib.rs:3:43
  |
3 | pub fn pow(base: i64, exponent: usize) -> i6 {
  |                                           ^^ did you mean `i16`?

error: aborting due to previous error

For more information about this error, try `rustc --explain E0412`.
error: Could not compile `myexponent`.
```

This will be a very similar experience if you know about the watchman or nodemon packages from the Node.js ecosystem.

cargo-edit

The cargo-edit subcommand is used to automatically add dependencies to your Cargo.toml file. It can add dependencies of all kinds, including dev dependencies and build dependencies, and also lets you add a specific version of any dependency. It can be installed by running cargo install cargo-edit. This subcommand provides four commands: cargo add, cargo rm, cargo edit, and cargo upgrade.

cargo-deb

This is another useful community developed subcommand that can create Debian packages (.deb) for the easy distribution of Rust executables on Debian Linux. We can install it by running cargo install cargo-deb. We'll use this tool at the end of this chapter to package our imgtool command-line executable as a .deb package.

cargo-outdated

This command shows the outdated crate dependencies in your Cargo project. This can be installed by running cargo install cargo-outdated. Once installed, you can see the outdated crates (if any) by running cargo outdated within the project directory.

Now, the way these subcommands work seamlessly with Cargo is that developers create these binary crates with a naming convention, such as cargo-[cmd], and when you cargo install that binary crate, Cargo exposes the installed binary to your $PATH variable, which can then be invoked with cargo <cmd>. It's a simple and effective way that's been adopted by Cargo to extend itself with community developed subcommands. There are many other such extensions for Cargo. You can find a list of all community curated subcommands at `https://github.com/rust-lang/cargo/wiki/Third-party-cargo-subcommands`.

cargo install is also used to install any binary crates or executables/applications that are developed in Rust. They are installed in the /home/<user>/.cargo/bin/ directory by default. We'll use this to install our imgtool application—which we will build at the end of this chapter – to make it available system wide.

Linting code with clippy

Linting is a practice that helps maintain the quality of your library and have it adhere to standard coding idioms and practices. The de facto linting tool in the Rust ecosystem is clippy. Clippy provides us with a bunch of lints (about 291 at the time of writing this book) to ensure high quality Rust code. In this section, we'll install clippy and try it out on our libawesome library, add some dummy code to it, and see what suggestions we get from clippy. There are various ways of using clippy on your project, but we will use the cargo clippy subcommand way as that's simple. Clippy can perform analysis on code because it's a compiler plugin and has access to a lot of the compiler's internal APIs.

To use clippy, we need to install it by running rustup component add clippy. If you don't have it already, rustup will install it for you. Now, to demonstrate how clippy can point out bad style in our code, we have put some dummy statements within an if condition inside our pow function in the myexponent crate, as follows:

```
// myexponent/src/lib.rs

fn pow(base: i64, exponent: usize) -> i64 {
    ///////////////////// Dummy code for clippy demo
    let x = true;
    if x == true {
    }
    /////////////////////
```

```
        let mut res = 1;
            ...
    }
```

With those lines added, by running cargo clippy in our myexponent directory, we get the following output:

```
→  myexponent git:(master) X cargo clippy
    Checking myexponent v0.1.0 (/home/creativcoder/book/Mastering-RUST-Second-Edition/Chapter02/myexponent)
warning: equality checks against true are unnecessary
 --> src/lib.rs:6:8
  |
6 |       if x == true {
  |          ^^^^^^^^^ help: try simplifying it as shown: `x`
  |
  = note: #[warn(clippy::bool_comparison)] on by default
  = help: for further information visit https://rust-lang.github.io/rust-clippy/master/index.html#bool_comparison

    Finished dev [unoptimized + debuginfo] target(s) in 0.23s
```

Great! Clippy has found a common code style that is redundant, that is, checking for a Boolean value that is either true or false. Alternatively, we could have written the preceding if condition directly as if x {} . There are many more checks that clippy does, and some of them even point out potential mistakes in your code, such as `https://rust-lang-nursery.` `github.io/rust-clippy/master/index.html#absurd_extreme_comparisons`. To see all the available lints and various ways of configuring clippy, head over to `https://github.com/` `rust-lang/rust-clippy`.

Exploring the manifest file – Cargo.toml

Cargo heavily depends on the project's manifest file, the Cargo.toml file, to get all sorts of information for the project. Let's take a closer look at the structure of this file and what items it can contain. As you saw earlier, cargo new creates an almost empty manifest file, filled with just the necessary fields so that a project can be built. Every manifest file is divided into sections that specify the different properties of a project. We will take a look at the sections that are typically found in a moderate sized Cargo project's manifest file. Here's an imaginary Cargo.toml file from a larger application:

```
# cargo_manifest_example/Cargo.toml
# We can write comments with `#` within a manifest file

[package]
name = "cargo-metadata-example"
version = "1.2.3"
description = "An example of Cargo metadata"
documentation = "https://docs.rs/dummy_crate"
license = "MIT"
```

```
readme = "README.md"
keywords = ["example", "cargo", "mastering"]
authors = ["Jack Daniels <jack@danie.ls>", "Iddie Ezzard <iddie@ezzy>"]
build = "build.rs"
edition = "2018"

[package.metadata.settings]
default-data-path = "/var/lib/example"

[features]
default=["mysql"]

[build-dependencies]
syntex = "^0.58"

[dependencies]
serde = "1.0"
serde_json = "1.0"
time = { git = "https://github.com/rust-lang/time", branch = "master" }
mysql = { version = "1.2", optional = true }
sqlite = { version = "2.5", optional = true }
```

Let's go through the parts that we haven't explained yet, starting from the [package] section:

- description: It contains a longer, free-form text field about the project.
- license: It contains software license identifiers, as listed in `http://spdx.org/licenses/`.
- readme: It allows you to link to a file in your project's repository. This should be shown as the entry point to the project's introduction.
- documentation: It contains the link to the crate's documentation if it's a library crate.
- keywords: It is a list of single words that helps in discovering your project either through search engines or through the crates.io website.
- authors: It lists the project's key authors.
- build: It defines a piece of Rust code (typically build.rs) that is compiled and run before the rest of the program is compiled. This is often used to generate code or to build native libraries that the crate depends on.

- edition: This key specifies which edition to use when compiling your project. In our case, we are using the 2018 edition. The previous edition was 2015, which is assumed to be the default if no edition key exists. Note: projects created with the 2018 edition are backward compatible, which means that they can use 2015 crates as dependencies too.

Next is [package.metadata.settings]. Typically, Cargo complains about all of the keys and sections that it doesn't know about, but the sections with metadata in them are an exception. They are ignored by Cargo, so they can be used for any configurable key/value pairs you need for your project.

The [features], [dependencies], and [build-dependencies] sections tie in together. A dependency can be declared by version number, as stated in SemVer's guidelines:

```
serde = "1.0"
```

This means that serde is a mandatory dependency and that we want the newest version, 1.0.*. The actual version will be fixed in Cargo.lock.

Using the caret symbol broadens the version ranges that Cargo is allowed to look for:

```
syntex = "^0.58"
```

Here, we're saying that we want the latest major version, 0.*.*, which must be at least 0.58.*.

Cargo also allows you to specify dependencies directly to a Git repository, provided that the repository is a project that was created by Cargo and follows the directory structure that Cargo expects. We can specify the dependency from GitHub like so:

```
time = { git = "https://github.com/rust-lang/time", branch = "master" }
```

This also works for other online Git repositories such as GitLab. Again, the actual version (or in the case of Git, changeset revision) will be fixed in Cargo.lock by the cargo update command.

The manifest also has two optional dependencies, mysql and sqlite:

```
mysql = { version = "1.2", optional = true }
sqlite = { version = "2.5", optional = true }
```

This means that the program can be built without depending on either. The [features] section contains a list of the default features:

```
default = ["mysql"]
```

This means that if you do not manually override the feature set when building your program, only mysql, and not sqlite, will be pulled in. An example use of features is when your library has certain optimization tweaks. However, this would be costly on an embedded platform, so the library author can release them as features, which will only be available on capable systems. Another example is when you are building a command-line application and also provide a GUI frontend as an extra feature.

That was a quick brief tour on how to describe a Cargo project using the Cargo.toml manifest file. There's quite a lot more to explore on how to configure your project with Cargo. Take a look at `https://doc.rust-lang.org/cargo/reference/manifest.html` for more information.

Setting up a Rust development environment

Rust has decent support for most code editors out there, whether it be vim, Emacs, intellij IDE, Sublime, Atom, or Visual Studio Code. Cargo is also well supported by these editors, and the ecosystem has several tools that enhance the experience, such as the following:

- rustfmt: It formats code according to conventions that are mentioned in the Rust style guide.
- clippy: This warns you of common mistakes and potential code smells. Clippy relies on compiler plugins that are marked as unstable, so it is available with nightly Rust only. With rustup, you can switch to nightly easily.
- racer: It can do lookups into Rust standard libraries and provides code completion and tool tips.

Among the aforementioned editors, the most mature IDE experience is provided by Intellij IDE and Visual Studio Code (vscode). We will cover setting up the development environment for vscode in this chapter as it is more accessible and lightweight. For vscode, the Rust community has an extension known as rls-vscode, which we'll install here. This extension is consists of the Rust language server (RLS), which uses many of the tools that we listed previously internally. We will be setting it up on Visual Studio Code 1.23.1 (d0182c341) with Ubuntu 16.04.

Installing vscode is beyond the scope of this book. You may look for your operating system's package repositories and go to `https://code.visualstudio.com` for more information on the same.

Let's actually open our imgtool application we created at the start of this chapter in vscode:

```
cd imgtool
code .                 # opens the current directory in vscode
```

Once we open our project, vscode recognizes our project automatically as a Rust project and gives us recommendations to download the vscode extension. It will look something like this:

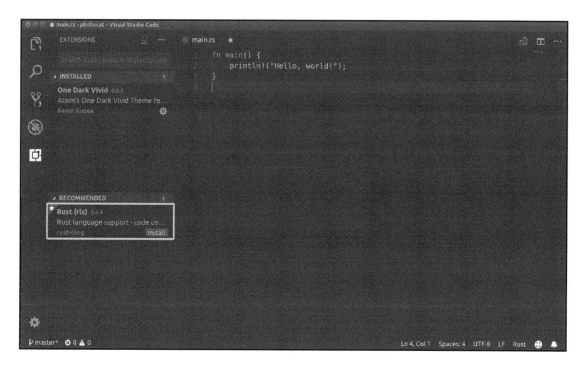

 If you don't get recommendations, you can always type Rust in the search bar on the top left. We can then click on Install and press Reload on the extension page, which restarts vscode and makes it available for use in our project:

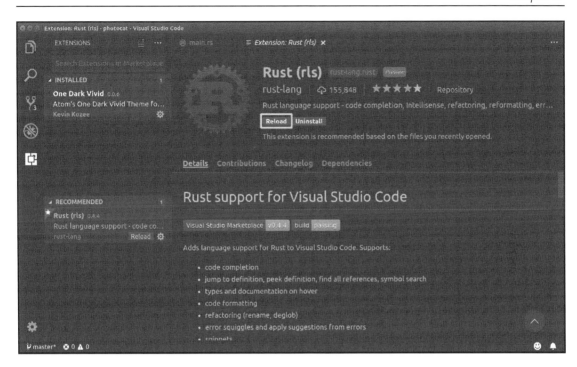

Next time you open the main.rs file in the project and start typing, the extension will kick in and prompt you to install any missing toolchains related to Rust that you can click install. It then starts downloading that toolchain:

After a few minutes, the status will change, like so:

Now, we are good to go.

Note: Since RLS is still in its preview phase, you may experience RLS getting stuck when installing on its first go. By restarting vscode and reinstalling RLS again after removing it, it should work. If it doesn't, feel free to raise an issue on its GitHub page: `rls-vscode`.

With our imgtool project opened, let's see how RLS responds when we try to import a module:

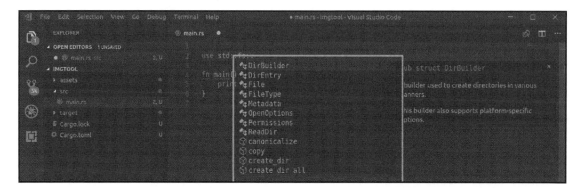

As you can see, it performs auto completion for the items that are available in the fs module in the Rust standard library. Finally, let's take a look at how RLS handles formatting code for us. Let's put all of the code on the same line to demonstrate this:

Let's save the file. We can then use Ctrl + Shift + I or Ctrl + Shift + P and select Format Document. This will instantly format the document and run cargo check against your code once you hit Save:

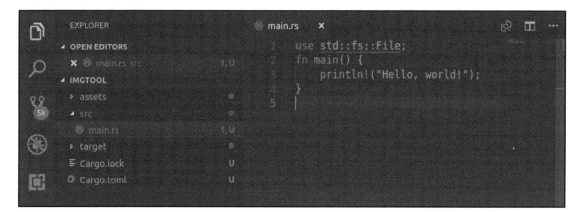

For more information on other code editors, Rust has a page called `https://areweideyet.com` that lists the status of all editors, along with the categories, showing the extent of support they have for the language. Do check them out!

Now, let's continue to implement our imgtool application.

Building a project with Cargo – imgtool

We now have a fairly good understanding of how to manage projects using Cargo. To drive the concepts in, we will build a command-line application that uses a third-party crate. The whole point of this exercise is to become familiar with the usual workflow of building projects by using third-party crates, so we're going to skip over a lot of details about the code we write here. You are encouraged to check out the documentation of the APIs that are used in the code, though.

We'll use a crate called image from crates.io. This crate provides various image manipulation APIs. Our command-line application will be simple; it will take a path to an image file as its argument, rotate it by 90 degrees, and write back to the same file, every time when run.

We'll cd into the imgtool directory, which we created previously. First, we need to tell Cargo that we want to use the image crate. We can use the cargo add image@0.19.0 command to add the image crate with version 0.19.0 from the command line. Here's our updated Cargo.toml file:

```
[package]
name = "imgtool"
version = "0.1.0"
authors = ["creativcoder"]
edition = "2018"

[dependencies]
image = "0.19.0"
```

Then, we'll invoke cargo build. This pulls the image crate from crates.io and pulls its dependencies, before finally compiling our project. Once that is done, we are ready to use it in our main.rs file. For our app, we'll provide an image path as an argument. In our main.rs file, we want to read this image's path:

```
// imgtool/src/main.rs

use std::env;
use std::path::Path;
```

```
fn main() {
    let image_path = env::args().skip(1).next().unwrap();
    let path = Path::new(&image_path);
}
```

First, we read the argument that was passed to imgtool by invoking the args() function from the env module. This returns a string as a path to the image file. We then take the image path and create a Path instance out of it. Next comes the rotate functionality that comes from the image crate. Note that if you're running Rust 2015 edition, you will need an additional extern crate image; declaration on top of main.rs for you to be able to access the image crate's APIs. With Rust 2018 edition, this is not needed:

```
// imgtool/src/main.rs

use std::env;
use std::path::Path;

fn main() {
    let image_path = env::args().skip(1).next().unwrap();
    let path = Path::new(&image_path);
    let img = image::open(path).unwrap();
    let rotated = img.rotate90();
    rotated.save(path).unwrap();
}
```

From the image crate, we use the open function to open our image and store it in img. We then call rotate90 on img. This returns an image buffer as rotated, which we just save back to the original image path by calling save and passing the path. Most of the function calls in the preceding code return a wrapper value called Result, and so we call unwrap() on Result values to tell the compiler that we don't care whether the function call failed, assuming that it has succeeded, and we just want to get the wrapped value from the Result type. We will learn about the Result type and proper error handling methods in Chapter 6, *Error Handling*. For the demo, under the project's asset folder, you will find an image of Ferris the crab (assets/ferris.png). Before running the code, we will see the following image:

Time to run our application with this image as an argument. Now, there are two ways you can run the imgtool binary and pass the image as an argument:

- By doing a cargo build and then invoking the binary manually as ./target/debug/imgtool assets/ferris.png.
- By directly running cargo run -- assets/ferris.png. The double dashes mark the end of the parameters for Cargo's own arguments. Anything after it is passed to our executable (here, this is imgtool).

After running cargo run -- assets/ferris.png, we can see that Ferris has taken a tumble:

Great! Our application works. We can now install our tool by running cargo install inside our imgtool directory and then use it from anywhere in our terminal. Also, if you are on Ubuntu, we can use the cargo deb subcommand to create a deb package so that you can distribute it to other consumers. Running the cargo deb command produces the .deb file, as shown in the following screenshot:

```
→ imgtool git:(master) x cargo deb
warning: description field is missing in Cargo.toml
warning: license field is missing in Cargo.toml
   Compiling nodrop v0.1.12
   Compiling cfg-if v0.1.4
   Compiling num-traits v0.2.5
   Compiling scopeguard v0.3.3
   Compiling memoffset v0.2.1
   Compiling lazy_static v1.0.1
   Compiling rayon-core v1.4.0
   Compiling num-integer v0.1.39
   Compiling unicode-xid v0.1.0
   Compiling libc v0.2.42
   Compiling rayon v1.0.1
   Compiling jpeg-decoder v0.1.15
   Compiling num-derive v0.2.2
   Compiling image v0.19.0
   Compiling imgtool v0.1.0 (/home/creativcoder/book/Mastering-RUST-Second-Edition/Chapter02/imgtool)
    Finished release [optimized] target(s) in 1m 04s
/home/creativcoder/book/Mastering-RUST-Second-Edition/Chapter02/imgtool/target/debian/imgtool_0.1.0_amd64.deb
```

Summary

In this chapter, we got acquainted with the standard Rust build tool, Cargo. We took a cursory look at initializing, building, and running tests using Cargo. We also explored tools beyond Cargo that make developer experience smoother and more efficient, such as RLS and clippy. We saw how these tools can be integrated with the Visual Studio Code editor by installing the RLS extension. Finally, we created a small CLI tool to manipulate images by using a third-party crate from Cargo.

In the next chapter, we will be talking about testing, documenting, and benchmarking our code.

3
Tests, Documentation, and Benchmarks

In this chapter, we will continue with Cargo and learn how to write tests, how to document our code, and how to measure the performance of our code with benchmark tests. We'll then put those skills to use and build a simple crate that simulates logic gates, giving you an end- to-end experience of writing unit and integration tests, as well as documentation tests.

In this chapter, we'll cover the following topics:

- Motivation on testing
- Organizing tests and testing primitives
- Unit tests and integration tests
- Documentation tests
- Benchmark tests
- Continuous integration with Travis CI

Motivation for testing

"Things that are impossible just take longer."

- Ian Hickson

Software systems are like machines with small cogs and gears. If any of the individual gears malfunctions, the machine as a whole is most likely to behave in an unreliable manner. In software, the individual gears are functions, modules, or any libraries that you use. Functional testing of the individual components of a software system is an effective and practical way of maintaining high quality code. It doesn't prove that bugs don't exist, but it helps in building confidence when deploying the code to production and maintaining the sanity of the code base when the project is to be maintained for a long time. Furthermore, large-scale refactoring in software is hard to do without unit tests. The benefits of the smart and balanced use of unit testing in software are profound. During the implementation phase, a well-written unit test becomes an informal specification for components of the software. In the maintenance phase, the existing unit tests serve as a harness against regressions in the code base, encouraging an immediate fix. In compiled languages like Rust, this gets even better as the refactors involved (if any) for regressions from unit tests are more guided due to helpful error diagnostics from the compiler.

Another good side effect of unit tests is that they encourage the programmer to write modular code that is mostly dependent on the input parameters, that is, stateless functions. It moves the programmer away from writing code that depends on a global mutable state. Writing tests that depend on a global mutable state are hard to write. Moreover, the act of simply thinking about writing tests for a piece of code helps the programmer figure out silly mistakes in their implementation. They also act as very good documentation for any newcomer trying to understand how different parts of the code base interact with each other.

The takeaway is that tests are indispensable for any software project. Now, let's look at how we can write tests in Rust, starting by learning about organizing tests!

Organizing tests

At a minimum, there are two kinds of tests that we usually write when developing software: unit tests and integration tests. They both serve different purposes and interact differently with the code base under test. Unit tests are always meant to be lightweight, testing individual components so that the developer can run them often, thus providing a shorter feedback loop, while integration tests are heavy and are meant to simulate real-world scenarios, making assertions based on their environment and specification. Rust's built-in testing framework provides us with sane defaults for writing and organizing these tests:

- **Unit tests**: Unit tests are usually written within the same module that contains the code to be tested. When these tests increase in number, they are organized into one entity as a nested module. One usually creates a child module within the current module, names it `tests` (by convention) with an annotation of the `#[cfg(test)]` attribute over it, and puts all the test-related functions inside of it. This attribute simply tells the compiler to include code within the tests module, but only when `cargo test` is run. More on attributes in a moment.
- **Integration tests**: Integration tests are written separately in a `tests/` directory at the crate root. They are written as if the tests are the consumer of the crate being tested. Any `.rs` file within the `tests/` directory can add a `use` declaration to bring in any public API that needs to be tested.

To write any of the aforementioned tests, there are some testing primitives we need to be familiar with.

Testing primitives

Rust's built-in testing framework is based on a bunch of primitives that are mainly composed of attributes and macros. Before we write any actual tests, it's important that we get familiar with how to use them effectively.

Attributes

An attribute is an annotation on an item in Rust code. Items are top-level language constructs in a crate such as functions, modules, structs, enums, and constant declarations, and other things that are meant to be defined only at the crate root. Attributes are usually compiler built-ins, but can also be created by users through compiler plugins. They instruct the compiler to inject extra code or meaning for the item that appears below them, or for the module if they apply to a module. We'll cover more on these in Chapter 7, *Advanced Concepts*. For the sake of keeping things in scope, we will talk about two forms of attributes here:

- `#[<name>]`: This applies per item and usually appears above them in their definition. For example, test functions in Rust are annotated with the `#[test]` attribute. It signifies that the function is to be treated as part of the test harness.
- `#![<name>]`: This applies to the whole crate. Notice that it has an extra ! there. It usually goes at the very top of your crate root.

 If we are creating a library crate, the crate root is basically `lib.rs`, whereas when creating a binary crate, the crate root would be the `main.rs` file.

There are also other forms of attributes such as `#[cfg(test)]` that are used when writing tests within a module. This attribute is added on top of test modules to hint to the compiler to conditionally compile the module, but only when code is compiled in test mode. Attributes are not just limited to being used in testing code; they are widely used in Rust. We'll get to see more of them in upcoming chapters.

Assertion macros

In testing, when given a test case, we try to assert the expected behavior of our software component on a given range of inputs. Languages usually provide functions called assertion functions to perform these assertions. Rust provides us with assertion functions, implemented as macros, that help us achieve the same thing. Let's take a look at some of the commonly used ones:

```
assert!(true);
assert!(a == b, "{} was not equal to {}", a, b);
```

- `assert!`: This is the simplest assertion macro that takes a Boolean value to assert against. If the value is `false`, the test panics, showing the line where the failure happened. This can additionally take in a format string, followed by a corresponding number of variables, for providing custom error messages:

```
let a = 23;
let b = 87;
assert_eq!(a, b, "{} and {} are not equal", a, b);
```

- `assert_eq!`: This takes in two values and fails if they are not equal. This can also take in a format string for custom error messages.
- `assert_ne!`: This is similar to `assert_eq!` since it takes two values, but only asserts when the values are not equal to each other.
- `debug_assert!`: This is similar to `assert!`. Debug assertion macros can be also be used in code other than test code. This is mostly used in code to assert for any contract or invariant that should be held by the code during runtime. These assertions are only effective on debug builds and help catch assertion violations when run in debug mode. When the code is compiled in optimized mode, these macro invocations are completely ignored and optimized away to a no-op. There are similar variants to this such as `debug_assert_eq!` and `debug_assert_ne!`, which work just like the `assert!` class of macros.

To compare the values within these assertion macros, Rust relies on traits. For example, the `==` inside `assert!(a == b)` actually turns into a method call, `a.eq(&b)`, which returns a `bool` value. The `eq` method comes from the `PartialEq` trait. Most built-in types in Rust implement the `PartialEq` and `Eq` traits so that they can be compared. The details of these traits and the difference between `PartialEq` and `Eq` are discussed in `Chapter 4`, *Types, Generics, and Traits*.

For user-defined types, however, we need to implement these traits. Fortunately, Rust provides us with a convenient macro called **derive**, which takes one or more trait names to implement. It can be used by putting the `#[derive(Eq, PartialEq)]` annotation over any user-defined type. Notice the trait names within parentheses. Derive is a procedural macro that simply generates code for `impl` blocks for the type on which it appears and implements the trait's methods or any associated functions. We'll discuss these macros when we get to `Chapter 9`, *Metaprogramming with Macros*.

With that aside, let's start writing some tests!

Unit tests

In general, a unit test is a function that instantiates a small portion of an application and verifies its behavior independently from other parts of the code base. In Rust, unit tests are usually written within a module. Ideally, they should only aim to cover the module's functionality and its interfaces.

First unit test

The following is our very first unit test:

```
// first_unit_test.rs

#[test]
fn basic_test() {
    assert!(true);
}
```

A unit test is written as a function and is marked with a `#[test]` attribute. There's nothing complex in the preceding `basic_test` function. We have a basic `assert!` call passing in `true`. For better organization, you may also create a child module called **tests** (by convention) and put all related test code inside it.

Running tests

The way we run this test is by compiling our code in test mode. The compiler ignores the compilation of test annotated functions unless it's told to build in test mode. This can be achieved by passing the `--test` flag to `rustc` when compiling the test code. Following that, tests can be run by simply executing the compiled binary. For the preceding test, we'll compile it in test mode by running this:

```
rustc --test first_unit_test.rs
```

With the `--test` flag, `rustc` puts a `main` function with some test harness code and invokes all your defined test functions as threads in parallel. All tests are run in parallel by default unless told to do so with the environment variable `RUST_TEST_THREADS=1`. This means that if we want to run the preceding test in single thread mode, we can execute with `RUST_TEST_THREADS=1 ./first_unit_test`.

Now, Cargo already has support for running tests, and all of this is usually done internally by invoking `cargo test`. This command compiles and runs the test annotated functions for us. In the examples that follow, we will mostly use Cargo to run our tests.

Isolating test code

When our tests grow in complexity, there may be additional helper methods that we might create that only gets used within the context of our test code. In such situations, it is beneficial to isolate the test-related code from the actual code. We can do this by encapsulating all of our test-related code inside a module and putting a `#[cfg(test)]` annotation over it.

The `cfg` in the `#[cfg(...)]` attribute is generally used for conditional compilation and not just limited to test code. It can include or exclude code for different architectures or configuration flags. Here, the configuration flag is `test`. You might remember that the tests in the previous chapter were already using this form. This has the advantage that your test code is only compiled and included in the compiled binary when you run `cargo test`, and otherwise ignored.

Say you want to programmatically generate test data for your tests, but there's no reason to have that code in the release build. Let's create a project by running `cargo new unit_test --lib` to demonstrate this. In `lib.rs`, we have defined some tests and functions:

```
// unit_test/src/lib.rs

// function we want to test
fn sum(a: i8, b: i8) -> i8 {
    a + b
}

#[cfg(test)]
mod tests {
    fn sum_inputs_outputs() -> Vec<((i8, i8), i8)> {
        vec![((1, 1), 2), ((0, 0), 0), ((2, -2), 0)]
    }

    #[test]
    fn test_sums() {
        for (input, output) in sum_inputs_outputs() {
            assert_eq!(crate::sum(input.0, input.1), output);
        }
    }
}
```

We can run these tests by running `cargo test`. Let's go through the preceding code. We generate known input and output pairs in the `sum_inputs_outputs` function, which is used by the `test_sums` function. The `#[test]` attribute keeps the `test_sums` function out of our release compilation. However, `sum_inputs_outputs` is not marked with `#[test]`, and will get included in compilation if it's declared outside the `tests` module. By using `#[cfg(test)]` with a `mod tests {}` child module and encapsulating all the test code and its related functions inside this module, we get the benefit of keeping both the code and the resulting binary clean of the test code.

We also had our `sum` function defined as private without the `pub` visibility modifier, which means that unit tests within modules also allow you to test private functions and methods. Quite convenient!

Failing tests

There are also test cases where you will want your API methods to fail based on some input, and you want the test framework to assert this failure. Rust provides an attribute called #[should_panic] for this. Here's a test that panics and uses this attribute:

```
// panic_test.rs

#[test]
#[should_panic]
fn this_panics() {
    assert_eq!(1, 2);
}
```

The #[should_panic] attribute can be paired with a #[test] attribute to signify that running the this_panics function should cause a non-recoverable failure, which is called a **panic** in Rust.

Ignoring tests

Another useful attribute for writing tests is #[ignore]. If your test code is exceedingly heavy, the #[ignore] annotation enables the test harness to ignore such test functions when running cargo test. You can then choose to individually run those tests by supplying an --ignored parameter to either your test runner or the cargo test command. Here's the code containing a silly loop that, when run using cargo test, is ignored by default:

```
// silly_loop.rs

pub fn silly_loop() {
    for _ in 1..1_000_000_000 {};
}

#[cfg(test)]
mod tests {
    #[test]
    #[ignore]
    pub fn test_silly_loop() {
        ::silly_loop();
    }
}
```

Note the `#[ignore]` attribute over the `test_silly_loop` test function. Here's the output from the ignored test:

```
→  Chapter03 git:(master) x rustc --test ignored_test.rs
→  Chapter03 git:(master) x ./ignored_test

running 1 test
test tests::test_silly_loop ... ignored

test result: ok. 0 passed; 0 failed; 1 ignored; 0 measured; 0 filtered out

→  Chapter03 git:(master) x time ./ignored_test --ignored

running 1 test
test tests::test_silly_loop ... ok

test result: ok. 1 passed; 0 failed; 0 ignored; 0 measured; 0 filtered out

./ignored_test --ignored  42.32s user 0.00s system 99% cpu 42.349 total
→  Chapter03 git:(master) x █
```

Note: A single test can also be run by supplying the test function name to Cargo, for example, `cargo test some_test_func`.

Integration tests

While unit tests can test the private interface of your crate and individual modules, integration tests are kind of like black box tests that aim to test the end-to-end use of the public interface of your crate from a consumer's perspective. In terms of writing code, there is not a lot of difference between writing integration tests and unit tests. The only difference lies in the directory structure and that the items need to be made public, which is already exposed by the developer as per the design of the crate.

First integration test

As we stated previously, Rust expects all integration tests to live in the `tests/` directory. Files within the `tests/` directory are compiled as if they are separate binary crates while using our library under test. For the following example, we'll create a new crate by running `cargo new integration_test --lib`, with the same function, `sum`, as in the previous unit test, but now we have added a `tests/` directory, which has an integration test function defined as follows:

```
// integration_test/tests/sum.rs

use integration_test::sum;

#[test]
fn sum_test() {
    assert_eq!(sum(6, 8), 14);
}
```

We first bring the function `sum` in scope. Second, we have a function, `sum_test`, that calls `sum` and asserts on the return value. When we try to run `cargo test`, we are presented with the following error:

```
→  integration_test git:(master) ✗ cargo test
   Compiling integration_test v0.1.0 (/home/creativcoder/book/Mastering-
error[E0603]: function `sum` is private
 --> tests/sum.rs:3:23
  |
3 | use integration_test::sum;
  |                       ^^^

error: aborting due to previous error

For more information about this error, try `rustc --explain E0603`.
error: Could not compile `integration_test`.
```

This error seems reasonable. We want the users of our crate to use the `sum` function, but in our crate we have it defined as a private function by default. So, after adding the `pub` modifier before the `sum` function and running `cargo test`, our test is green again:

```
   Running target/debug/deps/sum-7332a92ecb202aed

running 1 test
test sum_test ... ok

test result: ok. 1 passed; 0 failed; 0 ignored; 0 measured; 0 filtered out
```

Here's a view of the directory tree of our `integration_test` example crate:

```
.
├──── Cargo.lock
├──── Cargo.toml
├──── src
│     └──── lib.rs
└──── tests
      └──── sum.rs
```

As an example of an integration test, this was very trivial, but the gist of it is that when we write integration tests, we use the crate that's being tested, like any other user of a library would use it.

Sharing common code

As is often the case with integration tests, there is some setup and teardown-related code that we might need to put in place before we can actually run our tests. You usually want them to be shared by all of the files in the `tests/` directory. For sharing code, we can use modules by either creating them as a directory that shares common code, or use a module `foo.rs` and declare in our `integration` test files that we depend on it by putting a `mod` declaration. So, in our preceding `tests/` directory, we added a `common.rs` module that has two functions called `setup` and `teardown`:

```
// integration_test/tests/common.rs

pub fn setup() {
    println!("Setting up fixtures");
}

pub fn teardown() {
    println!("Tearing down");
}
```

In both of our functions, we can have any kind of fixture-related code. Consider that you have an integration test that relies on the existence of a text file. In our function `setup`, we can create the text file, while in our functi0n `teardown`, we can clean up our resources by deleting the file.

To use these functions in our integration test code in `tests/sum.rs`, we put in the `mod` declarations like so:

```
// integration_test/tests/sum.rs

use integration_test::sum;

mod common;

use common::{setup, teardown};

#[test]
fn sum_test() {
    assert_eq!(sum(6, 8), 14);
}

#[test]
fn test_with_fixture() {
    setup();
    assert_eq!(sum(7, 14), 21);
    teardown();
}
```

We have added another function, `test_with_fixture`, that includes calls to `setup` and `teardown`. We can run this test with `cargo test test_with_fixture`. As you may have noticed from the output, we don't get to see our `println!` calls anywhere from within the `setup` or `teardown` functions. This is because, by default, the test harness hides or captures print statements within test functions to make the test results tidier, and only shows the test harness's outputs. If we want to view print statements within our tests, we can run the test with `cargo test test_with_fixture -- --nocapture`, which gives us the following output:

```
     Running target/debug/deps/sum-7332a92ecb202aed

running 1 test
Setting up fixtures
Tearing down
test test_with_fixture ... ok

test result: ok. 1 passed; 0 failed; 0 ignored; 0 measured; 1 filtered out
```

We can see our print statements now. We needed the `--` in `cargo test test_with_fixture -- --nocapture` because we actually want to pass the `--nocapture` flag to our test runner. `--` marks the end of arguments for `cargo` itself, and any argument following that is passed to the binary being invoked by cargo, which is our compiled binary with test harness.

That's about it for integration tests. At the end of this chapter, we'll create a project where we get to see both unit tests and integration tests work in tandem. Next, we'll learn about documenting Rust code, an overlooked but quite important part of software development.

Documentation

Documentation is a very crucial aspect of any open source software aiming for wide adoption by the programmer community. While your code, which should be readable, tells you how it works, the documentation should tell you about the why and how of the design decisions and example usage of the public APIs of your software. Well documented code with a comprehensive README.md page boosts the discoverability of your project many times over.

The Rust community takes documentation very seriously and has tools at various levels to make it easy to write documentation for code. It also makes it presentable and consumable for its users. For writing documentation, it supports the markdown dialect. Markdown is a very popular markup language and is the standard these days for writing docs. Rust has a dedicated tool called **rustdoc** that parses markdown doc comments, converts them to HTML, and generates beautiful and searchable documentation pages.

Writing documentation

To write documentation, we have special symbols for marking the start of documentation comments (doc comments hereafter). Docs are written in a similar fashion, the way we write comments, but they are treated differently compared to ordinary comments and are parsed by rustdoc. The doc comments are divided into two levels and use separate symbols to mark the start of the doc comment:

- **Item level**: These comments are meant for items within the module such as structs, enum declarations, functions, trait constants, and so on. They should appear above the item. For single-line comments, they start with ///, while multi-line comments begin with /** and end with */.
- **Module level**: These are comments that appear at the root level, i.e., main.rs, lib.rs, or any other module, and use //! to mark the start of a line comment – or /*! for multi-line comments – before ending them with */. They are suitable for giving a general overview of your crate and example usage.

Within the doc comment, you can write docs using the usual markdown syntax. It also supports writing valid Rust code within backticks (```let a = 23;```), which becomes part of documentation tests.

The preceding notation for writing comments is actually a syntatic sugar for the `#[doc="your doc comment"]` attribute. These are called **doc attributes**. When rustdoc parses the `///` or `/**` lines, it converts them into these doc attributes. Alternatively, you can also write docs using these doc attributes.

Generating and viewing documentation

To generate documentation, we can use the `cargo doc` command in our project directory. It generates docs in the `target/doc/` directory with a bunch of HTML files and predefined stylesheets. By default, it generates docs for a crate's dependencies too. We can tell Cargo to ignore generating docs for dependencies by running `cargo doc --no-deps`.

To view the documentation, one can spawn a HTTP server by navigating inside the `target/doc` directory. Python's simple HTTP server can come in handy here. However, there's a better way to do this! Passing the `--open` option to `cargo doc` will open the documentation page directly in your default browser.

 `cargo doc` can be combined with `cargo watch` to get a seamless experience in writing documentation and getting live feedback on the generated page for any documentation changes you do on your project.

Hosting documentation

After your documentation has been generated, you will need to host it somewhere for the public to view and use. There are three possibilities here:

- **docs.rs**: Crates that are hosted on `crates.io` get their documentation page automatically generated and hosted on `https://docs.rs`.
- **GitHub pages**: You can host your documentation on the `gh-pages` branch if your crate is on GitHub.
- **External website:** You can manage your own web server for hosting documentation. Rust's standard library documentation is a fine example of this: `https://doc.rust-lang.org/std/`.

As an added note, if your project's documentation spans more than two to three pages and requires a detailed introduction, then there's a better option to generate book-like documentation. This is done by using the `mdbook` project. For more information on that, check out their GitHub page at `https://github.com/rust-lang-nursery/mdBook`.

Doc attributes

We mentioned that the doc comments that we write get converted into doc attributes form. Apart from those, there are other doc attributes for documentation that can tweak the generated documentation page, and these are applied either at the crate level or at the item level. They are written like `#[doc(key = value)]`. Some of the most useful doc attributes are as follows:

Crate-level attributes:

- `#![doc(html_logo_url = "image url")]`: Allows you to add a logo to the top-left of your documentation page.
- `#![doc(html_root_url = "https://docs.rs/slotmap/0.2.1")]`: Allows you to set the URL for the documentation page.

- `#![doc(html_playground_url = "https://play.rust-lang.org/")]`: Allows you to put a run button near the code example in your documentation so that you can run it directly in the online Rust playground.

Item-level attributes:

- `#[doc(hidden)]`: Say you have written the documentation for a public function, `foo`, as a note to yourself. However, you don't want your consumers to view the documentation. You can use this attribute to tell rustdoc to ignore generating docs for `foo`.
- `#[doc(include)]`: This can be used to include documentation from other files. This helps you separate your documentation from code if it's really long.

For more attributes like these ones, head over to `https://doc.rust-lang.org/beta/rustdoc/the-doc-attribute.html`.

Documentation tests

It's often a good practice to include code examples with any documentation for your crate's public APIs. There's a caveat in maintaining such examples, though. Your code might change and you might forget to update your examples. Documentation tests (doctests) are there to remind you to update your example code as well. Rust allows you to embed code in backticks within doc comments. Cargo can then run this example code that's been embedded within your documentation, and treats it as part of the unit test suite. This means that documentation examples run every time you run your unit tests, forcing you to update them. Quite amazing!

Documentation tests are also executed via Cargo. We have created a project called `doctest_demo` to illustrate documentation tests. In `lib.rs`, we have the following code:

```
// doctest_demo/src/lib.rs

//! This crate provides functionality for adding things
//!
//! # Examples
//! ```
//! use doctest_demo::sum;
//!
//! let work_a = 4;
//! let work_b = 34;
//! let total_work = sum(work_a, work_b);
//! ```

/// Sum two arguments
///
/// # Examples
///
/// ```
/// assert_eq!(doctest_demo::sum(1, 1), 2);
/// ```
pub fn sum(a: i8, b: i8) -> i8 {
    a + b
}
```

As you can see, the difference between module-level and function-level doctests is not much. They are used in pretty much the same way. It is just that the module-level doctests show the overall usage of the crate, covering more than one API surface, while function-level doctests cover just the particular function over which they appear.

Documentation tests run with all the other tests when you run `cargo test`. Here's the output when we run `cargo test` in our `doctest_demo` crate:

```
→  doctest_demo git:(master) x cargo test
   Compiling doctest_demo v0.1.0
    Finished dev [unoptimized + debuginfo] target(s) in 0.59s
     Running target/debug/deps/doctest_demo-5fd75d54d0921516

running 0 tests

test result: ok. 0 passed; 0 failed; 0 ignored; 0 measured; 0 filtered out

   Doc-tests doctest_demo

running 2 tests
test src/lib.rs -   (line 6) ... ok
test src/lib.rs - sum (line 18) ... ok

test result: ok. 2 passed; 0 failed; 0 ignored; 0 measured; 0 filtered out
```

Benchmarks

When business needs change and your program gets a requirement to perform more efficiently, the first step to take is to find out the areas that are slow in the program. How can you tell where the bottlenecks are? You can tell by measuring individual parts of your program on various expected ranges or on a magnitude of inputs. This is known as benchmarking your code. Benchmarking is usually done at the very last stage of development (but does not have to be) to provide insights on areas where there are performance pitfalls in code.

There are various ways to perform benchmark tests for a program. The trivial way is to use the Unix tool time to measure the execution time of your program after your changes. But that doesn't provide precise micro-level insights. Rust provides us with a built-in micro benchmarking framework. By micro benchmarking, we mean that it can be used to benchmark individual parts of the code in isolation and remains unbiased from external factors. However, it also means that we should not rely solely on micro benchmarks since the real world results can be skewed. Thus, a micro benchmark is often followed by profiling and macro benchmarking of the code. Nonetheless, micro benchmarking is often a starting point for improving the performance of your code as the individual parts contribute a lot to the overall running time of your program.

In this section, we will discuss the tool that Rust provides as a built in for performing micro benchmarks. Rust lowers the bar for writing benchmarking code right from the initial stages of development, rather than doing it as a last resort. The way you run benchmarks is similar to how tests are run, but uses the `cargo bench` command instead.

Built-in micro-benchmark harness

Rust's built-in benchmarking framework measures the performance of code by running it through several iterations and reports the average time taken for the operation in question. This is facilitated by two things:

- The `#[bench]` annotation on a function. This marks the function as a benchmark test.
- The internal compiler crate `libtest` with a `Bencher` type, which the benchmark function uses for running the same benchmark code in several iterations. This type resides under the `test` crate, which is internal to the compiler.

Now, we'll write and run a simple benchmark test. Let's create a new Cargo project by running `cargo new --lib bench_example`. No changes to `Cargo.toml` are needed for this. The contents of `src/lib.rs` is as follows:

```
// bench_example/src/lib.rs

#![feature(test)]
extern crate test;

use test::Bencher;

pub fn do_nothing_slowly() {
    print!(".");
    for _ in 1..10_000_000 {};
}

pub fn do_nothing_fast() {
}

#[bench]
fn bench_nothing_slowly(b: &mut Bencher) {
    b.iter(|| do_nothing_slowly());
}

#[bench]
fn bench_nothing_fast(b: &mut Bencher) {
```

```
        b.iter(|| do_nothing_fast());
    }
```

Note that we had to specify the internal crate `test` with the `external crate` declaration, along with the `#[feature(test)]` attribute. The `extern` declaration is needed for crates internal to the compiler. In future versions of the compiler, this might not be needed and you will be able to `use` them like normal crates.

If we run our benchmarks by running `cargo bench`, we will see the following:

```
→  bench_example git:(master) x cargo bench
    Compiling bench_example v0.1.0
error[E0554]: #![feature] may not be used on the stable release channel
 --> src/lib.rs:2:1
  |
2 | #![feature(test)]
  | ^^^^^^^^^^^^^^^^^

error: aborting due to previous error

For more information about this error, try `rustc --explain E0554`.
error: Could not compile `bench_example`.

To learn more, run the command again with --verbose.
→  bench_example git:(master) x
```

Unfortunately, benchmark tests are an unstable feature, so we'll have to use the nightly compiler for these. Fortunately, with `rustup`, moving between different release channels of the Rust compiler is easy. First, we'll make sure that the nightly compiler is installed by running `rustup update nightly`. Then, within our `bench_example` directory, we will override the default toolchain for this directory by running `rustup override set nightly`. Now, running `cargo bench` will give the following output:

```
→  bench_example git:(master) x rustup override set nightly
info: using existing install for 'nightly-x86_64-unknown-linux-gnu'
info: override toolchain for '/home/creativcoder/book/Mastering-RUST-Second-Edition/Chapter
ly-x86_64-unknown-linux-gnu'

  nightly-x86_64-unknown-linux-gnu unchanged - rustc 1.33.0-nightly (ceb251214 2019-01-16)

→  bench_example git:(master) x cargo bench
    Finished release [optimized] target(s) in 0.01s
     Running target/release/deps/bench_example-60d11240637eefb7

running 2 tests
test bench_nothing_fast   ... bench:           0 ns/iter (+/- 0)
test bench_nothing_slowly ... bench:          69 ns/iter (+/- 4)

test result: ok. 0 passed; 0 failed; 0 ignored; 2 measured; 0 filtered out
```

Those are nanoseconds per iteration, with the figure inside the parentheses showing the variation between each run. Our slower implementation was quite slow and variable in running time (as shown by the large +/- variation).

Inside our functions marked with #[bench], the parameter to iter is a closure with no parameters. If the closure had parameters, they would be inside ||. This essentially means that iter is passed a function that the benchmark test can run repeatedly. We print a single dot in the function so that Rust won't optimize the empty loop away. If the println!() was not there, then the compiler would have optimized away the loop to a no-op, and we would get false results. There are ways to get around this, and this is done by using the black_box function from the test module. However, even using that does not guarantee that the optimizer won't optimize your code. Now, we also have other third-party solutions for running benchmarks on stable Rust.

Benchmarking on stable Rust

The built-in benchmarking framework provided by Rust is unstable, but fortunately there are community developed benchmarking crates that work on stable Rust. One such popular crate that we'll explore here is criterion-rs. This crate is designed to be easy to use while at the same time providing detailed information on the benchmarked code. It also maintains the state of the last run, reporting performance regressions (if any) on every run. Criterion.rs generates more statistical reports than the built-in benchmark framework, and also generates helpful charts and graphs using *gnuplot* to make it understandable to the user.

To demonstrate using this crate, we'll create a new crate called cargo new criterion_demo --lib. We will add the criterion crate to Cargo.toml as a dependency under the dev-dependencies section:

```
[dev-dependencies]
criterion = "0.1"

[[bench]]
name = "fibonacci"
harness = false
```

We have also added a new section known as [[bench]], which indicates to cargo that we have a new benchmark test named fibonacci and that it does not use the built-in benchmark harness (harness = false), since we are using the criterion crate's test harness.

Now, in `src/lib.rs`, we have a fast and a slow version of a function that computes the nth `fibonacci` number (with initial values of $n_0 = 0$ and $n_1 = 1$):

```rust
// criterion_demo/src/lib.rs

pub fn slow_fibonacci(nth: usize) -> u64 {
    if nth <= 1 {
        return nth as u64;
    } else {
        return slow_fibonacci(nth - 1) + slow_fibonacci(nth - 2);
    }
}

pub fn fast_fibonacci(nth: usize) -> u64 {
    let mut a = 0;
    let mut b = 1;
    let mut c = 0;
    for _ in 1..nth {
        c = a + b;
        a = b;
        b = c;
    }
    c
}
```

`fast_fibonacci` is the bottom-up iterative solution to get the nth **fibonacci** number, whereas the `slow_fibonacci` version is the slow recursive version. Now, criterion-rs requires us to place our benchmarks inside a `benches/` directory, which we created at the crate root. Within the `benches/` directory, we have also created a file named `fibonacci.rs`, which matches our name under the `[[bench]]` in `Cargo.toml`. It has the following content:

```rust
// criterion_demo/benches/fibonacci.rs

#[macro_use]
extern crate criterion;
extern crate criterion_demo;

use criterion_demo::{fast_fibonacci, slow_fibonacci};
use criterion::Criterion;

fn fibonacci_benchmark(c: &mut Criterion) {
    c.bench_function("fibonacci 8", |b| b.iter(|| slow_fibonacci(8)));
}

criterion_group!(fib_bench, fibonacci_benchmark);
criterion_main!(fib_bench);
```

There's quite a lot going on here! In the preceding code, we first declare our required crates and import our the `fibonacci` functions that we need to benchmark (`fast_fibonacci` and `slow_fibonacci`). Also, there is a `#[macro_use]` attribute above `extern crate criterion`, which means to use any macros from a crate, we need to opt for it using this attribute as they are not exposed by default. It's similar to a `use` statement, which is used to expose module items.

Now, criterion has this notion of benchmark groups that can hold related benchmark code. Accordingly, we created a function named `fibonacci_benchmark`, which we then pass on to the `criterion_group!` macro. This assigns a name of `fib_bench` to this benchmark group. The `fibonacci_benchmark` function takes in a mutable reference to a `criterion` object, which holds the state of our benchmark runs. This exposes a method called `bench_function`, which we use to pass in our benchmark code to run in a closure with a given name (above `fibonacci 8`). Then, we need to create the main benchmark harness, which generates code with a `main` function to run all of it by using `criterion_main!`, before passing in our benchmark group, `fib_bench`. Now, it's time to run `cargo bench` with the first `slow_fibonacci` function inside the closure. We get the following output:

```
    Finished release [optimized] target(s) in 2.80s
     Running target/release/deps/criterion_demo-ab08d384846d9c62

running 1 test
test tests::test_exponent ... ignored

test result: ok. 0 passed; 0 failed; 1 ignored; 0 measured; 0 filtered out

     Running target/release/deps/fibonacci-f246ca3e49a531a4
fibonacci 8             time:   [106.78 ns 106.95 ns 107.16 ns]
Found 7 outliers among 100 measurements (7.00%)
  7 (7.00%) high severe

→  criterion_demo git:(master) ✗ 
```

We can see that the recursive version of our `fibonacci` function takes about **106.95 ns** to run on average. Now, within the same benchmark closure, if we replace our `slow_fibonacci` with our `fast_fibonacci` and run `cargo bench` again, we'll get the following output:

```
    Finished release [optimized] target(s) in 2.67s
    Running target/release/deps/criterion_demo-ab08d384846d9c62

running 1 test
test tests::test_exponent ... ignored

test result: ok. 0 passed; 0 failed; 1 ignored; 0 measured; 0 filtered out

    Running target/release/deps/fibonacci-f246ca3e49a531a4
fibonacci 8            time:   [7.8309 ns 7.8460 ns 7.8637 ns]
                       change: [-92.639% -92.615% -92.591%] (p = 0.00 < 0.05)
                       Performance has improved.
Found 3 outliers among 100 measurements (3.00%)
  2 (2.00%) high mild
  1 (1.00%) high severe

→  criterion_demo git:(master) x ▮
```

Great! The `fast_fibonacci` version takes just **7.8460 ns** to run on average. That's obvious, but the great thing about this is the detailed benchmark report, which also shows a human-friendly message: **Performace has improved**. The reason criterion is able to show this regression report is that it maintains the previous state of benchmark runs and uses their history to report changes in performance.

Writing and testing a crate – logic gate simulator

Armed with all of this knowledge, let's start things off with our logic gate simulation crate. We'll create a new project by running `cargo new logic_gates --lib`. Starting with primitive gates implemented as functions such as `and`, `xor`, and so on, we will write unit tests for these gates. Following that, we'll write integration tests by implementing a half adder that uses our primitive gates. During this process, we'll also get to write documentation for our crate.

First off, we'll start with some unit tests. Here's the initial crate code in its entirety:

```
//! This is a logic gates simulation crate built to demonstrate writing
unit tests and integration tests

// logic_gates/src/lib.rs

pub fn and(a: u8, b: u8) -> u8 {
    unimplemented!()
}

pub fn xor(a: u8, b: u8) -> u8 {
    unimplemented!()
}

#[cfg(test)]
mod tests {
    use crate::{xor, and};
    #[test]
    fn test_and() {
        assert_eq!(1, and(1, 1));
        assert_eq!(0, and(0, 1));
        assert_eq!(0, and(1, 0));
        assert_eq!(0, and(0, 0));
    }

    #[test]
    fn test_xor() {
        assert_eq!(1, xor(1, 0));
        assert_eq!(0, xor(0, 0));
        assert_eq!(0, xor(1, 1));
        assert_eq!(1, xor(0, 1));
    }
}
```

We have started with two logic gates, and and xor, which have been implemented as functions. We also have tests cases against those that fail when run because they haven't been implemented yet. Note that to represent bit 0 and 1, we are using a u8 as Rust does not have a native type to represent bits. Now, let's fill in their implementation, along with some documentation:

```
/// Implements a boolean `and` gate taking as input two bits and returns a
bit as output
pub fn and(a: u8, b: u8) -> u8 {
    match (a, b) {
        (1, 1) => 1,
        _ => 0
```

```
        }
    }

    /// Implements a boolean `xor` gate taking as input two bits and returning
    a bit as output
    pub fn xor(a: u8, b: u8) -> u8 {
        match (a, b) {
            (1, 0) | (0, 1) => 1,
            _ => 0
        }
    }
```

In the preceding code, we just expressed the truth tables of the and and xor gates using match expressions. We can see how concise match expressions can be in expressing our logic. Now, we can run the tests by running cargo test:

```
    Finished dev [unoptimized + debuginfo] target(s) in 1.43s
     Running target/debug/deps/logic_gates-0907bf0fe044c345

running 2 tests
test tests::test_xor ... ok
test tests::test_and ... ok
```

All green! We are now ready to write integration tests by implementing a half adder using these gates. A half adder fits in perfectly as an integration test example as it tests the individual components of our crate while they're being used together. Under the tests/ directory, we'll create a file called half_adder.rs that includes the following code:

```
// logic_gates/tests/half_adder.rs

use logic_gates::{and, xor};

pub type Sum = u8;
pub type Carry = u8;

pub fn half_adder_input_output() -> Vec<((u8, u8), (Sum, Carry))> {
    vec![
        ((0, 0), (0, 0)),
        ((0, 1), (1, 0)),
        ((1, 0), (1, 0)),
        ((1, 1), (0, 1)),
    ]
}

/// This function implements a half adder using primitive gates
fn half_adder(a: u8, b: u8) -> (Sum, Carry) {
    (xor(a, b), and(a, b))
```

```
}

#[test]
fn one_bit_adder() {
    for (inn, out) in half_adder_input_output() {
        let (a, b) = inn;
        println!("Testing: {}, {} -> {}", a, b, out);
        assert_eq!(half_adder(a, b), out);
    }
}
```

In the preceding code, we import our primitive gate functions `xor` and `and`. Following that, we have something like `pub type Sum = u8`, which is known as a **type alias**. They are helpful in situations where you either have a type that is cumbersome to write every time or when you have types with complex signatures. It gives another name to our original type and is purely for readability and disambiguation; it has no implications in the way Rust analyzes those types. We then use the `Sum` and `Carry` in our `half_adder_input_output` function, which implements the truth table for the half adder. This is a convenient helper function to test our `half_adder` function that follows it. This function takes in two one-bit inputs and calculates the `Sum` and `Carry` from them before returning them as a tuple of (`Sum`, `Carry`). Further ahead, we have our `one_bit_adder` integration test function, in which we iterate over our half adder input output pairs and assert against the output of the `half_adder`. By running `cargo test`, we get the following output:

```
→  logic_gates git:(master) x cargo test
    Finished dev [unoptimized + debuginfo] target(s) in 0.00s
     Running target/debug/deps/logic_gates-ea0cb9231ae0bb72

running 2 tests
test tests::test_and ... ok
test tests::test_xor ... ok

test result: ok. 2 passed; 0 failed; 0 ignored; 0 measured; 0 filtered out

     Running target/debug/deps/half_adder-9d928a564423f6e0

running 1 test
test one_bit_adder ... ok

test result: ok. 1 passed; 0 failed; 0 ignored; 0 measured; 0 filtered out

   Doc-tests logic_gates

running 0 tests

test result: ok. 0 passed; 0 failed; 0 ignored; 0 measured; 0 filtered out
```

Great ! Let's also generate documentation for our crate by running `cargo doc --open`. The `--open` flag opens the page for us to view in a browser. To customize our documentation, we'll also add an icon to our crate docs page. To do this, we need to add the following attribute at the top of `lib.rs`:

```
#![doc(html_logo_url =
"https://d30y9cdsu7xlg0.cloudfront.net/png/411962-200.png")]
```

After generation, the documentation page looks like this:

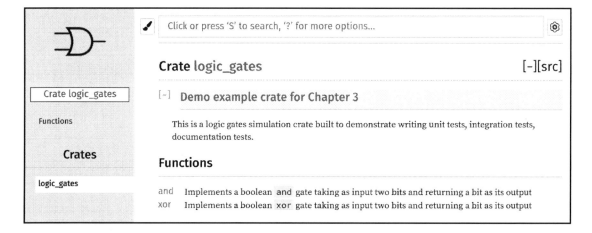

This is great! We have come a long way in our testing journey. Next, let's look at the aspect automating out test suites.

Continuous integration with Travis CI

It is often the case in large software systems that for every change to our code, we want both our unit and integration tests to run automatically. Moreover, in a collaborative project, the manual way is just not practical. Fortunately, Continuous Integration is a practice that aims to automate those aspects of software development. Travis CI is a public continuous integration service that allows you to run your project's tests automatically in the cloud, based on event hooks. One example of an event hook is when new commits are pushed.

Travis is generally used to automate running builds and tests and to report failed builds, but can also be used for creating releases and even deploying them in staging or production environments. We'll focus on one aspect of Travis in this section, performing automated runs of our tests for our project. GitHub already has integration with Travis that can run tests for new commits in our project. To make this happen, we need the following:

- Our project on GitHub
- An account in Travis, which is made by logging in with GitHub
- Your project enabled for builds in Travis
- A `.travis.yml` file at the root of your repository that tells Travis what to run on

The first step is to go to `https://travis-ci.org/` and log in with your GitHub credentials. From there, we can add our GitHub repository in Travis. Travis has good native support for Rust projects and keeps its Rust compiler continuously up to date. It provides a basic version of the `.travis.yml` file for Rust projects, which is as follows:

```
language: rust
rust:
  - stable
  - beta
  - nightly
matrix:
  allow_failures:
  - rust: nightly
```

The Rust project recommends testing against beta and nightly channels too, but you may choose to target just a single version by removing the corresponding lines. This recommended setup runs the tests on all three versions, but allows the fast-moving nightly compiler to fail.

With this `.travis.yml` file in your repository, GitHub will inform Travis CI every time you push your code and run your tests automatically. We can also attach build status badges to our repository's `README.md` file, which shows a green badge when tests pass and a red badge in when tests fail.

Let's integrate Travis with our `logic_gates` crate. For this, we have to add a `.travis.yml` file at our crate root. The following is the contents of the `.travis.yml` file:

```
language: rust
rust:
  - stable
  - beta
  - nightly
matrix:
```

```
    allow_failures:
      - rust: nightly
    fast_finish: true
cache: cargo

script:
  - cargo build --verbose
  - cargo test --verbose
```

After pushing this to GitHub, we then need to enable Travis for our project on their page, as follows:

The preceding screenshot is from my TravisCI account. Now, we'll make a commit to our `logic_gates` repository by adding a simple `README.md` file to trigger the Travis build runner. While we do this, let's also add a build badge to our `README.md` file that will show the status of our repository to consumers. To do this, we'll click the build passing badge on the right:

This opens up a popup menu with the badge link:

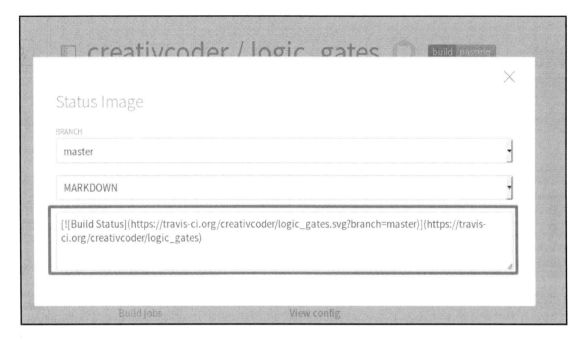

We will copy this link and add it to the top in our README.md file as follows:

```
[![Build
Status](https://travis-ci.org/$USERNAME/$REPO_NAME.svg?branch=master)](http
s://travis-ci.org/creativcoder/logic_gates)
```

You need to replace $USERNAME and $REPO_NAME with your details.

After this change and committing the `README.md` file, we will start to see the Travis build starting and succeeding:

Awesome! If you are feeling more ambitious, you can also try hosting the `logic_gates` crate's documentation on your repository's `gh-pages` branch on GitHub. You can do this by using the `cargo-travis` project, which is available at `https://github.com/roblabla/cargo-travis\`.

For an even more versatile CI setup that covers major platforms, you can use the template provided by the trust project, which is available at `https://github.com/japaric/trust`.

Finally, to publish your crate on *crates.io*, you can follow the directions given in Cargo's reference documentation: `https://doc.rust-lang.org/cargo/reference/publishing.html`.

Summary

In this chapter, we got acquainted with writing unit tests, integration tests, documentation tests, and benchmarks using both `rustc` and the `cargo` tool. We then implemented a logic gate simulator crate and got to experience the whole crate development workflow. Later, we learned how to integrate Travis CI for our GitHub project.

In the next chapter, we'll explore Rust's type system and how to use it to express proper semantics in our program at compile time.

Types, Generics, and Traits

4

Rust's type system is one of the striking features of the language. In this chapter, we'll go into detail on some of the notable aspects of the language such as traits, generics, and how to use them to write expressive code. We'll also explore some of the standard library traits that help with writing idiomatic Rust libraries. Expect lots of interesting material in this chapter!

We'll cover the following topics:

- Type systems and why they matter
- Generic programming
- Augmenting types using traits
- Exploring standard library traits
- Composing traits and generics for writing expressive code

Type systems and why they matter

"Be conservative in what you send, be liberal in what you accept."

- John Postel

Why do we need types in a language? That's a good question to ask as a motivation to understand type systems in programming languages. As programmers, we know that programs written for computers are represented in binary as combinations of 0s and 1s at the lowest level. In fact, the earliest computers had to be programmed manually in machine code. Eventually, programmers realized that this is very error-prone, tedious, and time-consuming. It's not practical for a human to manipulate and reason about these entities at the binary level. Later, during the 1950s, the programming community came up with machine code mnemonics, which turned into the assembly language we know of today. Following that, programming languages came into existence, which compiled down to assembly code and allowed programmers to write code that is human readable yet easy for computers to compile down to machine code. However, the languages that we humans speak can be quite ambiguous, so a set of rules and constraints needed to be put in place to convey what is possible and what is not in a computer program written in a human-like language, that is, the semantics. This brings us to the idea of types and type systems.

A type is a named set of possible values. For example, u8 is a type that can contain only positive values from 0 to 255. Types provide us with a way to bridge the gap between the lower-level representation and the mental model we create of these entities. Apart from this, types also provide us with a way to express intent, behavior, and constraints for an entity. They define what we can and cannot do with types. For example, it is undefined to add a value of a type string to a value of a type number. From types, language designers built type systems, which are sets of rules that govern how different types interact with one another in a programming language. They act as a tool for reasoning about programs and help ensure that our programs behave correctly and according to the specification. Type systems are qualified based on their expressiveness, which simply means the extent to which you can express your logic, as well as invariants in the program using only the type system. For example, Haskell, a high-level language, has a very expressive type system, while C, a low-level language, provides us with very few type-based abstractions. Rust tries to draw a fine line between these two extremes.

Rust's type system is inspired quite a bit by functional languages such as Ocaml and Haskell with their ADTs such as enums and structs, traits (akin to haskell typeclasses), and error handling types (Option and Result). The type system is characterized as a strong type system, which simply means that it performs more type checks at compile time rather than throwing them at runtime. Furthermore, the type system is static, which means that variables that are, for example, bound to an integer value, cannot be changed to point to a string later. These features enable robust programs that rarely break the invariants at runtime, with the cost that writing programs requires a bit of planning and thinking from the programmer. Rust tries to put more planning on your plate when designing programs, which can put off some programmers looking to prototype things fast. However, it is a good thing from the long-term perspective of maintaining software systems.

With that aside, let's start by exploring how Rust's type system enables code reuse.

Generics

From the dawn of high-level programming languages, the pursuit of better abstraction is something that language designers have always strived for. As such, many ideas concerning code reuse emerged. The very first of them was functions. Functions allow you to chunk away a sequence of instructions within a named entity that can be called later many times, optionally accepting any arguments for each invocation. They reduce code complexity and amplify readability. However, functions can only get you so far. If you have a function, say `avg`, that calculates the average of a given list of integer values and later you have a use case where you need to calculate the average for a list of float values too, then the usual solution is to create a new function that can average float values from the list of floats. What if you wanted to accept a list of double values too? We probably need to write another function again. Writing the same function over and over again that differs only by its arguments is a waste of precious time for programmers. To reduce this repetition, language designers wanted a way to express code so that the `avg` function can be written in a way that accepts multiple types, a generic function, and thus the idea of generic programming, or generics, was born. Having functions that can take more than one type is one of the features of generic programming, and there are other places that generics can be used. We'll explore all of them in this section.

Generic programming is a technique that is only applicable in the case of statically typed programming languages. They first appeared in ML, a statically typed functional language. Dynamic languages such as Python use duck typing, where APIs treat arguments based on what they can do rather than what they are, so they don't rely on generics. Generics are part of the language design feature that enables code reuse and the **Don't repeat yourself** (DRY) principle. Using this technique, you can write algorithms, functions, methods, and types with placeholders for types, and specify a type variable (with a single letter, which is usually `T`, `K`, or `V` by convention) on these types, telling the compiler to fill in the actual types later when any code instantiates them. These types are referred to as generic types or items. The single letter symbols such as `T` on type are called **generic type parameters**. They are substituted with concrete types such as `u32` when you use or instantiate any generic item.

Note: By substitution, we mean that every time a generic item is used with a concrete type, a specialized copy of that code is generated at compile time with the type variable T, getting replaced with the concrete type. This process of generating specialized functions with concrete types at compile time is called **monomorphization**, which is the procedure of doing the opposite of polymorphic functions.

Let's look at some of the existing generic types from the Rust standard library.

The Vec<T> type from the standard library is a generic type that is defined as follows:

```
pub struct Vec<T> {
    buf: RawVec<T>,
    len: usize,
}
```

We can see that the type signature of Vec contains a type parameter T after its name, surrounded by a pair of angle brackets < >. Its member field, buf, is a generic type as well, and so the Vec itself has to be generic. If we don't have T on our generic type Vec<T>, even though we have a T on its buf field, we get the following error:

```
error[E0412]: cannot find type `T` in this scope
```

This T needs to be part of the type definition for Vec. So, when we denote a Vec, we always refer to it by using Vec<T> when denoting generically or by using Vec<u64> when we know the concrete type. Next, let's look at how to create our own generic types.

Creating generic types

Rust allows us to declare many things as generics such as structs, enums, functions, traits, methods, and implementation blocks. One thing that they have in common is that the generic type parameters are separated by and enclosed within a pair of < > brackets. Within them, you can put any number of comma-separated generic type parameters. Let's go through how you might create generics, starting by looking at generic functions.

Generic functions

To create a generic function, we place the generic type parameter immediately after the function name and before the parenthesis, like so:

```
// generic_function.rs

fn give_me<T>(value: T) {
    let _ = value;
}

fn main() {
    let a = "generics";
    let b = 1024;
    give_me(a);
    give_me(b);
}
```

In the preceding code, `give_me` is a generic function with `<T>` after its name, and the `value` parameter is of type `T`. In `main`, we can call this function with any argument. During compilation, our compiled object file will contain two specialized copies of this function. We can confirm this in our generated binary object file by using the `nm` command, like so:

```
→  Chapter04 git:(master) ✗ nm generic_function | grep "give"
0000000000005f20 t _ZN16generic_function7give_me17h29bb3e742e0dfeacE
0000000000005f40 t _ZN16generic_function7give_me17h5322ff805bab030bE
```

`nm` is a utility from the GNU binutils package for viewing symbols from compiled object files. By passing `nm` our binary, we pipe and grep for the prefix of our `give_me` function. As you can see, we have two copies of the function with random IDs appended to them to distinguish them. One of them takes a `&str` and the other a `i32`, because of two invocations with different arguments.

Generic functions are a cheap way to give the illusion of polymorphic code. I say illusion because after compilation, it is all duplicated code with concrete types as parameters. They come with a downside though, which is an increase in the size of the compiled object file due to code duplication. This is proportional to the number of concrete types that are used. In later sections, when we get to traits, we'll see the true form of polymorphism, trait objects. Still, polymorphism through generics is preferred in most cases because it has no runtime overhead, as is the case with trait objects. Trait objects should only be used when generics don't cater to the solution and cases where you need to store a bunch of types together in a collection. We'll see those examples when we get to trait objects. Next, we'll look at how we can make our structs and enums generic. We'll only explore how to declare them first. Creating and using these types are covered in the later sections.

Generic types

Generic structs: We can declare tuple structs and normal structs generically like so:

```
// generic_struct.rs

struct GenericStruct<T>(T);

struct Container<T> {
    item: T
}

fn main() {
    // stuff
}
```

Generic structs contain the generic type parameter after the name of the struct, as shown in the preceding code. With this, whenever we denote this struct anywhere in our code, we also need to type the <T> part together with the type.

Generic enums: Similarly, we can create generic enums as well:

```
// generic_enum.rs

enum Transmission<T> {
    Signal(T),
    NoSignal
}

fn main() {
    // stuff
}
```

Our Transmission enum has a variant called Signal, which holds a generic value, and a variant called NoSignal, which is a no value variant.

Generic implementations

We can also write impl blocks for our generic types too, but it gets verbose here because of the extra generic type parameters, as we'll see. Let's implement a new() method on our Container<T> struct:

```
// generic_struct_impl.rs

struct Container<T> {
```

```
        item: T
    }

    impl Container<T> {
        fn new(item: T) -> Self {
            Container { item }
        }
    }

    fn main() {
        // stuff
    }
```

Let's compile this:

```
→  Chapter04 git:(master) x rustc generic_struct.rs
error[E0412]: cannot find type `T` in this scope
 --> generic_struct.rs:7:16
  |
7 |  impl Container<T> {
  |                 ^ not found in this scope

error[E0412]: cannot find type `T` in this scope
 --> generic_struct.rs:8:18
  |
8 |      fn new(item: T) -> Self {
  |                   ^ not found in this scope

error: aborting due to 2 previous errors

For more information about this error, try `rustc --explain E0412`.
```

The error message cannot find our generic type T. When writing an `impl` block for any generic type, we need to declare the generic type parameter before using it within our type. T is just like a variable—a type variable—and we need to declare it. Therefore, we need to modify the implementation block a bit by adding `<T>` after `impl`, like so:

```
    impl<T> Container<T> {
        fn new(item: T) -> Self {
            Container { item }
        }
    }
```

With that change, the preceding code compiles. The previous `impl` block basically means that we are implementing these methods for all types `T`, which appear in `Container<T>`. This `impl` block is a generic implementation. Therefore, every concrete `Container` that ever gets generated will have these methods. Now, we could have also written a more specific `impl` block for `Container<T>` by putting any concrete type in place of `T`. This is what it would look like:

```
impl Container<u32> {
    fn sum(item: u32) -> Self {
        Container { item }
    }
}
```

In the preceding code, we implemented a method called `sum`, which is only present on `Container<u32>` types. Here, we don't need the `<T>` after `impl` because of the presence of `u32` as a concrete type. This is another nice property of `impl` blocks, which allows you to specialize generic types by implementing methods independently.

Using generics

Now, the way we instantiate or use generic types is also a bit different than their non-generic counterparts. Any time we instantiate them, the compiler needs to know the concrete type in place of `T` in their type, signature, which gives it the type information to monomorphize the generic code. Most of the time, the concrete type is inferred based on the instantiation of the type or by calling any method that takes a concrete type in the case of generic functions. In rare cases, we need to help the compiler by specifically typing out the concrete type in place of the generic type by using the turbofish (`::<>`) operator. We'll see how that is used in a moment.

Let's look at the case of instantiating `Vec<T>`, a generic type. Without any type signature, the following code does not compile:

```
// creating_generic_vec.rs

fn main() {
    let a = Vec::new();
}
```

Compiling the preceding code, gives the following error:

```
→ Chapter04 git:(master) x rustc vec.rs
error[E0282]: type annotations needed
 --> vec.rs:2:13
  |
2 |     let a = Vec::new();
  |         ^^^^^^^^ cannot infer type for `T`
  |         |
  |         consider giving `a` a type

error: aborting due to previous error
```

This is because the compiler doesn't know what type a would contain until we specify it manually or call one of its methods, thereby passing in a concrete value. This is shown in the following snippet:

```rust
// using_generic_vec.rs

fn main() {
    // providing a type
    let v1: Vec<u8> = Vec::new();

    // or calling method
    let mut v2 = Vec::new();
    v2.push(2);    // v2 is now Vec<i32>

    // or using turbofish
    let v3 = Vec::<u8>::new();    // not so readable
}
```

In the second code snippet, we specified the type of v1 to be a Vec of u8, and it compiles fine. Another way, as with v2, is to call a method that accepts any concrete type. After the push method call, the compiler can infer that v2 is a Vec<i32>. The other way to create the Vec is to use the turbofish operator, as is the case with v3 binding in the preceding code.

The turbofish operator in generic functions appears right after the function name and before the parenthesis. Another example of this is the generic parse function from the std::str module. parse can parse values from a string, and many types are able to parse from it, such as i32, f64, usize, and so on, so it's a generic type. So, when using parse, you really need to use the turbofish operator, like so:

```rust
// using_generic_func.rs

use std::str;

fn main() {
```

```
        let num_from_str = str::parse::<u8>("34").unwrap();
        println!("Parsed number {}", num_from_str);
}
```

Something to take note of is that only types that implement the `FromStr` interface or trait can be passed to the `parse` function. `u8` has an implementation of `FromStr`, and so we were able to parse it in the preceding code. The `parse` function uses the `FromStr` trait to limit types that can be passed to it. We'll get to know how we can mix generics and traits after we're done exploring traits.

With the idea of generics under our belt, let's focus on one of the most ubiquitous features in Rust, traits!

Abstracting behavior with traits

From a polymorphism and code reuse perspective, it is often a good idea to separate shared behavior and common properties of types from themselves in code and only have methods that are unique to themselves. In doing so, we allow different types to relate to each other with these common properties, which allows us to program for APIs that are more general or inclusive in terms of their parameters. This means that we can accept types that have those shared properties while not being restricted to one particular type.

In object-oriented languages such as Java or C#, interfaces convey the same idea, where we can define shared behavior that many types can implement. For example, instead of having multiple `sort` functions, which take in a list of integer values, and other functions that take in a list of string values, we can have a single `sort` function that can take a list of items that implement the `Comparable` or `Comparator` interface. This allows us to pass anything that is `Comparable` to our `sort` function.

Rust also has a similar yet powerful construct known as **traits**. There are many forms of traits in Rust, and we'll look at most of them and the ways we can interact with them briefly. Also, when traits are mixed with generics, we can restrict the range of parameters that we can pass to our APIs. We'll see how that happens when we learn more about trait bounds.

Traits

A trait is an item that defines a set of contracts or shared behavior that types can opt to implement. Traits are not usable by themselves and are meant to be implemented by types. Traits have the power to establish relationships between distinct types. They are the backbone to many language features such as closures, operators, smart pointers, loops, compile-time data race checks, and much more. Quite a few of the high-level language features in Rust boil down to some type calling a trait method that it implements. With that said, let's look at how we can define and use a trait in Rust!

Let's say we are modeling a simple media player application that can play audio and video files. For this demo, we'll create a project by running `cargo new super_player`. To convey the idea of traits and to make this simple, in our `main.rs` file, we have represented our audio and video media as tuple structs with the name of the media as a `String`, like so:

```
// super_player/src/main.rs

struct Audio(String);
struct Video(String);

fn main() {
    // stuff
}
```

Now, at the very minimum, both the `Audio` and `Video` structs need to have a `play` and `pause` method. It's a functionality that's shared by both of them. It's a good opportunity for us to use a trait here. Here, we'll define a trait called `Playable` with two methods in a separate module called `media.rs`, like so:

```
// super_player/src/media.rs

trait Playable {
    fn play(&self);
    fn pause() {
        println!("Paused");
    }
}
```

We use the `trait` keyword to create a trait, followed by its name and a pair of braces. Within the braces, we can provide zero or more methods that any type implementing the trait should fulfill. We can also define constants within traits, which all of the implementers can share. The implementer can be any struct, enum, primitive, function, closure, or even a trait.

You may have noticed the signature of `play`; it takes a reference to a symbol, `self`, but does not have a body, and ends with a semicolon. `self` is just a type alias to `Self`, which refers to the type on which the trait is being implemented. We'll cover these in detail in `Chapter 7`, *Advanced Concepts*. This means that the methods within the traits are like an abstract method from Java. It is up to the types to implement this trait and define the function according to their use case. However, methods declared within a trait can also have default implementations, as is the case with the `pause` function in the preceding code. `pause` does not take `self`, and so it's akin to a static method that does not require an instance of the implementer to invoke it.

We can have two kinds of methods within a trait:

- **Associated methods**: These are methods that are available directly on the type implementing the trait and do not need an instance of the type to invoke them. There are also known as static methods in mainstream languages, for example, the `from_str` method from the `FromStr` trait in the standard library. It is implemented for a `String` and thus allows you to create a `String` from a `&str` by calling `String::from_str("foo")`.
- **Instance methods**: These are methods that have their first parameter as `self`. These are only available on instances of the type that are implementing the trait. `self` points to the instance of the type implementing the trait. It can be of three types: `self` methods, which consume the instance when called; `&self` methods, which only have read access to the instance its members (if any); and `&mut self` methods, which have mutable access to its members and can modify them or even replace them with another instance. For example, the `as_ref` method from the `AsRef` trait in the standard library is an instance method that takes `&self`, and is meant to be implemented by types that can be converted to a reference or a pointer. We'll cover references and the `&` and `&mut` parts of the type signature in these methods when we get to `Chapter 5`, *Memory Management and Safety*.

Now, we'll implement the preceding `Playable` trait on our `Audio` and `Video` types, like so:

```
// super_player/src/main.rs

struct Audio(String);
struct Video(String);

impl Playable for Audio {
    fn play(&self) {
        println!("Now playing: {}", self.0);
```

```
        }
    }

    impl Playable for Video {
        fn play(&self) {
            println!("Now playing: {}", self.0);
        }
    }

    fn main() {
        println!("Super player!");
    }
```

We write trait implementations with the `impl` keyword followed by the trait name, followed by the `for` keyword and the type we want to implement the trait for, followed by a pair of braces. Within these braces, we are required to provide the implementations of methods, and optionally override any default implementation that exists in the trait. Let's compile this:

```
→  super_player git:(master) ✗ cargo run
   Compiling super_player v0.1.0 (/home/creativcoder/book/Mastering-RUST-Second-Edition,
error[E0405]: cannot find trait `Playable` in this scope
 --> src/main.rs:8:6
  |
8 |  impl Playable for Audio {
  |       ^^^^^^^^ not found in this scope
help: possible candidate is found in another module, you can import it into scope
  |
3 |  use media::Playable;
  |
```

The preceding error highlights an important feature of traits: traits are private by default. To be usable by other modules or across crates, they need to be made public. There are two steps to this. First, we need to expose our trait to the outside world. To do that, we need to prepend our `Playable` trait declaration with the `pub` keyword:

```
// super_player/src/media.rs

pub trait Playable {
    fn play(&self);
    fn pause() {
        println!("Paused");
    }
}
```

After we have exposed our trait, we need to use the `use` keyword to bring the trait into scope in the module we want to use the trait in. This will allow us to call its methods, like so:

```
// super_player/src/main.rs

mod media;

struct Audio(String);
struct Video(String);

impl Playable for Audio {
    fn play(&self) {
        println!("Now playing: {}", self.0);
    }
}

impl Playable for Video {
    fn play(&self) {
        println!("Now playing: {}", self.0);
    }
}

fn main() {
    println!("Super player!");
    let audio = Audio("ambient_music.mp3".to_string());
    let video = Video("big_buck_bunny.mkv".to_string());
    audio.play();
    video.play();
}
```

With that, we can play our audio and video media:

```
→  super_player git:(master) ✗ cargo run
    Finished dev [unoptimized + debuginfo] target(s) in 0.00s
     Running `target/debug/super_player`
Super player!
♪ Now playing: ambient_music.mp3
♪ Now playing: big_buck_bunny.mkv
→  super_player git:(master) ✗
```

This is very far from any actual media player implementation, but our aim was to explore the use case for traits.

Traits can also specify in their declaration that they depend on other traits; this is a feature known as trait inheritance. We can declare inherited traits like so:

```
// trait_inheritance.rs

trait Vehicle {
    fn get_price(&self) -> u64;
}

trait Car: Vehicle {
    fn model(&self) -> String;
}

struct TeslaRoadster {
    model: String,
    release_date: u16
}

impl TeslaRoadster {
    fn new(model: &str, release_date: u16) -> Self {
        Self { model: model.to_string(), release_date }
    }
}

impl Car for TeslaRoadster {
    fn model(&self) -> String {
        "Tesla Roadster I".to_string()
    }
}

fn main() {
    let my_roadster = TeslaRoadster::new("Tesla Roadster II", 2020);
    println!("{} is priced at ${}", my_roadster.model,
my_roadster.get_price());
}
```

In the preceding code, we declared two traits: a `Vehicle` (a more general) trait and a `Car` (more specific) trait, which depends on `Vehicle`. Since `TeslaRoadster` is a car, we implemented the `Car` trait for it. Also, notice the body of the method `new` on `TeslaRoadster`, which uses `Self` as the return type. This is also substituted for the `TeslaRoadster` instance that we return from `new`. `Self` is just a convenient type alias for the implementing type within the trait's impl blocks. It can also be used to create other types, such as tuple structs and enums, and also in match expressions. Let's try compiling this code:

```
→  Chapter04 git:(master) ✗ rustc trait_inheritance.rs
error[E0277]: the trait bound `TeslaRoadster: Vehicle` is not satisfied
 --> trait_inheritance.rs:16:6
    |
16  | impl Car for TeslaRoadster {
    |      ^^^ the trait `Vehicle` is not implemented for `TeslaRoadster`

error: aborting due to previous error

For more information about this error, try `rustc --explain E0277`.
→  Chapter04 git:(master) ✗ ▊
```

See that error? In its definition, the `Car` trait specifies the constraint that any type that implements the trait must also implement the `Vehicle` trait, `Car: Vehicle`. We did not implement `Vehicle` for our `TeslaRoadster`, and Rust caught and reported it for us. Therefore, we must implement the `Vehicle` trait like so:

```
// trait_inheritance.rs

impl Vehicle for TeslaRoadster {
    fn get_price(&self) -> u64 {
        200_000
    }
}
```

With that implementation satisfied, our program compiles fine with the following output:

```
Tesla Roadster II is priced at $200000
```

The underscore in `200_200` in the `get_price` method is a handy syntax to create readable numeric literals.

As an analogy to object-oriented languages, traits and their implementations are similar to interfaces and classes that implement those interfaces. However, it is to be noted that traits are very different from interfaces:

- Even though traits have a form of inheritance in Rust, implementations do not. This means that a trait called `Panda` can be declared, which requires another trait called `KungFu` to be implemented by types that implement `Panda`. However, the types themselves don't have any sort of inheritance. Therefore, instead of object inheritance, type composition is used, which relies on trait inheritance to model any real-world entity in code.
- You can write trait implementation blocks anywhere, without having access to the actual type.
- You can also implement your own traits on any type ranging from built-in primitive types to generic types.
- You cannot implicitly have return types as traits in a function like you can return an *interface* as a return type in Java. You have to return something called a trait object, and the syntax to do that is explicit. We'll see how to do that when we get to trait objects.

The many forms of traits

In the preceding examples, we had a glimpse of the simplest form of trait. But there's more to traits than meets the eye. As you start interacting with traits in bigger code bases, you will encounter different forms of them. Depending on the complexity of the program and the problem to be solved, the simple form of traits might not be suitable. Rust provides us with other forms of traits that model the problem well. We'll take a look at some of the standard library traits and try to classify them so that we have a good idea when to use what.

Marker traits

Traits defined in the `std::marker` module are called **marker traits**. These traits don't have any method, and simply have their declaration with their name with an empty body. Examples from the standard library include `Copy`, `Send`, and `Sync`. They are called marker traits because they are used to simply mark a type as belonging to a particular family for to gain some compile time guarantees. Two such examples from the standard library are the `Send` and `Sync` traits that are auto-implemented by the language for most types whenever appropriate, and convey which values are safe to send and share across threads. We'll get to know more about them in `Chapter 8`, *Concurrency*.

Simple traits

This is the simplest form a trait definition could possibly be. We already discussed this as an introduction to traits:

```
trait Foo {
    fn foo();
}
```

An example from the standard library would be the `Default` trait, which is implemented for types that can be initialized with a default value. It is documented at `https://doc.rust-lang.org/std/default/trait.Default.html`.

Generic traits

Traits can also be generic. This is useful in scenarios where you want to implement a trait for a wide variety of types:

```
pub trait From<T> {
    fn from(T) -> Self;
}
```

Two such examples are is the `From<T>` and `Into<T>` traits, which allow from conversion from a type to a type `T` and vice versa. Their use becomes prominent when these traits are used as trait bounds in function parameters. We'll see what trait bounds are and how they work in a moment. However, generic traits can get quite verbose when they are declared with three or four generic types. For those cases, we have associated type traits.

Associated type traits

```
trait Foo {
    type Out;
    fn get_value(self) -> Self::Out;
}
```

These are a better alternative to generic traits due to their ability to declare associated types within the trait, like the `Out` type in the declaration of `Foo` in the preceding code. They have a less verbose type signature. The advantage of them is that, in the implementation, they allow us to declare the associated type once and use `Self::Out` as the return type or parameter type in any of the trait methods or functions. This removes the redundant specification of types, as is the case with generic traits. One of the finest examples of associated type traits is the `Iterator` trait, which is used for iterating over the values of a custom type. Its documentation can be found at `https://doc.rust-lang.org/std/iter/trait.Iterator.html`. We'll dig deeper into iterators when we get to `Chapter 8`, *Advanced Concepts*.

Inherited traits

We already saw these traits in our `trait_inheritance.rs` code example. Unlike types in Rust, traits can have an inheritance relationship, for instance:

```
trait Bar {
    fn bar();
}

trait Foo: Bar {
    fn foo();
}
```

In the preceding snippet , we declared a trait, `Foo`, that depends on a super trait, `Bar`. The definition of `Foo` mandates implementing `Bar` whenever you are implementing `Foo` for your type. One such example from the standard library is the `Copy` trait, which requires the type to also implement the `Clone` trait.

Using traits with generics – trait bounds

Now that we have a decent idea about generics and traits, we can explore ways in which we can combine them to express more about our interfaces at compile time. Consider the following code:

```
// trait_bound_intro.rs

struct Game;
struct Enemy;
struct Hero;

impl Game {
```

```
        fn load<T>(&self, entity: T) {
            entity.init();
        }
    }

    fn main() {
        let game = Game;
        game.load(Enemy);
        game.load(Hero);
    }
```

In the preceding code, we have a generic function, load, on our Game type that can take any game entity and load it in our game world by calling init() on all kinds of T. However, this example fails to compile with the following error:

```
→  Chapter04 git:(master) ✗ rustc trait_bound_intro.rs
error[E0599]: no method named `init` found for type `T` in the current scope
--> trait_bound_intro.rs:9:16
  |
9 |            entity.init();
  |                   ^^^^
  |

error: aborting due to previous error

For more information about this error, try `rustc --explain E0599`.
```

So, a generic function taking any type T cannot know or assume by default the init method exists on T. If it did, it wouldn't be generic at all, and would only be able to accept types that have the init() method on them. So, there is a way that we can let the compiler know of this and constrain the set of types that load can accept using traits. This is where trait bounds come into the picture. We can define a trait called Loadable and implement it on our our Enemy and Hero types. Following that, we have to put a couple of symbols beside our generic type declaration to specify the trait. We call this a trait bound. The changes to the code are as follows:

```
// trait_bounds_intro_fixed.rs

struct Game;
struct Enemy;
struct Hero;

trait Loadable {
    fn init(&self);
}

impl Loadable for Enemy {
    fn init(&self) {
```

```
        println!("Enemy loaded");
    }
}

impl Loadable for Hero {
    fn init(&self) {
        println!("Hero loaded");
    }
}

impl Game {
    fn load<T: Loadable>(&self, entity: T) {
        entity.init();
    }
}

fn main() {
    let game = Game;
    game.load(Enemy);
    game.load(Hero);
}
```

In this new code, we implement Loadable for both `Enemy` and `Hero` and we also modified the load method as follows:

```
fn load<T: Loadable>(&self, entity: T) { .. }
```

Notice the : `Loadable` part. This is how we specify a trait bound. Trait bounds allow us to constrain the range of parameters that a generic API can accept. Specifying a trait bound on a generic item is similar to how we specify types for variables, but here the variable is the generic type `T` and the type is some trait, such as `T: SomeTrait`. Trait bounds are almost always needed when defining generic functions. If one defines a generic function that takes `T` without any trait bounds, we cannot call any of the methods since Rust does not know what implementation to use for the given method. It needs to know whether `T` has the `foo` method or not to monomorphize the code. Take a look at another example:

```
// trait_bounds_basics.rs

fn add_thing<T>(fst: T, snd: T) {
    let _ = fst + snd;
}

fn main() {
    add_thing(2, 2);
}
```

We have a method, `add_thing`, that can add any type T. If we compile the preceding snippet, it does not compile and gives the following error:

```
→  Chapter04 git:(master) X rustc trait_bound_basics.rs
error[E0369]: binary operation `+` cannot be applied to type `T`
 --> trait_bound_basics.rs:4:5
  |
4 |     fst + snd;
  |     ^^^^^^^^^
  |
  = note: `T` might need a bound for `std::ops::Add`

error: aborting due to previous error

For more information about this error, try `rustc --explain E0369`.
```

It says to add a trait bound Add on T. The reason for this is that the addition operation is dictated by the Add trait, which is generic, and different types have different implementations that might even return a different type altogether. This means that Rust needs our help to annotate that for us. Here, we need to modify our function definition like so:

```
// trait_bound_basics_fixed.rs

use std::ops::Add;

fn add_thing<T: Add>(fst: T, snd: T) {
    let _ = fst + snd;
}

fn main() {
    add_thing(2, 2);
}
```

We added the : Add after T and with that change, our code compiles. Now, there are two ways to specify trait, bounds depending on how complex the type signature gets when defining generic items with trait bounds:

In-between generics:

```
fn show_me<T: Display>(val: T) {
    // can use {} format string now, because of Display bound
    println!("{}", val);
}
```

This is the most common syntax to specify trait bounds on generic items. We read the preceding function as follows `show_me` is a method that takes any type that implements the `Display` trait. This is the usual syntax used to declare the trait bound when the length of the type signature of the generic function is small. This syntax also works when specifying trait bounds on types. Now, let's look at the second way to specify trait bounds.

Using where clauses:

This syntax is used when the type signature of any generic item becomes too large to fit on a line. For example, there is a `parse` method in the standard library's `std::str` module, which has the following signature:

```
pub fn parse<F>(&self) -> Result<F, <F as FromStr>::Err>
where F: FromStr { ... }
```

Notice the `where F: FromStr` part. This tells us that our `F` type must implement the `FromStr` trait. The `where` clause decouples the trait bound from the function signature and makes it readable.

Having seen how to write trait bounds, it's important to know where can we specify these bounds. Trait bounds are applicable in all of the places where you can use generics.

Trait bounds on types

We can specify trait bounds on types too:

```
// trait_bounds_types.rs

use std::fmt::Display;

struct Foo<T: Display> {
    bar: T
}

// or

struct Bar<F> where F: Display {
    inner: F
}

fn main() {}
```

However, trait bounds on types are discouraged as it places restrictions on types themselves. Generally, we want types to be as generic as possible, allowing us to create instances using any type, and instead place restrictions on their behavior using traits bounds in functions or methods.

Trait bounds on generic functions and impl blocks

This is the most common place where trait bounds are used. We can specify trait bounds on functions and also on generic implementations, as shown in the following example:

```
// trait_bounds_functions.rs

use std::fmt::Debug;

trait Eatable {
    fn eat(&self);
}

#[derive(Debug)]
struct Food<T>(T);

#[derive(Debug)]
struct Apple;

impl<T> Eatable for Food<T> where T: Debug {
    fn eat(&self) {
        println!("Eating {:?}", self);
    }
}

fn eat<T>(val: T) where T: Eatable {
    val.eat();
}

fn main() {
    let apple = Food(Apple);
    eat(apple);
}
```

We have a generic type `Food` and a specific food type `Apple` that we put into a `Food` instance and bind to variable `apple`. Next, we call the generic method `eat`, passing `apple`. Looking at the signature of `eat`, the type `T` has to be `Eatable`. To make `apple` eatable, we implement the `Eatable` trait for `Food`, also specifying that our type has to be `Debug` to make it printable to the console inside our method. This is a dumb example but demonstrates the idea.

Using + to compose traits as bounds

We can also specify multiple trait bounds to a generic type using the + symbol. Let's take a look at the impl block for the `HashMap` type from the standard library:

```
impl<K: Hash + Eq, V> HashMap<K, V, RandomState>
```

Here, we can see that `K`, denoting the type of the `HashMap` key, has to implement the `Eq` trait, as well as the `Hash` trait.

We can also combine traits to create a new trait, that represents all of them:

```
// traits_composition.rs

trait Eat {
    fn eat(&self) {
        println!("eat");
    }
}
trait Code {
    fn code(&self) {
        println!("code");
    }
}
trait Sleep {
    fn sleep(&self) {
        println!("sleep");
    }
}

trait Programmer : Eat + Code + Sleep {
    fn animate(&self) {
        self.eat();
        self.code();
        self.sleep();
        println!("repeat!");
    }
}
```

```
struct Bob;
impl Programmer for Bob {}
impl Eat for Bob {}
impl Code for Bob {}
impl Sleep for Bob {}

fn main() {
    Bob.animate();
}
```

In the preceding code, we created a new trait `Programmer`, that is a composition of three traits, `Eat` `Code` and `Sleep`. In this way, we have put constraints on the type, so that if a type `T` implements `Programmer`, it has to implement all the other traits. Running the code produces the following output:

```
eat
code
sleep
repeat!
```

Trait bounds with impl trait syntax

The other syntax for declaring trait bounds is the impl trait syntax, which is a recent addition to the compiler. Using this syntax, you can also write a generic function with trait bounds like this:

```
// impl_trait_syntax.rs

use std::fmt::Display;

fn show_me(val: impl Display) {
    println!("{}", val);
}

fn main() {
    show_me("Trait bounds are awesome");
}
```

Instead of specifying `T: Display`, we directly use `impl Display`. This is the impl trait syntax. This provides advantages in cases where we want to return a complex or unrepresentable type, such as a closure from a function. Without this syntax, you had to return it by putting it behind a pointer using the `Box` smart pointer type, which involves heap allocation. Closures under the hood are implemented as structs that implement a family of traits. One of these traits is the `Fn(T) -> U` trait. So, using the impl trait syntax, it's now possible to write functions where we can write something like this:

```
// impl_trait_closure.rs

fn lazy_adder(a:u32, b: u32) -> impl Fn() -> u32 {
    move || a + b
}

fn main() {
    let add_later = lazy_adder(1024, 2048);
    println!("{:?}", add_later());
}
```

In the preceding code, we created a function, `lazy_adder`, that takes in two numbers and returns a closure that adds two numbers. We then call `lazy_adder`, passing in two numbers. This creates a closure in `add_later` but does not evaluate it. In `main`, we called `add_later` in the `println!` macro. We can even have this syntax in both places, like so:

```
// impl_trait_both.rs

use std::fmt::Display;

fn surround_with_braces(val: impl Display) -> impl Display {
    format!("{{{{}}}}", val)
}

fn main() {
    println!("{}", surround_with_braces("Hello"));
}
```

`surround_with_braces` takes in anything that is `Display` and returns a string surrounded with `{}`. Here, both our return types are `impl Display`.

The extra braces are there to escape the brace itself, as `{}` has a special meaning in string formatting for string interpolation.

The impl trait syntax for trait bounds is mostly recommended to be used as return types from functions. Using it in parameter position means that we can't use the turbofish operator. This can cause API incompatibility if some dependent code uses the turbofish operator to invoke one of your crate's methods. It should only be used when we don't have a concrete type available to us, as is the case with closures.

Exploring standard library traits

Rust's standard library has a lot of built-in traits. Most of the syntatic sugar in Rust is due to traits. These traits also provide a nice baseline upon which crate authors can provide an idiomatic interface to their libraries. In this section, we'll explore some of the abstractions and conveniences of the standard library traits that enhance the experience for a crate author and the consumer. We'll base our exploration from a library author's perspective and create a library that provides support for complex number types. This example serves well to introduce the common traits you have to implement if you are creating a crate of your own.

We'll create a new project by running `cargo new complex --lib`. To start with, we need to represent our complex number as a type. We'll use a struct for this. Our complex number struct has two fields: the *real* and *imaginary* part of a complex number. Here's how we have defined it:

```
// complex/src/lib.rs

struct Complex<T> {
    // Real part
    re: T,
    // Complex part
    im: T
}
```

We're making it generic over `T`, as `re` and `im` can both be a float or an integer value. For this type to be of any use, we want ways to create instances of it. The usual way to do this is to implement the associated method `new`, where we pass the values for `re` and `im`. What if we also wanted to initialize a complex value with defaults (say `re = 0`, `im = 0`)? For this, we have a trait called `Default`. Implementing `Default` is very simple for a user-defined type; we can just put a `#[derive(Default)]` attribute over the `Complex` structure to automatically implement the `Default` trait for it.

Note: `Default` can only be implemented for structs, enums, or unions whose members and fields themselves implement `Default`.

Now, our updated code with the method `new` and the `Default` annotation looks like this:

```
// complex/src/lib.rs

#[derive(Default)]
struct Complex<T> {
    // Real part
    re: T,
    // Complex part
    im: T
}

impl<T> Complex<T> {
    fn new(re: T, im: T) -> Self {
        Complex { re, im }
    }
}

#[cfg(test)]
mod tests {
    use Complex;
    #[test]
    fn complex_basics() {
        let first = Complex::new(3,5);
        let second: Complex<i32> = Complex::default();
        assert_eq!(first.re, 3);
        assert_eq!(first.im, 5);
        assert!(second.re == second.im);
    }
}
```

We also added a simple initialization test case at the bottom under the `tests` module. The `#[derive(Default)]` attribute functionality is implemented as a procedural macro that can automatically implement traits for the type on which it appear. This auto-deriving requires that the fields of any custom type, such as a struct or an enum, also implement the `Default` trait themselves. Deriving a trait using them is only applicable to structs, enums, and unions. We'll look at how to write our own deriving procedural macros in Chapter 9, *Metaprogramming with Macros*. Also, the function `new` is not really a special constructor function (if you are familiar with languages with constructors), but just a conventional name adopted by the community as a method name to create new instances of types.

Now, before we get into more complex trait implementations, we need to auto-derive some more built-in traits that will help us implement more high-level functionality. Let's look at some of them:

- `Debug`: We have already seen this before. As the name suggests, this trait helps types to be printed on the console for debugging purposes. In the case of a composite type, the types will be printed in a JSON-like format with braces and parentheses, and quotes if the type is a string. This is implemented for most built-in types in Rust.
- `PartialEq` and `Eq`: These traits allow two items to be compared to each other for equality. For our complex type, only `PartialEq` makes sense, because when our complex type contains `f32` or `f64` values, we cannot compare them since `Eq` is not implemented for `f32` and `f64` values. `PartialEq` defines partial ordering. whereas `Eq` requires a total ordering, Total ordering is undefined for floats, as NaN is not equal to NaN. NaN is a type in floating point types that represents an operation whose result is undefined, such as `0.0 / 0.0`.
- `Copy` and `Clone`: These traits define how types get duplicated. We have a separate section for them in Chapter 6, *Memory Management and Safety*. In brief, when auto-derived on any custom type, these traits allow you to create a new copy from the instance, either implicitly when `Copy` is implemented or explicitly by calling `clone()` on them when `Clone` is implemented. Please note that the `Copy` trait depends on `Clone` being implemented on types.

With those explanations out of the way, we'll add auto-derives for these built-in traits, like so:

```
#[derive(Default, Debug, PartialEq, Copy, Clone)]
struct Complex<T> {
    // Real part
    re: T,
    // Complex part
    im: T
}
```

Next, let's enhance our `Complex<T>` type more so that we have better ergonomics in terms of its use. Some additional traits we'll implement (in no particular order) are as follows:

- The `Add` trait from the `std::ops` module ,which will let us use the + operator to add `Complex` types
- The `Into` and `From` traits from the `std::convert` module ,which will give us the ability to create `Complex` types from other types

- The `Display` trait, will let us print a human readable version of our `Complex` type

Let's start with the implementation of the `Add` trait. It is documented at `https://doc.rust-lang.org/std/ops/trait.Add.html`, and the trait is declared like so:

```
pub trait Add<RHS = Self> {
    type Output;
    fn add(self, rhs: RHS) -> Self::Output;
}
```

Let's go through it line by line:

- `pub trait Add<RHS = Self>` says that `Add` is a trait that has a generic type, `RHS`, that is set to `Self` by default. Here, `Self` is an alias for the type that implements this trait, which is `Complex` in our case. It's a convenient way to refer to the implementer within the trait.
- `Output` is an associated type that the implementer needs to declare.
- `fn add(self, rhs: RHS) -> Self::Output` is the core functionality that's provided by the `Add` trait and is the method that gets invoked whenever we use + operator between two implementing types. It's an instance method, takes `self` by value and takes in an `rhs` as a parameter, which is `RHS` in the trait definition. In our case, the left-hand side and the right-hand side around the + operator are of the same type by default, but `RHS` can be changed to any other type when we are writing impl blocks. For example, we can have an implementation that adds the `Meter` and `Centimeter` types. In that case, we'll write `RHS=Centimeter` in our impl block. Finally, it says that the `add` method must return the `Output` type that we declared on the second line with the `Self::Output` syntax.

OK, let's try implementing this. Here's the code, along with the tests:

```
// complex/src/lib.rs

use std::ops::Add;

#[derive(Default, Debug, PartialEq, Copy, Clone)]
struct Complex<T> {
    // Real part
    re: T,
    // Complex part
    im: T
}

impl<T> Complex<T> {
```

```
        fn new(re: T, im: T) -> Self {
            Complex { re, im }
        }
    }

    impl<T: Add<T, Output=T>> Add for Complex<T> {
        type Output = Complex<T>;
        fn add(self, rhs: Complex<T>) -> Self::Output {
            Complex { re: self.re + rhs.re, im: self.im + rhs.im }
        }
    }

    #[cfg(test)]
    mod tests {
        use Complex;
        #[test]
        fn complex_basics() {
            let first = Complex::new(3,5);
            let second: Complex<i32> = Complex::default();
        }

        fn complex_addition() {
            let a = Complex::new(1,-2);
            let b = Complex::default();
            let res = a + b;
            assert_eq!(res, a);
        }
    }
```

Let's dig into the `impl` block for `Complex<T>`:

```
impl<T: Add<T, Output=T> Add for Complex<T>
```

The impl block for `Add` seems more complex. Let's go through this piece by piece:

- The `impl<T: Add<T, Output=T>` part says that we are implementing `Add` for a generic type T, where T implements `Add<T, Output=T>`. The `<T, Output=T>` part says that the implementation of the `Add` trait must have the same input and output types.
- `Add for Complex<T>` says that we are implementing the `Add` trait for the `Complex<T>` type.
- `T: Add` has to implement the `Add` trait. If it doesn't, we can't use the + operator on it.

Then comes the `From` trait. It would be convenient if we could also construct `Complex` types from a built-in primitive type such as a two-element tuple, where the first element is the real part and the second is the imaginary part. We can do this by implementing the `From` trait. This trait defines a `from` method, giving us a general way to do conversions between types. Its documentation can be found at `https://doc.rust-lang.org/std/convert/trait.From.html`.

Here's the trait definition:

```
pub trait From<T> {
    fn from(self) -> T;
}
```

This is a bit simpler than the previous one. It's a generic trait, where `T` specifies what type to convert from. When we implement this, we just need to substitute the `T` with the type we want to implement it for and implement the `from` method. Then, we can use the method on our type. Here's an implementation that converts our `Complex` value into a two-element tuple type, which is natively known to Rust:

```
// complex/src/lib.rs

// previous code omitted for brevity

use std::convert::From;

impl<T> From<(T, T)> for Complex<T> {
    fn from(value: (T, T)) -> Complex<T> {
        Complex { re: value.0, im: value.1 }
    }
}

// other impls omitted

#[cfg(test)]
mod tests {
    // other tests
     use Complex;
     #[test]
     fn complex_from() {
         let a = (2345, 456);
         let complex = Complex::from(a);
         assert_eq!(complex.re, 2345);
         assert_eq!(complex.im, 456);
     }
}
```

Let's look at the `impl` line for this one. This is similar to the `Add` trait, except that we don't have to constrain our generic by any special output type, since `From` does not have that:

```
impl<T> From<(T, T)> for Complex<T> {
    fn from(value: (T, T)) -> Complex<T> {
        Complex { re: value.0, im: value.1 }
    }
}
```

The first `<T>` is a declaration of the generic type `T`, and the second and third are the uses of it. We are creating it from a `(T, T)` type.

Finally, to be able to let the users view the complex type as in mathematical notation, we should implement the `Display` trait. It's documented at `https://doc.rust-lang.org/std/fmt/trait.Display.html`, and here's the trait's type signature:

```
pub trait Display {
    fn fmt(&self, &mut Formatter) -> Result<(), Error>;
}
```

The following code shows the implementation of `Display` for the `Complex<T>` type:

```
// complex/src/lib.rs

// previous code omitted for brevity

use std::fmt::{Formatter, Display, Result};

impl<T: Display> Display for Complex<T> {
    fn fmt(&self, f: &mut Formatter) -> Result {
        write!(f, "{} + {}i", self.re, self.im)
    }
}

#[cfg(test)]
mod tests {
    // other tests
    use Complex;
    #[test]
    fn complex_display() {
        let my_imaginary = Complex::new(2345,456);
        println!("{}", my_imaginary);
    }
}
```

The `Display` trait has an `fmt` method, which takes in a `Formatter` type that we write into using the `write!` macro. Like before, because our `Complex<T>` type uses a generic type for both the `re` and `im` fields, we need to specify that it also must satisfy the `Display` trait.

Running `cargo test -- --nocapture`, we get the following output:

```
    Finished dev [unoptimized + debuginfo] target(s) in 0.77s
     Running target/debug/deps/complex-cd1ab394f2b278f3

running 4 tests
test tests::complex_addition ... ok
2345 + 456i
test tests::complex_display ... ok
test tests::complex_from ... ok
test tests::complex_basics ... ok

test result: ok. 4 passed; 0 failed; 0 ignored; 0 measured; 0 filtered out
```

We can see that our complex type is printed in a readable format as `2345 + 456i` and that all of our tests are green. Next, let's look at the idea of polymorphism and how Rust traits model this.

True polymorphism using trait objects

Rust allows a true form of polymorphism through special forms of types implementing a trait. These are known as *trait objects*. Before we explain how Rust achieves polymorphism using trait objects, we need to understand the idea of **dispatch**.

Dispatch

Dispatch is a concept that emerged from the object-oriented programming paradigm, mainly in the context of one of its features called polymorphism. In the context of OOP, when APIs are generic or take parameters implementing an interface, it here has to figure out what method implementation to invoke on an instance of a type that's passed to the API. This process of method resolution in a polymorphic context is called **dispatch**, and invoking the method is called dispatching.

In mainstream languages that support polymorphism, the dispatch may happen in either of the following ways:

- **Static dispatch:** When the method to invoke is decided at compile time, it is known as static dispatch or early binding. The method's signature is used to decide the method to call, and all of this is decided at compile time. In Rust, generics exhibit this form of dispatch because even though the generic function can accept many arguments, a specialized copy of the function is generated at compile time with that concrete type.
- **Dynamic dispatch:** In object-oriented languages, there are times when the method call can't be decided until runtime. This is because the concrete type is hidden and only interface methods are available to call on the type. In Java, this is the case when a function has an argument, which is known as an **interface**. Such a scenario can only be handled by dynamic dispatch. In dynamic dispatch, the method is determined dynamically by navigating through the list of implementations of the interface from the `vtable` and invoking the method. The `vtable` is a list of function pointers that point to each type's implemented method. This has a bit of overhead because of the extra pointer indirection in method invocation.

Let's explore trait objects next.

Trait objects

Now, up until this point, we have mostly seen traits being used in a static dispatch context, where we specified trait bounds in generic APIs. However, we also have another way to create polymorphic APIs, where we can specify parameters as something that implements a trait rather than a generic or a concrete type. This form of type, specified as implementing a trait API, is known as a trait object. Trait objects are similar to C++ virtual methods. A trait object is implemented as a fat pointer and is an unsized type, which means that they can only be used behind references (`&`). We explain unsized types in Chapter 7, *Advanced Concepts*. A trait object fat pointer has the first pointer pointing points to the actual data associated with the object while the second pointer to a virtual table (vtable), which is a structure holding one function pointer per method for the object, at a fixed offset.

Trait objects are Rust's way of performing dynamic dispatch where we don't have the actual concrete type information. Method resolution is done by hopping down to the vtable and invoking the appropriate method. One of the use cases for trait objects is that they allow you to operate on a collection that can have multiple types, but with an extra pointer indirection at runtime. To illustrate this, consider the following program:

```rust
// trait_objects.rs

use std::fmt::Debug;

#[derive(Debug)]
struct Square(f32);
#[derive(Debug)]
struct Rectangle(f32, f32);

trait Area: Debug {
    fn get_area(&self) -> f32;
}

impl Area for Square {
    fn get_area(&self) -> f32 {
        self.0 * self.0
    }
}

impl Area for Rectangle {
    fn get_area(&self) -> f32 {
        self.0 * self.1
    }
}

fn main() {
    let shapes: Vec<&dyn Area> = vec![&Square(3f32), &Rectangle(4f32,
2f32)];
    for s in shapes {
        println!("{:?}", s);
    }
}
```

As you can see, the elements of shapes are of type `&dyn Area`, a type that is represented as a trait. The trait object is represented by `dyn Area`, denoting that it's a pointer to some implementation of the `Area` trait. A type in the form of a trait object allows you to store different types within a collection type such as `Vec`. In the preceding example, `Square` and `Rectangle` were converted into trait objects implicitly because we pushed a reference to them. We can also make a type, a trait object by casting it manually. This is an advanced case, though, and is used when the compiler cannot cast the type as a trait object by itself.

Do note that we can only create trait objects of types whose sizes we know at compile time. A `dyn Trait` is an unsized type and can only be created as a reference. We can also create trait objects by putting them behind other pointer types such as `Box`, `Rc`, `Arc`, and so on.

 In the older Rust 2015 edition, trait objects are referred to as just the name of the trait, for a trait object `dyn Foo`, it is represented as `Foo`. This syntax is confusing and it deprecated in the latest 2018 edition.

In the following code, we are illustrating the use of `dyn Trait` as a parameters in functions:

```
// dyn_trait.rs

use std::fmt::Display;

fn show_me(item: &dyn Display) {
    println!("{}", item);
}

fn main() {
    show_me(&"Hello trait object");
}
```

Traits, along with generics, provide both kinds of code reuse, either through monomorphization (early binding) or through runtime polymorphism (late binding). The decision on when to use which depends on the context and the needs of the application in question. Often, error types are taken toward the dynamic dispatch train as they are supposed to be code paths that rarely get executed. Monomorphization can be handy for small use cases, but the downside to it is that it introduces code bloat and duplication, which affects the cache line and increases binary size. However, of these two options, static dispatch should be preferred unless there is a hard constraint on binary size.

Summary

Types are one of the most beautiful aspects of any statically typed language. They allow you to express so much at compile time. This chapter might not be the most advanced in this book, but the content was probably the heaviest. We now have a working knowledge of the different ways to reuse code. We also got to know about the mighty traits and how Rust's standard library makes heavy use of them.

In the next chapter, we'll learn about how programs use memory and how Rust provides compile-time memory management.

5
Memory Management and Safety

Memory management is a fundamental concept to understand for anyone working with a low-level programming language. Low-level languages don't come with automatic memory reclamation solutions like a built-in garbage collector, and it's the responsibility of the programmer to manage memory that's used by the program. Having knowledge of where and how memory gets used in a program enables programmers to build efficient and safe software systems. A lot of bugs in low-level software are due to improper handling of memory. At times, it's the programmer's mistake. The other times, it's the side effect of the programming language used, such as C and C++, which are infamous for a lot of memory vulnerability reports in software. Rust offers a better, compile-time solution to memory management. It makes it hard to write software that leaks memory unless you explicitly intend to! Programmers who have done a fair amount of development with Rust eventually come to the realization that it discourages bad programming practices and directs the programmer toward writing software that uses memory safely and efficiently.

In this chapter, we go into the nitty-gritty details of how Rust tames the memory that's used by resources in a program. We'll give a brief introduction to processes, memory allocation, memory management, and what we mean by memory safety. Then, we'll go through the memory safety model provided by Rust and understand the concepts that enable it to track memory usage at compile time. We'll see how traits are used to control where types reside in memory and when they get freed. We'll also delve into various smart pointer types that provide abstractions to manage resources in the program.

The topics that are covered in this chapter are as follows:

- Programs and memory
- Memory allocations and safety
- Memory management
- Stack and Heap
- Trifecta of safety—Ownership, borrowing, and lifetimes
- Smart pointer types

Programs and memory

"If you're willing to restrict the flexibility of your approach, you can almost always do something better."

– John Carmack

As a motivation to understand memory and its management, it's important for us to have a general idea of how programs are run by the operating system and what mechanisms are in place that allow it to use memory for its requirements.

Every program needs memory to run, whether it's your favorite command-line tool or a complex stream processing service, and they have vastly different memory requirements. In major operating system implementations, a program in execution is implemented as a process. A process is a running instance of a program. When we execute `./my_program` in a shell in Linux or double-click on `my_program.exe` on Windows, the OS loads `my_program` as a process in memory and starts executing it, along with other processes, giving it a share of CPU and memory. It assigns the process with its own virtual address space, which is distinct from the virtual address space of other processes and has its own view of memory.

During the lifetime of a process, it uses many system resources. First, it needs memory to store its own instructions, then it needs space for resources that are demanded at runtime during instruction execution, then it needs a way to keep track of function calls, any local variables, and the address to return to after the last invoked function. Some of these memory requirements can be decided ahead at compile time, like storing a primitive type in a variable, while others can only be satisfied at runtime, like creating a dynamic data type such as `Vec<String>`. Due to the various tiers of memory requirements, and also for security purposes, a process's view of memory is divided into regions known as the memory layout.

Here, we have an approximate representation of the memory layout of a process in general:

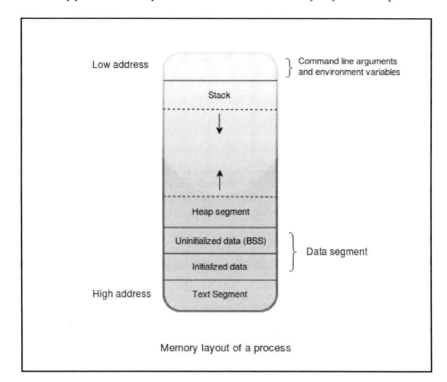

Memory layout of a process

This layout is divided into various regions based on the kind of data they store and the functionality they provide. The major parts we are concerned with are as follows:

- **Text segment**: This section contains the actual code to be executed in the compiled binary. The text segment is a read-only segment and any user code is forbidden to modify it. Doing so can result in a crash of the program.
- **Data segment**: This is further divided into subsections, that is, the initialized data segment and uninitialized data segment, which is historically known as **Block Started by Symbol (BSS)**, and holds all global and static values declared in the program. Uninitialized values are initialized to zero when they are loaded into memory.
- **Stack segment**: This segment is used to hold any local variables and the return addresses of functions. All resources whose sizes are known in advance and any temporary/intermediary variables that a program creates are implicitly stored on the stack.

- **Heap segment**: This segment is used to store any dynamically allocated data whose size is not known up front and can change at runtime depending on the needs of the program. This is the ideal allocation place when we want values to outlive their declaration within a function.

How do programs use memory?

So, we know that a process has a chunk of memory dedicated for its execution. But, how does it access this memory to perform its task? For security purposes and fault isolation, a process is not allowed to access the physical memory directly. Instead, it uses a virtual memory, which is mapped to the actual physical memory by the OS using an in-memory data structure called **pages**, which are maintained in **page tables**. The process has to request memory from the OS for its use, and what it gets is a virtual address that is internally mapped to a physical address in the RAM. For performance reasons, this memory is requested and processed in chunks. When virtual memory is accessed by the process, the memory management unit does the actual conversion from virtual to physical memory.

The whole series of steps through which memory is acquired by a process from the OS is known as **memory allocation**. A process requests a chunk of memory from the OS by using *system calls*, and the OS marks that chunk of memory in use by that process. When the process is done using the memory, it has to mark the memory as free so other processes can use it. This is called **de-allocation** of memory. Major operating system implementations provide abstractions through system calls (such as `brk` and `sbrk` in Linux), which are functions that talk directly to the OS kernel and can allocate memory requested by the process. But these kernel-level functions are very low-level, so they are further abstracted by system libraries such as the **glibc** library, which is C's standard library in Linux including the implementation of the POSIX APIs, facilitating low-level interactions with the OS from the C language.

POSIX is an acronym for Portable Operating System Interface, a term coind by Richard Stallman. It is a set of standards that emerged with the need to standardize what functionality, a Unix-like operating system should provide, what low level APIs they should expose to languages such as C, what command-line utilities they should include, and many other aspects.

Glibc also provides a memory allocator API, exposing functions such as `malloc`, `calloc`, and `realloc` for allocating memory and the `free` function for de-allocating memory. Even though we have a fairly high-level API for allocating/de-allocating memory, we still have to manage memory ourselves when using low-level programming languages.

Memory management and its kinds

The RAM in your computer is a limited resource and is shared by all running programs. It's a necessity that when a program is done executing its instructions, it is expected to release any memory used so that the OS can reclaim it and hand it to other processes. When we talk about memory management, a prominent aspect we care about is the reclamation of used memory and how that happens. The level of management required in deallocating used memory is different in different languages. Up until the mid-1990s, the majority of programming languages relied on manual memory management, which required the programmer to call memory allocator APIs such as `malloc` and `free` in code to allocate and deallocate memory, respectively. Around 1959, *John McCarthy*, the creator of *Lisp*, invented **Garbage Collectors** (**GC**), a form of automatic memory management and Lisp was the first language to use one. A GC runs as a daemon thread as part of the running program and analyzes the memory that is no longer being referenced by any variable in the program and frees it automatically at certain points in time along with program execution.

However, low-level languages don't come with a GC as it introduces non-determinism and a runtime overhead due to the GC thread running in the background, which in some cases pauses the execution of the program. This pause sometimes reaches to a milisecond of latency. This might violate the hard time and space constraints of system software. Low-level languages put the programmer in control of managing memory manually. However, languages such as C++ and Rust take some of this burden off from programmers, through type system abstractions like smart pointers, which we'll cover later in the chapter.

Given the difference between languages, we can classify the memory management strategies that are used by them into three buckets:

- **Manual**: *C* has this form of memory management, where it's completely the programmers responsibility to put `free` calls after the code is done using memory. C++ automates this to some extent using smart pointers where the `free` call is put in a class's deconstructor method definition. Rust also has smart pointers, which we will cover later in this chapter.

- **Automatic**: Languages with this form of memory management include an additional runtime thread,that is the Garbage Collector, that runs alongside the program as a daemon thread. Most dynamic languages based on a virtual machine such Python, Java, C# and Ruby rely on automatic memory management. Automatic memory management is one of the reasons that writing code in these languages is easy.
- **Semi-automatic**: Languages such as Swift fall into this category. They don't have a dedicated GC built in as part of the runtime, but offer a reference counting type, which does automatic management of memory at a granular level. Rust also provides the reference counting types `Rc<T>` and `Arc<T>`. We'll get to them when we explain about *smart pointers*, later in this chapter.

Approaches to memory allocation

At runtime, memory allocations in a process happens either on the *stack* or on the *heap*. They are storage locations that are used to store values during the execution of the program. In this section, we'll take a look at both of these allocation approaches.

The stack is used for short-lived values whose sizes are known as compile time, and is the ideal storage location for function calls and their associated context, which needs to go away once the function returns. The heap is for anything that needs to live beyond function calls. As mentioned in `Chapter 1`, *Getting Started with Rust*, Rust prefers stack allocation by default. Any value or instance of a type that you create and bind to a variable gets stored on the stack by default. Storing on the heap is explicit and is done by using smart pointer types, which are explained later in this chapter.

The stack

Any time we call a function or a method, the stack is used for allocating space for values that are created within the function. All of the `let` bindings in your functions are stored in the stack, either as values themselves or as pointers to memory locations on the heap. These values constitute the **stack frame** for the active function. A stack frame is a logical block of memory in the stack that stores the context of a function call. This context may include function arguments, local variables, return addresses, and any saved register's values that need to be restored after returning from the function. As more and more functions get called, their corresponding stack frames are pushed onto the stack. Once a function returns, the stack frame corresponding to the function goes away, along with all values declared within that frame.

These values are removed in the reverse order of their declaration, following the **Last In First Out** (**LIFO**) order.

Allocation on the stack is fast because allocating and deallocating memory here requires just one CPU instruction: incrementing/decrementing the stack frame pointer. The stack frame pointer (esp) is a CPU register that always points to the top of the stack. The stack frame pointer keeps on updating as functions get called, or when they return. When a function returns, its stack frame is discarded by restoring the stack frame pointer to where it was before entering the function. Using stacks is a temporary memory allocation strategy, but it is reliable in terms of releasing used memory because of its simplicity. However, the same property of a stack makes it unsuitable for cases where we need longer living values beyond the current stack frame.

Here's a piece of code to roughly illustrate how the stack gets updated in a program during function calls:

```
// stack_basics.rs

fn double_of(b: i32) -> i32 {
    let x = 2 * b;
    x
}

fn main() {
    let a = 12;
    let result = double_of(a);
}
```

We'll represent the state of the stack for this program by an empty array []. Let's explore the stack contents by doing a dry run of this program. We'll use [] to also represent stack frames within our parent stack. When this program is run, the following are the sequence of steps that happens:

1. When the main function is invoked, it creates the stack frame, which holds a and result (initialized to zero). The stack is now [[a=12, result=0]].
2. Next, the double_of function is called and a new stack frame is push onto the stack to hold its local values. The stack's contents is now [[a=12, result=0], [b=12, temp_double=2*x, x=0]]. temp_double is a temporary variable that's created by the compiler to store the result of 2 * x, which is then assigned to the x that's variable declared within the double_of function. This x is then returned to the caller, which is our main function.

3. Once `double_of` returns, its stack frame is popped off the stack and the stack contents are now `[[a=12, result=24]`.

4. Following that, `main` ends and its stack frame is popped out, leaving the stack empty: `[]`.

There are more details to this, though. We just gave a very high level overview of a function call and its interaction with the stack memory. Now, if all we had were local values staying valid only for the lifetime of the function call, it would be very limiting. While the stack is simple and powerful, to be practical, a program also needs longer-living variables, and for that we need the heap.

The heap

The heap is for the more complicated and dynamic memory allocation requirements. A program might allocate on the heap at some point and may release it at some other point, and there need not be a strict boundary between these points, as is the case with stack memory. In the case of stack allocation, you get deterministic allocation and deallocation of values. Also, a value in the heap may live beyond the function where it was allocated and it may later get deallocated by some other function. In that case, the code fails to call `free`, so it may not get deallocated at all, which is the worst case.

Different languages use the heap memory differently. In dynamic languages such as Python, everything is an object and they are allocated on the heap by default. In C, we allocate memory on the heap using manual `malloc` calls, while in C++, we allocate using the `new` keyword. To deallocate memory, we need to call free in C and delete in C++. In C++, to avoid manual `delete` calls, programmers often use smart pointer types such as `unique_ptr` or `shared_ptr`. These smart pointer types have deconstructor methods, which get invoked when they go out of scope internally, calling `delete`. This paradigm of managing memory is called the RAII principle, and was popularized by C++.

 RAII stands for Resource Acquisition Is Initialization; a paradigm suggesting that resources must be acquired during initialization of objects and must be released when they are deallocated or their destructors are called.

Rust also has similar abstractions to how C++ manages heap memory. Here, the only way to allocate memory on the heap is through smart pointer types. Smart pointer types in Rust implement the Drop trait, which specifies how memory used by the value should be deallocated, and are semantically similar to deconstructor methods in C++. Unless someone writes their own custom smart pointer type, you never need to implement Drop on their types. More on the Drop trait in a separate section.

To allocate memory on the heap, languages rely on dedicated memory allocators, which hide all the low-level details like allocating memory on aligned memory, maintaining free chunks of memory to reduce system call overheads, and reducing fragmentation while allocating memory and other optimizations. For compiling programs, the compiler rustc itself uses the jemalloc allocator, whereas the libraries and binaries that are built from Rust use the system allocator. On Linux, it would be the glibc memory allocator APIs. Jemalloc is an efficient allocator library for use in multithreaded environments and it greatly reduces the build time of Rust programs. While jemalloc is used by the compiler, it's not used by any applications that are built with Rust because it increases the size of the binary. So, compiled binaries and libraries always use the system allocators by default.

Rust also has a pluggable allocator design, and can use the system allocator or any user implemented allocator that implements the GlobalAlloc trait from the std::alloc module. This is often implemented by the #[global_allocator] attribute, which can be put on any type to declare it as an allocator.

Note: If you have a use case where you want to use the jemalloc crate for your programs too, you can use the https://crates.io/crates/jemallocator crate.

In Rust, most dynamic types with sizes not known in advance are allocated on the heap. This excludes primitive types. For instance, creating a String internally allocates on the heap:

```
let s = String::new("foo");
```

String::new allocates a Vec<u8> on the heap and returns a reference to it. This reference is bound to the variable s, which is allocated on the stack. The string in the heap lives for as long as s is in scope. When s goes out of scope, the Vec<u8> is deallocated from the heap and its drop method is called as part of the Drop implementation. For rare cases where you need to allocate a primitive type on the heap, you can use the Box<T> type, which is a generic smart pointer type.

In the next section, let's look at the pitfalls when using a language such as C that doesn't have all the comforts of automatic memory management.

Memory management pitfalls

In languages with a GC, dealing with memory is abstracted away from the programmer. You declare and use the variables in your code, and how they get deallocated is an implementation detail you don't have to worry about. A low-level system programming language such as C/C++, on the other hand, does nothing to hide these details from the programmer, and provides nearly no safety. Here, programmers are given the responsibility of deallocating memory via manual free calls. Now, if we look at the majority of **Common Vulnerabilities & Exposure (CVEs)** in software related to memory management, it shows that we humans are not very good at this! Programmers can easily create hard-to-debug errors by allocating and deallocating values in the wrong order, or may even forget to deallocate used memory, or cast pointers illegally. In C, nothing stops you from creating a pointer out of an integer and dereferencing it somewhere, only to see the program crash later. Also, it's quite easy to create vulnerabilities in C because of the minimal compiler checks.

The most concerning case is freeing heap allocated data. The heap memory is to be used with care. Values in the heap can possibly live forever during the lifetime of the program if not freed, and may eventually lead to the program being killed by the **Out Of Memory (OOM)** killer in the kernel. At runtime, a bug in the code or mistake from the developer can also cause the program to either forget to free the memory, or access a portion of memory that is outside the bounds of its memory layout, or dereference a memory address in the protected code segment. When this happens, the process receives a trap instruction from the kernel, which is what you see as a `segmentation fault` error message, followed by the process getting aborted. As such, we must ensure that processes and their interactions with memory need to be safe! Either we as programmers need to be critically aware of our `malloc` and `free` calls, or use a memory safe language to handle these details for us.

Memory safety

But what do we mean by a program being memory safe? Memory safety is the idea that your program never touches a memory location it is not supposed to, and that the variables declared in your program cannot point to invalid memory and remain valid in all code paths. In other words, safety basically boils down to pointers having valid references all of the time in your program, and that the operations with pointers do not lead to undefined behavior. Undefined behavior is the state of a program where it has entered a situation that has not been accounted for in the compiler's because the compiler specification does not clarify what happens in that situation.

An example of undefined behavior in C is accessing out of bound and uninitialized array elements:

```c
// uninitialized_reads.c

#include <stdio.h>
int main() {
    int values[5];
    for (int i = 0; i < 5; i++)
        printf("%d ", values[i]);
}
```

In the preceding code, we have an array of 5 elements and we loop and print the values in the array. Running this program with `gcc -o main uninitialized_reads.c &&` `./main` gives me the following output:

```
4195840 0 4195488 0 609963056
```

On your machine, this could print any value, or might even print an address of an instruction, which can be exploited. This is an undefined behavior where anything can happen. Your program might crash immediately, which is the best case scenario as you get to know it then and there. It may also continue to work, clobbering any internal state of the program that might later give faulty outputs from the application.

Another example of memory safety violation is the iterator invalidation problem in C++:

```cpp
// iterator_invalidation.cpp

#include <iostream>
#include <vector>

int main() {
    std::vector <int> v{1, 5, 10, 15, 20};
    for (auto it=v.begin();it!=v.end();it++)
        if ((*it) == 5)
            v.push_back(-1);
    for (auto it=v.begin();it!=v.end();it++)
        std::cout << (*it) << " ";
    return 0;
}
```

In this C++ code, we create a vector of integers v and we are trying to iterate using an iterator called `it` in the `for` loop. The problem with the preceding code, is that we have an `it` iterator pointer to v, while at the same time we iterate and push to v.

Now, because of the way vectors are implemented, they internally reallocate to some other place in memory if their size reaches their capacity. When this happens, this would render the `it` pointer pointing to some garbage value, which is called the iterator invalidation problem, because the pointer is now pointing to invalid memory.

Another example of memory unsafety are buffer overflows in C. The following is a simple piece of code to demonstrate this idea:

```c
// buffer_overflow.c

int main() {
    char buf[3];
    buf[0] = 'a';
    buf[1] = 'b';
    buf[2] = 'c';
    buf[3] = 'd';
}
```

This compiles fine and even runs without errors, but the last assignment went over the allocated buffer and might have overwritten other data or instructions in the address. Also, specially crafted malicious input values, adapted to the architecture and environment, could yield arbitrary code execution. These kind of errors have happened in actual code in less obvious ways and has led to vulnerabilities affecting businesses worldwide. On recent versions of gcc compilers, this is detected as a stack smash attack where gcc halts the program by sending a `SIGABRT` (abort) signal.

Memory safety bugs lead to memory leaks, hard crashes in the form of segmentation faults, or in the worst case, security vulnerabilities. To create correct and safe programs in C, a programmer has to be discrete in correctly placing `free` calls when they are done using the memory. Modern C++ safeguards against some of the problems associated with manual memory management by providing smart pointer types, but this does not completely eliminate them. Languages based on virtual machines (Java's JVM being the most prominent example) use garbage collection to eliminate whole classes of memory safety issues. While Rust doesn't have a built-in GC, it relies on the same RAII built into the language and makes freeing used memory automatic for us based on the scope of variables and is much more safer than C or C++. It provides us with several fine-grained abstractions that you can choose according to your needs and pay only for what you use. To see how all of this works in Rust, let's explore the principles that helps Rust provide compile-time memory management to programmers.

Trifecta of memory safety

The concepts that we will explore next are the core tenets of Rust's memory safety and its zero cost abstraction principle. They enable Rust to detect memory safety violations in a program at compile time, provide automatic freeing of resources when their scope ends, and much more. We call these concepts ownership, borrowing, and lifetimes. Ownership is kind of like the core principle, while borrowing and lifetimes are type system extensions to the language, enforcing and sometimes relaxing the ownership principle in different contexts in code to ensure compile-time memory management. Let's elaborate on these ideas.

Ownership

The notion of a true owner of a resource in a program differs across languages. Here, by resource, we collectively refer to any variable holding a value on the heap or the stack, or a variable holding an open file descriptor, a database connection socket, a network socket, and similar things. All of them occupy some memory from the time they exist until the time they are done being used by the program. An important responsibility of being the owner of a resource is to judiciously free the memory used by them, as not being able to perform deallocations at proper places and times can lead to memory leaks.

When programming in dynamic languages such as Python, it's fine to have multiple owners or aliases to a `list` object where you can add to or remove items from the list using one of the many variables pointing to the object. The variables don't need to care about freeing the memory used by the object because the GC takes care of this and will free the memory once all references to the object are gone.

For compiled languages such as C/C++, before smart pointers were a thing, libraries had an opinionated take on whether the callee or the caller of an API was responsible for deallocating the memory after the code is done with a resource. These opinions existed because ownership is not enforced by the compiler in these languages. There's still a possibility of goofing up by not using smart pointers in C++. It's totally fine in C++ to have more than one variable pointing to a value on the heap (though we advise against it), and that is called *aliasing*. The programmer runs into all sorts of ill effects with the flexibility of having multiple pointers or aliases to a resource, one being the iterator invalidation problem in C++, which we explained previously. Specifically, problems arise when there is at least one mutable alias to a resource among other immutable aliases in a given scope.

Rust, on the other hand, tries to bring proper semantics regarding the ownership of values in a program. The ownership rule of Rust states the following principles:

- When you create a value or a resource using the `let` statement and assign it to a variable, the variable becomes the owner of the resource
- When the value is reassigned from one variable to another, the ownership of the value moves to the other variable and the older variable becomes invalid for further use
- The value and the variable are deallocated at the end of their scope

The takeaway is that values in Rust have a single owner, that is, the variables that created them. The principle is quite simple, but the implications of it are what surprises programmers coming from other languages. Consider the following code, which demonstrates the ownership principle in its most basic form:

```rust
// ownership_basics.rs

#[derive(Debug)]
struct Foo(u32);

fn main() {
    let foo = Foo(2048);
    let bar = foo;
    println!("Foo is {:?}", foo);
    println!("Bar is {:?}", bar);
}
```

We create two variables, `foo` and `bar`, that points to a `Foo` instance. As someone familiar with mainstream imperative languages that allow multiple owners to a value, we expect this program to compile just fine. But in Rust, we get the following error upon compilation:

```
→  Chapter06 git:(master) ✗ rustc ownership_basics.rs
error[E0382]: use of moved value: `foo`
  --> ownership_basics.rs:44:29
   |
43 |     let bar = foo;
   |         --- value moved here
44 |     println!("Foo is {:?}", foo);
   |                             ^^^ value used here after move
   |
   = note: move occurs because `foo` has type `Foo`, which does not implement the `Copy` trait

error: aborting due to previous error
```

Here, we created a `Foo` instance and assigned it to the `foo` variable. According to the ownership rule, `foo` is now the owner of the `Foo` instance. In the next line, we then assign `foo` to `bar`. On executing the second line in `main`, `bar` becomes the new owner of the `Foo` instance and the older `foo` is now an abandoned variable, which cannot be used anywhere after the move. This is evident from the `println!` call on the third line. Rust moves values pointed to by a variable by default any time we assign it to some other variable or read from the variable. The ownership rule prevents you from having multiple points of access for modifying the value, which can lead to use after free situations, even in single threaded contexts with languages that permit multiple mutable aliases for values. The classic example is the iterator invalidation problem in C++. Now, to analyze when a value goes out of scope, the ownership rule also takes into account the scope of variables. Let's understand scopes next.

A brief on scopes

Before we go further into ownership, we need to get a brief idea of scopes, which might be familiar to you already if you know C, but we'll recap it here in the context of Rust, as ownership works in tandem with scopes. So, a scope is nothing but an environment where variables and values come into existence. Every variable you declare is associated with a scope. Scopes are represented in code by braces `{}`. A scope is created whenever you use a *block expression*, that is, any expression that starts and ends with braces `{}`. Also, scopes can nest within each other and can access items from the parent scope, but not the other way around.

Here's some code that demonstrates multiple scopes and values:

```
// scopes.rs

fn main() {
    let level_0_str = String::from("foo");
    {
        let level_1_number = 9;
        {
            let mut level_2_vector = vec![1, 2, 3];
            level_2_vector.push(level_1_number);    // can access
        } // level_2_vector goes out of scope here

        level_2_vector.push(4);    // no longer exists
    } // level_1_number goes out of scope here
} // level_0_str goes out of scope here
```

To help with this explanation, will assume that our scopes are numbered, starting from 0. With this assumption, we have created variables that have the `level_x` prefix in their name. Let's run through the preceding code, line by line. As functions can create new scopes, the `main` function introduces a root scope level 0 with a `level_0_str` defined within it. Inside the level 0 scope, we create a new scope, level 1, with a bare block { }, which contains the variable `level_1_number`. Within level 1, we create another block expression, which becomes level 2 scope. In level 2, we declare another variable, `level_2_vector`, to which we push `level_1_number`, which comes from the parent scope,that is, level 1. Finally, when the code reaches the end of }, all of the values get destructed and the respective scopes come to an end. Once the scope ends, we cannot use any values defined within them.

Scopes are an important property to keep in mind when reasoning about the ownership rule. They are also used to reason about borrowing and lifetimes, as we'll see later. When a scope ends, any variable that owns a value runs code to deallocate the value and itself becomes invalid for use outside the scope. In particular, for heap allocated values, a `drop` method is placed right before the end of the scope }. This is akin to calling the `free` function in C, but here it's implicit and saves the programmer from forgetting to deallocate values. The `drop` method comes from the `Drop` trait, which is implemented for most heap allocated types in Rust and makes automatic freeing of resources a breeze.

Having learned about scopes, let's look at an example similar to the one we previously saw in `ownership_basics.rs`, but this time, let's use a primitive value:

```
// ownership_primitives.rs

fn main() {
    let foo = 4623;
    let bar = foo;
    println!("{:?} {:?}", foo, bar);
}
```

Try compiling and running this program. You might be in for a surprise as this program compiles and runs just fine. What gives? In the program, the ownership of 4623 does not move from `foo` to `bar`, but `bar` gets a separate copy of 4623. It appears that primitive types are treated specially in Rust, where they get copied instead of moved. This means that there are different semantics of ownership depending on what types we use in Rust, which brings us to the concept of move and copy semantics.

Move and copy semantics

In Rust, variable bindings have move semantics by default. But what does this really mean? To understand that, we need to think about how variables are used in a program. We create values or resources and assign them to variables to easily refer to them later in our program. These variables are names that point to the memory location where the value resides. Now, operations with variables such as reading, assignment, addition, passing them to functions, and so on can have different semantics or meaning around how the value being pointed to by the variable is accessed. In statically typed languages, these semantics are broadly classified as move semantics and copy semantics. Let's define both.

Move semantics: A value that gets moved to the receiving item when accessed through a variable or reassigning to a variable exhibits move semantics. Rust has move semantics by default due to its **affine type system**. A highlighting part of affine type systems is that values or resources can only be used once, and Rust exhibits this property with the ownership rule.

Copy semantics: A value that gets copied (as in a bitwise copy) by default when assigned or accessed through a variable or passed to/returned from a function exhibits copy semantics. This means that the value can be used any number of times and each value is completely new.

These semantics are familiar to people from the C++ community. C++ has copy semantics by default. Move semantics were added later with the C++11 release.

Move semantics in Rust can be limiting at times. Fortunately, a type's behavior can be changed to follow copy semantics by implementing the `Copy` trait. This is implemented by default for primitives and other stack-only data types and is the reason why the previous code using primitives works. Consider the following snippet that tries to make a type `Copy` explicitly:

```
// making_copy_types.rs

#[derive(Copy, Debug)]
struct Dummy;

fn main() {
    let a = Dummy;
    let b = a;
    println!("{}", a);
    println!("{}", b);
}
```

On compiling this, we get the following error:

```
→  Chapter05 git:(master) X rustc making_copy_types.rs
error[E0277]: the trait bound `Dummy: std::clone::Clone` is not satisfied
 --> making_copy_types.rs:3:10
  |
3 | #[derive(Copy)]
  |          ^^^^ the trait `std::clone::Clone` is not implemented for `Dummy`

error: aborting due to previous error

For more information about this error, try `rustc --explain E0277`.
```

Interesting! It appears that Copy depends on the Clone trait. This is because Copy is defined in the standard library as follows:

```
pub trait Copy: Clone { }
```

Clone is a super trait of Copy, and any type implementing Copy must also implement Clone. We can make this example compile by adding the Clone trait beside Copy in the derive annotation:

```
// making_copy_types_fixed.rs

#[derive(Copy, Clone, Debug)]
struct Dummy;

fn main() {
    let a = Dummy;
    let b = a;
    println!("{}", a);
    println!("{}", b);
}
```

The program works now. But it's not quite clear of the differences between Clone and Copy. Let's differentiate them next.

Duplicating types via traits

The Copy and Clone traits convey the idea of how types gets duplicated when they are used in code.

Copy

The Copy trait is usually implemented for types that can be completely represented on the stack. This is to say that they don't have any part of themselves that lives on the heap. If that were the case, Copy would be a heavy operation as it would also have to go down the heap to copy the values. It directly affects how the = assignment operator works. If a type implements Copy, an assignment from one variable to another would copy the data implicitly.

Copy is an auto trait that is implemented automatically on most stack data types such as primitives and immutable references, that is, &T. The way Copy duplicates types is very similar to how the memcpy function works in C, which is used to copy values bitwise. Copy for user-defined types is not implemented by default as Rust wants to be explicit about copying and the developer has to opt in to implement the trait. Copy also depends on the Clone trait when anyone wants to implement Copy on their types.

Types that don't implement Copy are Vec<T>, String, and mutable references. To make copies of these values, we use the more explicit Clone trait.

Clone

The Clone trait is for explicit duplication and comes with a clone method that a type can implement to obtain a copy of itself. The Clone trait is defined like so:

```
pub trait Clone {
    fn clone(&self) -> Self;
}
```

It has a method called clone that takes an immutable reference to the receiver, that is, &self, and returns a new value of the same type. User defined types or any wrapper types that need to provide the ability to duplicate themselves should implement the Clone trait by implementing the clone method.

But unlike Copy types where assignment implicitly copies the value, to duplicate a Clone value, we have to explicitly call the clone method. The clone method is a more general duplication mechanism and Copy is a special case of it, which is always a bitwise copy. Items such as String and Vec that are heavy to copy, only implements the Clone trait. Smart pointer types also implement the Clone trait where they just copy the pointer and extra metadata such as the reference count while pointing to the same heap data.

This is one of those examples of being able to decide how we want to copy types, and the `Clone` trait gives us that flexibility.

Here's a program that demonstrates using `Clone` to duplicate a type:

```
// explicit_copy.rs

#[derive(Clone, Debug)]
struct Dummy {
    items: u32
}

fn main() {
    let a = Dummy { items: 54 };
    let b = a.clone();
    println!("a: {:?}, b: {:?}", a, b);
}
```

We added a `Clone` in the derive attribute. With that, we can call `clone` on `a` to get a new copy of it.

Now, you are probably wondering when you should one implement either of these types. The following are a few guidelines.

When to implement `Copy` on a type:

Small values that can be represented solely in the stack as follows:

- If the type depends only on other types that have `Copy` implemented on them; the `Copy` trait is implicitly implemented for it.
- The `Copy` trait implicitly affects how the assignment operator = works. The decision on whether to make your own externally visible types using the `Copy` trait requires some consideration due to how it affects the assignment operator. If at an early point of development your type is a `Copy` and you remove it afterwards, it affects every point where values of that type are assigned. You can easily break an API in that manner.

When to implement `Clone` on a type:

- The `Clone` trait merely declares a `clone` method, which needs to be called explicitly.
- If your type also contains a value on the heap as part of its representation, then opt for implementing `Clone`, which makes it explicit to users that will also be cloning the heap data.

- If you are implementing a smart pointer type such as a reference counting type, you should implement `Clone` on your type to only copy the pointers on the stack.

Now that we know the basics of `Copy` and `Clone`, let's move on to see how ownership affects various places in code.

Ownership in action

Apart from the `let` binding example, there are other places where you will find ownership in effect, and it's important to recognize these and the errors the compiler gives us.

Functions: If you pass parameters to functions, the same ownership rules are in effect:

```
// ownership_functions.rs

fn take_the_n(n: u8) { }

fn take_the_s(s: String) { }

fn main() {
    let n = 5;
    let s = String::from("string");

    take_the_n(n);
    take_the_s(s);

    println!("n is {}", n);
    println!("s is {}", s);
}
```

The compilation fails in a similar way:

```
→  Chapter06 git:(master) ✗ rustc ownership_functions.rs
error[E0382]: use of moved value: `s`
  --> ownership_functions.rs:15:25
   |
12 |        take_the_s(s);
   |                   - value moved here
...
15 |        println!("s is {}", s);
   |                            ^ value used here after move
   |
   = note: move occurs because `s` has type `std::string::String`, which does not implement the
`Copy` trait

error: aborting due to previous error

For more information about this error, try `rustc --explain E0382`.
```

String does not implement the Copy trait, so the ownership of the value is moved inside the take_the_s function. When that function returns, the scope of the value comes to an end and drop is called on s, which frees the heap memory used by s. Therefore, s cannot be used after the function call anymore. However, since String implements Clone, we can make our code work by adding a .clone() call at the function call site:

```
take_the_s(s.clone());
```

Our take_the_n works fine as u8 (a primitive type) implements Copy.

This is to say that, after passing move types to a function, we cannot use that value later. If you want to use the value, we must clone the type and send a copy to the function instead. Now, if we only need read access to variable s, another way we could have made this code work is by passing the string s back to main. This looks something like this:

```
// ownership_functions_back.rs

fn take_the_n(n: u8) { }

fn take_the_s(s: String) -> String {
    println!("inside function {}", s);
    s
}

fn main() {
    let n = 5;
    let s = String::from("string");

    take_the_n(n);
    let s = take_the_s(s);

    println!("n is {}", n);
    println!("s is {}", s);
}
```

We added a return type to our take_the_s function and return the passed string s back to the caller. In main, we receive it in s. With this, the last line of code in main works.

Match expressions: Within a match expression, a move type is also moved by default, as shown in the following code:

```
// ownership_match.rs

#[derive(Debug)]
enum Food {
    Cake,
```

```
        Pizza,
        Salad
    }

    #[derive(Debug)]
    struct Bag {
        food: Food
    }

    fn main() {
        let bag = Bag { food: Food::Cake };
        match bag.food {
            Food::Cake => println!("I got cake"),
            a => println!("I got {:?}", a)
        }
        println!("{:?}", bag);
    }
```

In the preceding code, we create a `Bag` instance and assign it to `bag`. Next, we match on its `food` field and print some text. Later, we print the `bag` with `println!`. We get the following error upon compilation:

```
→ Chapter05 git:(master) ✗ rustc ownership_match.rs
error[E0382]: use of partially moved value: `bag`
  --> ownership_match.rs:20:22

17 |         a => println!("I got {:?}", a)
   |         - value moved here
...
20 |     println!("{:?}", bag);
   |                      ^^^ value used here after move
   |
   = note: move occurs because `bag.food` has type `Food`, which does not implement the `Copy` trait

error: aborting due to previous error

For more information about this error, try `rustc --explain E0382`.
```

As you can clearly read, the error message says that `bag` has already been moved and consumed by the `a` variable in the match expression. This invalidates the variable `bag` for any further use. We'll see how to make this code work when we get to the concept of borrowing.

Methods: Within an `impl` block, any method with `self` as the first parameter takes ownership of the value on which the method is called. This means that after you call the method on the value, you cannot use that value again. This is shown in the following code:

```
// ownership_methods.rs

struct Item(u32);
```

```
impl Item {
    fn new() -> Self {
        Item(1024)
    }

    fn take_item(self) {
        // does nothing
    }
}

fn main() {
    let it = Item::new();
    it.take_item();
    println!("{}", it.0);
}
```

Upon compilation, we get the following error:

```
→  Chapter05 git:(master) ✗ rustc ownership_methods.rs
error[E0382]: use of moved value: `it.0`
  --> ownership_methods.rs:18:20

17 |        it.take_item();
   |        -- value moved here
18 |        println!("{}", it.0);
   |                       ^^^^ value used here after move
   |
   = note: move occurs because `it` has type `Item`, which does not implement the `Copy` trait
```

`take_item` is an instance method that takes `self` as the first parameter. After its invocation, `it` is moved inside the method and deallocated when the function scope ends. We cannot use `it` again later. We'll make this code work when we get to the borrowing concept.

Ownership in closures: A similar thing happens with closures. Consider the following code snippet:

```
// ownership_closures.rs

#[derive(Debug)]
struct Foo;

fn main() {
    let a = Foo;

    let closure = || {
        let b = a;
    };
```

```
        println!("{:?}", a);
    }
```

As you can already guess, the ownership of `Foo` is moved to `b` inside the closure by default on assignment, and we can't access `a` again. We get the following output when compiling the preceding code:

```
→  Chapter05 git:(master) ✗ rustc ownership_closures.rs
error[E0382]: use of moved value: `a`
  --> ownership_closures.rs:13:22
   |
9  |        || {
   |        -- value moved (into closure) here
...
13 |        println!("{:?}", a);
   |                         ^ value used here after move
   |
   = note: move occurs because `a` has type `Foo`, which does not implement the `Copy` trait

error: aborting due to previous error

For more information about this error, try `rustc --explain E0382`.
```

To have a copy of `a`, we can call `a.clone()` inside the closure and assign it to `b` or place a move keyword before the closure, like so:

```
let closure = move || {
    let b = a;
};
```

This will make our program compile.

 Note: Closures take values differently depending on how a variable is used inside the closure.

With these observations, we can already see that the ownership rule can be quite restrictive as it allows us to use a type only once. If a function needs only read access to a value, then we either need to return the value back again from the function or clone it before passing it to the function. The latter might not be possible if the type does not implement `Clone`. Cloning the type might seem like an easy thing to get around the ownership principle, but it defeats the whole point of the zero-cost promise as `Clone` always duplicates types always, possibly making a call to the memory allocator APIs, which is a costly operation involving system calls.

With move semantics and the ownership rule in effect, it soon gets unwieldy to write programs in Rust. Fortunately, we have the concept of borrowing and reference types that relax the restrictions imposed by the rules but still maintains the ownership guarantees at compile time.

Borrowing

The concept of borrowing is there to circumvent the restrictions with the ownership rule. Under borrowing, you don't take ownership of values, but only lend data for as long as you need. This is achieved by borrowing values, that is, taking a reference to a value. To borrow a value, we put the & operator before the variable & is the *address of* operator . We can borrow values in Rust in two ways.

Immutable borrows: When we use the & operator before a type, we create an immutable reference to it. Our previous example from the ownership section can be re-written using borrowing:

```
// borrowing_basics.rs

#[derive(Debug)]
struct Foo(u32);

fn main() {
    let foo = Foo;
    let bar = &foo;
    println!("Foo is {:?}", foo);
    println!("Bar is {:?}", bar);
}
```

This time, the program compiles, as the second line inside `main` has changed to this:

```
    let bar = &foo;
```

Notice the & before the variable `foo`. We are borrowing `foo` and assigning the borrow to `bar`. `bar` has a type of &Foo, which is a reference type. Being an immutable reference, we cannot mutate the value inside Foo from `bar`.

Mutable borrows: Mutable borrows to a value can be taken using the &mut operator. With mutable borrows, you can mutate the value. Consider the following code:

```
// mutable_borrow.rs

fn main() {
    let a = String::from("Owned string");
```

```
        let a_ref = &mut a;
        a_ref.push('!');
    }
```

Here, we have a `String` instance declared as `a`. We also create a mutable reference to it with `b` using `&mut a`. This does not move `a` to `b`,- only borrows it mutably. We then push a `'!'` character to the string. Let's compile this program:

```
→   Chapter05 git:(master) ✗ rustc mutable_borrow.rs
error[E0596]: cannot borrow immutable local variable `a` as mutable
 --> mutable_borrow.rs:5:22
  |
4 |     let a = String::from("Owned string");
  |         - help: make this binding mutable: `mut a`
5 |     let a_ref = &mut a;
  |                      ^ cannot borrow mutably

error: aborting due to previous error

For more information about this error, try `rustc --explain E0596`.
```

We have an error. The compiler says that we cannot borrow `a` mutably. This is because mutable borrows require the owning variable itself to be declared with the `mut` keyword. This should be obvious, as we can't mutate something that's behind an immutable binding. Accordingly, we'll change our declaration of `a` to this:

```
    let mut a = String::from("Owned string");
```

This makes the program compile. Here, `a` is a stack variable that points to a heap allocated value, and `a_ref` is a mutable reference to the value owned by `a`. `a_ref` can mutate the `String` value but it cannot drop the value, as it's not the owner. The borrow becomes invalid if `a` is dropped before the line that takes a reference.

Now, we add a `println!` at the end of the previous program to print the modified `a`:

```
    // exclusive_borrow.rs

    fn main() {
        let mut a = String::from("Owned string");
        let a_ref = &mut a;
        a_ref.push('!');
        println!("{}", a);
    }
```

Compiling this gives us the following error:

```
→  Chapter05 git:(master) ✗ rustc exclusive_borrow.rs
error[E0502]: cannot borrow `a` as immutable because it is also borrowed as mutable
 --> exclusive_borrow.rs:7:20
  |
5 |      let a_ref = &mut a;
  |                       - mutable borrow occurs here
6 |      a_ref.push('!');
7 |      println!("{}", a);
  |                     ^ immutable borrow occurs here
8 | }
  | - mutable borrow ends here

error: aborting due to previous error

For more information about this error, try `rustc --explain E0502`.
```

Rust forbids this, thus borrowing the value immutably as a mutable borrow with `a_ref` already is present in the scope. This highlights another important rule with borrowing. Once a value is borrowed mutably, we cannot have any other borrows of it. Not even an immutable borrow. Having explored borrowing, let's highlight the exact borrowing rules in Rust.

Borrowing rules

Similar to the ownership rule, we also have borrowing rules that maintain the single ownership semantics with references, too. These rules are as follows:

- A reference may not live longer than what it referred to. This is obvious, since if it did, it would be referring to a garbage value.
- If there's a mutable reference to a value, no other references, either mutable or immutable references, are allowed to the same value in that scope. A mutable reference is an exclusive borrow.
- If there is no mutable reference to a thing, any number of immutable references to the same value are allowed in the scope.

 The borrowing rules in Rust are analyzed by a component of the compiler called the borrow checker. The Rust community amusingly calls dealing with borrowing errors as fighting the borrow checker.

Now that we're familiar with the rules, let's see what happens if we go against the borrow checker by violating them.

Borrowing in action

Rust's error diagnostics around the borrowing rules are really helpful when we go against the borrow checker. In the following few examples, we'll see them in various contexts.

Borrowing in functions: As you saw previously, moving ownership when making function calls does not make much sense if you are only reading the value, and is very limiting. You don't get to use the variable after you call the function. Instead of taking parameters by value, we can take them by references. We can fix the previous code example that was presented in the ownership section to pass the compiler without cloning, like so:

```
// borrowing_functions.rs

fn take_the_n(n: &mut u8) {
    *n += 2;
}

fn take_the_s(s: &mut String) {
    s.push_str("ing");
}

fn main() {
    let mut n = 5;
    let mut s = String::from("Borrow");

    take_the_n(&mut n);
    take_the_s(&mut s);

    println!("n changed to {}", n);
    println!("s changed to {}", s);
}
```

In the preceding code, `take_the_s` and `take_the_n` now take mutable references. With this, we needed to modify three things in our code. First, the variable binding will have to be made mutable:

```
let mut s = String::from("Borrow");
```

Second, our function changes to the following:

```
fn take_the_s(n: &mut String) {
    s.push_str("ing");
}
```

Third, the call site would also need to change to this form:

```
take_the_s(&mut s);
```

Again, we can see that everything in Rust is explicit. Mutability is very visible in Rust code for obvious reasons, especially when multiple threads come into play.

Borrowing in match: In match expressions, a value is moved by default in the match arms, unless it's a `Copy` type. The following code, which was presented in the previous section on ownership, compiles by borrowing in match arms:

```rust
// borrowing_match.rs

#[derive(Debug)]
enum Food {
    Cake,
    Pizza,
    Salad
}

#[derive(Debug)]
struct Bag {
    food: Food
}

fn main() {
    let bag = Bag { food: Food::Cake };
    match bag.food {
        Food::Cake => println!("I got cake"),
        ref a => println!("I got {:?}", a)
    }
    println!("{:?}", bag);
}
```

We made a slight change to the preceding code, which might be familiar to you from the ownership section. For the second match arm, we prefixed a with `ref`. The `ref` keyword is a keyword that can match items by taking a reference to them instead of capturing them by value. With this change, our code compiles.

Returning a reference from a function: In the following code example, we have a function that tries to return a reference to a value declared within the function:

```rust
// return_func_ref.rs

fn get_a_borrowed_value() -> &u8 {
    let x = 1;
    &x
```

```
}

fn main() {
    let value = get_a_borrowed_value();
}
```

This code fails to pass the borrow checker, and we are met with the following error:

```
error[E0106]: missing lifetime specifier
 --> return_func_ref.rs:3:30

3 | fn get_a_borrowed_value() -> &u8 {
                                 ^ help: consider giving it a 'static lifetime: `&'static`

  = help: this function's return type contains a borrowed value, but there is no value for it to be borrowed from

error: aborting due to previous error

For more information about this error, try `rustc --explain E0106`.
```

The error message says that we are missing a lifetime specifier. That doesn't help much in regards to explaining what is wrong with our code. This is where we need to acquaint ourselves with the concept of lifetimes, which we will cover in the next section. Before that, let's expound on the kind of functions that we can can have based on borrowing rules.

Method types based on borrowing

The borrowing rules also dictate how inherent methods on types are defined and also instance methods from traits. The following are how they receive the instance, presented by least restrictive to most restrictive:

- `&self` methods: These methods only have immutable access to its members
- `&mut self` methods: These methods borrows the self instance mutably
- `self` methods: These methods takes ownership of the instance on which it is called and the type is not available to be called later

In the case of user defined types, the same kind of borrowing applies also to its field members.

 Note: Unless you're deliberately writing a method that should move or drop `self` at the end, always prefer immutable borrowing methods that is, having `&self` as the first parameter.

Lifetimes

The third piece in Rust's compile time memory safety puzzle is the idea of lifetimes and the related syntactic annotation for specifying lifetimes in code. In this section, we'll explain lifetimes by stripping them down to the basics.

When we declare a variable by initializing it with a value, the variable has a certain lifetime, beyond which it is invalid to use it. In general programming parlance, the lifetime of a variable is the region in code in which the variable points to a valid memory. If you have ever programmed in C, you should be acutely aware of the case with lifetimes of variables: every time you allocate a variable with `malloc`, it should have an owner, and that owner should reliably decide when that variable's life ends and when the memory gets freed. But the worst thing is, it's not enforced by the C compiler; rather, it's the programmer's responsibility.

For data allocated on the stack, we can easily reason by looking at the code and figure out whether a variable is alive or not. For heap allocated values, though, this isn't clear. Lifetimes in Rust is a concrete construct and not a conceptual idea as in C. They do the same kind of analysis that a programmer does manually, that is, by examining the scope of value and any variable that references it.

When talking about lifetimes in Rust, you only need to deal with them when you have a reference. All references in Rust have an implicit lifetime information attached to them. A lifetime defines how long the reference lives in relation to the original owner of the value and also the extent of the scope of the reference. Most of the time, it is implicit and the compiler figures out the lifetime of the variables by looking at the code. But in some cases, the compiler cannot and then it needs our help, or better said, it asks you to specify your intent.

So far, we have been dealing with references and borrowing quite easily in the previous code examples, but let see what happens when we try to compile the following code:

```
// lifetime_basics.rs

struct SomeRef<T> {
    part: &T
}

fn main() {
    let a = SomeRef { part: &43 };
}
```

This code is very simple. We have a `SomeRef` struct, which stores a reference to a generic type, `T`. In `main`, we create an instance of the struct, initializing the `part` field with a reference to an `i32`, that is, `&43`.

It gives the following error upon compilation:

```
→  Chapter05 git:(master) X rustc lifetime_basics.rs
error[E0106]: missing lifetime specifier
 --> lifetime_basics.rs:4:11
  |
4 |     part: &T
  |           ^ expected lifetime parameter

error: aborting due to previous error

For more information about this error, try `rustc --explain E0106`.
```

In this case, the compiler asks us to put in something called a lifetime parameter. A lifetime parameter is very similar to a generic type parameter. Where a generic type `T` denotes any type, lifetime parameters denote the region or the span where the reference is valid to be used. It's just there for the compiler to fill in with the actual region information later when the code is analyzed by the borrow checker.

A lifetime is purely a compile time construct that helps the compiler to figure out the extent to which a reference can be used within a scope, and ensures that it follows the borrowing rules. It can keep track of things like the origin of references and whether they outlive the borrowed value. Lifetimes in Rust ensure that a reference can't outlive the value it points to. Lifetimes are not something that you as a developer will use, but it's for the compiler to use and reason about validity of references.

Lifetime parameters

For cases where the compiler can't figure out the lifetime of values by examining the code, we need to tell Rust by using some annotations in code. To distinguish from identifiers, lifetime annotations are denoted by a quirky symbol of prefixing a letter with `'`. So, to make our previous example compile with a parameter, we have added a lifetime annotation on our `StructRef`, like so:

```
// using_lifetimes.rs

struct SomeRef<'a, T> {
    part: &'a T
}
```

```
fn main() {
    let _a = SomeRef { part: &43 };
}
```

A lifetime is denoted by a ', followed by any sequence of valid identifiers. But, by convention, most lifetimes used in the Rust code uses 'a, 'b and 'c as lifetime parameters. If you have multiple lifetimes on a type, you can use longer descriptive lifetime names such as 'ctx, 'reader, 'writer, and so on. It is declared at the same place and in the same way as generic type parameters.

We saw examples where the lifetimes acted as a generic parameter for resolving valid references later, but there's a lifetime that has a concrete value. It is shown in the following code:

```
// static_lifetime.rs

fn main() {
    let _a: &'static str = "I live forever";
}
```

The static lifetime means that these references are valid for the entire duration of the program. All literal strings in Rust have a lifetime of 'static and they go to the data segment of the compiled object code.

Lifetime elision and the rules

Any time there's a reference in a function or a type definition, there's a lifetime involved. Most of the time, you don't need to use explicit lifetime annotation is you code as the compiler is smart to infer them for you as a lot of information is already available at compile time about references.

In other words, these two function signatures are identical:

```
fn func_one(x: &u8) → &u8 { .. }

fn func_two<'a>(x: &'a u8) → &'a u8 { .. }
```

In the usual case, the compiler has elided the lifetime parameter for func_one and we don't need to write it as func_two.

But the compiler can elide lifetimes only in restricted places and there are rules for elision. Before we talk about these rules, we need to talk about input and output lifetimes. These are only discussed when functions that take references are involved.

Input lifetime: Lifetime annotations on function parameters that are references are referred to as input lifetimes.

Output lifetimes: Lifetime annotations on function return values that are references are referred to as output lifetimes.

It's import to note that any output lifetime originates from input lifetimes. We cannot have a output lifetime that is independent and distinct from the input lifetime. It can only be a lifetime that is smaller than or equal to the output lifetime.

The following are the rules that are followed when eliding lifetimes:

- If the input lifetime contains only a single reference, the output lifetime is assumed to be the same
- For methods involving `self` and `&mut self`, the input lifetime is inferred for the `&self` parameter

But sometimes in ambiguous situations, the compiler doesn't try to assume things. Consider the following code:

```
// explicit_lifetimes.rs

fn foo(a: &str, b: &str) -> &str {
    b
}

fn main() {
    let a = "Hello";
    let b = "World";
    let c = foo(a, b);
}
```

In the preceding code, `RefItem` stores a reference to any type, `T`. In this case, the lifetime of the return value isn't obvious as there are two input references involved. But, sometimes, the compiler is not able to figure out the lifetimes of references, and then it needs our help and asks us to specify lifetime parameters. Consider the following code, which does not compile:

```
→ Chapter05 git:(master) ✗ rustc explicit_lifetimes.rs
error[E0106]: missing lifetime specifier
 --> explicit_lifetimes.rs:3:29
  |
3 | fn foo(a: &str, b: &str) -> &str {
  |                             ^ expected lifetime parameter
  |
  = help: this function's return type contains a borrowed value, but the signature does not say whether it is borrowed fro
m `a` or `b`
```

The preceding program doesn't compile because Rust is unable to figure out the lifetime of the return value and it needs our help here.

Now, there are various places where we have to specify lifetimes when Rust cannot figure them out for us:

- Function signatures
- Structs and struct fields
- impl blocks

Lifetimes in user defined types

If a struct definition has fields that are reference to any type, we need to explicitly specify how long those references will live. The syntax is similar to that of function signatures: we first declare the lifetime names on the struct line, and then use them in the fields.

Here's what the syntax looks like in its simplest form:

```
// lifetime_struct.rs

struct Number<'a> {
    num: &'a u8
}

fn main() {
    let _n = Number {num: &545};
}
```

The definition of Number lives as long as the reference for num.

Lifetime in impl blocks

When we create impl blocks for structs with references, we need to repeat the lifetime declarations and definitions again. For instance, if we made an implementation for the struct Foo we defined previously, the syntax would look like this:

```
// lifetime_impls.rs

#[derive(Debug)]
struct Number<'a> {
    num: &'a u8
}
```

```
impl<'a> Number<'a> {
    fn get_num(&self) -> &'a u8 {
        self.num
    }
    fn set_num(&mut self, new_number: &'a u8) {
        self.num = new_number
    }
}

fn main() {
    let a = 10;
    let mut num = Number { num: &a };
    num.set_num(&23);
    println!("{:?}", num.get_num());
}
```

In most of these cases, this is inferred from the types themselves and then, we can omit the signatures with <'_> syntax.

Multiple lifetimes

Just like generic type parameters, we can specify multiple lifetimes if we have more than one reference that has different lifetimes. However, it can quickly become hairy when you have to juggle with more than one lifetime in your code. Most of the time, we can get away with just one lifetime in our structs or any of our functions. But there are cases where we'll need more than one lifetime annotations. For example, say we are building a decoder library that can parse binary files according to a schema and a given encoded stream of bytes. We have a Decoder object, which has a reference to a Schema object and a reference to a Reader type. Our Decoder definition will then look something like this:

```
// multiple_lifetimes.rs

struct Decoder<'a, 'b, S, R> {
    schema: &'a S,
    reader: &'b R
}

fn main() {}
```

In the preceding definition, it is quite possible that we get Reader from the network while the Schema is local, and so their lifetimes in code can be different. When we provide implementations for this Decoder, we can specify relations with it by lifetime subtyping, which we will explain next.

Lifetime subtyping

We can specify relation between lifetimes that specifies whether two references can be used in the same place. Continuing with our `Decoder` struct example, we can specify the lifetimes' relations with each other in the `impl` block, like so:

```
// lifetime_subtyping.rs

struct Decoder<'a, 'b, S, R> {
    schema: &'a S,
    reader: &'b R
}

impl<'a, 'b, S, R> Decoder<'a, 'b, S, R>
where 'a: 'b {
}

fn main() {
    let a: Vec<u8> = vec![];
    let b: Vec<u8> = vec![];
    let decoder = Decoder {schema: &a, reader: &b};
}
```

We specified the relation in the impl block using the where clause as: 'a: 'b . This is read as the lifetime 'a outlives 'b or in other words 'b should never live longer than 'a.

Specifying lifetime bounds on generic types

Apart from using traits to constrain the types that can be accepted by a generic function, we can also constrain generic type parameters using lifetime annotations. For instance, consider we have a logger library where the `Logger` object is defined as follows:

```
// lifetime_bounds.rs

enum Level {
    Error
}

struct Logger<'a>(&'a str, Level);

fn configure_logger<T>(_t: T) where T: Send + 'static {
    // configure the logger here
}

fn main() {
    let name = "Global";
```

```
        let log1 = Logger(name, Level::Error);
        configure_logger(log1);
}
```

In the preceding code, we have a `Logger` struct with its name and a `Level` enum. We also have a generic function called `configure_logger` that takes a type `T` that is constrained with `Send + 'static`. In main, we create a logger with a `'static`, string `"Global"`, and call `configure_logger` passing it.

Along with the `Send` bound, which says that this thread can be sent to threads, we also say that the type must live as long as the `'static` lifetime. Let's say we were to use a Logger that references a string of shorter lifetimes, like so:

```
// lifetime_bounds_short.rs

enum Level {
    Error
}

struct Logger<'a>(&'a str, Level);

fn configure_logger<T>(_t: T) where T: Send + 'static {
    // configure the logger here
}

fn main() {
    let other = String::from("Local");
    let log2 = Logger(&other, Level::Error);
    configure_logger(&log2);
}
```

This will fail with the following error:

```
→  Chapter05 git:(master) ✗ rustc lifetime_bounds_short.rs
error[E0597]: `other` does not live long enough
  --> lifetime_bounds_short.rs:15:24
   |
15 |      let log2 = Logger(&other, Level::Error);
   |                         ^^^^^ borrowed value does not live long enough
16 |      configure_logger(&log2);
17 |  }
   |  - borrowed value only lives until here
   |
   = note: borrowed value must be valid for the static lifetime...

error[E0597]: `log2` does not live long enough
  --> lifetime_bounds_short.rs:16:23
   |
16 |      configure_logger(&log2);
   |                        ^^^^^ borrowed value does not live long enough
17 |  }
   |  - borrowed value only lives until here
   |
   = note: borrowed value must be valid for the static lifetime...

error: aborting due to 2 previous errors

For more information about this error, try `rustc --explain E0597`.
```

The error message clearly say, that the borrowed value must be valid for the static lifetime, but we have passed it a string, which has a lifetime called `'a` from main, which is a shorter lifetime than `'static`.

With the concept of lifetimes under our belt, let's revisit pointer types in Rust.

Pointer types in Rust

Our tale about memory management would be incomplete if we didn't include pointers in the discussion, which are the primary way to manipulate memory in any low level language. Pointers are simply variables that point to memory locations in the process's address space. In Rust, we deal with three kinds of pointers.

References – safe pointers

These pointers are already familiar to you from the borrowing section. References are like pointers in C, but they are checked for correctness. They can never be null and always point to some data owned by any variable. The data they point to can either be on the stack or on the heap, or the data segment of the binary. They are created using the & or the &mut operator. These operators, when prefixed on a type T, create a reference type that is denoted by &T for immutable references and &mut T for mutable references. Let's recap on these again:

* &T: It's an immutable reference to a type T. A &T pointer is a Copy type, which simply means you can have many immutable references to a value T. If you assign this to another variable, you get a copy of the pointer, which points to the same data. It is also fine to have a reference to a reference, such as &&T.
* &mut T: It's an immutable pointer to a type T. Within any scope, you cannot have two mutable references to a value T, due to the borrowing rule. This means that &mut T types do not implement the Copy trait. They also cannot be sent to threads.

Raw pointers

These pointers have a quirky type signature of being prefixed with a *, which also happens to be the dereference operator. They are mostly used in unsafe code. One needs an unsafe block to dereference them. There are two kinds of raw pointers in Rust:

* *const T: An immutable raw pointer to a type T. They are also Copy types. They are similar to &T, it's just that *const T can also be null.
* *mut T: A mutable raw pointer to a value T, which is non-Copy.

As an added note, a reference can be cast to a raw pointer, as shown in the following code:

```
let a = &56;
let a_raw_ptr = a as *const u32;
// or
let b = &mut 5634.3;
let b_mut_ptr = b as *mut T;
```

However, we can't cast a `&T` to a `*mut T`, as it would violate the borrowing rules that allow only one mutable borrow.

For mutable references, we can cast them to `*mut T` or even `*const T`, which is called pointer weakening, as we go from a more capable pointer `&mut T` to a less capable `*const T` pointer. For immutable references, we can only cast them to `*const T`.

However, dereferencing a raw pointer is an unsafe operation. We'll see how raw pointers are useful when we get to `Chapter 10`, *Unsafe Rust and Foreign Function Interfaces*.

Smart pointers

Managing raw pointers is highly unsafe and developers need to be careful about a lot of details when using them. Uninformed usage may lead to issues such as memory leaks, dangling references, and double frees in large code bases in non-obvious ways. To alleviate from these issues, we can use smart pointers, which were popularized by C++.

Rust also has many kinds of smart pointers. They are called smart because they also have extra metadata and code associated with them that gets executed when they are created or destroyed. Being able to automatically free the underlying resource when a smart pointer goes out of scope is one of the major reasons to use smart pointers.

Much of the smartness in smart pointers comes from two traits, called the `Drop` trait and the `Deref` trait. Before we explore the available smart pointer types in Rust, let's understand these traits in detail.

Drop

This is the trait we've been referring to quite a few times which does all the magic of automatically freeing up the resources that are used when a value goes out of scope. The `Drop` trait is akin to what you would call an `object destructor` method in other languages. It contains a single method, `drop`, which gets called when the object goes out of scope. The method takes in a `&mut self` as parameter. Freeing of values with drop is done in **last in, first out**. That is, whatever was constructed the last, gets destructed first. The following code illustrates this:

```
// drop.rs

struct Character {
    name: String,
}
```

```rust
impl Drop for Character {
    fn drop(&mut self) {
        println!("{} went away", self.name)
    }
}

fn main() {
    let steve = Character {
        name: "Steve".into(),
    };
    let john = Character {
        name: "John".into(),
    };
}
```

The output is as follows:

```
→  Chapter05 git:(master) x rustc drop.rs
warning: unused variable: `steve`
  --> drop.rs:14:9
   |
14 |      let steve = Character {
   |          ^^^^^ help: consider using `_steve` instead
   |
   = note: #[warn(unused_variables)] on by default

warning: unused variable: `john`
  --> drop.rs:17:9
   |
17 |      let john = Character {
   |          ^^^^ help: consider using `_john` instead

→  Chapter05 git:(master) x ./drop
John went away
Steve went away
```

The drop method is an ideal place for you to put any cleanup code for your own structs, if
needed. It's especially handy for types where the cleanup is less clearly deterministic, such
as when using reference counted values or garbage collectors. When we instantiate any
`Drop` implementing value (any heap allocated type), the Rust compiler inserts `drop` method
calls after every end of scope, after compilation. So, we don't need to manually call `drop` on
these instances. This kind of automatic reclamation based on scope is inspired by the RAII
principle of C++.

Deref and DerefMut

To provide similar behavior as normal pointers, that is, to be able to dereference the call methods on the underlying type being pointed to, smart pointer types often implement the Deref trait, which allows us to use the * dereferencing operator with these types. While Deref gives you read-only access, there is also DerefMut, which can give you a mutable reference to the underlying type. Deref has the following type signature:

```
pub trait Deref {
    type Target: ?Sized;
    fn deref(&self) -> &Self::Target;
}
```

If defines a single method called Deref that takes self by reference and returns a immutable reference to the underlying type. This combined with the deref coercion feature of Rust, reduces a lot of code that you have to write. Deref coercion is when a type automatically gets converted from one type of reference to some other reference. We'll look at them in Chapter 7, *Advanced Concepts*.

Types of smart pointers

Some of the smart pointer types from the standard library as follows:

- Box<T>: This provides the simplest form of heap allocation. The Box type owns the value inside it, and can thus be used for holding values inside structs or for returning them from functions.
- Rc<T>: This is for reference counting. It increments a counter whenever somebody takes a new reference, and decrements it when someone releases a reference. When the counter hits zero, the value is dropped.
- Arc<T>: This is for atomic reference counting. This is like the previous type, but with atomicity to guarantee multithread safety.
- Cell<T>: This gives us internal mutability for types that implement the Copy trait. In other words, we gain the possibility to get multiple mutable references to something.
- RefCell<T>: This gives us internal mutability for types, without requiring the Copy trait. It uses runtime locking for safety.

Box<T>

The generic type `Box` in the standard library gives us the simplest way to allocate values in the heap. It's simply declared as a tuple struct in the standard library, and wraps any type given to it and puts it on heap. If you're familiar with the concept of boxing and unboxing from other languages, such as Java where you have Boxed integers as the *Integer* class, this provides a similar abstraction. The ownership semantics with `Box` type depends on the wrapped type. If the underlying type is `Copy`, the Box instance becomes copy, otherwise it moves by default.

To create a heap allocated value of type `T` using a `Box`, we simply call the associated `new` method, passing in the value. Creating the `Box` value wrapping a type `T` gives back the `Box` instance, which is a pointer on the stack that points to `T`, which is allocated on the heap. The following example shows how to use `Box`:

```
// box_basics.rs

fn box_ref<T>(b: T) -> Box<T> {
    let a = b;
    Box::new(a)
}

struct Foo;

fn main() {
    let boxed_one = Box::new(Foo);
    let unboxed_one = *boxed_one;
    box_ref(unboxed_one);
}
```

In our main function, we created a heap allocated value in boxed_one by calling `Box::new(Foo)`.

The `Box` type can be used in the following situations:

- It can be used to create recursive type definitions. For example, here is a Node type that represents a node in a singly linked list:

```
// recursive_type.rs

struct Node {
    data: u32,
    next: Option<Node>
}

fn main() {
```

```
        let a = Node { data: 33, next: None };
    }
```

On compiling, we are presented with this error:

```
→  Chapter05 git:(master) X rustc recursive_type.rs
error[E0072]: recursive type `Node` has infinite size
 --> recursive_type.rs:3:1
  |
3 |  struct Node {
  |  ^^^^^^^^^^^ recursive type has infinite size
4 |      data: u32,
5 |      next: Option<Node>
  |      ------------------ recursive without indirection
  |
  = help: insert indirection (e.g., a `Box`, `Rc`, or `&`) at some point to make `Node` representable
```

We cannot have this definition of the Node type because next has a type that refers to itself. If this definition is allowed, there is no end for the compiler to analyze our Node definition as it will keep evaluating it until it hits out of memory. This is better illustrated with the following snippet:

```
struct Node {
    data: u32,
    next: Some(Node {
            data: u32,
            next: Node {
                    data: u32,
                    next: ...
            }
        })
}
```

This evaluation of the Node definition will keep on continuing until the compiler runs out of memory. Also, as every piece of data needs to have a statically known size at compile time, this is a non-representable type in Rust. We need to make the next field something that has a fixed size. We can do this by putting next behind a pointer because pointers are always fixed size. If you see the error message, the compiler, we'll use the Box type Our new Node definition changes like so:

```
struct Node {
    data: u32,
    next: Option<Box<Node>>
}
```

The `Box` type is also used when defining recursive types that need to be hidden behind a `Sized` indirection. So, an enum consisting of a variant with a reference to itself could use the `Box` type to tuck away the variant in the following situations:

- When you need to store types as trait objects
- When you need to store functions in a collection

Reference counted smart pointers

The ownership rule allows only one owner to exist at a time in a given scope. However, there are cases where you need to share the type with multiple variables. For instance, in a GUI library, each of the child widgets needs to have a reference to its parent container widget for things like communicating to layout the child widget based on resize events from the user. While lifetimes allow you to reference the parent node from the child nodes by storing the parent as a `& 'a  Parent` (say), it's often limited by the lifetime `'a` of the value. Once the scope ends, your reference is invalid. In such cases, we need more flexible approaches, and that calls for using reference counting types. These smart pointer types provide shared ownership of values in the program.

Reference counting types enables garbage collection at a granular level. In this approach, a smart pointer type allows you to have multiple references to the wrapped value. Internally, the smart pointer keeps a count of how many references it has given out and are active using a reference counter (hereby refcount), which is just an integral value. As variables that reference the wrapped smart pointer value go out of scope, the refcount value decrements. Once all of the references to the object are gone and the refcount reaches `0`, the value is deallocated. This is how reference counted pointers work in general.

Rust provides us with two kinds of reference counting pointer types:

- `Rc<T>` : This is mainly for use in single threaded environments
- `Arc<T>` is meant to be used in multi-threaded environments

Let's explore the single threaded variant here. We'll take a visit to its multi-threaded counterparts in `Chapter  8`, *Concurrency*.

Rc<T>

When we interact with an Rc type, the following changes happen to it internally:

- When you take a new shared reference to Rc by calling Clone(), Rc increments its internal reference count. Rc internally uses the Cell type for its reference counts
- When the reference goes out of scope, it decrements it
- When all shared references go out of scope, the refcount becomes zero. At this point, the last drop call on Rc does its deallocation

Using reference counted containers gives us more flexibility in the implementation: we can hand out copies of our value as if it were a new copy without having to keep exact track of when the references go out of scope. That doesn't mean that we can mutably alias the inner values.

Rc<T> is mostly used via two methods:

- The static method Rc::new makes a new reference counted container.
- The clone method increments the strong reference count and hands out a new Rc<T>.

Rc internally keeps two kinds of references: strong (Rc<T>) and weak (Weak<T>). Both keep a count of how many references of each type have been handed out, but only when the strong reference count reaches zero so that the values get deallocated. The motivation for this is that an implementation of a data structure may need to point to the same thing multiple times. For instance, an implementation of a tree might have references to both the child nodes and the parent, but incrementing the counter for each reference would not be correct and would lead to reference cycles. The following diagram illustrates the reference cycle situation:

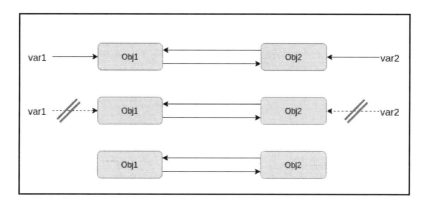

In the preceding diagram, we have two variables, `var1` and `var2`, that reference two resources, `Obj1` and `Obj2`. Along with that, `Obj1` also has a reference to `Obj2` and `Obj2` has a reference to `Obj1`. Both `Obj1` and `Obj2` have reference count of 2 when `var1` and `var2` goes out of scope, the reference count of `Obj1` and `Obj2` reaches 1. They won't get freed because they still refer to each other.

The reference cycle can be broken using weak references. As another example, a linked list might be implemented in such a way that it maintains links via reference counting to both the next item and to the previous. A better way to do this would be to use strong references to one direction and weak references to the other.

Let's see how that might work. Here's a minimal implementation of possibly the least practical but best learning data structure, the singly linked list:

```
// linked_list.rs

use std::rc::Rc;

#[derive(Debug)]
struct LinkedList<T> {
    head: Option<Rc<Node<T>>>
}

#[derive(Debug)]
struct Node<T> {
    next: Option<Rc<Node<T>>>,
    data: T
}

impl<T> LinkedList<T> {
    fn new() -> Self {
        LinkedList { head: None }
    }

    fn append(&self, data: T) -> Self {
        LinkedList {
            head: Some(Rc::new(Node {
                data: data,
                next: self.head.clone()
            }))
        }
    }
}

fn main() {
    let list_of_nums = LinkedList::new().append(1).append(2);
```

```
    println!("nums: {:?}", list_of_nums);

    let list_of_strs = LinkedList::new().append("foo").append("bar");
    println!("strs: {:?}", list_of_strs);
}
```

The linked list is formed of two structs: LinkedList provides a reference to the first element of the list and the list's public API, and Node contains the actual elements. Notice how we're using Rc and cloning the next data pointer on every append. Let's walk through what happens in the append case:

1. LinkedList::new() gives us a new list. Head is None.
2. We append 1 to the list. Head is now the node that contains 1 as data, and next is the previous head: None.
3. We append 2 to the list. Head is now the node that contains 2 as data, and next is the previous head, the node that contains 1 as data.

The debug output from println! confirms this:

```
nums: LinkedList { head: Some(Node { next: Some(Node { next: None, data: 1
}), data: 2 }) }
strs: LinkedList { head: Some(Node { next: Some(Node { next: None, data:
"foo" }), data: "bar" }) }
```

This is a rather functional form of this structure; every append works by just adding data at the head, which means that we don't have to play with references and actual list references can stay immutable. That changes a bit if we want to keep the structure this simple but still have a double-linked list, since then we actually have to change the existing structure.

You can downgrade an Rc<T> type into a Weak<T> type with the downgrade method, and similarly a Weak<T> type can be turned into Rc<T> using the upgrade method. The downgrade method will always work. In contrast, when calling upgrade on a weak reference, the actual value might have been dropped already, in which case you get a None.

So, let's add a weak pointer to the previous node:

```
// rc_weak.rs

use std::rc::Rc;
use std::rc::Weak;

#[derive(Debug)]
struct LinkedList<T> {
    head: Option<Rc<LinkedListNode<T>>>
}
```

```
#[derive(Debug)]
struct LinkedListNode<T> {
    next: Option<Rc<LinkedListNode<T>>>,
    prev: Option<Weak<LinkedListNode<T>>>,
    data: T
}

impl<T> LinkedList<T> {
    fn new() -> Self {
        LinkedList { head: None }
    }

    fn append(&mut self, data: T) -> Self {
        let new_node = Rc::new(LinkedListNode {
            data: data,
            next: self.head.clone(),
            prev: None
        });

        match self.head.clone() {
            Some(node) => {
                node.prev = Some(Rc::downgrade(&new_node));
            },
            None => {
            }
        }

        LinkedList {
            head: Some(new_node)
        }
    }
}

fn main() {
    let list_of_nums = LinkedList::new().append(1).append(2).append(3);
    println!("nums: {:?}", list_of_nums);
}
```

The `append` method grew a bit; we now need to update the previous node of the current
head before returning the newly created head. This is almost good enough, but not quite.
The compiler doesn't let us do invalid operations:

```
→  Chapter05 git:(master) ✗ rustc rc_weak.rs
error[E0594]: cannot assign to field of immutable binding
 --> rc_weak.rs:32:17
   |
32 |                 node.prev = Some(Rc::downgrade(&new_node));
   |                 ^^^^^^^^^^^^^^^^^^^^^^^^^^^^^^^^^^^^^^^^^^^ cannot mutably borrow field of immutable binding

error: aborting due to previous error
```

We could make `append` take a mutable reference to `self`, but that would mean that we could only append to the list if all the nodes' bindings were mutable, forcing the whole structure to be mutable. What we really want is a way to make just one small part of the whole structure mutable, and fortunately we can do that with a single `RefCell`.

1. Add a use for the `RefCell`:

   ```
   use std::cell::RefCell;
   ```

2. Wrap the previous field in `LinkedListNode` in a `RefCell`:

   ```
   // rc_3.rs
   #[derive(Debug)]
   struct LinkedListNode<T> {
       next: Option<Rc<LinkedListNode<T>>>,
       prev: RefCell<Option<Weak<LinkedListNode<T>>>>,
       data: T
   }
   ```

3. We change the `append` method to create a new `RefCell` and update the previous reference via the `RefCell` mutable borrow:

   ```
   // rc_3.rs

   fn append(&mut self, data: T) -> Self {
       let new_node = Rc::new(LinkedListNode {
           data: data,
           next: self.head.Clone(),
           prev: RefCell::new(None)
       });

       match self.head.Clone() {
           Some(node) => {
               let mut prev = node.prev.borrow_mut();
               *prev = Some(Rc::downgrade(&new_node));
           },
           None => {
           }
       }

       LinkedList {
           head: Some(new_node)
       }
   }
   ```

Whenever we're using `RefCell` borrows, it's a good practice to think carefully that we're using it in a safe way, since making mistakes there may lead to runtime panics. In this implementation, however, it's easy to see that we have just the single `borrow`, and that the closing block immediately discards it.

Apart from shared ownership, we can also get shared mutability at runtime with Rust's concept of interior mutability, which are modeled by special wrapper smart pointer types.

Interior mutability

As we saw previously, Rust protects us at compile time from the pointer aliasing problem by allowing only a single mutable reference at any given scope. However, there are cases where it becomes too restrictive, making code that we know is safe not pass the compiler because of the strict borrow checking. For these situations, one of the solutions is to move the borrow checking from compile time to runtime, which is achieved with *interior mutability*. Before we talk about the types that enable interior mutability, we need to understand the concept of interior mutability and inherited mutability:

- **Inherited mutability**: This is the default mutability you get when you take a `&mut` reference to some struct. This also implies that you can modify any of the fields of the struct.
- **Interior mutability**: In this kind of mutability, even if you have a `&SomeStruct` reference to some type, you can modify its fields if the fields have the type as `Cell<T>` or `RefCell<T>`.

Interior mutability allows for bending the borrowing rules a bit, but it also puts the burden on the programmer to ensure that no two mutable borrows are present at runtime. These types offload the detection of multiple mutable references from compile time to runtime and undergo a panic if two mutable references to a value exist. Interior mutability is often used when you want to expose an immutable API to users, despite having mutable parts to the API internally. The standard library has two generic smart pointer types that provide shared mutability: `Cell` and `RefCell`.

Cell<T>

Consider this program, where we have a requirement to mutate `bag` with two mutable references to it:

```
// without_cell.rs

use std::cell::Cell;
```

```
#[derive(Debug)]
struct Bag {
    item: Box<u32>
}

fn main() {
    let mut bag = Cell::new(Bag { item: Box::new(1) });
    let hand1 = &mut bag;
    let hand2 = &mut bag;
    *hand1 = Cell::new(Bag {item: Box::new(2)});
    *hand2 = Cell::new(Bag {item: Box::new(2)});
}
```

But, of course, this does not compile due to the borrow checking rules:

```
→ Chapter05 git:(master) ✗ rustc without_cell.rs
error[E0499]: cannot borrow `bag` as mutable more than once at a time
  --> without_cell.rs:13:22
   |
12 |         let hand1 = &mut bag;
   |                          --- first mutable borrow occurs here
13 |         let hand2 = &mut bag;
   |                          ^^^ second mutable borrow occurs here
...
16 | }
   | - first borrow ends here

error: aborting due to previous error
```

We can make this work by encapsulating the bag value inside a Cell. Our code is updated as follows:

```
// cell.rs

use std::cell::Cell;

#[derive(Debug)]
struct Bag {
    item: Box<u32>
}

fn main() {
    let bag = Cell::new(Bag { item: Box::new(1) });
    let hand1 = &bag;
    let hand2 = &bag;
    hand1.set(Bag { item: Box::new(2)});
    hand2.set(Bag { item: Box::new(3)});
}
```

This works as you would expect, and the only added cost is that you have to write a bit more. The additional runtime cost is zero, though, and the references to the mutable things remain immutable.

The `Cell<T>` type is a smart pointer type that enables mutability for values, even behind an immutable reference. It provides this capability with very minimal overhead and has a minimal API:

- `Cell::new` method allows you to create new instances of the `Cell` type by passing it any type `T`.
- `get`: The `get` method allows you to copy of the value in the cell. This method is only available if the wrapped type `T` is `Copy`.
- `set`: Allows you to modify the inner value, even behind a immutable reference.

RefCell<T>

If you need Cell-like features for non-Copy types, there is the `RefCell` type. It uses a read/write pattern similar to how borrowing works, but moves the checks to runtime, which is convenient but not zero-cost. RefCell hands out references to the value, instead of returning things by value as is the case with the `Cell` type. Here's a sample program that

```
// refcell_basics.rs

use std::cell::RefCell;

#[derive(Debug)]
struct Bag {
    item: Box<u32>
}

fn main() {
    let bag = RefCell::new(Bag { item: Box::new(1) });
    let hand1 = &bag;
    let hand2 = &bag;
    *hand1.borrow_mut() = Bag { item: Box::new(2) };
    *hand2.borrow_mut() = Bag { item: Box::new(3) };
    let borrowed = hand1.borrow();
    println!("{:?}", borrowed);
}
```

As you can see, we can borrow `bag`, mutably from `hand1` and `hand2` even though they are declared as immutable variables. To modify the items in bag, we called `borrow_mut` on `hand1` and `hand2`. Later, we borrow it immutably and print the contents.

The `RefCell` type provides us with the following two borrowing methods:

- The `borrow` method takes a new immutable reference
- The `borrow_mut` method takes a new mutable reference

Now, if we try to call both of the methods in the same scope: by changing the last line in the preceding code to this:

```
println!("{:?} {:?}", hand1.borrow(), hand1.borrow_mut());
```

We get to see the following upon running the program:

```
thread 'main' panicked at 'already borrowed: BorrowMutError',
src/libcore/result.rs:1009:5
note: Run with `RUST_BACKTRACE=1` for a backtrace.
```

A runtime panic ! This is because of the same ownership rule of having exclusive mutable access. But, for `RefCell` this is checked at runtime instead. For situations like this, one has to explicitly use bare blocks to separate the borrows or use the drop method to drop the reference.

 Note: The Cell and RefCell types are not thread safe. This simply means that Rust won't allow you to share these types in multiple threads.

Uses of interior mutability

In the previous section, the examples on using `Cell` and `RefCell` were simplified, and you most probably won't need to use them in that form in real code. Let's take a look at some actual benefits that these types would give us.

As we mentioned previously, the mutability of a binding is not fine-grained; a value is either immutable or mutable, and that includes all of its fields if it's a struct or an enum. `Cell` and `RefCell` can turn an immutable thing into something that's mutable, allowing us to define parts of an immutable struct as mutable.

The following piece of code augments a struct with two integers and a `sum` method to cache the answer of the `sum` and return the cached value if it exists:

```
// cell_cache.rs

use std::cell::Cell;
```

```
struct Point {
    x: u8,
    y: u8,
    cached_sum: Cell<Option<u8>>
}

impl Point {
    fn sum(&self) -> u8 {
        match self.cached_sum.get() {
            Some(sum) => {
                println!("Got from cache: {}", sum);
                sum
            },
            None => {
                let new_sum = self.x + self.y;
                self.cached_sum.set(Some(new_sum));
                println!("Set cache: {}", new_sum);
                new_sum
            }
        }
    }
}

fn main() {
    let p = Point { x: 8, y: 9, cached_sum: Cell::new(None) };
    println!("Summed result: {}", p.sum());
    println!("Summed result: {}", p.sum());
}
```

The following is the output of this program:

```
→  Chapter05 git:(master) ✗ rustc cell_cache.rs
→  Chapter05 git:(master) ✗ ./cell_cache
Set cache: 17
Summed result: 17
Got from cache: 17
Summed result: 17
```

Summary

Rust takes a low-level systems programming approach to memory management, promising C-like performance, sometimes even better. It does this without requiring a garbage collector through its use of ownership, lifetimes, and borrow semantics. We covered a whole lot of ground here in a subject that's probably the heaviest to grasp for a new Rustacean. That's what people familiar with Rust like to call themselves, and you are getting close to becoming one! Getting fluent in this shift of thinking of ownership at compile time takes a bit of time, but the investment in learning these concepts pays off in the form of reliable software with a small memory footprint.

Our next chapter will concern how fallible situations are handled in Rust. See you there!

6
Error Handling

In this chapter, we'll take a look at how fallible and unexpected situations are handled in Rust, gain an understanding of the error handling with errors as types, and look at how to design interfaces that compose well with error types. We aim to cover the first two error scenarios as they are under our control and languages generally provide mechanisms for handling these errors. If fatal errors occur, our program gets aborted by the operating system kernel and so we don't have much control over them.

In this chapter, we will cover the following topics:

- Error handling prelude
- Recovering from errors using the `Option` and `Result` types
- Combinator methods for `Option` and `Result`
- Propagating errors
- Non-recoverable errors
- Custom errors and the `Error` trait

Error handling prelude

"From then on, when anything went wrong with a computer, we said it had bugs in it."

- Grace Hopper

Writing programs that behave well under expected conditions is a good start. It's when a program encounters unexpected situations where it gets really challenging. Proper error handling is an important but often overlooked practice in software development. Most error handling, in general, falls into three categories:

- Recoverable errors that are expected to happen due to the user and the environment interacting with the program, for example, a **file not found** error or a number parse error.
- Non-recoverable errors that violate the contracts or invariants of the program, for example, **index out of bounds** or **divide by zero**.
- Fatal errors that abort the program immediately. Such situations include running out of memory, and stack overflow.

Programming in the real world often entails dealing with errors. Examples include malicious input to a web application, connection failures in network clients, filesystem corruption, and integer overflow errors in numerical applications. In the event of there being no error handling, the program just crashes or is aborted by the OS when it hits an unexpected situation. Most of the time, this is not the behavior we want our programs to exhibit in unexpected situation. Consider, for example, a real-time stream processing service that fails to receive messages from clients at some point in time due to a failure in parsing messages from a client who is sending malformed messages. If we have no way to handle this, our service will abort every time we have parsing errors. This is not good from a usability perspective and is definitely not a characteristic of network applications. The ideal way for the service to handle this situation is to catch the error, act upon it, pass the error log to a log-aggregation service for later analysis and continue receiving messages from other clients. That's when a recoverable way of handling errors comes into the picture, and is often the practical way to model error handling. In this case, the language's error handling constructs enable programmers to intercept errors and take action against them, which saves the program from being aborted.

Two paradigms that are quite popular when approaching error handling are return codes and exceptions. The C language embraces the return code model. This is a very trivial form of error handling, where functions use integers as return values to signify whether an operation succeeded or failed. A lot of C functions return a -1 or NULL in the event of an error. For errors when invoking system calls, C sets the global `errno` variable upon failure. But, being a global variable, nothing stops you from modifying the `errno` variable from anywhere in the program. It's then for the programmer to check for this error value and handle it. Often, this gets really cryptic, error-prone, and is not a very flexible solution. The compiler does not warn us if we forget to check the return value either, unless you use a static analysis tool.

Another approach to handling errors is via exceptions. Higher-level programming languages such as Java and C# use this form of error handling. In this paradigm, code that might fail should be wrapped in a `try {}` block and any failure within the `try{}` block must be caught in a `catch {}` block (ideally, with the `catch` block immediately after the `try` block). But, exceptions also have their downsides. Throwing an exception is expensive, as the program has to unwind the stack, find the appropriate exception handler, and run the associated code. To avoid this overhead, programmers often adopt the defensive code style of checking for exception-throwing code and then proceeding forward. Also, the implementation of exceptions is flawed in many languages, because it allows ignorant programmers to swallow exceptions with a catch all block with a base exception class such as a throwable in Java, thereby resulting in a possibly inconsistent state in the program if they just log and ignore the exception. Also, in these languages, there is no way for a programmer to know by looking at the code whether a method could throw an exception, unless they are using methods with checked exceptions. This makes it hard for programmers to write safe code. Due to this, programmers often need to rely on the documentation (if it exists at all) of methods to figure out whether they could throw an exception.

Rust, on the other hand, embraces type-based error handling, which is seen in functional languages such as OCaml and Haskell, and at the same time also appears similar to C's returning error code model. But in RUST, the return values are proper error types and can be user-defined, The language's type system mandates handling error states at compile time. If you know Haskell, it is quite similar to its `Maybe` and `Either` types; Rust just has different names for them, that is, `Option` and `Result` for recoverable errors. For non-recoverable errors, there's a mechanism called **panic**, which is a fail-hard error handling strategy and it is advisable to use it as a last resort when there is a bug or violation of an invariant in the program.

Why did Rust choose this form of error handling? Well, as we have already said, exceptions and their associated stack unwinding have an overhead. This goes against Rust's central philosophy of zero runtime costs. Secondly, exception-style error handling, as it is typically implemented, allows ignoring these errors via catch-all exception handlers. This creates the potential for program state inconsistency, which goes against Rust's safety tenet.

With the prelude aside, let's dig into some recoverable error handling strategies!

Recoverable errors

As we have already said, the majority of error handling in Rust is done via two generic types, Option and Result. They act as wrapper types in the sense that it is recommended that APIs that can fail return the actual values by putting them inside these types. These types are built with a combination of enums and generics. As an enum, they get the ability to store a success state and an error state, while generics allow them to specialize at compile time so that they store any value in either state. These types also come with a lot of convenient methods (commonly known as **combinators**) implemented on them, allowing you to consume, compose, or transform the inner values easily. One thing to note about the Option and Result types is that they are ordinary types from the standard library in the sense that they aren't compiler built-ins that are treated differently by the compiler. Anyone can create a similar error abstraction using the power of enums and generics. Let's start exploring them by first looking at the simplest one, that is, Option.

Option

In languages that have the notion of nullable values, there is a defensive code style that programmers adopt to perform operations on any value that can possibly be null. Taking an example from Kotlin/Java, it appears something like this:

```kotlin
// kotlin pseudocode

val container = collection.get("some_id")

if (container != null) {
    container.process_item();
} else {
    // no luck
}
```

First, we check that container is not null and then call process_item on it. If we forget the null safety check, we'll get the infamous NullPointerException when we try to invoke container.process_item() – you only get to know this at runtime when it throws the exception. Another downside is the fact that we can't deduce right away whether container is null just by looking at the code. To save against that, the code base needs to be sprinkled with these null checks, which hinder its readability to a great extent.

Rust does not have the notion of null values, which is infamously quoted as being the billion-dollar mistake by *Tony Hoare*, who introduced `null` references in the ALGOL W language back in 1965. In Rust, APIs that might fail and want to indicate a missing value are meant to return `Option`. This error type is suitable when any of our APIs, along with a succeeding value, want to signify the absence of a value. To put it simply, it's quite analogous to nullable values, but here, the `null` check is explicit and is enforced by the type system at compile time.

`Option` has the following type signature:

```
pub enum Option<T> {
    /// No value
    None,
    /// Some value `T`
    Some(T),
}
```

It's an enum with two variants and is generic over `T`. We create an `Option` value by using either `let wrapped_i32 = Some(2);` or `let empty: Option<i32> = None;`.

Operations that succeed can use the `Some(T)` variable to store any value, `T`, or use the `None` variable to signify that the value is `null` in the case of a failed state. Though we are less likely to create `None` values explicitly, when we need to create a `None` value, we need to specify the type on the left, as Rust is unable to infer the type from the right-hand side. We could have also initialized it on the right, as `None::<i32>;` using the `turbofish` operator, but specifying the type on the left is identified as idiomatic Rust code.

As you may have noticed, we didn't create the `Option` values through the full syntax, that is, `Option::Some(2)`, but directly as `Some(2)`. This is because both of its variants are automatically re-exported from the `std` crate (Rust's standard library crate) as part of the prelude module (`https://doc.rust-lang.org/std/prelude/`). The prelude module contains re-exports of most commonly used types, functions, and any modules from the standard library. These re-exports are just a convenience that's provided by the `std` crate. Without them, we would have to write the full syntax every time we needed to use these frequently used types. As a result, this allows us to instantiate `Option` values directly through the variants. This is also the case with the `Result` type.

So, creating them is easy, but what does it look like when you are interacting with an `Option` value? From the standard library, we have the `get` method on the `HashMap` type, which returns an `Option`:

```
// using_options.rs

use std::collections::HashMap;

fn main() {
    let mut map = HashMap::new();
    map.insert("one", 1);
    map.insert("two", 2);

    let value = map.get("one");
    let incremented_value = value + 1;
}
```

Here, we create a new `HashMap` map of `&str` as the key and `i32` as the value, and later, we retrieve the value for the `"one"` key and assign it to the `value` . After compiling, we get the following error message:

```
→  Chapter06 git:(master) x rustc using_options.rs
error[E0369]: binary operation `+` cannot be applied to type `std::option::Option<&{integer}>`
  --> using_options.rs:10:29
   |
10 |     let incremented_value = value + 1;
   |                             ^^^^^^^^^
   |
   = note: an implementation of `std::ops::Add` might be missing for `std::option::Option<&{integer}>`

error: aborting due to previous error

For more information about this error, try `rustc --explain E0369`.
```

Why can't we add 1 to our `value`? As someone familiar with imperative languages, we expect `map.get()` to return an `i32` value if the key exists or a null otherwise. But here, `value` is an `Option<&i32>`. The `get()` method returns an `Option<&T>`, and not the inner value (a `&i32`) because there is also the possibility that we might not have the key we are looking for and so `get` can return `None` in that case. It gives a misleading error message, though, because Rust doesn't know how to add an `i32` to a `Option<&i32>`, as no such implementation of the `Add` trait exists for these two types. However, it indeed exists for two i32's or two &i32's.

So, to add 1 to our `value`, we need to extract `i32` from `Option`. Here, we can see Rust's explicit error handling behavior spring into action. We can only interact with the inner `i32` value after we check whether `map.get()` is a `Some` variant or a `None` variant.

To check for the variants, we have two approaches; one of which is pattern matching or `if let`:

```
// using_options_match.rs

use std::collections::HashMap;

fn main() {
    let mut map = HashMap::new();
    map.insert("one", 1);
    map.insert("two", 2);

    let incremented_value = match map.get("one") {
        Some(val) => val + 1,
        None => 0
    };
    println!("{}", incremented_value);
}
```

With this approach, we match against the return value of `map.get()` and take actions based on the variant. In the case of `None`, we simply assign 0 to `incremented_value`. Another way we could have done this is by using `if let`:

```
let incremented_value = if let Some(v) = map.get("one") {
    v + 1
} else {
    0
};
```

This is recommended for cases where we are only interested in one variant of our value and want to do a common operation for other variants. In those cases, `if let` is much cleaner.

Unwrapping: The other, less safe, approach is to use unwrapping methods on `Option`, that is, the `unwrap()` and the `expect()` methods. Calling these methods will extract the inner value if it's a `Some`, but will panic if it's a `None`. These methods are recommended only when we are really sure that the `Option` value is indeed a `Some` value:

```
// using_options_unwrap.rs

use std::collections::HashMap;

fn main() {
```

```
    let mut map = HashMap::new();
    map.insert("one", 1);
    map.insert("two", 2);
    let incremented_value = map.get("three").unwrap() + 1;
    println!("{}", incremented_value);
}
```

Running the preceding code panics, showing the following message because we unwrapped a None value as we don't have any value for the three key:

```
thread 'main' panicked at 'called `Option::unwrap()` on a `None` value',
libcore/option.rs:345:21
note: Run with `RUST_BACKTRACE=1` for a backtrace.
```

Between the two, expect() is preferred because it allows you to pass a string as a message to be printed upon panic, and shows the exact line number in your source file where the panic happened, whereas unwrap() does not allow you to pass debug messages as arguments and shows a line number in the standard library source file where the unwrap() method of Option is defined, which is not very helpful. These methods are also present on the Result type.

Next, let's look at the Result type.

Result

Result is similar to Option, but with the added advantage of storing arbitrary error values with more context on the error, instead of just None. This type is suitable when we want the user to know why an operation failed. Here's the type signature of Result:

```
enum Result<T, E> {
    Ok(T),
    Err(E),
}
```

It has two variants, both of which are generic. Ok(T) is the variant we use for the success state putting in any value, T, while Err(E) is what we use in the error state putting in any error value, E. We can create them like so:

```
// create_result.rs

fn main() {
    let my_result = Ok(64);
    let my_err = Err("oh no!");
}
```

However, this does not compile, and we receive the following error message:

```
→  Chapter06 git:(master) ✗ rustc create_result.rs
error[E0282]: type annotations needed
  --> create_result.rs:4:21
   |
4  |     let my_result = Ok(64);
   |         ---------    ^^ cannot infer type for `E`
   |         |
   |         consider giving `my_result` a type

error: aborting due to previous error
```

As `Result` has two generic variants and we gave the concrete type for only the `Ok` variant for `my_result`; it doesn't know the concrete type of `E`. This is similar for the `my_err` value. We need to specify concrete types for both, like so:

```
// create_result_fixed.rs

fn main() {
    let _my_result: Result<_, ()> = Ok(64);
    // or
    let _my_result = Ok::<_, ()>(64);

    // similarly we create Err variants

    let _my_err = Err::<(), f32>(345.3);
    let _other_err: Result<bool, String> = Err("Wait, what ?".to_string());
}
```

In the first case of creating values of the rgw `Ok` variant, we used `()` to specify the type, `E`, of the `Err` variant. In the second part of the snippet, we created values of the `Err` variant in a similar way, this time specifying a concrete type for the `Ok` variant. We can use underscores to ask Rust to infer types for us in obvious cases.

Next, we'll see how we can interact with `Result` values. Many file manipulation APIs in the standard library return a `Result` type, because there can be different reasons for failure such as **file not found**, **directory does not exists**, and **permission errors**. These can be put into the `Err` variant to let the user know of the exact cause. For the demo, we'll try to open a file, read its contents into a `String`, and print the contents, as shown in the following snippet:

```
// result_basics.rs

use std::fs::File;
use std::io::Read;
use std::path::Path;
```

```
fn main() {
    let path = Path::new("data.txt");
    let file = File::open(&path);
    let mut s = String::new();
    file.read_to_string(&mut s);
    println!("Message: {}", s);
}
```

This is how the compiler responds:

```
→  Chapter06 git:(master) x rustc result_basics.rs
error[E0599]: no method named `read_to_string` found for type `std::result::Result<std::fs::File, std::
  --> result_basics.rs:11:10

11 |         file.read_to_string(&mut s);
                 ^^^^^^^^^^^^^^^^

error: aborting due to previous error

For more information about this error, try `rustc --explain E0599`.
```

We created a new file by calling `open` from `File`, providing our path to `data.txt`, which doesn't exist. When we call `read_to_string` on `file`, and try to read it into `s`, we get the preceding error. Examining the error message, it appears that `file` has a type of `Result<File, Error>`. From its documentation, the `open` method is defined like so:

```
fn open<P: AsRef<Path>>(path: P) -> Result<File>
```

To astute observers, there may be a source of confusion, as it looks like `Result` is missing the generic `E` type for the error variant, but it's simply hidden away by a type alias. If we look at the `type` alias definition in the `std::io` module, it is defined as follows:

```
type Result<T> = Result<T, std::io::Error>;
```

So, it is type aliased with a common error type of `std::io::Error`. This is because a lot of APIs in the standard library use this as an error type. This is another benefit of type aliases, where we can extract common parts from our type signature. Putting that tip aside, to be able to call the `read_to_string` method on our `file`, we need to extract the inner `File` instance, that is, perform pattern matching on variants. By doing this, the preceding code changes, as follows:

```
// result_basics_fixed.rs

use std::fs::File;
use std::io::Read;
use std::path::Path;

fn main() {
```

```
        let path = Path::new("data.txt");
        let mut file = match File::open(&path) {
            Ok(file) => file,
            Err(err) => panic!("Error while opening file: {}", err),
        };

        let mut s = String::new();
        file.read_to_string(&mut s);
        println!("Message: {}", s);
    }
```

Here, we made two changes. First, we made the file variable mutable. Why? Because the function signature of read_to_string is as follows:

```
        fn read_to_string(&mut self, buf: &mut String) -> Result<usize>
```

The first parameter being `&mut self` means that the instance we are calling this method on needs to be mutable because reading the file changes, internal pointers of the file handle. Secondly, we handled both the variants, where, in the Ok case, we return the actual File object if everything was good, but crash when we get an Err value and display an error message.

With this change, let's compile and run this program:

```
warning: unused `std::result::Result` which must be used
  --> result_basics.rs:15:5
   |
15 |       file.read_to_string(&mut s);
   |       ^^^^^^^^^^^^^^^^^^^^^^^^^^^^
   |
   = note: #[warn(unused_must_use)] on by default
   = note: this `Result` may be an `Err` variant, which should be handled

→ Chapter05 git:(master) x ./result_basics
thread 'main' panicked at 'Error while opening file: No such file or directory (os error 2)', result_basics.rs:11:21
note: Run with `RUST_BACKTRACE=1` for a backtrace.
```

This panics because we don't have a file named data.txt in our directory. Try creating a file with the same name with any arbitrary text in it and run this program again to see it succeed. First, though, let's do something about that warning. Warnings are always a sign of poor code quality, and we ideally want to have none of them. The warning is there because File::read_to_string (a method from the Read trait) returns a value of type Result<usize>. Rust warns you whenever a return value from a function call is ignored. Here, the usize value in Result<usize> tells us how many bytes were read into the string.

We have two ways of handling this warning:

- Handle both the Ok and Err cases as before for the Result value returned by the read_to_string method
- Assign the return value to a special variable _ (**underscore**), which lets the compiler know that we want to ignore the value

For cases where we don't care about the value, we can use the second approach and so the read_to_string line changes as follows:

```
let _ = file.read_to_string(&mut s);
```

With that change, the code compiles without warnings. However, you should handle the return value and try not to use the catch all underscore variable.

Combinators on Option/Result

As Option and Result are wrapper types, the only way to safely interact with their inner values is either through pattern matching or if let. This paradigm of using matching and then acting on the inner values is a very common operation and, as such, it becomes very tedious having to write them every time. Fortunately, these wrapper types come with lots of helper methods, also known as combinators, implemented on them that allow you to manipulate the inner values easily.

These are generic methods and there are many kinds depending on the use case. Some methods act on success values, such as Ok(T)/Some(T), while some of them act on failed values, such as Err(E)/None. Some methods unwrap and extract the inner value, while some preserve the structure of the wrapper type modifying just the inner values.

 Note: In this section, when we talk about success values, we are commonly referring to Ok(T)/Some(T) variants and when we talk about failed values, we are referring to Err(T)/None variants.

Common combinators

Let's look at some of the useful combinators that are available for both the `Option` and `Result` types:

> `map`: This method allows you to transform the success value, `T`, to another value, `U`. The following is the type signature of `map` for the `Option` type:

```
pub fn map<U, F>(self, f: F) -> Option<U>
where F: FnOnce(T) -> U {
    match self {
        Some(x) => Some(f(x)),
        None => None,
    }
}
```

The following is the signature for the `Result` type:

```
pub fn map<U, F>(self, f: F) -> Option<U>
where F: FnOnce(T) -> U {
    match self {
        Ok(t) => Ok(f(t)),
        Err(e) => Err(e)
    }
}
```

This method's type signature can be read as follows: `map` is a generic method over `U` and `F`, and takes `self` by value. It then takes a parameter, `f`, of type `F` and returns an `Option<U>`, where `F` is constrained by the `FnOnce` trait, which has an input parameter, `T`, and a return type of `U`. Phew! That was quite a mouthful.

Let's make this simpler to understand. There are two parts to understand about the `map` method. First, it takes a parameter as `self`, which means the value on which this method is called is consumed after the call. Second, it takes in a parameter, `f`, of type `F`. This is a closure that's provided to `map`, which tells it how to do the conversion from `T` to `U`. The closure is generically represented as `F` and the `where` clause says that `F` is `FnOnce(T) -> U`. This is a special type of trait that is only applicable to closures and hence has a function like the signature of `(T) -> U`. The `FnOnce` prefix just means that this closure takes ownership of the input parameter, `T`, signifying that we can only call this closure once with `T` as `T` will be consumed upon invocation. We'll look into closures in more depth in `Chapter 7`, *Advanced Concepts*. The `map` method does nothing if the value is a failed value.

Using combinators

Using the `map` method is simple:

```
// using_map.rs

fn get_nth(items: &Vec<usize>, nth: usize) -> Option<usize> {
    if nth < items.len() {
        Some(items[nth])
    } else {
        None
    }
}

fn double(val: usize) -> usize {
    val * val
}

fn main() {
    let items = vec![7, 6, 4, 3, 5, 3, 10, 3, 2, 4];
    println!("{}", items.len());
    let doubled = get_nth(&items, 4).map(double);
    println!("{:?}", doubled);
}
```

In the preceding code, we have a method called `get_nth` that gives us the `nth` element
from `Vec<usize>` and returns `None` if it couldn't find one. We then have a use case where
we want to double the value. We can use the `map` method on the return value of `get_nth`,
passing in the `double` function we defined previously. Alternatively, we could have
provided a closure written inline, like the following:

```
let doubled = get_nth(&items, 10).map(|v| v * v);
```

This is quite a concise way to chain operations! This is less verbose than using `match` or `if
let`.

The preceding explanation of the `map` method is very much applicable to the next set of methods that we'll look at, so we'll skip explaining their type signature as it would be too noisy for us to go through every one of them. Instead, we'll just explain briefly the functionality that's provided by these methods. You are encouraged to read and become familiar with their type signature by referring to their documentation:

- `map_err`: This method acts only on `Result` types and allows transforming the failed value from `E` to some other type, `H`, but only if the value is an `Err` value. `map_err` is not defined for `Option` types, as doing anything with `None` would be pointless.
- `and_then`: In the case of a failed value, this returns the value as is, but in the case of a successful value, this takes in a closure as the second argument, which acts on the wrapped value and returns the wrapped type. This is useful when you need to perform transformations on the inner values, one after another.
- `unwrap_or`: This method extracts the inner success value, or returns a default one if it's a failed value. You provide the default value to it as a second argument.
- `unwrap_or_else`: This method acts the same as the preceding method but computes a different value when it is a failed value by taking a closure as the second argument.
- `as_ref`: This method converts the inner value to a reference and returns the wrapped value, that is, an `Option<&T>` or a `Result<&T, &E>`.
- `or`/ `or_else`: These methods return the value as is if it's a success value, or returns an alternative `Ok`/`Some` value, which is provided as the second argument. `or_else` accepts a closure within which you need to return a success value.
- `as_mut`: This method converts the inner value into a mutable reference and returns the wrapped value, that is, an `Option<&mut T>` or a `Result<&mut T, &mut E>`.

There are many more that are unique to the `Option` and `Result` types.

Converting between Option and Result

We also have methods where one wrapper type can be converted into another, depending on how you want to compose those values with your APIs. They become really handy in situations where we are interacting with third-party crates, where we have a value as an Option, but the crate's method we are using accepts a Result as a type, as follows:

- ok_or: This method converts an Option value to a Result value, by taking in an error value as a second parameter. A similar variant to this is the ok_or_else method, which should be preferred over this, as it computes the value lazily by taking in a closure.
- ok: This method converts a Result into an Option consuming self, and discards the Err value.

Early returns and the ? operator

This is another pattern that is quite common when we interact with Result types. The pattern goes as follows: when we have a success value, we immediately want to extract it, but when we have an error value, we want to make an early return and propagate the error to the caller. To illustrate this pattern, we will use the following snippet, which uses the usual match expression to act on the Result type:

```
// result_common_pattern.rs

use std::string::FromUtf8Error;

fn str_upper_match(str: Vec<u8>) -> Result<String, FromUtf8Error> {
    let ret = match String::from_utf8(str) {
        Ok(str) => str.to_uppercase(),
        Err(err) => return Err(err)
    };

    println!("Conversion succeeded: {}", ret);
    Ok(ret)
}

fn main() {
    let invalid_str = str_upper_match(vec![197, 198]);
    println!("{:?}", invalid_str);
}
```

The ? operator abstracts this pattern, making it possible to write the `bytes_to_str` method in a more concise way:

```
// using_question_operator.rs

use std::string::FromUtf8Error;

fn str_upper_concise(str: Vec<u8>) -> Result<String, FromUtf8Error> {
    let ret = String::from_utf8(str).map(|s| s.to_uppercase())?;
    println!("Conversion succeeded: {}", ret);
    Ok(ret)
}

fn main() {
    let valid_str = str_upper_concise(vec![121, 97, 89]);
    println!("{:?}", valid_str);
}
```

This operator becomes even nicer if you have a sequence of `Result`/`Option` returning method calls, where a failure in each operator should mean a failure of the whole. For instance, we could write the whole operation of creating a file and writing to it as follows:

```
let _ = File::create("foo.txt")?.write_all(b"Hello world!")?;
```

It works pretty much as a replacement for the `try!` macro, which does the same thing as before ? was implemented in the compiler. Now, ? is a replacement for that, but there are some plans to make it more generic and usable for other cases, too.

Bonus tip: The `main` function also allows you to return `Result` types. Specifically, it allows you to return types that implement the `Termination` trait. This means that we can also write `main` as follows:

```
// main_result.rs

fn main() -> Result<(), &'static str> {
    let s = vec!["apple", "mango", "banana"];
    let fourth = s.get(4).ok_or("I got only 3 fruits")?;
    Ok(())
}
```

Next, let's move on to dealing with non-recoverable errors.

Non-recoverable errors

When code that's in the execution phase encounters a bug, or one of its variants is violated, it has the potential to corrupt the program state in unexpected ways if it's ignored. These situations are deemed non-recoverable because of their inconsistent program state, which may lead to faulty outputs or unexpected behavior later. This means that a fail-stop approach is the best way to recover from them so as to not harm other parts or systems indirectly. For these kinds of cases, Rust provides us with a mechanism called **panic**, which aborts the thread on which it is invoked and does not affect any other threads. If the main thread is the one facing the panic, then the program aborts with a non-zero exit code of 101. If it's a child thread, the panic does not propagate to the parent thread and halts at the thread boundary. A panic in one thread does not affect the other threads and is isolated, except in cases where they corrupt a mutex lock on some shared data; it is implemented as a macro by the same panic! mechanism.

When panic! is called, the panicking thread starts unwinding the function call stack, starting from the place at which it was invoked, all the way until the entry point in the thread. It also generates a stack trace or a backtrace for all functions that are invoked in this process, just like exceptions. But in this case, it does not have to look for any exception handlers, as they don't exist in Rust. Unwinding is the process of moving up the function call chain while cleaning up or freeing resource, from each function call stack. These resources can be stack allocated or heap allocated. Stack allocated resources automatically get released once the function ends. For variables pointing to heap allocated resources, Rust calls the drop method on them, which frees up the memory used by the resource. This cleanup is necessary to avoid memory leaks. Apart from code calling panic explicitly, Result/Option error types also call panic if any code does unwrap on failed values, that is, Err/None. panic is also the choice that's used for failing assertions in unit tests, and it's encouraged to fail tests with panics by using the #[should_panic] attribute.

In the case of single-threaded code having panics on the main thread, unwinding doesn't provide much of a benefit, as the operating system reclaims all the memory after the process aborts. Fortunately, there are options to turn off unwinding in panic, which may be required on platforms such as embedded systems, where we have a single main thread doing all the work and where unwinding is an expensive operation that isn't of much use.

To figure out the sequence of calls that led to the panic, we can view the backtrace from the thread by running any panicking program and setting the RUST_BACKTRACE=1 environment variable from our command-line shell. Here's an example where we have two threads, where both of them panic:

```rust
// panic_unwinding.rs

use std::thread;

fn alice() -> thread::JoinHandle<()> {
    thread::spawn(move || {
        bob();
    })
}

fn bob() {
    malice();
}

fn malice() {
    panic!("malice is panicking!");
}

fn main() {
    let child = alice();
    let _ = child.join();

    bob();
    println!("This is unreachable code");
}
```

alice spawns a new thread using thread::spawn and calls bob within the closure. bob calls malice, which in turn panics. main also calls bob, which panics.

Here's the output of running this program:

```
→  Chapter06 git:(master) x RUST_BACKTRACE=1 ./panic_unwinding
thread '<unnamed>' panicked at 'malice is panicking!', panic_unwinding.rs:16:5
note: Some details are omitted, run with `RUST_BACKTRACE=full` for a verbose backtrace.
stack backtrace:
   0: std::sys::unix::backtrace::tracing::imp::unwind_backtrace
             at libstd/sys/unix/backtrace/tracing/gcc_s.rs:49
   1: std::sys_common::backtrace::print
             at libstd/sys_common/backtrace.rs:71
             at libstd/sys_common/backtrace.rs:59
   2: std::panicking::default_hook::{{closure}}
             at libstd/panicking.rs:211
   3: std::panicking::default_hook
             at libstd/panicking.rs:227
   4: std::panicking::rust_panic_with_hook
             at libstd/panicking.rs:475
   5: std::panicking::begin_panic
   6: panic_unwinding::malice
   7: panic_unwinding::bob
   8: panic_unwinding::alice::{{closure}}
thread 'main' panicked at 'malice is panicking!', panic_unwinding.rs:16:5
stack backtrace:
   0: std::sys::unix::backtrace::tracing::imp::unwind_backtrace
             at libstd/sys/unix/backtrace/tracing/gcc_s.rs:49
   1: std::sys_common::backtrace::print
             at libstd/sys_common/backtrace.rs:71
             at libstd/sys_common/backtrace.rs:59
   2: std::panicking::default_hook::{{closure}}
             at libstd/panicking.rs:211
   3: std::panicking::default_hook
             at libstd/panicking.rs:227
   4: std::panicking::rust_panic_with_hook
             at libstd/panicking.rs:475
   5: std::panicking::begin_panic
   6: panic_unwinding::malice
   7: panic_unwinding::bob
   8: panic_unwinding::main
   9: std::rt::lang_start::{{closure}}
  10: std::panicking::try::do_call
```

We join the thread by calling `join()` and expect everything to go fine in our child thread, which is definitely not the case. We get two backtraces, one for the panic that happened in the child thread and the other from calling `bob` in the main thread.

If you need more control over how unwinding in panics is handled in a thread, you can use the `std::panic::catch_unwind` function. Even though it's recommended to handle errors via the `Option/Result` mechanism, you can use this method to handle fatal errors in worker threads; you can do this by restoring any violated invariants, letting the workers die, and restarting them. However, `catch_unwind` doesn't prevent the panic – it only allows you to customize the unwind behavior associated with panic. `panic` with `catch_unwind` is not recommended as a general error handling method for Rust programs.

The `catch_unwind` function takes a closure and handles any panics that happen inside it. Here's its type signature:

```
fn catch_unwind<F: FnOnce() -> R + UnwindSafe, R>(f: F) -> Result<R>
```

As you can see, the return value of `catch_unwind` has an additional constraint, `UnwindSafe`. This means that the variables in the closure must be exception-safe, which most types are, but notable exceptions are mutable references (`&mut T`). A value is exception safe if exception-throwing code cannot lead to the value being left in an inconsistent state. This means that the code inside the closure must not `panic!()` itself.

Here's a simple example that uses `catch_unwind`:

```
// catch_unwind.rs

use std::panic;

fn main() {
    panic::catch_unwind(|| {
        panic!("Panicking!");
    }).ok();

    println!("Survived that panic.");
}
```

Here's the output after running the preceding program:

```
→  Chapter06 git:(master) ✗ rustc catch_unwind.rs
→  Chapter06 git:(master) ✗ ./catch_unwind
thread 'main' panicked at 'Panicking!', catch_unwind.rs:7:9
note: Run with `RUST_BACKTRACE=1` for a backtrace.
Survived that panic.
```

As you can see, `catch_unwind` does not prevent the panic from happening; it just stops the unwinding associated with the panicking thread. Note again that `catch_unwind` is not the recommended method for error management in Rust. It is not guaranteed to catch all panics, such as panics that abort the program. Catching panic unwinding is necessary in situations where Rust code is communicating with other languages such as C, where unwinding to C code is an undefined behavior. In those cases, the programmer has to handle the unwind and do what C expects by returning an error code. The program can then resume the unwind by using the `resume_unwind` function from the same `panic` module.

For rare cases where the default unwinding behavior of panic can get too expensive, such as when writing programs for microcontrollers, there's a compiler flag that can be configured to turn all panics into aborts. To do that, your project's `Cargo.toml` needs to have the following attribute under the `profile.release` section:

```
[profile.release]
panic = "abort"
```

User-friendly panics

As we saw in the preceding code, panic messages and backtraces can be very cryptic, but it does not have to be like that. If you are an author of a command-line tool, `human_panic` is a crate from the community that replaces verbose, cryptic panic messages with human-readable messages. It also writes the backtrace to a file to allow it to be reported to the tool author by users. More information about `human_panic` can be found on the project repository page: `https://github.com/rust-clique/human-panic`.

Custom errors and the Error trait

A non-trivial project that has varied functionality is often spread across modules. With an organization, it's more informative to provide module-specific error messages and information for the user. Rust allows us to create custom error types that can help us achieve more granular error reports from our application. Without custom errors that are specific to our project, we might have to use existing error types in the standard library, which may not be relevant to our API's operations and will not give precise information to users if things go wrong with an operation in our module.

In languages that have exceptions, such as Java, the way you create custom exceptions is by inheriting from the base `Exception` class and overriding its methods and member variables. While Rust doesn't have type-level inheritance, it has trait inheritance and provides us with the `Error` trait that any type can implement, making the type a custom error type. This type can now be composed with existing standard library error types when using a trait object such as `Box<dyn Error>` as the return type of functions returning `Result` for the `Err` variant. Here's the type signature of the `Error` trait:

```
pub trait Error: Debug + Display {
    fn description(&self) -> &str { ... }
    fn cause(&self) -> Option<&dyn Error> { ... }
}
```

To create our own error type, the type must implement the `Error` trait. If we look at the trait's definition, it also requires that we implement the `Debug` and `Display` traits for our type. The `description` method returns a string slice reference, which is a human-readable form describing what the error is about. The `cause` method returns an optional reference to another `Error` trait object, representing a possible lower-level reason for the error. The cause method from custom error types allows you to get information on the chain of errors right from the source, making precise logging of the error possible. For instance, let's take an HTTP query as an example of a fallible operation. Our hypothetical library has a `get` method that can perform `GET` requests. The query might fail due to a lot of different reasons:

- The DNS query might fail because of networking failures or because of an incorrect address
- The actual transfer of packets might fail
- The data might be received correctly, but there could be something wrong with the received HTTP headers, and so on and so forth

If it were the first case, we might imagine three levels of errors, chained together by the `cause` fields:

- The UDP connection failing due to the network being down (`cause` = `None`)
- The DNS lookup failing due to a UDP connection failure (`cause` = `UDPError`)
- The `GET` query failing due to a DNS lookup failure (`cause` = `DNSError`)

The `cause` method comes in handy when the developer wants to know the root cause of a failure.

Now, to demonstrate integrating a custom error type in to a project, we have created a crate called `todolist_parser` using cargo, which exposes an API to parse a list of todos from a text file. The parsing of todos can fail in different ways, such as **file not found**, an empty todo, or because it contains non-text characters. We'll use a custom error type to model these situations. Under `src/error.rs`, we have defined the following error types:

```
// todolist_parser/src/error.rs

use std::error::Error;
use std::fmt;
use std::fmt::Display;

#[derive(Debug)]
pub enum ParseErr {
    Malformed,
    Empty
```

```
    }

    #[derive(Debug)]
    pub struct ReadErr {
        pub child_err: Box<dyn Error>
    }

    // Required by error trait
    impl Display for ReadErr {
        fn fmt(&self, f: &mut fmt::Formatter) -> fmt::Result {
            write!(f, "Failed reading todo file")
        }
    }

    // Required by error trait
    impl Display for ParseErr {
        fn fmt(&self, f: &mut fmt::Formatter) -> fmt::Result {
            write!(f, "Todo list parsing failed")
        }
    }

    impl Error for ReadErr {
        fn description(&self) -> &str {
            "Todolist read failed: "
        }

        fn cause(&self) -> Option<&dyn Error> {
            Some(&*self.child_err)
        }
    }

    impl Error for ParseErr {
        fn description(&self) -> &str {
            "Todolist parse failed: "
        }

        fn cause(&self) -> Option<&Error> {
            None
        }
    }
```

As of now, we are modelling two errors, which are very basic:

- Failing to read the list of todos modeled as `ReadErr`
- Failing to parse the todos modeled as `ParseErr`, which has two variants, where it can fail either due to the file being `Empty` or the file containing non-text/binary symbols, which means that it's `Malformed`

Following that, we implement the `Error` trait and the required super traits, `Display` and `Debug`. `lib.rs` contains the required parsing methods, as well as the declaration of the `TodoList` struct, as shown in the following code:

```rust
// todolist_parser/src/lib.rs

//! This crate provides an API to parse list of todos

use std::fs::read_to_string;
use std::path::Path;

mod error;
use error::ParseErr;
use error::ReadErr;

use std::error::Error;

/// This struct contains a list of todos parsed as a Vec<String>
#[derive(Debug)]
pub struct TodoList {
    tasks: Vec<String>,
}

impl TodoList {
    pub fn get_todos<P>(path: P) -> Result<TodoList, Box<dyn Error>>
    where
    P: AsRef<Path>, {
        let read_todos: Result<String, Box<dyn Error>> = read_todos(path);
        let parsed_todos = parse_todos(&read_todos?)?;
        Ok(parsed_todos)
    }
}

pub fn read_todos<P>(path: P) -> Result<String, Box<dyn Error>>
where
    P: AsRef<Path>,
{
    let raw_todos = read_to_string(path)
        .map_err(|e| ReadErr {
            child_err: Box::new(e),
        })?;
    Ok(raw_todos)
}

pub fn parse_todos(todo_str: &str) -> Result<TodoList, Box<dyn Error>> {
    let mut tasks: Vec<String> = vec![];
    for i in todo_str.lines() {
        tasks.push(i.to_string());
```

```
    }
    if tasks.is_empty() {
        Err(ParseErr::Empty.into())
    } else {
        Ok(TodoList { tasks })
    }
}
```

We have two top-level functions, `read_todos` and `parse_todos`, which are invoked by the `get_todos` method of `TodoList`.

We have an example usage of `TodoList` under `examples/basics.rs`, as follows:

```
// todolist_parser/examples/basics.rs

extern crate todolist_parser;

use todolist_parser::TodoList;

fn main() {
    let todos = TodoList::get_todos("examples/todos");
    match todos {
        Ok(list) => println!("{:?}", list),
        Err(e) => {
            println!("{}", e.description());
            println!("{:?}", e)
        }
    }
}
```

If we run our `basics.rs` example via the `cargo run --example basics` command, we get the following output:

```
→  todolist_parser git:(master) ✗ cargo run --example basics
    Finished dev [unoptimized + debuginfo] target(s) in 0.00s
     Running `target/debug/examples/basics`
Todolist read failed:
ReadErr { child_err: Os { code: 2, kind: NotFound, message: "No such file or directory" } }
→  todolist_parser git:(master) ✗ 
```

If you look at the error value being printed, it wraps the actual cause of error within the `ReadErr` value.

Rust has decent built-ins for defining custom error types. If you're writing your own crates, you should define your own error types to make debugging easier. However, implementing the `Error` trait for all of your types can often become redundant and time-consuming. Fortunately, we have a crate from the Rust community called **failure** (`https://github.com/rust-lang-nursery/failure`), which automates the creation of custom error types, along with the necessary implementation of traits that are auto-derived through the use of procedural macros. If you are feeling more ambitious, you are encouraged to refactor this library to use the `failure` crate.

Summary

In this chapter, we have learned that, error handling in Rust is explicit: operations that can fail have a two-part return value via the `Result` or `Option` generic types. You must handle errors in some way, either by unpacking the `Result`/`Option` values with a `match` statement, or by using combinator methods. Unwrapping should be avoided on error types. Instead, use combinators or match expressions to take appropriate action or propagate the error to the caller by using the `?` operator. It is okay to panic when programming errors are so fatal that recovery would be impossible. Panics are mostly non-recoverable, which means that they crash your thread. Their default behavior is unwinding, which can be expensive and can be turned off if programs don't want this overhead. It is advised to be as descriptive as possible when communicating errors, and authors are encouraged to use custom error types in their crates.

In the next chapter, we'll cover some of the advanced aspects of the language and explore more of the guts of the type system.

Advanced Concepts 7

Quite a few concepts we learned in the previous chapters really deserve close attention so we can appreciate the design of Rust. Learning these advanced topics will also help you further when you need to understand complex code bases. These concepts are also helpful when you want to create libraries that provide idiomatic Rust APIs.

We'll cover the following topics in this chapter:

- Type system tidbits
- Strings
- Iterators
- Closures
- Modules

Type system tidbits

"An algorithm must be seen to be believed"

– Donald Knuth

Before we go into more dense topics in this chapter, we'll first discuss some of the type system tidbits in statically typed programming languages in general, with focus on Rust. Some of these topics may already be familiar to you from Chapter 1, *Getting Started with Rust*, but we're going to dig into the details here.

Blocks and expressions

Despite being a mix of statements and expressions, Rust is primarily an expression-oriented language. This means that most constructs are expressions that return a value. It's also a language that uses C-like braces { }, to introduce new scope for variables in a program. Let's get these concepts straight before we talk more about them later in this chapter.

A **block expression** (hereby referred as blocks) is any item that starts with { and ends with }. In Rust, they include if else expressions, match expressions, while loops, loops, bare { } blocks, functions, methods, and closures, and all of them return a value which is the last line of the expression. If you put a semicolon in the last expression, the block expressions default to a return value of the unit () type.

A related concept to blocks is the **scope**. A scope is introduced whenever a new block is created. When we a new block and create any variable bindings within it, the bindings are confined to that scope and any reference to them is valid only within the scope bounds. It's like a new environment for variables to live in, isolated from the others. Items such as functions, impl blocks, bare blocks, if else expressions, match expressions, functions, and closures introduce new scope in Rust. Within a block/scope, we can declare structs, enums, modules, traits and their implementations, and even blocks. Every Rust program starts with one root scope, which is the scope introduced by the main function. Within that, many nested scopes can be created. The main scope becomes the parent scope for all inner scopes declared. Consider the following snippet:

```
// scopes.rs

fn main() {
    let mut b = 4;
    {
        let mut a = 34 + b;
        a += 1;
    }

    b = a;
}
```

We used a bare block { }, to introduce a new inner scope and created a variable a. Following the end of the scope, we are trying to assign b to the value of a, which comes from the inner scope. Rust throws a compile time error saying cannot find value `a` in this scope. The parent scope from main does not know anything about a as it comes from the inner scope. This property of scopes is also used sometimes to control how long we want a reference to be valid, as we saw in Chapter 5, *Memory Management and Safety*.

But the inner scope can access values from their parent scope. Because of that, it is possible to write `34 + b` within our inner scope.

Now we come to expressions. We can benefit from their property of returning a value and that they must be of the same type in all branches. This results in very concise code. For example, consider this snippet:

```
// block_expr.rs

fn main() {
    // using bare blocks to do multiple things at once
    let precompute = {
        let a = (-34i64).abs();
        let b = 345i64.pow(3);
        let c = 3;
        a + b + c
    };

    // match expressions
    let result_msg = match precompute {
        42 => "done",
        a if a % 2 == 0 => "continue",
        _ => panic!("Oh no !")
    };

    println!("{}", result_msg);
}
```

We can use bare blocks to chunk several lines of code together and assign the value at the end with an implicit return of the `a + b + c` expression to `precompute` as shown previously. Match expressions can also assign and return values from their match arms directly.

 Note: Being similar to the `switch` statement in C, match arms in Rust do not suffer from the `case fall through` side effect that results in lots of bugs in C code.

The C switch case requires every `case` statement within the `switch` block to have a `break` if we want to bail out after running the code in that `case`. If the `break` is not present, any `case` statement following that is also executed, which is called the fall-through behavior. A match expression, on the other hand, is guaranteed to evaluate only one of the match arms.

If `else` expressions provide the same conciseness:

```
// if_expr.rs

fn compute(i: i32) -> i32 {
    2 * i
}

fn main() {
    let result_msg = "done";
    // if expression assignments
    let result = if result_msg == "done" {
        let some_work = compute(8);
        let stuff = compute(4);
        compute(2) + stuff // last expression gets assigned to result
    } else {
        compute(1)
    };

    println!("{}", result);
}
```

In statement-based languages such as Python, you would write something like this for the preceding snippet:

```
result = None
if (state == "continue"):
    let stuff = work()
    result = compute_next_result() + stuff
else:
    result = compute_last_result()
```

In the Python code, we had to declare `result` beforehand, followed by doing separate assignments in the if else branch. Rust is more concise here, with the assignment being done as a result of the if else expression. Also, in Python, you can forget to assign a value to a variable in either of the branches and the variable may be left uninitialized. Rust will report at compile time if you return and assign something from the `if` block and either miss or return a different type from the `else` block.

As an added note, Rust also supports declaring uninitialized variables:

```
fn main() {
    let mut a: i32;
    println!("{:?}", a);     // error
    a = 23;
    println!("{:?}", a);     // fine now
}
```

But they need to be initialized before we use them. If an uninitialized variable is attempted to be read from later, Rust will forbid that and report at compile time that the variable must be initialized:

```
   Compiling playground v0.0.1 (file:///playground)
error[E0381]: use of possibly uninitialized variable: `a`
 --> src/main.rs:7:22
  |
7 |     println!("{:?}", a);
  |                      ^ use of possibly uninitialized `a`
```

Let statements

In `Chapter 1`, *Getting Started with Rust*, we briefly introduced `let`, which is used to create new variable bindings—but `let` is more than that. In fact, `let` is a pattern-matching statement. Pattern matching is a construct mostly seen in functional languages such as Haskell and allows us to manipulate and make decisions about values based on their internal structure or can be used to extract values out of algebraic data types. We had already

```
let a = 23;
let mut b = 403;
```

Our first line is `let` in its simplest form and it declares an immutable variable binding, `a`. In the second line, we have `mut` after the `let` keyword for `b`. `mut` is part of the `let` pattern, which binds `b` mutably to `i32` types in this case. `mut` enables `b` to bind again to some other `i32` type. Another keyword that's seen less frequently with `let` is the `ref` keyword. Now, we generally use the `&` operator to create a reference/pointer to any value. The other way to create a reference to any value is to use the `ref` keyword with `let`. To illustrate `ref` and `mut`, we have a snippet:

```
// let_ref_mut.rs

#[derive(Debug)]
struct Items(u32);

fn main() {
    let items = Items(2);
    let items_ptr = &items;
    let ref items_ref = items;

    assert_eq!(items_ptr as *const Items, items_ref as *const Items);

    let mut a = Items(20);
```

```
    // using scope to limit the mutation of `a` within this block by b
    {
        // can take a mutable reference like this too
        let ref mut b = a; // same as: let b = &mut a;
        b.0 += 25;
    }

    println!("{:?}", items);

    println!("{:?}", a);    // without the above scope
                            // this does not compile. Try removing the scope
}
```

Here, `items_ref` is a reference created using the usual `&` operator. The next line also creates the `items_ref` reference to the same `items` value using `ref`. We can confirm, with the `assert_eq!` call following it, that the two pointer variables point to the same `items` value. The cast to `*const Items` is used to compare whether two pointers point to the same memory location, where `*const Items` is a raw pointer type to `Items`. Additionally, by combining `ref` and `mut` as shown in the second to last part of the code, we can get a mutable reference to any owned value other than the usual way of doing so with the `&mut` operator. But we have to use an inner scope to modify a from b.

Languages using pattern matching are not just limited to having identifiers on the left hand side of `=` but can additionally have patterns referring to the structure of types. So, another convenience `let` provides us with is the ability to extract values from fields of an algebraic data type, such as a struct or enum as new variables. Here, we have a snippet that demonstrates this:

```
// destructure_struct.rs

enum Food {
    Pizza,
    Salad
}

enum PaymentMode {
    Bitcoin,
    Credit
}

struct Order {
    count: u8,
    item: Food,
    payment: PaymentMode
}
```

```
fn main() {
    let food_order = Order { count: 2,
                             item: Food::Salad,
                             payment: PaymentMode::Credit };

    // let can pattern match inner fields into new variables
    let Order { count, item, .. } = food_order;
}
```

Here, we created an instance of `Order`, which is bound to `food_order`. Let's assume we got `food_order` from some method call and we want to access the `count` and `item` values. We can extract the individual fields, `count` and `item`, directly using `let`. `count` and `item` become new variables that hold the corresponding field values from the `Order` instance. This is technically called the **destructuring syntax** of `let`. The way the variables get destructured depends on whether the value on the right is an immutable reference, mutable reference, or an owned value or by how we reference it on the left-hand side using the `ref` or `mut` patterns. In the previous code, it was captured by the value because `food_order` owns the `Order` instance and we matched the members on the left-hand side without any `ref` or `mut` keyword. If we want to destructure the members by immutable reference, we would put an `&` symbol before `food_order` or use `ref` or `mut` alternatively:

```
let Order { count, item, .. } = &food_order;
// or
let Order { ref count, ref item, .. } = food_order;
```

The first style is generally preferred as it's concise. If we want to have a mutable reference, we have to place `&mut` after making `food_order` itself mutable:

```
let mut food_order = Foo { count: 2,
                           item: Food::Salad,
                           payment: PaymentMode::Credit };
let Order { count, item, .. } = &mut food_order;
```

Fields that we don't care about can be ignored by using the `..`, as shown in the code. Also, a slight restriction of `let` destructuring is that we are not free to choose the mutability of individual fields. All variables must have the the same mutability—either all are immutable or all are mutable. Note that `ref` isn't generally used to declare variable bindings and is mostly used in match expressions in cases where we want to match against a value by reference because the `&` operator does not work within match arms, as demonstrated here:

```
// match_ref.rs

struct Person(String);

fn main() {
```

```
        let a = Person("Richard Feynman".to_string());
        match a {
            Person(&name) => println!("{} was a great physicist !", name),
            _ => panic!("Oh no !")
        }

        let b = a;
    }
```

If we want to use the inner value from `Person` struct by an immutable reference, our intuition would say to use something like `Person(&name)` in the match arm to match by reference. But we get this error upon compilation:

```
→  Chapter07 git:(master) X rustc match_ref.rs
error[E0308]: mismatched types
  --> match_ref.rs:8:16
   |
8  |            Person(&name) => println!("{} was a great physicist !", name),
   |                   ^^^^^ expected struct `std::string::String`, found reference
   |
   = note: expected type `std::string::String`
              found type `&_`
   = help: did you mean `name: &std::string::String`?

error: aborting due to previous error
```

This gives us a misleading error because `&name` is creating a reference out of `name` (`&` is an operator) and the compiler thinks that we want to match against `Person(&String)` but the `a` value is actually `Person(String)`. So, in this case `ref` has to be used to destructure it as a reference. To make it compile, we change it accordingly to `Person(ref name)` on the left-hand side.

The destructuring syntax is also applicable to enum types as well:

```
// destructure_enum.rs

enum Container {
    Item(u64),
    Empty
}

fn main() {
    let maybe_item = Container::Item(0u64);
    let has_item = if let Container::Item(0) = maybe_item {
        true
    } else {
        false
    };
}
```

Here, we have `maybe_item` as a `Container` enum. Combining `if let` and pattern matching, we can conditionally assign the value to `has_item` variable using the `if let <destructure pattern> = expression {}` syntax.

The destructuring syntax can be used in function parameters as well. For example, in the case of custom types, such as a struct when used in a function as arguments:

```
// destructure_func_param.rs

struct Container {
    items_count: u32
}

fn increment_item(Container {mut items_count}: &mut Container) {
    items_count += 1;
}

fn calculate_cost(Container {items_count}: &Container) -> u32 {
    let rate = 67;
    rate * items_count
}

fn main() {
    let mut container = Container {
        items_count: 10
    };

    increment_item(&mut container);
    let total_cost = calculate_cost(&container);
    println!("Total cost: {}", total_cost);
}
```

Here, `calculate_cost` function has a parameter that's destructured as a struct with fields bound to the `items_count` variable. If we want to destructure mutably, we add the `mut` keyword before the member field as is the case with the `increment_item` function.

Refutable patterns: Refutable pattern are `let` patterns where the left-hand side and the right-hand side are not compatible for pattern matching and, in those cases one has to use the exhaustive match expression instead. Up until now, all forms of `let` patterns we've seen were irrefutable patterns. Irrefutable means that they're able to properly match against the value on the right side of `'='` as a valid pattern.

But sometimes, pattern matching with `let` may fail because of invalid patterns, for example, when matching an enum `Container` that has two variants:

```
// refutable_pattern.rs

enum Container {
    Item(u64),
    Empty
}

fn main() {
    let mut item = Container::Item(56);
    let Container::Item(it) = item;
}
```

Ideally, we expect `it` to store `56` as the value, after being destructured from `item`. If we try compiling this, we get the following:

```
→  Chapter07 git:(master) ✗ rustc refutable_pattern.rs
error[E0005]: refutable pattern in local binding: `Empty` not covered
  --> refutable_pattern.rs:10:9
   |
10 |     let Container::Item(it) = item;
   |         ^^^^^^^^^^^^^^^^^^^ pattern `Empty` not covered

error: aborting due to previous error
```

The reason this match does not succeed is because `Container` has two variants, `Item(u64)` and `Empty`. Even though we know that `item` contains the `Item` variant, `let` patterns can't rely on this fact, because if `item` is mutable, some code can assign an `Empty` variant there later, which would render the destructure an undefined operation. We have to cover all possible cases. Destructuring directly against a single variant violates the semantics of exhaustive pattern matching and hence our match fails.

Loop as an expression

In Rust, a loop is also an expression that returns `()` by default when we `break` out of it. The implication of this is that `loop` can also be used to assign value to a variable with `break`. For example, it can be used in something like this:

```
// loop_expr.rs

fn main() {
    let mut i = 0;
    let counter = loop {
```

```
        i += 1;
        if i == 10 {
            break i;
        }
    };
    println!("{}", counter);
}
```

Following the `break` keyword, we include the value we want to return and this gets assigned to `counter` variable when the loop breaks (if at all). This is really handy in cases where you assign the value of any variable within the loop after breaking from the loop and need to use it afterward.

Type clarity and sign distinction in numeric types

While mainstream languages differentiate between numeric primitives such as an integer, a double, and a byte, a lot of newer languages such as Golang have started adding distinction between signed and unsigned numeric types too. Rust follows in the same footsteps by distinguishing signed and unsigned numeric types, providing them as separate types altogether. From a type-checking perspective, this adds another layer of safety to our programs. This allows us to write code that exactly specifies its requirements. For example, consider a database connection pool struct:

```
struct ConnectionPool {
    pool_count: usize
}
```

For languages that provide a common integer type that incorporates both signed and unsigned values, you would specify the type of `pool_count` as an integer, which can also store negative values. It does not make sense for `pool_count` to be negative. With Rust, we can specify this clearly in code by using an unsigned type instead, such as `u32` or `usize`.

One more aspect to note about primitive types is that Rust does not perform automatic casts when mixing signed and unsigned types in arithmetic operations. You have to be explicit about this and cast the value manually. An example of an unintended auto cast in C/C++ would be the following:

```
#include <iostream>
int main(int argc, const char * argv[]) {
    uint foo = 5;
    int bar = 6;
    auto difference = foo - bar;
    std::cout << difference;
    return 0;
}
```

The preceding code prints 4294967295. Here, the difference won't be −1 on subtracting foo and bar; instead C++ does its own thing without the programmer's consent. int (signed integer) is auto cast to uint (unsigned integer) and wraps to a maximum value of uint being 4294967295. This code continues to run without complaining about underflow here.

Translating the same program in Rust, we get the following:

```
// safe_arithmetic.rs

fn main() {
    let foo: u32 = 5;
    let bar: i32 = 6;
    let difference = foo - bar;
    println!("{}", difference);
}
```

Following will be the output:

Rust won't compile this, showing an error message. You have to explicitly cast either of the values according to your intent. Also, if we perform overflow/underflow operations on two unsigned or signed types, Rust will `panic!()` and abort your program when you build and run in `debug` mode. When built in `release` mode, it does a wrapping arithmetic.

 By wrapping arithmetic, we mean that adding `1` to `255` (a `u8`) will result in `0`.

Panicking in debug mode is the right thing to do here because if such arbitrary values are allowed to propagate to other parts of code, they can taint your business logic and introduce further hard-to-track bugs in the program. So, a fail-stop approach is better in these cases where the user accidentally performs an overflow/underflow operation and this gets caught in debug mode. When the programmer wants to allow wrapping semantics on arithmetic operations, then they may choose to ignore the panic and proceed to compile in release mode. That's another aspect of safety that the language provides you.

Type inference

Type inference is useful in statically typed languages as it makes the code easier to write, maintain, and refactor. Rust's type system can figure out types for fields, methods, local variables, and most generic type arguments when you don't specify them. Under the hood, a component of the compiler called the type checker uses the *Hindley Milner* type inference algorithm to decide what the types of local variables should be. It is a set of rules about establishing types of expressions based on their usage. As such, it can infer types based on the environment and the way a type is used. One such example is the following:

```
let mut v = vec![];
v.push(2);    // can figure type of `v` now to be of Vec<i32>
```

With only the first line initializing the vector, Rust's type checker is unsure of what the type for `v` should be. It's only when it reaches the next line, `v.push(2)`, that it knows that `v` is of the type, `Vec<i32>`. Now the type of `v` is frozen to `Vec<i32>`.

If we added another line, `v.push(2.4f32);`, then the compiler will complain of type mismatch as it already had inferred it from the previous line to be of `Vec<i32>`. But sometimes, the type checker cannot figure out types of variables in complex situations. But with some help from the programmer, the type checker is able to infer types. For example, for the next snippet, we read a file `foo.txt`, containing some text and read it as bytes:

```
// type_inference_iterator.rs

use std::fs::File;
use std::io::Read;

fn main() {
    let file = File::open("foo.txt").unwrap();
    let bytes = file.bytes().collect();
}
```

Compiling this gives us this error:

```
→ Chapter07 git:(master) X rustc type_inference_iterator.rs
error[E0282]: type annotations needed
  --> type_inference_iterator.rs:8:9
   |
8  |         let bytes = file.bytes().collect();
   |             ^^^^^
   |             |
   |             cannot infer type
   |             consider giving `bytes` a type

error: aborting due to previous error

For more information about this error, try `rustc --explain E0282`.
```

The `collect` method on iterators is basically an `aggregator` method. We'll look at iterators later in this chapter. The resulting type it collects into can be any collection type. It can either be `LinkedList`, `VecDeque`, or `Vec`. Rust does not know what the programmer intends and, due to such ambiguity, it needs our help here. We made the following change for the second line in `main`:

```
    let bytes: Vec<Result<u8, _>> = file.bytes().collect();
```

Calling `bytes()` returns `Result<u8, std::io::Error>`. After adding some type hint as to what to collect into (here, `Vec`), the program compiles fine. Note the _ on the `Result` error variant. It was enough for Rust to hint that we need a `Vec` of `Result` of `u8`. The rest, it is able to figure out—the error type in `Result` needs to be of `std::io::Error` type. It was able to figure that out because there is no such ambiguity here. It gets the information from the `bytes()` method signature. Quite smart!

Type aliases

Type aliases are a feature not unique to Rust. C has the `typedef` keyword, while Kotlin has `typealias` for the same. They are there to make your code more readable and remove the type signature cruft that often piles up in statically typed languages, for example, if you have an API from your crate where you return a `Result` type, wrapping a complex object as depicted below:

```
// type_alias.rs

pub struct ParsedPayload<T> {
    inner: T
}

pub struct ParseError<E> {
    inner: E
}

pub fn parse_payload<T, E>(stream: &[u8]) -> Result<ParsedPayload<T>,
ParseError<E>> {
    unimplemented!();
}

fn main() {
    // todo
}
```

As you can see, for some of the methods, such as `parse_payload`, the type signature gets too large to fit in a line. Also, having to type `Result<ParsedPayload<T>, ParseError<E>>` every time they are used becomes cumbersome. What if we could refer to this type by a simpler name? This is the exact use case type aliases serve. They enable us to give another (desirably simpler) name to types with a complex type signature.

So, we can give an alias to the return type of `parse_payload` as follows:

```
// added a type alias
type ParserResult<T, E> = Result<ParsedPayload<T>, ParseError<E>>;

// and modify parse_payload function as:
pub fn parse_payload<T, E>(stream: &[u8]) -> ParserResult<T, E> {
    unimplemented!();
}
```

This makes it more manageable if we later want to change the actual inner types. We can type alias any simple types too:

```
type MyString = String;
```

So, now we can use `MyString` anywhere we use `String`. But this doesn't mean that `MyString` is of a different type. During compilation, this just gets substituted/expanded to the original type. When creating type aliases for generic types, the type alias also needs a generic type parameter (`T`). So aliasing `Vec<Result<Option<T>>>` becomes the following:

```
type SomethingComplex<T> = Vec<Result<Option<T>>>;
```

Let's assume you have a lifetime in your type, as in `SuperComplexParser<'a>`:

```
struct SuperComplexParser<'s> {
    stream: &'a [u8]
}

type Parser<'s> = SuperComplexParser<'s>;
```

When creating type aliases for them, we need to specify the lifetime as well, as is the case with the `Parser` type alias.

With those type system niceties out of the way, let's talk about strings again!

Strings

In `Chapter 1`, *Getting Started with Rust*, we mentioned that strings are of two types. In this section, we'll give a clearer picture on strings, their peculiarities, and how they differ from strings in other languages.

While other languages have a pretty straightforward story on string types, the `String` type in Rust is one of the tricky and uneasy types to handle. As we know, Rust places distinction on whether a value is allocated on the heap or on the stack. Due to that, there are two kinds of strings in Rust: owned strings (`String`) and borrowed strings (`&str`). Let's explore both of them.

Owned strings – String

The `String` type comes from the standard library and is a heap-allocated UTF-8 encoded sequence of bytes. They are simply `Vec<u8>` under the hood but have extra methods that are applicable to only strings. They are owned types, which means that a variable that holds a `String` value is its owner. You will usually find that `String` types can be created in multiple ways, as shown in the following code:

```
// strings.rs

fn main() {
    let a: String = "Hello".to_string();
    let b = String::from("Hello");
    let c = "World".to_owned();
    let d = c.clone();
}
```

In the preceding code, we created four strings in four different ways. All of them create the same string type and have the same performance characteristics. The first variable, a, creates the string by calling the `to_string` method, which comes from the `ToString` trait with the string literal, `"Hello"`. A string literal such as `"Hello"` by itself also has a type of `&str`. We'll explain them when we get to borrowed versions of strings. We then create another string, b, by calling the `from` method, which is an associated method on `String`. The third string c, is created by calling a trait method, `to_owned`, from the `ToOwned` trait, which is implemented for `&str` types—literal strings. The fourth string, d, is created by cloning an existing string, c. The fourth way of creating strings is an expensive operation , which we should avoid as it involves copying the underlying bytes by iterating over them.

As `String` is allocated on heap, it can be mutated and can grow at runtime. This means that strings have an associated overhead when manipulating them because they might possibly get reallocated as you keep adding bytes to them. Heap allocation is a relatively expensive operation but, fortunately, the way allocation happens for `Vec` (doubled every capacity limit), means this cost is amortized over usage.

Strings also have a lot of convenient methods in the standard library. Following are the important ones:

- `String::new()` allocates an empty `String` type.
- `String::from(s: &str)` allocates a new `String` type and populates it from a string slice.

- `String::with_capacity(capacity: usize)` allocates an empty `String` type with a preallocated size. This is performant when you know the size of your string beforehand.
- `String::from_utf8(vec: Vec<u8>)` tries to allocate a new `String` type from `bytestring`. The contents of the parameter must be UTF-8 or this will fail. It returns the `Result` wrapper type.
- The `len()` method on string instances gives you the length of the `String` type, taking Unicode into account. As an example, a `String` type containing the word yö has a length of two, even though it takes three bytes in memory.
- The `push(ch: char)` and `push_str(string: &str)` methods add a character or a string slice to the string.

This is, of course, a non-exhaustive list. A complete list of all the operations can be found at `https://doc.rust-lang.org/std/string/struct.String.html`.

Here's an example that uses all of the aforementioned methods:

```
// string_apis.rs

fn main() {
    let mut empty_string = String::new();
    let empty_string_with_capacity = String::with_capacity(50);
    let string_from_bytestring: String = String::from_utf8(vec![82, 85, 83,
84]).expect("Creating String from bytestring failed");

    println!("Length of the empty string is {}", empty_string.len());
    println!("Length of the empty string with capacity is {}",
    empty_string_with_capacity.len());
    println!("Length of the string from a bytestring is {}",
    string_from_bytestring.len());

    println!("Bytestring says {}", string_from_bytestring);

    empty_string.push('1');
    println!("1) Empty string now contains {}", empty_string);
    empty_string.push_str("2345");
    println!("2) Empty string now contains {}", empty_string);
    println!("Length of the previously empty string is now {}",
    empty_string.len());
}
```

With `String` explored, let's look at the borrowed version of strings known as string slices or the `&str` type.

Borrowed strings – &str

We can also have strings as references called string slices. These are denoted by `&str` (pronounced as *stir*), which is a reference to a `str` type. In constrast to the `String` type, `str` is a built-in type known to the compiler and is not something from the standard library. String slices are created as `&str` by default—a pointer to a UTF-8 encoded byte sequence. We cannot create and use values of the bare `str` type, as it represents a contiguous sequence of UTF-8 encoded bytes with a finite but unknown size. They are technically called unsized types. We'll explain unsized types later in this chapter.

`str` can only be created as a reference type. Let's assume we try to create a `str` type forcibly by providing the type signature on the left:

```
// str_type.rs

fn main() {
    let message: str = "Wait, but why ?";
}
```

We'll be presented with a confusing error:

```
→  Chapter04 git:(master) ✗ rustc unusable_str.rs
error[E0308]: mismatched types
 --> unusable_str.rs:4:24
  |
4 |     let message: str = "Wait, but why ?";
  |                        ^^^^^^^^^^^^^^^^^^ expected str, found reference
  |
  = note: expected type `str`
             found type `&'static str`

error[E0277]: the trait bound `str: std::marker::Sized` is not satisfied
 --> unusable_str.rs:4:9
  |
4 |     let message: str = "Wait, but why ?";
  |         ^^^^^^^ `str` does not have a constant size known at compile-time
  |
  = help: the trait `std::marker::Sized` is not implemented for `str`
  = note: all local variables must have a statically known size

error: aborting due to 2 previous errors

Some errors occurred: E0277, E0308.
For more information about an error, try `rustc --explain E0277`.
→  Chapter04 git:(master) ✗ █
```

It says: **all local variables must have a statically known size**. This basically means that every local variable we define using a `let` statement needs to have a size as they are allocated on the stack and the stack has a fixed size. As we know, all variable declarations go on the stack either as values themselves or as pointers to heap allocated types. All stack-allocated values need to have a proper size known and, due to this, `str` cannot be initialized.

`str` basically means a fixed-sized sequence of strings that's agnostic to the location where it resides. It could either be a reference to a heap-allocated string, or it could be a `&'static str` string residing on the data segment of the process that lives for the entire duration of the program, which is what the `'static` lifetime denotes.

We can, however, create a borrowed version of `str`, as in `&str`, which is what gets created by default when we write a string literal. So string slices are only created and used behind a pointer—`&str`. Being a reference, they also have different lifetimes associated with them based on the scope of their owned variable. One of them is of `'static` lifetime, which is the lifetime of string literals.

String literals are any sequence of characters you declare within double quotes. For example, we create them like so:

```
// borrowed_strings.rs

fn get_str_literal() -> &'static str {
    "from function"
}

fn main() {
    let my_str = "This is borrowed";
    let from_func = get_str_literal();
    println!("{} {}", my_str, from_func);
}
```

In the preceding code, we have a `get_str_literal` function that returns a string literal. We also create a string literal `my_str` in `main`. `my_str` and the string returned by `get_str_literal` has the type, `&'static str`. The `'static` lifetime annotation denotes that the string stays for the entire duration of the program. The `&` prefix says that it's a pointer to the string literal, while `str` is the unsized type. Any other `&str` type you encounter are **borrowed string slices** of any owned `String` type on the heap. The `&str` types, once created, can't be modified as they are created immutable by default.

We can also take a mutable slice to the string, and the type changes to &mut str, though it's uncommon to use them in this form except with a few methods in the standard library. The &str type is the recommended type to be used when passing strings around, either to functions or to other variables.

Slicing and dicing strings

All strings in Rust are guaranteed to be UTF-8 by default, and indexing on string types in Rust does not work as you would use them in other languages. Let's try accessing the individual characters of our string:

```
// strings_indexing.rs

fn main() {
    let hello = String::from("Hello");
    let first_char = hello[0];
}
```

On compiling this, we get the following error:

```
→  Chapter07 git:(master) ✗ rustc string_indexing.rs
error[E0277]: the type `std::string::String` cannot be indexed by `{integer}`
 --> string_indexing.rs:5:22
  |
5 |     let first_char = hello[0];
  |                      ^^^^^^^^ `std::string::String` cannot be indexed by `{integer}`
  |
  = help: the trait `std::ops::Index<{integer}>` is not implemented for `std::string::String`

error: aborting due to previous error

For more information about this error, try `rustc --explain E0277`.
```

That's not a very helpful message. But it refers to something called the Index trait. The Index trait is implemented on collection types whose elements can be accessed by the indexing operator [] using index type as a usize value. Strings are valid UTF-8-encoded byte sequences and a single byte does not equate to a single character. In UTF-8, a single character may also be represented by multiple bytes. So, indexing does not work on strings.

Instead, we can have slices of strings. This can either be done as follows:

```
// string_range_slice.rs

fn main() {
    let my_str = String::from("Strings are cool");
    let first_three = &my_str[0..3];
    println!("{:?}", first_three);
}
```

But, as is the case with all indexing operation, this panics if the start or the end index is not on a valid char boundary.

Another way to iterator over all characters of a string is to use the chars() method, which turns the string into an iterator over its characters. Let's change our code to use chars instead:

```
// strings_chars.rs

fn main() {
    let hello = String::from("Hello");
    for c in hello.chars() {
        println!("{}", c);
    }
}
```

The chars method returns characters of the string at proper Unicode boundaries. We can also call other iterator methods on this to either skip or get a range of characters.

Using strings in functions

It's idiomatic and performant to pass string slices to functions. Here's an example:

```
// string_slices_func.rs

fn say_hello(to_whom: &str) {
    println!("Hey {}!", to_whom)
}

fn main() {
    let string_slice: &'static str = "you";
    let string: String = string_slice.into();
    say_hello(string_slice);
    say_hello(&string);
}
```

To the astute observer, the `say_hello` method also worked with a `&String` type. Internally, `&String` automatically coerces to `&str`, due to the type coercion trait `Deref` implemented for `&String` to `&str`. This is because `String` implements `Deref` for the `str` type.

Here, you can see why I stressed the point earlier. A string slice is an acceptable input parameter not only for actual string slice references but also for `String` references! So, once more: if you need to pass a string to your function, use the string slice, `&str`.

Joining strings

Another source of confusion when dealing with strings in Rust is when concatenating two strings. In other languages, you have a very intuitive syntax for joining two strings. You just do `"Foo" + "Bar"` and you get a `"FooBar"`. Not quite the case with Rust:

```
// string_concat.rs

fn main() {
    let a = "Foo";
    let b = "Bar";
    let c = a + b;
}
```

If we compile this, we get the following error:

```
→  Chapter07 git:(master) ✗ rustc string_concat.rs
error[E0369]: binary operation `+` cannot be applied to type `&str`
 --> string_concat.rs:6:13
  |
6 |     let c = a + b;
  |             ^^^^^  `+` can't be used to concatenate two `&str` strings
  |
help: `to_owned()` can be used to create an owned `String` from a string reference. String concatenation appends the strin
g on the right to the string on the left and may require reallocation. This requires ownership of the string on the left
  |
6 |     let c = a.to_owned() + b;
  |             ^^^^^^^^^^^^

error: aborting due to previous error

For more information about this error, try `rustc --explain E0369`.
```

The error message is really helpful here. The concatenation operation is a two step process. First, you need to allocate a string and then iterate over both of them to copy their bytes to this newly allocated string. As such, there's an implicit heap allocation involved, hidden behind the + operator. Rust discourages implicit heap allocation. Instead, the compiler suggests that we can concatenate two string literals by explicitly making the first one an owned string. So our code changes, like so:

```
// string_concat.rs

fn main() {
    let foo = "Foo";
    let bar = "Bar";
    let baz = foo.to_string() + bar;
}
```

So we made `foo` a `String` type by calling the `to_string()` method. With that change, our code compiles.

The main difference between both `String` and `&str` is that `&str` is natively recognized by the compiler, while `String` is a custom type from the standard library. You could implement your own similar `String` abstraction on top of `Vec<u8>`.

When to use &str versus String ?

To a programmer coming to Rust, often the confusion is around which one to use. Well, the best practice is to use APIs that take a `&str` type when possible, as when the string is already allocated somewhere, you can save copying and allocation costs just by referencing that string. Passing `&str` around your program is nearly free: it incurs nearly no allocation costs and no copying of memory.

Global values

Apart from variable and type declarations, Rust also allows us to define global values that can be accessed from anywhere in the program. They follow the naming convention of every letter being uppercase. These are of two kinds: constants and statics. There are also constant functions, which can be called to initialize these global values. Let's explore constants first.

Constants

The first form of global values are constants. Here's how we can define one:

```
// constants.rs

const HEADER: &'static [u8; 4] = b"Obj\0";

fn main() {
    println!("{:?}", HEADER);
}
```

We use the `const` keyword to create constants. As constants aren't declared with the `let` keyword, specifying types is a must when creating them. Now, we can use `HEADER` where we would use the byte literal, `Obj\`. `b""` is a convenient syntax to create a sequence of bytes of the `&'static [u8; n]` type, as in a `'static` reference to a fixed-sized array of bytes. Constants represent concrete values and don't have any memory location associated with them. They are inlined wherever they are used.

Statics

Statics are proper global values, as in they have a fixed memory location and exist as a single instance in the whole program. These can also be made mutable. However, as global variables are a breeding ground for the nastiest bugs out there, there are some safety mechanisms in place. Both reading and writing to statics has to be done inside an `unsafe` `{}` block. Here's how we crate and use statics:

```
// statics.rs

static mut BAZ: u32 = 4;
static FOO: u8 = 9;

fn main() {
    unsafe {
        println!("baz is {}", BAZ);
        BAZ = 42;
        println!("baz is now {}", BAZ);
        println!("foo is {}", FOO);
    }
}
```

In the code, we've declared two statics BAZ and FOO. We use the static keyword to create them along with specifying the type explicitly. If we want them to be mutable, we add the mut keyword after static. Statics aren't inlined like constants. When we read or write the static values, we need to use an unsafe block. Statics are generally combined with synchronization primitives for any kind of thread-safe use. They are also used to implement global locks and when integrating with C libraries.

Generally, if you don't need to rely on singleton property of statics and its predefined memory location and just want a concrete value, you should prefer using consts. They allow the compiler to make better optimizations and are more straightforward to use.

Compile time functions – const fn

We can also define constant functions that evaluate their argument during compile time. This means that a const value declaration can have a value that's from an invocation of a const function. const functions are pure functions and must be reproducible. This means that they cannot take mutable arguments to any type. They also cannot include operations that are dynamic such as a heap allocation. They can be called in non-const places where they act just like normal functions. But when they are called in const contexts, they are evaluated at compile time. Here's how we define a const function:

```
// const_fns.rs

const fn salt(a: u32) -> u32 {
    0xDEADBEEF ^ a
}

const CHECKSUM: u32 = salt(23);

fn main() {
    println!("{}", CHECKSUM);
}
```

In the code, we defined a const function, salt, that takes a u32 value as parameter and does a xor operation with the hex value, 0xDEADBEEF. Const functions are quite useful for operations that can be performed at compile time. For instance, let's say you are writing a binary file parser and you need to read the first four bytes of the file as an initialization and validation step for the parser. The following code demonstrates how we can do this entirely at runtime:

```
// const_fn_file.rs

const fn read_header(a: &[u8]) -> (u8, u8, u8, u8) {
```

```
        (a[0], a[1], a[2], a[3])
    }

    const FILE_HEADER: (u8,u8,u8,u8) =
    read_header(include_bytes!("./const_fn_file.rs"));

    fn main() {
        println!("{:?}", FILE_HEADER);
    }
```

In the code, the `read_header` function receives a file as a bytes array using the `include_bytes!` macro, which also reads the file at compile time. We then pull 4 bytes out of it and return it as a four-element tuple. Without the `const` function, all this would be done at runtime.

Dynamic statics using the lazy_static! macro

As we have seen, global values can only be declared for types that are non-dynamic in their initialization and have a known size on the stack at compile time. For example, you can't create a `HashMap` as a static value because it requires a heap allocation. Fortunately, we can have `HashMap` and other dynamic collection types such as `Vec` as global statics too, using a third-party crate called `lazy_static`. This crate exposes the `lazy_static!` macro, which can be used to initialize any dynamic type that's accessible globally from anywhere in the program. Here's a snippet of how to initialize a Vec that can be mutated from multiple threads:

```
// lazy_static_demo

use std::sync::Mutex;

lazy_static! {
    static ref ITEMS: Mutex<Vec<u64>> = {
        let mut v = vec![];
        v.push(9);
        v.push(2);
        v.push(1);
        Mutex::new(v)
    }
}
```

Items declared within the `lazy_static!` macro are required to implement the Sync trait. This means if we want a mutable static, we have to use a multithreaded type such as `Mutex` or `RwLock` instead of `RefCell`. We'll explain these types when we get to `Chapter 8, Concurrency`. We'll be using this macro frequently in future chapters. Head over to the crate repository to learn more about using `lazy_static`.

Iterators

We glimpsed iterators in `Chapter 1`, *Getting Started with Rust*. To recap, an iterator is any ordinary type that can walk over elements of a collection type in one of three ways: via `self`, `&self`, or `&mut self`. They are not a new concept and mainstream language such as C++ and Python have them already though that in Rust, they can appear surprising at first due to their form as an associated type trait. Iterators are used quite frequently in idiomatic Rust code when dealing with collection types.

To understand how they work, let's look at the definition of the `Iterator` trait from the `std::iter` module:

```
pub trait Iterator {
    type Item;
    fn next(&mut self) -> Option<Self::Item>;
    // other default methods omitted
}
```

The `Iterator` trait is an associated type trait which mandates the two items, to be defined for any implementing type. First is the associated type, `Item`, which specifies what item the iterator yields. Second is the `next` method, which is called every time we need to read a value from the type being iterated over. There are also other methods that we've omitted here, as they have default implementations. To make a type iterable, we only need to specify the `Item` type and implement the `next` method and all other methods with default implementations become available for the type. In this way, iterators are a really powerful abstraction. You can see the full set of default methods at: `https://doc.rust-lang.org/std/iter/trait.Iterator.html`.

The `Iterator` trait has a sibling trait called `IntoIterator`, which is implemented by types that want to convert in to an iterator. It provides the `into_iter` method that takes the implementing type via `self` and consumes the elements of the type.

Let's implement the `Iterator` trait for a custom type. Identify what you want to iterate over in your data type if it's not a collection. Then, create a wrapper struct holding any state of the iterator. Often, we' will find iterators being implemented for some wrapper type that references the collection type's element either by ownership or by an immutable or mutable reference. The methods to convert a type in to an iterator are also named conventionally:

- `iter()` takes elements by reference.
- `iter_mut()` takes mutable reference to elements.
- `into_iter()` takes ownership of the values and consumes the actual type once iterated completely. The original collection can no longer be accessed.

The type that implements the `Iterator` trait can be used in a `for` loop and under the hood, the next method of the item gets called. Consider the for loop as shown in the following:

```
for i in 0..20 {
    // do stuff
}
```

The preceding code would get de-sugared as follows:

```
let a = Range(..);
while let Some(i) = a.next() {
    // do stuff
}
```

It' will repeatedly call `a.next()` until it matches a `Some(i)` variant. When it matches `None`, the iteration stops.

Implementing a custom iterator

To understand iterators more thoroughly, we'll implement an iterator that generates prime numbers up to a certain limit that's customizable by the user. First, let's clarify the API expectations that we'll need from our iterator:

```
// custom_iterator.rs

use std::usize;
```

```
struct Primes {
    limit: usize
}

fn main() {
    let primes = Primes::new(100);
    for i in primes.iter() {
        println!("{}", i);
    }
}
```

So, we have a type called `Primes` that we can instantiate with the `new` method, providing the upper bound on the number of primes to generate. We can call `iter()` on this instance to convert it in to an iterator type, which can then be used in a `for` loop. With that said, let's add the `new` and `iter` methods on it:

```
// custom_iterator.rs

impl Primes {
    fn iter(&self) -> PrimesIter {
        PrimesIter {
            index: 2,
            computed: compute_primes(self.limit)
        }
    }

    fn new(limit: usize) -> Primes {
        Primes { limit }
    }
}
```

The `iter` method takes the `Primes` type via `&self` and returns a `PrimesIter` type containing two fields: `index`, which stores the `index` in the vector, and a `computed` field that stores the pre-computed primes in a vector. The `compute_primes` method is defined as follows:

```
// custom_iterator.rs

fn compute_primes(limit: usize) -> Vec<bool> {
    let mut sieve = vec![true; limit];
    let mut m = 2;
    while m * m < limit {
        if sieve[m] {
            for i in (m * 2..limit).step_by(m) {
                sieve[i] = false;
            }
        }
    }
```

```
            m += 1;
        }
        sieve
    }
}
```

This function implements the sieve of the eratosthenes algorithm for efficiently generating prime numbers up to a given limit. Next, there's the definition of the `PrimesIter` struct along with its `Iterator` implementation:

```
// custom_iterator.rs

struct PrimesIter {
    index: usize,
    computed: Vec<bool>
}

impl Iterator for PrimesIter {
    type Item = usize;
    fn next(&mut self) -> Option<Self::Item> {
        loop {
            self.index += 1;
            if self.index > self.computed.len() - 1 {
                return None;
            } else if self.computed[self.index] {
                return Some(self.index);
            } else {
                continue
            }
        }
    }
}
```

In the `next` method, we loop and get the next prime number if the value at `self.index` is `true` in the `self.computed` Vec. If we went past the elements in our `computed` Vec, then we return `None` to signify that we are done. Here's the complete code with the main function that generates `100` prime numbers:

```
// custom_iterator.rs

use std::usize;

struct Primes {
    limit: usize
}

fn compute_primes(limit: usize) -> Vec<bool> {
    let mut sieve = vec![true; limit];
```

```rust
        let mut m = 2;
        while m * m < limit {
            if sieve[m] {
                for i in (m * 2..limit).step_by(m) {
                    sieve[i] = false;
                }
            }
            m += 1;
        }
        sieve
    }

impl Primes {
    fn iter(&self) -> PrimesIter {
        PrimesIter {
            index: 2,
            computed: compute_primes(self.limit)
        }
    }

    fn new(limit: usize) -> Primes {
        Primes { limit }
    }
}

struct PrimesIter {
    index: usize,
    computed: Vec<bool>
}

impl Iterator for PrimesIter {
    type Item = usize;
    fn next(&mut self) -> Option<Self::Item> {
        loop {
            self.index += 1;
            if self.index > self.computed.len() - 1 {
                return None;
            } else if self.computed[self.index] {
                return Some(self.index);
            } else {
                continue
            }
        }
    }
}

fn main() {
    let primes = Primes::new(100);
```

```
        for i in primes.iter() {
            print!("{},", i);
        }
    }
```

We get the following output:

```
3,5,7,11,13,17,19,23,29,31,37,41,43,47,53,59,61,67,71,73,79,83,89,97
```

Great! Apart from `Vec`, there are a lot of types that implement the `Iterator` trait in the standard library, such as `HashMap`, `BTreeMap`, and `VecDeque`.

Advanced types

In this section, we'll look at some of the advanced types in Rust. Let's first start with unsized types.

Unsized types

Unsized types are categories of types that are first encountered if one tries to create a variable of the type, `str`. We know that we can create and use string references only behind references such as `&str`. Let's see what error message we get if we try to create a `str` type:

```
// unsized_types.rs

fn main() {
    let a: str = "2048";
}
```

We get the following error upon compilation:

```
→  Chapter08 git:(master) X rustc unsized_types.rs
error[E0308]: mismatched types
 --> unsized_types.rs:4:18
  |
4 |     let a: str = "2048";
  |                  ^^^^^^ expected str, found reference
  |
  = note: expected type `str`
             found type `&'static str`

error[E0277]: the size for values of type `str` cannot be known at compilation time
 --> unsized_types.rs:4:9
  |
4 |     let a: str = "2048";
  |         ^ doesn't have a size known at compile-time
  |
  = help: the trait `std::marker::Sized` is not implemented for `str`
  = note: to learn more, visit <https://doc.rust-lang.org/book/second-edition/ch19-04-advanced-t
ypes.html#dynamically-sized-types-and-the-sized-trait>
  = note: all local variables must have a statically known size
  = help: unsized locals are gated as an unstable feature
```

By default, Rust creates a reference type of `str` as `'static str`. The error message mentions that all local variables—values that live on the stack—must have a statically known size at compile time. This is because the stack memory is finite and we cannot have infinite- or dynamic-sized types. Similarly, there are other instances of types that are unsized:

- `[T]`: This is a slice of type, `T`. They can only be used as `&[T]` or `&mut [T]`.
- `dyn Trait`: This is a trait object. They can only be used as a `&dyn Trait` or `&mut dyn Trait` type.
- Any struct that has an unsized type as its last field is also considered an unsized type as well.
- There's `str`, which we already explored. `str` internally is just a `[u8]` but with the added guarantee that the bytes are valid UTF-8.

Function types

Functions in Rust also have a concrete type and they differ in terms of their argument types and also in their `arity`, as in how many arguments they take, as in the example:

```
// function_types.rs

fn add_two(a: u32, b: u32) -> u32 {
    a + b
}
```

```
fn main() {
    let my_func = add_two;
    let res = my_func(3, 4);
    println!("{:?}", res);
}
```

Functions in Rust are first class citizens. This means they can be stored in variables or passed to other functions or returned from functions. The preceding code declares a function add_two, which we store in my_func and later invoke with 3 and 4.

 Function types are not to be confused with Fn closures as they both have fn as their type signature prefix.

Never type ! and diverging functions

We used a macro called unimplemented!(), which helps in letting the compiler ignore any unimplemented function and to compile our code. This works because the unimplemented macro returns something called a never type, denoted by !.

Unions

For interoperability with C code, Rust also supports the union type, which maps directly to a C union. Unions are unsafe to read from. Let's see an example of how to create and interact with them:

```
// unions.rs

#[repr(C)]
union Metric {
    rounded: u32,
    precise: f32,
}

fn main() {
    let mut a = Metric { rounded: 323 };
    unsafe {
        println!("{}", a.rounded);
    }
    unsafe {
        println!("{}", a.precise);
    }
}
```

```
        a.precise = 33.3;
        unsafe {
            println!("{}", a.precise);
        }
    }
```

We created a union type, Metric, that has two fields rounded and precise, and represents some measurement. In main, we initialize an instance of it in the a variable.

We can only initialize one of the variables, otherwise the compiler complains with the following message:

```
error: union expressions should have exactly one field
  --> unions.rs:10:17
   |
10 |      let mut a = Metric { rounded: 323, precise:23.0 };
```

We also had to use unsafe blocks to print fields of our union. Compiling and running the previous code gives us the following output:

```
323
0.000000000000000000000000000000000000000000000453
33.3
```

As you can see, we get a garbage value for the uninitialized field, precise. At the time of writing this book, union types only allow Copy types as their fields. They share the same memory space with all of their fields, exactly like C unions.

Cow

Cow is a smart pointer type that provides two versions of strings. It stands for Clone on Write. It has the following type signature:

```
pub enum Cow<'a, B> where B: 'a + ToOwned + 'a + ?Sized,  {
    Borrowed(&'a B),
    Owned(<B as ToOwned>::Owned),
}
```

First, we have the two variants:

- Borrowed that represents the borrowed version of some type B. This B has to implement the ToOwned trait.
- There is also owned variant which contains the owned version of the type.

This type is suitable for cases where one needs to avoid allocations where it's not needed. A real world example is the JSON parser crate called serde_json.

Advanced traits

In this section, we'll discuss some of the advanced traits that are important to know when we are dealing with complex code bases.

Sized and ?Sized

The Sized trait is a marker trait that represents types whose sizes are known at compile time. It is implemented for most types in Rust except for unsized types. All type parameters have an implicit trait bound of Sized in their definition. We can also specify optional trait bounds using the ? operator before a trait, but the ? operator with traits only works for marker traits as the time of writing this book. It may be extended to other types in future.

Borrow and AsRef

These are special traits that carry the notion of able to construct a out of any type.

ToOwned

This trait is meant to be implemented for types that can be converted in to an owned version. For example, the &str type has this trait implemented for String. This means the &str type has a method called to_owned() on it that can convert it in to a String type, which is an owned type.

From and Into

To convert one type into another, we have the `From` and `Into` traits. The interesting part about both of these traits is that we only need to implement the `From` trait and we get the implementation of the `Into` trait for free, because of the following impl:

```
#[stable(feature = "rust1", since = "1.0.0")]
impl<T, U> Into<U> for T where U: From<T> {
    fn into(self) -> U {
        U::from(self)
    }
}
```

Trait objects and object safety

Object safety is a set of rules and restrictions that does not allow trait objects to be constructed. Consider the following code:

```
// object_safety.rs

trait Foo {
    fn foo();
}

fn generic(val: &Foo) {

}

fn main() {

}
```

We get the following error upon compilation:

```
→  Chapter07 git:(master) X rustc object_safety.rs
error[E0038]: the trait `Foo` cannot be made into an object
 --> object_safety.rs:8:1
  |
8 | fn generic(val: &Foo) {
  | ^^^^^^^^^^^^^^^^^^^^^ the trait `Foo` cannot be made into an object
  |
  = note: method `foo` has no receiver

error: aborting due to previous error

For more information about this error, try `rustc --explain E0038`.
```

This brings us to the idea of object safety, which is a set of restrictions that forbids creating a trait object from a trait. In this example, since our type doesn't have a self reference, it's not possible to create a trait object out of it. In this case, to convert any type into a trait object, methods on the type need to be an instance—one that takes `self` by reference. So, we change our trait method declaration, `foo`, to the following:

```
trait Foo {
    fn foo(&self);
}
```

This makes the the compiler happy.

Universal function call syntax

There are times when you are using a type that has the same set of methods as one of its implemented traits. In those situations, Rust provides us with the uniform function call syntax that works for calling methods that are either on types themselves or come from a trait. Consider the following code:

```
// ufcs.rs

trait Driver {
    fn drive(&self) {
        println!("Driver's driving!");
    }
}

struct MyCar;

impl MyCar {
    fn drive(&self) {
        println!("I'm driving!");
    }
}

impl Driver for MyCar {}

fn main() {
    let car = MyCar;
    car.drive();
}
```

The preceding code has two methods with the same name, `drive`. One of them is an inherent method and the other comes from the trait, `Driver`. If we compile and run this, we get the following output:

```
I'm driving
```

Well, what if we wanted to call the `Driver` trait's `drive` method? Inherent methods on types are given higher priority than other methods with the same name. To call a trait method, we can use the **Universal Function Call Syntax (UFCS)**.

Trait rules

Traits also have special properties and restrictions, which are important to know about when you are using them.

An important property of the type system in the context of traits is the **trait coherence** rule. The idea of trait coherence is that there should be exactly one implementation of a trait on a type that implements it. This should be quite obvious since, with two implementations there would be ambiguity in what to choose between the two.

Another rule that might confuse many about traits is the **orphan rule**. The orphan rule, in simple words, states that we cannot implement external traits on external types.

To word it in another way, either the trait must be defined by you if you are implementing something on an external type, or your type should be defined by you when you are implementing an external trait. This rules out the possibility of having conflicts in overlapping trait implementations across crates.

Closures in depth

As we know already, closures are a fancier version of functions. They are also first-class functions, which means that they can be put into variables or can be passed as an argument to functions or even returned from a function. But what sets them apart from functions is that they are also aware of the environment they are declared within and can reference any variable from their environment. The way they reference variables from their environment is determined by how the variable is used inside the closure.

A closure, by default, will try to capture the variable in the most flexible way possible. Only when the programmer needs a certain way of capturing the value will they coerce to the programmer's intent. That won't make much sense unless we see different kinds of closures in action. Closures under the hood are anonymous structs that implement three traits that represent how closures access their environment. We will look at the three traits (ordered from least restrictive to most restrictive) next.

Fn closures

Closures that access variables only for read access implement the `Fn` trait. Any value they access are as reference types (`&T`). This is the default mode of borrowing the closures assumes. Consider the following code:

```
// fn_closure.rs

fn main() {
    let a = String::from("Hey!");
    let fn_closure = || {
        println!("Closure says: {}", a);
    };
    fn_closure();
    println!("Main says: {}", a);
}
```

We get the following output upon compilation:

```
Closure says: Hey!
Main says: Hey!
```

The `a` variable was still accessible even after invoking the closure as the closure used `a` by reference.

FnMut closures

When the compiler figures out that a closure mutates a value referenced from the environment, the closure implements the `FnMut` trait. Adapting the same code as before, we have the following:

```
// fn_mut_closure.rs

fn main() {
    let mut a = String::from("Hey!");
    let fn_mut_closure = || {
```

```
        a.push_str("Alice");
    };
    fn_mut_closure();
    println!("Main says: {}", a);
}
```

The previous closure adds the `"Alice"` string to `a`. `fn_mut_closure` mutates its environment.

FnOnce closures

Closures that take ownership of the data they read from their environment get implemented with `FnOnce`. The name signifies that this closure can only be called once and, because of that, the variables are available only once. This is the least recommended way to construct and use closures, because you cannot use the referenced variables later:

```
// fn_once.rs

fn main() {
    let mut a = Box::new(23);
    let call_me = || {
        let c = a;
    };

    call_me();
    call_me();
}
```

This fails with the following error:

```
→  Chapter07 git:(master) X rustc fn_once.rs
error[E0382]: use of moved value: `call_me`
  --> fn_once.rs:10:5
   |
9  |     call_me();
   |     ------- value moved here
10 |     call_me();
   |     ^^^^^^^ value used here after move
   |
note: closure cannot be invoked more than once because it moves the variable `a` out of its environment
  --> fn_once.rs:6:18
   |
6  |         let _c = a;
   |                  ^
error: aborting due to previous error
```

But there are use cases where FnOnce closures are the only applicable closures. One such example is the thread::spawn method in the standard library used for spawning new threads.

Consts in structs, enums, and traits

Structs, enums, and traits definitions can also be provided with constant field members. They can be used in cases where you need to share a constant among them. Take, for example, a scenario where we have a Circle trait that's is meant to be implemented by different circular shape types. We can add a PI constant to the Circle trait, which can be shared by any type that has an area property and relies on value of PI for calculating the area:

```
// trait_constants.rs

trait Circular {
    const PI: f64 = 3.14;
    fn area(&self) -> f64;
}

struct Circle {
    rad: f64
}

impl Circular for Circle {
    fn area(&self) -> f64 {
        Circle::PI * self.rad * self.rad
    }
}

fn main() {
    let c_one = Circle { rad: 4.2 };
    let c_two = Circle { rad: 75.2 };
    println!("Area of circle one: {}", c_one.area());
    println!("Area of circle two: {}", c_two.area());
}
```

We can also have consts in structs and enums:

```
// enum_struct_consts.rs

enum Item {
    One,
    Two
}
```

```
struct Food {
    Cake,
    Chocolate
}

impl Item {
    const DEFAULT_COUNT: u32 = 34;
}

impl Food {
    const FAVORITE_FOOD: &str = "Cake";
}

fn main() {
}
```

Next, let's look at some of the advanced aspects of modules.

Modules, paths, and imports

Rust provides us with a lot of flexibility in terms of how we organize our project, as we saw in Chapter 2, *Managing Projects with Cargo*. Here, we'll go into some of the advanced aspects of modules and different ways to introduce more privacy in our code.

Imports

We can do **nested imports** of items from modules. This helps in reducing the taken up by imports. Consider the following code:

```
// nested_imports.rs

use std::sync::{Mutex, Arc, mpsc::channel};

fn main() {
    let (tx, rx) = channel();
}
```

Re-exports

Re-exports allows one to selectively expose items from a module. We were already using the convenience of reexports when we used the `Option` and `Result` types. Re-exports also helps in reducing the import path one has to write if the module is created a nested directory containing many submodules.

For example, here we have a sub module named `bar.rs` from a cargo project we created called `reexports`:

```
// reexports_demo/src/foo/bar.rs

pub struct Bar;
```

The `Bar` is a publicly exposed struct module under `src/foo/bar.rs`. If the user wants to use `Bar` in their code, they will have to write something like the following:

```
// reexports_demo/src/main.rs

use foo::bar::Bar;

fn main() {
}
```

The above `use` statement is quite verbose. When you have a lot of nested sub-modules in your project, this gets awkward and redundant. Instead, we can reexport `Bar` from the `bar` module all of the way to our crate root, like so, in our `foo.rs`:

```
// reexports_demo/src/foo.rs

mod bar;
pub use bar::Bar;
```

To re-export, we use the `pub use` keyword. Now we can easily use `Bar` as well as using `foo::Bar`.

By default, Rust recommends **absolute imports** within root modules. Absolute imports are done starting with the `crate` keyword, whereas **relative imports** are done using the `self` keyword. When re-exporting sub-modules to their parent modules, we might benefit from relative imports, as using absolute imports becomes long and redundant.

Selective privacy

The privacy of items in Rust starts at the module level. As a library author, to expose things to users from a module, we use the `pub` keyword. But there are items that we only want to expose to other modules within the crate, but not to the users. In such cases, we can use the `pub(crate)` modifier for the item, which allows the item to be exposed only within the crate.

Consider the following code:

```
// pub_crate.rs

fn main() {
}
```

Advanced match patterns and guards

In this section, we'll take a look at some of the advanced usage of match and let patterns. First, let's look at match.

Match guards

We can also use match guards on arms (`if code > 400 || code <= 500`) to match on a subset of values. They start with an `if` expression.

Advanced let destructure

We have the following complex data that we want to match against:

```
// complex_destructure.rs

enum Foo {
    One, Two, Three
}

enum Bar(Foo);

struct Dummy {
    inner: Bar
}
```

```
struct ComplexStruct {
    obj: Dummy
}

fn get_complex_struct() -> ComplexStruct {
    ComplexStruct {
        obj: Dummy { inner: Bar(Foo::Three) }
    }
}

fn main() {
    let a = get_complex_struct();
}
```

Casting and coercion

Casting is a mechanism of downgrading or upgrading a type to some other type. When the casting happens implicitly, it is called coercion. Rust also allows for casting types at various levels. The very obvious candidates are primitive numeric types. You may have the need to cast a u8 type to promote to u64 or to truncate i64 to i32. To perform trivial casts, we use the as keyword, like so:

```
let a = 34u8;
let b = a as u64;
```

It's not only primitive types—casting is supported at higher-level types too. We can also cast a reference of a type to its trait object, if it implements that particular trait. So we can do something like the following:

```
// cast_trait_object.rs

use std::fmt::Display;

fn show_me(item: &Display) {
    println!("{}", item);
}

fn main() {
    let a = "hello".to_string();
    let b = &a;
    show_me(b);
    // let c = b as &Display;
}
```

There are other classes of casting supported by various pointer types:

- Converting a `*mut T` to `*const T`. The other method is forbidden in safe Rust and requires an `unsafe` block
- Converting `&T` in to `*const T` and vice versa

There is also another explicit and unsafe version of casting called `transmutes` and, because it's unsafe, it is very dangerous to use when you are unaware of the consequences. When used ignorantly, it leads you into situations similar to one where you create a pointer from an integer in C.

Types and memory

In this section, we'll touch on some aspects and low-level details of types in programming languages that are important to know if you are someone writing systems software and care about performance.

Memory alignment

This is one of those aspects of memory management that you will rarely have to care about unless performance is a strict requirement. Due to data access latency between memory and the processor, when the processor accesses data from memory, it does so in a chunk and not byte by byte. This is to help reduce the number of memory accesses. This chunk size is called the memory access granularity of the CPU. Usually, the chunk sizes are one word (32 bit), two word, four word, and so on, and they depend on the target architecture. Due to this access granularity, it is desired that the data resides in memory which is aligned to a multiple of the word size. If that is not the case, then the CPU has to read and then perform left or right shifts on the data bits and discard the unneeded data to read a particular value. This wastes CPU cycles. In most cases, the compiler is smart enough to figure out the data alignment for us, but in some cases, we need to tell it. There are two important terms we need to understand:

- **Word size:** Word size means the number of bits of data processed by the microprocessor as a unit.
- **Memory access granularity:** The minimum chunk of data accessed by the CPU from the memory bus is called the memory access granularity.

Data types in all programming languages have both a size and an alignment. The alignment of primitive types is equal to their size. So, usually, all primitive types are aligned and the CPU has no problem doing an aligned read for these. But when we create custom data types, compilers usually insert padding between our struct fields if they are not aligned to allow the CPU to access memory in an aligned manner.

Having known about data type size and alignment, let's explore the `std::mem` module from the standard library that allows us to introspect data types and their sizes.

Exploring the std::mem module

In regard to types and their size in memory, the `mem` module from the standard library provides us with convenient APIs to inspect sizes and alignment of types and functionalities for initializing raw memory. Quite a few of these functions are unsafe and must only be used when the programmer knows what they are doing. We'll restrict our exploration to these APIs:

- `size_of` returns the size of a type given via a generic type
- `size_of_val` returns the size of a value given as a reference

Being generic, these methods are meant to be called using the turbofish `::<>` operator. We are not actually giving these methods a type as a parameter; we're just explicitly calling them against a type. If we were skeptical about the zero-cost claims of some of the preceding generic types, we could use these functions to check the overhead. Let's take a look at some sizes of types in Rust:

```
// mem_introspection.rs

use std::cell::Cell;
use std::cell::RefCell;
use std::rc::Rc;

fn main() {
    println!("type u8: {}", std::mem::size_of::<u8>());
    println!("type f64: {}", std::mem::size_of::<f64>());
    println!("value 4u8:  {}", std::mem::size_of_val(&4u8));
    println!("value 4:  {}", std::mem::size_of_val(&4));
    println!("value 'a': {}", std::mem::size_of_val(&'a'));

    println!("value \"Hello World\" as a static str slice: {}",
std::mem::size_of_val("Hello World"));
    println!("value \"Hello World\" as a String: {}",
std::mem::size_of_val("Hello World").to_string());
```

```
        println!("Cell(4)): {}", std::mem::size_of_val(&Cell::new(84)));
        println!("RefCell(4)): {}", std::mem::size_of_val(&RefCell::new(4)));

        println!("Rc(4): {}", std::mem::size_of_val(&Rc::new(4)));
        println!("Rc<RefCell(8)>): {}",
    std::mem::size_of_val(&Rc::new(RefCell::new(4))));
    }
```

Another observation that's important to notice, is the size of various pointers. Consider the following code:

```
// pointer_layouts.rs

trait Position {}

struct Coordinates(f64, f64);

impl Position for Coordinates {}

fn main() {
    let val = Coordinates(1.0, 2.0);
    let ref_: &Coordinates = &val;
    let pos_ref: &Position = &val as &Position;
    let ptr:        *const Coordinates = &val as *const Coordinates;
    let pos_ptr: *const Position  = &val as *const Position;
    println!("ref_: {}", std::mem::size_of_val(&ref_));
    println!("ptr: {}", std::mem::size_of_val(&ptr));
    println!("val: {}", std::mem::size_of_val(&val));
    println!("pos_ref: {}", std::mem::size_of_val(&pos_ref));
    println!("pos_ptr: {}", std::mem::size_of_val(&pos_ptr));
}
```

We create pointers to a Coordinate struct in a bunch of different ways and we print their sizes by casting them as different kind of pointers. Compiling and running the code above, gives us the following output:

```
ref_: 8
ptr: 8
val: 16
pos_ref: 16
pos_ptr: 16
```

This clearly shows that trait objects and references to traits are fat pointers double the size of a normal pointer.

Serialization and deserialization using serde

Serialization and deserialization are important concepts to understand for any kind of application needs to transfer or store data in a compact manner. **Serialization** is the process by which an in-memory data type can be converted into a sequence of bytes, while **deserilization** is the opposite of that, meaning it can read data. Many programming languages provide support for converting a data structure into a sequence of bytes. The beautiful part about serde is that it generates the serialization of any supported type at compile time, relying heavily on procedural macros. Serialization and deserialization is a zero cost operation with serde most of the time.

In this demo, we'll explore the serde crate to serialize and deserialize a user defined type. Let's create a new project by running cargo new serde_demo with the following contents in Cargo.toml:

```
# serde_demo/Cargo.toml

[dependencies]
serde = "1.0.84"
serde_derive = "1.0.84"
serde_json = "1.0.36"
```

Following are the contents in main.rs:

```
serde_demo/src/main.rs

use serde_derive::{Serialize, Deserialize};

#[derive(Debug, Serialize, Deserialize)]
struct Foo {
    a: String,
    b: u64
}

impl Foo {
    fn new(a: &str, b: u64) -> Self {
        Self {
            a: a.to_string(),
            b
        }
    }
}

fn main() {
    let foo_json = serde_json::to_string(Foo::new("It's that simple",
101)).unwrap();
```

```
    println!("{:?}", foo_json);
    let foo_value: Foo = serde_json::from_str(foo_json).unwrap();
    println!("{:?}", foo_value);
}
```

To serialize any native data type to a JSON-like format, we simply need to put a derive annotation over our types, which is the case of for our struct, `Foo`.

`serde` supports a lot of serializers implemented as crates. Popular examples are `serde_json`, `bincode` and `TOML`. More supported formats can be found at: `https://github.com/TyOverby/bincode`. These serialization implementors, such as the `serde_json` crate, provide methods such as `to_string` to convert

Summary

In this chapter, we covered quite a bit of detail on some of the advanced aspects of Rust's type system. We got to know the various traits that make writing ergonomic Rust code. We also saw advanced pattern matching constructs. In the end, we looked at the serde crate that is blazing fast in performing data serialization. The next chapter will be about how to do multiple things at the same time using concurrency.

8
Concurrency

Modern day software is rarely written to perform tasks sequentially. It is more important today to be able to write programs that do more than one thing at a time and do it correctly. As transistors keep getting smaller, computer architects are unable to scale CPU clocks frequency due to quantum effects in the transistors. This has shifted focus more towards building concurrent CPU architectures that employ multiple cores. With this shift, developers need to write highly concurrent applications to maintain performance gains that they had for free when Moore's law was in effect.

But writing concurrent code is hard and languages that don't provide better abstractions make the situation worse. Rust attempts to make things better and safer in this space. In this chapter, we will go through the concepts and primitives that enable Rust to provide fearless concurrency to developers, allowing them to easily express their programs in a way that can safely do more than one thing at a time.

The topics covered in this chapter are as follows:

- Program execution models
- Concurrency and associated pitfalls
- Threads as unit of concurrency
- How Rust provides thread-safety
- Concurrency primitives in Rust
- Other libraries for concurrency

Program execution models

"An evolving system increases its complexity unless work is done to reduce it."

- Meir Lehman

In the early 1960s, before multitasking was even a thing, programs written for computers were limited to a sequential execution model, where they were able to run instructions one after the other in chronological order. This was mainly due to limitations in how many instructions the hardware could process during that time. As we shifted from vacuum tubes to transistors, then to integrated chips, the modern day computer opened up possibilities to support multiple points of execution in programs. Gone are the days of sequential programming model where computers had to wait for an instruction to finish before executing the next one. Today, it's more common for computers to be able to do more than one thing at a time and do it correctly.

The modern day computer models a concurrent execution model, where a bunch of instructions can execute independently of each other with overlapping time periods. In this model, instructions need not wait for each other and run nearly at the same time, except when they need to share or coordinate with some data. If you look at the modern day software, it does many things that appear to happen at the same time, as in the following examples:

- The user interface of a desktop application continues to work normally even though the application connects to the network in the background
- A game updates the state of thousands of entities at the same time, while playing a soundtrack in the background and keeping a consistent frame rate
- A scientific, compute-heavy program splits computation in order to take full advantage of all of the cores in the machine
- A web server handles more than one request at a time in order to maximize throughput

These are some really compelling examples that propel the need to model our program as concurrent processes. But what does concurrency really mean? In the next section, let's define that.

Concurrency

The ability of a program to manage more than one thing at a time while giving an illusion of them happening at the same time is called concurrency, and such programs are called concurrent programs. Concurrency allows you to structure your program in a way that it performs faster if you have a problem that can be split into multiple sub-problems. When talking about concurrency, another term called parallelism is often thrown in the discussion, and it is important we know the differences as the usage of these terms often overlap. Parallelism is when each task runs simultaneously on separate CPU cores with non-overlapping time periods. The following diagram illustrates the difference between concurrency and parallelism:

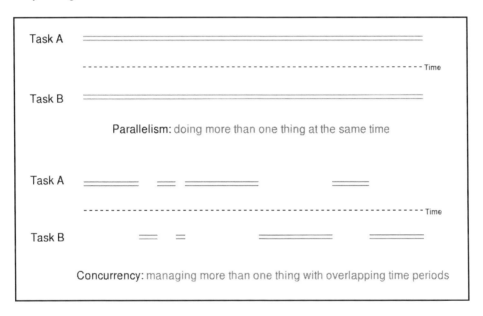

To put it another way, concurrency is about structuring your program to manage more than one thing at a time, while parallelism is about putting your program on multiple cores to increase the amount of work it does in a period of time. With this definition, it follows that concurrency when done right, does a better utilization of the CPU while parallelism might not in all cases. If your program runs in parallel but is only dealing with a single dedicated task, you aren't gaining much throughput. This is to say that we gain the best of both worlds when a concurrent program is made to run on multiple cores.

Usually, the support for concurrency is already provided at the lower levels by the operating system, and developers mostly program against the higher level abstractions provided by programming languages. On top of the low level support, there are different approaches to concurrency.

Approaches to concurrency

We use concurrency to offload parts of our program to run independently. At times, these parts may depend on each other and are progressing towards a common goal or they may be embarrassingly parallel, which is a term used to refer to problems that can be split into independent stateless tasks, for instance, transforming each pixel of an image in parallel. As such, the approaches used to make a program concurrent depend on what level we are leveraging concurrency and the nature of the problem we are trying to solve. In the next section, let's discuss the available approaches to concurrency.

Kernel-based

With multitasking being the norm these days, modern operating systems need to deal with more than one processes. As such, your operating system kernel already provides primitives for writing concurrent programs in one of the following forms:

- **Processes**: In this approach, we can run different parts of a program by spawning separate replicas of themselves. On Linux, this can be achieved using the `fork` system call. To communicate any data with the spawned processes, one can use various **Inter Process Communication** (**IPC**) facilities such as pipes and FIFOs. Process based concurrency provides you with features such as fault isolation, but also has the overhead of starting a whole new process. There's a limited number of processes you can spawn before the OS runs out of memory and kills them. Process-based concurrency is seen in Python's multiprocessing module.

- **Threads**: Processes under the hood are just threads, specifically called the main thread. A process can launch or spawn one or more threads. A thread is the smallest schedulable unit of execution. Every process starts with a main thread. In addition to that, it can spawn additional threads using the APIs provided by the OS. To allow a programmer to use threads, most languages come with threading APIs in their standard library. They are lightweight compared to processes. Threads share the same address space with the parent process. They don't need to have a separate entry in the **Process Control Block (PCB)** in the kernel, which is updated every time we spawn a new process. But taming multiple threads within a process is a challenge because, unlike processes, they share the address space with their parent process and other child threads and, because scheduling of threads is decided by the OS, we cannot rely on the order the threads will execute and what memory they will read from or write to. These operations suddenly become hard to reason about when we go from a single-threaded program to a multi-threaded one.

> **Note**: The implementation of threads and processes differ between operating systems. Under Linux, they are treated the same by the kernel, except that threads don't have their own process control block entry in the kernel and they share the address space with their parent process and any other child threads.

User-level

Process- and thread-based concurrency are limited by how many of them we can spawn. A lighter and more efficient alternative is to use user space threads, popularly known as green threads. They first appeared in Java with the code name *green* and the name has stuck since then. Other languages such as Go (goroutines), and Erlang also have green threads. The primary motivation in using green threads is to reduce the overhead that comes with using process- and thread-based concurrency. Green threads are very lightweight to spawn and use less space than a thread. For instance, in Go, a goroutine takes only 4 KiB of space compared to the usual 8MB by a thread.

User space threads are managed and scheduled as part of the language runtime. A runtime is any extra bookeeping or managing code that's executed with every program you run. This would be your garbage collector or the thread scheduler. Internally, user space threads are implemented on top of native OS threads. Rust had green threads before the 1.0 version, but they were later removed before the language hit stable release. Having green threads would have steered away Rust's guarantee and its principle of having no runtime costs.

User space concurrency is more efficient, but hard to get right in its implementation. Thread-based concurrency, however, is a tried and tested approach and has been popular since multi-process operating systems came into existence and it's the go- to approach for concurrency. Most mainstream languages provide threading APIs that allows users to create threads and easily offload a portion of their code for independent execution.

Leveraging concurrency in a program follows a multi-step process. First, we need to identify parts of our problem that can be run independently. Then, we need to look for ways to co-ordinate threads that are split into multiple sub-tasks to accomplish a shared goal. In the process, threads might also need to share data and they need synchronization for accessing or writing to shared data. With all of the benefits that concurrency brings with it, there are a new set of challenges and paradigms that developers need to care and plan for. In the next section, let's discuss the pitfalls of concurrency.

Pitfalls

The advantages of concurrency abound, but it brings a whole lot of complexity and pitfalls that we have to deal with. Some issues when writing concurrent programs code are as follows:

- **Race conditions**: As threads are scheduled by the operating system, we don't have a say in what order and how threads will access a shared data. A common use case in multi-threaded code is about updating a global state from multiple threads. This follows a three step process—read, modify, and write. If these three operations aren't performed atomically by threads, we may end up with a race condition.

A set of operations is atomic if they execute together in an indivisble manner. For a set of operations to be atomic, it must not be pre-empted in the middle of its execution. It must execute completely or not at all.

If two threads try to update a value at a memory location at the same time, they might end up overwriting each other's values and only one of the updates will ever be written to memory or the value might not get updated at all. This is a classic example of a race condition. Both threads are racing to update the value without any co-ordination with each other. This leads to other issues such as data races.

- **Data race**: When multiple threads try to write data to a certain location in memory and when both of them write at the same time, it's hard to predict what values will get written. The end result in the memory could also be garbage value. Data race is a consequence of a race condition, as read-modify-update operation must happen atomically by any thread to ensure that consistent data gets read or written by any thread.

- **Memory unsafety and undefined behavior**: Race conditions can also lead to undefined behavior. Consider the following pseudocode:

```
// Thread A

Node get(List list) {
    if (list.head != NULL) {
        return list.head
    }
}

// Thread B
list.head = NULL
```

We have two threads, A and B, that act on a linked list. `Thread A` tries to retrieve the head of the list. For doing this safely, it first checks the head of the list is not `NULL` and then returns it. `Thread B` sets the head of the list to a `NULL` value. Both of these run at nearly the same time and might get scheduled by the OS in different order. For instance, in one of the execution instances, the point where `Thread A` runs first and asserts that `list.head`, is not `NULL`. Right after that, `Thread A` is preempted by the OS and `Thread B` is scheduled to run. Now, `Thread B` sets `list.head` to `NULL`. Following that, when `Thread A` gets the chance to run, it will try to return `list.head` which is a `NULL` value. This would result in a segmentation fault when `list.head` is read from. In this case, memory unsafety happens because ordering is not maintained for these operations.

There is a common solution to the previously mentioned problems—synchronizing or serializing access to shared data or code or ensuring that the threads run critical sections atomically. This is done using synchronization primitives such as a mutex, semaphores, or conditional variables. But even using these primitives can lead to other issues such as deadlocks.

Deadlocks: Apart from race conditions, another issue that threads face is getting starved of resources while holding a lock on a resource. Deadlock is a condition where a **Thread A** holding a **resource a** and waiting for **resource b**. Another **Thread B** is holding a resource b and is waiting for **resource a.** The following diagram depicts the situation:

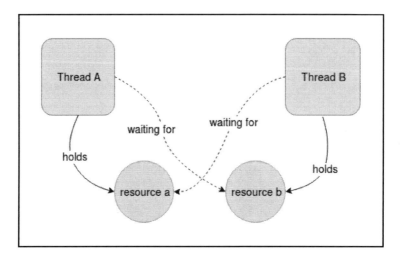

Deadlocks are hard to detect but they can be solved by taking locks in the correct order. In the preceding case, if both Thread A and Thread B try to take the lock first, we can ensure that the locks are released properly.

With the advantages and pitfalls explored, let's go through the APIs that Rust provides to write concurrent programs.

Concurrency in Rust

Rust's concurrency primitives rely on native OS threads. It provides threading APIs in the `std::thread` module in the standard library. In this section, we'll start with the basics on how to create threads to perform tasks concurrently. In subsequent sections, we'll explore how threads can share data with each other.

Thread basics

As we said, every program starts with a main thread. To create an independent execution point from anywhere in the program, the main thread can spawn a new thread, which becomes its child thread. Child threads can further spawn their own threads. Let's look at a concurrent program in Rust that uses threads in the simplest way possible:

```rust
// thread_basics.rs

use std::thread;

fn main() {
    thread::spawn(|| {
        println!("Thread!");
        "Much concurrent, such wow!".to_string()
    });
    print!("Hello ");
}
```

In `main`, we call the `spawn` function from the `thread` module which takes a no parameter closure as an argument. Within this closure, we can write any code that we want to execute concurrently as a separate thread. In our closure, we simply print some text and return `String`. Compiling and running this program gives us the following output:

```
$ rustc thread_basics.rs
$ ./thread_basics
Hello
```

Strange! We only get to see `"Hello"` being printed. What happened to `println!("Thread");` from the child thread ? A call to `spawn` creates the thread and returns immediately and the thread starts executing concurrently without blocking the instructions after it. The child thread is created in the detached state. Before the child thread has any chance to run its code, the program reaches the `print!("Hello");` statement and exits the program when it returns from `main`. As a result, code within the child thread doesn't execute at all. To allow the child thread to execute its code, we need to wait on the child thread. To do that, we need to first assign the value returned by `spawn` to a variable:

```rust
let child = thread::spawn(|| {
    print!("Thread!");
    String::from("Much concurrent, such wow!")
});
```

The `spawn` function returns a `JoinHandle` type, which we store in the `child` variable. This type is a handle to the child thread, which can be used to join a thread—in other words, wait for its termination. If we ignore the `JoinHandle` type of a thread, there is no way to wait for the thread. Continuing with our code, we call the `join` method on the child before exiting from `main` as in the following:

```
let value = child.join().expect("Failed joining child thread");
```

Calling `join` blocks the current thread and waits for the child thread to finish before executing any line of code following the `join` call. It returns a `Result` value. Since we know that this thread does not panic, we call `expect` to unwrap the `Result` type giving us the string. Joining the thread can fail if a thread is joining itself or gets deadlocked, and, in that case, it returns an `Err` variant with the value that was passed to the `panic!` call though, in this case, the returned value is of the `Any` type which must be downcasted to a proper type. Our updated code is as follows:

```
// thread_basics_join.rs

use std::thread;

fn main() {
    let child = thread::spawn(|| {
        println!("Thread!");
        String::from("Much concurrent, such wow!")
    });

    print!("Hello ");
    let value = child.join().expect("Failed joining child thread");
    println!("{}", value);
}
```

Here's the output of the program:

```
$ ./thread_basics_join
Hello Thread!
Much concurrent, such wow!
```

Great ! We wrote our first concurrent *hello world* program. Let's explore other APIs from the `thread` module.

Customizing threads

We also have APIs that can be used to configure threads by setting their properties such as the name or their stack size. For this, we have the `Builder` type from the `thread` module. Here's a simple program that creates a thread and spawns it using the `Builder` type:

```
// customize_threads.rs

use std::thread::Builder;

fn main() {
    let my_thread = Builder::new().name("Worker Thread".to_string())
                                  .stack_size(1024 * 4);
    let handle = my_thread.spawn(|| {
        panic!("Oops!");
    });
    let child_status = handle.unwrap().join();
    println!("Child status: {}", child_status);
}
```

In the preceding code, we use the `Builder::new`, method followed by calling the `name` and `stack_size` methods to add a name to our thread and its stack size respectively. We then call `spawn` on `my_thread`, which consumes the builder instance and spawns the thread. This time, within our closure, we `panic!` with an "Oops" message. Following is the output of this program:

```
$ ./customize_threads
thread 'Worker Thread' panicked at 'Oops!', customize_threads.rs:9:9
note: Run with `RUST_BACKTRACE=1` for a backtrace.
Child status: Err(Any)
```

We get to see that the thread has the same name we gave it - "`Worker Thread`". Also, notice the "`Child status`" message that's returned as an `Any` type. Values returned from panic call in a thread are returned as an `Any` type and must be downcasted to a specific type. That's all on the basics of spawning threads.

But the threads we spawned in the preceding code examples aren't doing much. We use concurrency to solve problems that can be split into multiple sub-tasks. In simple cases, these sub-tasks are independent of each other such as applying a filter to each pixel of an image in parallel. In other situations, the sub-tasks running in threads might want want to co-ordinate on some shared data.

They might also be contributing to a computation whose end result depends on the individual results from the threads, for instance, downloading a file from multiple threads in blocks and communicating it to a parent manager thread. Other problems might be dependent on a shared state such as an HTTP client sending a POST request to a server that has to update the database. Here, the database is the shared state common to all threads. These are some of the most common use cases of concurrency and it's important that threads are able to share or communicate data back and forth between each other and with their parent thread.

Let's step up the game a bit and look at how we can access existing data from parent threads within child threads.

Accessing data from threads

A thread that doesn't communicate or access data from the parent thread is not much. Let's take a very common pattern of using multiple threads to concurrently access items in a list to perform some computation. Consider the following code:

```
// thread_read.rs

use std::thread;

fn main() {
    let nums = vec![0, 1, 2, 3, 4];
    for n in 0..5 {
        thread::spawn(|| {
            println!("{}", nums[n]);
        });
    }
}
```

In the preceding code, we have 5 numbers in values and we spawn 5 threads where each one of them accesses the data in values. Let's compile this program:

```
→ Chapter08 git:(master) X rustc thread_read.rs
error[E0373]: closure may outlive the current function, but it borrows `nums`, which is owned by the current function
 --> thread_read.rs:8:23

8  |           thread::spawn(|| {
   |                         ^^ may outlive borrowed value `nums`
9  |               println!("{}", nums[n]);
   |                              ---- `nums` is borrowed here
help: to force the closure to take ownership of `nums` (and any other referenced variables), use the `move` keyword

8  |           thread::spawn(move || {
   |                         ^^^^^^^
```

Interesting ! The error makes sense if you think about it from a borrowing perspective. `nums` comes from the main thread. When we spawn a thread, it is not guaranteed to exit before the parent thread and may outlive it. When the parent thread returns, the `nums` variable is gone and `Vec` it's pointing to is freed. If the preceding code was allowed by Rust, the child thread could have accessed `nums` which might have some garbage value after `main` returns and it would have undergone a segmentation fault.

If you look at the help message from from the compiler, it suggests us to move or capture `nums` inside the closure. This way the referenced a `nums` variable from `main` is moved inside `closure` and it won't be available in the `main` thread.

Here's the code that uses the `move` keyword to move the value from the parent thread in its child thread:

```rust
// thread_moves.rs

use std::thread;

fn main() {
    let my_str = String::from("Damn you borrow checker!");
    let _ = thread::spawn(move || {
        println!("In thread: {}", my_str);
    });
    println!("In main: {}", my_str);
}
```

In the preceding code, we are trying to accessed `my_str` again. This fails with the following error:

```
→  Chapter08 git:(master) ✗ rustc thread_moves.rs
error[E0382]: use of moved value: `my_str`
  --> thread_moves.rs:10:29

7  |         let _ = thread::spawn(move || {
   |                               ------- value moved (into closure) here
...
10 |         println!("In main: {}", my_str);
   |                                 ^^^^^^ value used here after move

= note: move occurs because `my_str` has type `std::string::String`, which does not implement the `Copy` trait
```

As you can see from the preceding error message, with `move`, you don't get to use the data again, even if we are only reading `my_str` from our child thread. Here too, we are saved by the compiler. If the child thread frees the data and we access `my_str` from `main`, we'll access a freed value which is a use after free issue.

As you saw, the same rules of ownership and borrowing work in multi-threaded contexts too. This is one of the novel aspects of its design that doesn't require additional constructs to enforce correct concurrent code. But, how do we achieve the preceding use case of accessing data from threads? Because threads are more likely to outlive their parent, we can't have references in threads. Instead, Rust provides us with synchronization primitives that allow us to safely share and communicate data between threads. Let's explore these primitives. These types are usually composed in layers depending on the needs and you only pay for what you use.

Concurrency models with threads

We mainly use threads to perform a task that can be split into sub-problems, where the threads might need to communicate or share data with each other. Now, using the threading model as the baseline, there are different ways to structure our program and control access to shared data. A concurrency model specifies how multiple threads interact with instructions and data shared between them and how they make progress over time and space (here, memory).

Rust does not prefer any opinionated concurrency model and frees the developer in using their own models depending on the problem they are trying to solve through third party crates. So, other models of concurrency exist that includes the actor model implemented as a library in the `actix` crate. There are other models too, such as the work stealing concurrency model implemented by the `rayon` crate. Then, there is the `crossbeam` crate, which allows concurrent threads to share data from their parent stack frame and are guaranteed to return before the parent stack is deallocated.

There are two popular built-in concurrency models with which Rust provides us: sharing data with synchronization and sharing data by message passing.

Shared state model

Using shared state to communicate values to a thread is the most widely used approach, and the synchronization primitives to achieve this exist in most mainstream languages. Synchronization primitives are types or language constructs that allow multiple threads to access or manipulate a value in a thread-safe way. Rust also has many synchronization primitives that we can wrap around types to make them thread-safe.

As we saw in the previous section, we cannot have shared access to any value from multiple threads. We need shared ownership here. Back in Chapter 5, *Memory Management and Safety*, we introduced the Rc type. that can provide shared ownership of values. Let's try using this type with our previous example of reading data from multiple threads:

```
// thread_rc.rs

use std::thread;
use std::rc::Rc;

fn main() {
    let nums = Rc::new(vec![0, 1, 2, 3, 4]);
    let mut childs = vec![];
    for n in 0..5 {
        let ns = nums.clone();
        let c = thread::spawn(|| {
            println!("{}", ns[n]);
        });
        childs.push(c);
    }

    for c in childs {
        c.join().unwrap();
    }
}
```

This fails with the following error:

```
→  Chapter08 git:(master) ✗ rustc thread_rc.rs
error[E0277]: `std::rc::Rc<std::vec::Vec<i32>>` cannot be shared between threads safely
  --> thread_rc.rs:10:9
   |
10 |          thread::spawn(|| {
   |          ^^^^^^^^^^^^^ `std::rc::Rc<std::vec::Vec<i32>>` cannot be shared between threads safely
   |
   = help: the trait `std::marker::Sync` is not implemented for `std::rc::Rc<std::vec::Vec<i32>>`
   = note: required because of the requirements on the impl of `std::marker::Send` for `&std::rc::Rc<std::vec::Vec<i32>>`
   = note: required because it appears within the type `[closure@thread_rc.rs:10:23: 12:10 ns:&std::rc::Rc<std::vec::Vec<i32>>, n:&usize]`
   = note: required by `std::thread::spawn`

error: aborting due to previous error
```

Rust saves us here too. This is because an Rc type is not thread-safe as mentioned previously, as the reference count update operation is not atomic. We can only use Rc in single-threaded code. If we want to have the same kind of shared ownership across multi-threaded contexts, we can use the Arc type, which is just like Rc, but has atomic reference counting capability.

Shared ownership with Arc

The preceding code can be made to work with the multi-threaded `Arc` type as follows:

```
// thread_arc.rs

use std::thread;
use std::sync::Arc;

fn main() {
    let nums = Arc::new(vec![0, 1, 2, 3, 4]);
    let mut childs = vec![];
    for n in 0..5 {
        let ns = Arc::clone(&nums);
        let c = thread::spawn(move || {
            println!("{}", ns[n]);
        });

        childs.push(c);
    }

    for c in childs {
        c.join().unwrap();
    }
}
```

In the preceding code, we simply replaced the wrapper of the vector from `Rc` to the `Arc` type. Another change is that, before we reference `nums` from a child thread, we need to clone it with `Arc::clone()`, which gives us an owned `Arc<Vec<i32>>` value that refers to the same `Vec`. With that change, our program compiles and provides safe access to the shared `Vec`, with the following output:

```
$ rustc thread_arc.rs
$ ./thread_arc
0
2
1
3
4
```

Now, another use case in multi-threaded code is to mutate a shared value from multiple threads. Let's see how to do that next.

Mutating shared data from threads

We'll take a look at a sample program where five threads push data to a shared Vec. The following program tries to do the same:

```
// thread_mut.rs

use std::thread;
use std::sync::Arc;

fn main() {
    let mut nums = Arc::new(vec![]);
    for n in 0..5 {
        let mut ns = nums.clone();
        thread::spawn(move || {
            nums.push(n);
        });
    }
}
```

We have the same nums wrapped with Arc. But we cannot mutate it, as the compiler gives the following error:

```
→  Chapter08 git:(master) ✗ rustc thread_mut.rs
error[E0596]: cannot borrow immutable borrowed content as mutable
  --> thread_mut.rs:11:13
   |
11 |             ns.push(n);
   |             ^^ cannot borrow as mutable

warning: variable does not need to be mutable
  --> thread_mut.rs:7:9
   |
7  |     let mut nums = Arc::new(vec![]);
   |         ----^^^^
   |         |
   |         help: remove this `mut`
   |
   = note: #[warn(unused_mut)] on by default

error: aborting due to previous error

For more information about this error, try `rustc --explain E0596`.
```

This doesn't work as cloning `Arc` hands out immutable reference to the inner value. To mutate data from multiple threads, we need to use a type that provides shared mutability just like `RefCell`. But similar to `Rc`, `RefCell` cannot be used across multiple threads. Instead, we need to use their thread-safe variants such as the `Mutex` or `RwLock` wrapper types. Let's explore them next.

Mutex

When safe mutable access to a shared resource is required, the access can be provided by the use of mutex. Mutex is a portmanteau for mutual exclusion, a widely used synchronization primitive for ensuring that a piece of code is executed by only one thread at a time. A `mutex` in general is a guard object which a thread acquires to protect data that is meant to be shared or modified by multiple threads. It works by prohibiting access to a value from more than one thread at a time by locking the value. If one of the threads has a lock on the `mutex` type, no other thread can run the same code until the thread that holds the lock is done with it.

The `std::sync` module from the standard library contains the `Mutex` type allowing one to mutate data from threads in thread-safe manner.

The following code example shows how to use the `Mutex` type from a single child thread:

```
// mutex_basics.rs

use std::sync::Mutex;
use std::thread;

fn main() {
    let m = Mutex::new(0);
    let c = thread::spawn(move || {
        {
            *m.lock().unwrap() += 1;
        }
        let updated = *m.lock().unwrap();
        updated
    });
    let updated = c.join().unwrap();
    println!("{:?}", updated);
}
```

Running this works as expected. But, this won't work when multiple threads try to access the value as `Mutex` doesn't provide shared mutability. To allow a value inside a `Mutex` to be mutated from multiple threads, we need to compose it it the `Arc` type. Let's see how to do that next.

Shared mutability with Arc and Mutex

Having explored the basics of Mutex in single threaded contexts, we'll revisit the example from the previous section. The following code modifies a value using a `Mutex` wrapped in an `Arc` from the multiple threads:

```
// arc_mutex.rs

use std::sync::{Arc, Mutex};
use std::thread;

fn main() {
    let vec = Arc::new(Mutex::new(vec![]));
    let mut childs = vec![];
    for i in 0..5 {
        let mut v = vec.clone();
        let t = thread::spawn(move || {
            let mut v = v.lock().unwrap();
            v.push(i);
        });
        childs.push(t);
    }

    for c in childs {
        c.join().unwrap();
    }

    println!("{:?}", vec);
}
```

In the preceding code, we created a `Mutex` value in m. We then spawn a thread. The output on your machine may vary.

Calling `lock` on a mutex will block other threads from calling `lock` until the lock is gone. As such, it is important that we structure our code in such a way that the is granular. Compiling and running this gives the following output:

```
$ rustc arc_mutex.rs
$ ./arc_mutex
Mutex { data: [0,1,2,3,4] }
```

There is another similar alternative to `Mutex`, which is the `RwLock` type that is more aware on the kind of lock you have on your type, and can be more performant when reads are more often than writes. Let's explore it next.

RwLock

While Mutex is fine for most use cases, for some multi-threaded scenarios, reads happen more often than writes from multiple threads. In that case, we can use the RwLock type, which also provides shared mutability but can do so at a more granular level. RwLock stands for Reader-Writer lock. With `RwLock`, we can have many readers at the same but only one writer in a given scope. This is much better than a Mutex which agnostic of the kind of access a thread wants. Using RwLock

RwLock exposes two methods:

- `read`: Gives read access to the thread. There can be many read invocations.
- `write`: Gives exclusive access to thread for writing data to the wrapped type. There can be one write access from an `RwLock` instance to a thread.

Here's a sample program that demonstrates using the `RwLock` instead of `Mutex`:

```
// thread_rwlock.rs

use std::sync::RwLock;
use std::thread;

fn main() {
    let m = RwLock::new(5);
    let c = thread::spawn(move || {
        {
            *m.write().unwrap() += 1;
        }
        let updated = *m.read().unwrap();
        updated
    });
    let updated = c.join().unwrap();
```

```
    println!("{:?}", updated);
}
```

But `RwLock` on some systems such as Linux, suffers from the writer starvation problem. It's a situation when readers continually access the shared resource, and writer threads never get the chance to access the shared resource.

Communicating through message passing

Threads can also communicate with each other through a more high level abstraction called message passing. This model of thread communication removes the need to use explicit locks by the user.

The standard library's `std::sync::mpsc` module provides a lock-free multi-producer, single-subscriber queue, which serves as a shared message queue for threads wanting to communicate with one another. The `mpsc` module standard library has two kinds of channels:

- `channel`: This is an asynchronous, infinite buffer channel.
- `sync_channel`: This is a synchronous, bounded buffer channel.

Channels can be used to send data from one thread to another. Let's look at asynchronous channels first.

Asynchronous channels

Here is an example of a simple producer-consumer system, where the main thread produces the values `0`, `1`, `...`, `9` and the spawned thread prints them:

```
// async_channels.rs

use std::thread;
use std::sync::mpsc::channel;

fn main() {
    let (tx, rx) = channel();
    let join_handle = thread::spawn(move || {
        while let Ok(n) = rx.recv() {
            println!("Received {}", n);
        }
    });

    for i in 0..10 {
```

```
        tx.send(i).unwrap();
    }

    join_handle.join().unwrap();
}
```

We first call the `channel` method. This returns two values, `tx` and `rx`. `tx` is the transmitter end, having type `Sender<T>` and `rx` is the receiver end having type `Receiver<T>`. Their names are just a convention and you can name them anything. Most often, you will see code bases use these names as they are concise to write.

Next, we spawn a thread that will receive values from the `rx` side:

```
let join_handle = thread::spawn(move || {
    // Keep receiving in a loop, until tx is dropped!
    while let Ok(n) = rx.recv() { // Note: `recv()` always blocks
        println!("Received {}", n);
    }
});
```

We use a `while let` loop. This loop will receive `Err` when `tx` is dropped. The drop happens when `main` returns.

In the preceding code, first, to create the `mpsc` queue, we call the `channel` function, which returns to us `Sender<T>` and `Receiver<T>`.

`Sender<T>` is a `Clone` type, which means it can be handed off to many threads, allowing them to send messages into the shared queue.

The **multi producer, single consumer (mpsc)** approach provides multiple writers but only a single reader. Both of these functions return a pair of generic types: a sender and a receiver. The sender can be used to push new things into the channel, while receivers can be used to get things from the channel. The sender implements the `Clone` trait while the receiver does not.

With the default asynchronous channels, the `send` method never blocks. This is because the channel buffer is infinite, so there's always space for more. Of course, it's not really infinite, just conceptually so: your system may run out of memory if you send gigabytes to the channel without receiving anything.

Synchronous channels

Synchronous channels have a bounded buffer and, when it's full, the `send` method blocks until there's more space in the channel. The usage is otherwise quite similar to asynchronous channels:

```rust
// sync_channels.rs

use std::thread;
use std::sync::mpsc;

fn main() {
    let (tx, rx) = mpsc::sync_channel(1);
    let tx_clone = tx.clone();

    let _ = tx.send(0);

    thread::spawn(move || {
        let _ = tx.send(1);
    });

    thread::spawn(move || {
        let _ = tx_clone.send(2);
    });

    println!("Received {} via the channel", rx.recv().unwrap());
    println!("Received {} via the channel", rx.recv().unwrap());
    println!("Received {} via the channel", rx.recv().unwrap());
    println!("Received {:?} via the channel", rx.recv());
}
```

The synchronous channel size is 1, which means that we can't have more than one item in the channel. Any send call after the first send will block in such a case. However, in the preceding code, we don't get blocks (at least, the long ones) as the two sending threads work in the background and the main thread gets to receive it without being blocked on the send call. For both these channel types, the `recv` call returns an `Err` value if the channel is empty.

thread-safety in Rust

In the previous section, we saw how the compiler stops us from sharing the data. If a child thread accesses data mutably, it is moved because Rust won't allow it to be used in the parent thread as the child thread might deallocate it, leading to a dangling pointer dereference in the main thread. Let's explore the idea of thread-safety and how Rust's type systems achieves that.

What is thread-safety?

thread-safety is the property of a type or a piece of code that, when executed or accessed by multiple threads, does not lead to unexpected behavior. It refers to the idea that data is consistent for reads while being safe from corruption when multiple threads write to it.

Rust only protects you from data races. It doesn't aim to protect against deadlocks as they are difficult to detect. It instead offloads this to third-party crates such as the `parking_lot` crate.

Rust has a novel approach to protecting against data races. Most of the thread-safety bits are already embedded in the `spawn` method's type signature. Let's look at its type signature:

```
fn spawn<F, T>(f: F) -> JoinHandle<T>
    where F: FnOnce() -> T,
        F: Send + 'static,
        T: Send + 'static
```

That's a scary-looking type signature. Let's make it less scary by explaining what each of the parts mean.

`spawn` is a generic function over `F` and `T` and takes a parameter, `f`, and returns a generic type called `JoinHandle<T>`. Following that, the `where` clause specifies multiple trait bounds:

- `F: FnOnce() -> T`: This says that `F` implements a closure that can be called only once. In other words, `f` is a closure that takes everything by value and moves items referenced from the environment.

- `F: Send + 'static`: This means that the closure must be `Send` and must have the `'static` lifetime, implying that any type referenced from within the closure in its environment must also be Send and must live for the entire duration of the program.
- `T: Send + 'static`: The return type, `T`, from the closure must also implement the `Send + 'static` trait.

As we know, `Send` is a marker trait. It is just used as a type-level marker that implies that the value is safe to be sent across threads; most types are Send. Types that don't implement `Send` are pointers, references, and so on. In addition, `Send` is an auto trait or an automatically derived trait whenever applicable. Compound data types such as a struct implement `Send` if all of the fields in a struct are `Send`.

Traits for thread-safety

Thread-safety is the idea that, if you have data that you want to data from multiple threads, any read or write operation on that value does not lead to inconsistent results. The problem with updating a value, even with a simple increment operation such as `a += 1` is that it roughly translates in to a three-step process—`load increment store`. Data that can be safely updated is meant to be wrapped in thread-safe types such as `Arc` and `Mutex` to ensure that we have data consistency in a program.

In Rust, you get compile-time guarantees on types that can be safely used and referenced within a thread. These guarantees are implemented as traits, which are the `Send` and `Sync` trait.

Send

A Send type is safe to send to multiple threads. This implies that the type is a `move` type. Types that aren't Send are pointer types such as `&T`, unless `T` is `Sync`.

The `Send` trait has the following type signature in the standard library's `std::marker` module:

```
pub unsafe auto trait Send { }
```

There are three important things to notice in its definition: first, it's a marker trait without any body or item. Second, it's prefixed with the `auto` keyword as it is implemented implicitly for most types when appropriate. Thirdly, it's an unsafe trait because Rust wants to make the developer sure that they opt in explicitly and ensure that their type has thread-safe synchronization built in.

Sync

The `Sync` trait has a similar type signature:

```
pub unsafe auto trait Sync { }
```

This trait signifies that types that implement this trait are safe to be shared between threads. If something is `Sync` then a reference to it in other words, `&T` is `Send`. This means that we can pass references to it to many threads.

Concurrency using the actor model

Another model of concurrency that is quite similar to the message passing model is the actor model. The actor model became popular with Erlang, a functional programming language popular in the telecom industry, known for its robustness and distributed by default nature.

The actor model is a conceptual model that implements concurrency at the type level using entities called actors. It was first introduced by Carl Eddie Hewitt in 1973. It removes the need for locks and synchronization and provides a cleaner way to introduce concurrency in a system. The actor model consists of three things:

- **Actor:** This is a core primitive in the actor model. Each actor consists of its address, using which we can send messages to an actor's and mailbox, which is just a queue to store the messages it has received. The queue is generally a **First In, First Out (FIFO)** queue. The address of an actor is needed so that other actors can send messages to it. The supervisor actor can create child actors that can create other child actors.
- **Messages:** Actors communicate only via messages. They are processed asynchronously by actors. The `actix-web` framework provides a nice wrapper for synchronous operations in an asynchronous wrapper.

In Rust, we have the `actix` crate that implements the actor model. The `actix` crate, uses the tokio and futures crate which we'll cover in `Chapter 12`, *Network Programming in Rust*. The core objects to that crate is the Arbiter type which is simply a thread which spawns an event loop underneath and provides a handle to the event loop as an `Addr` type. Once created, we can use this handle to send messages to the actor.

In `actix`, creation of actor follows a simple step of creating a type, defining a message and implementing the handler for the message for the actor type. Once that is done, we can create the actor and spawn them into one of the created arbiters.

Each actor runs within an arbiter.

When we create an actor, they don't execute right away. It's when we put these actors into arbiter threads, they then start executing.

To keep the code example simple and to show how to setup actors and run them in actix, we'll create a actor that can add two numbers. Let's create a new project by running `cargo new actor_demo` with the following dependencies in `Cargo.toml`:

```
# actor_demo/Cargo.toml

[dependencies]
actix = "0.7.9"
futures = "0.1.25"
tokio = "0.1.15"
```

Our `main.rs` contains the following code:

```
// actor_demo/src/main.rs

use actix::prelude::*;
use tokio::timer::Delay;
use std::time::Duration;
use std::time::Instant;
use futures::future::Future;
use futures::future;

struct Add(u32, u32);

impl Message for Add {
    type Result = Result<u32, ()>;
}

struct Adder;

impl Actor for Adder {
```

```rust
        type Context = SyncContext<Self>;
}

impl Handler<Add> for Adder {
        type Result = Result<u32, ()>;

        fn handle(&mut self, msg: Add, _: &mut Self::Context) -> Self::Result {
            let sum = msg.0 + msg.0;
            println!("Computed: {} + {} = {}",msg.0, msg.1, sum);
            Ok(msg.0 + msg.1)
        }
}

fn main() {
        System::run(|| {
            let addr = SyncArbiter::start(3, || Adder);
            for n in 5..10 {
                addr.do_send(Add(n, n+1));
            }

            tokio::spawn(futures::lazy(|| {
                Delay::new(Instant::now() + Duration::from_secs(1)).then(|_| {
                    System::current().stop();
                    future::ok::<(),()>(())
                })
            }));
        });
}
```

In the preceding code, we have created an actor named Adder. This actor can send and receive messages of type Add. This is a tuple struct that encapsulates two numbers to be added. To allow Adder to receive and process Add messages, we implement the Handler trait for Adder parameterized over the Add message type. In the Handler implementation, we print the computation being performed and return the sum of the given numbers.

Following that, in main, we first create a System actor by calling its run method which takes in a closure. Within the closure, we start a SyncArbiter with 3 threads by calling its start method. This create 3 actors ready to receive messages. It returns a Addr type which is a handle to the event loop to which we can send messages to the Adder actor instance. We then send 5 messages to our arbiter address addr. As the System::run is an parent event loop that runs forever, we spawn a future to stop the System actor after a delay of 1 second. We can ignore the details of this part of the code as it is simply to shutdown the System actor in an asynchronous way.

With that said, let's take this program for a spin:

```
$ cargo run
Running `target/debug/actor_demo`
Computed: 5 + 6 = 10
Computed: 6 + 7 = 12
Computed: 7 + 8 = 14
Computed: 8 + 9 = 16
Computed: 9 + 10 = 18
```

Similar to the `actix` crate, there are other crates in the Rust ecosystem that implements various concurrency models suitable for different use cases.

Other crates

Apart from `actix`, we have a crate named `rayon` which is a work stealing based data parallelism library that makes it dead simple to write concurrent code.

Another notable crate to mention is the `crossbeam` crate which allows one to write multi-threaded code that can access data from its parent stack frame and are guaranteed to terminate before the parent stack frame goes away.

`parking_lot` is another crate that provides a faster alternative to concurrency primitives present in the standard library. If you have a use case where the standard library `Mutex` or `RwLock` is not performant enough, then you can use this crate to gain significant speedups.

Summary

It is quite astonishing that the same ownership principle that prevents memory safety violations in single-threaded contexts also works for multithreaded contexts in composition with marker traits. Rust has easy and safe ergonomics for integrating concurrrency in your application with minimal runtime cost. In this chapter, we learned how to use the `threads` API provided by Rust's standard library and got to know how copy and move types work in the context of concurrency. We covered channels, the atomic reference counting type, `Arc`, and how to use `Arc` with `Mutex` and also explored the actor model of concurrency.

In the next chapter, we'll dive into metaprogramming which is all about generating code from code.

Metaprogramming with Macros

9

Metaprogramming is a concept that changes the way you look at instructions and data in a program. It allows you to generate new code by treating instructions like any other piece of data. Many languages have support for metaprogramming, for example, Lisp's macros, C's `#define` construct, and Python's metaclasses. Rust is no different and provides many forms of metaprogramming, which we'll explore in this chapter.

In this chapter, we will look at the following topics:

- What is metaprogramming?
- Macros in Rust and their forms
- Declarative macros, macro variables, and types
- Repeating constructs
- Procedural macros
- Macro use case
- Available macro crates

What is metaprogramming?

"Lisp isn't a language, it's a building material."

– Alan Kay

Any program, regardless of the language used, contains two entities: data and instructions that manipulate the data. The usual flow of a program is mostly concerned with manipulating data. The issue with instructions, though, is that once you write them, it's like they've been carved into stone, and so they are non-malleable. It would be more enabling if we could treat instructions as data and generate new instructions using code. Metaprogramming provides exactly that!

It's a programming technique where you can write code that has the ability to generate new code. Depending on the language, it can be approached in two ways: at runtime or at compile time. Runtime metaprogramming is available in dynamic languages such as Python, Javascript, and Lisp. For compiled languages, it's not possible to generate instructions at runtime because these languages perform the ahead of time compilation of programs. However, you have the option of generating code at compile time, which is what C macros provide. Rust also provides compile time code generation capabilities, and these are more capable and sound than C macros.

In many languages, metaprogramming constructs are often denoted by the umbrella term **macros**, which for some languages are a built-in feature. For others, they are provided as a separate compilation phase. In general, a macro takes an arbitrary sequence of code as input and outputs valid code that can be compiled or executed by the language, along with other code. The input to the macro doesn't need to be a valid syntax and you are free to define your own custom syntax for the macro input. Also, how you invoke a macro and the syntax for defining them is different across languages. For instance, C macros works at the preprocessor stage, which reads tags starting with #define and expands them before forwarding the source file to the compiler. Here, expanding means generating code by substituting inputs that are provided to the macro. Lisp, on the other hand, provides function-like macros that are defined with defmacro (a macro itself), which takes the name of the macro being created and one or more parameters, and returns new Lisp code. However, C and Lisp macros lack a property that's referred to as hygiene. They are non-hygienic in the sense that they can capture and interfere with code outside the macro upon expansion, which can lead to unexpected behavior and logical errors when the macro is invoked at certain places in the code.

To demonstrate the problem with a lack of hygiene, we'll take the example of a C macro. These macros simply copy/paste code with simple variable substitutions and are not context aware. Macros written in C are not hygienic in the sense that they can refer to variables defined anywhere, as long as those variables are in scope at the macro invocation site. For instance, the following is a macro SWITCH defined in C that can swap two values, but ignorantly modifies other values in doing so:

```c
// c_macros.c

#include <stdio.h>

#define SWITCH(a, b) { temp = b; b = a; a = temp; }

int main() {
    int x=1;
    int y=2;
    int temp = 3;
```

```
        SWITCH(x, y);
        printf("x is now %d. y is now %d. temp is now %d\n", x, y, temp);
}
```

Compiling this with `gcc c_macros.c -o macro && ./macro` gives the following output:

```
x is now 2. y is now 1. temp is now 2
```

In the preceding code, unless we declare our own `temp` variable inside the `SWITCH` macro, the original `temp` variable in `main` is modified by the expansion of the `SWITCH` macro. This unhygienic nature makes C macros unsound and brittle, and can easily make a mess unless special precautions are taken, such as using a different name for the `temp` variable within the macro.

Rust macros on the other hand are hygienic and also more context aware than just performing simple string substitution and expansion. They are aware of the scope of the variables that have been referenced within the macro and do not shadow any identifiers that have already been declared outside. Consider the following Rust program, which tries to implement the macro we used previously:

```
// c_macros_rust.rs

macro_rules! switch {
    ($a:expr, $b:expr) => {
        temp = $b; $b = $a; $a = temp;
    };
}

fn main() {
    let x = 1;
    let y = 2;
    let temp = 3;
    switch!(x, y);
}
```

In the preceding code, we created a macro called `switch!` and later invoked that in `main` with two values, x and y. We'll skip explaining the details in the macro definition, as we will cover them in detail later in this chapter.

However, to our surprise, this doesn't compile and fails with the following error:

```
→  Chapter09 git:(master) ✗ rustc c_macros.rs
error[E0425]: cannot find value `temp` in this scope
  --> c_macros.rs:5:9

5  |          temp = $b; $b = $a; $a = temp;
   |          ^^^^ not found in this scope
...
13 |          switch!(x, y);
   |          ------------- in this macro invocation
```

From the error message, our `switch!` macro doesn't know anything about the `temp` variable that's declared in `main`. As we can see, Rust macros don't capture variables from their environment as they work differently compared to C macros. Even if it would have, we will be saved from modification as `temp` is declared immutable in the preceding program. Neat!

Before we get into writing more macros like these in Rust, it's important to have an idea of when to use a macro-based solution for your problem and when not to!

When to use and not use Rust macros

One of the advantages of using macros is that they don't evaluate their arguments eagerly like functions do, which is one of the motivations to use macros other than functions.

 By eager evaluation, we mean that a function call like `foo(bar(2))` will first evaluate `bar(2)` and then pass its value to `foo`. Contrary to that, this is a lazy evaluation, which is what you see in iterators.

A general *rule of thumb* is that macros can be used in situations where functions fail to provide the desired solution, where you have code that is quite repetitive, or in cases where you need to inspect the structure of your types and generate code at compile time. Taking examples from real use cases, Rust macros are used in a lot of cases, such as the following:

- Augmenting the language syntax by creating custom **Domain-Specific Languages (DSLs)**
- Writing compile time serialization code, like serde does
- Moving computation to compile-time, thereby reducing runtime overhead
- Writing boilerplate test code and automating test cases
- Providing zero cost logging abstractions such as the log crate

At the same time, macros should be used sparingly as they make the code difficult to maintain and reason about, as they work at the meta level and not many developers will be comfortable using them. They make the code harder to read and from a maintainability perspective, readability should always be preferred. Also, heavy use of macros can result in performance penalties due to a lot of duplicate code generation, which affects the CPU instruction cache.

Macros in Rust and their types

Rust macros do their magic of code generation before the program compiles to a binary object file. They take input, known as **token trees**, and are expanded at the end of the second pass of parsing during **Abstract Syntax Tree (AST)** construction. These are pieces of jargon from the compiler world and need some explanation, so let's do that. To understand how macros work, we need to be familiar with how source code is processed by the compiler to understand a program. This will help us in understanding how a macro processes its input and the error messages they emit when we use them incorrectly. We'll only cover parts that are relevant to our understanding of macros.

First, the compiler reads the source code byte by byte and groups characters into meaningful chunks, which are called **tokens**. This is done by a component of the compiler that's generally referred to as the **tokenizer**. Therefore, an `a + 3 * 6` expression gets converted to `"a"`, `"+"`, `"3"`, `"*"`, `"6"`, which is a sequence of tokens. Other tokens can be the `fn` keyword, any identifier, braces `{}` `()`, an assignment operator `=`, and so on. These tokens are called **token trees** in macro parlance. There are also tokens trees such as `"("`, `")"`, `"}"`, `"{"`, which can group other tokens. Now, at this stage, the token sequences by themselves don't convey any meaning on how to process and interpret the program. For that, we need a **parser**.

A parser converts this flat stream of tokens into a hierarchical structure that guides the compiler on how to interpret the program. The token trees are passed on to the parser, which constructs an in-memory representation of the program called the Abstract Syntax Tree. For instance, our sequence of tokens, `a + 3 * 6`, which is an expression, can be evaluated with the value `20` when `a` is `2`.

However, the compiler doesn't know how to evaluate this expression correctly unless we separate the precedence of operators (that is, * comes before +) and represent them with a tree structure, as shown in the following diagram:

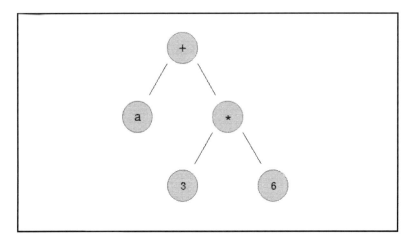

When we have represented the expression as a tree structure in code so that multiplication happens before addition, we can do a post order traversal of this tree to correctly evaluate the expression. So, given that explanation, where does our macro expansion fit here? Rust macros are parsed at the end of the second phase of Abstract Syntax Tree construction, which is a phase where name resolution happens. Name resolution is the stage where variables that are defined in the expression are looked up for their existence in the scope. In the preceding expression, name resolution will happen for the a variable. Now, if the a variable in our preceding expression was assigned a value from a macro invocation such as let a = foo!(2 + 0);, then the parser goes on to expand the macro before proceeding to the name resolution. The name resolution phase catches errors in the program, such as using a variable that is not in scope. However, there are more complex cases than this.

This entails Rust macros being context aware and, depending on what your macro expands into, they can only appear in supported places, as defined in the language's grammar. For example, you cannot write a let statement at the item level, that is, within a module.

 Grammar defines valid ways to write programs, just like grammar in a spoken language guides construction of meaningful sentences. For those who are curious, Rust's grammar is defined at https://doc.rust-lang. org/grammar.html.

One instance of macros that we've seen several times already is the `println!` macro. It is implemented as a macro because it allows Rust to check at compile time that its arguments are valid and that the string interpolation variables that have been passed to it are correct in number. Another advantage of using a macro for printing strings is that it allows us to pass as many arguments to `println!` as possible, which would not have been possible if it were implemented as a regular function. This is because Rust does not support variadic arguments for functions. Consider the following example:

```
println("The result of 1 + 1 is {}", 1 + 1);
println!("The result of 1 + 1 is {}");
```

As you already know, the second form will fail at compile time because it's missing an argument that matches the format string. This is reported at compile time. In this way, it is far safer than C's `printf` function, which can lead to memory vulnerabilities such as the format string attack. Other feature of the `println!` macro is that we can customize how we want to print values within strings:

```
// print_formatting.rs

use std::collections::HashMap;

fn main() {
    let a = 3669732608;
    println!("{:p}", &a);
    println!("{:x}", a);

    // pretty printing
    let mut map = HashMap::new();
    map.insert("foo", "bar");
    println!("{:#?}", map);
}
```

In the preceding code, we can print the memory address and hexadecimal representation of the value stored in a via `"{:p}"` and `"{:x}"`, respectively. These are called **format specifiers**. We can also print non-primitive types in more of a JSON-like format with the `"{:#?}"` format specifier within `println!`. Let's compile and run our preceding program:

```
error[E0277]: the trait bound `{integer}: std::fmt::Pointer` is not
satisfied
  --> print_formatting.rs:7:22
   |
7  |     println!("{:p}", a);
   |                      ^ the trait `std::fmt::Pointer` is not implemented
for `{integer}`
```

Ok, we have an error. As you may have noticed, in the first `println!` macro call, we are trying to print the address of `a` using the `"{:p}"` specifier, but the variable we mentioned is a number. We need to pass a reference such as `&a` to the format specifier. With that change, the preceding program compiles. All of this formatting and checking for proper values for string interpolation happens at compile time, thanks to the implementation of macros as part of the parsing phase.

Types of macros

There are different forms of macros in Rust. Some allow you to call them like functions, while others allow you to conditionally include code, depending on compile-time conditions. Another class of macros allows you to implement traits on methods at compile time. They can be broadly divided into two forms:

- **Declarative macros:** These are the simplest form of macros. These are created using `macro_rules!`, which itself is a macro. They provide the same ergonomics of a calling a function, but are easily distinguished by a `!` at the end. They are the go-to approach for writing quick small macros within a project. The syntax for defining them is very similar to how you would write match expressions. They are called **declarative** in the sense that you already have a mini DSL, along with recognized token types and repetition constructs, using which you can declaratively express what code you want to generate. You don't write how you generate the code as that is taken care of by the DSL.
- **Procedural macros:** Procedural macros are a more advanced form of macros and give complete control over the manipulation and generation of code. These macros don't come with any DSL support and are procedural in the sense that you have to write how you want the code to be generated or transformed for a given token tree input. The downside is that they are complex to implement and require a bit of understanding of compiler internals and how a program is represented in memory within the compiler. While `macro_rules!` can be defined anywhere in your project, procedural macros as of now are required to be created as separate crates with the special attribute of `proc-macro = true` in `Cargo.toml`.

Creating your first macro with macro_rules!

Let's start with declarative macros first by building one using the `macro_rules!` macro. Rust already has the `println!` macro, which is used to print things to the standard output. However, it doesn't have an equivalent macro for reading input from the standard input. To read from the standard input, you have to write something like the following:

```
let mut input = String::new();
io::stdin().read_line(&mut input).unwrap();
```

These lines of code can be easily abstracted away with a macro. We'll name our macro `scanline!`. Here's the code that shows us how we want to use this macro:

```
// first_macro.rs
fn main() {
    let mut input = String::new();
    scanline!(input);
    println!("{:?}", input);
}
```

We want to be able to create a `String` instance and just pass it to `scanline!`, which handles all the details of reading from standard input. If we compile the preceding code by running `rustc first_macro.rs`, we get the following error:

```
error: cannot find macro `scanline!` in this scope
 --> first_macro.rs:5:5
  |
5 |     scanline!(input);
  |     ^^^^^^^^

error: aborting due to previous error
```

`rustc` cannot find the `scanline!` macro, because we haven't defined it yet, so let's do that:

```
// first_macro.rs

use std::io::stdin;
// A convenient macro to read input as string into a buffer
macro_rules! scanline {
    ($x:expr) => ({
        stdin().read_line(&mut $x).unwrap();
        $x.trim();
    });
}
```

To create the `scanline!` macro, we use the `macro_rules!` macro, followed by the macro name `scanline!`, followed by a pair of braces. Within the braces, we have things that look similar to match arms. These are called **matching rules**. Every matching rule consists of three parts. The first is the pattern matcher, that is, the `($x:expr)` part, followed by a `=>`, and then the code generation block, which can be delimited either with `()`, `{}`, or even `[]`. A matching rule has to end with a semicolon when there is more than one rule to match.

In the preceding code, the notation on the left, `($x:expr)`, within parentheses is the rules, where `$x` is a token tree variable that needs to have a type specified after the colon `:`, which is an `expr` token tree type. Their syntax is similar to how we specify parameters in functions. When we invoke the `scanline!` macro with any token sequence as input, it gets captured in `$x` and is referred to by the same variable within the code generation block on the right. The `expr` token type means that this macro can only accept things that are expressions. We'll cover other kinds of token types that are accepted by `macro_rules!` in a moment. In the code generation block, we have multi-line code to generate, so we have a pair of braces, which are there to account for multi-line expressions. The matching rule ends with a semicolon. We can also omit braces if we have a single line of code that needs to be generated. The generated code we want is as follows:

```
io::stdin().read_line(&mut $x).unwrap();
```

Notice that `read_line` accepts something that doesn't look like a proper mutable reference to some identifier, that is, it's a `&mut $x`. The `$x` gets substituted with an actual expression that we pass to our macro on invocation. That's it; we just wrote our first macro! The complete code is as follows:

```
// first_macro.rs
use std::io;
// A convenient macro to read input as string into a buffer
macro_rules! scanline {
    ($x:expr) => ({
        io::stdin().read_line(&mut $x).unwrap();
    });
}

fn main() {
    let mut input = String::new();
    scanline!(input);
    println!("I read: {:?}", input);
}
```

In `main`, we first create our `input` string, which will store our input from the user. Next, our `scanline!` macro is invoked where we pass the `input` variable. Within this macro, this is then referred to as `$x`, as we saw in the preceding definition. With the invocation of `scanline`, when the compiler sees the invocation, it replaces that with the following:

```
io::stdin().read_line(&mut input).unwrap();
```

Here's the output on running the preceding code with an input string of `Alice` from the standard input:

```
$ Alice
I read: "Alice\n"
```

Following code generation, the compiler also checks whether the generated code makes any sense. For example, if we were to invoke `scanline!` with some other item that is not accounted for in the matching rules (say, passing an `fn` keyword, such as `scanline!(fn)`), we would get the following error:

```
→  Chapter09 git:(master) ✗ rustc first_macro.rs
error: no rules expected the token `fn`
  --> first_macro.rs:14:15
   |
14 |        scanline!(fn);
   |                  ^^

error: aborting due to previous error
```

Also, even if we pass an expression (say, `2`), which is valid to pass (as it's also an `expr`) to this macro but doesn't make sense in this context, Rust will catch this and report as follows:

```
→  Chapter09 git:(master) ✗ rustc first_macro.rs
error[E0308]: mismatched types
  --> first_macro.rs:8:31
   |
8  |           io::stdin().read_line(&mut $x).unwrap();
   |                                 ^^^^^^^^ expected struct `std::string::String`, found integral variable
...
14 |       scanline!(3);
   |       ------------- in this macro invocation
   |
   = note: expected type `&mut std::string::String`
              found type `&mut {integer}`

error: aborting due to previous error

For more information about this error, try `rustc --explain E0308`.
```

This is neat! Now, we can also add multiple matching rules to our macro. So, let's add an empty rule that covers the case where we just want `scanline!` to allocate the `String` for us, read from `stdin`, and return the string back. To add a new rule, we modify the code like so:

```
// first_macro.rs

macro_rules! scanline {
    ($x:expr) => ({
        io::stdin().read_line(&mut $x).unwrap();
    });
    () => ({
        let mut s = String::new();
        stdin().read_line(&mut s).unwrap();
        s
    });
}
```

We added an empty match rule, `() => {}`. Within the braces, we generate a bunch of code where we first create a `String` instance in s, call `read_line`, and pass `&mut` s. Finally, we return s to the caller. Now, we can call our `scanline!` without a pre-allocated `String` buffer:

```
// first_macro.rs

fn main() {
    let mut input = String::new();
    scanline!(input);
    println!("Hi {}",input);
    let a = scanline!();
    println!("Hi {}", a);
}
```

It's also important to note that we cannot invoke this macro anywhere outside functions. For instance, the `scanline!` invocation at the root of a module will fail, as it is invalid to write a `let` statement within a `mod {}` declaration.

Built-in macros in the standard library

Apart from `println!`, there are other useful macros in the standard library that are implemented using the `macro_rules!` macro. Knowing about them will help us appreciate the places and situations where using a macro is a cleaner solution, while not sacrificing readability.

Some of these macros are as follows:

- `dbg!`: This allows you to print the value of expressions with their values. This macro moves whatever is passed to it, so if you only want to give read access to their types, you need to pass a reference to this macro instead. It's quite handy as a tracing macro for expressions during runtime.
- `compile_error!`: This macro can be used to report an error from code at compile time. This is a handy macro to use when you are building your own macro and want to report any syntactic or semantic errors to the user.
- `concat!`: This macro can be used to concatenate any number of literals passed to it and returns the concatenated literals as a `&'static str`.
- `env!`: This inspects an environment variable at compile time. In a lot of languages, accessing values from the environment variable is mostly done at runtime. In Rust, by using this macro, you can resolve environment variables at compile time. Note that this method panics when it cannot find the variable that's defined, so a safe version of this is the `option_env!` macro.
- `eprint!` and `eprintln!`: This is similar to `println!`, but outputs messages to the standard error stream.
- `include_bytes!`: This macro can be used as a quick way to read files as an array of bytes, such as `&'static [u8; N]`. The file path given to it is resolved relative to the current file in which this macro is invoked.
- `stringify!`: This macro is useful if you want to get a literal translation of a type or a token as a string. We'll use this when we write our own procedural macro.

If you want to explore the full set of macros that are available in the standard library, they can be found at `https://doc.rust-lang.org/std/#macros`.

macro_rules! token types

Before we build more complex macros, it's important to become familiar with the valid inputs that `macro_rules!` can take. Since `macro_rules!` work at the syntactic level, it needs to provide users, a handle to these syntactic elements, and distinguish what can and cannot be included within a macro and how we can interact with them.

The following are some important token tree types that you can pass into a macro as input:

- `block`: This is a sequence of statements. We have already used `block` in the debugging example. It matches any sequence of statements, delimited by braces, such as what we were using before:

  ```
  { silly; things; }
  ```

This block includes the statements `silly` and `things`.

- `expr`: This matches any expression, for example:
  - `1`
  - `x + 1`
  - `if x == 4 { 1 } else { 2 }`
- `ident`: This matches an identifier. Identifiers are any unicode strings that are not keywords (such as `if` or `let`). As an exception, the underscore character alone is not an identifier in Rust. Examples of identifiers are as follows:
  - `x`
  - `long_identifier`
  - `SomeSortOfAStructType`
- `item`: This matches an item. Module-level things are idenitified as items. These include functions, use declarations, type definitions, and so on. Here are some examples:
  - `use std::io;`
  - `fn main() { println!("hello") }`
  - `const X: usize = 8;`

These do not have to be one-liners, of course. The `main` function could be a single item, even if it spanned several lines.

- `meta`: A `meta` item. The parameters inside attributes are called meta items, which are captured by `meta`. The attributes themselves look as follows:
  - `#![foo]`
  - `#[baz]`
  - `#[foo(bar)]`
  - `#[foo(bar="baz")]`

- Meta items are the things that are found inside brackets. So, for each of the preceding attributes, the corresponding meta items are as follows:

  - `foo`
  - `baz`
  - `foo(baz)`
  - `foo(bar="baz")`

- `pat`: This is a pattern. Match expressions have patterns on the left-hand side of each match, which `pat` captures. Here are some examples:

  - `1`
  - `"x"`
  - `t`
  - `*t`
  - `Some(t)`
  - `1 | 2 | 3`
  - `1 ... 3`
  - `_`

- `path`: It matches a qualified name. Paths are qualified names, that is, names with a namespace attached to them. They're quite similar to identifiers, except that they allow the double colon in their names because they signify paths. Here are some examples:

  - `foo`
  - `foo::bar`
  - `Foo`
  - `Foo::Bar::baz`

This is useful in cases where you need to capture the path of some type so that you can use it later in code generation, such as when aliasing complex types with paths.

- `stmt`: This is a statement. Statements are like expressions, except that more patterns are accepted by `stmt`. The following are some examples of this:

  - `let x = 1`
  - `1`
  - `foo`
  - `1+2`

In contrast to the first example, `let x = 1` wouldn't be accepted by `expr`.

- `tt`: This is a token tree, which is a sequence of other tokens. The `tt` keyword captures a single token tree. A token tree is either a single token (such as `1`, `+`, or `"foo bar"`) or several tokens surrounded by any of the braces, `()`, `[]`, or `{}`. The following are some examples:

  - `foo`

  - `{ bar; if x == 2 { 3 } else { 4 }; baz }`

  - `{ bar; fi x == 2 ( 3 ] ulse ) 4 {; baz }`

As you can see, the insides of the token tree do not have to make semantic sense; they just have to be a sequence of tokens. Specifically, what does not match this are two or more tokens not enclosed in braces (such as `1 + 2`). This is the most general sequence of code or tokens `macro_rules!` can capture.

- `ty`: This is a Rust type. The `ty` keyword captures things that look like types. Here are some examples:

  - `u32`

  - `u33`

  - `String`

No semantic checking that the type is actually a type is done in the macro expansion phase, so `"u33"` is accepted just as well as `"u32"`. However, once the code gets generated and goes to the semantic analysis phase, the type is checked, giving an error message of `error: expected type, found `u33``. This is used when you are generating code to create a function or implementing methods of a trait on a type.

- `vis`: This represents a visibility modifier. This captures visibility modifiers `pub`, `pub(crate)`, and so on. This is helpful when you are generating module-level code and need to capture privacy modifiers in code fragments that have been passed to the macro.
- `lifetime`: Identifies a lifetime such as `'a`, `'ctx`, `'foo`, and so on.
- `literal`: A literal that can be any token, like a string literal such as `"foo"` or an identifier such as `bar`.

Repetitions in macros

Apart from token tree types, we also need a way to repeatedly generate certain parts of our code. One of the practical examples from the standard library is the `vec![]` macro, which relies on repetition to give an illusion of variadic arguments, and allows you to create Vecs in any of the following manners:

```
vec![1, 2, 3];
vec![9, 8, 7, 6, 5, 4];
```

Let's see how `vec!` does this. Here's vec's `macro_rules!` definition from the standard library:

```
macro_rules! vec {
    ($elem:expr; $n:expr) => (
        $crate::vec::from_elem($elem, $n)
    );
    ($($x:expr),*) => (
        <[_]>::into_vec(box [$($x),*])
    );
    ($($x:expr,)*) => (vec![$($x),*])
}
```

By ignoring the details to the right of `=>` and focusing on the last two matching rules on the left-hand side, we can see something new in these rules:

```
($($x:expr),*)
($($x:expr,)*)
```

These are repeating rules. The repeating pattern rule follows:

- **pattern**: `$($var:type)*`. Notice the `$()*`. For the sake of referring to them, we'll call them **repeaters**. Also, let's denote the inner `($x:expr)` as X. Repeaters come in three forms:
    - `*`, meaning the repetition needs to happen zero or more times
    - `+`, meaning the repetition needs to happen at least one or more times
    - `?`, meaning the token can repeat once at most

Repeaters can also include extra literal characters that can be part of the repetition. In the case of `vec!`, there is the comma character, which we need to support to distinguish each element in `Vec` in the macro invocation.

In the first matching rule, the comma character is after x. This allows for expressions such as `vec![1, 2, 3,]`.

The second matching rule has the comma inside x after the elements. This is a typical case and will match sequences such as 1, 2, 3. We needed two rules here because the first rule cannot account for cases such as where we don't have the trailing comma, which is the common case. Also, the patterns in `vec!` use *, which implies that `vec![]` is also an allowed invocation of the macro. With +, it wouldn't be.

Now, let's look at how the captured repetition rule is forwarded on the right-hand side in the code generation block. In the second matching rule, the `vec!` macro just forwards them into a `Box` type using an identical syntax:

```
($($x:expr),*) => (<[_]>::into_vec(box [$($x),*]));
```

The only difference we can see between the token tree variable declaration on the left-hand side and the usage on the right-hand side is that the right-hand side does not include the type (`expr`) of the token variable. The third matching rule just piggybacks on the second rule's code generation block and calls `vec![$($x),*]`, thus changing the comma placement and calling it again. This means that we can also call a macro within a macro, which is a really powerful feature. All of this can get pretty meta-level and you should aim for simpler maintainable macros as much as possible.

Now, let's take a look at how to build a macro that uses repetitions.

A more involved macro – writing a DSL for HashMap initialization

Armed with the knowledge of repetitions and token tree types, let's build something practical using repetitions in `macro_rules!`. In this section, we'll build a crate that exposes a macro that allows you to create HashMaps such as the following:

```
let my_map = map! {
    1 => 2,
    2 => 3
};
```

This is more concise and readable compared to manually calling `HashMap::new()`, followed by one or more `insert` calls. Let's create a new `cargo` project by running `cargo new macro_map --lib` with the initial block for `macro_rules!`:

```
// macro_map/lib.rs

#[macro_export]
macro_rules! map {
    // todo
}
```

Since we want the users to use our macros, we need to add a `#[macro_export]` attribute on this macro definition. Macros are private by default in a module, which is similar to other items. We'll call our macro `map!` and since we are building our own syntax to initialize HashMap, we'll go with the `k => v` syntax, where `k` is the key and `v` is the value in our HashMap. Here's our implementation within `map! {}`:

```
macro_rules! map {
    ( $( $k:expr => $v:expr ),* ) => {
        {
            let mut map = ::std::collections::HashMap::new();
            $(
                map.insert($k, $v);
            )*
            map
        }
    };
}
```

Let's understand the matching rule here. First, we'll examine the inner part, which is `( $k:expr => $v:expr )`. Let's denote this part of the rule as `Y`. So, `Y` captures our key `k` and value `v` literals as `expr` with a `=>` in between them. Surrounding `Y`, we have `($(Y),*)`, which denotes the repetition of `Y` zero or more times, delimited by a comma. On the right of the matching rule within braces, we first create a `HashMap` instance. Then, we write the repeaters `$()*`, which have our `map.insert($k, $v)` code fragment within them, which will be repeated the same number of times as in our macro input.

Let's quickly write a test for that:

```
// macro_map/lib.rs

#[cfg(test)]
mod tests {
    #[test]
    fn test_map_macro() {
        let a = map! {
            "1" => 1,
            "2" => 2
        };

        assert_eq!(a["1"], 1);
        assert_eq!(a["2"], 2);
    }
}
```

By running a cargo test, we get the following output:

```
running 1 test
test tests::test_map_macro ... ok
```

Nice! Our test passes and we can now initialize HashMaps in a convenient way using our shiny new `map!` macro!

Macro use case – writing tests

Macros are used quite a lot when writing test cases for unit tests. Let's say you were writing a HTTP client library and you would like to test your client on various HTTP verbs such as GET or POST and on a variety of different URLs. The usual way you would write your tests is to create functions for each type of request and the URL. However, there's a better way to do this. Using macros, you can cut down your testing time by many folds by building a small DSL to perform the tests, which is readable and can also be type checked at compiled time. To demonstrate this, let's create a new crate by running `cargo new http_tester --lib`, which contains our macro definition. This macro implements a small language that's designed for describing simple HTTP GET/POST tests to a URL. Here's a sample of what the language looks like:

```
http://duckduckgo.com GET => 200
http://httpbin.org/post POST => 200, "key" => "value"
```

The first line makes a GET request to duckduckgo.com, and expects a return code of 200 (Status Ok). The second one makes a POST request to httpbin.org, along with form parameters "key"="value" with a custom syntax. It also expects a return code of 200. This is very simplistic but sufficient for demonstration purposes.

We'll assume that we already have our library implemented and will use a HTTP request library called reqwest. We'll add a dependency on reqwest in our Cargo.toml file:

```
# http_tester/Cargo.toml

[dependencies]
reqwest = "0.9.5"
```

Here's lib.rs:

```
// http_tester/src/lib.rs

#[macro_export]
macro_rules! http_test {
    ($url:tt GET => $code:expr) => {
        let request = reqwest::get($url).unwrap();
        println!("Testing GET {} => {}", $url, $code);
        assert_eq!(request.status().as_u16(), $code);
    };
    ($url:tt POST => $code:expr, $($k:expr => $v:expr),*) => {
        let params = [$(($k, $v),)*];
        let client = reqwest::Client::new();
        let res = client.post($url)
            .form(&params)
            .send().unwrap();
        println!("Testing POST {} => {}", $url, $code);
        assert_eq!(res.status().as_u16(), $code);
    };
}

#[cfg(test)]
mod tests {
    #[test]
    fn test_http_verbs() {
        http_test!("http://duckduckgo.com" GET => 200);
        http_test!("http://httpbin.org/post" POST => 200, "hello" =>
"world", "foo" => "bar");
    }
}
```

Within the macro definition, we just match on the rules, which is where GET and POST are treated as literal tokens. Within the arms, we create our request client and assert on the status code that's returned by the input, which is provided to the macro. The POST test case also has a custom syntax for providing query parameters such as key => value, which is collected as an array in the params variable. This is then passed to the form method of the reqwest::post builder method. We'll explore the request library more when we get to Chapter 13, *Building Web Applications in Rust*.

Let's run cargo test and see the output:

```
running 1 test
test tests::test_http_verbs ... ok
```

Take a moment to think about what the benefit of using a macro here is. This could be implemented as a #[test] annotated function call as well, but the macro has a few benefits, even in this basic form. One benefit is that the HTTP verb is checked at compile time and our tests are now more declarative. If we try to invoke the macro with a test case that is not accounted for (say, HTTP DELETE), we'll get the following error:

```
error: no rules expected the token `DELETE`
```

Apart from using them for enumerating tests cases, macros are also used to generate Rust code based on some outside environmental state (such as database tables, time and date, and so on). They can be used to decorate structures with custom attributes, generating arbitrary code for them at compile time, or to create new linter plugins for making additional static analysis that the Rust compiler itself does not support. A great example is the clippy lint tool, which we've used already. Macros are also used to generate code that invokes native C libraries. We'll see how that happens when we get to Chapter 10, *Unsafe Rust and Foreign Function Interfaces*.

Exercises

If you are already finding macros empowering, here are some exercises for you to try so that you can tinker with macros some more:

1. Write a macro that accepts the following language:

```
language = HELLO recipient;
recipient = <String>;
```

For instance, the following strings would be acceptable in this language:

```
HELLO world!
HELLO Rustaceans!
```

Make the macro generate code that outputs a greeting that's directed to the recipient.

2. Write a macro that takes an arbitrary number of elements and outputs an unordered HTML list in a literal string, for instance, `html_list!([1, 2]) => <ul><li>1/<li><li>2</li></ul>`.

Procedural macros

Declarative macros can become tedious to read and maintain when your code generation logic becomes complex, as you need to write your logic with its own DSL to manipulate tokens. There are better, more flexible ways than using `macro_rules!`. For complex problems, you can leverage procedural macros as they are better suited to writing something non-trivial. They are suitable for cases where you need full control of code generation.

These macros are implemented as functions. These functions receive the macro input as a `TokenStream` type and return the generated code as a `TokenStream` after undergoing any transformation at compile time. To mark a function as a procedural macro, we need to annotate it with the `#[proc_macro]` attribute. At the time of writing this book, procedural macros come in three forms, which are categorized by how they are invoked:

*   **Function-like procedural macros:** These use `#[proc_macro]` attribute on functions. The `lazy_static!` macro from the `lazy_static` crate uses function-like macros.
*   **Attribute-like procedural macros:** These use `#[proc_macro_attribute]` attribute on functions. The `#[wasm-bindgen]` attribute in the `wasm-bindgen` crate uses this form of macro.
*   **Derive procedural macros:** These use `#[proc_macro_derive]`. These are the most frequently implemented macros in the majority of Rust crates, such as `serde`. They are also known as **derive macros** or **macros 1.1** due to the name of the RFC that introduced them.

At the time of writing this book, the procedural macro API is very limited on what can be done with a `TokenStream`, so we need to use third-party crates such as `syn` and `quote` to parse the input as a Rust code data structure, which can then be analyzed according to your needs for code generation. Also, procedural macros need to be created as a separate crate with the special crate attribute of `proc-macro = true`, which is specified in `Cargo.toml`. To use the macro, we can depend on the macro in the same way as other crates by specifying it under dependencies in `Cargo.toml` and importing the macro with `use` statements.

Among all three forms, derive macros are the most widely used form of procedural macros. We'll take a deep dive into them next.

Derive macros

We already saw that we can write `#[derive(Copy, Debug)]` on any struct, enum, or union type to get the `Copy` and `Debug` traits implemented for it, but this auto-derive feature is limited only to a few built-in traits in the compiler. With derive macros or macros 1.1, you get the ability to derive your own custom trait on any struct or enum or union type, thereby reducing the amount of boilerplate code that you would have written by hand. This may seem like a niche use case, but it is the most used procedural macro form, which high performance crates such as `serde` and `diesel` use. The derive macros only apply to data types such as structs, enums, or unions. Creating a custom derive macro for implementing a trait on a type requires the following steps:

1. First, you need your type and the trait that you want to implement on the type. These can come from any crate, either locally defined or from a third party, provided that one of them has to be defined by you, because of the orphan rule.
2. Next, we need to create a new crate with the `proc-macro` attribute set to `true` in `Cargo.toml`. This marks the crate as a procedural macro crate. This is done because procedural macros need to live in their own crate, as per the current implementation. This separation as a crate might change in the future, though.
3. Then, within this crate, we need to create a function that's annotated with the `proc_macro_derive` attribute. To the `proc_macro_derive` attribute, we pass in the trait name `Foo` as an argument. This function is what will get called when we write `#[derive(Foo)]` on any `struct`, `enum`, or `union`.

Only functions that have the `proc_macro_derive` attribute are allowed to be exported from this crate.

However, all of this is a bit vague until we see it in real code. So, let's build our own derive macro crate. The macro that we are going to build will be able to convert any given struct to a dynamic map of key values, such as `BTreeMap<String, String>`. The choice of `BtreeMaps` is just to have a sorted iteration on the fields, which is not the case with `HashMap`, though you can use hashmaps too.

We'll also make use of two crates, `syn` and `quote`, which will allow us to parse our code into a convenient data structure that we can examine and manipulate. We'll build three crates for this project. First, we'll create a binary crate by running `cargo new into_map_demo`, which uses our library crate and the derive macro crate. The following are the dependencies in our `Cargo.toml` file:

```
# into_map_demo/Cargo.toml

[dependencies]
into_map = { path = "into_map" }
into_map_derive = { path = "into_map_derive" }
```

The preceding `into_map` and `into_map_derive` crates are specified as local to this crate as path dependencies. However, we don't have them yet, so let's create them in the same directory by running the following commands:

- `cargo new into_map`: This crate will contain our trait as a separate library
- `cargo new into_map_derive`: This is our derive macro crate

Now, let's examine our `main.rs`, which contains the following initial code:

```
// into_map_demo/src/main.rs

use into_map_derive::IntoMap;

#[derive(IntoMap)]
struct User {
    name: String,
    id: usize,
    active: bool
}

fn main() {
    let my_bar = User { name: "Alice".to_string(), id: 35, active: false };
```

```
        let map = my_bar.into_map();
        println!("{:?}", map);
}
```

In the preceding code, we have our `User` struct annotated with
`#[derive(IntoMap)]`. `#[derive(IntoMap)]` will invoke our procedural macro from the
`into_map_derive` crate. This does not compile as we don't have the `IntoMap` derive
macro implemented yet. However, this shows us how we want to use the macro as a
consumer of this crate. Next, let's see what we have in our `into_map` crate's `lib.rs` file:

```
// into_map_demo/into_map/src/lib.rs

use std::collections::BTreeMap;

pub trait IntoMap {
    fn into_map(&self) -> BTreeMap<String, String>;
}
```

Our `lib.rs` file simply contains an `IntoMap` trait definition with a single method named
`into_map` that takes a reference to `self` and returns a `BTreeMap<String, String>`. We
want to derive the `IntoMap` trait for our `User` struct through our derive macro.

Let's examine our `into_map_derive` crate next. In this crate, we have the following
dependencies in `Cargo.toml`:

```
# into_map_demo/into_map_derive/src/Cargo.toml

[lib]
proc-macro = true

[dependencies]
syn = { version = "0.15.22", features = ["extra-traits"] }
quote = "0.6.10"
into_map = { path="../into_map" }
```

As we mentioned previously, we annotate the `[lib]` section with the `proc-macro`
attribute set to `true`. We also use `syn` and `quote` as they help us parse Rust code from the
`TokenStream` instance. The `syn` crate creates an in-memory data structure called the AST,
which represents a piece of Rust code. We can then use this structure to examine our source
code and extract information programmatically. The `quote` crate is a complement to the
`syn` crate in the sense that it allows you to generate Rust code within the provided `quote!`
macro, and also allows you to substitute values from `syn` data types. We also depend on
the `into_map` crate, from where we bring the `IntoMap` trait into scope within our macro
definition.

The code we want this macro to generate will look something like the following:

```
impl IntoMap for User {
    fn into_map(&self) -> BTreeMap<String, String> {
        let mut map = BTreeMap::new();
        map.insert("name".to_string(), self.name.to_string());
        map.insert("id".to_string(), self.id.to_string());
        map.insert("active".to_string(), self.active.to_string());
        map
    }
}
```

We want to implement the `into_map` method on our `User` struct, but we want it to be generated automatically for us. This is something that is quite tedious to hand code for cases where we have a struct with lots of fields. Derive macros are tremendously helpful in such cases. Let's look at an implementation.

At a high level, the code generation in the `into_map_derive` crate is divided into two phases. In the first phase, we iterate over the fields of the struct and collect code for inserting items into the `BTreeMap`. The generated `insert` code tokens will look something like this:

```
map.insert(field_name, field_value);
```

This will be collected into a vector. In the second phase, we take all of the generated `insert` code tokens and expand them into another token sequence, which is the `impl` block for the `User` struct.

Let's start by exploring the implementation in `lib.rs`:

```
// into_map_demo/into_map_derive/src/lib.rs

extern crate proc_macro;
use proc_macro::TokenStream;
use quote::quote;
use syn::{parse_macro_input, Data, DeriveInput, Fields};

#[proc_macro_derive(IntoMap)]
pub fn into_map_derive(input: TokenStream) -> TokenStream {
    let mut insert_tokens = vec![];
    let parsed_input: DeriveInput = parse_macro_input!(input);
    let struct_name = parsed_input.ident;
    match parsed_input.data {
        Data::Struct(s) => {
            if let Fields::Named(named_fields) = s.fields {
                let a = named_fields.named;
                for i in a {
```

```
                    let field = i.ident.unwrap();
                    let insert_token = quote! {
                        map.insert(
                            stringify!(#field).to_string(),
                            self.#field.to_string()
                        );
                    };
                    insert_tokens.push(insert_token);
                }
            }
        }
        other => panic!("IntoMap is not yet implemented for: {:?}", other),
    }
```

Whew, that's a lot of strange looking code! Let's go through this line by line. First, we have our `into_map_derive` function annotated with the `#[proc_macro_derive(IntoMap)]` attribute. We can give any name this function, though. This function receives a `TokenStream` as input, which will be our `User` struct declaration. We then create an `insert_tokens` list to store our input tokens, which is part of the actual code generation. We'll explain that in a moment.

We then call the `parse_macro_input!` macro from the `syn` crate, passing the `input` token stream. This gives us back a `DeriveInput` instance in the `parsed_input` variable. `parsed_input` represents our `User` struct definition as a token data structure. From that, we pull out the struct name with the `parsed_input.ident` field. Next, we match on the `parsed_input.data` field, which returns what kind of item it is: struct, enum, or union.

To keep our implementation simpler, we are only implementing the `IntoMap` trait for structs, so we match only when our `parsed_input.data` is a `Data::Struct(s)`. The inner `s` is, again, a struct that represents the items that constitute a struct definition. We are interested in what fields `s` has, particularly named fields, so we use an `if let` to specifically match for that. Inside the `if` block, we get a reference to all the fields of our struct and then iterate over them. For each field, we generate an insert code for our `btree` map using the `quote!` macro from the `quote` crate:

```
map.insert(
    stringify!(#field).to_string(),
    self.#field.to_string()
);
insert_tokens.push(insert_token);
```

Notice the #field symbol. Within the quote! macro, we can have template variables that will be substituted with their value in the generated code. In this case, #field gets replaced with whatever field is present in our struct. First, we convert #field to a string literal by using the stringify! macro, which is an Ident type from the syn crate. We then push this generated chunk of code into the insert_tokens vec.

Following that, we come to our final phase of code generation:

```
let tokens = quote! {
    use std::collections::BTreeMap;
    use into_map::IntoMap;

    impl IntoMap for #struct_name {
        /// Converts the given struct into a dynamic map
        fn into_map(&self) -> BTreeMap<String, String> {
            let mut map = BTreeMap::new();
            #(#insert_tokens)*
            map
        }
    }
};

proc_macro::TokenStream::from(tokens)
}
```

Here, we are finally generating our final impl block for our struct. Within the quote! block, whatever we write will be generated exactly as written, including the indentation and code comments. First, we do the imports of the BtreeMap type and the IntoMap trait. Then, we have the IntoMap implementation. Within that, we create our map, and just expand out the insert_tokens that we collected in the first phase of code generation. Here, the outer #()* repeater tells the quote! macro to repeat the same code zero or more times. For iterable items such as our insert_tokens, this will repeat all the items within it. This generates code for inserting the field name and field value from the struct into the map. Finally, we take the whole implementation code that's stored in the tokens variable and return this as a TokenStream by calling TokenStream::from(tokens). That's it! Let's try this macro in main.rs:

```
// into_map_demo/src/main.rs

use into_map_derive::IntoMap;

#[derive(IntoMap)]
struct User {
    name: String,
    id: usize,
```

```
        active: bool
    }

fn main() {
    let my_bar = User { name: "Alice".to_string(), id: 35, active: false };
    let map = my_bar.into_map();
    println!("{:?}", map);
}
```

Running `cargo run` gives us the following output:

```
{"active": "false", "id": "35", "name": "Alice"}
```

Great! It works. Next, let's look at how we can debug macros.

Debugging macros

When developing complex macros, most of the time you need ways to analyze how your code expands to the inputs you gave to the macro. You can always use `println!` or `panic!` at the places you want to see the generated code, but it's a very crude way to debug it. There's are better way, though. The Rust community provides us with a subcommand called `cargo-expand`. This subcommand was developed by David Tonlay at `https://github.com/dtolnay/cargo-expand`, who is also the author of the `syn` and `quote` crates. This command internally calls the nightly compiler flag `-Zunstable-options -- pretty=expanded`, but the design of the subcommand was done in such a way that it doesn't require you to manually switch to the nightly tool chain as it finds and switches to it automatically. To demonstrate this command, we'll take the example of our `IntoMap` derive macro and observe what code it generated for us. By switching into the directory and running `cargo expand`, we get the following output:

```
    Checking map_struct_demo v0.1.0
    Finished dev [unoptimized + debuginfo] target(s) in 0.14s
#![feature(prelude_import)]
#![no_std]
#[prelude_import]
use ::std::prelude::v1::*;
#[macro_use]
extern crate std;
// into_map_demo/src/main.rs

extern crate into_map;

#[macro_use]
extern crate into_map_derive;

struct User {
    name: String,
    id: usize,
    active: bool,
}
use std::collections::BTreeMap;
use into_map::IntoMap;
impl IntoMap for User {
    #[doc = r" Converts the given struct into a dynamic map"]
    fn into_map(&self) -> BTreeMap<String, String> {
        let mut map = BTreeMap::new();
        map.insert("name".to_string(), self.name.to_string());
        map.insert("id".to_string(), self.id.to_string());
        map.insert("active".to_string(), self.active.to_string());
        map
    }
}
```

As you can see, the `impl` block at the bottom is what was generated by the `IntoMap` derive macro. `cargo-expand` also includes pretty printed syntax highlighted output. This command is a must-have tool for someone writing complex macros.

Useful procedural macro crates

As procedural macros can be distributed as crates, a lot of emerging helpful macro crates are available, which can be found at `crates.io`. Using them can greatly reduce the boilerplate you need to write for generating Rust code. Some of them are as follows:

- `derive-new`: A derive macro provides a default all-fields constructor for structs and is quite customizable.
- `derive-more`: A derive macro that circumvents the limitation where we wrap a type for which we already have a lot of traits auto-implemented, but lose the ability to create our own type wrapping for it. This crate helps us provide the same set of traits, even on these wrapper types.
- `lazy_static`: This crate provides a function-like procedural macro called `lazy_static!`, where you can declare `static` values that require dynamically initialized types. For example, you can declare a configuration object as a `HashMap` and can access it globally across the code base.

Summary

In this chapter, we covered the metaprogramming abilities of Rust and looked at many kinds of macros. The most frequently used macro is `macro_rules!`, which is a declarative macro. Declarative macros work at the abstract syntax tree level, which means that they do not support arbitrary expansions, but require that the macro expansions are well-formed in the AST. For more complex use cases, you can use procedural macros where you get complete control of manipulating the input and generating the desired code. We also looked at ways to debug macros using the cargo subcommand `cargo-expand`.

Macros are indeed a powerful tool, but not something that should be used heavily. Only when the more usual mechanisms of abstraction such as functions, traits, and generics do not suffice for the problem at hand should we turn to macros. Also, macros make the code less readable for newcomers to a code base and should be avoided. Having said that, they are quite useful in writing test case conditions and are widely used by developers.

In the next chapter, we'll get a glimpse of another side of Rust, the unsafe bits, which are less recommended but unavoidable if you want to interoperate Rust with different languages.

10
Unsafe Rust and Foreign Function Interfaces

Rust is a language that has two modes: safe mode (the default) and unsafe mode. In safe mode, you get all sorts of safety features to protect you from serious mistakes, but there are times when you're required to shake off the safety harness provided by the compiler and get that extra level of control. One use case is interfacing with other languages, such as C, which can be very unsafe. In this chapter, you will get to know what sort of extra work is required when Rust has to interact with other languages and how unsafe mode is used to facilitate and make this interaction explicit.

In this chapter, we will cover the following topics:

- Understanding the safe and unsafe modes
- Operations that are unsafe in Rust
- Foreign function interface, talking to C, and vice versa
- Interfacing with Python using PyO3
- Interfacing with Node.js using Neon

What is safe and unsafe really?

"You are allowed to do this, but you had better know what you are doing."

- A Rustacean

When we talk about safety in programming languages, it is a property that spans different levels. A language can be memory-safe, type-safe, or it can be concurrent-safe. Memory safety means that a program doesn't write to a forbidden memory address and it doesn't access invalid memory. Type safety means that a program doesn't allow you to assign a number to a string variable and that this check happens at compile time, while concurrent-safe means that the program does not lead to race conditions when multiple threads are executing and modifying a shared state. If a language provides all of these levels of safety by itself, then it is said to be safe. To put it more generally, a program is deemed safe if, in all possible executions of the program and for all possible inputs, it gives correct outputs, does not lead to crashes, and does not clobber or corrupt its internal or external state. With Rust in safe mode, this is indeed true!

An unsafe program is one that violates an invariant at runtime or triggers an undefined behavior. These unsafe effects may be local to a function, or may have propagated later as a global state in the program. Some of them are inflicted by programmers themselves, such as logic errors, while some of them are due to the side effects of the compiler implementation that's used, and sometimes from the language specification itself. **Invariants** are conditions that must always be true during the execution of the program in all code paths. The simplest example would be that a pointer pointing to an object on the heap should never be null within a certain section of code. If that invariant breaks, code that is dependent on that pointer might dereference it and undergo a crash. Languages such as C/C++ and languages based on them are unsafe because quite a few operations are categorized as an undefined behavior in the compiler specification. An undefined behavior is an effect of hitting a situation in a program for which the compiler specification does not specify what happens at lower levels, and you are free to assume that anything can happen. One example of undefined behavior is using an uninitialized variable. Consider the following C code:

```c
// both_true_false.c

int main(void) {
    bool var;
    if (var) {
        fputs("var is true!\n");
    }
    if (!var) {
        fputs("var is false!\n");
    }
    return 0;
}
```

The output of this program is not the same with all C compiler implementations because using an uninitialized variable is an undefined operation. On some C compilers with some optimizations enabled, you may even get the following output:

```
var is true
var is false
```

Having your code take unpredictable code paths like this is something you don't want to see happen in production. Another example of undefined behavior in C is writing past the end of an array of size n. When the write happens to n + 1 offset in memory, the program may either crash or it may modify a random memory location. In the best case scenario, the program would crash immediately and you would get to know about this. In the worst case scenario, the program would continue running but may later corrupt other parts of the code and give faulty results. Undefined behaviors in C exist in the first place to allow compilers to optimize code for performance and go with the assumption that a certain corner case never happens and to not add error-checking code for these situations, just to avoid the overhead associated with error handling. It would be great if undefined behavior could be converted to compile time errors, but detecting some of these behaviors at compile time sometimes becomes resource intensive, and so not doing so keeps the compiler implementation simple.

Now, when Rust has to interact with these languages, it knows very little about how function calls and how types are represented at lower levels in these languages and because undefined behavior can occur at unexpected places, it sidesteps from all of these gotchas and instead provides us with a special unsafe {} block for interacting with things that come from other languages. In unsafe mode, you get some extra abilities to do things, which would be considered undefined behavior in C/C++. However, with great power comes great responsibility. A a developer who uses unsafe in their code has to be careful of the operations that are performed within the unsafe block. With Rust in unsafe mode, the onus is on you. Rust places trust in the programmer to keep operations safe. Fortunately, this unsafe feature is provided in a very controlled manner and is easily identifiable by reading the code, because unsafe code is always annotated with the unsafe keyword or unsafe {} blocks. This is unlike C, where most things are likely to be unsafe.

Now, it's important to mention that, while Rust offers to protect you from major unsafe situations in programs, there are also cases where Rust can't save you, even if the program you wrote is safe. These are the cases where you have logical errors such as the following:

- A program uses floating point numbers to represent currency. However, floating-point numbers are not precise and lead to rounding errors. This error is somewhat predictable (since, given the same input, it always manifests itself in the same way) and easy to fix. This is a logic and implementation error, and Rust offers no protection for such errors.

- A program to control a spacecraft uses primitive numbers as parameters in functions to calculate distance metrics. However, a library may be providing an API where the distances are interpreted in the metric system, and the user might provide numbers in the imperial system, leading to invalid measurements. A similar error occurred in 1999, in NASA's Mars Climate Orbiter spacecraft, and caused nearly $125 million worth of loss. Rust won't fully protect you from such mistakes, although, with the help of type system abstractions such as enums and the newtype pattern, we can isolate different units from each other and restrict the API's surface to only valid operations, making this error much less likely.

- A program writes to shared data from multiple threads without the appropriate locking mechanisms. The error manifests itself unpredictably, and finding it can be very difficult since it is non-deterministic. In this case, Rust fully protects you against data races with its ownership and borrowing rules, which are applicable to concurrent code too, but it cannot detect deadlocks for you.

- A program accesses an object through a pointer, which, in some situations, is a null pointer, causing the program to crash. In safe mode, Rust fully protects you against null pointers. However, when using unsafe mode, the programmer has to make sure that operations with a pointer from other languages are safe.

The unsafe feature of Rust is also needed for situations where the programmer knows better than the compiler and has to implement some of the tricky parts in their code, where the compile-time ownership rules become too restrictive and get in the way. For instance, let's say there's a case where you need to convert a sequence of bytes into a `String` value and you know that your `Vec<u8>` is a valid UTF-8 sequence. In this case, you can directly use the unsafe `String::from_utf_unchecked` method instead of the usual safe `String::from_utf8` method to bypass the extra overhead in checking for valid UTF-8 in the `from_utf8` method and can gain a bit of speedup. Also, when doing low-level embedded system development or any program that interfaces with the operating system kernel, you need to switch to unsafe mode. However, not everything requires unsafe mode and there are a few select operations that the Rust compiler sees as unsafe. They are as follows:

- Updating a mutable static variable
- Dereferencing raw pointers, such as `*const T` and `*mut T`
- Calling an unsafe function
- Reading values from a union type
- Invoking a declared function in `extern` blocks – items from other languages

Some of the memory-safety guarantees are relaxed in the aforementioned situations, but the borrow checker is still active in these operations and all the scoping and ownership rules still apply. The Rust reference about unsafety at `https://doc.rust-lang.org/stable/reference/unsafety.html` distinguishes between what is considered undefined and what is not unsafe. To easily distinguish this when you are performing the aforementioned operations, Rust requires you to use the `unsafe` keyword. It allows only a handful of places to be marked as `unsafe`, such as the following:

- Functions and methods
- Unsafe block expressions, such as `unsafe {}`
- Traits
- Implementation blocks

Unsafe functions and blocks

Let's look at unsafe functions and blocks, starting with unsafe functions:

```
// unsafe_function.rs

fn get_value(i: *const i32) -> i32 {
    *i
}

fn main() {
    let foo = &1024 as *const i32;
    let _bar = get_value(foo);
}
```

We defined a `get_value` function that takes in a pointer to an `i32` value, which simply returns the pointed value back by dereferencing it. In `main`, we are passing `foo` to `get_value`, which is a reference to an `i32` value that `1024` cast to `*const i32`. If we try running this, the compiler says the following:

```
error[E0133]: dereference of raw pointer is unsafe and requires unsafe function
  or block
  --> unsafe_function.rs:4:5
   |
4  |     *i
   |     ^^ dereference of raw pointer
   |
   = note: raw pointers may be NULL, dangling or unaligned; they can violate ali
asing rules and cause data races: all of these are undefined behavior
```

As we already said, we need an `unsafe` function or block to dereference a raw pointer. Let's go with the first suggestion and add `unsafe` before our function:

```
unsafe fn get_value(i: *const i32) -> i32 {
    *i
}
```

Now, let's try running this again:

```
error[E0133]: call to unsafe function is unsafe and requires unsafe function or
block
  --> unsafe_function.rs:9:15
   |
9  |         let bar = get_value(foo);
   |                   ^^^^^^^^^^^^^^ call to unsafe function
   |
   = note: consult the function's documentation for information on how to avoid
undefined behavior
```

Interesting! We got rid of the error on our get_value function, but now another error is shown at the call site in main. Calling an unsafe function requires us to wrap it within an unsafe block. That's because unsafe functions, apart from Rust's unsafe functions, can also be functions in other languages that are declared in extern blocks. These might or might not return values that the caller expects or a totally malformed value. As such, we need the unsafe block when calling unsafe functions. We modify our code to invoke get_value within an unsafe block like so:

```
fn main() {
    let foo = &1024 as *const i32;
    let bar = unsafe { get_value(foo) };
}
```

unsafe blocks are expressions, so we remove the semi-colon after get_value, and instead move it outside the unsafe block so that our return value from get_value gets assigned to bar. With that change, our program compiles.

Unsafe functions behave like regular functions, except that the aforementioned operations are allowed in it and that declaring your function as unsafe makes it non-callable from regular, safe functions. However, we could have written get_value the other way around:

```
fn get_value(i: *const i32) -> i32 {
    unsafe {
        *i
    }
}
```

This looks similar to before but contains a significant change. We moved the `unsafe` keyword from the function signature to an inner `unsafe` block. The function now does the same unsafe operation but wraps it inside a function that appears just like a regular `safe` function. Now, this function can be called without requiring unsafe blocks on the caller side. This technique is often used to provide interfaces from libraries that look safe, even though they are doing unsafe operations internally. Obviously, if you do this, you should take special care that the `unsafe` blocks are correct. There are quite a lot of APIs in the standard library that use this paradigm of tucking away operations within `unsafe` blocks while providing a safe API on the surface. For example, the `insert` method on the `String` type, which inserts a character, `ch`, at a given index, `idx`, is defined like so:

```
// https://doc.rust-lang.org/src/alloc/string.rs.html#1277-1285

pub fn insert(&mut self, idx: usize, ch: char) {
    assert!(self.is_char_boundary(idx));
    let mut bits = [0; 4];
    let bits = ch.encode_utf8(&mut bits).as_bytes();
    unsafe {
        self.insert_bytes(idx, bits);
    }
}
```

First, it does an assertion if the `idx` passed to it lies at the start or the end of a UTF-8 encoded code-point sequence. Then, it encodes the `ch` passed to it as a sequence of bytes. Finally, it calls an `unsafe` method, `insert_bytes`, in an `unsafe` block, passing in `idx` and `bits`.

There are many such APIs in the standard library that have similar implementations where they rely on an unsafe block internally, either to gain speedups or when they need mutable access to individual parts of a value because ownership gets in the way.

Now, if we call our `get_value` function from our previous snippet, with a number as an argument, and cast it to a pointer, you can already guess what's going to happen:

```
unsafe_function(4 as *const i32);
```

Running this gives us the following output:

```
→  Chapter10 git:(master) ✗ ./unsafe_function
[1]    21025 segmentation fault (core dumped)  ./unsafe_function
```

This is an obvious segmentation fault message! The takeaway from this observation is that the `unsafe` function, even though appearing safe on the outside, can be ignorantly or intentionally misused if the user supplies a malformed value. Therefore, if there is the need to expose an unsafe API from your library where the safety of your operations is dependent on user-supplied arguments, the author should document this clearly to ensure they are not passing an invalid value and mark the function with `unsafe` rather than using `unsafe` blocks internally.

Safe wrapper functions behind `unsafe` blocks should not really be exposed to consumers and instead are to be used mostly to hide implementation details in libraries, as is the case with many standard library API implementations. If you're not certain that you have managed to create a safe wrapper around the unsafe part, you should mark the function as `unsafe`.

Unsafe traits and implementations

Apart from functions, traits can also be marked as unsafe. It isn't obvious why we would need unsafe traits. One of the primary motivations for unsafe traits existing in the first place is to mark types that cannot be sent to or shared between threads. This is achieved via the unsafe `Send` and `Sync` marker traits. These types are also auto traits, which means that they are implemented for most types in the standard library whenever appropriate. However, they are also explicitly opted out for certain types, for instance, the `Rc<T>`. An `Rc<T>` does not have an atomic reference counting mechanism and if it were to implement `Sync` and later be used in multiple threads, then we might end up with the wrong reference counts on the type, which could lead to early frees and dangling pointers. Making `Send` and `Sync` unsafe puts the onus on the developer to only implement it, that is, if they have proper synchronization in place for their custom types. `Send` and `Sync` are marked as `unsafe` because it's incorrect to implement them for types that have no clear semantics on how types behave when mutated from multiple threads.

Another motivation for marking traits as unsafe is to encapsulate operations that are likely to have an undefined behavior by a family of types. As we've already mentioned, traits, by their nature, are used to specify a contract that implementing types must hold. Now, let's say your types contain entities from FFI boundaries, that is, a field that contains a reference to a C string, and you have many of these types. In this case, we can abstract away the behavior of such types by using an unsafe trait and then we can have a generic interface that takes types that implement this unsafe trait. One such example from Rust's standard library is the `Searcher` trait, which is an associated type of the `Pattern` trait, which is defined at `https://doc.rust-lang.org/std/str/pattern/trait.Pattern.html`. The `Searcher` trait is an unsafe trait that abstracts the notion of searching an item from a given byte sequence. One of the implementers of `Searcher` is the `CharSearcher` struct. Marking it as `unsafe` removes the burden on the `Pattern` trait to check for valid slices on valid UTF-8 byte boundaries and can give you some performance gains in string matching.

With the motivation for unsafe traits covered, let's look at how we can define and use unsafe traits. Marking a trait as unsafe doesn't make your methods unsafe. We can have unsafe traits that have safe methods. The opposite is also true; we can have a safe trait that can have unsafe methods within it, but that doesn't signify that the trait is unsafe. Unsafe traits are denoted in the same way as functions by simply prepending them with the `unsafe` keyword:

```
// unsafe_trait_and_impl.rs

struct MyType;

unsafe trait UnsafeTrait {
    unsafe fn unsafe_func(&self);
    fn safe_func(&self) {
        println!("Things are fine here!");
    }
}

trait SafeTrait {
    unsafe fn look_before_you_call(&self);
}

unsafe impl UnsafeTrait for MyType {
    unsafe fn unsafe_func(&self) {
        println!("Highly unsafe");
    }
}

impl SafeTrait for MyType {
    unsafe fn look_before_you_call(&self) {
        println!("Something unsafe!");
```

```
    }
}

fn main() {
    let my_type = MyType;
    my_type.safe_func();
    unsafe {
        my_type.look_before_you_call();
    }
}
```

In the preceding code, we have all kinds of variations with unsafe traits and methods. First, we have two trait declarations: UnsafeTrait, which is an unsafe trait and SafeTrait, which is safe. We also have a unit struct called MyType, which implements them. As you can see, unsafe traits require the unsafe prefix to implement MyType, letting the implementer know that they have to uphold the contracts that are expected by the trait. In the second implementation of the SafeTrait on MyType, we have an unsafe method that we need to call within the unsafe block, as we can see in the main function.

In the following sections, we'll be exploring a handful of languages and how Rust interoperates with them. All of the related APIs and abstractions that Rust provides to communicate safely back and forth between languages is colloquially termed the **Foreign Function Interface** (**FFI**). As part of the standard library, Rust provides us with built-in FFI abstractions. Wrapper libraries on top of these provide seamless cross-language interaction.

Calling C code from Rust

First, we'll take a look at an example of calling C code from Rust. We'll create a new binary crate from which we'll call our C function that's defined in a separate C file. Let's create a new project by running cargo new c_from_rust. Within the directory, we'll also add our C source, that is, the mystrlen.c file, which has the following code inside it:

```
// c_from_rust/mystrlen.c

unsigned int mystrlen(char *str) {
    unsigned int c;
    for (c = 0; *str != '\0'; c++, *str++);
    return c;
}
```

It contains a simple function, `mystrlen`, which returns the length of a string passed to it. We want to invoke `mystrlen` from Rust. To do that, we'll need to compile this C source into a static library. There's one more example in the upcoming section, where we cover linking dynamically to a shared library. We'll use the `cc` crate as a build dependency in our `Cargo.toml` file:

```
# c_from_rust/Cargo.toml

[build-dependencies]
cc = "1.0"
```

The `cc` crate does all the heavy lifting of compiling and linking our C source file with our binary with correct linker flags. To specify our build commands, we need to put a `build.rs` file at the crate root, which has the following contents:

```
// c_from_rust/build.rs

fn main() {
    cc::Build::new().file("mystrlen.c")
                    .static_flag(true)
                    .compile("mystrlen");
}
```

We created a new `Build` instance and passed the C source filename with the static flag set to `true` before giving a name to our static object file to the `compile` method. Cargo runs the contents of any `build.rs` file before any project files get compiled. Upon running code from `build.rs`, the `cc` crate automatically appends the conventional `lib` prefix in C libraries, so our compiled static library gets generated at `target/debug/build/c_from_rust-5c739ceca32833c2/out/libmystrlen.a`.

Now, we also need to tell Rust about the existence of our `mystrlen` function. We do this by using `extern` blocks, where we can specify items that come from other languages. Our `main.rs` file is as follows:

```
// c_from_rust/src/main.rs

use std::os::raw::{c_char, c_uint};
use std::ffi::CString;

extern "C" {
    fn mystrlen(str: *const c_char) -> c_uint;
}

fn main() {
    let c_string = CString::new("C From Rust").expect("failed");
```

```
    let count = unsafe {
        mystrlen(c_string.as_ptr())
    };
    println!("c_string's length is {}", count);
}
```

We have a couple of imports from the `std::os::raw` module that contain types that are compatible with primitive C types and have names close to their C counterparts. For numeric types, a single letter before the type says whether the type is unsigned. For instance, the unsigned integer is defined as `c_uint`. In our `extern` declaration of `mystrlen`, we take a `*const c_char` as input, which is equivalent to `char *` in C, and return a `c_uint` as output, which maps to `unsigned int` in C. We also import the `CString` type from the `std::ffi` module, as we need to pass a C-compatible string to our `mystrlen` function. The `std::ffi` module contains common utilities and types that make it easy to perform cross language interactions.

As you may have noticed, in the `extern` block, we have a string, `"C"`, following it. This `"C"` specifies that we want the compiler's code generator to confirm to the C ABI (`cdecl`) so that the function-calling convention follows exactly as a function call that's done from C. An **Application Binary Interface (ABI)** is basically a set of rules and conventions that dictate how types and functions are represented and manipulated at the lower levels. The function-calling convention is one aspect of an ABI specification. It's quite analogous to what an API means for a library consumer. In the context of functions, an API specifies what functions you can call from the library, while the ABI specifies the lower-level mechanism by which a function is invoked. A calling convention defines things such as whether function parameters are stored in registers or on the stack, and whether the caller clears the register/stack state or the caller when the function returns, and other details. We could have also ignored specifying this, as `"C"` (`cdecl`) is the default ABI in Rust for items that are declared in an `extern` block. The `cdecl` is a calling convention that's used by most C compilers for function calls. There are also other ABIs that Rust supports such as `fastcall`, `cdecl`, `win64`, and others, and these need to be put after the `extern` block based on what platform you are targeting.

In our `main` function, we use a special version of a `CString` string from the `std::ffi` module because strings in C are null terminated, while Rust one's aren't. `CString` does all the checks for us to give us a C-compatible version of strings where we don't have a null 0 byte character in the middle of the string and ensures that the ending byte is a 0 byte. The `ffi` module contains two major string types:

- `std::ffi::CStr` represents a borrowed C string that's analogous to `&str`. It can be used to reference a string that has been created in C.
- `std::ffi::CString` represents an owned string that is compatible with foreign C functions. It is often used to pass strings from Rust code to foreign C functions.

Since we want to pass a string from the Rust side to the function we just defined, we used the `CString` type here. Following that, we call `mystrlen` in an unsafe block, passing in the `c_string` as a pointer. We then print the string length to standard output.

Now, all we need to do is run `cargo run`. We get the following output:

```
→  c_from_rust git:(master) ✗ cargo run
    Finished dev [unoptimized + debuginfo] target(s) in 0.01s
     Running `target/debug/c_from_rust`
c_string's length is 11
```

The `cc` crate automatically figures out the correct C compiler to call. In our case, on Ubuntu, it automatically invokes `gcc` to link our C library. Now, there are a couple of improvements to be made here. First, it is awkward that we have to be in an `unsafe` block to call the function as we know it's not unsafe. We know our C implementation is sound, at least for this small function. Second, we will panic if `CString` creation fails. To solve this, we can create a safe wrapper function. In a simplistic form, this just means creating a function that calls the external function inside an unsafe block:

```rust
fn safe_mystrlen(str: &str) -> Option<u32> {
    let c_string = match CString::new(str) {
        Ok(c) => c,
        Err(_) => return None
    };

    unsafe {
        Some(mystrlen(c_string.as_ptr()))
    }
}
```

Our `safe_mystrlen` function returns an `Option` now, where it returns `None` if `CString` creation fails and, following that, calls `mystrlen` wrapped in an `unsafe` block, which is returned as `Some`. Calling `safe_mystrlen` feels exactly like calling any other Rust function. If possible, it's recommended to make safe wrappers around external functions, taking care that all exceptional cases happening inside the `unsafe` block are handled properly so that library consumers don't use unsafe in their code.

Calling Rust code from C

As we stated in the previous section, when Rust libraries expose their functions to other languages using the `extern` block, they expose the C ABI (`cdecl`) by default. As such, it becomes a very seamless experience of calling Rust code from C. To C, they appear just like regular C functions. We'll take a look at an example of calling Rust code from a C program. Let's create a cargo project for this by running `cargo new rust_from_c --lib`.

In our `Cargo.toml` file, we have the following items:

```
# rust_from_c/Cargo.toml

[package]
name = "rust_from_c"
version = "0.1.0"
authors = ["Rahul Sharma <creativcoders@gmail.com>"]
edition = "2018"

[lib]
name = "stringutils"
crate-type = ["cdylib"]
```

Under the `[lib]` section, we specified the crate as `cdylib`, which indicates that we want a dynamically loadable library to be generated, which is more commonly known as a shared object file (`.so`) in Linux. We specified an explicit name for our `stringutils` library, and this will be used to create the shared object file.

Now, let's move on to our implementation in `lib.rs`:

```
// rust_from_c/src/lib.rs

use std::ffi::CStr;
use std::os::raw::c_char;

#[repr(C)]
pub enum Order {
```

```
        Gt,
        Lt,
        Eq
    }

    #[no_mangle]
    pub extern "C" fn compare_str(a: *const c_char, b: *const c_char) -> Order
    {
        let a = unsafe { CStr::from_ptr(a).to_bytes() };
        let b = unsafe { CStr::from_ptr(b).to_bytes() };
        if a > b {
            Order::Gt
        } else if a < b {
            Order::Lt
        } else {
            Order::Eq
        }
    }
```

We have a single function, `compare_str`. We prepend it with the `extern` keyword to expose it to C, followed by specifying the `"C"` ABI for the compiler to generate code appropriately. We also need to add a `#[no_mangle]` attribute, as Rust adds random characters to function names by default to prevent the clashing of names of types and functions across modules and crates. This is called name mangling. Without this attribute, we won't be able to call our function by the name `compare_str`. Our function lexicographically compares two C strings passed to it and returns an enum, `Order`, accordingly, which has three variants: `Gt` (Greater than), `Lt` (Less than), and `Eq` (Equal). As you may have noticed, the enum definition has a `#[repr(C)]` attribute. Because this enum is being returned to the C side, we want it to be represented in the same way as a C enum. The `repr` attribute allows us to do that. On the C side, we will get a `uint_32` type as the return type of this function as enums variants are represented as 4 bytes in Rust, as well as in C. Do note that at the time of writing this book, Rust follows the same data layout for enums that have associated data as it does for C enums. However, this may change in the future.

Now, let's create a file called `main.c` that uses our exposed function from Rust:

```c
// rust_from_c/main.c

#include <stdint.h>
#include <stdio.h>

int32_t compare_str(const char* value, const char* substr);

int main() {
```

```
    printf("%d\n", compare_str("amanda", "brian"));
    return 0;
}
```

We declared the prototype of our `compare_str` function, just like any normal prototype declaration. Following that, we called `compare_str` in `main`, passing in our two string values. Do note that if we were passing strings that were allocated on the heap, we would need to also free it from the C side. In this case, we are passing a C string literal that goes to the data segment of the process, and so we don't need to do any free calls. Now, we'll create a simple `Makefile` that builds our `stringutils` crate and also compiles and links with our `main.c` file:

```
# rust_from_c/Makefile

main:
    cargo build
    gcc main.c -L ./target/debug -lstringutils -o main
```

We can now run `make` to build our crate and then run `main` by first setting our `LD_LIBRARY_PATH` to where our generated `libstringutils.so` resides. Following that, we can run `main` like so:

```
$ export LD_LIBRARY_PATH=./target/debug
$ ./main
```

This gives us an output of 1, which is the value of the `Lt` variant from the `Order` enum on the Rust side. The takeaway from this example is that when you are invoking a Rust function from C/C++ or any other language that has a supported ABI in Rust, we cannot pass Rust-specific data types to the FFI boundary. For instance, passing `Option` or `Result` types, that ha've associated data with them is meaningless, as C cannot interpret and extract values out of them, as it has no way of knowing about that. In such cases, we need to pass primitive values as return types from functions to the C side or convert our Rust type to some format that C can understand.

Now, consider our previous case of calling C code from Rust. In the manual way, we needed to write `extern` declarations for all of our APIs that have been declared in header files. It would be great if this could be automated for us. Let's see how we can do that next!

Using external C/C++ libraries from Rust

Given the amount of software written over the last three decades, a lot of system software is written in C/C++. It's more likely that you may want to link to an existing library written in C/C++ for use in Rust, as rewriting everything in Rust (though desirable) is not practical for complex projects. But at the same time, writing manual FFI bindings for these libraries is also painful and error-prone. Fortunately, there are tools for us to automatically generate bindings to C/C++ libraries. For this demo, the required code on the Rust side is much simpler than the previous example of calling C/C++ code from Rust, as, this time, we'll use a neat crate called **bindgen** that automatically generates FFI bindings from C/C++ libraries. Bindgen is the recommended tool if someone wants to integrate a complex library with lots of APIs. Writing these bindings manually can be very error-prone and bindgen helps us by automating this process. We'll use this crate to generate bindings for a simple C library, `levenshtein.c`, which can be found at `https://github.com/wooorm/levenshtein.c`, which is used to find the minimum edit distance between two strings. The edit distance is used in a wide variety of applications, such as in fuzzy string matching, natural language processing, and in spell checkers. Anyway, let's create our cargo project by running `cargo new edit_distance --lib`.

Before we use bindgen, we need to install a few dependencies as bindgen needs them:

```
$ apt-get install llvm-3.9-dev libclang-3.9-dev clang-3.9
```

Next, in our `Cargo.toml` file, we'll add a `build` dependency on `bindgen` and the `cc` crate:

```
# edit_distance/Cargo.toml

[build-dependencies]
bindgen = "0.43.0"
cc = "1.0"
```

The `bindgen` crate will be used to generate bindings from the `levenshtein.h` header file, while the `cc` crate will be used to compile our library as a shared object so that we can use it from Rust. Our library-related files reside in the `lib` folder at the crate root.

Next, we'll create our `build.rs` file, which will be run before any of our source files are compiled. It will do two things: first, it will compile `levenshtein.c` to a shared object (`.so`) file, and second, it will generate bindings to the APIs defined in the `levenshtein.h` file:

```
// edit_distance/build.rs

use std::path::PathBuf;

fn main() {
    println!("cargo:rustc-rerun-if-changed=.");
    println!("cargo:rustc-link-search=.");
    println!("cargo:rustc-link-lib=levenshtein");

    cc::Build::new()
        .file("lib/levenshtein.c")
        .out_dir(".")
        .compile("levenshtein.so");

    let bindings = bindgen::Builder::default()
        .header("lib/levenshtein.h")
        .generate()
        .expect("Unable to generate bindings");

    let out_path = PathBuf::from("./src/");
    bindings.write_to_file(out_path.join("bindings.rs")).expect("Couldn't
write bindings!");
}
```

In the preceding code, we tell Cargo that our library search path is our current directory and that the library we are linking against is called `levenshtein`. We also tell Cargo to rerun code in `build.rs` if any of our files in our current directory change:

```
println!("cargo:rustc-rerun-if-changed=.");
println!("cargo:rustc-link-search=.");
println!("cargo:rustc-link-lib=levenshtein");
```

Following that, we create a compilation pipeline for our library by creating a new `Build` instance and provide the appropriate C source file for the `file` method. We also set the output directory to `out_dir` and our library name to the `compile` method:

```
cc::Build::new().file("lib/levenshtein.c")
                .out_dir(".")
                .compile("levenshtein");
```

Next, we create a bindgen `Builder` instance, pass our header file location, call `generate()`, and then write it to a `bindings.rs` file before calling `write_to_file`:

```
let bindings = bindgen::Builder::default().header("lib/levenshtein.h")
                                          .generate()
                                          .expect("Unable to generate
bindings");
```

Now, when we run `cargo build`, a `bindings.rs` file will be generated under `src/`. As we mentioned previously, it's good practice for all libraries that are exposing FFI bindings to provide a safe wrapper. So, under `src/lib.rs`, we'll create a function named `levenshtein_safe` that wraps the unsafe function from `bindings.rs`:

```
// edit_distance/src/lib.rs

mod bindings;

use crate::bindings::levenshtein;
use std::ffi::CString;

pub fn levenshtein_safe(a: &str, b: &str) -> u32 {
    let a = CString::new(a).unwrap();
    let b = CString::new(b).unwrap();
    let distance = unsafe { levenshtein(a.as_ptr(), b.as_ptr()) };
    distance
}
```

We import the unsafe function from `bindings.rs`, wrap it within our `levenshtein_safe` function, and call our `levenshtein` function in an `unsafe` block, passing C-compatible strings. It's time to test our `levenshtein_safe` function. We'll create a `basic.rs` file in an `examples/` directory in our crate root, which has the following code:

```
// edit_distance/examples/basic.rs

use edit_distance::levenshtein_safe;

fn main() {
    let a = "foo";
    let b = "fooo";
    assert_eq!(1, levenshtein_safe(a, b));
}
```

We can run this with `cargo run --example basic` and we should see no assertion failures as the value should be 1 from the `levenshtein_safe` call. Now, it's a recommended naming convention for these kind of crates to have the suffix `sys` appended to them, which only houses FFI bindings. Most crates on `crates.io` follow this convention. This was a whirlwind tour on how to use bindgen to automate cross-language interaction. If you want similar automation for reverse FFI bindings, such as Rust in C, there is also an equivalent project called `cbindgen` at `https://github.com/eqrion/cbindgen`, which can generate C header files for Rust crates. For instance, `Webrender` uses this crate to expose its APIs to other languages. Given the legacy of C, it's the lingua franca of programming languages and Rust has first-class support for it. A lot of other languages also call into C. This implies that your Rust code can be called from all other languages that target C. Let's make other languages talk to Rust.

Creating native Python extensions with PyO3

In this section, we'll see how Python can also call Rust code. The Python community has always been a heavy user of native modules such as numpy, lxml, opencv, and so on, and most of them have their underlying implementations in either C or C++. Having Rust as an alternative to native C/C++ modules is a major advantage both in terms of speed and safety for a lot of Python projects out there. For the demo, we'll build a native Python module that's implemented in Rust. We'll be using `pyo3`, a popular project that provides Rust bindings for the Python interpreter and hides all the low-level details, thus providing a very intuitive API. The project is on GitHub at `https://github.com/PyO3/pyo3`. It supports both Python 2 and Python 3 versions. `pyo3` is a fast-moving target and only works on nightly at the time of writing this book. So, we'll use a specific version of `pyo3`, that is, `0.4.1`, along with a specific nightly version of the Rust compiler.

Let's create a new cargo project by running `cargo new word_suffix --lib`. This library crate will expose a Python module called `word_suffix`, which contains a single function, `find_words`, which accepts a comma-separated string of words and returns all the words in that text that end with a given suffix. Once we build our module, we'll be able to import this module like a normal Python module.

Before we go ahead with the implementation, we'll need to switch to a specific nightly Rust toolchain for this project, that is, `rustc 1.30.0-nightly (33b923fd4 2018-08-18)`. We can override the toolchain to use this specific nightly version for this project by running `rustup override set nightly-2018-08-19` in our current directory (`word_suffix/`).

To start things off, we'll specify our dependencies in our `Cargo.toml` file:

```
# word_suffix/Cargo.toml

[package]
name = "word_suffix"
version = "0.1.0"
authors = ["Rahul Sharma <creativcoders@gmail.com>"]

[dependencies]
pyo3 = "0.4"

[lib]
crate-type = ["cdylib"]
```

We added our only dependency here on `pyo3`. As you can see, in the `[lib]` section, we specified the `crate-type` as `cdylib`, which means that the generated library is similar to a C shared library (`.so` in linux), which Python already knows how to call.

Now, let's start the implementation in our `lib.rs` file:

```rust
// word_suffix/src/lib.rs

//! A demo python module in Rust that can extract words
//! from a comma seperated string of words that ends with the given suffix

#[macro_use]
extern crate pyo3;
use pyo3::prelude::*;

/// This module is a python module implemented in Rust.
#[pymodinit]
fn word_suffix(_py: Python, module: &PyModule) -> PyResult<()> {
    module.add_function(wrap_function!(find_words))?;
    Ok(())
}

#[pyfunction]
fn find_words(src: &str, suffix: &str) -> PyResult<Vec<String>> {
    let mut v = vec![];
    let filtered = src.split(",").filter_map(|s| {
        let trimmed = s.trim();
        if trimmed.ends_with(&suffix) {
            Some(trimmed.to_owned())
        } else {
            None
        }
    });
```

```
    for s in filtered {
        v.push(s);
    }
    Ok(v)
}
```

First, we imported our `pyo3` crate, along with all the Python-related types from the `prelude` module. Then, we defined a `word_suffix` function, annotating it with the `#[pymodinit]` attribute. This becomes our Python module, which we can import in any `.py` file. This function receives two arguments. The first argument is `Python`, a marker type that is required for most Python related operations in `pyo3`. This is used to indicate that a particular operation modifies the Python interpreter state. The second argument is a `PyModule` instance, which represents a Python module object. Through this instance, we then add our `find_words` function, wrapped inside the `wrap_function` macro by calling `add_function`. The `wrap_function` macro does some manipulation to the provided Rust function to convert it into a Python-compatible function.

Next, is our `find_words` function, which is the important piece here. We wrap it with a `#[pyfunction]` attribute, which performs conversions on the argument and return type of our function so that it's compatible with a Python function. Our `find_words` implementation is simple. First, we create a vector, `v`, to hold the list of filtered words. Then, we filter our `src` string by splitting on `", "`, followed by a `filter` and `map` operation. The `split(",")` call returns an iterator on which we call the `filter_map` method. This method receives a closure as an argument containing the split word `s`. We first remove any white space from our `s` by calling `s.trim()`, followed by checking whether it `ends_with` our provided `suffix` string. If it does, it converts `trimmed` to an owned `String` wrapping in `Some`; otherwise, it returns `None`. We then iterate over all the filtered words (if any), push them to our `v`, and return it.

With that explanation out of the way, it's time to build our Python module. To do that, we have `pyo3-pack`: another tool from the same `pyo3` project that automates the whole process of making a native Python module. This tool also has the ability to publish the built packages to the **Python Package Index (PyPI)**. Let's install `pyo3-pack` by running `cargo install pyo3-pack`. Now, we can generate the package as a Python wheel (`.whl`), followed by installing the package locally using `pyo3-pack develop`. But before we do that, we need to be in a Python virtual environment, since the `py3-pack develop` command requires that.

We can create our virtual environment by running the following code:

```
virtualenv -p /usr/bin/python3.5 test_word_suffix
```

We are using Python 3.5 here. After that, we need to activate our environment by running the following code:

```
source test_word_suffix/bin/activate
```

If you don't have `pip` or `virtualenv` installed, you can install them by running the following code:

```
sudo apt-get install python3-pip
sudo pip3 install virtualenv
```

Now, we can run `pyo3-pack develop`, which creates the *wheel* files for both Python 2 and Python 3 versions and also installs them locally inside our virtual environment.

Now, we'll create a simple `main.py` file in our `word_suffix` directory and import this module to see if we can use our module:

```
# word_suffix/main.py

import word_suffix

print(word_suffix.find_words("Baz,Jazz,Mash,Splash,Squash", "sh"))
```

Running it via `python main.py`, we get the following output:

```
(test_word_suffix) ➜  word_suffix git:(master) ✗ python main.py
['Mash', 'Splash', 'Squash']
(test_word_suffix) ➜  word_suffix git:(master) ✗ ▮
```

Great! This was a very simple example, though. For complex cases, there are lots of details that you need to know about. To explore more about `pyo3`, head over to their excellent guide at `https://pyo3.rs`.

Creating native extensions in Rust for Node.js

There are times when the performance of JavaScript in the Node.js runtime is not enough, so developers reach out to other low-level languages to create native Node.js modules. Often, C and C++ are used as the implementation language for these native modules. Rust can also be used to create native Node.js modules via the the same FFI abstractions that we saw for C and Python. In this section, we'll explore a high-level wrapper for these FFI abstractions, called the `neon` project, which was created by Dave Herman from Mozilla.

The neon project is a set of tools and glue code that makes the life of Node.js developers easier, allowing them to write native Node.js modules in Rust and consume them seamlessly in their JavaScript code. The project resides at `https://github.com/neon-bindings/neon`. It's partially written in JavaScript: there's a command-line tool called `neon` in the `neon-cli` package, a JavaScript-side support library, and a Rust-side support library. Node.js itself has good support for loading native modules, and neon uses that same support.

In the following demo, we will be building a native Node.js module in Rust as an npm package, exposing a function that can count occurrences of a given word in a chunk of text. We will then import this package and test the exposed function in a `main.js` file. This demo requires Node.js (version `v11.0.0`) to be installed, along with its package manager, `npm` (version `6.4.1`). If you don't have Node.js and `npm` installed, head over to `https://www.digitalocean.com/community/tutorials/how-to-install-node-js-on-ubuntu-16-04` to set them up. After you are done installing them, you need to install the `neon-cli` tool using `npm` by running the following command:

```
npm install --global neon-cli
```

Since we want this tool to be available globally to create new projects from anywhere, we pass the `--global` flag. The `neon-cli` tool is used to create a Node.js project with skeleton neon support included. Once it is installed, we create our project by running `neon new native_counter`, which prompts for basic information for the project, as shown in the following screenshot:

```
→  Chapter10 neon new native_counter
This utility will walk you through creating the native_counter Neon project.
It only covers the most common items, and tries to guess sensible defaults.

Press ^C at any time to quit.
? version 0.1.0
? description A native nodejs module in Rust to count words in a given text
? node entry point lib/index.js
? git repository
? author Rahul Sharma
? email creativcoders@gmail.com
? license MIT

Woo-hoo! Your Neon project has been created in: native_counter

The main Node entry point is at: native_counter/lib/index.js
The main Rust entry point is at: native_counter/native/src/lib.rs

To build your project, just run npm install from within the native_counter directory.
Then you can test it out with node -e 'require("./")'.

Happy hacking!
```

Here's the directory structure this command created for us:

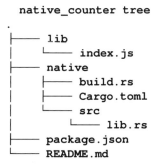

```
native_counter tree
.
├──── lib
│      └──── index.js
├──── native
│      ├──── build.rs
│      ├──── Cargo.toml
│      └──── src
│            └──── lib.rs
├──── package.json
└──── README.md
```

The project structure neon created for us is the same npm package structure that we get with the usual `lib` directory and `package.json`. In addition to the Node.js package structure, it has also created a cargo project for us under the `native` directory with some initial code in it. Let's see what the contents of this directory are, starting with `Cargo.toml`:

```
# native_counter/native/Cargo.toml

[package]
name = "native_counter"
version = "0.1.0"
authors = ["Rahul Sharma <creativcoders@gmail.com>"]
license = "MIT"
build = "build.rs"
exclude = ["artifacts.json", "index.node"]

[lib]
name = "native_counter"
crate-type = ["dylib"]

[build-dependencies]
neon-build = "0.2.0"

[dependencies]
neon = "0.2.0"
```

The prominent thing to note is the [lib] section, which specifies the crate type as dylib, which means we require Rust to create a shared library. There is also an autogenerated build.rs file at the root level, which does some initial build environment configuration by calling neon_build::setup() inside it. Next, we'll remove the existing code in our lib.rs file and add the following code:

```
// native_counter/native/src/lib.rs

#[macro_use]
extern crate neon;

use neon::prelude::*;

fn count_words(mut cx: FunctionContext) -> JsResult<JsNumber> {
    let text = cx.argument::<JsString>(0)?.value();
    let word = cx.argument::<JsString>(1)?.value();
    Ok(cx.number(text.split(" ").filter(|s| s == &word).count() as f64))
}

register_module!(mut m, {
    m.export_function("count_words", count_words)?;
    Ok(())
});
```

First, we import the neon crate, along with the macros and all the items from the prelude module. Following that, we define a function, count_words, which takes in a FunctionContext instance. This contains information in JavaScript regarding the active function that's invoked, such as the argument list, length of arguments, the this binding, and other details. We expect the caller to pass two arguments to our count_words function. Firstly, the text, and secondly, the word to search for in the text. These values are extracted by calling the argument method on the cx instance and passing in the respective index to it. We also use the turbofish operator to ask it to give a value of the JsString type. On the returned JsString instance, we call the value method to get a Rust String value.

After we're done extracting the arguments, we split our text with white space and filter only the chunks that contain the given `word` before calling `count()` on the iterator chain to count the number of matched occurrences:

```
text.split(" ").filter(|s| s == &word).count()
```

`count()` returns `usize`. However, we need to cast `usize` to `f64` because of the `Into<f64>` trait bound on our `number` method on `cx`. Once we do that, we wrap this expression with a call to `cx.number()`, which creates a JavaScript-compatible `JsNumber` type. Our `count_words` method returns a `JsResult<JsNumber>` type, as accessing the arguments might fail and returning a proper *JavaScript* type might also fail. This error variant in the `JsResult` type represents any exception that's thrown from the JavaScript-side.

Next, we register our `count_words` function with the `register_module!` macro. This macro gets a mutable reference to a `ModuleContext` instance, `m`. Using this instance, we export our function by calling the `export_function` method, passing in the name of the function as string and the actual function type as the second parameter.

Now, here's our updated `index.js` file's contents:

```
// native_counter/lib/index.js

var word_counter = require('../native');
module.exports = word_counter.count_words;
```

As `index.js` is the root of an npm package, we require our native module and must export the function directly at the root of the module using `module.exports`. We can now build our module using the following code:

```
neon build
```

Once the package has been built, we can test it by creating a simple `main.js` file in the `native_counter` directory with the following code:

```
// native_counter/main.js

var count_words_func = require('.');
var wc = count_words_func("A test text to test native module", "test");
console.log(wc);
```

We'll run this file by running the following code:

```
node main.js
```

This gives us an output of 2. That concludes our awesome journey on making Rust and other languages talk to each other. It turns out that Rust is quite smooth at this interaction. There are rough edges in cases where other languages don't understand Rust's complex data types, but this is to be expected, as every language is different in its implementation.

Summary

Rust provides us with convenient FFI abstractions to interface with different languages and has first-class support for C, as it exposes the C ABI (cdecl) for functions marked as extern. As such, it's a good candidate for bindings for a lot of C/C++ libraries. One of the prominent examples of this is the SpiderMonkey JavaScript engine that's implemented in C++, which is used in the Servo project. The Servo engine calls into C++ using the bindings that are generated via the bindgen crate.

But, when we are interacting with cross-language boundaries, the language constructs and data representation that one language has don't need to match with the other language. As such, we need to put extra annotations, along with unsafe blocks, in Rust code to let the compiler know of our intent. We saw this when we used the #[repr(C)] attribute. The **Foreign Function Interface** (**FFI**), like many other Rust features, is zero-cost, which means that a minimal runtime cost is incurred when linking to code from other languages. We took a look at Python and Node.js, which have nice wrapper crates for these low-level FFI abstractions. For languages that don't have such wrappers, interfacing with other languages is always possible by using the bare FFI APIs that Rust's standard library provides.

The aim up until this chapter was to cover the topics that are core to the language, and I hope you are up to speed with most of the core language features. The remaining chapters will cover case studies of various Rust frameworks and crates, and will be heavily oriented toward applying Rust to practical projects.

11
Logging

Logging is an important, yet overlooked, practice in the software development life cycle. It is often integrated as an afterthought on facing the consequences of latent invalid states and errors that accumulate over time in software systems. Any moderate sized project should have logging support from the initial days of development.

In this chapter, we'll get to know why setting up logging in an application is important, the need for a logging framework, how to approach logging, and what crates are available in the Rust ecosystem to enable programmers to leverage the power of logging in their applications.

In this chapter, we will cover the following topics:

- What is logging and why do we need it?
- The need for logging frameworks
- Logging frameworks and their features
- Exploring logging crates in Rust

What is logging and why do we need it?

"Generally, a program should say nothing unless and until it has something to say."

- Kernighan and Plauger

Before we talk about the importance of logging, let's define the term so that we have a better context for it. Logging is the practice of making an application record its activity at runtime to any output, where the individual record is called an **event log** or simply a **log**. This is often associated with a timestamp describing when the event occurred. The event could be anything that changes the state of the program internally or externally. Logs help you in gaining insights on an application's runtime behavior over the course of time, or in getting more context on the application state when debugging a bug. They also find their use in generating analytics reports for business purposes. This is to say that the degree of utility logging provides to a user depends mainly on the application and consumers' needs.

Now, in an application without any kind of logging integration, there are limited options for us to know about the behavior of our program at runtime. We could use external utilities such as *htop* in Linux to monitor our program, but this gives us a view of the program from the outside and provides limited information regarding the internals.

Information from within a program while it's running is useful for debugging purposes or can be used for runtime performance analysis. In the case of fatal failures in our program, we can get to know about the whereabouts of our program when it crashes. At the very least, the program will leave a stack trace, thus providing a bit of context on where the program went wrong. However, there are classes of bugs and events that do not cause immediate problems but later turn into fatal errors, especially in long running systems. In these cases, event logs can help quickly narrow down the issue in the program. That's where adding logging capabilities to a program becomes tremendously helpful.

Systems that benefit greatly from logging and need to rely on event logs are web services, network servers, stream processing services, and similar long running systems. In these systems, individual event logs combined with subsequent logs over the course of time, when ingested and put into analysis by a log aggregation service, can provide useful statistics about the system.

For a commercial application such as a shopping website, you can leverage log analytics to get business insights, leading to better sales. In network servers, you can find useful activity logs to track any malicious attempts made to the server such as a distributed denial of service (DDoS) attack. Developers can assess the performance of their web API endpoints by getting request-response latency figures from the collected API request logs.

Logs also serve as an important debugging context and can minimize the time that's taken in performing root cause analysis during a debugging session, where you have time constraints to fix issues that happen in production.

Sometimes, logging is the only way to do this because debuggers are not always available or applicable. This is usually the case in distributed systems and multi-threaded applications. Anyone who has done a fair amount of development within these systems is quite aware of why logging is such an important part of the software development pipeline.

There are three broad categories of users who benefit greatly from the practice of application logging:

- **System administrators**: They need to monitor server logs for any malfunction, for example, a hard disk crash or network failures.
- **Developers**: During development, integrating logs in the project can help cut down development time by a lot and can later be used to get insights into the way users use their application.
- **Network security teams**: In the case of any attack on a remote server, the security folks benefit greatly from logging as they can get to know how a certain attack was carried out by tracing the event logs that the victim server logged.

Being a functional component in software development practices, and providing great value in the long run, integrating logging in a system demands dedicated frameworks, and we'll see why in the next section.

The need for logging frameworks

We now know why logs are important. The next question however is how do we integrate logging capabilities in our application? The simplest and most straightforward way to get your application to log events is to have a bunch of print statements sprinkled in code at the required places. This way, we easily get our event logs to the standard output on our Terminal console, which gets our job done, but there's more to be desired. In quite a few cases, we also want our logs to persist for analysis at a later point in time. So, if we want to collect the output from our print statements to a file, we have to look for additional ways such as piping the output to a file using the shell output redirection facility, which is basically plumbing a different set of tools to get to the goal of getting logs from our application to different outputs. As it turns out, there are limitations to this approach.

You don't get to filter or turn off your print statements for cases where you don't need to log for a particular module. For that, you either have to comment them out or remove them and redeploy your services. Another limitation is that when your logging commands become large, you have to write and maintain shell scripts for collecting logs for multiple outputs. All of this gets unwieldy and less maintainable very quickly. Using a print statement is a quick and dirty logging practice and is not a very scalable solution. What we need is a better and more customizable architecture for application logging. The scalable and cleaner way is to have a dedicated logger that removes all of these limitations, and that is why logging frameworks exist. In addition to basic logging needs, these frameworks also provide additional features such as log file rotations when reaching a certain size limit, setting logging frequency, granular log configuration per module, and much more.

Logging frameworks and their key features

There are a wide variety of logging frameworks offered by mainstream languages. Some notable ones to mention include *Log4j* from Java, *Serilog* from C#, and *Bunyan* from Node.js. From the time of proliferation of these frameworks, and from their use cases, there are similarities in what features a logging framework should provides to its users. The following are the most desirable properties that logging frameworks should have:

- **Fast**: Logging frameworks must ensure that they are not doing expensive operations when logging and should be able to process efficiently using as few CPU cycles as possible. For instance, in Java, if your log statements contain objects with lots of `to_string()` calls to them to just interpolate the object within the log message, then that's an expensive operation. This is considered an inefficient practice in Java.
- **Configurable outputs**: It's very limiting to have the ability to log messages only to standard output. It stays only until the shell session and you need to manually paste the logs to a file to use them later. Logging frameworks should provide the ability to support multiple outputs, such as a file or even a network socket.
- **Log levels:** The prominent feature of logging frameworks that makes them stand out from normal print-based logging is the ability to control what and when things get logged. This is usually implemented using the idea of *log levels*. A log level is a configurable filter that's usually implemented as a type that is checked for before sending the log output anywhere. The levels are usually in the following order, from lowest priority to highest priority:
    - **Error**: This level is suitable for logging events that are critical and those that may lead to invalid outputs from the application.

- **Warn**: This level is suitable for events for which you have taken measures, but also want to know when it happens to take actions later if they occur frequently.
- **Info**: This level can be used for normal events such as printing the application version, user logins, connection successful messages, and so on.
- **Debug**: As the name suggests, this is used to support debugging. It is useful for monitoring the values of variables and how they get manipulated in different code paths when debugging.
- **Trace**: This level is used when you want a step-by-step execution of your algorithm or any non-trivial function that you wrote. Method invocations with parameter and return values are things that can be put as trace logs.

Some of these names might differ slightly across frameworks, but the priorities they signify are mostly the same. In major logging frameworks, these levels are set by the logger during its initialization and any subsequent logging invocations check for the set level and filters out the logs accordingly. For example, a `Logger` object with the call to `Logger.set_level(INFO)` would allow all logs using levels above `Info` to be logged, while ignoring `Debug` and `Trace` logs.

- **Log filtering**: It should be easy to log only the desired places in code and to turn off other logs based on the severity/importance of events.
- **Log Rotation**: When logging to a file, it is imminent that prolonged logging will fill up disk space. A logging framework should provide facilities to limit the log file size and allow for the deletion of older log files.
- **Asynchronous logging**: Logging invocations on the main thread have the possibility of blocking the main code from making progress. Even though an efficient logger would do as little as possible, it still does a blocking I/O call between the actual code. As such, it is desirable that most logging invocations are offloaded to a dedicated logger thread.
- **Log message attributes**: Another thing worth mentioning are the attributes on log messages that get sent to the logging API. At a minimum, a logging framework should provide the following attributes to log messages:
  - **Timestamp**: The time at which the event happened
  - **Log Severity**: The importance of the message, for example, Error, Warning, Information, Debug, and so on

- **Event location**: The place in the source code where the event happened
- **Message**: The actual event message that describes what happened

Depending on these features, there are differences in how logging frameworks approach logging. Let's explore them next.

Approaches to logging

When integrating logging in an application, we need to decide what information to log and how granular it should be. If there are too many logs, we lose the ability of easily finding relevant information in the sea of noise and if there's not enough log messages, we risk missing that one important event. We also need to think about how to organize information in our log message so that it becomes easier to search and analyze it later. These questions lead to logging frameworks that are broadly divided into two categories: unstructured logging and structured logging.

Unstructured logging

The usual way to approach logging is the practice of logging events as plain strings and shoving any fields from required values into the log message by converting them into strings. This form of logging is called unstructured logging as the information in the log message doesn't have any predefined structure or order. Unstructured logging serves well for most use cases, but it has its downsides too.

After collecting log messages, a common use case with them is to be able search for them for a particular event at a later point in time. However, the retrieval of unstructured logs from a collection of logs can be a pain. The problem with unstructured log messages is that they don't have any predictable format and it becomes quite resource heavy for a log aggregation service to sift through all of the raw log messages using simple text matching queries. You need to write regular expressions that match on a chunk of text or grep them from the command line to get that particular event. With an increasing amount of logs, this approach eventually becomes a bottleneck in getting useful information from log files. The other approach is to log messages that have a predefined structure and for that we have structured logging.

Structured logging

Structured logging is a scalable and better alternative to unstructured logging. As the name suggests, structured logging defines a structure and formatting to your log messages and every log message is guaranteed to have this format. The advantage of this is that it becomes very easy for log aggregation services to build a search index and present any particular event to the user, regardless of the amount of messages they have. There are quite a few structured logging frameworks such as Serilog in C# that provide support for structured logging. These frameworks provide a plugin-based log output abstraction called *Sinks*. Sinks are how you direct where you want your logs to be sent. A Sink can be your Terminal, a file, a database, or a log aggregation service such as logstash.

Structured logging frameworks know how to serialize a certain object and can do so in a proper format. They also automate the formatting of log messages by providing hierarchical log outputs, depending on which component the log is emitted from. The downside to structured logging is that it can be a bit time-consuming to integrate it into your application as you have to decide on the hierarchy and the format of your logs beforehand.

It's often a trade-off when choosing between structured logging and unstructured logging. Complex projects that log heavily can benefit from structured logging as they can get semantic and efficiently searchable logs from their modules, while small to moderate size projects can make do with unstructured logging. Ultimately, it's the application's needs that should decide how you integrate logging in your application. In the next section, we'll explore a couple of unstructured logging frameworks as well as structure logging frameworks in Rust that you can use for getting your application to log events.

Logging in Rust

Rust has quite a few flexible and extensive logging solutions. Like popular logging frameworks in other languages, the logging ecosystem here is split into two parts:

- **Logging facade**: This part is implemented by the `log` crate and provides an implementation agnostic logging API. While other frameworks implement logging APIs as functions or methods on some object, the log crate provides us with macro-based logging APIs, which are categorized by log levels to log events to a configured log output.

- **Logging implementations**: These are community developed crates that provide actual logging implementation in terms of where the output goes and how it happens. There are many such crates, such as env_logger, simple_logger, log4rs, and fern. We'll visit a couple of them in a moment. Crates that come under this category are meant to be used only by binary crates, that is, executables.

This separation of concerns between the logging API and the underlying mechanism by which logs go to an output is done so that developers don't need to change their log statements in code and can easily swap the underlying logging implementation on an as-needed basis.

log – Rust's logging facade

The log crate comes from the *rust-lang nursery* organization on GitHub and is managed by the community at https://github.com/rust-lang-nursery/log. It provides separate macros for logging at different log levels such as error!, warn!, info!, debug!, and trace!, in the order of the most priority to the least priority. These macros are major points of interaction for consumers of this crate. They internally call the log! macro in this crate, which does all the bookkeeping such as checking for the log level and formatting log messages. The core component of this crate is the log trait that other backend crates implement. The trait defines operations that are required for a logger and has other APIs, such as for checking whether logging is enabled or for flushing any buffered logs.

The log crate also provides a maximum log level constant called STATIC_MAX_LEVEL, which can be configured project wide at compile time. With this constant, you can set the log level of an application statically using cargo feature flags, which allows for the compile time filtering of logs for the application and all of its dependencies. These level filters can be set in Cargo.toml separately for debug and release builds: max_level_<LEVEL> (debug) and release_max_level_<LEVEL> (release). In binary projects, you can specify the dependency on the log crate with compile time log levels as follows:

```
[dependencies]
log = "0.4.6", features = ["release_max_level_error", "max_level_debug"] }
```

It's a good practice to set this constant to a desired value as, by default, the level is set to Off. It also allows the log macros to optimize away any log invocations at disabled levels. Libraries should only link to the log crate and not any logger implementation crate as binary crates should have control over what to log and how to log it. Using this crate solely in your application won't produce any log output as you need to use logging crates such as env_logger or log4rs along with it.

To see the `log` crate in action, we'll build a library crate by running `cargo new user_auth --lib` and adding `log` as a dependency in our `Cargo.toml` file:

```
# user_auth/Cargo.toml

[dependencies]
log = "0.4.6"
```

This crate simulates a dummy user sign-in API. Our `lib.rs` file has a `User` struct, which has a method called `sign_in`:

```
// user_auth/lib.rs

use log::{info, error};

pub struct User {
    name: String,
    pass: String
}

impl User {
    pub fn new(name: &str, pass: &str) -> Self {
        User {name: name.to_string(), pass: pass.to_string()}
    }

    pub fn sign_in(&self, pass: &str) {
        if pass != self.pass {
            info!("Signing in user: {}", self.name);
        } else {
            error!("Login failed for user: {}", self.name);
        }
    }
}
```

In the `sign_in` method, we have a couple of log invocations on whether the sign in succeeded or failed. We'll use this library crate together with a binary crate thats creates a `User` instance and calls the `sign_in` method. Since depending on the `log` crate itself won't produce any log output, we'll use the `env_logger` as the logging backend for this example. Let's explore `env_logger` first.

The env_logger

env_logger is a simple logging implementation that allows you to control logs to stdout or stderr through the RUST_LOG environment variable. The values of this environment variable are comma-separated logger strings that correspond to module names and log levels. To demonstrate env_logger, we'll create a new binary crate by running cargo new env_logger_demo and specifying dependencies for log, env_logger, and our user_auth library, which we created in the previous section. Here's our Cargo.toml file:

```
# env_logger_demo/Cargo.toml

[dependencies]
env_logger = "0.6.0"
user_auth = { path = "../user_auth" }
log = { version = "0.4.6", features = ["release_max_level_error",
"max_level_trace"] }
```

Here's our main.rs file:

```
// env_logger_demo/src/main.rs

use log::debug;

use user_auth::User;

fn main() {
    env_logger::init();
    debug!("env logger demo started");
    let user = User::new("bob", "super_sekret");
    user.sign_in("super_secret");
    user.sign_in("super_sekret");
}
```

We create our User instance and call sign_in, passing in our password. The first sign in attempt is a failed one, which will get logged as an error. We can run it by setting the RUST_LOG environment variable, followed by cargo run:

```
RUST_LOG=user_auth=info,env_logger_demo=info cargo run
```

We set the logs from the user_auth crate to info and the levels above it, while logs from our env_logger_demo crate are set to debug and above.

Running this gives us the following output:

```
→  env_logger_demo git:(master) X RUST_LOG=user_auth=info,env_logger_demo=debug cargo run
    Finished dev [unoptimized + debuginfo] target(s) in 0.03s
     Running `target/debug/env_logger_demo`
 2018-11-25T19:18:51Z DEBUG env_logger_demo  env logger demo started
 2018-11-25T19:18:51Z INFO  user_auth  Signing in user: bob
 2018-11-25T19:18:51Z ERROR user_auth  Login failed for user: bob
```

The `RUST_LOG` accepts the `RUST_LOG=path::to_module=log_level[,]` pattern, where `path::to_module` specifies the logger and should be a path to any module with the crate name as the base. The `log_level` is any of the log levels that are defined in the log crate. `[,]` at the end indicates that we can optionally have as many of these logger specifications separated by a comma.

An alternative way to run the preceding program is by setting the environment variable within the code itself using the `set_var` method from the `env` module in the standard library:

```
std::env::set_var("RUST_LOG", "user_auth=info,env_logger_demo=info cargo
run");
env_logger::init();
```

This produces the same output as before. Next, let's take a look at a more complex and highly configurable logging crate.

log4rs

The `log4rs` crate, as the name suggests, is inspired by the popular `log4j` library from Java. This crate is much more powerful than `env_logger` and allows for granular logger configuration via YAML files.

We'll build two crates to demonstrate integrating logging via the `log4rs` crate. One will be a library crate, `cargo new my_lib --lib`, and the other will be our binary crate, `cargo new my_app`, which uses `my_lib`. A cargo workspace directory, called `log4rs_demo`, contains both of our crates.

Our `my_lib` crate has the following contents in the `lib.rs` file:

```
// log4rs_demo/my_lib/lib.rs

use log::debug;

pub struct Config;
```

```
impl Config {
    pub fn load_global_config() {
        debug!("Configuration files loaded");
    }
}
```

It has a struct called `Config` with a dummy method called `load_global_config`, which logs a message at the debug level. Next, our `my_app` crate contains the following contents in the `main.rs` file:

```
// log4rs_demo/my_app/src/main.rs

use log::error;

use my_lib::Config;

fn main() {
    log4rs::init_file("config/log4rs.yaml", Default::default()).unwrap();
    error!("Sample app v{}", env!("CARGO_PKG_VERSION"));
    Config::load_global_config();
}
```

In the preceding code, we initialize our `log4rs` logger via the `init_file` method, passing in the path to the `log4rs.yaml` config file. Next, we log a dummy error message, thus printing the app version. Following that, we call `load_global_config`, which logs another message. The following is the content of the `log4rs.yaml` configuration file:

```
# log4rs_demo/config/log4rs.yaml

refresh_rate: 5 seconds

root:
  level: error
  appenders:
    - stdout
appenders:
  stdout:
    kind: console
  my_lib_append:
    kind: file
    path: "log/my_lib.log"
    encoder:
      pattern: "{d} - {m}{n}"

loggers:
  my_lib:
    level: debug
```

```
appenders:
  - my_lib_append
```

Let's go through this line by line. The first line, `refresh_rate`, specifies the time interval after which `log4rs` reloads the configuration file to account for any changes that are made to this file. This means that we can modify any value in our YAML file and `log4rs` will dynamically reconfigure its loggers for us. Then, we have the `root` logger, which is the parent of all loggers. We specify the default level as `error` and the appender as `stdout`, which is defined below it.

Next, we have the `appenders` section. Appenders are places where logs go. We have specified two appenders: `stdout`, which is of `console` type, and `my_lib_append`, which is a `file` appender, which includes information about the path of the file and the log pattern to use under the `encoder` section.

Next, there is the section of `loggers` where we can define loggers based on the crates or modules with different levels. We defined a logger called `my_lib`, which corresponds to our `my_lib` crate, with the `debug` level and appender as `my_lib_append`. This means that any logs from the `my_lib` crate will go to the `my_lib.log` file, as specified by the `my_lib_append` appender.

By running `cargo run` in the `log4rs_demo` directory, we get the following output:

```
→  log4rs_demo git:(master) ✗ cargo run
    Finished dev [unoptimized + debuginfo] target(s) in 0.04s
     Running `target/debug/my_app`
2018-11-26T03:52:52.052338058+05:30 ERROR my_app - Sample app v0.1.0
2018-11-26T03:52:52.052507189+05:30 DEBUG my_lib - Configuration files loaded
```

That was a brief intro to `log4rs`. If you want to explore more on configuring these logs, head over to the documentation page at `https://docs.rs/log4rs`.

Structured logging using slog

All of the aforementioned crates are quite useful and are ideal for most use cases, but they do not support structured logging. In this section, we'll see how structured logging can be integrated into our application using the `slog` crate, one of the few popular structured logging crates in the Rust ecosystem. For this demo, we'll create a new project by running `cargo new slog_demo`, which simulates a shooting game.

We'll need the following dependencies in our `Cargo.toml` file:

```
# slog_demo/Cargo.toml

[dependencies]
rand = "0.5.5"
slog = "2.4.1"
slog-async = "2.3.0"
slog-json = "2.2.0"
```

The `slog` framework is ideal for moderate to big projects where there is lot of interplay between modules as it helps to integrate detailed logs for the long-term monitoring of events. It works on the idea of providing hierarchical and composable logging configuration in the application and allows for semantic event logging. There are two important concepts under `slog` that you need to be aware of to successfully use the crate: *Loggers* and *Drains*. Logger objects are used to log events while a Drain is an abstraction specifying a place where the log messages go and how they get there. This can be your standard output, a file, or a network socket. Drains are similar to what you would call a `Sink` in the *Serilog* framework in C#.

Our demo simulates game events from dummy game entities based on their actions. The entities have a parent-child relationship in the game, where we can attach the hierarchical logging capability in them quite easily with `slog` framework's structural logging configuration. We'll get to know about this when we see the code. At the root level, we have the `Game` instance, for which we can define a root logger to provide a baseline context in our log messages, such as the game name and version. So, we'll create a root logger attached to the `Game` instance. Next, we have the `Player` and `Enemy` types, which are child entities to the `Game`. These become child loggers of the root logger. Then, we have weapons for both the enemy and the player, which become the child logger for the player and the enemy logger. As you can see, setting up `slog` is a bit more involved than the previous frameworks we looked at.

Along with `slog` as the base crate, we'll also use the following crates in our demo:

- `slog-async`: Provides an asynchronous logging drain that decouples logging calls from the main thread.
- `slog-json`: A drain that outputs messages to any `Writer` as JSON. We'll use `stdout()` as the `Writer` instance for this demo.

Let's take a look at our `main.rs` file:

```
// slog_demo/main.rs

#[macro_use]
extern crate slog;

mod enemy;
mod player;
mod weapon;

use rand::Rng;
use std::thread;
use slog::Drain;
use slog::Logger;
use slog_async::Async;
use std::time::Duration;
use crate::player::Player;
use crate::enemy::Enemy;

pub trait PlayingCharacter {
    fn shoot(&self);
}

struct Game {
    logger: Logger,
    player: Player,
    enemy: Enemy
}

impl Game {
    fn simulate(&mut self) {
        info!(self.logger, "Launching game!");
        let enemy_or_player: Vec<&dyn PlayingCharacter> = vec![&self.enemy,
&self.player];
        loop {
            let mut rng = rand::thread_rng();
            let a = rng.gen_range(500, 1000);
            thread::sleep(Duration::from_millis(a));
            let player = enemy_or_player[{
                if a % 2 == 0 {1} else {0}
            }];
            player.shoot();
        }
    }
}
```

In the preceding code, we have a bunch of `use` statements, followed by our `PlayingCharacter` trait, which is implemented by our `Player` and `Enemy` structs. Our `Game` struct has a `simulate` method, which simply loops and randomly sleeps, thereby selecting at random either the player or the enemy before calling the `shoot` method on them. Let's continue down the same file:

```
// slog_demo/src/main.rs

fn main() {
    let drain = slog_json::Json::new(std::io::stdout()).add_default_keys()
                                                       .build()
                                                       .fuse();
    let async_drain = Async::new(drain).build().fuse();
    let game_info = format!("v{}", env!("CARGO_PKG_VERSION"));
    let root_log_context = o!("Super Cool Game" => game_info);
    let root_logger = Logger::root(async_drain, root_log_context);
    let mut game = Game { logger: root_logger.clone(),
                          player: Player::new(&root_logger, "Bob"),
                          enemy: Enemy::new(&root_logger, "Malice") };
    game.simulate()
}
```

In `main`, we first create our `drain` using `slog_json::Json`, which can log messages as JSON objects, followed by passing it to another drain, `Async`, which will offload all log invocations to a separate thread. Then, we create our `root_logger` by passing in our `drain` with an initial context for our log messages using the convenient `o!` macro. In this macro, we simply print the name and version of our game using the `CARGO_PKG_VERSION` environment variable. Next, our `Game` struct takes our root logger and `enemy` and `player` instances. To the `Player` and `Enemy` instances, we pass a reference to the `root_logger`, using which they create their child loggers. Then, we call `simulate` on our game instance.

The following is the content of `player.rs`:

```
// slog_demo/src/player.rs

use slog::Logger;

use weapon::PlasmaCannon;
use PlayingCharacter;

pub struct Player {
    name: String,
    logger: Logger,
    weapon: PlasmaCannon
}
```

```
impl Player {
    pub fn new(logger: &Logger, name: &str) -> Self {
        let player_log = logger.new(o!("Player" => format!("{}", name)));
        let weapon_log = player_log.new(o!("PlasmaCannon" => "M435"));
        Self {
            name: name.to_string(),
            logger: player_log,
            weapon: PlasmaCannon(weapon_log),
        }
    }
}
```

Here, our `new` method on `Player` gets the root `logger`, to which it adds its own context with the `o!` macro. We also create a logger for `weapon` and pass the player logger to it, which add its own information such as the ID of the weapon. Finally, we return our configured `Player` instance:

```
impl PlayingCharacter for Player {
    fn shoot(&self) {
        info!(self.logger, "{} shooting with {}", self.name, self.weapon);
        self.weapon.fire();
    }
}
```

We also implement the `PlayingCharacter` trait for our `Player`.

Next is our `enemy.rs` file, which is identical to everything we had in `player.rs`:

```
// slog_demo/src/enemy.rs

use weapon::RailGun;
use PlayingCharacter;
use slog::Logger;

pub struct Enemy {
    name: String,
    logger: Logger,
    weapon: RailGun
}

impl Enemy {
    pub fn new(logger: &Logger, name: &str) -> Self {
        let enemy_log = logger.new(o!("Enemy" => format!("{}", name)));
        let weapon_log = enemy_log.new(o!("RailGun" => "S12"));
        Self {
            name: name.to_string(),
            logger: enemy_log,
            weapon: RailGun(weapon_log)
```

```
                }
            }
        }

    impl PlayingCharacter for Enemy {
        fn shoot(&self) {
            warn!(self.logger, "{} shooting with {}", self.name, self.weapon);
            self.weapon.fire();
        }
    }
```

Then, we have our `weapon.rs` file, which contains two weapons that are used by the enemy and player instances:

```
// slog_demo/src/weapon.rs

use slog::Logger;
use std::fmt;

#[derive(Debug)]
pub struct PlasmaCannon(pub Logger);

impl PlasmaCannon {
    pub fn fire(&self) {
        info!(self.0, "Pew Pew !!");
    }
}

#[derive(Debug)]
pub struct RailGun(pub Logger);

impl RailGun {
    pub fn fire(&self) {
        info!(self.0, "Swoosh !!");
    }
}

impl fmt::Display for PlasmaCannon {
    fn fmt(&self, f: &mut fmt::Formatter) -> fmt::Result {
        write!(f, stringify!(PlasmaCannon))
    }
}

impl fmt::Display for RailGun {
    fn fmt(&self, f: &mut fmt::Formatter) -> fmt::Result {
        write!(f, stringify!(RailGun))
    }
}
```

That's all that is required for our game simulation. We can now run it by invoking `cargo run`. Here's the output on my machine:

```
→  slog_demo git:(master) ✗ cargo run
    Finished dev [unoptimized + debuginfo] target(s) in 0.03s
     Running `target/debug/slog_demo`
{"msg":"Launching game!","level":"INFO","ts":"2018-11-25T01:38:11.037367223+05:30","Super Cool G
ame":"v0.1.0"}
{"msg":"Enemy shooting with RailGun","level":"WARN","ts":"2018-11-25T01:38:11.913014535+05:30","
Enemy":"Malice","Super Cool Game":"v0.1.0"}
{"msg":"Swoosh !!","level":"INFO","ts":"2018-11-25T01:38:11.913264517+05:30","RailGun":"S12","En
emy":"Malice","Super Cool Game":"v0.1.0"}
{"msg":"Enemy shooting with RailGun","level":"WARN","ts":"2018-11-25T01:38:12.642179832+05:30","
Enemy":"Malice","Super Cool Game":"v0.1.0"}
{"msg":"Swoosh !!","level":"INFO","ts":"2018-11-25T01:38:12.642374457+05:30","RailGun":"S12","En
emy":"Malice","Super Cool Game":"v0.1.0"}
{"msg":"Enemy shooting with RailGun","level":"WARN","ts":"2018-11-25T01:38:13.445342834+05:30","
Enemy":"Malice","Super Cool Game":"v0.1.0"}
{"msg":"Swoosh !!","level":"INFO","ts":"2018-11-25T01:38:13.445551682+05:30","RailGun":"S12","En
emy":"Malice","Super Cool Game":"v0.1.0"}
```

As you can see, our game entities send log messages, which are then formatted and output as JSON with the help of `slog` and its drains. Similar to the JSON drain we used previously, there are many such drains that have been built by the community for `slog`. We can have a drain that outputs log messages directly to a log aggregation service, which knows how to handle JSON data and can easily index them for the efficient retrieval of logs. The pluggable and composable nature of `slog` makes it stand out from other logging solutions. With this demo, we have come to the end of the logging story in Rust. However, there are other more interesting logging frameworks for you to explore, and you can find them at `http://www.arewewebyet.org/topics/logging/`.

Summary

In this chapter, we learned about the importance of logging in software development and the ways of approaching it, including what characteristics to look for when choosing a logging framework. We also got to know about unstructured and structured logging, their pros and cons, and explored the available crates in the Rust ecosystem to integrate logging into our applications.

The next chapter will be about network programming, where we will explore the built-in facilities and crates that Rust provides to create efficient applications that communicate with one another.

Network Programming in Rust

12

In this chapter, we'll take a look at what Rust has to offer for network programming. We'll start by exploring existing networking primitives in the standard library by building a simple Redis clone. This will help us get familiar with the default synchronous network I/O model and its limitations. Next, we'll explain how asynchrony is a better approach when dealing with network I/O on a large scale. In the process, we'll get to know about the abstractions provided by the Rust ecosystem for building asynchronous network applications and refactor our Redis server to make it asynchronous using third-party crates.

In this chapter, we will cover the following topics:

- Network programming prelude
- Synchronous network I/O
- Building a simple Redis server
- Asynchronous network I/O
- An introduction to `futures` and `tokio` crates

Network programming prelude

"A program is like a poem: you cannot write a poem without writing it."

– E. W. Dijkstra

Building a medium through which machines can communicate with each other over the internet is a complicated task. There are different kinds of devices that communicate over the internet, running different OS and different versions of applications, and they need a set of agreed upon rules to exchange messages with one another. These rules of communication are called network protocols and the messages devices send to each other are referred to as network packets.

For the separation of concerns of various aspects, such as reliability, discoverability, and encapsulation, these protocols are divided into layers with higher-layer protocols stacked over the lower-layers. Each network packet is composed of information from all of these layers. These days, modern operating systems already ship with a network protocol stack implementation. In this implementation, each layer provides support for the layers above it.

At the lowest layer, we have the Physical layer and the Data Link layer protocol for specifying how packets are transmitted through wires across nodes on the internet and how they move in and out of network cards in computers. The protocols on this layer are the Ethernet and Token Ring protocols. Above that, we have the IP layer, which employs the concept of unique IDs, called IP addresses, to identify nodes on the internet. Above the IP layer, we have the Transport layer, which is a protocol that provides point-to-point delivery between two processes on the internet. Protocols such as TCP and UDP exist at this layer. Above the Transport layer, we have Application layer protocols such as HTTP and FTP, both of which are used to build rich applications. This allows for a higher level of communication, such as a chat application running on mobile devices. The entire protocol stack works in tandem to facilitate these kinds of complex interactions between applications running on computers, spread across the internet.

With devices connecting to each other over the internet and sharing information, distributed application architectures started to proliferate. Two models emerged: the decentralized model, popularly known as the peer-to-peer model, and the centralized model, which is widely known as the client-server model. The later is more common out of the two these days. Our focus in this chapter will be on the client-server model of building network applications, especially on the Transport layer.

In major operating systems, the Transport layer of the network stack is exposed to developers under a family of APIs named **Sockets**. It includes a set of interfaces, which are used to set up a communication link between two processes. Sockets allow you to communicate data back and forth between two processes, either locally or remotely, without requiring the developer to have an understanding of the underlying network protocol.

The Socket API's roots lie in the **Berkley Software Distribution (BSD)**, which was the first operating system to provide a networking stack implementation with a socket API in 1983. It serve as the reference implementation for networking stacks in major operating systems today. In Unix-like systems, a socket follows the same philosophy of *everything is a file* and exposes a file descriptor API. This means that one can read and write data from a socket just like files.

Sockets are file descriptors (an integer) that point to a descriptor table of the process that's managed by the kernel. The descriptor table contains a mapping of file descriptors to **file entry** structures, which contains the actual buffer for the data that's sent to the socket.

The Socket API acts primarily at the TCP/IP layer. On this layer, the sockets that we create are categorized on various levels:

- **Protocol**: Depending on the protocol, we can either have a TCP socket or a UDP socket. TCP is a stateful streaming protocol that provides the ability to deliver messages in a reliable fashion, whereas UDP is a stateless and unreliable protocol.
- **Communication kind**: Depending on whether we are communicating with processes on the same machine or processes on remote machines, we can either have internet sockets or Unix domain sockets. Internet sockets are used for exchanging messages between processes on remote machines. It is represented by a tuple of an IP address and a port. Two processes that want to communicate remotely must use IP sockets. Unix domain sockets are used for communication between processes that run on the same machine. Here, instead of an IP address-port pair, it takes a filesystem path. For instance, databases use Unix domain sockets to expose connection endpoints.
- **I/O model**: Depending on how we read and write data to a socket, we can create sockets of two kinds: blocking sockets and non-blocking sockets.

Now that we know more about sockets, let's explore the client-server model a bit more. In this model of networking, the usual flow of setting up two machines to communicate with each other follows this process: the server creates a socket and binds it to an IP address-port pair before specifying a protocol, which can be TCP or UDP. It then starts listening for connections from clients. The client, on the other hand, creates a connecting socket and connects to the given IP address and port. In Unix, processes can create a socket using the `socket` system. This call gives back a file descriptor that the program can use to perform read and write calls to the client or to the server.

Rust provides us with the `net` module in the standard library. This contains the aforementioned networking primitives on the Transport layer. For communicating over TCP, we have the `TcpStream` and `TcpListener` types. For communicating over UDP, we have the `UdpSocket` type. The `net` module also provides proper data types for representing IP addresses and supports both v4 and v6 versions.

Building network applications that are reliable involves several considerations. If you are okay with few of the packets getting dropped between message exchanges, you can go with UDP sockets, but if you cannot afford to have packets dropped or want to have message delivery in sequence, you must use TCP sockets. The UDP protocol is fast and came much later to cater to needs where you require minimal latency in the delivery of packets and can deal with a few packets being dropped. For example, a video chat application uses UDP, but you aren't particularly affected if a few of the frames drop from the video stream. UDPs are used in cases where you are tolerant of no delivery guarantees. We'll focus our discussion on TCP sockets in this chapter, as it's the most used protocol by the majority of network applications that need to be reliable.

Another factor to consider, is how well and efficient your application is able to serve clients. From a technical standpoint, this translates to choosing the I/O model of sockets.

 I/O is an acronym for Input/Output, and in this context, it is a catch-all phrase that simply denotes reading and writing bytes to sockets.

Choosing between blocking and non-blocking sockets changes its architecture, the way we write our code, and how it scales to clients. Blocking sockets give you a **synchronous I/O** model, while non-blocking sockets let you do **asynchronous I/O**. On platforms that implement the Socket API, such as Unix, sockets are created in blocking mode by default. This entails the default I/O model in major network stacks following the synchronous model. Let's explore both of these models next.

Synchronous network I/O

As we said previously, a socket is created in blocking mode by default. A server in blocking mode is synchronous in the sense that each read and write call on the socket blocks and waits until it is complete. If another client tries to connect to the server, it needs to wait until the server is done serving the previous client. This is to say that until the TCP read and write buffers are full, your application blocks on the respective I/O operation and any new client connections must wait until the buffers are empty and full again.

 The TCP protocol implementation contains its own read and write buffers on the kernel level, apart from the application maintaining any buffers of its own.

Rust's standard library networking primitives provide the same synchronous API for sockets. To see this model in action, we'll implement something more than an echo server. We'll build a stripped down version of Redis. Redis is a data structure server and is often used as an in-memory data store. Redis clients and servers speak the RESP protocol, which is a simple line-based protocol. While the protocol is agnostic of TCP or UDP, Redis implementations mostly use the TCP protocol. TCP is a stateful stream-based protocol with no way for servers and clients to identify how many bytes to read from the socket to construct a protocol message. To account for that, most protocols follow this pattern of using a length byte, followed by the same length of payload bytes.

A message in the RESP protocol is similar to most line-based protocols in TCP, with the initial byte being a marker byte followed by the length of the payload, followed by the payload itself. The message ends with a terminating marker byte. The RESP protocol supports various kinds of messages, ranging from simple strings, integers, arrays, and bulk strings and so on. A message in the RESP protocol ends with a \r\n byte sequence. For instance, a success message from the server to the client is encoded and sent as +OK\r\n (without quotes). + indicates a success reply, and then follows the strings. The command ends with \r\n. To indicate if a query has failed, the Redis server replies with – Nil\r\n.

Commands such as get and set are sent as arrays of bulk strings. For instance, a get foo command will be sent as follows:

```
*2\r\n$3\r\nget\r\n$3\r\nfoo\r\n
```

In the preceding message, *2 indicates that we have an array of 2 commands and is delimited by \r\n. Following that, $3 indicates that we have a string of length 3, i.e., the GET command followed by a $3 for the string foo. The command ends with \r\n. That's the basics on RESP. We don't have to worry about the low-level details of parsing RESP messages, as we'll be using a fork of a crate called resp to parse incoming byte streams from our client into a valid RESP message.

Building a synchronous redis server

To make this example short and easy to follow, our Redis clone will implement a very small subset of the RESP protocol and will be able to process only SET and GET calls. We'll use the official redis-cli that comes with the official *Redis* package to make queries against our server. To use the redis-cli, we can install Redis on Ubuntu by running apt-get install redis-server.

Let's create a new project by running `cargo new rudis_sync` and adding the following dependencies in our `Cargo.toml` file:

```
rudis_sync/Cargo.toml

[dependencies]
lazy_static = "1.2.0"
resp = { git = "https://github.com/creativcoder/resp" }
```

We have named our project `rudis_sync`. We depend on two crates:

- `lazy_static`: We'll use this to store our in-memory database.
- `resp`: This is a forked crate that resides on my GitHub repository. We'll use this to parse the stream of bytes from the client.

To make the implementation easier to follow, `rudis_sync` has very minimal error-handling integration. When you are done experimenting with the code, you are encouraged to implement better error-handling strategies.

Let's start with the contents of our `main.rs` file:

```rust
// rudis_sync/src/main.rs

use lazy_static::lazy_static;
use resp::Decoder;
use std::collections::HashMap;
use std::env;
use std::io::{BufReader, Write};
use std::net::Shutdown;
use std::net::{TcpListener, TcpStream};
use std::sync::Mutex;
use std::thread;

mod commands;
use crate::commands::process_client_request;

type STORE = Mutex<HashMap<String, String>>;

lazy_static! {
    static ref RUDIS_DB: STORE = Mutex::new(HashMap::new());
}

fn main() {
    let addr = env::args()
        .skip(1)
        .next()
        .unwrap_or("127.0.0.1:6378".to_owned());
```

```
let listener = TcpListener::bind(&addr).unwrap();
println!("rudis_sync listening on {} ...", addr);

for stream in listener.incoming() {
    let stream = stream.unwrap();
    println!("New connection from: {:?}", stream);
    handle_client(stream);
}
}
```

We have a bunch of imports, followed by an in-memory RUDIS_DB hashmap that's declared in a lazy_static! block. We are using this as an in-memory database to store key and value pairs that are sent by clients. In our main function, we create a listening address in addr from the user-provided argument or use 127.0.0.1:6378 as the default. We then create a TcpListener instance by calling the associated bind method, passing the addr. This creates a TCP listening socket. Later, we call the incoming method on listener, which then returns an iterator of new client connections. For each client connection stream that is of the TcpStream type (a client socket), we call the handle_client function, passing in the stream.

In the same file, the handle_client function is responsible for parsing queries that are sent from the client, which would be one of the GET or SET queries:

```
// rudis_sync/src/main.rs

fn handle_client(stream: TcpStream) {
    let mut stream = BufReader::new(stream);
    let decoder = Decoder::new(&mut stream).decode();
    match decoder {
        Ok(v) => {
            let reply = process_client_request(v);
            stream.get_mut().write_all(&reply).unwrap();
        }
        Err(e) => {
            println!("Invalid command: {:?}", e);
            let _ = stream.get_mut().shutdown(Shutdown::Both);
        }
    };
}
```

The `handle_client` function receives the client `TcpStream` socket in the `stream` variable. We wrap our client `stream` in a `BufReader`, which is then passed as a mutable reference to the `Decoder::new` method from the `resp` crate. The `Decoder` reads bytes from the `stream` to create a RESP `Value` type. We then have a match block to check whether our decoding succeeded. If it fails, we print an error message and close the socket by calling `shutdown()` and requesting both the reader part and writer part of our client socket connection to be closed with the `Shutdown::Both` value. The `shutdown` method needs a mutable reference, so we call `get_mut()` before that. In a real-world implementation, you obviously need to handle this error gracefully.

If the decoding succeeds, we call `process_client_request`, which returns the `reply` to send back to the client. We write this `reply` to the client by calling `write_all` on the client `stream`. The `process_client_request` function is defined in `commands.rs` as follows:

```
// rudis_sync/src/commands.rs

use crate::RUDIS_DB;
use resp::Value;

pub fn process_client_request(decoded_msg: Value) -> Vec<u8> {
    let reply = if let Value::Array(v) = decoded_msg {
        match &v[0] {
            Value::Bulk(ref s) if s == "GET" || s == "get" =>
handle_get(v),
            Value::Bulk(ref s) if s == "SET" || s == "set" =>
handle_set(v),
            other => unimplemented!("{:?} is not supported as of now",
other),
        }
    } else {
        Err(Value::Error("Invalid Command".to_string()))
    };

    match reply {
        Ok(r) | Err(r) => r.encode(),
    }
}
```

This function takes the decoded `Value` and matches it on the parsed query. In our implementation, we expect the client to send an array of bulk strings, so we match on the `Value::Array` variant of `Value`, using `if let`, and store the array in v. If we match as an `Array` value in the `if` branch, we take that array and match on the first entry in v, which will be our command type, that is, GET or SET. This is again a `Value::Bulk` variant that wraps the command as a string.

We take the reference to the inner string as s and match only if the string has a GET or SET as a value. In the case of GET, we call handle_get, passing the v array, and in the case of SET, we call handle_set. In the else branch, we simply send a Value::Error reply to the client with invalid Command as the description.

The value that's returned by both branches is assigned to the reply variable. It is then matched for the inner type r and turned into Vec<u8> by invoking the encode method on it, which is then returned from the function.

Our handle_set and handle_get functions are defined in the same file as follows:

```
// rudis_sync/src/commands.rs

use crate::RUDIS_DB;
use resp::Value;

pub fn handle_get(v: Vec<Value>) -> Result<Value, Value> {
    let v = v.iter().skip(1).collect::<Vec<_>>();
    if v.is_empty() {
        return Err(Value::Error("Expected 1 argument for GET
command".to_string()))
    }
    let db_ref = RUDIS_DB.lock().unwrap();
    let reply = if let Value::Bulk(ref s) = &v[0] {
        db_ref.get(s).map(|e|
Value::Bulk(e.to_string())).unwrap_or(Value::Null)
    } else {
        Value::Null
    };
    Ok(reply)
}

pub fn handle_set(v: Vec<Value>) -> Result<Value, Value> {
    let v = v.iter().skip(1).collect::<Vec<_>>();
    if v.is_empty() || v.len() < 2 {
        return Err(Value::Error("Expected 2 arguments for SET
command".to_string()))
    }
    match (&v[0], &v[1]) {
        (Value::Bulk(k), Value::Bulk(v)) => {
            let _ = RUDIS_DB
                .lock()
                .unwrap()
                .insert(k.to_string(), v.to_string());
        }
        _ => unimplemented!("SET not implemented for {:?}", v),
    }
}
```

```
        Ok(Value::String("OK".to_string()))
    }
```

In `handle_get()`, we first check whether the GET command has no key present in the
query and fails with an error message. Next, we match on `v[0]`, which is the key for the
GET command, and check whether it exists in our database. If it exists, we wrap it
in `Value::Bulk` using the map combinator, otherwise we return a `Value::Null` reply:

```
        db_ref.get(s).map(|e| Value::Bulk(e.to_string())).unwrap_or(Value::Null)
```

We then store it in a `reply` variable and return it as a `Result` type, that is, `Ok(reply)`.

A similar thing happens in `handle_set`, where we bail out if we don't have enough
arguments to the SET command. Next, we match on our key and value using `&v[0]` and
`&v[1]` and insert it into `RUDIS_DB`. As an acknowledgement of the SET query., we reply
with `Ok`.

Back in our `process_client_request` function, once we create the reply bytes, we match
on the `Result` type and convert them into a `Vec<u8>` by calling `encode()`, which is then
written to the client. With that walk-through out of the way, it's time to test our client with
the official `redis-cli` tool. We'll run it by invoking `redis-cli -p 6378`:

```
→  rudis_sync git:(master) ✗ redis-cli -p 6378
127.0.0.1:6378> GET foo
(error) NIL
127.0.0.1:6378> SET foo bar
OK
127.0.0.1:6378> GET foo
"bar"
127.0.0.1:6378>
```

In the preceding session, we did a few GET and SET queries with an expected reply from
`rudis_sync`. Also, here's our output log from the `rudis_server` of our new
connection(s):

```
→  rudis_sync git:(master) ✗ cargo run
    Finished dev [unoptimized + debuginfo] target(s) in 0.01s
     Running `target/debug/rudis_sync`
rudis_sync server listening on 127.0.0.1:6378 ...
New client connnection from TcpStream { addr: V4(127.0.0.1:6378), peer: V4(127.0.0.1:49912), fd: 4 }
```

But the problem with our server is that we have to wait until the initial client has finished being served. To demonstrate this, we'll introduce a bit of delay in our `for` loop that handles new client connections:

```
for stream in listener.incoming() {
    let stream = stream.unwrap();
    println!("New connection from: {:?}", stream);
    handle_client(stream);
    thread::sleep(Duration::from_millis(3000));
}
```

The `sleep` call simulates a delay in request processing. To see the latencies, we'll start two clients at almost the same time, where one of them makes a `SET` request and the other one makes a `GET` request on the same key. Here's our first client, which does the `SET` request:

```
→  rudis_sync git:(master) ✗ redis-cli -p 6378
127.0.0.1:6378> SET foo bar
OK
127.0.0.1:6378>
```

Here's our second client, which does a `GET` request on the same key, `foo`:

```
→  rudis_sync git:(master) ✗ redis-cli -p 6378
127.0.0.1:6378> GET foo
"bar"
(2.51s)
127.0.0.1:6378>
```

As you can see, the second client had to wait for almost three seconds to get the second `GET` reply.

Due to its nature, the synchronous mode becomes a bottleneck when you need to process more than 100,000 (say) clients at the same time, with each client taking varying amounts of processing time. To get around this, you usually need to spawn a thread for handling each client connection. Whenever a new client connection is made, we spawn a new thread and offload the `handle_client` invocation from the main thread, allowing the main thread to accept other client connections. We can achieve this by using a single line change in our `main` function, like so:

```
for stream in listener.incoming() {
    let stream = stream.unwrap();
    println!("New connection from: {:?}", stream);
    thread::spawn(|| handle_client(stream));
}
```

This removes the blocking nature of our server, but introduces the overhead of spawning a new thread every time a new client connection is received. First, there is an overhead of spawning threads and, second, the context switch time between threads adds another overhead.

As we can see, our `rudis_sync` server works as expected. But it will soon be bottlenecked by the amount of threads our machine can handle. This threading model of handling connections worked well until the internet began gaining a wider audience and more and more clients connecting to the internet became the norm. Today, however, things are different and we need highly efficient servers that can handle millions of requests at the same time. It turns out that we can tackle the problem of handling more clients on a more foundational level, that is, by using non-blocking sockets. Let's explore them next.

Asynchronous network I/O

As we saw in our `rudis_sync` server implementation, the synchronous I/O model can be a major bottleneck in handling multiple clients in a given period of time. One has to use threads to process more clients. However, there's a better way to scale our server. Instead of coping with the blocking nature of sockets, we can make our sockets non-blocking. With non-blocking sockets, any read, write, or connect operation, on the socket will return immediately, regardless of whether the operation completed successfully or not, that is, they don't block the calling code if the read and write buffers are partially filled. This is the asynchronous I/O model as no client needs to wait for their request completion, and is instead notified later of the completion or failure of the request.

The asynchronous model is very efficient compared to threads, but it adds more complexity to our code. In this model, because an initial read or write call on the socket is unlikely to succeed, we need to retry the interested operation again at a later time. This process of retrying the operation on the socket is called polling. We need to poll the sockets from time to time to see if any of our read/write/connect operations can be completed and also maintain state on how many bytes we have read or written so far. With large number of incoming socket connections, using non-blocking sockets entails having to deal with polling and maintenance of state.This soon blows up as a complex state machine. In addition to that polling is a very in-efficient operation. Even if we don't have any events on our sockets. There are better approaches, though.

On Unix-based platforms, polling mechanism on sockets is done through `poll` and `select` system calls, which are available on all Unix platforms. Linux has a better `epoll` API in addition to them. Instead of polling the sockets by ourselves, which is an inefficient operation, these APIs can tell us when the socket is ready to read or write. Where poll and select run a for loop on each requested socket, `epoll` runs in `O(1)` to notify any interested party of a new socket event.

The asynchronous I/O model allows you to handle a considerably larger amount of sockets than would be possible with the synchronous model, because we are doing operations in small chunks and quickly switching to serving other clients. Another efficiency is that we don't need to spawn threads, as everything happens in a single thread.

To write asynchronous network applications with non-blocking sockets, we have several high quality crates in the Rust ecosystem.

Async abstractions in Rust

The async network I/O is advantageous, but programming them in their raw form is hard. Fortunately, Rust provides us with convenient abstractions in the form of third-party crates for working with asynchronous I/O. It alleviates the developer from most of the complex state machine handling when dealing with non-blocking sockets and the underlying socket polling mechanism. Two of the lower-layer abstractions that are available as crates are the `futures` and `mio` crates. Let's understand them in brief.

Mio

When working with non-blocking sockets, we need a way to check whether the socket is ready for the desired operation. The situation is worse when we have thousands, or more, sockets to manage. We can use the very inefficient way of running a loop, checking for the socket state, and performing the operation once it's ready. But there are better ways to do this. In Unix, we had the `poll` system call, to which you give the list of file descriptors you want to be monitored for events. It was then replaced by the `select` system call, which improved things a bit. However, both `select` and `poll` were not scalable as they were basically for loops under the hood and the iteration time went up linearly as more and more sockets were added to its monitor list.

Under Linux, then came `epoll`, which is the current and most efficient file descriptor multiplexing API. This is used by most network and I/O applications that want to do asynchronous I/O. Other platforms have similar abstractions, such as **kqueue** in macOS and BSD. On Windows, we have **IO Completion Ports (IOCP)**.

It is these low-level abstractions that `mio` abstracts over, providing a cross-platform, highly efficient interface to all of these I/O multiplexing APIs. Mio is quite a low-level library, but it provides a convenient way to set up a reactor for socket events. It provides the same kind of networking primitives such as the `TcpStream` type as the standard library does, but these are non-blocking by default.

Futures

Juggling with mio's socket polling state machine is not very convenient. To provide a higher-level API that can be used by application developers, we have the `futures` crate. The `futures` crate provides a trait named `Future`, which is the core component of the crate. A `future` represents the idea of a computation that is not immediately available, but might be available later. Let's look at its type signature of the `Future` trait to get more information about it:

```
pub trait Future {
    type Item;
    type Error;
    fn poll(&mut self) -> Poll<Self::Item, Self::Error>;
}
```

A `Future` is an associated type trait that defines two types: an `Item` type representing the value that the `Future` will resolve to and an `Error` type that specifies what error type the future will fail with. They are quite similar to the `Result` type in the standard library, but instead of getting the result right away, they don't compute the immediately.

A `Future` value on its own cannot be used to build asynchronous applications. You need some kind of reactor and an event loop to progress the future toward completion. By design, the only way to have them succeed with a value or fail with an error is to poll them. This operation is represented by the single require method known as `poll`. The method `poll` specifies what should be done to progress the future. A future can be composed of several things, chained one after another. To progress a future, we need a reactor and an event loop implementation, and that is provided by the `tokio` crate.

Tokio

Combining both of the above mentioned abstractions, and along a work stealing scheduler, event loop and a timer implementation we have the `tokio` crate, which provides a runtime for driving these futures to completion. With the `tokio` framework, you can spawn many futures and have them run concurrently.

The `tokio` crate was born to provide a go-to solution for building robust and high-performance asynchronous networking applications that are agnostic of the protocol, yet provides abstractions for general patterns that are common in all networking applications. The `tokio` crate is technically a runtime consisting of a thread pool, and event loop, and a reactor for I/O events based on mio. By runtime, we mean that every web application developed with tokio will have the mentioned components above running as part of the application.

Futures in the tokio framework run inside a task. A task is similar to a user space thread or a green thread. An executor is responsible for scheduling tasks for execution.

When a future does not have any data to resolve or is waiting for data to arrive at the socket in case of a `TcpStream` client read, it returns a `NotReady` status. But, in doing this it also needs to register interest with the reactor to be notified again of any new data on the server.

When a future is created, no work is performed. For the work defined by the future to happen, the future must be submitted to an executor. In tokio, tasks are user-level threads that can execute futures. In its implementation of the `poll` method, a task has to arrange itself to be polled later in case no progress can be made. For doing this it has to pass its task handler to the reactor thread. The reactor in case of Linux is mio the crate.

Building an asynchronous redis server

Now that we're familiar with the asynchronous I/O solutions that the Rust ecosystem provides, it's time to revisit our Redis server implementation. We'll port our `rudis_sync` server to the asynchronous version using the `tokio` and `futures` crates. As with any asynchronous code, using `futures` and `tokio` can be daunting at first, and it can take time getting used to its API. However, We'll try to make things easy to understand here. Let's start by creating our project by running `cargo new rudis_async` with the following dependencies in `Cargo.toml`:

```
# rudis_async/Cargo.toml

[dependencies]
tokio = "0.1.13"
futures = "0.1.25"
lazy_static = "1.2.0"
resp = { git = "https://github.com/creativcoder/resp" }
tokio-codec = "0.1.1"
bytes = "0.4.11"
```

We are using a bunch of crates here:

- `futures`: Provides a cleaner abstraction for dealing with async code
- `tokio`: Encapsulates mio and provides a runtime for running asynchronous code
- `lazy_static`: Allows us to create a dynamic global variable that can be mutated
- `resp`: A crate that can parse Redis protocol messages
- `tokio-codec`: This allows you to convert a stream of bytes from the network into a given type, which is parsed as a definite message according to the specified codec. A codec converts stream of bytes into a parsed message termed as a **Frame** in the tokio ecosystem.
- `bytes`: This is used with the tokio codec to efficiently convert a stream of bytes into a given *Frame*

Our initial code in `main.rs` follows a similar structure:

```
// rudis_async/src/main.rs

mod codec;
use crate::codec::RespCodec;

use lazy_static::lazy_static;
use std::collections::HashMap;
use std::net::SocketAddr;
use std::sync::Mutex;
use tokio::net::TcpListener;
use tokio::net::TcpStream;
use tokio::prelude::*;
use tokio_codec::Decoder;
use std::env;

mod commands;
use crate::commands::process_client_request;

lazy_static! {
    static ref RUDIS_DB: Mutex<HashMap<String, String>> =
Mutex::new(HashMap::new());
}
```

We have a bunch of imports and the same `RUDIS_DB` in a `lazy_static!` block. We then have our function `main`:

```
// rudis_async/main.rs

fn main() -> Result<(), Box<std::error::Error>> {
    let addr = env::args()
```

```
            .skip(1)
            .next()
            .unwrap_or("127.0.0.1:6378".to_owned());
    let addr = addr.parse::<SocketAddr>()?;

    let listener = TcpListener::bind(&addr)?;
    println!("rudis_async listening on: {}", addr);

    let server_future = listener
        .incoming()
        .map_err(|e| println!("failed to accept socket; error = {:?}", e))
        .for_each(handle_client);

    tokio::run(server_future);
    Ok(())
}
```

We parse the string that's been passed in as an argument or use a default address of
127.0.0.1:6378. We then create a new TcpListener instance with addr. This returns us
a future in listener. We then chain on this future by calling incoming on and invoke
for_each on it which takes in a closure and call handle_client on it. This future gets
stored as server_future.In the end, we call tokio::run passing in server_future.
This creates a main tokio task and schedules the future for execution.

In the same file, our handle_client function is defined like so:

```
// rudis_async/src/main.rs

fn handle_client(client: TcpStream) -> Result<(), ()> {
    let (tx, rx) = RespCodec.framed(client).split();
    let reply = rx.and_then(process_client_request);
    let task = tx.send_all(reply).then(|res| {
        if let Err(e) = res {
            eprintln!("failed to process connection; error = {:?}", e);
        }
        Ok(())
    });

    tokio::spawn(task);
    Ok(())
}
```

In `handle_client`, we first split our `TcpStream` into a writer (`tx`) and reader (`rx`) half by first converting the stream to a framed future calling framed on `RespCodec` receives the `client` connection and converts it into a framed future by calling framed on `RudisFrame`. Following that, we call `split` on it, which converts the frame into a `Stream` and `Sink` future, respectively. This simply gives us a `tx` and `rx` to read and write from the client socket. However, when we read this, we get the decoded message. When we write anything to `tx`, we write the encoded byte sequence.

On `rx`, we call `and_then` passing the `process_client_request` function, which will resolve the future to a decoded frame. We then take the writer half `tx`, and call `send_all` with the `reply`. We then spawn the future task by calling `tokio::spawn`.

In our `codec.rs` file, we have defined `RudisFrame`, which implements `Encoder` and `Decoder` traits from the `tokio-codec` crate:

```
// rudis_async/src/codec.rs

use std::io;
use bytes::BytesMut;
use tokio_codec::{Decoder, Encoder};
use resp::{Value, Decoder as RespDecoder};
use std::io::BufReader;
use std::str;

pub struct RespCodec;

impl Encoder for RespCodec {
    type Item = Vec<u8>;
    type Error = io::Error;

    fn encode(&mut self, msg: Vec<u8>, buf: &mut BytesMut) ->
io::Result<()> {
        buf.reserve(msg.len());
        buf.extend(msg);
        Ok(())
    }
}

impl Decoder for RespCodec {
    type Item = Value;
    type Error = io::Error;

    fn decode(&mut self, buf: &mut BytesMut) -> io::Result<Option<Value>> {
        let s = if let Some(n) = buf.iter().rposition(|b| *b == b'\n') {
            let client_query = buf.split_to(n + 1);
```

```
            match str::from_utf8(&client_query.as_ref()) {
                Ok(s) => s.to_string(),
                Err(_) => return Err(io::Error::new(io::ErrorKind::Other,
    "invalid string")),
            }
        } else {
            return Ok(None);
        };

        if let Ok(v) = RespDecoder::new(&mut
    BufReader::new(s.as_bytes())).decode() {
            Ok(Some(v))
        } else {
            Ok(None)
        }
    }
}
```

The `Decoder` implementation specify how to parse incoming bytes into a `resp::Value` type, whereas the `Encoder` trait specifies how to encode a `resp::Value` to a stream of bytes to the client.

Our `commands.rs` file implementation is the same as the previous one so we'll skip going through that. With that said, let's try our new server by running `cargo run`:

```
    Running `target/debug/rudis_async`
rudis_async listening on: 127.0.0.1:6378
```

With the official redis-cli client, we can connect to our server by running:

```
$ redis-cli -p 6378
```

Here's a session of running `redis-cli` against `rudis_async` server:

```
→  rudis_async git:(master) ✗ redis-cli -p 6378
127.0.0.1:6378> set foo bar
OK
127.0.0.1:6378> get foo
bar
```

Summary

Rust is very well-equipped and suitable for providing higher-performance, quality, and security for network applications. While built-in primitives are well-suited to a synchronous application model, for asynchronous I/O, Rust provides rich libraries with well-documented APIs that help you build high-performance applications.

In the next chapter, we'll step up the network protocol stack and and learn how to build web applications with Rust.

Building Web Applications with 13 Rust

In this chapter, we'll explore building web applications with Rust. We'll get to know the benefits of a static type system and the speed of a compiled language when building web applications with it. We'll also explore Rust's strongly typed HTTP libraries and build a URL shortener as an exercise. Following that, we'll look at a very popular framework called Actix-web and build a bookmark API server with it.

In this chapter, we will cover the following topics:

- Web applications in Rust
- Building a URL shortener with Hyper Crate
- The need for web frameworks
- Understanding the Actix-web framework
- Building an HTTP Rest API using Actix-web

Web applications in Rust

"The most important property of a program is whether it accomplishes the intention of its user."

– C. A. R. Hoare

It's rare for a low-level language to enable developers to write web applications with it while providing thekind of high-level ergonomics that dynamic languages do. With Rust, it's quite the opposite. Developing web applications with Rust is a similar experience one might expect from dynamic languages such as Ruby or Python, due to its high-level abstractions.

Web applications developed in dynamic languages can only get you so far though. A lot of developers find to what, as their code base reaches about a 100,000 lines of code, they start seeing the brittle nature of dynamic languages. With every small change you make, you need to have tests in place to let you know what parts of the application are affected. As the application grows, it becomes a whack-a-mole situation in terms of testing and updating.

Building web applications in a statically typed language such as Rust is another level of experience. Here, you get compile-time checks on your code, thus reducing the amount of unit tests you have to write by a large amount. You don't have the overhead of a language runtime such as an interpreter either, as is the case with dynamic languages that run a GC along with your application. Web applications written in a statically typed language can be compiled as a single static binary that can be deployed with minimal setup needed. Besides, you get speed and accuracy guarantees from the type system and there is a lot of help from the compiler during code refactoring. Rust gives you all of these guarantees, along with the same high-level feel of dynamic languages.

Web applications primarily sit on the application layer protocol and speak the HTTP protocol. HTTP is a stateless protocol where each message is either a request or a response from the client or the server. A message in the HTTP protocol consists of a header and a payload. The header provides context for the kind of HTTP message, such as its origin or the length of the payload, while the payload contains the actual data. HTTP is a text-based protocol, and we generally use libraries to do the hard work of parsing strings as proper HTTP messages. These libraries are further used to build high-level abstractions on top of them, such as a web framework.

To speak HTTP in Rust, we have the `hyper` crate, which we'll explore next.

Typed HTTP with Hyper

The **hyper** crate can parse HTTP messages, and has an elegant design with focus on strongly typed APIs. It is designed as a type-safe abstraction for raw HTTP requests, as opposed to a common theme in HTTP libraries: describing everything as strings. For example, HTTP status codes in Hyper are defined as enums, for example, the type `StatusCode`. The same goes for pretty much everything that can be strongly typed, such as HTTP methods, MIME types, HTTP headers, and so on.

Hyper has both client and server functionality split into separate modules. The client side allows you to build and make HTTP requests with a configurable request body, headers, and other low-level configurations. The server side allows you to open a listening socket and attach request handlers to it. However, it does not include any request route handler implementation – that is left to web frameworks. It is designed to be used as a foundational crate to build higher-level web frameworks. It uses the same `tokio` and `futures` async abstractions under the hood and thus is very performant.

At its core, Hyper has the concept `Service` trait concept:

```
pub trait Service {
    type ReqBody: Payload;
    type ResBody: Payload;
    type Error: Into<Box<dyn StdError + Send + Sync>>;
    type Future: Future<Item = Response<Self::ResBody>, Error =
Self::Error>;
    fn call(&mut self, req: Request<Self::ReqBody>) -> Self::Future;
}
```

The `Service` trait represents a type that handles HTTP requests that are sent from any client and returns a `Response`, which is a future. The core API of this trait that types need to implement is the `call` method, which takes in a `Request` that's parameterized over a generic type `Body` and returns a `Future` that resolves to a `Response`, which is parameterized over the associated type `ResBody`. We don't need to manually implement this trait, as hyper includes a bunch of factory methods that can implement the `Service` trait for you. You simply need to provide a function that takes HTTP requests and returns responses.

In the following section, we'll explore both the client and server APIs of hyper. Let's start by exploring the server APIs by building a URL shortener from scratch.

Hyper server APIs – building a URL shortener

In this section, we'll build a URL shortener server that exposes a `/shorten` endpoint. This endpoint accepts a `POST` request, with the body containing the URL to be shortened. Let's fire up a new project by running `cargo new hyperurl` with the following dependencies in `Cargo.toml`:

```
# hyperurl/Cargo.toml

[dependencies]
hyper = "0.12.17"
serde_json = "1.0.33"
```

```
futures = "0.1.25"
lazy_static = "1.2.0"
rust-crypto = "0.2.36"
log = "0.4"
pretty_env_logger = "0.3"
```

We'll name our URL shortening server, **hyperurl**. A URL shortener service is a service that provides the functionality to create a shorter URL for any given URL. When you have a really long URL, it becomes tedious to share it with someone. A lot of URL shortening services exist today, such as *bit.ly*. If you have used Twitter, users use short URL in tweets quite often, to save space.

Here's our initial implementation in `main.rs`:

```
// hyperurl/src/main.rs

use log::{info, error};
use std::env;

use hyper::Server;
use hyper::service::service_fn;

use hyper::rt::{self, Future};

mod shortener;
mod service;
use crate::service::url_service;

fn main() {
    env::set_var("RUST_LOG","hyperurl=info");
    pretty_env_logger::init();

    let addr = "127.0.0.1:3002".parse().unwrap();
    let server = Server::bind(&addr)
        .serve(|| service_fn(url_service))
        .map_err(|e| error!("server error: {}", e));
    info!("URL shortener listening on http://{}", addr);
    rt::run(server);
}
```

In main, we create a Server instance and bind it to our loopback address and port string "127.0.0.1:3002". This returns a builder instance on which we call serve before passing in the function url_service which implements the Service trait. The function url_service maps a Request to a future of Response. service_fn is a factory function that has the following signature:

```
pub fn service_fn<F, R, S>(f: F) -> ServiceFn<F, R> where
    F: Fn(Request<R>) -> S,
    S: IntoFuture,
```

As you can see, F needs to be a Fn closure that

Our function url_service implements the Service trait. Next, let's see the code in service.rs:

```rust
// hyperurl/src/service.rs

use std::sync::RwLock;
use std::collections::HashMap;
use std::sync::{Arc};
use std::str;
use hyper::Request;
use hyper::{Body, Response};
use hyper::rt::{Future, Stream};

use lazy_static::lazy_static;

use crate::shortener::shorten_url;

type UrlDb = Arc<RwLock<HashMap<String, String>>>;
type BoxFut = Box<Future<Item = Response<Body>, Error = hyper::Error> +
Send>;

lazy_static! {
    static ref SHORT_URLS: UrlDb = Arc::new(RwLock::new(HashMap::new()));
}

pub(crate) fn url_service(req: Request<Body>) -> BoxFut {
    let reply = req.into_body().concat2().map(move |chunk| {
        let c = chunk.iter().cloned().collect::<Vec<u8>>();
        let url_to_shorten = str::from_utf8(&c).unwrap();
        let shortened_url = shorten_url(url_to_shorten);
        SHORT_URLS.write().unwrap().insert(shortened_url,
url_to_shorten.to_string());
        let a = &*SHORT_URLS.read().unwrap();
        Response::new(Body::from(format!("{:#?}", a)))
    });
```

```
        Box::new(reply)
    }
```

This module exposes a single function `url_service`, which implements the `Service` trait. Our `url_scrvice` method implements the method `call` by taking in a req of the `Request<Body>` type and returns a future that is behind a `Box`.

Next, is our `shortener` module:

```
// hyperurl/src/shortener.rs

use crypto::digest::Digest;
use crypto::sha2::Sha256;

pub(crate) fn shorten_url(url: &str) -> String {
    let mut sha = Sha256::new();
    sha.input_str(url);
    let mut s = sha.result_str();
    s.truncate(5);
    format!("https://u.rl/{}", s)
}
```

Our `shorten_url` function takes in a URL to shorten as a `&str`. It then computes the SHA-256 hash of the URL and truncates it to a string of length five. This is obviously not how a real URL shortener works and is not a scalable solution either. However, it's fine for our demonstration purposes.

Let's take this for a spin:

```
     Running `target/debug/hyperurl`
 INFO  hyperurl > hyperurl is listening at 127.0.0.1:3002
```

Our server is running. At this point we can either send requests POST through curl. We'll do this the other way by building a command-line client for sending URLs to shorten this server.

While Hyper is recommended for complex HTTP applications, it's quite cumbersome every time to create a handler service, register it, and run it in a runtime. Often, for to build smaller tools such as a CLI application that needs to make a couple of GET requests, this becomes overkill. Fortunately, we have another opinionated wrapper over hyper called the `reqwest` crate. As the name suggests, it is inspired by Python's Requests library. We'll use this to build our hyperurl client that sends URL shorten requests.

hyper as a client – building a URL shortener client

Now that we have our URL shortener service ready, let's explore the client side of hyper. Although we can build a web UI that we can use for shortening URLs, we'll keep it simple and build a **Command-Line Interface (CLI)** tool. The CLI can be used to pass any URL that needs to be shortened. In response, we'll get back the shortened URL from our hyperurl server.

While hyper is recommended for building complex web applications, a lot of setup is involved every time you need to create a handler service, register it, and run it in a runtime instance. When building smaller tools, such as a CLI application that needs to make a few GET requests, all of these steps become overkill. Fortunately, we have a convenient wrapper crate over hyper called **reqwest** that abstracts hyper's client APIs. As the name suggests, it is inspired by Python's Requests library.

Let's create a new project by running `cargo new shorten` with the following dependencies in our `Cargo.toml` file:

```
# shorten/Cargo.toml

[dependencies]
quicli = "0.4"
structopt = "0.2"
reqwest = "0.9"
serde = "1"
```

To build the CLI tool, we'll use the `quicli` framework, which is a collection of high-quality crates that help build CLI tools. The `structopt` crate is used along with `quicli`, while the `serde` crate is used by the `structopt` crate for the derive macro. To make POST requests to our hyperurl server, we'll use the `reqwest` crate.

Our `main.rs` has the following code inside it:

```
// shorten/src/main.rs

use quicli::prelude::*;
use structopt::StructOpt;

const CONN_ADDR: &str = "127.0.0.1:3002";

/// This is a small CLI tool to shorten urls using the hyperurl
/// url shortening service
#[derive(Debug, StructOpt)]
struct Cli {
    /// The url to shorten
    #[structopt(long = "url", short = "u")]
    url: String,
    // Setting logging for this CLI tool
    #[structopt(flatten)]
    verbosity: Verbosity,
}

fn main() -> CliResult {
    let args = Cli::from_args();
    println!("Shortening: {}", args.url);
    let client = reqwest::Client::new();
    let mut res = client
        .post(&format!("http://{}/shorten", CONN_ADDR))
        .body(args.url)
        .send()?;
    let a: String = res.text().unwrap();
    println!("http://{}", a);
    Ok(())
}
```

With our hyperurl server still running, we'll open a new terminal window and invoke shorten with `cargo run -- --url https://rust-lang.org`:

```
  shorten git:(master) X cargo run -- --url https://rust-lang.org
    Finished dev [unoptimized + debuginfo] target(s) in 0.18s
      Running `target/debug/shorten --url 'https://rust-lang.org'`
Shortening: https://rust-lang.org
http://127.0.0.1:3002/abf27
```

Let's head over to a browser with the shortened URL, that is, `http://127.0.0.1:3002/abf27`:

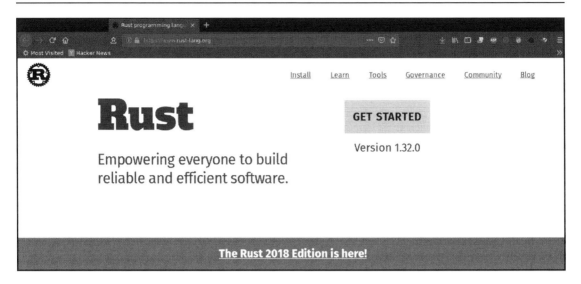

Having explored hyper, let's get a bit more high level. In the next section, we'll explore Actix-web, a fast web application framework based on the actor model implementation in the `actix` crate. But, first let's talk about why we need web frameworks.

Web frameworks

Before we begin exploring `actix-web`, we need to get some motivation as to why we need web frameworks in the first place. The web, as many of us know, is a complex, evolving space. There are lots of details to take care of when writing web applications. You need to set up routing rules and authentication policies. On top of that, as applications evolve, there are best practices and similar patterns that one will have to repeat implementing, if you're not using a web framework.

It's quite tedious having to reinvent these foundational attributes of web applications every time you want to build a web application yourself. A concrete example is when you are providing different routes in your application. In a web application built from scratch, you would have to parse the resource path from the request, do some matching on it, and act on the request. A web framework automates the matching of routes and route handlers by providing DSLs to allow you to configure routing rules in a cleaner way. Web frameworks also abstract all the best practices, common patterns, and idioms around building web applications, and give developers a head start, allowing them to focus on their business logic rather than reinventing solutions for problems that has already been solved.

The Rust community has seen a lot of web frameworks in the works, lately such as Tower, Tide, Rocket, `actix-web`, Gotham, and so on. At the time of writing this book, the most feature-rich and active frameworks are Rocket and `actix-web`. While Rocket is quite concise and a polished framework, it requires a nightly version of the Rust compiler. This restriction will soon be removed, though, as the APIs that Rocket depends on get stabilized. Its direct competitor at the moment is `actix-web`, which runs on stable Rust and is quite close to the ergonomics that are provided by the Rocket framework. We will be covering `actix-web` next.

Actix-web basics

The Actix-web framework builds upon the actor model that's implemented by the actix crate, which we already covered in `Chapter 7`, *Advanced Concepts*. Actix-web advertises itself as a small, fast, and pragmatic HTTP web framework. It's primarily an asynchronous framework that relies internally on tokio and the futures crate but also provides a synchronous API and both of these APIs can be composed together seamlessly.

The entry point of any web application written using `actix-web` is the `App` struct. On an `App` instance, we can configure various route handlers and middlewares. We can also initialize our `App` with any state that we need to maintain across a request response. The route handlers that are provided on `App` implement the `Handler` trait and are simply functions that map a request to a response. They can also include request filters, which can forbid access to a particular route based on a predicate.

Actix-web internally spawns a number of worker threads, each with its own tokio runtime.

That's the basics out of the way, so let's dive right in, and go through the implementation of a REST API server using Actix-web.

Building a bookmarks API using Actix-web

We'll create a REST API server that allows you to store bookmarks and links to any blog or website that you wish to read later. We'll name our server `linksnap`. Let's create a new project by running `cargo new linksnap`. In this implementation, we won't be using a database for persistence for any link that is sent to our API, and will simply use an in-memory `HashMap` to store our entries. This means that every time our server restarts, all of the stored bookmarks will get removed.

Under the `linksnap/` directory, we have the following contents in `Cargo.toml`:

```
# linksnap/Cargo.toml

[dependencies]
actix = "0.7"
actix-web = "0.7"
futures = "0.1"
env_logger = "0.5"
bytes = "0.4"
serde = "1.0.80"
serde_json = "1.0.33"
serde_derive = "1.0.80"
url = "1.7.2"
log = "0.4.6"
chrono = "0.4.6"
```

We'll implement the following endpoints in our API server:

- `/links` is a GET method that retrieves a list of all links stored on the server.
- `/add` is a POST method that stores an entry of the link and returns a type `LinkId` as a response. This can be used to remove the link from the server.
- `/rm` is a DELETE method that removes a link with a given `LinkId`.

We have divided our server implementation into three modules:

- `links`: This module provides the `Links` and `Link` types, which represent a collection of links and a link, respectively
- `route_handlers`: This module contains all of our route handlers
- `state`: This module contains the implementation of an actor and all the messages it can receive on our `Db` struct.

An example flow of our app from the user request to the actor goes like this on the /links endpoint:

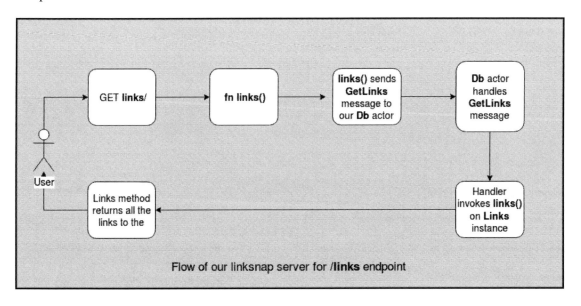

Flow of our linksnap server for **/links** endpoint

Let's go through the implementation, starting by looking at the contents in main.rs:

```
// linksnap/src/main.rs

mod links;
mod route_handlers;
mod state;

use std::env;
use log::info;
use crate::state::State;
use crate::route_handlers::{index, links, add_link, rm_link};
use actix_web::middleware::Logger;
use actix_web::{http, server, App};

fn init_env() {
    env::set_var("RUST_LOG", "linksnap=info");
    env::set_var("RUST_BACKTRACE", "1");
    env_logger::init();
    info!("Starting http server: 127.0.0.1:8080");
}

fn main() {
```

```
init_env();
let system = actix::System::new("linksnap");
let state = State::init();

let web_app = move || {
    App::with_state(state.clone())
        .middleware(Logger::default())
        .route("/", http::Method::GET, index)
        .route("/links", http::Method::GET, links)
        .route("/add", http::Method::POST, add_link)
        .route("/rm", http::Method::DELETE, rm_link)
};

server::new(web_app).bind("127.0.0.1:8080").unwrap().start();
let _ = system.run();
}
```

In main, we first call init_env, which sets up our environment for getting logs from the server, turns on the RUST_BACKTRACE variable for printing a detailed trace of any error, and initializes our logger by invoking env_logger::init().We then create our System actor which is the parent actor for all actors in the actor model. We then create our server state by calling State::init() and store it in state. This encapsulates our in-memory database actor type Db in state.rs. We'll go through this later.

We then create our App instance within a closure by calling App::with_state, thereby passing in our clone of our application state. The clone call on state is important here, as we need to have a single shared state across multiple actix worker threads. Actix-web internally spawns multiple threads with new App instances to handle requests, and each invocation of this state will have its own copy of the application state. If we don't share a reference to a single source of truth, then each App will have its own copy of the HashMap entries, which we don't want.

Next, we chain on our App with the method middleware by passing in a Logger. This will log any requests when a client hits one of our provisioned endpoints. We then add a bunch of route method calls. The route method takes an HTTP path as a string, an HTTP method, and a handler function that maps an HttpRequest to a HttpResponse. We'll explore handler functions later.

With our App instance configured and stored in web_app, we pass it to server::new(), followed by binding it to the address string "127.0.0.1:8080". We then call start to start the app in a new Arbiter instance, which is simply a new thread. According to actix, an Arbiter is a thread where actors are run and can access the event loop. Finally, we run our system actor by calling system.run(). The run method internally spins up a tokio runtime and starts all the arbiter threads.

Next, let's look at our route handlers in `route_handlers.rs`. This module defines all kinds of routes that are available in our server implementation:

```
// linksnap/src/route_handlers.rs

use actix_web::{Error, HttpRequest, HttpResponse};

use crate::state::{AddLink, GetLinks, RmLink};
use crate::State;
use actix_web::AsyncResponder;
use actix_web::FromRequest;
use actix_web::HttpMessage;
use actix_web::Query;
use futures::Future;

type ResponseFuture = Box<Future<Item = HttpResponse, Error = Error>>;

macro_rules! server_err {
    ($msg:expr) => {
        Err(actix_web::error::ErrorInternalServerError($msg))
    };
}
```

First, we have a bunch of imports followed by a couple of helper types defined. `ResponseFuture` is a convenient type alias for a boxed `Future` which resolves to an `HttpResponse`. We then have a helper macro named `server_err!`, which returns an `actix_web::error` type with the given description. We use this macro as a convenient way to return error whenver any of our client request processing fails.

Next, we have our simplest router handler for handling get requests on the / endpoint:

```
linksnap/src/route_handlers.rs

pub fn index(_req: HttpRequest<State>) -> HttpResponse {
    HttpResponse::from("Welcome to Linksnap API server")
}
```

The `index` function takes an `HttpRequest` and simply returns a `HttpResponse` constructed from a string. The `HttpRequest` type can be parameterized over any type. By default, it is a `()`. For our route handlers, we have parameterized it over our `State` type. This `State` encapsulates our in-memory database, which is implemented as an actor. `State` is a wrapper over `Addr<Db>`, which is an address to our `Db` actor.

This is a reference to our in-memory database. We'll use this to send messages to our in-memory database to insert, remove, or get links. We'll explore those APIs later. Let's look at some other handlers that are in the same file:

```
// linksnap/src/route_handlers.rs

pub fn add_link(req: HttpRequest<State>) -> ResponseFuture {
    req.json()
        .from_err()
        .and_then(move |link: AddLink| {
            let state = req.state().get();
            state.send(link).from_err().and_then(|e| match e {
                Ok(_) => Ok(HttpResponse::Ok().finish()),
                Err(_) => server_err!("Failed to add link"),
            })
        })
        .responder()
}
```

Our `add_link` function handles `POST` requests for adding a link. This handler expects a JSON body of this format:

```
{
    title: "Title of the link or bookmark",
    url: "The URL of the link"
}
```

In this function, we first get the request body as JSON by calling `req.json()`. This returns a future. We then map any error originated from the json method to an actix compatible error using the `from_err` method. The `json` method can extract typed information from a request's payload, thereby returning a `JsonBody<T>` future. This `T` is inferred by the next method chain `and_then` as `AddLink` where we take the parsed value and send it to our `Db` actor. Sending a message to our actor can fail, so if this happens, we again match on the returned value. In the case of `Ok`, we reply with an empty HTTP response of success, otherwise we fail with our `server_err!` macro passing in an error description.

Next, we have our `"/links"` endpoint:

```
// linksnap/src/route_handlers.rs

pub fn links(req: HttpRequest<State>) -> ResponseFuture {
    let state = &req.state().get();
    state
        .send(GetLinks)
        .from_err()
        .and_then(|res| match res {
```

```
            Ok(res) => Ok(HttpResponse::Ok().body(res)),
            Err(_) => server_err!("Failed to retrieve links"),
        })
        .responder()
    }
```

The `links` handler simply sends a `GetLinks` message to the `Db` actor and returns the received response before sending it back to the client using the `body` method. We then have our `rm_link` handler, which is defined as follows:

```
// linksnap/src/route_handlers.rs

pub fn rm_link(req: HttpRequest<State>) -> ResponseFuture {
    let params: Query<RmLink> = Query::extract(&req).unwrap();
    let state = &req.state().get();
    state
        .send(RmLink { id: params.id })
        .from_err()
        .and_then(|e| match e {
            Ok(e) => Ok(HttpResponse::Ok().body(format!("{}", e))),
            Err(_) => server_err!("Failed to remove link"),
        })
        .responder()
    }
```

To remove a link, we need to pass the link ID (an `i32`) as a query parameter. The `rm_link` method extracts the query parameters into a `RmLink` type using the convenient `Query::extract` method, which takes in the `HttpRequest` instance. Next, we get a reference to our `Db` actor and send an `RmLink` message to it with the ID. We return the reply as a string by constructing the `HttpRespnse` with the `body` method.

Here's our `State` and `Db` types in `state.rs`:

```
// linksnap/src/state.rs

use actix::Actor;
use actix::SyncContext;
use actix::Message;
use actix::Handler;
use actix_web::{error, Error};
use std::sync::{Arc, Mutex};
use crate::links::Links;
use actix::Addr;
use serde_derive::{Serialize, Deserialize};
use actix::SyncArbiter;

const DB_THREADS: usize = 3;
```

```
#[derive(Clone)]
pub struct Db {
    pub inner: Arc<Mutex<Links>>
}

impl Db {
    pub fn new(s: Arc<Mutex<Links>>) -> Db {
        Db { inner: s }
    }
}

impl Actor for Db {
    type Context = SyncContext<Self>;
}

#[derive(Clone)]
pub struct State {
    pub inner: Addr<Db>
}

impl State {
    pub fn init() -> Self {
        let state = Arc::new(Mutex::new(Links::new()));
        let state = SyncArbiter::start(DB_THREADS, move ||
Db::new(state.clone()));
        let state = State {
            inner: state
        };
        state
    }

    pub fn get(&self) -> &Addr<Db> {
        &self.inner
    }
}
```

First, we have set our DB_THREADS to a value of 3 which we have chosen arbitrarily. We'll have a thread pool through which we'll be making requests to the in-memory database.

Next, we have the `Db` struct definition that wraps the `Links` type in a thread safe wrapper of `Arc<Mutex<Links>`. We then implement the `Actor` trait on it, where in we specify the associated type `Context` as `SyncContext<Self>`.

We then have a `State` struct definition which is a `Addr<Db>`, i.e., a handle to an instance of the `Db` actor. We also have two methods on State - `init` which creates a new `State` instance and `get` which returns a reference to the handle to the `Db` actor.

Next, we have a bunch of message types that will be sent to our `Db` actor. Our `Db` is an actor and will receive three messages:

GetLinks: This is sent by the `/links` route handler to retrieve all links stored on the server. It is defined as follows:

```
// linksnap/src/state.rs

pub struct GetLinks;

impl Message for GetLinks {
    type Result = Result<String, Error>;
}

impl Handler<GetLinks> for Db {
    type Result = Result<String, Error>;
    fn handle(&mut self, _new_link: GetLinks, _: &mut Self::Context) ->
Self::Result {
        Ok(self.inner.lock().unwrap().links())
    }
}
```

First is the `GetLinks` message, which is sent to the `Db` actor from the `/links` route handler. To make this an actor message, we'll implement the `Message` trait for it. The `Message` trait defines an associated type `Result`, which is the type returned from the handler of the message. Next, we implement the `Handler` trait that is parameterized over the message `GetLinks` for the `Db` actor.

```
// linksnap/src/state.rs

pub struct GetLinks;

impl Message for GetLinks {
    type Result = Result<String, Error>;
}

impl Handler<GetLinks> for Db {
    type Result = Result<String, Error>;
```

```
        fn handle(&mut self, _new_link: GetLinks, _: &mut Self::Context) ->
    Self::Result {
            Ok(self.inner.lock().unwrap().links())
        }
    }
```

We implement the `Message` trait for it, which returns the string of all the links as the response.

AddLink: This is sent by the `/add` route handler on any new link that's sent by the client. It is defined as follows:

```
// linksnap/src/state.rs

#[derive(Debug, Serialize, Deserialize)]
pub struct AddLink {
    pub title: String,
    pub url: String
}

impl Message for AddLink {
    type Result = Result<(), Error>;
}

impl Handler<AddLink> for Db {
    type Result = Result<(), Error>;

    fn handle(&mut self, new_link: AddLink, _: &mut Self::Context) ->
    Self::Result {
        let mut db_ref = self.inner.lock().unwrap();
        db_ref.add_link(new_link);
        Ok(())
    }
}
```

Th `AddLink` type performs a double duty. With the `Serialize` and `Deserialize` traits implemented, it acts as a type that can be extracted from the incoming json response body in the `add_link` route. Second, it also implements the `Message` trait, which we can send to our `Db` actor.

RmLink: This is sent by the `/rm` route handler. It is defined as follows:

```
// linksnap/src/state.rs

#[derive(Serialize, Deserialize)]
pub struct RmLink {
    pub id: LinkId,
```

```
}

impl Message for RmLink {
    type Result = Result<usize, Error>;
}

impl Handler<RmLink> for Db {
    type Result = Result<usize, Error>;
    fn handle(&mut self, link: RmLink, _: &mut Self::Context) ->
Self::Result {
        let db_ref = self.get_conn()?;
        Link::rm_link(link.id, db_ref.deref())
            .map_err(|_| error::ErrorInternalServerError("Failed to remove
links"))
    }
}
```

This is the message sent when one wants to remove a link entry. It takes the RmLink message and forwards it

We can insert a link with the following curl command:

```
curl --header "Content-Type: application/json" \
  --request POST \
  --data '{"title":"rust blog","url":"https://rust-lang.org"}' \
  127.0.0.1:8080/add
```

To view the inserted links, we can issue:

```
curl 127.0.0.1:8080/links
```

To remove a link, given its Id, we can send a DELETE request using curl as:

```
curl -X DELETE 127.0.0.1:8080/rm?id=1
```

Summary

In this chapter, we explored a lot about building web applications with Rust and how easy it is to get started, given the high-quality crates that are available to us. Being a compiled language, web applications written in Rust are many times smaller than other frameworks that are written in dynamic languages. Most of the web framework space is dominated by interpreted dynamic languages that can hog a lot of CPU but aren't very resource-efficient. However, people use them because web applications are very convenient to write with them.

Web applications that are written with Rust take up a lot less space at runtime. Rust also takes up less memory during runtime, as no interpreter is needed, as is the case with dynamic languages. With Rust, you get the best of both worlds, that is, the same feel of dynamic languages while at the same time being performant, like C. This is a great deal for the web.

In the next chapter, we'll dive deeper into lists.

14
Lists, Lists, and More Lists

Lists are everywhere: shopping lists, to-do lists, recipes, street numbers in western countries... simply everywhere. Their defining characteristic, storing things in a linear, defined relationship with each other, helps us keep track of stuff and find it again later on. From a data structure perspective, they are also essential to almost any program and come in various shapes and forms. While some lists are tricky to implement in Rust, the general principles can be found here as well, along with some valuable lessons on the borrow checker! After this chapter, we want you to know more about the following:

- (Doubly) linked lists and when you should use them
- Array lists, better known as Rust's vector
- Skip lists and, ideally, the New York metro subway system
- Implementing a simple transaction log

 As a final note, this chapter will build *safe* implementations of various lists, even though unsafe versions could be faster and require less code. This decision is due to the fact that, when working on regular use cases, unsafe is almost never a solution. Check out the links in the *Further reading* section of this chapter for unsafe lists.

Linked lists

To keep track of a bunch of items, there is a simple solution: with each entry in the list, store a pointer to the next entry. If there is no next item, store null/nil/None and so on, and keep a pointer to the first item. This is called a **singly linked list**, where each item is connected with a single link to the next, as shown in the following diagram—but you already knew that:

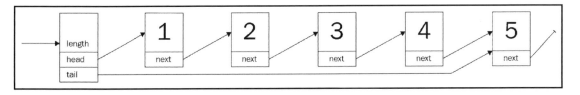

What are the real use cases for a linked list though? Doesn't everyone just use a dynamic array for everything?

Consider a transaction log, a typical append-only structure. Any new command (such as a SQL statement) is simply appended to the existing chain and is eventually written to a persistent storage. Thus, the initial requirements are simple:

- Append a command to an existing list
- Replay every command from the beginning to the end—in that order

In other words, its a queue (or **LIFO**—short for **Last In First Out**) structure.

A transaction log

First, a list has to be defined—in Rust, lacking a null type, each item is chained to the next by an Option property. The Option instances are enumerations that wrap either the value, in this case a heap reference (such as a Box, Rc, and so on), or none—Rust's typed null equivalent. Why? Let's find out!

Creating a prototypical implementation to explore a certain aspect is always a good idea, especially since the compiler often provides excellent feedback. Accordingly, an implementation of an integer list is the first step. How about this struct for each list element?

Have a look at the following code snippet:

```
struct Node {
    value: i32,
    next: Option<Node>
}
```

For practical considerations, it needs a way to know where to start and the length of the list. Considering the planned `append` operation, a reference to the end (tail) would be useful too:

```
struct TransactionLog {
    head: Option<Node>,
    tail: Option<Node>,
    pub length: u64
}
```

That looks great! Does it work though?

```
error[E0072]: recursive type `Node` has infinite size
  --> ch4/src/lib.rs:5:1
   |
5  | struct Node {
   | ^^^^^^^^^^^^^ recursive type has infinite size
6  | value: i32,
7  | next: Option<Node>
   | ------------------ recursive without indirection
   |
   = help: insert indirection (e.g., a `Box`, `Rc`, or `&`) at some point to
make `Node` representable
```

Unfortunately, it doesn't work—and, thinking back to the previous chapters, it becomes clear why: the compiler cannot be certain of the data structure's size, since the entire list would have to be nested into the first element. However, as we know, the compiler cannot compute and therefore allocate the required amount of memory this way—which is why reference types are required.

Reference types (such as `Box`, `Rc`, and so on) are a good fit, since they allocate space on the heap and therefore allow for larger lists. Here's an updated version:

```
use std::cell::RefCell;
use std::rc::Rc;

struct Node {
    value: i32,
    next: Option<Rc<RefCell<Node>>>
}
```

```
struct TransactionLog {
    head: Option<Rc<RefCell<Node>>>,
    tail: Option<Rc<RefCell<Node>>>,
    pub length: u64
}
```

Storing each node item in a `Rc<RefCell<T>>` provides the ability to retrieve and replace data as needed (the internal mutability pattern)—crucial when executing operations on the list. Another good practice is to alias types, especially if there are a lot of generics in play. This makes it easy to replace type implementations and provides a more readable definition:

```
type SingleLink = Option<Rc<RefCell<Node>>>;

#[derive(Clone)]
struct Node {
    value: i32,
    next: SingleLink,
}
```

Perfect! This is the base definition of the transaction log, but to use it there are many things missing. First of all, the value type has to be `String`:

```
#[derive(Clone)]
struct Node {
    value: String,
    next: SingleLink,
}

impl Node {
    // A nice and short way of creating a new node
    fn new(value: String) -> Rc<RefCell<Node>> {
        Rc::new(RefCell::new(Node {
            value: value,
            next: None,
        }))
    }
}
```

In addition to that, it is going to be useful to create an empty list, so the `impl` block of the list has a single function for now—`new_empty()`:

```
impl TransactionLog {
    pub fn new_empty() -> TransactionLog {
        TransactionLog { head: None, tail: None, length: 0 }
```

```
        }
    }
```

Still, there is a lot missing. To recap, the transaction log has two requirements:

- `Append` entries at the end
- `Remove` entries from the front

Let's start with the first requirement: appending items to the back of the list!

Adding entries

The transaction log can now be created and hold entries, but there is no way to add anything to the list. Typically, a list has the ability to add elements to either end—as long as there is a pointer to that end. If that was not the case, any operation would become computationally expensive, since every item has to be looked at to find its successor. With a pointer to the end (tail) of the list, this won't be the case for the append operation; however, to access a random index on the list, it would require some time to go through everything.

Naming is—especially if English is your second language—often tricky. Operations have different names by the language or library used. For example, common names for adding items to a list include `push` (can add to the front or back), `push_back`, `add`, `insert` (usually comes with a positional parameter), or `append`. On top of being able to guess method names, some imply completely different processes than others! If you design an interface or library, find the most descriptive and simple name possible and reuse whenever you can!

This is one of the things that a linked list does really well—adding items to either end. There are a few critical things that should not be overlooked, though:

- Creating the `Node` object within the method makes for a nicer API and better ownership handling.
- Edge cases such as empty lists.
- Incrementing the length is a good idea.
- The `RefCell` is used to retrieve mutable ownership for setting a new successor using its `borrow_mut()` function (interior mutability).

Once that is thought of, the actual implementation is not too bad. Rust's `Option` type offers a method to retrieve ownership of a value it contains, replacing it with `None` (see also the documentations for `Option.take()`—https://doc.rust-lang.org/std/option/enum.Option.html#method.take and `mem::replace()`—https://doc.rust-lang.org/stable/std/mem/fn.replace.html), which conveniently shortens the code required to append a new node:

```
pub fn append(&mut self, value: String) {
    let new = Node::new(value);
    match self.tail.take() {
        Some(old) => old.borrow_mut().next = Some(new.clone()),
        None => self.head = Some(new.clone())
    };
    self.length += 1;
    self.tail = Some(new);
}
```

With that, it's now possible to create a log of any string commands passing through. However, there is something important missing here as well: log replay.

Log replay

Typically in databases, transaction logs are a resilience measure if something bad happens that the database must be restored—or to keep a replica up to date. The principle is fairly simple: the log represents a timeline of commands that have been executed in this exact order. Thus, to recreate that final state of a database, it is necessary to start with the oldest entry and apply every transaction that follows in that very order.

You may have caught how that fits the capabilities of a linked list nicely. So, what is missing from the current implementation?

The ability to remove elements starting at the front.

Since the entire data structure resembles a queue, this function is going to be called `pop`, as it's the typical name for this kind of operation. Additionally, `pop` will consume the item that was returned, making the list a single-use structure. This makes sense, to avoid replaying anything twice!

This looks a lot more complex than it is: the interior mutability pattern certainly adds complexity to the implementation. However, it makes the whole thing safe—thanks to RefCells checking borrowing rules at runtime. This also leads to the chain of functions in the last part—it retrieves the value from within its wrappers:

```
pub fn pop(&mut self) -> Option<String> {
    self.head.take().map(|head| {
        if let Some(next) = head.borrow_mut().next.take() {
            self.head = Some(next);
        } else {
            self.tail.take();
        }
        self.length -= 1;
        Rc::try_unwrap(head)
            .ok()
            .expect("Something is terribly wrong")
            .into_inner()
            .value
    })
}
```

Calling this function in sequence returns the commands in the order they were inserted, providing a nice replay feature. For a real-world usage, it's important to provide the ability to serialize this state to disk as well, especially since this operation consumes the list entirely. Additionally, handling errors gracefully (instead of panicking and crashing) is recommended.

After use

Whenever the list needs to be disposed of, Rust calls a drop() method that is automatically implemented. However, since this is an automated process, each member is dropped recursively—which works OK until the level of nested next pointers exceeds the stack for executing the drop() method and crashes the program with an unexpected stack overflow message.

As a consequence, it is a good idea for production usage to also implement the Drop trait and dispose of the list elements iteratively. By the way, a stack overflow also happens while using the derived Debug implementation to print a Node—for the same reason.

Wrap up

A (transaction) log is a great use case for a linked list: They often grow to unexpected sizes, and indexing is not required. While a linked list is often a very simple type in other languages, it harbors a surprising amount of challenges in Rust. This is mostly due to the borrowing and ownership concepts which require a programmer to think about what goes where in great detail. For real-world use cases, however, it's better to use Rust's standard library linked list (`std::collections::LinkedList`). From a performance perspective, finding a particular item in the singly linked list requires looking at the entire list in the worst case, resulting in a runtime complexity of `O(n)`, with n being the number of items in the list (more on the topic of runtime complexity in `Chapter 18`, *Algorithm Evaluation*).

Upsides

The main benefits of a linked list are the abilities to grow very large in size cheaply, always maintain a certain direction, and allow to access items individually. What makes this data structure unique?

There are a few points:

- Low overhead allocation per item.
- Item count is only limited by heap memory.
- Mutation while iterating is possible.
- A direction is strictly enforced—there is no going back.
- Implementation is fairly simple (even in Rust).
- Efficient append, prepend, delete, and insert operations—compared to an array (no shifting required).

Generally, the linked list performs well in an environment where limited memory does not allow overhead allocation (as dynamic arrays do), or as a basis for an exotic lock-free data structure.

Downsides

The linked list has some obvious shortcomings:

- Indexing is inefficient, since every node has to be looked at.
- Iteration in general involves a lot of jumping around on the heap, which takes more time and makes the operation hard to cache.
- Reversing a list is *very* inefficient.

The last point is important, so, commonly, a linked-list implementation will have a link back as well, which makes it a doubly linked list.

Doubly linked list

The transaction log of the previous section is due for an upgrade. The product team wants to enable users to be able to examine the log by going through it **forward and backward** to see what each step does. This is bad news for the regular linked list, as it's really inefficient to go anywhere other than forward. So, how is this rectified?

It is rectified using the doubly linked list. The doubly linked list introduces the link `back`. While this sounds like a minor change, it allows to work on that list backward as well as forward, which significantly improves the ability to look up items. By augmenting the previous singly linked list item with a back pointer, the doubly linked list is almost created:

```
#[derive(Debug, Clone)]
struct Node {
    value: String,
    next: Link,
    prev: Link,
}

type Link = Option<Rc<RefCell<Node>>>;

#[derive(Debug, Clone)]
pub struct BetterTransactionLog {
    head: Link,
    tail: Link,
    pub length: u64,
}
```

Similar to the singly linked list, the list itself only consists of a head and a tail pointer, which makes accessing either end of the list cheap and easy. Additionally, the nodes now also feature a pointer back to the preceding node, making the list look like this:

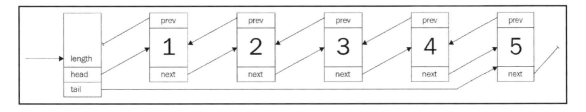

This is also the point that makes the doubly linked list tricky in Rust. The ownership principle is great if there is a hierarchy of ownership: a customer has an address, a text file has several lines of text, and so on. However, a node in a doubly linked list doesn't have clear ownership of either of its neighbors.

A better transaction log

So, the list of requirements got expanded:

- Move forward through the log
- Move backward through the log
- Moves don't consume the log

A nice fit for the doubly linked list, so the existing transaction log can be upgraded! With the pointers to both neighbors of a node, it can solve the problem. However, what about moving through the list without removing elements?

For that, another concept is required: **iterators**. Rust's iterators are leaning on the functional side of programming and provide a versatile interface for integrating with all kinds of other data structures and commands across the language. For example, `for` loops will pick up on the iterator and behave as expected.

 Iterators are pointers to the current item with a method called `next()` that produces the next item while moving the pointer forward! This concept is applied a lot when using a more functional approach to working with collections: by chaining them together and applying a function after invoking `next()`, going through a list can be very efficient. Check the *Further reading* section and the last chapter of this book for more information!

The data model is going to look like the singly linked list, so most of the operations can be used as they are—they only need to be upgraded to work with the back-pointer as well.

Examining the log

Looking at the list without consuming it is an iterator's job (see the info box), which—in Rust as well as in most other languages—is a simple implementation of an interface or trait. In fact, this is so common that the Rust docs have a great article (`https://doc.rust-lang.org/std/iter/index.html#implementing-iterator`), which is exactly what's required.

Since we are already working with heap references, the iterator can simply save an optional reference to a node and it's easy to move it forward and backward:

```
pub struct ListIterator {
    current: Link,
}

impl ListIterator {
    fn new(start_at: Link) -> ListIterator {
        ListIterator {
            current: start_at,
        }
    }
}
```

As the documentation states, a `for` loop uses two traits: `Iterator` and `IntoIterator`. Implementing the former is usually a good idea, as it provides access to the powerful methods in `Iterator`, such as `map`, `fold`, and so on, and nicely chains together with other—compatible—iterators:

```
impl Iterator for ListIterator {
    type Item = String;
    fn next(&mut self) -> Option<String> {
        let current = &self.current;
        let mut result = None;
        self.current = match current {
            Some(ref current) => {
                let current = current.borrow();
                result = Some(current.value.clone());
                current.next.clone()
            },
            None => None
        };
        result
    }
}
```

This iterator is responsible for moving one direction: forward. How can we walk back too?

Reverse

Now, since the requirement was also to go back, the iterator needs to go both ways. One easy way is to simply add a function to the structure that is called `reverse()`, but that would not integrate well and would require developers to read up on this API, and it creates additional work, since the forward/backward iterators are separate.

Rust's standard library offers an interesting concept for this: `DoubleEndedIterator`. Implementing this trait will provide the ability to reverse an iterator in a standardized way by offering a `next_back()` function to get the previous value—with the doubly linked list, this is only a matter of which property gets set to the current item! Therefore, both iterators share a large chunk of the code:

```
impl DoubleEndedIterator for ListIterator {
    fn next_back(&mut self) -> Option<String> {
        let current = &self.current;
        let mut result = None;
        self.current = match current {
            Some(ref current) => {
                let current = current.borrow();
                result = Some(current.value.clone());
                current.prev.clone()
            },
            None => None
        };
        result
    }
}
```

With this in place, an iterator can be created by calling the `iter()` function on the list type, and by calling `iter().rev()`, the iterator will be reversed, providing the ability to go back as well as forward.

Wrap up

Doubly linked lists are in many cases improved versions (and the default) over regular linked lists, thanks to the better flexibility at the cost of a single pointer per node and slightly more complex operations.

In particular, by keeping the code safe (in Rust terms, so no `unsafe {}` was used), the code gets riddled with `RefCells` and `borrow()` to create a data structure that the borrow checker is auditing at runtime. Looking at the Rust source code for `LinkedList`, this is not the case there (more on that in `Chapter 17`, *Collections in Rust*). The basic structure is similar, but the operations use a bunch of unsafe code underneath—something that requires a good experience writing Rust.

 `PhantomData<T>` is a zero-size type that informs the compiler about a range of things, such as drop behavior, sizes, and so on, when generics are involved.

As a quick preview, here is the Rust standard library's LinkedList<T> definition and implementation. It's a doubly linked list! Additionally, the push_front_node (prepend) function shows the use of an unsafe area to speed up inserts. For more information on that, check out the link to the online book *Learning Rust With Entirely Too Many Linked Lists* in the *Further reading* section at the end of the chapter:

```
pub struct LinkedList<T> {
    head: Option<Shared<Node<T>>>,
    tail: Option<Shared<Node<T>>>,
    len: usize,
    marker: PhantomData<Box<Node<T>>>,
}

struct Node<T> {
    next: Option<Shared<Node<T>>>,
    prev: Option<Shared<Node<T>>>,
    element: T,
}

[...]

impl<T> LinkedList<T> {
    /// Adds the given node to the front of the list.
    #[inline]
    fn push_front_node(&mut self, mut node: Box<Node<T>>) {
        unsafe {
            node.next = self.head;
            node.prev = None;
            let node = Some(Shared::from(Box::into_unique(node)));

            match self.head {
                None => self.tail = node,
                Some(mut head) => head.as_mut().prev = node,
            }

            self.head = node;
            self.len += 1;
        }
    }

// [...]  The remaining code was left out.

}
```

Whatever the implementation, there are general upsides and downsides to the doubly linked list.

Upsides

As a linked list, the principles are the same but slightly different. However, the major points of when the list is a good choice are shared with the singly linked list:

- Low overhead allocation per item (but more than the singly linked list).
- Item count is only limited by heap memory.
- Mutation while iterating is possible.
- Implementation is more complex but still fairly simple.
- Inserts, deletes, append, and prepend remain efficient.
- Efficient reversion.

This makes the doubly linked list a superior version of the two versions of linked lists, which is why it's usually the default `LinkedList` type.

Downsides

The doubly linked list shares a lot of the downsides of its less complex sibling and replaces the "no going back" with "more memory overhead" and "more complex implementation". Here's the list again:

- Indexing is still inefficient.
- Nodes are also allocated on the heap, which requires a lot of jumping around too.
- An additional pointer has to be stored per node.
- Implementation is more complex.

Inefficient indexing and iteration is something that a lot of developers wanted to get rid of, so they invented a more exotic version of a linked list: the **skip list**.

Skip lists

A lot of people love New York—and so do we. It has many qualities that are hard to describe; it is a crazy (in a good way), lively city that brings together many cultures, backgrounds, ethnicities, activities, and opportunities. New York also features a large public transport network, almost like cities in Europe.

What does any of this have to do with skip lists? A subway system can be expressed as a simple list of stops (expressed in street numbers, a common thing in the USA): `14 -> 23 -> 28 -> 33 -> 42 -> 51 -> 59 -> 68`. However, the New York subway system has something called **express trains** which reduce the number of stops to cover larger distances faster.

Suppose someone wants to go from stop 14 to stop 51. Instead of seeing the doors open and close five times, they can go there getting off at the third stop. In fact, this is how New Yorkers use the trains 4, 5, and 6 between 14th Street (Union Square) and 51st Street. Turned on its side, the subway plan looks roughly like this:

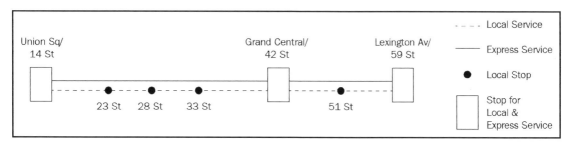

The local service trains stop at every stop along the way, but the express service trains skip certain smaller stops only to halt at shared stations where travelers can switch between the two. The skipping happens quite literally on some stops where trains simply drive through, sometimes confusing tourists and locals alike.

Expressed as a data structure, the list is essentially several lists, each at a different level. The lowest level contains *all* nodes, where the upper levels are their "express services" that can skip a number of nodes to get further ahead quicker. This results in a multilayered list, fused together only at certain nodes that have a connection on these particular levels:

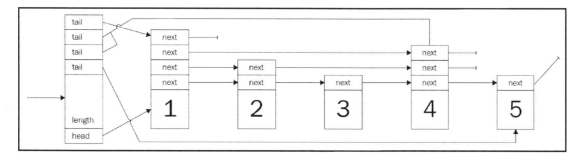

Ideally, each level has half the number of nodes that the previous level has, which means that there needs to be a decision-making algorithm that can work with a growing list and still maintain this constraint. If this constraint is not kept, search times get worse, and in the worst-case scenario it's a regular linked list with a lot of overhead.

 A node's level is decided using a probabilistic approach: increment the level as long as a coin flip comes out on the same side. While this produces the desired distribution, that's only meaningful if the higher-level nodes are evenly distributed. There are a few posts on improved versions in the *Further reading* section.

In addition to that, the skip list has to be ordered to function properly. After all, if the elements of the list are in a random order, how would the list know what it is skipping? In general, however, a node type for this—basic—skip list looks like this:

```
type Link = Option<Rc<RefCell<Node>>>;

struct Node {
    next: Vec<Link>,
    pub value: u64,
}
```

And to chain them together, a list type is also required:

```
struct SkipList {
    head: Link,
    tails: Vec<Link>,
    max_level: usize,
    pub length: u64,
}
```

What stands out is that the `struct` is very similar to the previous lists. Indeed—the relationship is undeniable, since they share almost all the properties. However, there are two differences: the `tails` is a `Vec<Link>` and the `max_level` is a property of the list.

The `tails` property being a vector is due to the fact that every level will have a tail end, meaning that whenever an append occurs, all tails may need to be updated. Additionally, the developer is responsible for providing an appropriate `max_level` value, since changing `max_level` would result in constructing a new list!

Going back to the previous example, the product team has requested more features! Users are confused by the lack of a clear direction in the list, and they are annoyed that there is no way to quickly skip the verbose but less-than-interesting parts in the beginning.

As a consequence, the product team wants the following:

- A time associated with the logged transaction
- To be able to quickly jump to an arbitrary time
- To start iterating from there

Doesn't this sound a lot like a skip list?

The best transaction log

To improve the transaction log in the way the product team describes, it's a perfect fit for a skip list. How about ordering the commands by a u32 number—a millisecond offset from the initial timestamp. The commands it contains are going to be stored as strings associated with the offset.

Nevertheless, the list and its nodes need to be implemented.

Compared to previous implementations (especially since the singly linked list is a close relative), there are two major differences in this declaration. Firstly, the next pointer is an array, which is due to the node having a different successor at every level.

Secondly, the content was previously named value, but to differentiate between the timestamp offset and the actual content, value has been replaced by offset and command:

```
#[derive(Clone)]
struct Node {
    next: Vec<Link>,
    pub offset: u64,
    pub command: String,
}
```

These nodes form the basis of this—improved—transaction log. As previously, with the singly linked list, this is done by creating a type that has a head pointer.

The list

Other than a simple pointer to the head, the list best stores the length as well as the maximum level that elements can have. This user-supplied parameter is critical, since if it's chosen too low, searching will approximate the search performance of a singly linked list (O(n)).

In contrast, choosing a maximum level that is too high will also result in an uneven distribution that could see as many vertical (levels down) as horizontal iterations ($O(n + h)$), none of which are good. The Big O notation ($O(n)$ and so on) will be discussed in `Chapter 18`, *Algorithm Evaluation*.

Consequently, this parameter has to be set to somewhat reflect the future size of the list and the highest level only contains two or three nodes at most:

```
#[derive(Clone)]
pub struct BestTransactionLog {
    head: Link,
    tails: Vec<Link>,
    max_level: usize,
    pub length: u64,
}
```

The `tails` property is a vector pointing to the tail of each level. When adding data, this is the primary place to update this transaction log, thanks to the append-only nature of our skip list.

Adding data

Having the basic data structures ready, a function to insert data is required. As previously stated, a skip list can only work if the values are somehow comparable and follow an ascending order. This makes sense: skipping ahead is only useful if you know where you are going!

A very efficient way to create a sorted list is by doing a **sorted insert** (sometimes called an **insertion sort**). Commonly, this would add some complexity to the insert logic to find the correct place for the node. However, since a timestamp is naturally ascending and a comparable value, this version of the transaction log works without a sophisticated insert, thereby requiring fewer tests and fewer headaches when reading it a year down the road.

In fact, this means reusing some code from earlier sections is entirely possible:

```
pub fn append(&mut self, offset: u64, value: String) {
    let level = 1 + if self.head.is_none() {
        self.max_level    // use the maximum level for the first node
    } else {
        self.get_level() // determine the level by coin flips
    };

    let new = Node::new(vec![None; level], offset, value);
```

```
    // update the tails for each level
    for i in 0..level {
        if let Some(old) = self.tails[i].take() {
            let next = &mut old.borrow_mut().next;
            next[i] = Some(new.clone());
        }
        self.tails[i] = Some(new.clone());
    }

    // this is the first node in the list
    if self.head.is_none() {
        self.head = Some(new.clone());
    }
    self.length += 1;
}
```

Yet, there is an important addition: deciding on the level a node should (also) be present at. This is what makes the list powerful and is done just before the node is created:

```
let level = 1 + if self.head.is_none() {
    self.max_level
} else {
    self.get_level()
};
let new = Node::new(vec![None; level], offset, value);
```

This snippet shows some important details:

- The first node is always present on all levels, which makes search considerably easier, since the algorithm only needs to descend. However, this is only possible thanks to the append-only approach!
- Each node's `next` vector has to store succeeding pointers at the level's index, which means that the actual length needs to be `highest level + 1`.

How do you decide on the level, though? This is a great question, since this is the heart of a well-performing skip list.

Leveling up

Since `search` in a skip list is very much like `search` in a binary search tree (the first section in `Chapter 15`, *Robust Trees*, will get more into those), it has to retain a certain distribution of nodes to be effective. The original paper by William Pugh proposes a way to create the desired distribution of nodes on a certain level by repeatedly flipping a coin (assuming $p = 0.5$).

This is the proposed algorithm (*William Pugh, Skip Lists: A Probabilistic Alternative to Balanced Trees, Figure 5*):

```
randomLevel()
    lvl := 1
    -- random() that returns a random value in [0...1)
    while random() < p and lvl < MaxLevel do
        lvl := lvl + 1
    return lvl
```

Since this is a simple and understandable implementation, the skip list in this chapter will use this as well. However, there are better ways to generate the required distribution, and this is left for you to explore further. For this task, the first external crate is going to be used: rand.

 rand is provided by the Rust project but published in its own repository. There certainly are discussions about why this is not part of the default standard library; however, it's not too bad having the choice of crates to import if it needs to be replaced by something more lightweight, or if the target platform is not supported.

This Rust code should do just fine and generate the required level on call:

```
fn get_level(&self) -> usize {
    let mut n = 0;
    // bool = p(true) = 0.5
    while rand::random::<bool>() && n < self.max_level {
        n += 1;
    }
    n
}
```

Regarding the algorithm, bear this in mind: a range of levels that come out are [0, max_level], including the level. Each time a value is inserted, this function is called to acquire the level for the resultant node, so jumps can actually make search faster.

Jumping around

The skip list only resembles a binary search tree, but it is able to achieve the same runtime complexity (O(log n)) without the need for expensive rebalancing. This is due to the jumps the skip list allows. Logically, it makes sense: by jumping over several nodes, these nodes don't need to be looked at to find out whether those are the values that are being searched for. Fewer nodes means fewer comparisons, leading to a reduced runtime.

The jumps are quickly implemented too and can be implemented in a function using a few loops:

```rust
pub fn find(&self, offset: u64) -> Option<String> {
    match self.head {
        Some(ref head) => {
            let mut start_level = self.max_level;
            let node = head.clone();
            let mut result = None;
            loop {
                if node.borrow().next[start_level].is_some() {
                    break;
                }
                start_level -= 1;
            }
            let mut n = node;
            for level in (0..=start_level).rev() {
                loop {
                    let next = n.clone();
                    match next.borrow().next[level] {
                        Some(ref next)
                            if next.borrow().offset <= offset =>
                                n = next.clone(),
                        _ => break
                    };
                }
                if n.borrow().offset == offset {
                    let tmp = n.borrow();
                    result = Some(tmp.command.clone());
                    break;
                }
            }
            result
        }
        None => None,
    }
}
```

These 30 lines of code allow you to search the list quickly within a few steps. First, a sensible starting level has to be found by starting at the highest possible level, to see which has a valid node that follows it. The following happens in this part:

```rust
let mut start_level = self.max_level;
let node = head.clone();
loop {
    if node.borrow().next[start_level].is_some() {
        break;
    }
}
```

```
            start_level -= 1;
    }
```

Once this level is figured out, the next step is to move vertically toward the desired node and move lower, as the potential next node is greater than the value we are looking for:

```
let mut n = node;
for level in (0..=start_level).rev() {
    loop {
        let next = n.clone();
        match next.borrow().next[level] {
            Some(ref next)
                if next.borrow().offset <= offset =>
                    n = next.clone(),
            _ => break
        };
    }
    if n.borrow().offset == offset {
        let tmp = n.borrow();
        result = Some(tmp.command.clone());
        break;
    }
}
result
```

Finally, the result of the search is returned as an Option that contains the command that was issued at the specified time—or None. Depending on the semantics of failure, it could be a better choice to use a Result with the appropriate message that informs the user about why there was no result (the list was empty, no value has been found, and so on).

Thoughts and discussion

skip list is a fascinating data structure, as it is fairly simple to implement and combines the benefits of tree-like structures within a list without the need for expensive inserts or rebalancing. To visualize the power of this data structure, here is a chart that compares the find() operation of skip lists and (std::collections::) LinkedList:

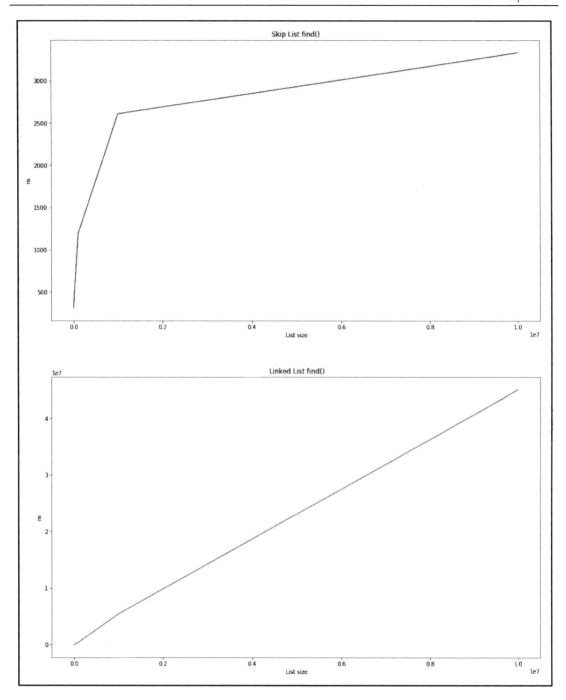

The graph output for Skip List find () and Linked List find ()

The first chart (higher) shows how the skip list behaves according to an `O(log n)` type function, which proves that the implementation works! The second (lower) chart shows the linear search in `LinkedList`, with the time required growing in `O(n)`. The raw numbers are even more impressive:

Size	Skip list [avg ns]	Linked list [avg ns]
1,000	311	825
10,000	438	17,574
100,000	1,190	428,259
1,000,000	2,609	5,440,420
10,000,000	3,334	45,157,562

These numbers reflect the **nanoseconds (ns)** required for a single call to the `find()` method averaged over a number of trials. This is truly a great data structure for search.

Upsides

In a word: `search`. The number of steps required to retrieve a single item is linear (it will take as many steps to find an item as there are items in the list), in the *worst case*. Commonly, the time would be at the level of a binary search tree!

In more practical terms, this would provide the ability to store large amounts of data in a list and quickly find the items that you were looking for. However, there is more; here is a list of upsides:

- The item count is only limited by heap memory
- The search is really efficient
- It is less complex to implement than many trees

Yet, there are downsides to this list.

Downsides

The memory efficiency of a skip list and its complexity can be an issue. With the append-only approach, the list implemented in this book avoids a few complexities such as sorted insert (we'll get there later). Other points include the following:

- Memory efficiency: lots and lots of pointers create overhead
- Implementation complexity
- Sorting required

- Updates are expensive
- Probabilistic approach to elevating nodes onto certain levels

Depending on the type of project, these might be prohibitive issues. However, there are other types of lists that might be suitable, one of them being the dynamic array.

Dynamic arrays

Arrays are another common way to store sequences of data. However, they lack a fundamental feature of lists: expansion. Arrays are efficient because they are a fixed-size container of length n, where every element has an equal size. Thus, any element can be reached by calculating the address to jump to using the simple formula `start_address + n * element_size`, making the entire process really fast. Additionally, this is very CPU cache-friendly, since the data is always at least one hop away.

The idea of using arrays to emulate list behavior has been around for a long time (Java 1.2 included an `ArrayList` class in 1998, but the idea is likely much older) and it is still a great way to achieve high performance in lists. Rust's `Vec<T>` uses the same technique. To start off, this is how an array list is built:

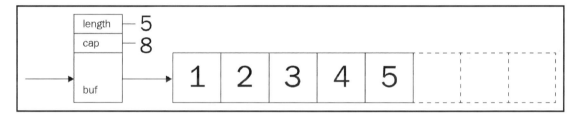

Consequently, this Rust implementation will have an array (actually a slice, but more on that later) as the main storage facility as well:

```
pub struct DynamicArray {
    buf: Box<[Option<u64>]>,
    cap: usize,
    pub length: usize,
}
```

The idea is that, dynamic list sizes can be emulated at the cost of memory and potentially excessive overallocation. Consequently, the critical point is when the currently allocated size is exceeded and the list needs to grow. The question becomes this: how much memory is going to be needed?

The consequence of too little memory is that reallocation is going to happen again quickly—which will remove any performance gains over regular lists. If the resizing was too large, a lot of memory would go to waste, and, depending on the program's target platform, this might be a huge issue. Thus, the strategy of acquiring more memory is essential. Rust's `Vec` follows a smart implementation and allows either an exact allocation and an amortized allocation of simply double (or more) the size of the current internal array.

Java's implementation grows the vector by simply creating a new array with the old capacity added to a bit-shifted version (to the right by one) of the old capacity. That is, of course, only if that is enough. Typically, that leads to adding half of the current capacity or more to the number of possible elements. Naturally, all existing elements are (shallow) copied to the new array before disposing of the original memory. In code, it looks as follows (from OpenJDK 8, class `ArrayList`, lines 237 to 247; new lines added for readability):

```java
private void grow(int minCapacity) {
    // overflow-conscious code
    int oldCapacity = elementData.length;
    int newCapacity = oldCapacity + (oldCapacity >> 1);

    if (newCapacity - minCapacity < 0)
        newCapacity = minCapacity;

    if (newCapacity - MAX_ARRAY_SIZE > 0)
        newCapacity = hugeCapacity(minCapacity);

    // minCapacity is usually close to size, so this is a win:
    elementData = Arrays.copyOf(elementData, newCapacity);
}
```

This code has a fascinating simplicity, and it's used by billions of programs worldwide, and the implementation of this book's dynamic array will use the same strategy.

Again, the product team has another feature request. Users liked the going-back-and-forth feature a lot, so they want to save a few noteworthy timestamps in a separate list.

Often, these kinds of requirements send developers straight to a hash table or dictionary type. However, these usually do not retain the order of the items that were inserted and, if iteration is a primary concern, they are perhaps not the most efficient way to do this.

Favorite transactions

To clean up the product team's demands, here is a list of the required features:

- Save a transaction's timestamp in a list
- Access the elements quickly by index, in any order
- Iterate the items in the order they were saved

A dynamic array utilizes an expanding array underneath and works really quickly, for accessing indices directly while still supporting iteration—great for saving a numbered list of noteworthy timestamps. The direct index access provides a way to fetch the stored data without having to go through the entire list, and since transaction timestamps are basically u64 numbers (milliseconds), the data structure can be a dynamic array of multiple u64.

Other than previous lists, this time, a node only stores data and can therefore be a type alias as well:

```
type Node = Option<u64>;
```

Making the node an Option type is necessary, since the capacity and actual length of the internal slice may differ—which means that an "empty" marker is needed:

```
pub struct TimestampSaver {
    buf: Box<[Node]>,
    cap: usize,
    pub length: usize,
}
```

Once the node type is declared, it can be used inside the new list's internal buffer. This construct is called a **boxed slice** (see the following section) and stores nodes in an array-like fashion.

Internal arrays

Arrays are defined as data structures that have a known size at compile time. Rust takes this very seriously, and the array constructor will only take constants to denominate size in an array. [0u8; 4] will work, but let my_array_size = 2 * 2; [0u8; my_array_size] won't.

So, how do you dynamically reallocate a new array then? In Rust, there is also something called `slices`, which are views into a sequence data structure, akin to an array. These are a great fit when stored inside a `Box` pointer: allocated on the heap, it has all the benefits of an array with a dynamic size.

As previously mentioned, this implementation goes with Java's `ArrayList` growth strategy and increases its size by at least 50% each time more capacity is required. While this has the unfortunate effect of exponential growth, it has worked for Java—a *very* popular language—for decades.

The Rust implementation is close to its Java pendant; in fact, only the oversized variety is missing:

```
fn grow(&mut self, min_cap: usize) {
    let old_cap = self.buf.len();
    let mut new_cap = old_cap + (old_cap >> 1);

    new_cap = cmp::max(new_cap, min_cap);
    new_cap = cmp::min(new_cap, usize::max_value());
    let current = self.buf.clone();
    self.cap = new_cap;
    self.buf = vec![None; new_cap].into_boxed_slice();
    self.buf[..current.len()].clone_from_slice(&current);
}
```

You will quickly see that the `vec![]` macro has been used—"*why is that?*" you might ask. Unfortunately, there is no great and safe way outside the `vec![]` macro to allocate this boxed slice. This use of the macro, however, allows to create an empty vector with the appropriate size and convert it into a boxed slice—a slice stored in a `Box`. This slice can afterward clone data from the previous slice.

This code works well up to the length of `usize`, which depends on the platform the program has been compiled for.

Quick access

Due to the underlying slice, accessing an index is cheap. In fact, it always takes the same amount of time, regardless of the index (which makes it different to previously discussed lists). A call to the `at()` function will therefore simply forward it accordingly:

```
pub fn at(&mut self, index: usize) -> Option<u64> {
    if self.length > index {
        self.buf[index]
```

```
    } else {
        None
    }
}
```

Here, again, the Rust implementation has to deal with sharing borrowed content or clone the data structure which might require more memory. Under the hood, a `u64` is implicitly cloned.

To fulfill all requirements, the `Iterator` trait has to be implemented as well. Unlike the doubly linked list, the iterator cannot store a single node and go forward or backward from there. It has to store a pointer to the entire list, along with the current index:

```
pub struct ListIterator {
    current: usize,
    data: Box<[Node]>,
}
```

This `struct` makes the implementation already obvious. Move the current pointer back and forth as needed:

```
impl Iterator for ListIterator {
    type Item = u64;

    fn next(&mut self) -> Option<u64> {
        if self.current < self.data.len() {
            let item = self.data[self.current];
            self.current += 1;
            item
        } else {
            None
        }
    }
}

impl DoubleEndedIterator for ListIterator {
    fn next_back(&mut self) -> Option<u64> {
        if self.current < self.data.len() {
            let item = self.data[self.current];
            if self.current == 0 {
                self.current = self.data.len() - 1;
            } else {
                self.current -= 1;
            }
            item
        } else {
            None
```

```
                }
            }
        }
```

This is a simple and clear iterator: no unpacking, explicit borrowing, and so on, just a simple counter that is incremented or decremented as it moves through the list.

Wrap up

The dynamic array is a very flexible way of using array-like structures as a list—and it's surprisingly easy to implement and use. In fact, adding other features (`prepend`, insert at a specified position, and so on) is only a matter of a few lines of code.

For Rust, the difference from the other list types is the clearly defined hierarchical ownership: the list `struct` owns the internal structure, which in turn owns the data in its elements. There are no links among the elements that could create ambiguity in who owns what, making the dynamic array a great example for how productive Rust code can be.

Upsides

Other than it being only a few lines of code, the dynamic array has quite a few upsides:

- Speed: arrays/slices make things really fast
- Simple and fast element access
- Clear ownership structures
- Fast append and iteration
- Very CPU cache-friendly

One thing is clear: it's fast in many cases. When is the dynamic array not the best choice, though?

Downsides

However, this type of list is also quite memory-inefficient, and its rigid structure can be a downside as well:

- Operations other than append will require to shift elements
- Growth strategy is not memory-efficient

- A single large chunk of memory is required
- Size is limited by `usize` type, which differs from platform to platform
- Growth speed decreases with list size

This concludes this journey into the realm of lists, hopefully in a successful manner. Before the next chapter begins, a quick summary highlights all the important parts.

Summary

Lists are everywhere! While this is true, it's a fact that makes everything harder. Which list is the right tool for the job? How well will it do at certain sizes to add and later find elements? What's the overhead if my payload size is really small?

These are all questions that programmers are faced with today, and the author hopes to provide some guidance on these decisions. To recap: the least complex is the singly linked list, upon which the doubly linked list is built. Skip lists are in essence multilayered singly linked lists that provide excellent search performance at the cost of memory overhead. Last, but not least, there is the dynamic array—a type of list that wraps and manages an array for storing data just like a list.

Implementing these structures in Rust requires many pointers to the heap, especially `Rc` and `RefCells`, which were companions from the beginning to the end of the chapter. When you consider the structure of a singly linked list, each item required access to the next—but with a predictable size. This fact requires programmers to work with references, but how would this work if the list gets passed around the program, possibly living on the heap itself? The consequence is to simplify things and put them on to the heap from the beginning and use an interior mutable `Rc` and `RefCell` construct to do that.

Similarly, is the doubly linked list. Other than the forward (next) pointer that the singly linked sibling provides, a doubly linked node has to point backward as well. Therefore, each item has two pointers in addition to the payload, enabling a set of powerful features such as instant list reversal.

Skip lists, on the other hand, have been implemented as singly linked lists in this chapter (but certainly can be doubly linked as well). Their main improvement is the great ability to search the contained data quickly—just like a binary search tree. This means that, almost regardless of the size, the look-up performance is vastly better than that of a regular list, both in absolute and relative terms. Unfortunately, this comes at the cost of many more pointers per node.

The most popular data structure is probably the dynamic array. Often dubbed `Vec<T>` (Rust), `ArrayList` (Java), `List<T>` (C#), or simply `list()` (Python), these are wrappers around an array that is allocated and reallocated intelligently as required. By doing this, they can accommodate the need for fast element access and quick iteration at the cost of a shallow copy on resize, as well as having a large chunk of memory available. These are the best choice for storing a limited amount of small- to medium-sized items.

The next chapter is going to delve deeper into less linear data structures: trees. These constructs provide interesting capabilities by the way they are built and are a great choice for read-heavy undertakings.

Further reading

You can refer to the following links for more information:

- *Learning Rust With Entirely Too Many Linked Lists* (`http://cglab.ca/~abeinges/blah/too-many-lists/book/README.html`)
- Implementing the `Iterator` trait (`https://doc.rust-lang.org/std/iter/index.html#implementing-iterator`)
- *Skip Lists: Done Right* (`https://doc.rust-lang.org/std/iter/index.html#implementing-iterator`)
- *Skip Lists: A Probabilistic Alternative to Balanced Trees*, William Pugh (`https://www.epaperpress.com/sortsearch/download/skiplist.pdf`)

15
Robust Trees

Lists are great for storing a bunch of items, but what about looking up specific elements? In the previous chapter, a skip list greatly outperformed a regular linked list when simply finding an item. Why? Because it was utilizing an iteration strategy that resembles that of a balanced tree structure: there, the internal order lets the algorithm strategically skip items. However, that's only the beginning. Many libraries, databases, and search engines are built on trees; in fact, whenever a program is compiled, the compiler creates an abstract syntax tree.

Tree-based data structures incorporate all kinds of smart ideas that we will explore in this chapter, so you can look forward to the following:

- Implementing and understanding a binary search tree
- Learning about self-balancing trees
- How prefix or suffix trees work
- What a priority queue uses internally
- Graphs, the most general tree structure

Binary search tree

A tree structure is almost like a linked list: each node has branches—in the case of a binary tree, there are two—which represent children of that node. Since these children have children of their own, the node count grows exponentially, building a hierarchical structure that looks like a regular tree turned on its head.

Binary trees are a subset of these structures with only two branches, typically called left and right. However, that does not inherently help the tree's performance. This is why using a *binary search tree*, where left represents the smaller or equal value to its parent, and right anything that's greater than that parent node, was established!

If that was confusing, don't worry; there will be code. First, some vocabulary though: what would you call the far ends of the tree? Leaves. Cutting off branches? Pruning. The number of branches per node? Branching factor (binary trees have a branching factor of 2).

Great, with that out of the way, the nodes can be shown—although they look a lot like the doubly linked list from the previous chapter:

```
type Tree = Option<Box<Node>>;

struct Node {
    pub value: u64,
    left: Tree,
    right: Tree,
}
```

Similarly, the tree structure itself is only a pointer to the root node:

```
pub struct BinarySearchTree {
    root: Tree,
    pub length: u64,
}
```

Yet before you can get comfortable with the new data structure, the product team from the previous chapter is back! You did a great job improving the transaction log and they want to continue that progress and build an **Internet of Things** (**IoT**) device management platform so users can register a device with a numerical name and later search for it. However, the search has to be fast or really fast, which is especially critical since many customers have announced the incorporation of more than 10,000 devices into the new system!

Isn't this a great opportunity to get more experience with a binary search tree?

IoT device management

Device management in the IoT space is mostly about storing and retrieving specific devices or device twins. These objects typically store addresses, configuration values, encryption keys, or other things for small devices so nobody has to connect manually. Consequently, keeping an inventory is critical!

For now, the product team settled on a numerical "name", to be available faster than the competition, and to keep the requirements short:

- Store IoT device objects (containing the IP address, numerical name, and type)
- Retrieve IoT objects by numerical name
- Iterate over IoT objects

A great use for a tree: the numerical name can be used to create a tree and search for it nice and quickly. The basic object for storing this IoT device information looks like this:

```
#[derive(Clone, Debug)]
pub struct IoTDevice {
    pub numerical_id: u64,
    pub address: String,
}
```

For simplicity, this object will be used in the code directly (adding generics isn't too tricky, but would go beyond the scope of this book):

```
type Tree = Option<Box<Node>>;
struct Node {
    pub dev: IoTDevice,
    left: Tree,
    right: Tree,
}
```

Starting with this basic implementation, the requisite operations, add and find, can be implemented.

More devices

Unlike lists, trees make a major decision on insert: which side does the new element go to? Starting at the root node, each node's value is compared to the value that is going to be inserted: is this greater than or less than that? Either decision will lead down a different subtree (left or right).

This process is (usually recursively) repeated until the targeted subtree is None, which is exactly where the new value is inserted—as a leaf of the tree. If this is the first value going into the tree, it becomes the root node. There are some problems with this, and the more experienced programmers will have had a strange feeling already: what happens if you insert numbers in ascending order?

These feelings are justified. Inserting in ascending order (for example, 1, 2, 3, 4) will lead to a tree that is basically a list in disguise! This is also called a (very) unbalanced tree and won't have any of the benefits of other trees:

```
      1
    /   \
        2
      /   \
          3
        /   \
            4
```

During this chapter, we are going to go a lot more things on balancing trees and why that is important in order to achieve high performance. In order to avoid this pitfall associated with binary search trees, the first value to insert should ideally be the median of all elements since it will be used as the root node, as is visible in the following code snippet:

```rust
pub fn add(&mut self, device: IoTDevice) {
    self.length += 1;
    let root = mem::replace(&mut self.root, None);
    self.root = self.add_rec(root, device);
}

fn add_rec(&mut self, node: Tree, device: IoTDevice) -> Tree {
    match node {
        Some(mut n) => {
            if n.dev.numerical_id <= device.numerical_id {
                n.left = self.add_rec(n.left, device);
                Some(n)
            } else {
                n.right = self.add_rec(n.right, device);
                Some(n)
            }
        }
        _ => Node::new(device),
    }
}
```

Split into two parts, this code walks the tree recursively to find the appropriate position and attaches the new value as a leaf there. Actually, the insert is not that different from a regular tree walk in search or iteration.

Recursion is when a function calls itself. Think of the movie Inception—having a dream inside a dream inside a dream. it's the same concept. There are a few implications in programming: the original function is disposed of last since it's only finished after all recursive calls return. This also means that everything lives on the much smaller stack, which may result in a stack overflow when there are too many calls! Typically, recursive algorithms can also be implemented iteratively, but they are much harder to understand—so choose wisely!

Finding the right one

Having the ability to add devices to the tree, it's even more important to retrieve them again. Just like the skip list in the previous chapter, this retrieval ideally runs in *O(log n)* time, meaning that the majority of elements are going to be skipped when searching.

Consequently, if the tree is skewed in one direction, the performance approaches *O(n)* and more elements are looked at, thereby making the search slower. Since a skewed tree is more like a list, the recursive insert algorithm can overflow the stack quickly thanks to the high number of "levels" with only a single item. Otherwise, the recursive algorithm is only called as many times as the tree's height, a considerably lower number in a balanced tree. The algorithm itself resembles the previously shown insert algorithm:

```
pub fn find(&self, numerical_id: u64) -> Option<IoTDevice> {
    self.find_r(&self.root, numerical_id)
}

fn find_r(&self, node: &Tree, numerical_id: u64) -> Option<IoTDevice> {
    match node {
        Some(n) => {
            if n.dev.numerical_id == numerical_id {
                Some(n.dev.clone())
            } else if n.dev.numerical_id < numerical_id {
                self.find_r(&n.left, numerical_id)
            } else {
                self.find_r(&n.right, numerical_id)
            }
        }
        _ => None,
    }
}
```

Although this snippet's purpose is to find a specific node, there is a close relationship to enumerating every device—something that the users of this service certainly will want to have.

Finding all devices

Walking a tree and executing a callback when visiting each node can be done in three ways:

- Pre-order, executing the callback *before descending*
- In-order, which executes the callback *after descending left, but before descending into the right subtree*
- Post-order, where the callback is executed *after descending*

Each of these traversal strategies yields a different order of tree elements, with in-order producing a sorted output, while pre- and post-order create a more structurally oriented sorting. For our users, the in-order walk will provide the best experience, since it also lets them reason better regarding the expected outcome, and, if displayed in a list, it's easier to navigate.

While implementing this walk is very easy to do recursively, providing an iterator is more user-friendly (just like the lists in the previous chapter) and it enables a number of added functions, such as map() and filter(). However, this implementation has to be iterative, which makes it more complex and removes some of the efficiency of the tree.

Therefore, this tree supports a walk() function which calls a provided function each time it encounters a node, which can be used to fill a vector for the iterator:

```
pub fn walk(&self, callback: impl Fn(&IoTDevice) -> ()) {
    self.walk_in_order(&self.root, &callback);
}

fn walk_in_order(&self, node: &Tree, callback: &impl Fn(&IoTDevice) -> ())
{
    if let Some(n) = node {
        self.walk_in_order(&n.left, callback);
        callback(&n.dev);
        self.walk_in_order(&n.right, callback);
    }
}
```

An example of how to build a vector using this walk method is shown here:

```
let my_devices: RefCell<Vec<IoTDevice>> = RefCell::new(vec![]);
tree.walk(|n| my_devices.borrow_mut().push(n.clone()));
```

With this walking ability, all requirements are satisfied for now.

Wrap up

Thanks to their simplicity, binary search trees are beautifully efficient. In fact, the entire tree implementation for this section was done in fewer than 90 lines of Rust code, with functions of about 10 lines each.

A binary tree's efficiency allows for recursion to be used a lot, which typically results in functions that are easier to understand compared to their iterative counterparts. In the ideal case, that is, when a tree is perfectly balanced, a function only has to process $log2(n)$ nodes (n being the total number of nodes)—19 in a tree of 1,000,000 elements!

Unbalanced trees will decrease performance significantly and they are easily created by accident. The most unbalanced tree is created by inserting values that are already sorted, creating a very large difference in search performance:

```
test tests::bench_sorted_insert_bst_find ... bench: 16,376 ns/iter (+/-
6,525)
test tests::bench_unsorted_insert_bst_find ... bench: 398 ns/iter (+/- 182)
```

These results reflect the differences between a skip list and a doubly linked list from the previous chapter.

Upsides

To recap, a binary search tree has a number of great benefits for its users:

- Simple implementation
- Efficient and fast search
- Traversal allows for different orderings
- Great for large amounts of unsorted data

Downsides

By using a binary search tree, its drawbacks become obvious quickly:

- Worst-case performance is that of a linked list
- Unbalanced trees are easy to create by accident
- Unbalanced trees cannot be "repaired"
- Recursive algorithms can overflow on unbalanced trees

Obviously, a lot of the deeper issues result from the tree being unbalanced in some way—for which there is a solution: self-balancing binary search trees.

Red-black tree

With the previous tree structure, there was a major downside: a previously unknown sequence of keys that is inserted into the tree cannot be sorted. Think of how most identifiers are generated; they are typically ascending numbers. Shuffling these numbers won't always work, especially when they are gradually added. Since this leads to an unbalanced tree (the extreme case behaves just like a list), Rudolf Bayer came up with the idea of a special, self-balancing tree: the red-black tree.

This tree is a binary search tree that adds logic to rebalance after inserts. Within this operation, it is crucial to know when to stop "balancing"—which is where the inventor thought to use two colors: red and black.

In literature, the red-black tree is described as a binary search tree that satisfies a set of rules:

- The root node is always black
- Each other node is either red or black
- All leaves (often `null`/`NIL` values) are considered black
- A red node can only have black children
- Any path from the root to its leaves has the same number of black nodes

By enforcing these rules, a tree can be programmatically verified to be balanced. How are these rules doing that? Rules 4 and 5 provide the answer: if each branch has to have the same number of black nodes, neither side can be significantly longer than the other unless there were lots of red nodes.

How many of those can there be? At most, as many as there are black nodes—because they cannot have red children. Thus, one branch cannot significantly exceed the other, making this tree balanced. The code of the validation function illustrates this very well:

```
pub fn is_a_valid_red_black_tree(&self) -> bool {
    let result = self.validate(&self.root, Color::Red, 0);
    let red_red = result.0;
    let black_height_min = result.1;
    let black_height_max = result.2;
    red_red == 0 && black_height_min == black_height_max
}


// red-red violations, min black-height, max-black-height
fn validate(
    &self,
    node: &Tree,
    parent_color: Color,
    black_height: usize,
) -> (usize, usize, usize) {
    if let Some(n) = node {
        let n = n.borrow();
        let red_red = if parent_color == Color::Red && n.color ==
Color::Red {
            1
        } else {
            0
        };
        let black_height = black_height + match n.color {
            Color::Black => 1,
            _ => 0,
        };
        let l = self.validate(&n.left, n.color.clone(), black_height);
        let r = self.validate(&n.right, n.color.clone(), black_height);
        (red_red + l.0 + r.0, cmp::min(l.1, r.1), cmp::max(l.2, r.2))
    } else {
        (0, black_height, black_height)
    }
}
```

Like the binary search tree, each node in a tree has two children, with a key either greater than, equal to, or less than that of the current node. In addition to the key (as in a key-value pair), the nodes store a color that is red on insert, and a pointer back to its parent. Why? This is due to the required rebalancing, which will be described later. First, this can be a typical node:

```
type BareTree = Rc<RefCell<Node>>;
type Tree = Option<BareTree>;
```

```
struct Node {
    pub color: Color,
    pub key: u32,
    pub parent: Tree,
    left: Tree,
    right: Tree,
}
```

Using these nodes, a tree can be created just like a binary search tree. In fact, the insert mechanism is exactly the same except for setting the parent pointer. Newly inserted nodes are always colored red and, once in place, the tree might violate the rules. Only then is it time to find and fix these issues.

After an insert, the tree is in an invalid state that requires a series of steps to restore the red-black tree's properties. This series, comprised of rotation and recolor, starts at the inserted node and goes up the tree until the root node is considered valid. In summary, a red-black tree is a binary search tree that is rotated and recolored until balance is restored.

Recolor is simply changing the color of a specified node to a specific color, which happens as a final step when doing tree rebalancing. **Rotation** is an operation of a set of three nodes: the current node, its parent, and its grandparent. It is employed to fold list-like chains into trees by rotating either left or right around a specified node. The result is a changed hierarchy, with either the left or right child of the center node on top, and its children adjusted accordingly:

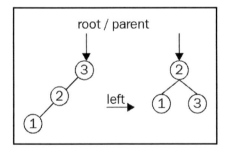

Clearly, this example is too simple and it can only happen within the first few inserts. Rotations require recolors after redefining the hierarchy of a set of nodes. To add further complexity, rotations regularly happen in succession:

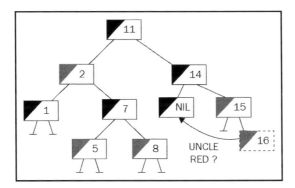

The preceding tree has had a node inserted and is now violating rule 4: *no red children on a red node*. The next step is to determine which steps are required to establish balance. For that, the parent's sibling's color (that is, the uncle's color) is examined. Red means that a simple recoloring of both siblings to black and their parent to red won't invalidate the tree and will fix the condition. This is not the case here (the uncle is None, which means black), and some rotation is required:

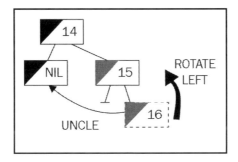

The first move is to align the nodes into a chain of left children (in this case), which is done by rotating around the center node, the insertee's parent:

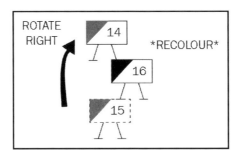

Once the chain is aligned, a right rotation of the third node (grandparent) creates a valid subtree by elevating the middle node (the "youngest" node/insertee), with the former parent and grandparent to the left and right, respectively. Then, the new constellation is recolored and the procedure begins anew, centered around the root of the new subtree (in this example, though, the tree is already valid):

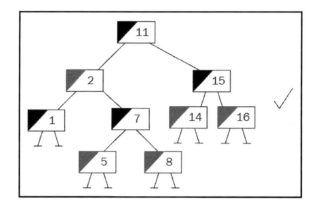

These steps can be repeated until the tree is valid and the root is reached (which might be different from what you started off with). This root node is heuristically painted black as well, which cannot violate the rules but shortcuts a potential red-red violation. For code on the fixing operation, see the following subsections.

The product team has even called this time to put emphasis on their new product ideas. The IoT platform is quite popular and customers have been using it a lot—and recognized a major slowdown when they kept adding their sequentially numbered devices. This resulted in angry calls to customer services, which then turned to the product team for help—and now it's time to implement the solution and replace the current tree for device management.

Better IoT device management

The problem that our users face is clear: if a binary search tree encounters sorted data (such as incremental IDs), it can only ever append to one side, creating an unbalanced tree. A red-black tree is able to handle this at the cost of more operations being executed during insert (such as rotating subtrees), which is acceptable for the users.

This tree has similar nodes to the binary search tree, with the addition of a color field and a parent field, the latter of which triggers a wider change compared to the binary search tree. Thanks to the pointer back, the tree nodes cannot exclusively own the pointers to the children and parent (because, who owns this value, the parent or the child?), which requires a well-known pattern in Rust: interior mutability. As discussed in an earlier chapter, RefCell owns the data's portion of the memory and handles borrow-checking at runtime so that mutable and immutable references can be obtained:

```
type BareTree = Rc<RefCell<Node>>;
type Tree = Option<BareTree>;

struct Node {
    pub color: Color,
    pub dev: IoTDevice,
    pub parent: Tree,
    left: Tree,
    right: Tree,
}

impl Node {
    pub fn new(dev: IoTDevice) -> Tree {
        Some(Rc::new(RefCell::new(Node {
            color: Color::Red,
            dev: dev,
            parent: None,
            left: None,
            right: None,
        })))
    }
}
```

With that in place, devices can be added.

Even more devices

Once the tree is created, an add() function lets the user add a device. The tree then proceeds to insert the new key just as if it were a binary search tree—only to check and fix any errors immediately afterward. Where a binary search tree could use a simple if condition to decide the direction it proceeds in, in the red-black tree, the direction has a larger impact, and nesting if conditions will result in chaotic, unreadable code.

Thus, let's create `enum` first, so any time the direction (example, insert, position of a node relative to another node, and so on) has to be decided, we can rely on that `enum`. The same goes for the tree's color:

```
#[derive(Clone, Debug, PartialEq)]
enum Color {
    Red,
    Black,
}

#[derive(PartialEq)]
enum RBOperation {
    LeftNode,
    RightNode,
}
```

Now, the `add()` function can use Rust's match clause to nicely structure the two branches:

```
pub fn add(&mut self, device: IoTDevice) {
    self.length += 1;
    let root = mem::replace(&mut self.root, None);
    let new_tree = self.add_r(root, device);
    self.root = self.fix_tree(new_tree.1);
}

fn add_r(&mut self, mut node: Tree, device: IoTDevice) -> (Tree, BareTree)
{
    if let Some(n) = node.take() {
        let new: BareTree;
        let current_device = n.borrow().dev.clone();

        match self.check(&current_device, &device) {
            RBOperation::LeftNode => {
                let left = n.borrow().left.clone();
                let new_tree = self.add_r(left, device);
                new = new_tree.1;
                let new_tree = new_tree.0.unwrap();
                new_tree.borrow_mut().parent = Some(n.clone());
                n.borrow_mut().left = Some(new_tree);
            }

            RBOperation::RightNode => {
                let right = n.borrow().right.clone();
                let new_tree = self.add_r(right, device);
                new = new_tree.1;
                let new_tree = new_tree.0.unwrap();

                new_tree.borrow_mut().parent = Some(n.clone());
```

```
                    n.borrow_mut().right = Some(new_tree);
            }
        }
        (Some(n), new)
    } else {
        let new = Node::new(device);
        (new.clone(), new.unwrap())
    }
}
```

One of the primary parts of the code is "checking" two devices, that is, comparing them in order to provide a direction that they should be appended to. This comparison is done in a separate function to improve maintainability:

```
fn check(&self, a: &IoTDevice, b: &IoTDevice) -> RBOperation {
    if a.numerical_id <= b.numerical_id {
        RBOperation::LeftNode
    } else {
        RBOperation::RightNode
    }
}
```

While this tree will append every larger item to the left (which seems unusual), the algorithms don't care; they will work regardless—and, by wrapping this into its own function, change is quick and easy.

Balancing the tree

After the node is added properly, `fix_tree()` takes care of restoring the red-black tree's properties—iteratively. While this is nicely descriptive and demonstrative it is long, so let's break it up into parts. Initially, the function determines whether it should stop (or not even start)—which only happens in two cases:

- When it's already the root node
- When the parent of the currently inspected node is red

Clearly, the former is the regular exit criterion as well, as the loop optimizes and moves the current pointer (n as in node) from the bottom toward the root of the tree to stop there:

```
fn fix_tree(&mut self, inserted: BareTree) -> Tree {
    let mut not_root = inserted.borrow().parent.is_some();

    let root = if not_root {
        let mut parent_is_red = self.parent_color(&inserted) == Color::Red;
        let mut n = inserted.clone();
```

```
while parent_is_red && not_root {
    if let Some(uncle) = self.uncle(n.clone()) {
```

Once started, the loop immediately goes for the uncle of a particular node (that is, the grandparent's second child) and its color. The uncle node can either be black (or None) or red, which are the two cases covered next. It is also important to find out *which* uncle it is, and therefore which node the current pointer points to: a left node or a right node. Let's take a look at the following code snippet:

```
if let Some(uncle) = self.uncle(n.clone()) {
    let which = uncle.1;
    let uncle = uncle.0;

    match which {
        RBOperation::LeftNode => {
            // uncle is on the left
            // ...

        RBOperation::RightNode => {
            // uncle is on the right
            // ...
```

This information is critical in determining the rotation order in this area of the tree. In fact, the two branches will execute the same steps, but mirrored:

```
// uncle is on the left
let mut parent = n.borrow().parent
                    .as_ref().unwrap().clone();
if uncle.is_some()
    && uncle.as_ref().unwrap().borrow()
        .color == Color::Red
{
    let uncle = uncle.unwrap();
    parent.borrow_mut().color = Color::Black;
    uncle.borrow_mut().color = Color::Black;
    parent.borrow().parent.as_ref()
      .unwrap().borrow_mut().color =
                                Color::Red;

    n = parent.borrow().parent.as_ref()
          .unwrap().clone();
} else {
    if self.check(&parent.borrow().dev,
            &n.borrow().dev)
                == RBOperation::LeftNode
    {
        // Do only if it's a right child
```

```
                    let tmp = n.borrow().parent.as_ref()
                                  .unwrap().clone();
                    n = tmp;
                    self.rotate(n.clone(),
                    Rotation::Right);
                    parent = n.borrow().parent.as_ref()
                                  .unwrap().clone();
                }
                // Until here. Then for all black uncles
                parent.borrow_mut().color = Color::Black;
                parent.borrow().parent.as_ref()
                  .unwrap().borrow_mut().color =
                                      Color::Red;
                let grandparent = n
                    .borrow()
                    .parent
                    .as_ref()
                    .unwrap()
                    .borrow()
                    .parent
                    .as_ref()
                    .unwrap()
                    .clone();
                self.rotate(grandparent, Rotation::Left);
            }
```

This code contains a large amount of unwrap(), clone(), and borrow() instances, a consequence of the interior mutability pattern. In this case, macros could help to reduce the code's verbosity.

Once the operations for one part of the tree finishes, the next iteration is prepared by checking for a red-red violation to see whether the loop needs to continue.

After the main loop exits, the pointer to the current node is moved up the tree to the root node (which is the function's return value, after all) and colored black. Why? This is a shortcut solution that would otherwise result in another iteration requiring many more expensive steps to be executed, and the rules of a red-black tree mandate a black root anyway:

```
        not_root = n.borrow().parent.is_some();
        if not_root {
            parent_is_red = self.parent_color(&n) == Color::Red;
        }
    }
    while n.borrow().parent.is_some() {
        let t = n.borrow().parent.as_ref().unwrap().clone();
        n = t;
```

```
        }
        Some(n)
    } else {
        Some(inserted)
    };
    root.map(|r| {
        r.borrow_mut().color = Color::Black;
        r
    })
```

With that shortcut, a valid tree is returned that can be set as the new root. However, the main purpose of the tree is to find stuff, which is not that different from a regular binary search tree.

Finding the right one, now

This piece of code can almost be reused from the binary search tree. Other than the borrow() calls (instead of a simple dereference or * operator) adding some amount of processing time, they provides a consistent search speed. For greater reuse of existing functions, the value to be found is wrapped into a dummy node. This way, no additional interface has to be created for comparing nodes:

```
pub fn find(&self, numerical_id: u64) -> Option<IoTDevice> {
    self.find_r(
        &self.root,
        &IoTDevice::new(numerical_id, "".to_owned(), "".to_owned()),
    )
}

fn find_r(&self, node: &Tree, dev: &IoTDevice) -> Option<IoTDevice> {
    match node {
        Some(n) => {
            let n = n.borrow();
            if n.dev.numerical_id == dev.numerical_id {
                Some(n.dev.clone())
            } else {
                match self.check(&n.dev, &dev) {
                    RBOperation::LeftNode => self.find_r(&n.left, dev),
                    RBOperation::RightNode => self.find_r(&n.right, dev),
                }
            }
        }
        _ => None,
    }
}
```

This is, again, a recursive walk of the tree until the specified value is found. Additionally, the "regular" tree walk was also added to the red-black tree variant:

```
pub fn walk(&self, callback: impl Fn(&IoTDevice) -> ()) {
    self.walk_in_order(&self.root, &callback);
}

fn walk_in_order(&self, node: &Tree, callback: &impl Fn(&IoTDevice) -> ())
{
    if let Some(n) = node {
        let n = n.borrow();

        self.walk_in_order(&n.left, callback);
        callback(&n.dev);
        self.walk_in_order(&n.right, callback);
    }
}
```

With these parts fixed, the platform performs consistently fast!

Wrap up

Red-black trees are great self-balancing binary trees, similar to **AVL** (short for **Adelson-Velsky and Landis**) trees. Both appeared around the same time, yet AVL trees are considered to be superior thanks to a lower height difference between the branches. Regardless of which tree structure is used, both are significantly faster than their less complex sibling, the binary search tree. Benchmarks using sorted data on insert (100,000 elements in this case) show how significant the difference between a balanced and unbalanced tree is:

```
test tests::bench_sorted_insert_bst_find ... bench: 370,185 ns/iter (+/-
265,997)
test tests::bench_sorted_insert_rbt_find ... bench: 900 ns/iter (+/- 423)
```

Another variation of a balanced tree is the 2-3-4 tree, a data structure that the red-black tree can be converted into. However, the 2-3-4 tree is, like the B-Tree (coming up later in this chapter), non-binary. Therefore, it is briefly discussed later in this chapter, but we encourage you to find other sources for details.

One major upside to implementing a red-black tree in Rust is the deep understanding of borrowing and ownership that follows the reference juggling when rotating, or "unpacking", a node's grandfather. It is highly recommended as a programming exercise to implement your own version!

Upsides

A red-black tree has a few desirable properties over a regular binary search tree:

- Balance makes searches consistently fast
- Predictable, low-memory usage
- Inserts are reasonably fast
- Simplicity of a binary tree
- Easy to validate

However, the data structure has some significant downsides as well, especially when planning to implement it!

Downsides

Speed is great, but can your implementation achieve it? Let's have a look at the downsides of red-black trees:

- Complex implementation, especially in Rust
- Concurrent writes require the entire tree to be locked
- Performance is great compared to binary search trees, but other trees perform better at the same complexity
- Skip lists (from the previous chapter) perform similarly with better concurrency and simpler implementations

In any case, the red-black tree is a great journey into sophisticated binary tree structures. A more exotic binary tree structure is the heap (not to be confused with the portion of main memory).

Heaps

Since binary trees are the most basic forms of trees, there are several variations designed for a specific purpose. Where the red-black tree is an advanced version of the initial tree, the binary heap is a version of the binary tree that does not facilitate search.

In fact, it has a specified purpose: finding the maximum or minimum value of a node. These heaps (min-heap or max-heap) are built in a way that the root node is always the value with the desired property (min or max) so it can be retrieved in constant time—that is, it always takes the same number of operations to fetch. Once fetched, the tree is restored in a way that the next operation works the same. How is this done though?

Heaps work, irrespective of whether they are min-heaps or max-heaps, because a node's children always have the same property as the entire tree. In a max-heap, this means that the root node is the maximum value of the sequence, so it has to be the greatest value of its children (it's the same with min-heaps, just in reverse). While there is no specific order to this (such as the left node being greater than the right node), there is a convention to prefer the right node for max-heaps and the left for min-heaps.

Upon inserting a new node, it is added last and then a place in the tree has to be determined. The strategy to do that is simple: look at the parent node; if it's greater (in a max-heap), swap the two, and repeat until this doesn't work or it becomes the root node. We call this operation **upheap**.

Similarly, this is how removals work. Once removed, the now-empty slot is replaced by a leaf of the tree—which is either the smallest (max-heap) or greatest (min-heap) value. Then, the same comparisons as with the insert are implemented, but in reverse. Comparing and swapping this node with the children restores the heap's properties and is called **downheap**.

If you paid attention to a node's journey, there is one detail that will be obvious to you: the tree is always "filled". This means that each level is fully populated (that is, every node has both children), making it a **complete binary tree** that maintains total order. This is a property that lets us implement this tree in an array (dynamic or not), making jumps cheap. It will all become clear once you see some diagram:

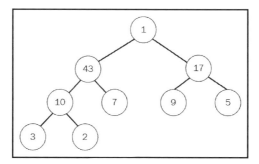

Commonly, the heap is used to create a priority queue of some kind, thanks to the ability to quickly retrieve the highest- or lowest-valued items. A very basic heap can be implemented in Rust as an array, which will provide everything necessary to make it work, but won't be as convenient as a `Vec`.

After the great success of the IoT device platform, an add-on has been planned. The product team is asking for a way to efficiently process messages that come from the devices, so that customers only have to deal with the actual handling of the message and skip the "plumbing" code. Since processing can be executed at (short) intervals, they require a way to order them quickly—ideally so that the device with the most messages can come first.

This sounds like the heap data structure, doesn't it? In fact, it can be a max-heap.

A huge inbox

Typically, heaps are used as priority queues of all kinds. Queues like that exist in any resource-constrained environment (and everywhere else, probably), but their purpose is to output things in an ordered fashion. By using the number of messages to determine the priority of a message notification, the heap can do the heavy lifting of this feature. Before jumping into the hard stuff, though, here are the bits containing the information:

```
#[derive(Clone, Debug)]
pub struct MessageNotification {
    pub no_messages: u64,
    pub device: IoTDevice,
}
```

The idea is to use the number of messages as an indicator of which device to poll first, which is why the device is required. Using this type, the heap does not require any specific node or link types to work:

```
pub struct MessageChecker {
    pub length: usize,
    heap: Vec<Box<MessageNotification>>,
}
```

There are two interesting points here: the underlying structure is a regular `Vec<T>`, which was chosen for its expansion capabilities (Rust's arrays are sized at compile time), and the functionality of `push` or `pop`.

Another noteworthy modification is that no `Option` is needed, which removes a check from the code and makes it easier to read. However, since many of the heap's operations work well with a direct, 1-index-based access, indices have to be translated before hitting `Vec<T>`.

So how does data get in?

Getting messages in

Once a message arrives, it is pushed to the back of the array when the upheap operation "bubbles up" the item until it finds its proper place. In Rust code, this is what that looks like:

```
pub fn add(&mut self, notification: MessageNotification) {
    self.heap.push(Box::new(notification));
    self.length = self.heap.len();
    if self.length > 1 {
        let mut i = self.length;
        while i / 2 > 0 && self.has_more_messages(i, i / 2) {
            self.swap(i, i / 2);
            i /= 2;
        }
    }
}
```

Initially, the new notification lives in a `Box` at the back of the `Vec<T>`, inserted via `push()`. A simple `while` loop then bubbles up the new addition by repeatedly swapping it whenever the `has_more_messages()` function is true. When is it true? Let's see the code:

```
fn has_more_messages(&self, pos1: usize, pos2: usize) -> bool {
    let a = &self.heap[pos1 - 1];
    let b = &self.heap[pos2 - 1];
    a.no_messages >= b.no_messages
}
```

By encapsulating this function, it's easily possible to change the heap into a min-heap should that be required—and the index translations are wrapped away here as well.

Getting data out requires doing this process in reverse in a function called `pop()`.

Taking messages out

Removing the first item in a Vec<T> is not difficult—in fact, Vec<T> ships with a swap_remove() function that does exactly what a heap needs: removing the first element of a Vec<T> by replacing it with the last element! This makes the code significantly shorter and therefore easier to reason about:

```
pub fn pop(&mut self) -> Option<MessageNotification> {
    if self.length > 0 {
        let elem = self.heap.swap_remove(0);
        self.length = self.heap.len();
        let mut i = 1;
        while i * 2 < self.length {
            let children = (i * 2, i * 2 + 1);
            i = if self.has_more_messages(children.0, children.1) {
                if self.has_more_messages(children.0, i) {
                    self.swap(i, children.0);
                    children.0
                } else {
                    break;
                }
            } else {
                if self.has_more_messages(children.1, i) {
                    self.swap(i, children.1);
                    children.1
                } else {
                    break;
                }
            }
        }
        Some(*elem)
    } else {
        None
    }
}
```

Obviously, this code is not short though—so what's amiss? The bubbling down. Swapping downward requires to look at the children (which are at the positions i * 2 and i * 2 + 1) to find out where (or if) the next iteration should proceed.

Wrap up

The heap data structure is surprisingly simple to implement. There are no lengthy unwraps, borrows, or other calls, and the pointer is owned by the `Vec` and can easily be swapped. Other than that, the upheap operation is only a `while` loop, just like the (slightly more complex) downheap function.

There is another typical use case for a heap though: sorting! Consider a bunch of numbers going into the heap instead of `MessageNotification` objects—they would come out sorted. Thanks to the efficiency of the upheap/downheap operations, the worst-case runtime of that sorting algorithm is great—but more on that in `Chapter 19`, *Ordering Things*.

Upsides

Compact and low-complexity implementation make the binary heap a great candidate for requiring any kind of sorting data structure. Other benefits include the following:

- An efficient way to sort lists
- Works well in concurrent situations
- A very efficient way to store a sorted array

Yet there are also downsides.

Downsides

Heaps are generally great, but have two caveats that limit their use:

- Use cases outside of queuing or sorting are rare
- There are better ways to sort

The binary heap was the last of the binary trees, and the next section will cover another rather exotic variation of a tree: the trie.

Trie

The trie is another interesting data structure—in particular, the way in which it is pronounced! Depending on your mother tongue, intuition might dictate a way, but—according to Wikipedia—the name was selected thanks to Edward Fredkin, who pronounced this type of tree differently, namely like **trie** in re**trie**val. Many English speakers resort to saying something along the lines of "try" though.

With that out of the way, what does the trie actually do for it to deserve a different name? It transpires that using retrieval was not a bad idea: tries store strings.

Imagine having to store the entire vocabulary of this book in a way to find out whether certain words are contained within the book. How can this be done efficiently?

After the previous sections, you should already have an answer, but if you think about strings—they are stored as arrays or lists of `char` instances—it would use a good amount of memory. Since each word has to use letters from the English alphabet, can't we use that?

Tries do something similar. They use characters as nodes in a tree where the parent node is the preceding character and all children (limited only by the size of the alphabet) are what follows. A trie storing the strings ABB, ABC, CAACB, CAACA, BBB, and BBA can be seen in the following trie diagram:

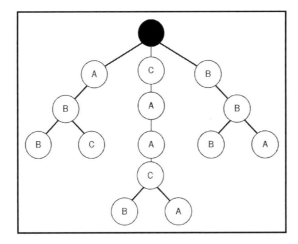

Storing strings like this enables a very efficient search. You only have to walk through the letters in the key that is to be stored to find out (or store) whether that string is contained in—for example—a set. In fact, if a string can only have a certain size, then the retrieval time is constant and it does not matter whether the trie stores 10 or 10 million words. Typically, this is useful for set data structures or key-value stores with string keys (such as hashes, but more on that later). Just like the binary search tree, this structure has a strong hierarchical memory management (that is, no pointers "back up"), making it a perfect fit for Rust.

Lately, the product team has looked into the user's device keys once again and found that the typical IoT device uses keys that represent a path, and they would often look like `countryA/cityB/factoryC/machine1/positionX/sensorY`. Reminded of the trees that worked so well earlier, they thought that you could use those to improve the directory as well. But you already have a better idea!

More realistic IoT device management

Paths like that tend to have a huge overlap, since there are countless sensors and devices in a single location. Additionally, they are unique thanks to the hierarchical properties and are human-readable in case the sensor needs to be found. A great fit for a trie!

The basis for this trie will be a node type that stores the children, current character, and, if it's a node that concludes a full key, the `IoTDevice` object from earlier in this chapter. This is what this looks like in Rust:

```
struct Node {
    pub key: char,
    next: HashMap<char, Link>,
    pub value: Option<IoTDevice>,
}
```

This time, the children is a different data structure as well: a `HashMap`. Maps (also called dictionaries, associative arrays) explicitly store a key alongside a value and the word "hash" hints at the method, which will be discussed in the next chapter. For now, the `HashMap` guarantees a single character to be associated with a Node type, leading the way for iteration. On top of that, this data structure allows for a get-or-add type operation, which significantly improves code readability.

Since the number of possible word beginnings is similar, the root is a `HashMap` as well, giving the trie multiple roots:

```
pub struct BestDeviceRegistry {
    pub length: u64,
    root: HashMap<char, Link>,
}
```

In order to fill up these maps with data, a method to add paths is required.

Adding paths

The algorithm for inserting a string into a trie can be described in only a few sentences: go through each character of the word and trace it down the trie. If a node does not yet exist, create it, and add the object with the last entry.

Of course, there are special cases that need to be decided as well: what happens when a string already exists? Overwrite or ignore? In the case of this implementation, the last write will win—that is, it's overwriting whatever existed previously:

```
pub fn add(&mut self, device: IoTDevice) {
    let p = device.path.clone();
    let mut path = p.chars();
    if let Some(start) = path.next() {
        self.length += 1;
        let mut n = self.root
                    .entry(start)
                    .or_insert(Node::new(start, None));
        for c in path {
            let tmp = n.next
                        .entry(c)
                        .or_insert(Node::new(c, None));
            n = tmp;
        }
        n.value = Some(device);
    }
}
```

Another special case is the root node, since it's not a real node but a `HashMap` right away. Once a trie is set up, the most important thing is to get stuff out again!

Walking

Add and search work in a very similar manner: follow the links to the characters of the key and return the "value" in the end:

```
pub fn find(&mut self, path: &str) -> Option<IoTDevice> {
    let mut path = path.chars();
    if let Some(start) = path.next() {
        self.root.get(&start).map_or(None, |mut n| {
            for c in path {
                match n.next.get(&c) {
                    Some(ref tmp) => n = tmp,
                    None => break,
                }
            }
            n.value.clone()
        })
    } else {
        None
    }
}
```

Since the trie does not store strings in any particular order (or even consistently), getting the same data out in a predictable way is tricky! Walking it like a binary tree works well enough, but will only be deterministic with respect to the insertion order, something that should be kept in mind when testing the implementation:

```
pub fn walk(&self, callback: impl Fn(&IoTDevice) -> ()) {
    for r in self.root.values() {
        self.walk_r(&r, &callback);
    }
}

fn walk_r(&self, node: &Link, callback: &impl Fn(&IoTDevice) -> ()) {
    for n in node.next.values() {
        self.walk_r(&n, callback);
    }
    if let Some(ref dev) = node.value {
        callback(dev);
    }
}
```

As previously mentioned, this walk is called a breadth-first traversal.

Wrap up

The trie data structure is a very efficient way of storing and finding strings by storing common prefixes, and they are often used in practice. One use case is the popular Java search engine Lucene, which uses this structure to store words in the search index, but there are plenty of other examples across different fields. Additionally, the simplicity is great for implementing a custom trie to store entire words or other objects instead of characters.

Upsides

The inherent prefix is great for efficient storage and, apart from that, there are the following benefits:

- Easy implementation facilitates customizing
- Minimal memory requirements for sets of strings
- Constant-time retrieval for strings with a known maximum length
- Exotic algorithms are available (for example, Burst Sort)

While the trie is great, it is also fairly simple, which comes with a number of downsides.

Downsides

Tries can work in a lot of shapes and forms, but can't handle every use case, unfortunately. Other disadvantages include the following:

- It has a name that's strange to pronounce
- There is no deterministic order on walking
- There are no duplicate keys

This concludes the more exotic tree varieties. Next up is the B-Tree, which is essentially a universal tree!

B-Tree

As you have noticed, restricting the number of children to 2 (like the binary trees earlier) yields a tree that only lets the algorithm decide whether to go left or right, and it's easily hardcoded. Additionally, storing only a single key-value pair in a node can be seen as a waste of space—after all, the pointers can be a lot larger than the actual payload!

B-Trees generally store multiple keys and values per node, which can make them more space-efficient (the payload-to-pointer ratio is higher). As a tree, each of these (key-value) pairs has children, which hold the values between the nodes they are located at. Therefore, a B-Tree stores triples of key, value, and child, with an additional child pointer to cover any "other" values. The following diagram shows a simple B-Tree. Note the additional pointer to a node holding smaller keys:

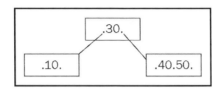

As depicted here, a B-Tree can have varying amounts of those key-value pairs (only the keys are visible), but they will have a maximum number of children—defined by the *order* parameter. Consequently, a binary search tree can be considered an order-2 B-Tree, without the added benefit of being self-balancing.

In order to achieve the self-balancing nature, a B-Tree has certain properties (as defined by Donald Knuth):

1. Each node can only have *order* children
2. Each node that is not a leaf node or root has at least *order/2* children
3. The root node has at least two children
4. All nodes hold *order - 1* keys when they have *order* children
5. All leaf nodes appear on the same level

How does self-balancing work? It is way simpler than a red-black tree. Firstly, new keys can only be inserted at the leaf level. Secondly, once the new key has found a node, the node is evaluated to the preceding rules—in particular, if there are now more than *order - 1* keys. If that is the case, the node has to be split, moving the center key to the parent node, as shown in the following diagram:

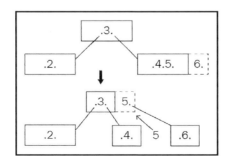

Next, the children are put in their intended position (especially important if the elevated node had children) and then the process is repeated up the tree until the root node is valid.

This process creates something that is called a **fat tree** (as opposed to a high tree), which means that adding height is only possible through splitting, which doesn't happen very often. In order to work with the nodes, they contain additional information about themselves:

```
type Tree = Box<Node>;

#[derive(Clone, PartialEq, Debug)]
enum NodeType {
    Leaf,
    Regular,
}

#[derive(Clone)]
struct Node {
    keys: Vec<Option<(u64, String, Option<Tree>)>>,
    left_child: Option<Tree>,
    pub node_type: NodeType,
}
```

In this case, the type of node is determined by a property, `node_type`, but the entire node could be wrapped into an enumeration as well. Furthermore, a special variable holding the "left child" has been attached in order to deal with keys lower than what is associated with the triples in the `keys` vector.

Like binary trees, the B-Tree exhibits logarithmic runtime complexity on search and insert ($O(log2(n))$) and, with the the simplified rebalancing, they make for a great choice for database indices. In fact, many SQL databases (such as SQLite and SQL Server) use B-Trees to store those search indices, and B+ Trees to store tables thanks to their smart ways of accessing the disk.

The product team has also heard about this and, since the previous attempts at the IoT device management solution have been a huge success, they thought about replacing the red-black tree with something better! They want to reduce the number of bugs by creating a more simplified version of the original database, so the requirements actually stay the same.

An IoT database

As in the previous implementation, this tree builds on the `numerical_id` property of `IoTDevice` as keys, and the device object as value. In code, a node looks very similar to the previous example:

```
type Tree = Box<Node>;
type KeyType = u64;

type Data = (Option<IoTDevice>, Option<Tree>);

#[derive(Clone, PartialEq, Debug)]
enum NodeType {
    Leaf,
    Regular,
}

#[derive(Clone, PartialEq)]
enum Direction {
    Left,
    Right(usize),
}

#[derive(Clone)]
struct Node {
    devices: Vec<Option<IoTDevice>>,
    children: Vec<Option<Tree>>,
    left_child: Option<Tree>,
    pub node_type: NodeType,
}
```

Instead of triples, this node type uses a synchronized index to find the children associated with a specified key-value pair. These pairs are also created ad hoc by evaluating the `numerical_id` property of the contained device, thereby also simplifying the code and eventual updates to the keys. Something that is missing from the node is a parent pointer, which made the entire red-black tree code significantly more complex.

The tree itself is stored as an `Option` on a boxed node (aliased as `Tree`), along with the `order` and `length` properties:

```
pub struct DeviceDatabase {
    root: Option<Tree>,
    order: usize,
    pub length: u64,
}
```

Finally, to check the validity of the tree, here's a `validate` method that recursively finds the minimum and maximum leaf height and checks whether the number of children is within bounds (as mentioned in the rules indicated earlier):

```
pub fn is_a_valid_btree(&self) -> bool {
    if let Some(tree) = self.root.as_ref() {
        let total = self.validate(tree, 0);
        total.0 && total.1 == total.2
    } else {
        false // there is no tree
    }
}

fn validate(&self, node: &Tree, level: usize) -> (bool, usize, usize) {
    match node.node_type {
        NodeType::Leaf => (node.len() <= self.order, level, level),
        NodeType::Regular => {
            // Root node only requires two children,
            //   every other node at least half the
            // order
            let min_children = if level > 0 {
                self.order / 2usize } else { 2 };
            let key_rules = node.len() <= self.order &&
                node.len() >= min_children;

            let mut total = (key_rules, usize::max_value(), level);
            for n in node.children.iter().chain(vec![&node.left_child]) {
                if let Some(ref tree) = n {
                    let stats = self.validate(tree, level + 1);
                    total = (
                        total.0 && stats.0,
                        cmp::min(stats.1, total.1),
                        cmp::max(stats.2, total.2),
                    );
                }
            }
            total
        }
    }
}
```

Having established these basic structures, we can move on to how to add new devices to the tree.

Adding stuff

B-Trees add new entries to their leaves, which then bubble up as nodes grow too large. In order to efficiently find a spot, this is done recursively, removing and replacing ownership as needed. Here is the `add()` function, which takes care of retrieving ownership of the root node and calling the recursive call with an existing or new node:

```
type Data = (Option<IoTDevice>, Option<Tree>);

pub fn add(&mut self, device: IoTDevice) {
    let node = if self.root.is_some() {
        mem::replace(&mut self.root, None).unwrap()
    } else {
        Node::new_leaf()
    };

    let (root, _) = self.add_r(node, device, true);
    self.root = Some(root);
}
```

Except in the case of the root node, the `add_r()` function (the recursive call) returns two pieces of information: the key it descended into and—in case of a "promotion"—the device and child that are to be added to whichever node it returns to. In principle, this function works as follows:

1. Recursively find the appropriate leaf and perform a sorted insert.
2. Increment the length if it's not a duplicate.
3. If the node now has more keys than are allowed: split.
4. Return the original node and the key with its new value to the caller.
5. Place the new node where it came from.
6. Add the promoted key.
7. Repeat from step 3 until at the root level:

```
fn add_r(&mut self, node: Tree, device: IoTDevice, is_root: bool)
-> (Tree, Option<Data>) {
    let mut node = node;
    let id = device.numerical_id;

    match node.node_type {
        NodeType::Leaf => {                          // 1
            if node.add_key(id, (Some(device), None)) {
                self.length += 1;              // 2
            }
        }
    }
```

```
                    NodeType::Regular => {
                        let (key, (dev, tree)) = node.remove_key(id).unwrap();
                        let new = self.add_r(tree.unwrap(), device, false);
                        if dev.is_none() {                    // 5
                            node.add_left_child(Some(new.0));
                        } else {
                            node.add_key(key, (dev, Some(new.0)));
                        }
                                                              // 6
                        if let Some(split_result) = new.1 {
                            let new_id = &split_result.0.clone().unwrap();
                            node.add_key(new_id.numerical_id, split_result);
                        }
                    }
                }

                if node.len() > self.order {                  // 3
                    let (new_parent, sibling) = node.split();

                    // Check if the root node is "full" and add a new level
                    if is_root {
                        let mut parent = Node::new_regular();
                        // Add the former root to the left
                        parent.add_left_child(Some(node));
                        // Add the new right part as well
                        parent.add_key(new_parent.numerical_id,
                                    (Some(new_parent), Some(sibling)));
                        (parent, None)
                    } else {
                                                              // 4
                        (node, Some((Some(new_parent), Some(sibling))))
                    }
                } else {
                    (node, None)
                }
            }
```

Since the root node is a special case where a new level is added to the tree, this has to be taken care of where the last split is happening—in the `add_r()` function. This is as simple as creating a new non-leaf node and adding the former root to the left and its sibling to the right, placing the new parent on top as the root node.

In this implementation, a lot of the heavy lifting is done by the node's implementation of several functions, including `split()`. While this is complex, it encapsulates the inner workings of the tree—something that should not be exposed too much so as to facilitate change:

```
pub fn split(&mut self) -> (IoTDevice, Tree) {
    let mut sibling = Node::new(self.node_type.clone());

    let no_of_devices = self.devices.len();
    let split_at = no_of_devices / 2usize;

    let dev = self.devices.remove(split_at);
    let node = self.children.remove(split_at);

    for _ in split_at..self.devices.len() {
        let device = self.devices.pop().unwrap();
        let child = self.children.pop().unwrap();
        sibling.add_key(device.as_ref().unwrap()
                        .numerical_id, (device, child));
    }

    sibling.add_left_child(node);
    (dev.unwrap(), sibling)
}
```

As described previously, splitting yields a new sibling to the original node and a new parent to both of them. The sibling will receive the upper half of the keys, the original node remains with the lower half, and the one in the center becomes the new parent.

Having added several devices, let's talk about how to get them back out.

Searching for stuff

A B-Tree's search works just the way binary tree searches do: recursively checking each node for the path to follow. In B-Trees, this becomes very convenient since it can be done in a loop, in this case, by the `get_device()` function:

```
pub fn get_device(&self, key: KeyType) -> Option<&IoTDevice> {
    let mut result = None;
    for d in self.devices.iter() {
        if let Some(device) = d {
            if device.numerical_id == key {
                result = Some(device);
                break;
            }
        }
```

```
            }
        }
        result
    }
```

This function is implemented at the node structure and does a regular linear search for the key itself. If it is unable to find that key, the `find_r()` function has to decide whether to continue, which it does by evaluating the node type. Since leaf nodes don't have any children, not finding the desired key will end the search, returning None. Regular nodes allow the search to continue on a deeper level of the tree:

```
pub fn find(&self, id: KeyType) -> Option<IoTDevice> {
    match self.root.as_ref() {
        Some(tree) => self.find_r(tree, id),
        _ => None,
    }
}

fn find_r(&self, node: &Tree, id: KeyType) -> Option<IoTDevice> {
    match node.get_device(id) {
        Some(device) => Some(device.clone()),
        None if node.node_type != NodeType::Leaf => {
            if let Some(tree) = node.get_child(id) {
                self.find_r(tree, id)
            } else {
                None
            }
        }
        _ => None,
    }
}
```

Another method for finding something within the tree's values is walking the tree.

Walking the tree

Similarly to the binary trees earlier in this chapter, walking can be done with different strategies, even if there are many more branches to walk. The following code shows an in-order tree walking algorithm, where the callback is executed between the left child and before descending into the child that is currently looked at:

```
pub fn walk(&self, callback: impl Fn(&IoTDevice) -> ()) {
    if let Some(ref root) = self.root {
        self.walk_in_order(root, &callback);
    }
}
```

```
fn walk_in_order(&self, node: &Tree, callback: &impl Fn(&IoTDevice) -> ())
{
    if let Some(ref left) = node.left_child {
        self.walk_in_order(left, callback);
    }

    for i in 0..node.devices.len() {
        if let Some(ref k) = node.devices[i] {
            callback(k);
        }

        if let Some(ref c) = node.children[i] {
            self.walk_in_order(&c, callback);
        }
    }
}
```

Thanks to the internal sorting, this walk retrieves the keys in an ascending order.

Wrap up

B-Trees are awesome. They are widely used in real-world applications, their implementation in Rust is not all that complex, and they maintain a great performance regardless of insertion order. Furthermore, the tree's order can dramatically improve performance by decreasing the tree's height. It is recommended to estimate the number of key-value pairs beforehand and adjust the order accordingly.

As a benchmark, let's evaluate the trees by inserting 100,000 unsorted, unique elements, and retrieving them using find(). Dot size represents the variance, while the values shown along the y axis are nanoseconds:

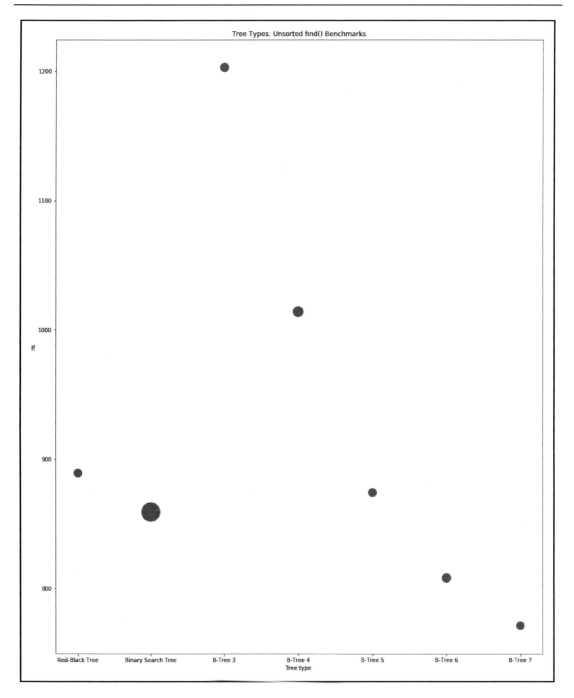

The chart output of Unsorted find ()

Other than that, it performs at the level of other trees, with vastly fewer lines of code and less code complexity, both of which impact readability and maintainability for other developers.

Upsides

This type of tree achieves great performance with the order parameter set accordingly:

- Less complex to implement than other self-balancing trees
- Widely used in database technology
- Predictable performance thanks to self-balancing
- Range queries are possible
- Variants that minimize disk access (B+ Tree)

The tree's downsides are few.

Downsides

Absolute performance depends significantly on the tree's order; other than that, this tree does not have many downsides.

Graphs

In their most generic form, trees are graphs—directed, acyclic graphs. A general graph can be described as a collection of connected nodes, sometimes referred to as vertices, with certain properties such as whether cycles are allowed. The connections between those also have their own name: edges. These edges can have certain properties as well, in particular, weights and directions (like one-way streets).

By enforcing these constraints, a model can be built that, just like trees, reflects a certain reality very well. There is one particular thing that is typically represented as a weighted graph: the internet. While, nowadays, this might be an oversimplification, with various versions of the Internet Protocol (IPv4 and IPv6) and **Network Address Translation** (**NAT**) technologies hiding large numbers of participants online, in its earlier days, the internet could be drawn as a collection of routers, computers, and servers (nodes) interconnected with links (edges) defined by speed and latency (weights).

The following diagram shows a random, undirected, unweighted graph:

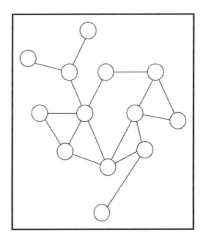

Other than humans, who can typically see and follow a reasonably efficient path through this mesh of interconnected nodes, computers require specific instructions to find anything in there! This called for new algorithms that allow for dealing with this complexity—which is especially tricky once the number of nodes in the mesh exceeds the number of nodes that can be looked at in time. This led to the development of many routing algorithms, techniques to finding cycles and segmenting the network, or popular NP-hard problems, such as the traveling salesman problem or the graph-coloring problem. The traveling salesman problem is defined as follows.

Find the optimal (shortest) path between cities without visiting one twice. On the left are some cities in Europe; on the right, two possible solutions (dotted versus solid lines):

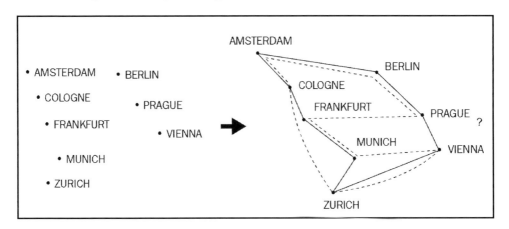

Today, there are many examples of graphs, the most obvious being a social graph (in social networks), but also as part of TensorFlow's deep learning API, state machines, and the rise of graph databases that offer a generic query language to traverse graphs. Even some less obvious use cases can be found, such as storing genetic sequences (nodes being the small parts of the DNA)!

To get out of theoretical constructs, how would you represent a graph in a program *efficiently*? As a node structure with a list of outbound vertices? How would you find a particular node then? A tricky problem! Graphs also have the habit of growing quite large, as anyone who ever wanted to serialize object graphs to JSON can testify: they run out of memory quite easily.

The best way to work with this data structure is surprisingly simple: a matrix. This matrix can either be sparse (that is, a list of lists with varying sizes), called an **adjacency list**, or a full-blown matrix (adjacency matrix). Especially for a matrix, the size is typically the number of nodes on either side and the weights (or Boolean values representing "connected" or "not connected") at each crossing. Many implementations will also keep the "real" nodes in its own list, using the indices as IDs. The following diagram shows how to display a graph as a matrix:

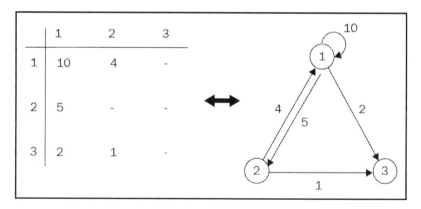

Rust provides many great tools for implementing really complex graph structures: enumerations and pattern-matching provide ways to operate on types of nodes and edges with low overhead, while iterators and functional approaches remove the need for verbose loops. Let's look at a generic graph structure in Rust:

```
struct ASimpleGraph {
    adjacency_list: Vec<Vec<usize>>,
}
```

This adjacency list can store nodes and whether they are connected, making this a finite, undirected, unweighted graph—great for storing simple relationships between objects. Already, a data structure such as this has the ability to implement sophisticated routing algorithms or run out of resources on a backtracking algorithm. In an adjacency list, each index in the list represents the origin of an edge and the contained elements (also lists) are any outbound edges. To traverse the graph, start at an origin index and find the next index by searching its edges. Then repeat until arriving at the destination node!

When the product team heard of this amazing data structure—and they are now well aware of your abilities—they came up with a new product: the literal Internet of Things (it's a working title). Their idea is to provide customers with a way to model complex sensor placements that would have distance built in! Customers can then go and evaluate all sensors that are within a certain range of each other, find single points of failure, or plan a route to inspect them quickly.

To summarize, customers should be able to do the following:

- Create or add a list of nodes
- Connect nodes with their physical distance to each other
- Find the shortest path between two nodes with respect to the distance provided
- Retrieve a list of neighbors of a specified node, up to a certain degree

Great idea, right? A great fit for graphs as well.

The literal Internet of Things

In order to get a head start on these requirements, the decision for a graph representation has to be made: list or matrix? Both work well, but for explanatory reasons, the examples will go with an adjacency list built on top of a vector of vectors:

```
pub struct InternetOfThings {
    adjacency_list: Vec<Vec<Edge>>,
    nodes: Vec<KeyType>,
}
```

As previously mentioned, it makes sense to keep the actual values, identifiers, or even entire objects in their own list and simply work with indices of the `usize` type. The edge structure in this example could be represented as a tuple just as well, but it's way more readable this way:

```
#[derive(Clone, Debug)]
struct Edge {
```

```
      weight: u32,
        node: usize,
}
```

Having those two structures in place, adding nodes (or... things) to the graph can be done with only a few lines:

```
fn get_node_index(&self, node: KeyType) -> Option<usize> {
    self.nodes.iter().position(|n| n == &node)
}

pub fn set_edges(&mut self, from: KeyType, edges: Vec<(u32, KeyType)>) {
    let edges: Vec<Edge> = edges.into_iter().filter_map(|e| {
        if let Some(to) = self.get_node_index(e.1) {
            Some(Edge { weight: e.0, node: to })
            } else {
                None
            }}).collect();
    match self.nodes.iter().position(|n| n == &from) {
        Some(i) => self.adjacency_list[i] = edges,
        None => {
            self.nodes.push(from);
            self.adjacency_list.push(edges)
        }
    }
}
```

Within that function, there is a crucial check that's made: every edge has to connect to a valid node, otherwise it will not be added to the graph. To achieve this, the code looks up the IDs provided in the `edges` parameter in its internal node storage to find the index it's at, something that is done by the `position()` function of Rust's iterator trait. It returns the position of when the provided predicate returns true! Similarly, the `filter_map()` function of the iterator will only include elements that evaluate to `Some()` (as opposed to `None`) in its result set. Therefore, the nodes have to have a setter that also initializes the adjacency list:

```
pub fn set_nodes(&mut self, nodes: Vec<KeyType>) {
    self.nodes = nodes;
    self.adjacency_list = vec![vec![]; self.nodes.len()]
}
```

Once that's done, the graph is ready to use. How about we go looking for neighbors first?

Neighborhood search

Neighborhood search is a very trivial algorithm: starting from the node provided, follow every edge and return what you find. In our case, the degree of the relationship is important.

Just like for the tree algorithms shown previously, recursion is a great choice for solving this problem. While an iterative solution will often be more memory-efficient (no stack overflows), recursion is way more descriptive once you get the hang of it. Additionally, some compilers (and partly `rustc`, but not guaranteed) will expand the recursion into a loop, providing the best of both worlds (look for tail call optimization)! Obviously, the most important thing is to have a projected growth in mind; 100,000 recursive calls are likely to fill up the stack.

However, the function to run the neighborhood is implemented two-fold. First, the public-facing function takes care of validating input data and sees whether the node actually exists:

```
pub fn connected(&self, from: KeyType, degree: usize) ->
Option<HashSet<KeyType>> {
    self.nodes.iter().position(|n| n == &from).map(|i| {
        self.connected_r(i, degree).into_iter().map(|n|
        self.nodes[n].clone()).collect()
    })
}
```

With that out of the way, the recursive call can create a list of all its neighbors and run the same call on each of them. Returning a set of nodes eliminates the duplicates as well:

```
fn connected_r(&self, from: usize, degree: usize) -> HashSet<usize> {
    if degree > 0 {
        self.adjacency_list[from]
            .iter()
            .flat_map(|e| {
                let mut set = self.connected_r(e.node, degree - 1);
                set.insert(e.node);
                set
            }).collect()
    } else {
        HashSet::new()
    }
}
```

Since the recursive call returns the internal representation (that is, indices), the outer function translates those back into data the user can understand. This function can serve as a basis for other features, such as intersecting the neighborhoods of two nodes, and vicinity search. Or, to make it more real, on a sensor outage, the company can check whether there is a common device that's responsible (intersection), or if other close-by sensors are reporting similar measurements to rule out malfunctions (neighborhood search). Now, let's move on to something more complex: finding the shortest path.

The shortest path

This algorithm has its roots in early networking: routers had to decide where to forward packets to, without having any knowledge of what's beyond. They simply had to make the best decision without having perfect information! Edsger Dijkstra, one of the pioneers of computer science, then came up with a graph-routing algorithm that has been named after him: Dijkstra's algorithm.

The algorithm works iteratively and goes over each node to add up their weights, thereby finding the distance (or cost) of reaching this node. It will then continue at the node with the lowest cost, which makes this algorithm a "greedy" algorithm. This continues until the desired node is reached or there are no more nodes to evaluate.

Algorithms that immediately converge toward what's best right now (**local optimum**) in order to find the best overall solution (**global optimum**) are called **greedy algorithms**. This, of course, is tricky, since the path to a global optimum might require the acceptance of an increased cost! There is no guaranteed way to finding the global optimum, so it's about reducing the probability of getting stuck in a local optimum. A well-known greedy algorithm in 2018 is stochastic gradient descent, which is used to train neural networks.

In code, this is what that looks like:

```
pub fn shortest_path(&self, from: KeyType, to: KeyType) -> Option<(u32,
Vec<KeyType>)> {
    let mut src = None;
    let mut dest = None;

    for (i, n) in self.nodes.iter().enumerate() {
        if n == &from {
            src = Some(i);
        }
        if n == &to {
            dest = Some(i);
```

```
        }
        if src.is_some() && dest.is_some() {
            break;
        }
    }
    if src.is_some() && dest.is_some() {
        let (src, dest) = (src.unwrap(), dest.unwrap());

        let mut distance: Vec<TentativeWeight> =
            vec![TentativeWeight::Infinite; self.nodes.len()];
        distance[src] = TentativeWeight::Number(0);

        let mut open: Vec<usize> =
                (0..self.nodes.len()).into_iter().collect();
        let mut parent = vec![None; self.nodes.len()];
        let mut found = false;
        while !open.is_empty() {
            let u = min_index(&distance, &open);
            let u = open.remove(u);

            if u == dest {
                found = true;
                break;
            }

            let dist = distance[u].clone();

            for e in &self.adjacency_list[u] {
                let new_distance = match dist {
                    TentativeWeight::Number(n) =>
                        TentativeWeight::Number(n + e.weight),
                    _ => TentativeWeight::Infinite,
                };
                let old_distance = distance[e.node].clone();

                if new_distance < old_distance {
                    distance[e.node] = new_distance;
                    parent[e.node] = Some(u);
                }
            }
        }
        if found {
            let mut path = vec![];
            let mut p = parent[dest].unwrap();
            path.push(self.nodes[dest].clone());
            while p != src {
                path.push(self.nodes[p].clone());
                p = parent[p].unwrap();
```

```
        }
        path.push(self.nodes[src].clone());

        path.reverse();
        let cost = match distance[dest] {
            TentativeWeight::Number(n) => n,
            _ => 0,
        };
        Some((cost, path))
    } else {
        None
    }
} else {
    None
}
}
```

Since this is a long one, let's break it down. This is boiler-plate code to ensure that both source and destination nodes are nodes in the graph:

```
pub fn shortest_path(&self, from: KeyType, to: KeyType) -> Option<(u32,
Vec<KeyType>)> {
    let mut src = None;
    let mut dest = None;

    for (i, n) in self.nodes.iter().enumerate() {
        if n == &from {
            src = Some(i);
        }
        if n == &to {
            dest = Some(i);
        }
        if src.is_some() && dest.is_some() {
            break;
        }
    }
    if src.is_some() && dest.is_some() {
        let (src, dest) = (src.unwrap(), dest.unwrap());
```

Then, each node gets a tentative weight assigned, which is infinite in the beginning, except for the origin node, which has zero cost to reach. The "open" list, which contains all the nodes yet to be processed, is conveniently created using Rust's range—as it corresponds to the indices we are working with.

The parent array keeps track of each node's parent once the lower cost is established, which provides a way to trace back the best possible path!

```
let mut distance: Vec<TentativeWeight> =
    vec![TentativeWeight::Infinite; self.nodes.len()];
distance[src] = TentativeWeight::Number(0);

let mut open: Vec<usize> =
            (0..self.nodes.len()).into_iter().collect();
let mut parent = vec![None; self.nodes.len()];
let mut found = false;
```

Now, let's plunge into the path-finding. The helper function, `min_index()`, takes the current distances and returns the index of the node that is easiest (as in lowest distance) to reach next. This node will then be removed from the open list. Here's a good point at which to also stop if the destination has been reached. For more thoughts on this, see the preceding information box on greedy algorithms. Setting `found` to `true` will help distinguish between no result and early stopping.

For each edge of this node, the new distance is computed and, if lower, inserted into a distance list (as seen from the source node). There are a lot of clones going on as well, which is due to ensuring not borrowing while updating the vector. With `u64` (or `u32`) types, this should not create a large overhead (pointers are typically that large too), but for other types, this can be a performance pitfall:

```
while !open.is_empty() {
    let u = min_index(&distance, &open);
    let u = open.remove(u);

    if u == dest {
        found = true;
        break;
    }

    let dist = distance[u].clone();

    for e in &self.adjacency_list[u] {
        let new_distance = match dist {
            TentativeWeight::Number(n) =>
                TentativeWeight::Number(n + e.weight),
            _ => TentativeWeight::Infinite,
        };
        let old_distance = distance[e.node].clone();

        if new_distance < old_distance {
            distance[e.node] = new_distance;
```

```
                parent[e.node] = Some(u);
            }
        }
    }
```

After this loop exits, there is a distance array and a parent array to be prepared for returning to the caller. First, trace back the path from the destination to the origin node in the parent array, which leads to the reverse optimal path between the two nodes:

```
    if found {
        let mut path = vec![];
        let mut p = parent[dest].unwrap();
        path.push(self.nodes[dest].clone());
        while p != src {
            path.push(self.nodes[p].clone());
            p = parent[p].unwrap();
        }
        path.push(self.nodes[src].clone());
        path.reverse();
        let cost = match distance[dest] {
            TentativeWeight::Number(n) => n,
            _ => 0,
        };
        Some((cost, path))
    } else {
        None
    }
} else {
    None
}
}
```

By strictly following the node with the lowest distance, Dijkstra's algorithm achieves a great runtime when stopping early, and runtime can even be improved by using more efficient data structures (such as a heap) to fetch the next node efficiently.

Modern approaches to shortest paths in a graph typically use the *A** (pronounced "a star") algorithm. While it operates on the same principles, it is also a bit more complex and would therefore go beyond the scope of this book.

Wrap up

A graph is surprisingly straightforward to implement: clear ownership in adjacency lists or matrices makes them almost effortless to work with! On top of that, there are two additional aspects that weren't yet covered in this implementation: an enumeration with an implementation, and using regular operations (here: comparison) with this implementation.

This shows how conforming to standard interfaces provides great ways to interface with the standard library or well-known operations in addition to the flexibility enumerations provide. With a few lines of code, infinity can be represented and worked with in a readable way. It was also a step toward more algorithmic aspects, which will be covered later in the book. For now, let's focus on graphs again.

Upsides

Graph structures are unique and there are rarely other ways of achieving the same outcome. Working in this environment enables you to focus deeply on relationships and think about problems differently. Following are some upsides of using graphs:

- Are amazing in modeling relationships
- Efficient retrieval of dependencies of a specific node
- Simplify complex abstractions
- Enable certain problems to be solved at all

Whether you choose a matrix or list representation is often a subjective choice and, for example, while the matrix provides easy deletes, a list stores edges more efficiently in the first place. It's all a trade-off.

Downsides

This leads us to the downsides of this particular data structure:

- Unable to solve certain problems efficiently (for example, a list of all nodes that have a certain property)
- More resource-inefficient

- Unsolved problems exist (for example, the traveling salesman problem with a high number of cities)
- Typically requires a problem to be reconsidered

With this, we can conclude this chapter about trees and their relatives after a summary.

Summary

This chapter went deep into trees, starting off with the simplest form: the binary search tree. This tree prepares the inserted data for search by creating a left and a right branch which hold smaller or greater values. A search algorithm can therefore just pick the direction based on the current node and the value coming in, thereby skipping a majority of the other nodes.

The regular binary search tree has a major drawback, however: it can become unbalanced. Red-black trees provide a solution for that: by rotating subtrees, a balanced tree structure is maintained and search performance is guaranteed.

Heaps are a more exotic use of the tree structure. With their primary use as a priority queue, they efficiently produce the lowest or highest number of an array in constant time. The upheap and downheap operations repair the structure upon insert or removal so that the root is again the lowest (min-heap) or highest (max-heap) number.

Another very exotic structure is the trie. They are specialized in holding strings and very efficiently find the data associated with a certain string by combining the characters as nodes with words "branching off" as required.

To go up in the generalization level, B-Trees are a generic form of a tree. They hold several values, with the ranges between them leading to a child node. Similar to red-black trees, they are balanced, and adding nodes only happens at the leaves where they may be "promoted" to a higher level. Typically, these are used in database indices.

Last but not least, the most generic form of a tree: the graph. Graphs are a flexible way to express constrained relationships, such as no cycles, and directionality. Typically, each node has weighted connections (edges) that provide some notion of cost of transitioning between the nodes.

With some of the essential data structures covered, the next chapter will explore sets and maps (sometimes called dictionaries). In fact, some of those have already been used in this chapter, so the next chapter will focus on implementing our own.

16
Exploring Maps and Sets

Up until this chapter, data structures have only become faster for searching, and this chapter is no different. What makes it different is why and how data can be found in two higher-level data structures: maps and sets. While the former is also known as dictionary, associative array, object, or hash table, the latter commonly crosses people's minds as a mathematical concept. Both can rely on hashing, a technique that allows for constant (or close to constant) time retrieval of items, checking whether they are contained in a set, or routing requests in distributed hash tables.

These data structures are also one level higher than the previous ones, since all of them build on existing structures, such as dynamic arrays or trees, and to top things off, the chapter starts with an algorithm. Understanding this chapter will be great preparation heading into the second part of the book, where algorithms are the main focus. Topics learned in this chapter include the following:

- Hashing functions and what they are good for
- How to implement a set based on different data structures
- What makes maps special

Hashing

The birthday paradox is a well-known phenomenon; two people share this special day that year, seemingly often, and we still get excited when it happens. Statistically speaking, the probability of meeting someone like this is really high, since in a room of just 23 people, the probability is already at 50%. While this may be an interesting fact, why is this introducing a section about hashing?

Birthdays can be considered a hash function—although a bad one. Hash functions are functions that map one value onto another value of a fixed size, like combining the day and month of a birthday into u64, shown as follows:

```
fn bd_hash(p: &Person) -> u64 {
    format!("{}{}", p.day, p.month) as u64
}
```

This function will prove very ineffective indeed, shown as follows:

- It is very hard to find out someone's birthday deterministically without asking them
- The space is limited to 366 unique values, which also makes collisions very likely
- They are not evenly distributed across the year

What makes a good hash function? It depends on the use case. There are many properties that can be associated with a hash function, such as the following:

- One way or two way (that is, given a hash, can one get the original value back?)
- Deterministic
- Uniform
- Fixed or variable range

Designing good hash functions is a *very* hard task in any field; there are countless algorithms that have been shown to be too weak for their designed purpose after several years of use, with SHA-1 being the latest prominent victim.

There is a wide variety of hashing algorithms for all kinds of use cases available, ranging from cryptographically secure to something akin to a parity bit to mitigate tampering. This section will focus on a few areas that we deemed interesting; for a wider picture, Wikipedia (https://en.wikipedia.org/wiki/List_of_hash_functions) provides a list that shows a number of available hashing algorithms and their articles.

Signatures are one of the most important fields for hashing algorithms and they can be as simple as the last digit on a credit card number (to validate the number) to 512-bit strong cryptographic digest functions, where a single collision is the end of that particular algorithm.

Outside of cryptography, hashing is used in completely different areas as well, such as peer-to-peer routing or encoding information in a tree-like structure. **GeoHashes** are a great example; instead of comparing longitude and latitude, these GeoHashes allow to quickly check if an area is located close to (or within) another area by comparing the first few characters of the hash. The algorithm was put into the public domain and can be found under http://geohash.org/. Collisions in this space can be ruled out since the entire space of possible input variations (coordinates on planet Earth) is known beforehand.

What are **collisions**? A collision occurs when two different input parameters lead to the same output, making the hash ambiguous. In cryptography, this fact will lead to a large scale crisis, just like it would if you found another key that matches your door lock. The main difference being that in the physical world, trying every door in your neighborhood is highly impractical, but with fully connected computers, this can be done in a matter of seconds. This means that the potential inputs are just as important as the quality of the hashing function itself—be it time and practicality (like physical items), or the applicable range (Earth coordinates, maximum number of nodes in a cluster)—transferring a function to a domain with a larger range leads to unexpected outcomes.

To summarize, collisions appear when the potential space of a key is either not large enough to withstand a full enumeration (brute force), or the outputs of the hash function are unevenly distributed.

Create your own

For the purpose of representing an object as a number (for use in a hash map or for comparison), most languages' built-in types come with a solid hash function for exactly that purpose, so building your own is almost never a good idea, unless a lot of time and effort goes into it. The better choice is to use what's built-in, or use a library that provides tested and proven methods.

It is important though to know how those functions are built, so let's create a trivial implementation to analyze the basic principles. The following example is one that uses the XOR operation on the previous and current byte to save their binary differences, then shifts it to the left up to four times (to fill up the u32 type):

```
pub fn hashcode(bytes: &[u8]) -> u32 {
    let mut a = 0_u32;
    for (i, b) in bytes.iter().enumerate() {
        a ^= *b as u32;
        a <<= i % 4;
```

```
        }
        a
    }
```

When this function is applied to a range of repeated letter strings, how are the values distributed? A histogram and a scatter plot tell the story, shown as follows:

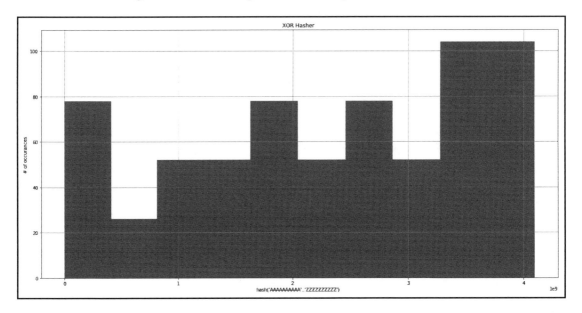

The output chart of the XOR Hasher

This histogram shows the distribution of the hash output, when the function is applied to all combinations of ten `AA-ZZ`, but each letter repeated ten times, so the first string is `AAAAAAAAAAAAAAAAAAAA` (20 letters), the last string is `ZZZZZZZZZZZZZZZZZZZZ`, yielding 675 combinations of 20 letter "words." This leads to a less optimal distribution, where the highest frequency is five times as high as the lowest. While speed can be a factor in using that function, it will clearly produce suboptimal results for cryptography.

In a scatter plot, this looks like the following:

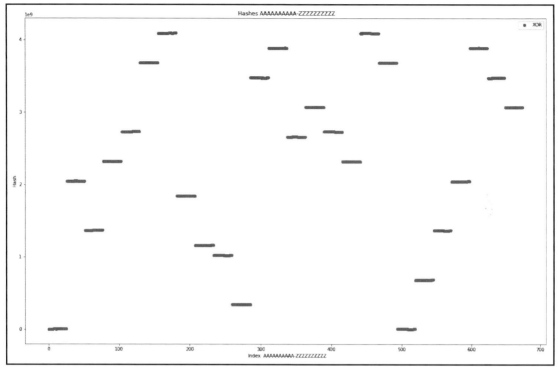

The output graph of the scatter plot

The scatter plot shows a different story. On the x axis, the index of each combination is shown, the y axis shows the hash output. Therefore, horizontal lines mean collisions, and they are all over the place! It can be interesting to explore further properties of a function like this, but the first results look quite dire, and searching for a better algorithm is the best use of anyone's time. Let's move on to checksums and digests.

Message digestion

Message digests are created as a way to guarantee authenticity; if a message was sent, a digest or signature of this message provides an ability to check whether the message has been tampered with. Typically, the signature will therefore be transmitted differently than the original message.

Obviously, this requires the hashing function to adhere to some basic rules to be considered good, listed as follows:

- A signature has to be quick and easy to obtain regardless of message size
- The signature can only have a fixed length
- The function has to minimize collisions

The hash functions contained in this group are the most popular ones and are the objective of many security researchers: MD5, SHA-1/2/3, or Adler 32. Adler 32 is prominently used in the `zlib` library to ensure the file's integrity, but should not be used to authenticate messages, thanks to the limited output space of 32-bit. However, it is easy to implement and understand, which makes it great for the purposes of this book:

```
const MOD_ADLER: u32 = 65521;

pub fn adler32(bytes: &[u8]) -> u32 {
    let mut a = 1_u32;
    let mut b = 0_u32;

    for byte in bytes {
        a = (a + byte as u32) % MOD_ADLER;
        b = (b + a) % MOD_ADLER;
    }

    (b << 16) | a
}
```

The algorithm sums up the bytes of any byte stream, and avoids an overflow by applying the modulo operation, using a large prime number (`65521`), which makes it harder for a byte to change without changing the final result. The algorithm has considerable weaknesses since there are many ways to change the operands of a sum without affecting the outcome!

Additionally, rolling over (after the modulo is applied) gives some weight to the order of bytes, so if the sum of bytes is not large enough, the algorithm is expected to produce even more collisions. Generally, this algorithm primarily protects against random transmission errors that cause bits to change, and is not useful in authenticating messages.

Wrap up

Hashing is a very useful tool that developers use every day—knowingly or unknowingly. Integer comparisons are fast, so checking the equality of two strings can be improved by comparing their hashes. Diverse keys can be made comparable by hashing—a method that is used in distributed databases to assign a partition to a row.

 Modulo hashing is a technique that lets a distributed database assign a row to a partition deterministically. Hash the row's key, then use the modulo operator with the maximum number of partitions to receive a destination to store the row.

Earlier, we explored some hash functions (XOR-based and Adler 32), but we never compared them. Additionally, Rust's standard library offers a hash function (built for `HashSet<K,V>`/`HashMap<K,V>`, and implemented for all standard types), which is a good baseline.

First, histograms—to show how many occurrences each hash has. As mentioned before, the XOR-based approach yields a very strange distribution, where some hashes clearly appear more often than others, shown as follows:

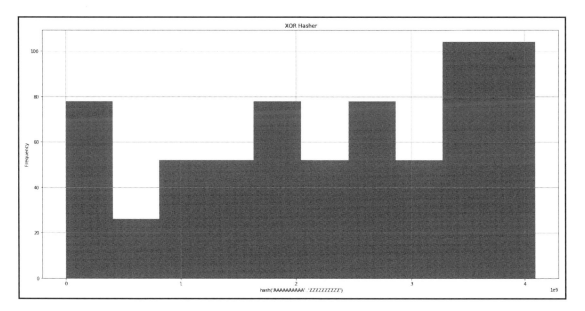

The output chart of the XOR Hasher

The Adler checksum creates a normal distribution in this case, which is probably due to the repetitive content, and the commutative nature of summing up numbers (*2 + 1 = 1 + 2*). Considering that transmission errors in compressed files are probably creating repetition, it looks like a solid choice for that use case. It would not do well in most other scenarios though:

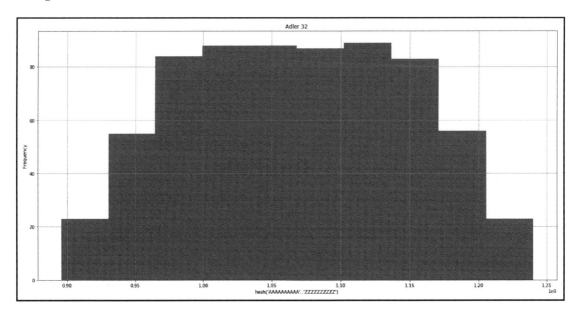

The output chart of Adler 32

The following is Rust's default choice, the `SipHash` based `DefaultHasher`:

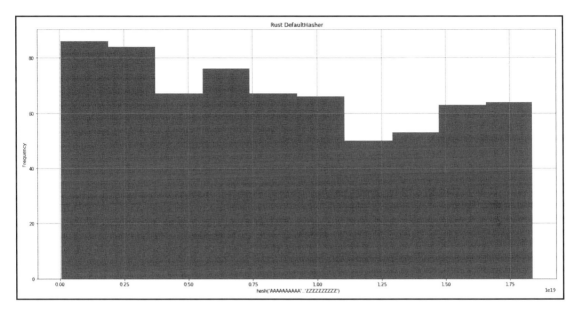

The output chart of the Rust DefaultHasher

Seeing the three distributions, their use in a hash table, where the frequency directly translates to the length of the lists at each bucket, becomes obvious. While it's best to have a length of one, lists of the same length at least yield the best performance if there is *any* collision. The Rust standard library clearly made a great choice with the `SipHash` based (https://link.springer.com/chapter/10.1007/978-3-642-34931-7_28) implementation.

A comparative scatter plot also sheds some light on the behavior of hash functions. Be aware that it is log-scaled to fit the results into a manageable plot, shown as follows:

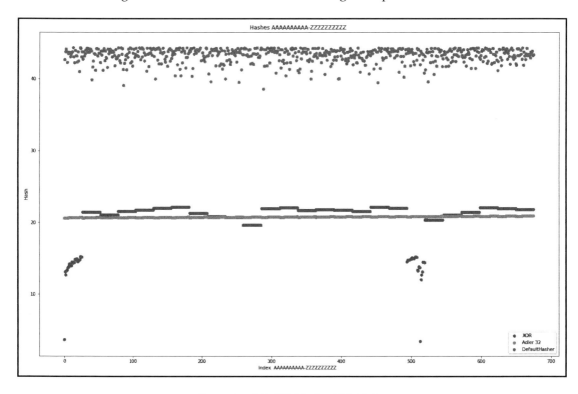

The comparison plot for XOR, Adler 32, and DefaultHasher

While the scale does not allow for a detailed judgment, what appears to be a line is always a collision-heavy behavior. As expected from the histograms, the Adler 32 and XOR-based approach both do not show a cloud. Since the y axis shows the actual hash (log-scaled), the more vertically spread it is, the better the distribution. Ideally, there would be a unique hash for each x value, but roughly the same number of dots for each y value predict a uniform hash function. Again, Rust's `DefaultHasher` looks very good in this plot, while both contenders show less optimal behaviors when used in similar cases.

A word of caution in the end. This is a software developer's perspective on hashing: security researchers and professionals know *a lot* more about hashing. It should be left to them to come up with new ways to create message signatures, so we can focus on building great software and use the best possible components to do that. In short: *do not build your own hash function for any production system.*

Now, for some practical application of hashing in a data structure: the map.

Maps

Index operations in arrays are fast, simple, and easy to understand, with one drawback: they only work with integers. Since an **array** is a continuous portion in memory that can be accessed by dividing it evenly, which makes the jumps between the elements easy, can this work with arbitrary keys as well? Yes! Enter maps.

Maps (also called dictionaries or associative arrays), are data structures that store and manage unique key-value pairs in an efficient way. These structures aim to quickly provide access to the values associated with the keys that are typically stored in one of the following two ways:

- A hashtable
- A tree

When key-value pairs are stored in a tree, the result is very similar to what was discussed in the previous chapter: self-balancing trees will provide consistent performance, avoiding the worst-case cost of a hash map.

Since trees have been discussed extensively in the previous chapter, the hash map is the main focus in this section. It uses a hashing function to translate the provided key into a number of some sort, which is in turn "mapped" on array buckets. This is where the entire pair is typically stored as a list (or tree) to deal with collisions effectively. Whenever a key is looked up, the map can search the associated bucket for the exact key. A key-value pair is inserted by hashing the key, using the modulo operation to find a spot in the array, and appending the pair to the list at the bucket.

If two or more elements are in that list, one or more collisions have occurred:

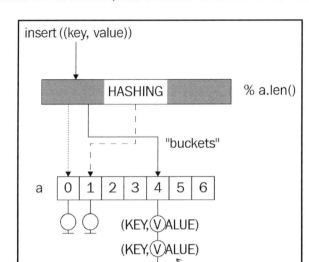

While this usually results in great access times, whenever similar hashes have to be stored (due to a bad hash function), the worst case scenario will be a search through an unordered list—with linear performance. This results in a boxed slice that holds all the data in the form of an Entry type, a vector of tuples. In this case, the implementation is even using generics:

```
type Entry<K, V> = Vec<(K, V)>;

pub struct HashMap<K, V>
where
 K: PartialEq + Clone,
 V: Clone,
{
    hash_fn: Box<dyn (Fn(&K) -> usize)>,
    store: Box<[Entry<K, V>]>,
    pub length: usize,
}
```

Additionally, the hash function can be freely chosen and is stored as a boxed function, which makes it handy to store within the object, and call whenever required. This also lets users customize the type of hashing for a particular use case.

By associating an index with a certain hash, a map lacks the ability to traverse its content in any kind of order. Therefore, keys and values cannot be iterated over in any kind of order, requiring sorting before any operation happens.

Once again, the product team is innovating and another feature would really add a lot of value to customers: associating postcodes with their factual data about the location. This way, a web service can cache commonly used data and reduce the load on the database, while serving customers a lot quicker! Since these locations are updated manually, an expiration is not required and the map can be filled on startup.

Customers provided a list of concise requirements as well to assist, shown as follows:

- Insert location information under their unique name
- Quickly retrieve information using their name
- Fetch all location names and associated information
- Update locations using their name

A hash table would do a great job here, would it not?

A location cache

Caching values is a typical use case for maps because even a large number of items won't affect the performance much, since the keys are always distinct. These keys can even carry information themselves!

For the use case defined in the last section, each customer uses postcodes within a country to identify locations; they typically cover an area that only holds a single office. Postal codes are stored as strings to cover the real world's wide variety of systems, and they are unique per country.

Thanks to a previous generic implementation, the entire `LocationCache` type can be an alias to a specialized `HashMap`, only requiring the hash function to be supplied on creation, shown as follows:

```
pub type LocationCache = HashMap<String, LocationInformation>;
```

The `HashMap` itself is a custom implementation that contains a key of type `K`, which has to also implement `PartialEq` (for comparing key instances directly), and `Clone` (for practical reasons).

The hash function

In addition to providing a generic data structure, the implementation lets the user supply a custom hash function that only maps a reference to the key type to a `usize` return type. The choice for the return type is arbitrary, and was chosen to avoid overflows.

Since the previously implemented hash function performed better than the Adler 32 checksum algorithm, the location cache will use this. To recall, the algorithm applies XOR between a byte and its predecessor and then bit shifts to the left, based on the byte's index. Alternatively, Rust's `DefaultHasher` is available as well:

```rust
pub fn hashcode(bytes: &[u8]) -> u32 {
    let mut a = 0_u32;
    for (i, b) in bytes.iter().enumerate() {
        a ^= *b as u32;
        a <<= i % 4;
    }
    a
}
```

Choosing a hashing algorithm is an important decision, as we will see in the *Wrap up* section. But first, locations need to be added!

Adding locations

In order to add a location, there are two important steps:

1. Compute the hash
2. Choose a bucket

Further operations, such as doing a sorted insert, will improve performance too, but they can be omitted by using a tree instead of a list within each bucket.

The location cache implementation uses a simple modulo operation between the hash and the length of the array to choose a bucket, which means that on top of regular hash collisions, choosing the size of the internal storage has a major influence on the performance as well. Choose a size too small and the buckets will overlap, regardless of the hash function!

In Rust code, the first part is done in the first line using the provided boxed `hashcode` function to create a hash. What follows is finding a bucket by applying something akin to the modulo operation (a binary AND operation between the hash and the highest index of the storage array) and a linear search of the attached list. If the key is found, the attached pair is updated and if not, it is added to the vector:

```
pub fn insert(&mut self, key: K, value: V) {
    let h = (self.hash_fn)(&key);
    let idx = h & (self.store.len() - 1);
    match self.store[idx].iter().position(|e| e.0 == key) {
        Some(pos) => self.store[idx][pos] = (key, value),
        None => {
            self.store[idx].push((key, value));
            self.length += 1
        }
    }
}
```

Once a location and the matching hash is stored, it can be retrieved again.

Fetching locations

Just like inserting, the retrieval process has the same steps. Whether the `get()` function to return a value or the `remove()` function, both go through the same steps: hash, match a bucket, do a linear search, and lastly, match with the expected return type. The `get()` function can utilize Rust's powerful iterators by using `find` to match the predicate within a bucket's vector and, since an `Option<Item>` is returned, its `map` function to extract the value instead of returning the entire pair:

```
pub fn get(&self, key: &K) -> Option<V> {
    let h = (self.hash_fn)(key);
    let idx = h & (self.store.len() - 1);
    self.store[idx]
        .iter()
        .find(|e| e.0 == *key)
        .map(|e| e.1.clone())
}

pub fn remove(&mut self, key: K) -> Option<V> {
    let h = (self.hash_fn)(&key);
    let idx = h & (self.store.len() - 1);
    match self.store[idx].iter().position(|e| e.0 == key) {
        Some(pos) => {
            self.length -= 1;
            Some(self.store[idx].remove(pos).1)
```

```
        }
        _ => None,
    }
}
```

The `remove` function is literally the inversion of an `insert` function; instead of updating the key-value pair if found, it is removed from the bucket and returned to the caller.

Wrap up

Hash maps are a great data structure, and often their value cannot be overstated, especially in caching or to simplify code that would otherwise have to match labels (or keys) to values using array indices. Their key breaking points are the hash function itself, and the bucket selection and organization, all of which warrant entire PhD theses and papers in computer science.

While a hash map is quick and easy to implement, the real question is: how does it perform? This is a valid question! Software engineers are prone to prefer their own implementation over learning what others already created, and while this is the premise for this entire book, benchmarks keep us honest and help us to appreciate the work that others have done.

How did this `HashMap` do, especially compared to `std::collections::HashMap<K,V>`? We have seen the hash function is far from ideal in some histograms, but what are the performance implications? Here is a scatter plot to answer all of these questions; it shows the `HashMap` implemented here with different hashing functions (Adler 32, `DefaultHasher`, XOR-based) compared to the `HashMap<K,V>` from the standard library (which uses `DefaultHasher` exclusively). The following benchmarks were performed on the same 1,000 to 10,000 randomly permuted strings between *A* and *Z* of lengths of 10 to 26 characters. The *y* axis shows the time required for a `get()` operation in nanoseconds, the *x* axis shows the number of items in the map. The sizes represent the deviation of the result:

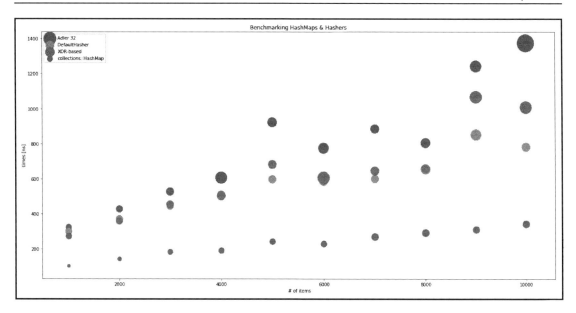

The scatter plot of the deviation of the result in Adler 32. DefaultHasher. XOR-based. collections-HashMap

This plot shows the real value and use of the particular hash functions, as they were all applied to this `HashMap,` and the work of the amazing Rust community with `std::collections::HashMap<K,V>,` which uses the `DefaultHasher`. Adler 32, as a checksum algorithm, did rather badly, which was expected, with even an increasing variance as the number of inserted items increased. Surprisingly, the XOR-based algorithm was not as bad as expected, but still had a high variance compared to the `DefaultHasher`, which performed consistently well.

All of them are a far cry off the `HashMap<K,V>` that comes with the standard library. This is great news, because the performance of this hash map implementation is also worse than the trees and skip lists presented in `Chapter 15`, *Robust Trees* and `Chapter 14`, *Lists, Lists, More Lists*.

This is proof that while the theory sounds great (constant time retrieval, best case)—implementation details can make or break a particular data structure, which is why we suspect that `collections::HashMap` sorts and inserts and use of traits instead of a boxed (hash) function to significantly improve performance.

Upsides

The hash map provides a great way to do key-value associations, which are highlighted as follows:

- Low overhead storage
- Hashed complex keys by default thanks to hashing
- Easy to understand
- Constant time retrieval

Yet, there are a few things that may be troublesome when compared to trees, or other efficient retrieval structures.

Downsides

Even though constant time retrieval sounds nice, the benchmarks show that it's not that simple. The downsides are as follows:

- Performance highly depends on the hash function and application
- Easy to implement naively, hard to get right
- Unordered storage

Some of these downsides could be mitigated by using a tree-based map, but that would be a tree as described in the previous chapter, and there is one data structure left to discuss here: the set.

Sets

Structured Query Language (SQL), is a declarative language invented to perform database operations. Its primary qualities are the ability to express *what* you want, rather than *how* you want it ("I want a set of items that conform to a predicate X" versus "Filter every item using predicate X"); this also allows non-programmers to work with databases, which is an aspect that today's NoSQL databases often lack.

You may think: how is that relevant? SQL allows us to think of the data as sets linked together with relations, which is what makes it so pleasant to work with. Understanding sets as a distinct collection of objects is sufficient to understand the language and how to manipulate the results. While this definition is also called the naive set theory, it is a useful definition for most purposes.

In general, a set has elements as members that can be described using a sentence or rule, like all positive integers, but it would contain every element only once and allow several basic operations: unions, intersections, differences, and the Cartesian product, which is the combination of two sets so that elements are combined in every possible way:

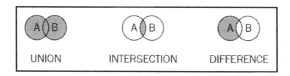

Since set elements are unique, any implementation of a set, therefore, has to make sure that each element is unique within the data structure, which is what makes the actual data structure special; it optimizes for uniqueness and retrieval.

What about using linear search on a vector to guarantee uniqueness? It works, but inserting in a populated set is going to take a lot longer than a new one. Additionally, the previous chapters talked about how trees are much better at finding things than lists, which is also why no good set implementation should use them.

The Rust collections in the standard library know two types of sets: BTreeSet<K,V> and HashSet<K,V>, both names that hint at their implementations. As mentioned in Chapter 15, *Robust Trees*, the B-Tree is a generic, self-balancing tree implementation that allows an arbitrary number of children per node, and makes search within its keys very efficient.

HashSet<K,V> is different. By storing a hash representation of the key, lookup can be done in constant time if the hashes are distributed uniformly. Since hash sets and hash maps have the same inner workings, this section will focus on a tree-based implementation and another section goes further into the depths of a hash map.

Other than inserting and checking whether a set contains a certain element, the main operations that a set should provide are union, intersect, and difference, as well as an iterator. Having these operations available will provide an efficient way to combine multiple sets in various ways, which is part of why they are useful.

In Rust code, a trie-based set could look like the following:

```
type Link<K> = Box<Node<K>>;

struct Node<K>
where
    K: PartialEq + Clone + Ord,
{
    pub key: K,
    next: BTreeMap<K, Link<K>>,
```

```
        ends_here: bool,
    }

    pub struct TrieSet<K>
    where
        K: PartialEq + Clone + Ord,
    {
        pub length: u64,
        root: BTreeMap<K, Link<K>>,
    }
```

This the trie implementation of `Chapter 15`, *Robust Trees*, with generics added and using a `BTreeMap<K,V>` root node to avoid creating too many trait dependencies. This allows arbitrary chains of simple data types to be stored as a trie, a highly efficient data structure where overlaps are kept together only to branch off once they diverge (read more on tries in `Chapter 15`, *Robust Trees*).

Can this store numbers? Yes, although they have to be converted to a byte array, but then anything can be stored in this set.

The product team has had an idea: they want to store network addresses for a network analysis software. They want to store these addresses in order to run some basic analysis on top of them: which network devices are in both networks, gathering all the addresses that are in either all or not in some specified networks. Since IP addresses are unique and consist of individual bytes that have to have common prefixes, wouldn't this be a great opportunity to use that trie set?

Storing network addresses

Storing network addresses is not a hard problem and there are many solutions out there. Their binary structure provides an opportunity to create something really specific—if time is not an issue.

In many cases, however, an off-the-shelf implementation of a data structure is enough to cover most basic use cases when that isn't your main concern. Hence, the network address storage can simple be a type alias that specifies the key type for the trie set, shown as follows:

```
    pub type NetworkDeviceStore = TrieSet<u8>;
```

Slight modifications to the `insert` (former `add`) function of the trie allows users to simply pass a slice of the key type into the function, shown in the following code:

```
    pub fn insert(&mut self, elements: &[K]) {
        let mut path = elements.into_iter();
```

```
        if let Some(start) = path.next() {
            let mut n = self
                .root
                .entry(start.clone())
                .or_insert(Node::new(start.clone(), false));
            for c in path {
                let tmp = n
                    .next
                    .entry(c.clone())
                    .or_insert(Node::new(c.clone(), false));
                n = tmp;
            }
            if !n.ends_here {
                self.length += 1;
            }
            n.ends_here = true;
        }
    }
```

This implementation differs only in a few details from what was done in the previous chapter. Firstly, it's important to avoid incrementing the length twice, which is avoided by checking if a key ends at the last node of the new key. This flag is also a new addition since the other implementation was specifically implemented to store instances of the IoTDevice type, and each node would have an optional device attached to it to signal the completion of a key.

A similar reasoning was applied to the walk and contains functions.

Networked operations

One key requirement of the product team was the ability to run simple analytics on top of this set. As a first step, these analytics can be comprised of set operations and comparing their lengths in order to create simple indicators.

One thing that is important, however, is to also get the addresses back out. For that, the implementation this time provides an iterator implementation that consumes the trie and stores it as a Vec<T>, shown as follows:

```
// [...] trie set implementation
    pub fn into_iter(self) -> SetIterator<K> {
        let v: RefCell<Vec<Vec<K>>> = RefCell::new(vec![]);
        self.walk(|n| v.borrow_mut().push(n.to_vec()));
        SetIterator::new(v.into_inner(), 0)
    }
}
```

```
pub struct SetIterator<K>
where
    K: PartialEq + Clone + Ord,
{
    data: Vec<Vec<K>>,
    last_index: usize,
}

impl<K> SetIterator<K>
where
    K: PartialEq + Clone + Ord,
{
    fn new(data: Vec<Vec<K>>, start_at: usize) -> SetIterator<K> {
        SetIterator {
            data: data,
            last_index: start_at,
        }
    }
}

impl<K> Iterator for SetIterator<K>
where
    K: PartialEq + Clone + Ord,
{
    type Item = Vec<K>;

    fn next(&mut self) -> Option<Vec<K>> {
        let result = self.data.get(self.last_index);
        self.last_index += 1;
        result.cloned()
    }
}
```

Once the vector is created, an index will do for keeping track of moving the iterator around. The set operations are actually not much more complex than that. However, all of them use the `walk()` function, which requires us to provide mutability in a lambda expression (or closure), and consequently a `RefCell` to take care of mutability management dynamically.

Union

The definition of a set union is that every element that occurs in either set is required to occur in the result. Therefore, the challenge is to insert elements from both sets into the resulting set, without creating duplicates.

Since this is handled by the `insert` process, a naive implementation could look like the following:

```
pub fn union(self, other: TrieSet<K>) -> TrieSet<K> {
    let new = RefCell::new(TrieSet::new_empty());
    self.walk(|k| new.borrow_mut().insert(k));
    other.walk(|k| new.borrow_mut().insert(k));
    new.into_inner()
}
```

This consumes both sets, returning only the result. The next operation, the intersection, looks very similar.

Intersection

To find the common elements of two sets, the intersection is a way of doing that. The definition also describes exactly that, which is why the naive implementation in Rust also follows that pattern, shown as follows:

```
pub fn intersection(self, other: TrieSet<K>) -> TrieSet<K> {
    let new = RefCell::new(TrieSet::new_empty());
    if self.length < other.length {
        self.walk(|k| {
            if other.contains(k) {
                new.borrow_mut().insert(k)
            }
        });
    } else {
        other.walk(|k| {
            if self.contains(k) {
                new.borrow_mut().insert(k)
            }
        });
    }
    new.into_inner()
}
```

As a last function, the difference is important, since it excludes common elements from the result set.

Difference

Instead of common elements, sometimes the opposite is required—removing elements that occur in both sets. This operation is also referred to as the complement of two sets, which only inserts elements into the result if they don't occur in the other set:

```
pub fn difference(self, other: TrieSet<K>) -> TrieSet<K> {
    let new = RefCell::new(TrieSet::new_empty());
    self.walk(|k| {
        if !other.contains(k) {
            new.borrow_mut().insert(k)
        }
    });
    new.into_inner()
}
```

With that, the set is finished, and all the desired functionality can be provided.

Wrap up

Sets are not complicated, but are useful. While database indices might be B-Trees, the result sets are the sets of primary keys that get moved around and operated on until the very last step, when the associated row information is fetched from disk. These are the moments when set data structures come in handy and provide a simple solution.

Similarly to everyday tasks, creating a list of unique elements can be very inefficient when a list is used; storing them in a set, however, requires no extra effort. In fact, most elements can then just be thrown into the set, which won't insert duplicates anyway.

Upsides

The set is a higher-level data structure that does the following:

- provides a simple interface for unique lists
- Implements a mathematical concept
- Has a very efficient way of storing and retrieving its elements

Downsides

The set has some downsides as well, primarily the following:

- Element order determinism depends on the implementation
- Does not always add a lot of value compared to maps
- Limited use cases

Since maps will be used a lot more often, let's dive into those.

Summary

Hashing is the art (and science) of creating a single representation (typically a number) from an arbitrary object, be it strings, `type` instances, or collections; there is a way to break them down into a number that should reflect a particular use case. The real question is what you want to achieve and what characteristics are expected from the outcome. Cryptographic hashing deals with minimizing collisions and creating signatures that create a very different hash from minor modifications, whereas GeoHashes are a way to hierarchically structure Earth's coordinates into a string. Whenever two (or more) inputs to a hash function lead to the same output, this is called a collision—a bad sign for any cryptographic hashing, but fine if it's mostly about storing something in a hash map, as long as the collisions are evenly distributed. Most importantly, however, software engineers should *never* come up with their own hash functions, especially if security is a concern.

Maps store and manage key-value pairs in an underlying data structure, which is typically either a tree or an array that maps hashes to key-value pairs called hash maps. By using a hash function to describe the key and sort the pair into buckets (array elements), hash maps are a great use case for hashing. These buckets are basically indices on an array that stores a list (or tree) for whenever different inputs lead to the same bucket. Consequently, the best case performance of a hash map is constant time ($O(1)$) to retrieve any value, whereas the worst case is linear time ($O(n)$) if the hash function returns a constant number. In reality, there are other uses that might be beneficial, such as caching, where the use case limits the potential inputs, and best case performance is always achieved.

Contrary to maps, **sets** are great data structures to store a unique collection of elements to perform set operations on. They can be implemented just like a hash map, using a hash function or a tree. In this chapter, we implemented a set based on a modified trie data structure from the previous chapter (*Robust Trees*), as well as the basic three operations: union, intersection, and difference.

In the next chapter, we will continue to explore Rust's `std::collections` library and its contents. This will include some benchmarking and looking into more implementation details, since these are the best implementations of all the concepts discussed in the book so far.

Further reading

Refer to the following links for more information:

- `http://geohash.org/`
- *Fletcher's checksum* (`https://en.wikipedia.org/wiki/Fletcher%27s_checksum`)
- Rust's `HashMap` **implementation reasoning** (`https://www.reddit.com/r/rust/comments/52grcl/rusts_stdcollections_is_absolutely_horrible/d7kcei2`)
- `https://doc.rust-lang.org/std/hash/`
- **Wikipedia's list of hash functions** (`https://en.wikipedia.org/wiki/List_of_hash_functions`)

17
Collections in Rust

In the previous chapters, we implemented a range of data structures, something that rarely happens in reality. Especially in Rust, the excellent Vec<T> covers a lot of cases, and if a map type structure is required, the HashMap<T> covers most of these too. So what else is there? How are they implemented? Why were they implemented if they won't be used? These are all great questions, and they'll get answered in this chapter. You can look forward to learning about the following:

- Sequence data types such as LinkedList<T>, Vec<T>, or VecDeque<T>
- Rust's BinaryHeap<T> implementation
- HashSet<T> and BTreeSet<T>
- How to map things with the BTreeMap<T> and HashMap<T>

Sequences

Lists of any kind are the most essential data structure in a typical program; they provide flexibility and can be used as a queue, as a stack, as well as a searchable structure. Yet the limitations and the operations make a huge of difference between different data structures, which is why the documentation for std::collections offers a decision tree to find out the collection type that is actually required to solve a particular problem.

The following were discussed in Chapter 14, *Lists, Lists, More Lists*:

- **Dynamic arrays** (Vec<T>) are the most universal and straightforward to use sequential data structure. They capture the speed and accessibility of an array, the dynamic sizing of a list, and they are the fundamental building block for higher order structures (such as stacks, heaps, or even trees). So, when in doubt a Vec<T> is always a good choice.

- VecDeque<T> is a close relative of the Vec<T>, implemented as a **ring buffer**—a dynamic array that wraps around the ends end, making it look like a circular structure. Since the underlying structure is still the same as Vec<T>, many of its aspects also apply here.
- The LinkedList<T> is very limited in its functionality in Rust. Direct index access will be inefficient (it's a counted iteration), which is probably why it can only iterate, merge and split, and insert or retrieve from the back and front.

This was a nice primer, so let's look deeper into each of Rust's data structures in std::collections!

Vec<T> and VecDeque<T>

Just like the dynamic array in Chapter 14, *Lists, Lists, More Lists*, Vec<T> and VecDeque<T> are growable, list-like data structures with support for indexing and based on a heap-allocated array. Other than the previously implemented dynamic array, it is generic by default without any constraints for the generic type, allowing literally any type to be used.

Vec<T> aims to have as little overhead as possible, while providing a few guarantees. At its core, it is a triple of (pointer, length, capacity) that provides an API to modify these elements. The capacity is the amount of memory that is allocated to hold items, which means that it fundamentally differs from length, the number of elements currently held. In case a zero-sized type or no initial length is provided, Vec<T> won't actually allocate any memory. The pointer only points to the reserved area in memory that is encapsulated as a RawVec<T> structure.

The main drawback of Vec<T> is its lack of efficient insertion at the front, which is what VecDeque<T> aims to provide. It is implemented as a ring, which wraps around the edges of the array, creating a more complex situation when the memory has to be expanded, or an element is to be inserted at a specified position. Since the implementations of Vec<T> and VecDeque<T> are quite similar, they can be used in similar contexts. This can be shown in their architecture.

Architecture

Both structures, Vec<T> and RawVec<T>, allocate memory in the same way: by using the RawVec<T> type. This structure is a wrapper around lower level functions to allocate, reallocate, or deallocate an array in the heap part of the memory, built for use in higher level data structures. Its primary goal is to avoid capacity overflows, out-of-memory errors, and general overflows, which saves the developer a lot of boilerplate code.

The use of this buffer by Vec<T> is straightforward. Whenever the length threatens to exceed capacity, allocate more memory and transfer all elements, shown in the following code:

```
#[stable(feature = "rust1", since = "1.0.0")]
pub fn reserve(&mut self, additional: usize) {
    self.buf.reserve(self.len, additional);
}
```

So this goes on to call the reserve() function, followed by the try_reserve(), followed by the amortized_new_size() of RawVec<T>, which also makes the decision about the size:

```
fn amortized_new_size(&self, used_cap: usize, needed_extra_cap: usize)
    -> Result<usize, CollectionAllocErr> {

    // Nothing we can really do about these checks :(
    let required_cap =
used_cap.checked_add(needed_extra_cap).ok_or(CapacityOverflow)?;
    // Cannot overflow, because `cap <= isize::MAX`, and type of `cap` is
`usize`.
    let double_cap = self.cap * 2;
    // `double_cap` guarantees exponential growth.
    Ok(cmp::max(double_cap, required_cap))
}
```

Let's take a look at VecDeque<T>. On top of memory allocation, VecDeque<T> has to deal with wrapping the data around the ring, which adds considerable complexity to inserting an element at a specified position, or when the capacity has to increase. Then, the old elements need to be copied to the new memory area, starting with the shortest part of a wrapped list.

Like the Vec<T>, the VecDeque<T> doubles its buffer in size if it is full, but uses the double() function to do so. *Be aware that doubling is not a guaranteed strategy and might change.*

However, whatever replaces it will have to retain the runtime complexities of the operations. The following are the functions used to determine whether the data structure is full and if it needs to grow in size:

```
#[inline]
fn is_full(&self) -> bool {
    self.cap() - self.len() == 1
}

#[inline]
fn grow_if_necessary(&mut self) {
    if self.is_full() {
        let old_cap = self.cap();
        self.buf.double();
        unsafe {
            self.handle_cap_increase(old_cap);
        }
        debug_assert!(!self.is_full());
    }
}
```

The `handle_cap_increase()` function will then decide where the new ring should live and how the copying into the new buffer is handled, prioritizing copying as little data as possible. Other than `Vec<T>`, calling the `new()` function on `VecDeque<T>` allocates at `RawVec<T>` with enough space for seven elements, which then can be inserted without growing the underlying memory, therefore it is not a zero-size structure when empty.

Insert

There are two ways to add elements to `Vec<T>`: `insert()` and `push()`. The former takes two parameters: an index of where to insert the element and the data. Before inserting, the position on the index will be freed by moving all succeeding elements towards the end (to the right). Therefore, if an element is inserted at the front, every element has to be shifted by one. `Vec<T>` code shows the following:

```
#[stable(feature = "rust1", since = "1.0.0")]
pub fn insert(&mut self, index: usize, element: T) {
    let len = self.len();
    assert!(index <= len);

    // space for the new element
    if len == self.buf.cap() {
        self.reserve(1);
    }
```

```
unsafe {
    // infallible
    // The spot to put the new value
    {
        let p = self.as_mut_ptr().add(index);
        // Shift everything over to make space. (Duplicating the
        // `index`th element into two consecutive places.)
        ptr::copy(p, p.offset(1), len - index);
        // Write it in, overwriting the first copy of the `index`th
        // element.
        ptr::write(p, element);
    }
    self.set_len(len + 1);
}
}
```

While shifting is done efficiently, by calling push(), the new item can be added without moving data around, shown as follows:

```
#[inline]
#[stable(feature = "rust1", since = "1.0.0")]
pub fn push(&mut self, value: T) {
    // This will panic or abort if we would allocate > isize::MAX bytes
    // or if the length increment would overflow for zero-sized types.
    if self.len == self.buf.cap() {
        self.reserve(1);
    }
    unsafe {
        let end = self.as_mut_ptr().offset(self.len as isize);
        ptr::write(end, value);
        self.len += 1;
    }
}
```

The main drawback of regular Vec<T> is the inability of efficiently adding data to the front, which is where VecDeque<T> excels. The code for doing this is nice and short, shown as follows:

```
#[stable(feature = "rust1", since = "1.0.0")]
pub fn push_front(&mut self, value: T) {
    self.grow_if_necessary();

    self.tail = self.wrap_sub(self.tail, 1);
    let tail = self.tail;
    unsafe {
        self.buffer_write(tail, value);
    }
}
```

With the use of `unsafe {}` in these functions, the code is much shorter and faster than it would be using safe Rust exclusively.

Look up

One major upside of using array-type data allocation is the simple and fast element access, which `Vec<T>` and `VecDeque<T>` share. The formal way to implement the direct access using brackets (`let my_first_element= v[0];`) is provided by the `Index<I>` trait.

Other than direct access, iterators are provided to search, fold, map, and so on the data. Some are equivalent to the `LinkedList<T>` part of this section.

As an example, the `Vec<T>`'s owning iterator (`IntoIter<T>`) owns the pointer to the buffer and moves a pointer to the current element forward. There is also a catch though: if the size of an element is zero bytes, how should the pointer be moved? What data is returned? The `IntoIter<T>` structure comes up with a clever solution (**ZSTs** are **zero-sized types**, so types that don't actually take up space):

```
pub struct IntoIter<T> {
    buf: NonNull<T>,
    phantom: PhantomData<T>,
    cap: usize,
    ptr: *const T,
    end: *const T,
}
// ...

#[stable(feature = "rust1", since = "1.0.0")]
impl<T> Iterator for IntoIter<T> {
    type Item = T;

    #[inline]
    fn next(&mut self) -> Option<T> {
        unsafe {
            if self.ptr as *const _ == self.end {
                None
            } else {
                if mem::size_of::<T>() == 0 {
                    // purposefully don't use 'ptr.offset' because for
                    // vectors with 0-size elements this would return the
                    // same pointer.
                    self.ptr = arith_offset(self.ptr as *const i8, 1) as
*mut T;

                    // Make up a value of this ZST.
```

```
                Some(mem::zeroed())
        } else {
            let old = self.ptr;
            self.ptr = self.ptr.offset(1);

            Some(ptr::read(old))
        }
    }
}
// ...
}
```

The comments already state what's happening, the iterator avoids returning the same pointer over and over again, and instead, increments it by one and returns a zeroed out memory. This is clearly something that the Rust compiler would not tolerate, so `unsafe` is a great choice here. Furthermore, the regular iterator (`vec![].iter()`) is generalized in the `core::slice::Iter` implementation, which works on generic, array-like parts of the memory.

Contrary to that, the iterator of `VecDeque<T>` resorts to moving an index around the ring until a full circle is reached. Here is its implementation, shown in the following code:

```
#[stable(feature = "rust1", since = "1.0.0")]
pub struct Iter<'a, T: 'a> {
    ring: &'a [T],
    tail: usize,
    head: usize,
}
// ...
#[stable(feature = "rust1", since = "1.0.0")]
impl<'a, T> Iterator for Iter<'a, T> {
    type Item = &'a T;

    #[inline]
    fn next(&mut self) -> Option<&'a T> {
        if self.tail == self.head {
            return None;
        }
        let tail = self.tail;
        self.tail = wrap_index(self.tail.wrapping_add(1), self.ring.len());
        unsafe { Some(self.ring.get_unchecked(tail)) }
    }
//...
}
```

Among other traits, both implement the `DoubleEndedIterator<T>` work on both ends, a special function called `DrainFilter<T>`, in order to retrieve items in an iterator only if a predicate applies.

Remove

`Vec<T>` and `VecDeque<T>` both remain efficient when removing items. Although, they don't change the amount of memory allocated to the data structure, both types provide a function called `shrink_to_fit()` to readjust the capacity to the length it has.

On `remove`, `Vec<T>` shifts the remaining elements toward the start of the sequence. Like the `insert()` function, it simply copies the entire remaining data with an offset, shown as follows:

```
#[stable(feature = "rust1", since = "1.0.0")]
pub fn remove(&mut self, index: usize) -> T {
    let len = self.len();
    assert!(index < len);
    unsafe {
        // infallible
        let ret;
        {
            // the place we are taking from.
            let ptr = self.as_mut_ptr().add(index);
            // copy it out, unsafely having a copy of the value on
            // the stack and in the vector at the same time.
            ret = ptr::read(ptr);

            // Shift everything down to fill in that spot.
            ptr::copy(ptr.offset(1), ptr, len - index - 1);
        }
        self.set_len(len - 1);
        ret
    }
}
```

For `VecDeque<T>`, the situation is much more complex: since the data can wrap around the ends of the underlying buffer (for example, the tail is on index three, head on index five, so the space from three to five is considered empty), it can't blindly copy in one direction. Therefore, there is some logic that deals with these different situations, but it is much too long to add here.

LinkedList<T>

Rust's `std::collection::LinkedList<T>` is a doubly linked list that uses an `unsafe` pointer operation to get around the `Rc<RefCell<Node<T>>>` unpacking we had to do in *Chapter 14*, *Lists, Lists, and More Lists*. While unsafe, this is a great solution to that problem, since the pointer operations are easy to comprehend and provide significant benefits. Let's look at the following code:

```
#[stable(feature = "rust1", since = "1.0.0")]
pub struct LinkedList<T> {
    head: Option<NonNull<Node<T>>>,
    tail: Option<NonNull<Node<T>>>,
    len: usize,
    marker: PhantomData<Box<Node<T>>>,
}

struct Node<T> {
    next: Option<NonNull<Node<T>>>,
    prev: Option<NonNull<Node<T>>>,
    element: T,
}
```

`NonNull` is a structure that originates from `std::ptr::NonNull`, which provides a non-zero pointer to a portion of heap memory in unsafe territory. Hence, the interior mutability pattern can be skipped at this fundamental level, eliminating the need for runtime checks.

Architecture

Fundamentally, `LinkedList` is built just the way we built the doubly linked list in *Chapter 14*, *Lists, Lists, and More Lists*, with the addition of a `PhantomData<T>` type pointer. Why? This is necessary to inform the compiler about the properties of the type that contains the marker when generics are involved. With it, the compiler can determine a range of things, including drop behavior, lifetimes, and so on. The `PhantomData<T>` pointer is a zero-size addition, and pretends to own type `T` content, so the compiler can reason about that.

Insert

The `std::collections::LinkedList` employs several unsafe methods in order to avoid the `Rc<RefCell<Node<T>>>` and `next.as_ref().unwrap().borrow()` calls that we saw when implementing a doubly linked list in a safe way. This also means that adding a node at either end entails the use of `unsafe` to set these pointers.

In this case, the code is easy to read and comprehend, which is important to avoid sudden crashes due to unsound code being executed. This is the core function to add a node in the front, shown as follows:

```
fn push_front_node(&mut self, mut node: Box<Node<T>>) {
    unsafe {
        node.next = self.head;
        node.prev = None;
        let node = Some(Box::into_raw_non_null(node));

        match self.head {
            None => self.tail = node,
            Some(mut head) => head.as_mut().prev = node,
        }

        self.head = node;
        self.len += 1;
    }
}
```

This code is wrapped by the publicly facing `push_front()` function, shown in the following code snippet:

```
#[stable(feature = "rust1", since = "1.0.0")]
pub fn push_front(&mut self, elt: T) {
    self.push_front_node(box Node::new(elt));
}
```

The `push_back()` function, which performs the same action but on the end of the list, works just like this. Additionally, the linked list can append another list just as easily, since it is almost the same as adding a single node, but with additional semantics (such as: is the list empty?) to take care of:

```
#[stable(feature = "rust1", since = "1.0.0")]
pub fn append(&mut self, other: &mut Self) {
    match self.tail {
        None => mem::swap(self, other),
        Some(mut tail) => {
            if let Some(mut other_head) = other.head.take() {
                unsafe {
                    tail.as_mut().next = Some(other_head);
                    other_head.as_mut().prev = Some(tail);
                }

                self.tail = other.tail.take();
                self.len += mem::replace(&mut other.len, 0);
            }
        }
    }
}
```

```
            }
        }
    }
```

Adding things is one of the strong suits of a linked list. But how about looking up elements?

Look up

The `collections::LinkedList` relies a lot on the `Iterator` trait to look up various items, which is great since it saves a lot of effort. This is achieved by extensively implementing various iterator traits using several structures, like the following:

- `Iter`
- `IterMut`
- `IntoIter`

Technically, `DrainFilter` also implements `Iterator`, but it's really a convenience wrapper. The following is the `Iter` structure declaration that the `LinkedList` uses:

```
#[stable(feature = "rust1", since = "1.0.0")]
pub struct Iter<'a, T: 'a> {
    head: Option<NonNull<Node<T>>>,
    tail: Option<NonNull<Node<T>>>,
    len: usize,
    marker: PhantomData<&'a Node<T>>,
}
```

If you remember the list's declaration earlier, it will become obvious that they are very similar! In fact, they are the same, which means that when iterating over a linked list, you are essentially creating a new list that gets shorter with every call to `next()`. As expected, this is a very efficient process that is employed here, since no data is copied and the `Iter` structures' head can move back and forth with the `prev`/`next` pointers of the current head.

`IterMut` and `IntoIter` have a slightly different structure, due to their intended purposes. `IntoIter` takes ownership of the entire list, and just calls `pop_front()` or `pop_back()` as requested.

`IterMut` has to retain a mutable reference to the original list in order to provide mutable references to the caller, but other than that, it's basically an `Iter` type structure.

The other structure that also does iteration is `DrainFilter`, which as the name suggests, removes items.

Remove

The linked list contains two functions: `pop_front()` and `pop_back()`, and they simply wrap around an "inner" function called `pop_front_node()`:

```
#[inline]
fn pop_front_node(&mut self) -> Option<Box<Node<T>>> {
    self.head.map(|node| unsafe {
        let node = Box::from_raw(node.as_ptr());
        self.head = node.next;

        match self.head {
            None => self.tail = None,
            Some(mut head) => head.as_mut().prev = None,
        }

        self.len -= 1;
        node
    })
}
```

This way, removing a specific element from `LinkedList<T>` has to be done either by splitting and appending the list (skipping the desired element), or by using `drain_filter()` function, which does almost exactly that.

Wrap up

`Vec<T>` and `VecDeque<T>` both build on a heap-allocated array, and perform very well on `insert` and `find` operations, thanks to the elimination of several steps. However, the dynamic array implementation from earlier in the book can actually hold its own against these.

The doubly-linked list implemented previously does not look good against the `LinkedList<T>` provided by `std::collections`, which is built far simpler and does not use `RefCells` that do runtime borrow checking:

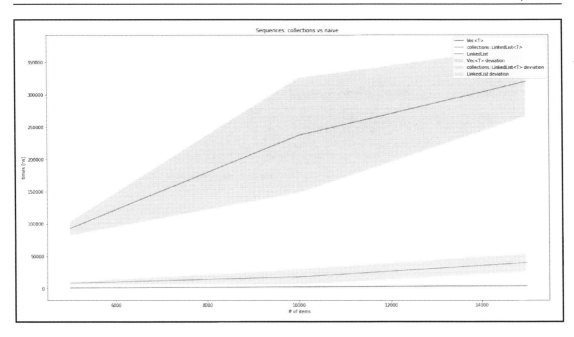

Clearly, if you need a linked list, do not implement it yourself, `std::collections::LinkedList<T>` is excellent as far as linked lists go. Commonly, `Vec<T>` will perform better while providing more features, so unless the linked list is absolutely necessary, `Vec<T>` should be the default choice.

Maps and sets

Rust's maps and sets are based largely on two strategies: B-Tree search and hashing. They are very distinct implementations, but achieve the same results: associating a key with a value (map) and providing a fast unique collection based on keys (set).

Hashing in Rust works with a `Hasher` trait, which is a universal, stateful hasher, to create a hash value from an arbitrary byte stream. By repeatedly calling the appropriate `write()` function, data can be added to the hasher's internal state and finished up with the `finish()` function.

Unsurprisingly the B-Tree in Rust is highly optimized. The `BTreeMap` documentation provides rich details on why the regular implementation (as previously shown) is cache inefficient and not optimized for modern CPU architectures. Hence, they provide a more efficient implementation, which is definitely fascinating, and you should check it out in the source code.

HashMap and HashSet

Both HashMap and HashSet use a hashing algorithm to produce the unique key required for storing and retrieving values. Hashes are created with an instance of the Hasher trait (DefaultHasher if nothing is specified) for each key that implements the Hash and Eq traits. They allow a Hasher instance to be passed into the Hash implementor to generate the required output and the data structure to compare keys for equality.

If a custom structure is to be used as a hashed key (for the map, or simply to store in the set), this implementation can be derived as well, which adds every field of the structure to the Hasher's state. In case the trait is implemented by hand, it has to create equal hashes whenever two keys are equal.

Since both data structures build on keys having implemented this trait, and both should be highly optimized, one question comes up: why bother with two variants?

Let's take a look into the source, shown as follows:

```
#[derive(Clone)]
#[stable(feature = "rust1", since = "1.0.0")]
pub struct HashSet<T, S = RandomState> {
    map: HashMap<T, (), S>,
}
```

The rest of this section will only talk about HashMap.

Architecture

HashMap is a highly optimized data structure that employs a performance heuristic called **Robin Hood hashing** to improve caching behavior, and thereby lookup times.

Robin Hood hashing is best explained together with the insertion algorithm linear probing, which is somewhat similar to the algorithm used in the hash map of the previous chapter. However, instead of an array of arrays (or Vec<Vec<(K, V)>>), the basic data structure is a flat array wrapped (together with all unsafe code) in a structure called RawTable<K, V>.

The table organizes its data into buckets (empty or full) that represent the data at a particular hash. Linear probing means that whenever a collision occurs (two hashes are equal without their keys being equal), the algorithm keeps looking into ("probing") the following buckets until an empty bucket is found.

The Robin Hood part is to count the steps from the original (ideal) position, and whenever an element in a bucket is closer to its ideal position (that is, richer), the bucket content is swapped, and the search continues with the element that was swapped out of its bucket. Thus, the search takes from the rich (with only a few steps removed from their ideal spot) and gives to the poor (those that are further away from their ideal spot).

This strategy organizes the array into clusters around the hash values and greatly reduces the key variance, while improving CPU cache-friendliness. Another main factor that influences this behavior is the size of the table and how many buckets are occupied (called **load factor**). `DefaultResizePolicy` of `HashMap` changes the table's size to a higher power of two at a load factor of 90.9%—a number that provides ideal results for the Robin Hood bucket stealing. There are also some great ideas on how to manage that growth without having to reinsert every element, but they would certainly exceed the scope of this chapter. It's recommended to read the source's comments if you are interested (see *Further reading* section).

Insert

The Robin Hood hashing strategy already describes a large portion of the `insert` mechanism: hash the key value, look for an empty bucket, and reorder elements along the way according to their probing distance:

```
pub fn insert(&mut self, k: K, v: V) -> Option<V> {
    let hash = self.make_hash(&k);
    self.reserve(1);
    self.insert_hashed_nocheck(hash, k, v)
}
```

This function only does the first step and expands the basic data structure—if needed. The `insert_hashed_nocheck()` function provides the next step by searching for the hash in the existing table, and returning the appropriate bucket for it. The element is responsible for inserting itself into the right spot. The steps necessary to do that depend on whether the bucket is full or empty, which is modeled as two different structures: `VacantEntry` and `OccupiedEntry`. While the latter simply replaces the value (this is an update), `VacantEntry` has to find a spot not too far from the assigned bucket:

```
pub fn insert(self, value: V) -> &'a mut V {
    let b = match self.elem {
        NeqElem(mut bucket, disp) => {
            if disp >= DISPLACEMENT_THRESHOLD {
                bucket.table_mut().set_tag(true);
            }
            robin_hood(bucket, disp, self.hash, self.key, value)
```

```
        },
        NoElem(mut bucket, disp) => {
            if disp >= DISPLACEMENT_THRESHOLD {
                bucket.table_mut().set_tag(true);
            }
            bucket.put(self.hash, self.key, value)
        },
    };
    b.into_mut_refs().1
}
```

The call to `robin_hood()` executes the search and swap described earlier. One interesting variable here is the `DISPLACEMENT_THRESHOLD`. Does this mean that there is an upper limit of how many displacements a value can have? Yes! This value is `128` (so `128` misses are required), but it wasn't chosen randomly. In fact, the code comments go into the details of why and how it was chosen, shown as follows:

```
// The threshold of 128 is chosen to minimize the chance of exceeding it.
// In particular, we want that chance to be less than 10^-8 with a load of
90%.
// For displacement, the smallest constant that fits our needs is 90, //
so we round that up to 128.
//
// At a load factor of α, the odds of finding the target bucket after
exactly n
// unsuccessful probes[1] are
//
// Pr_α{displacement = n} =
//      (1 - α) / α * ∑_{k≥1} e^(-kα) * (kα)^(k+n) / (k + n)! * (1 - kα /
(k + n + 1))
//
// We use this formula to find the probability of triggering the adaptive
behavior
//
// Pr_0.909{displacement > 128} = 1.601 * 10^-11
//
// 1. Alfredo Viola (2005). Distributional analysis of Robin Hood linear
probing // hashing with buckets.
```

As the comment states, the chance is *very* low that an element actually exceeds that threshold. Once a spot was found for every element, a look up can take place.

Lookup

Looking up entries is part of the insert process of HashMap and it relies on the same functions to provide a suitable entry instance to add data. Just like the insertion process, the lookup process does almost the same, save some steps in the end, listed as follows:

- Create a hash of the key
- Find the hash's bucket in the table
- Move away from the bucket comparing keys (linear search) until found

Since all of this has already been implemented for use in other functions, get() is pretty short, shown in the following code:

```
pub fn get<Q: ?Sized>(&self, k: &Q) -> Option<&V>
    where K: Borrow<Q>,
          Q: Hash + Eq
{
    self.search(k).map(|bucket| bucket.into_refs().1)
}
```

Similarly, the remove function requires search, and removal is implemented on the entry type.

Remove

The remove function looks a lot like the search function, shown as follows:

```
#[stable(feature = "rust1", since = "1.0.0")]
pub fn remove<Q: ?Sized>(&mut self, k: &Q) -> Option<V>
    where K: Borrow<Q>,
          Q: Hash + Eq
{
    self.search_mut(k).map(|bucket| pop_internal(bucket).1)
}
```

There is one major difference: search returns a mutable bucket from which the key can be removed (or rather, the entire bucket since it's now empty). HashMap turns out to be an impressive piece of code; can BTreeMap compete?

BTreeMap and BTreeSet

Talking about B-Trees in Chapter 15, *Robust Trees*, their purpose is storing key-value pairs—ideal for a map-type data structure. Their ability to find and retrieve these pairs is achieved by effectively minimizing the number of comparisons required to get to (or rule out) a key. Additionally, a tree keeps the keys in order, which means iteration is going to be implicitly ordered. Compared to HashMap, this can be an advantage since it skips a potentially expensive step.

Since—just like HashSet—BTreeSet simply uses BTreeMap with an empty value (only the key) underneath, only the latter is discussed in this section since the working is assumed to be the same. Again, let's start with the architecture.

Architecture

Rust's BTreeMap chose an interesting approach to maximize performance for search by creating large individual nodes. Recalling the typical sizes of nodes (that is, the number of children they have), they were more than two (root only), or half the tree's level to the tree's level number of children. In a typical B-Tree, the level rarely exceeds 10, meaning that the nodes stay rather small, and the number of comparisons within a node do too.

The implementors of the Rust BTreeMap chose a different strategy in order to improve caching behavior. In order to improve cache-friendliness and reduce the number of heap allocations required, Rusts' BTreeMap stores from *level - 1* to *2 * level - 1* number of elements per node, which results in a rather large array of keys.

While the opposite—small arrays of keys—fit the CPU's cache well enough, the tree itself has a larger number of them, so more nodes might need to be looked at. If the number of key-value pairs in a single node is higher, the overall node count shrinks, and if the key array still fits into the CPU's cache, these comparisons are as fast as they can be. The downside of larger arrays to search the key in is mitigated by using more intelligent searches (like binary search), so the overall performance gain of having fewer nodes outweighs the downside.

In general, when comparing the B-Tree from earlier in this book to BTreeMap, only a few similarities stand out, one of them being inserting a new element.

Insert

Like every B-Tree, inserts are done by first searching a spot to insert, and then applying the split procedure in case the node has more than the expected number of values (or children). Insertion is split into three parts and it starts with the first method to be called, which glues everything together and returns an expected result:

```
#[stable(feature = "rust1", since = "1.0.0")]
pub fn insert(&mut self, key: K, value: V) -> Option<V> {
    match self.entry(key) {
        Occupied(mut entry) => Some(entry.insert(value)),
        Vacant(entry) => {
            entry.insert(value);
            None
        }
    }
}
```

The second step is finding the handle for the node that the pair can be inserted into, shown as follows:

```
#[stable(feature = "rust1", since = "1.0.0")]
pub fn entry(&mut self, key: K) -> Entry<K, V> {
    // FIXME(@porglezomp) Avoid allocating if we don't insert
    self.ensure_root_is_owned();
    match search::search_tree(self.root.as_mut(), &key) {
        Found(handle) => {
            Occupied(OccupiedEntry {
                handle,
                length: &mut self.length,
                _marker: PhantomData,
            })
        }
        GoDown(handle) => {
            Vacant(VacantEntry {
                key,
                handle,
                length: &mut self.length,
                _marker: PhantomData,
            })
        }
    }
}
```

Once the handle is known, the entry (which is either a structure modeling a vacant or occupied spot) inserts the new key-value pair. If the entry was occupied before, the value is simply replaced—no further steps required. If the spot was vacant, the new value could trigger a tree rebalancing where the changes are bubbled up the tree:

```rust
#[stable(feature = "rust1", since = "1.0.0")]
pub fn insert(self, value: V) -> &'a mut V {
    *self.length += 1;

    let out_ptr;

    let mut ins_k;
    let mut ins_v;
    let mut ins_edge;

    let mut cur_parent = match self.handle.insert(self.key, value) {
        (Fit(handle), _) => return handle.into_kv_mut().1,
        (Split(left, k, v, right), ptr) => {
            ins_k = k;
            ins_v = v;
            ins_edge = right;
            out_ptr = ptr;
            left.ascend().map_err(|n| n.into_root_mut())
        }
    };

    loop {
        match cur_parent {
            Ok(parent) => {
                match parent.insert(ins_k, ins_v, ins_edge) {
                    Fit(_) => return unsafe { &mut *out_ptr },
                    Split(left, k, v, right) => {
                        ins_k = k;
                        ins_v = v;
                        ins_edge = right;
                        cur_parent = left.ascend().map_err(|n|
    n.into_root_mut());
                    }
                }
            }
            Err(root) => {
                root.push_level().push(ins_k, ins_v, ins_edge);
                return unsafe { &mut *out_ptr };
            }
        }
    }
}
```

Looking up keys is already part of the insert process, but it deserves a closer look too.

Look up

In a tree structure, inserts and deletes are based on looking up the keys that are being modified. In the case of `BTreeMap`, this is done by a function called `search_tree()` which is imported from the parent module:

```
pub fn search_tree<BorrowType, K, V, Q: ?Sized>(
    mut node: NodeRef<BorrowType, K, V, marker::LeafOrInternal>,
    key: &Q
) -> SearchResult<BorrowType, K, V, marker::LeafOrInternal, marker::Leaf>
        where Q: Ord, K: Borrow<Q> {

    loop {
        match search_node(node, key) {
            Found(handle) => return Found(handle),
            GoDown(handle) => match handle.force() {
                Leaf(leaf) => return GoDown(leaf),
                Internal(internal) => {
                    node = internal.descend();
                    continue;
                }
            }
        }
    }
}

pub fn search_node<BorrowType, K, V, Type, Q: ?Sized>(
    node: NodeRef<BorrowType, K, V, Type>,
    key: &Q
) -> SearchResult<BorrowType, K, V, Type, Type>
        where Q: Ord, K: Borrow<Q> {

    match search_linear(&node, key) {
        (idx, true) => Found(
            Handle::new_kv(node, idx)
        ),
        (idx, false) => SearchResult::GoDown(
            Handle::new_edge(node, idx)
        )
    }
}
```

The code itself is very easy to read, which is a good sign. It also avoids the use of recursion and uses a `loop{}` construct instead, which is a benefit for large lookups since Rust does not expand tail-recursive calls into loops (yet?). In any case, this function returns the node that the key resides in, letting the caller do the work of extracting the value and key from it.

Remove

The `remove` function wraps the occupied node's `remove_kv()` function, which removes a key-value pair from the handle that `search_tree()` unearthed. This removal also triggers a merging of nodes if a node now has less than the minimum amount of children.

Wrap up

As shown in this section, maps and sets have a lot in common and there are two ways that the Rust collections library provides them. `HashMap` and `HashSet` use a smart approach to finding and inserting values into buckets called Robin Hood hashing. Recalling the comparison benchmarks from `Chapter 16`, *Exploring Maps and Sets*, it provided a more stable and significantly better performance over a naive implementation:

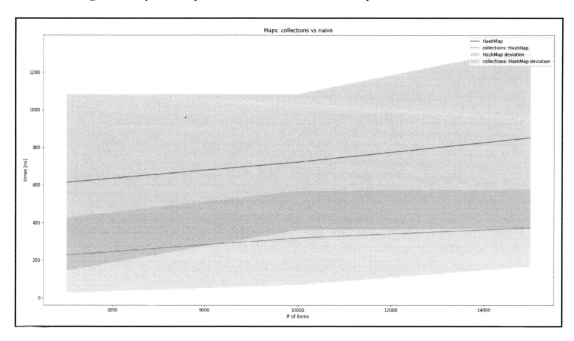

`BTreeMap` and `BTreeSet` are based on a different, more efficient implementation of a B-Tree. How much more efficient (and effective)? Let's find out!

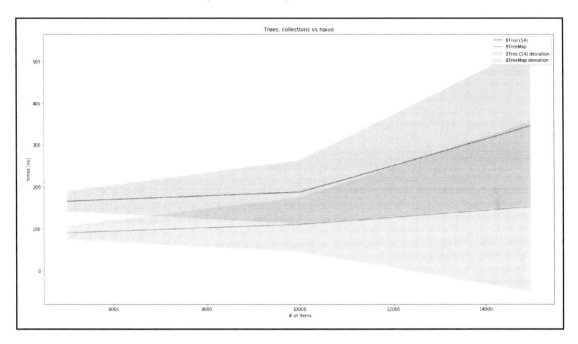

For a naive implementation of a B-Tree (from `Chapter 15`, *Robust Trees*), the performance is not that bad. However, while there might be some tweaks to be added here and there, evidence shows that there is a better and faster tree out there, so why not use that?

Summary

The Rust standard library features a great collections part, providing a few highly optimized implementations of basic data structures.

We started with `Vec<T>` and `VecDeque<T>`, both based on a heap-allocated array and wrapped in the `RawVec<T>` structure. They show excellent performance while memory efficiency remains high, thanks to the array base and `unsafe` operations based on pointers.

`LinkedList<T>` is a doubly-linked list that performs really well, thanks to direct data manipulation and the lack of runtime checking. While it excels at splitting and merging, most other operations are slower than `Vec<T>` and it lacks some useful features.

`HashSet` and `HashMap` are based on the same implementation (`HashMap`) and—unless specified differently—use `DefaultHasher` to generate a hashed key of an object. This key is stored (and later retrieved) using the Robin Hood hashing method, which provides major performance benefits over a naive implementation.

Alternatively, `BTreeSet` and `BTreeMap` use a B-Tree structure to organize keys and values. This implementation is also specialized and geared towards CPU-cache friendliness, and reducing the number of nodes (thereby minimizing the number of allocations) in order to create the high performance data structure that it is.

In the next chapter, we will decrypt the O notation, something that has been used sparingly up until this point, but is necessary for what follows: algorithms.

Further reading

You can refer to the following links for more information on topics covered in this chapter:

- `https://doc.rust-lang.org/std/collections/index.html`
- `http://cglab.ca/~abeinges/blah/rust-btree-case/`
- `https://doc.rust-lang.org/src/std/collections/hash/map.rs.html#148`

18
Algorithm Evaluation

When looking at algorithms as defined entities, what makes one algorithm better than the other? Is it the number of steps required to finish? The amount of memory that is committed? CPU cycles? How do they compare across machines and operating systems with different memory allocators?

There are a lot of questions here that need answers, since comparing work with others is important in order to find the best approach possible to solve a given problem. In this chapter, you can look forward to learning about the following:

- Evaluating algorithms in practice
- Classifying algorithm and data structure behaviors
- Estimating the plausibility of a better algorithm

The Big O notation

Physics is not a topic in this book, but its influence is far-reaching and powerful enough to be obeyed everywhere, even by virtual constructs such as algorithms! However great their design, they still are constrained by two important factors: time and space.

Time? Whenever anything needs to be done, a sequence of steps is required. By multiplying the number of steps by the time for each step, the total—absolute—time is easy to calculate. Or so we think. For computers, this is *mostly* true, but many questions make it very hard to really know, since modern CPUs go way beyond what previous generations were able to achieve. Is that only thanks to higher clock rates? What about the additional cores? SIMD? Simply taking the absolute time won't achieve real comparability between algorithms. Maybe the number of steps is what we should use.

Space (as in memory) has become a commodity in many domains over the last few years, even in the embedded space. While the situation has improved, it still pays to be mindful of how many bytes are stored in memory and how much that contributes to the goal of the algorithm. Or in other words, is this worth it? Many algorithmic tasks face a trade-off between what's stored in memory and what's computed on demand. The latter might be just enough to solve the problem, or it might not be; this is a decision the developer has to make.

Other people's code

Consequently, every algorithm must have a "number of steps required" and "bytes of memory required" property, right? Close: since they are ever-changing variables, a universal way of describing what other people have achieved is necessary.

Typically, programmers instinctively know how to do that: "is this thing really doing everything twice?!" should be a familiar outcry. What has been said here? Assuming it's a function that has an input parameter x, it sounds like the function is doing something with x twice. Mathematically speaking, this would be expressed as $f(x) = 2x$.

What this is really saying is that for every input, the required number of steps to fully execute the function is twice the input—isn't this exactly what we have been looking for? What would be a better way to write it down?

The Big O

Looking at that issue from a (mathematical) function perspective, this is a shared need across mathematics, computer science, physics, and so on: they all want to know how expensive a function is. This is why a common notation was invented by Edmund Landau: the Big O notation (or Landau notation) consisting of the uppercase letter O, which declares the *order* of a function. The main growth factor is then put into parentheses following the letter O.

There are other, related notations that use small *o*, Omegas, Theta, and others, but those are less relevant in practical terms. Check the *Further reading* section for an article by Donald Knuth on this.

Asymptotic runtime complexity

For computer science, the exact, absolute runtime is typically not important when implementing algorithms (you can always get a faster computer). Instead, the runtime complexity is more important since it directly influences performance as an overall measure of work, independent of details.

Since this is not an exact measurement and the actual performance is influenced by other factors, sticking with an asymptotic (read: rough) measure is the best strategy. In addition to that, algorithms have best and worst cases. Unless you are trying to improve on a particular case, the worst case is what's typically compared:

```
let my_vec = vec![5,6,10,33,53,77];
for i in my_vec.iter() {
    if i == 5 {
        break;
    }
    println!("{}", i);
}
```

Iterating over this, Vec<T> has a runtime complexity of $O(n)$ where n is the length of Vec<T>, regardless of the fact that the loop will break right away. Why? Because of pessimism. In reality, it is often hard to say what the input vector looks like and when it will actually exit, so the worst case is that it goes over the entire sequence without breaking, that is, n times. Now that we have seen how to write this down, let's see how to find out the runtime complexity of our own algorithms.

Making your own

There are only a few aspects that change the complexity of an algorithm, those that have been shown to proportionally increase the total time required of an algorithm.

These are as follows:

- An arithmetic operation (`10 + 30`)
- An assignment (`let x = 10`)
- A test (`x == 10`)
- A read or write of a basic type (`u32`, `bool`, and so on)

If a piece of code only does one of these operations, it is one step, that is, *O(1)*, and whenever there is a choice (`if` or `match`), the more complex branch has to be picked. Regardless of any input parameters, it will be the same number of steps—or constant time. If they are run in a loop, things get more interesting.

Loops

When in a loop, and the number of iterations is not known at compile time, it will be a major influence on runtime complexity. If an operation mentioned earlier is executed in the loop (for example, a `sum` operation), one could declare the complexity as *O(1 * n)* for the arithmetic operation. After adding another operation, we could express it as *O(2 * n)* and, while this would be correct, these are not the driving forces of the loop. Regardless of the number of operations that are executed *n* times, the main growth factor remains *n*. Hence, we simply say *O(n)*, unless you are trying to compare the same algorithm, where the number of iterations actually makes a difference. If there are subsequent loops, the most expensive one is picked.

However, upon nesting loops, the complexity changes considerably. Consider this (really bad) algorithm for comparing two lists:

```
let my_vec = vec![1,1,1,4,6,7,23,4];
let my_other_vec = vec![66,2,4,6,892];


for i in my_vec.iter() {
    for j in my_other_vec.iter() {
        if i == j {
            panic!();
        }
    }
}
```

For each element in the first collection, the second collection is fully iterated. In other words, each element is looked at $n * m$ times, resulting in a runtime complexity of $O(n*m)$, or, if both collections are the same size, $O(n^2)$.

Can it get even worse? Yes!

Recursion

Since all recursive algorithms can be unrolled into a loop, they can achieve the same results. However, recursion, or more specifically backtracking (which will be discussed in more detail in `Chapter 21`, *Random and Combinatorial*), makes it easier to create higher runtime complexities.

Typical combinatorial problems result in exponential runtimes, since there are a number of variations (such as different colors) that have to be enumerated n times so that a constraint is satisfied, which is only evaluated at the end. If there are two colors, the runtime complexity will therefore be $O(2^n)$ for a sequence of n colors, if no two colors can be adjacent to each other in a graph (graph coloring problem).

Recursive algorithms also make it hard to estimate runtime complexity quickly, since the branch development is hard to visualize.

Complexity classes

In general, all algorithms fall into one of a few classes. Let's look at these classes ordered by their growth speed. Depending on the literature, there might be more or fewer classes, but this is a good set to start with since they represent the major directions of growth behavior.

O(1)

Constant time, which means everything will take the same amount of time. Since this chart would be a horizontal line at the y value of 1, we will skip it in favor of sparing a tree.

O(log(n))

Growth is defined by the logarithmic function (in general, base 2), which is better than linear growth.

Here is the plot of the mathematical function:

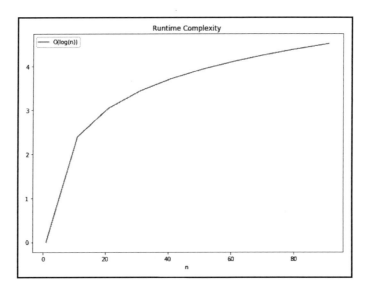

O(n)

Linear time, which means that the solution performance depends on the input in a linear way:

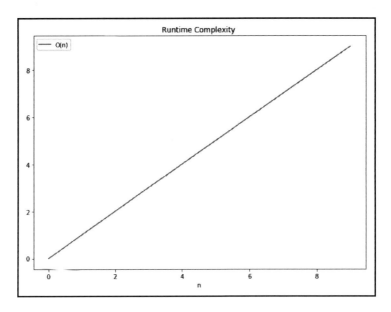

O(n log(n))

This is sometimes called quasilinear time and is the best achievable complexity for sorting:

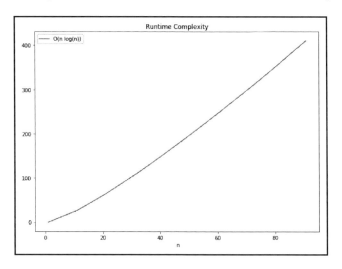

O(n²)

The squared runtime is typical for the naive implementation of search or sorting algorithms:

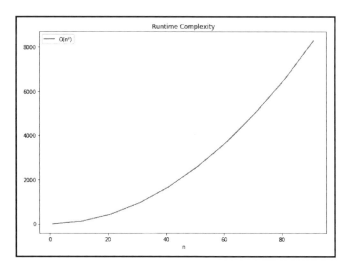

O(2ⁿ)

This is among the most expensive classes and can often be found in really hard-to-solve problems. This plot has a significantly smaller x value (*0 - 10*) and generates a higher y value (or runtime) than the `O(n log(n))` chart:

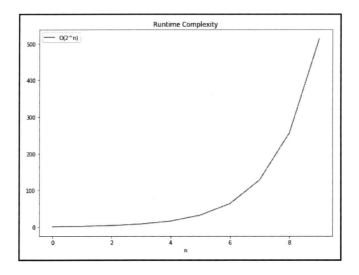

Comparison

Having individual charts is great for imagining the projected runtime and estimating what a task's performance could look like when its input is increased. If we plot all of these lines into a single chart, however, their performance will become obvious.

The typical comparison is against the linear time complexity (*O(n)*), since most naive solutions would be expected to achieve this performance:

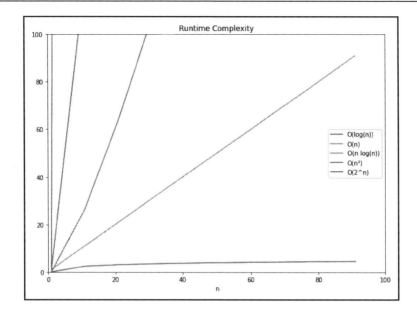

With this chart in mind, we can look at problems and their expected performance in the next section.

In the wild

In reality, there are a lot of factors that may influence the choice of space and runtime complexity. Typically, these factors are forms of resource constraints, such as power consumption on embedded devices, clock cycles in a cloud-hosted environment, and so on.

Since it is difficult to find out the complexities of a particular algorithm, it is helpful to know a few, so the choice comes intuitively. Often, the runtime complexity is not the only important aspect, but the absolute execution time counts. Under these conditions, a higher runtime complexity can be preferable if *n* is sufficiently small.

This is best demonstrated when Vec<T> contains only a few elements, where a linear search is a lot faster than sorting and then running a binary search. The overhead of sorting might just be too much compared to searching right away.

Getting this trade-off and the overall implementation right is hugely beneficial for the entire program and will outweigh any other optimizations. Let's take a look at a few runtime complexities that can be found in everyday life.

Data structures

Algorithms on lists of all kinds almost always exhibit $O(n)$ behavior, since most actions involve shifting or going through other elements. Hence, operations such as insert at or remove from a position, as well as finding elements (when unsorted), are $O(n)$. This is very visible, particularly in linked lists, with only a few exceptions: a dynamic array's element access ($O(1)$), prepending/appending elements or lists, and splitting lists appending elements in a linked list ($O(1)$).

Special cases of lists, such as **stacks** and **queues**, make use of these exceptions and let a user insert to or remove from only the ends of that list. **Skip lists** on the other hand employ a tree-like strategy for achieving great search performance, which speeds up inserts and removals too. But this comes at the expense of memory, since the additional elements are proportional ($log(n)$) to the list length.

For search, **trees** are great. Regular trees (that is, anything that can be a B-Tree) exhibit $O(log(n))$ complexities on many operations, including insert, remove, and find. This is particularly great since difference to $O(n)$ actually increases the more elements there are in the collection.

The only thing potentially better are **maps** and **sets**, if the underlying implementation uses an appropriate hashing algorithm. Any operation *should* be completed in constant time ($O(1)$), if there are no collisions. Typically, there will be some collisions, but the runtime complexity will not exceed $O(n)$ because, if all else fails, a linear search works. Consequently, real performance will be somewhere in between, with the hashing algorithm being the most important influence. For most libraries, hash maps (and sets) are faster than their tree-based counterparts.

Everyday things

Whenever something needs sorting, there are a lot of ways to achieve that, but the baseline is $O(n^2)$. It's the same way most people order their socks: pick one and find the match, then repeat (called **selection sort**). How else would one compare all elements to find their order? Better approaches, such as heap sort, merge sort, and so on, all exhibit $O(n\ log(n))$ behavior in the worst case, which is the best possible (consistent) performance for sorting algorithms. Additionally, since the best case for any sorting algorithm is $O(n)$—making sure everything was already in order—the average case matters the most. We will get into strategies about that later in this book.

Search (or lookup) is another topic that we will get into in `Chapter 20`, *Finding Stuff*, but the associated runtime complexities are great examples. Searching on any unsorted data structure will be *O(n)* most of the time, while sorted collections can utilize binary search (a tree's search strategy) and achieve *O(log(n))*. In order to save the cost of sorting, ideal hash tables provide the absolute best case for search: *O(1)*.

Exotic things

One class that was omitted from the earlier list is **polynomial time** (**P** in short). This class is quicker to solve than the exponential time class, but worse than $O(n^2)$. These problems include checking whether a number is a prime number, or solving a Sudoku. However, there are other problems in this class as well that actually have *no* "quick" (that is, solvable in P) solution, but a solution can be verified in P time. These are called **NP** (an abbreviation of **non-deterministic polynomial time**) problems and the hardest of them are NP-hard (see the information box).

The distinction between P, NP, NP-complete, and NP-hard is not intuitive. NP problems are problems that can be solved using a non-deterministic Turing machine in P time. **NP-hard** problems are problems without a solution that, if solved, would have a polynomial time solution and if it is also an NP problem, it is also considered NP-complete. Additionally, finding a solution for one of either class (NP-hard or NP-complete) would imply a solution for *all* NP-hard/NP-complete problems.

While there are no known algorithms to solve these problems quickly, there typically are naive approaches that result in *very* long runtimes. Popular problems in this space include the traveling salesman problem ($O(n!)$), the knapsack problem ($O(2^n)$, and the subset sum problem ($O(2^{n/2})$), all of which are currently solved (or approximated) using heuristics or programming techniques. For those interested, check the further reading section for links.

Summary

The Big O notation is a way to describe the time and space requirements of an algorithm (or data structure). This is not an exact science, however; it's about finding the primary growth factor of each of the things mentioned to answer this question: what happens when the problem space grows bigger?

Any algorithm will fall within a few relevant classes that describe that behavior. By applying the algorithm to one more element, how many more steps have to be taken? One easy way is to visualize the individual charts and think of whether it will be linear ($O(n)$), quasilinear ($O(n\ log(n))$), quadratic ($O(n^2)$), or even exponential ($O(2^n)$). Whatever the case may be, it is always best to do less work than there are elements to be looked at, such as constant ($O(1)$) or logarithmic ($O(log(n))$) behaviors!

Selecting the operations is typically done based on the worst-case behavior, that is, the upper limit of what is going to happen. In the next chapter, we will take a closer look at these behaviors in the cases of popular search algorithms.

Further reading

You can refer to the following links to get more information on the topics covered in this chapter:

- Wikipedia's list of best-, worst-, and average-case complexities (`https://en.wikipedia.org/wiki/Best,_worst_and_average_case`)
- Big O Cheatsheet (`http://bigocheatsheet.com/`)
- Heuristic algorithms at Northwestern University (`https://optimization.mccormick.northwestern.edu/index.php/Heuristic_algorithms`)
- Heuristic design and optimization at MIT (`http://www.mit.edu/~moshref/Heuristics.html`)
- *Big Omicron And Big Omega And Big Theta* by Donald Knuth (`http://www.phil.uu.nl/datastructuren/10-11/knuth_big_omicron.pdf`)

19
Ordering Things

Tidy house, tidy mind is a saying that, as in its German variation, implies that order plays an important part in our lives. Anyone who wants to maximize efficiency has to rely on order, or risk the occasional time-consuming search through the chaos that has slowly unfolded. Having things in a particular order is great; it's the process of getting there that is expensive.

This often does not feel like a good use of our time, or simply may not be worth it. While a computer does not exactly feel, the time required to sort things is of a similar cost. Minimizing this time is the goal of inventing new algorithms and improving their efficiency, which is necessary for a task as common as sorting. A call to `mycollection.sort()` is not expected to take seconds (or minutes or even hours), so this is also a matter of usability. In this chapter, we will explore several solutions for that, so you can look forward to learning about the following:

- Implementing and analyzing sorting algorithms
- Knowing more about (in)famous sorting strategies

From chaos to order

There are many sorting algorithms (and their individual variations), each with their individual characteristics. Since it is impossible to cover every algorithm in a single chapter, and considering their limited usefulness, this chapter covers a selected few.

The selection should show the different strategies that are common in sorting a collection of items, many of which have been implemented in various libraries across different languages. Since many of you will never implement any sorting algorithms for productive use, this section is supposed to familiarize you with what's behind the scenes when a call to `mycollection.sort()` is issued, and why this could take a surprising amount of time.

Sorting algorithms fall into a group on each of these properties:

- **Stable**: Maintains a relative order when comparing equal values
- **Hybrid**: Combines two or more sorting approaches (for example, by collection length)
- **In-place**: Uses indices instead of full copies for passing collections around

While stable and hybrid algorithms are more complex and, in many cases, at a higher level (because they combine various approaches), in-place sorting is common and reduces the space and amount of copying an algorithm has to do.

We have touched on a very basic sorting algorithm already: **insertion sort**. It is the exact algorithm most real life things are done with: when adding a new book to a bookshelf, most people will pick up the book, look at the property to order by (such as the author's last name), and find the spot in their current collection, starting from the letter *A*. This is a very efficient approach and is used to build a new collection with minimal overhead, but it does not warrant its own section.

Let's start off with an absolute classic that is always a part of any university's curriculum because of its simplicity: bubble sort.

Bubble sort

Bubble sort is the infamous algorithm that university students often learn as their first sorting algorithm. In terms of performance and runtime complexity, it is certainly among the worst ways to sort a collection, but it's great for teaching.

The principle is simple: walk through an array, scanning two elements and bringing them into the correct order by swapping. Repeat these steps until no swaps occur. The following diagram shows this process on the example array `[8, 9, 7, 6]`, where a total of four swaps establishes the order of `[6, 7, 8, 9]` by repeatedly comparing two succeeding elements:

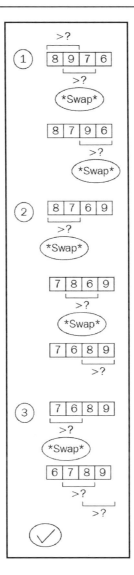

This diagram also shows an interesting (and name-giving) property of the algorithm: the "bubbling up" of elements to their intended position. The number 6 in the diagram travels, swap by swap, from the last position to the first position in the collection.

When this is transformed into Rust code, the simplicity remains: two nested loops iterate over the collection, whereas the outer loop could just as well run till infinity, since the inner portion does all the comparing and swapping.

Bubble sort is, infamously, a short snippet of code:

```
pub fn bubble_sort<T: PartialOrd + Clone>(collection: &[T]) -> Vec<T> {
    let mut result: Vec<T> = collection.into();
    for _ in 0..result.len() {
        let mut swaps = 0;
        for i in 1..result.len() {
            if result[i - 1] > result[i] {
                result.swap(i - 1, i);
                swaps += 1;
            }
        }
        if swaps == 0 {
            break;
        }
    }
    result
}
```

For easier handling, the algorithm creates a copy of the input array (using the Into<T> trait's into() method) and swaps around elements using the swap() method provided by Vec<T>.

The nested loops already hint toward the (worst case) runtime complexity: $O(n^2)$. However, thanks to the early stopping when there are no swaps in a run, a partially ordered collection will be sorted surprisingly quickly. In fact, the best case scenario is really fast with bubble sort, since it's basically a single run-through (in other words, $O(n)$ in this case).

The following chart shows three cases: sorting an already sorted collection (ascending numbers and descending numbers), as well as sorting a randomly shuffled array of distinct numbers:

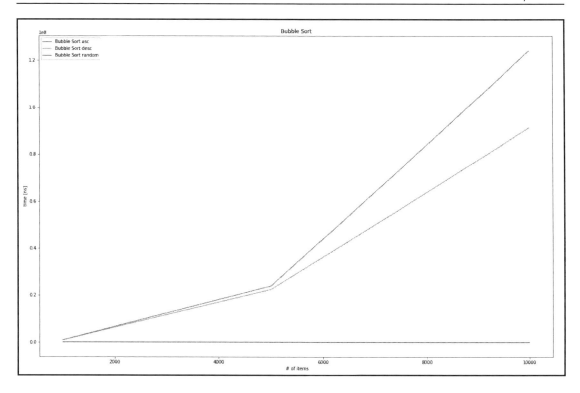

The output graph comparison between Bubble sort ascending, descending, and randomly sorted arrays

The algorithm will produce an ascending sequence, yet the shuffled collection shows a worse absolute runtime than the traditional worst case: a collection sorted in descending order. In any case, the exponential nature of these runtimes shows why bubble sort is not fit for real-world use.

Shell sort is sometimes dubbed as an optimized version of bubble sort!

Shell sort

Bubble sort always compares an element to the neighboring element, but is this important? Many would say that it depends on the pre-existing order of the unsorted collection: are these future neighbors far apart or close together?

Donald Shell, the inventor of shell sort, must have had a similar idea and used a "gap" between elements to make further jumps with the swapping approach adopted by bubble sort. By utilizing a specified strategy to choose those gaps, the runtime can change dramatically. Shell's original strategy is to start with half the collection's length and, by halving the gap size until zero, a runtime of $O(n^2)$ is achieved. Other strategies include choosing numbers based on some form of calculation of the current iteration k (for example, $2^k - 1$), or empirically collected gaps (http://sun.aei.polsl.pl/~mciura/publikacje/shellsort.pdf), which do not have a fixed runtime complexity yet!

The following diagram explains some of the workings of shell sort. First, the initial gap is chosen, which is n / 2 in the original paper. Starting at that gap (2, in this particular example), the element is saved and compared to the element *at the other end of the gap*, in other words, the current index minus the gap:

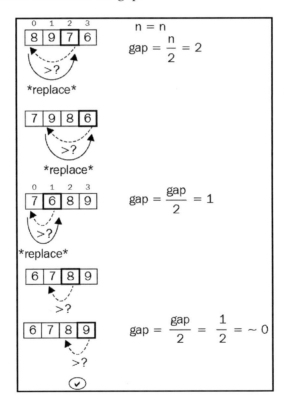

If the element at the other end of the gap is greater, it replaces the origin. Then, the process walks toward index zero with gap-sized steps, so the question becomes: what is going to fill that hole (7 is overwritten by 8, so the hole is where 8 was)—the original element, or element "gap" steps before it?

In this example, it's 7, since there is no preceding element. In longer collections, a lot more moving around can occur before the original element is inserted. After this insertion process has finished for index 2, it's repeated for index 3, moving from the gap toward the end of the collection. Following that, the gap size is reduced (in our case, by half) and the insertion steps are repeated until the collection is in order (and the gap size is zero).

Words, and even an image, make it surprisingly hard to understand what is going on. Code, however, shows the workings nicely:

```rust
pub fn shell_sort<T: PartialOrd + Clone>(collection: &[T]) -> Vec<T> {
    let n = collection.len();
    let mut gap = n / 2;
    let mut result: Vec<T> = collection.into();

    while gap > 0 {
        for i in gap..n {
            let temp = result[i].clone();

            let mut j = i;
            while j >= gap && result[j - gap] > temp {
                result[j] = result[j - gap].clone();
                j -= gap;
            }
            result[j] = temp;
        }
        gap /= 2;
    }
    result
}
```

This snippet shows the value of shell sort: with the correct gap strategy, it can achieve results that are similar to more sophisticated sorting algorithms, but it is a lot shorter to implement and understand. Because of this, it can be a good choice for embedded use cases, where no library and only limited space is available.

The actual performance on the test sets is good:

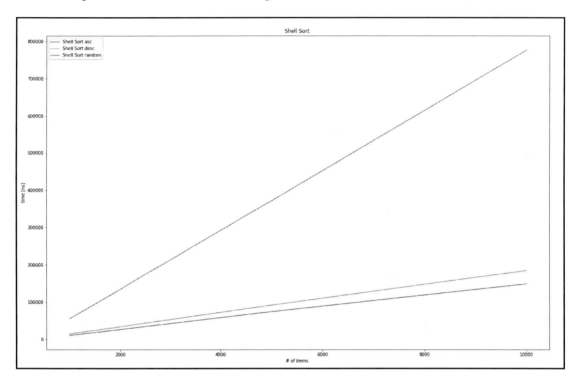

The output graph comparison between shell sort ascending, descending, and randomly sorted arrays

Even with the original gap strategy that is said to produce $O(n^2)$ runtimes, the random set produces something more akin to linear behavior. Definitely a solid performance, but can it compare to heap sort?

Heap sort

Ordering numbers was already a topic that we covered earlier in this book (Chapter 15, *Robust Trees*) while discussing trees: with heaps. A heap is a tree-like data structure with the highest (max-heap) or lowest number (min-heap) at the root that maintains order when inserting or removing elements. Hence, a sorting mechanism could be as simple as inserting everything into a heap and retrieving it again!

Since a (binary) heap has a known runtime complexity of $O(\log n)$, and the entire array has to be inserted, the estimated runtime complexity will be $O(n \log n)$, among the best sorting performances in sorting. The following diagram shows the binary heap in tree notation on the right, and the array implementation on the left:

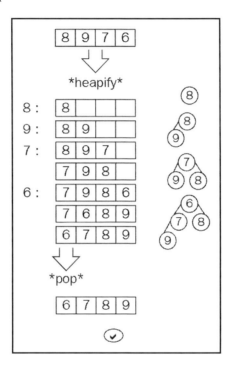

In the Rust standard library, there is a `BinaryHeap` structure available, which makes the implementation quick and easy:

```
pub fn heap_sort<T: PartialOrd + Clone + Ord>(collection: &[T]) -> Vec<T> {
    let mut heap = BinaryHeap::new();
    for c in collection {
        heap.push(c.clone());
    }
    heap.into_sorted_vec()
}
```

The fact that a heap is used to do the sorting will generate fairly uniform outcomes, making it a great choice for unordered collections, but an inferior choice for presorted ones. This is due to the fact that a heap is filled and emptied, regardless of the pre-existing ordering. Plotting the different cases shows almost no difference:

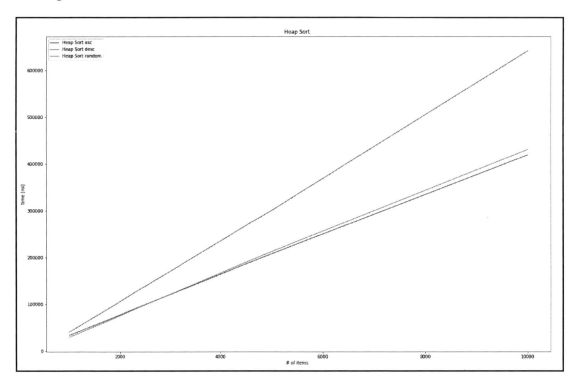

The output graph comparison between heap sort ascending, descending, and randomly sorted arrays

A very different strategy, called *divide and conquer*, is employed by an entire group of algorithms. This group is what we are going to explore now, starting with merge sort.

Merge sort

One fundamental strategy in battle, as well as in sorting collections, is to divide and conquer. Merge sort does exactly that, by splitting the collection in half recursively until only a single element remains. The merging operation can then put these single elements together in the correct order with the benefit of working with presorted collections.

What this does is reduce the problem size (in other words, the number of elements in the collection) to more manageable chunks that come presorted for easier comparison, resulting in a worst case runtime complexity of *O(n log n)*. The following diagram shows the split and merge process (note that comparing and ordering only starts at the merge step):

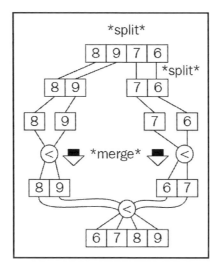

There are various implementations of this principle: bottom up, top down, using blocks, and other variations. In fact, as of 2018, Rust's default sorting algorithm is Timsort, a stable, hybrid algorithm that combines insertion sort (up until a certain size) with merge sort.

Implementing a vanilla merge sort in Rust is, again, a great place to use recursion. First, the left half is evaluated, then the right half of a sequence, and only then does merging begin, first by comparing the two sorted results (left and right) and picking elements from either side. Once one of these runs out of elements, the rest is simply appended since the elements are obviously larger. This result is returned to the caller, repeating the merging on a higher level until the original caller is reached.

Here's the Rust code for a typical merge sort implementation:

```rust
pub fn merge_sort<T: PartialOrd + Clone + Debug>(collection: &[T]) ->
Vec<T> {
    if collection.len() > 1 {
        let (l, r) = collection.split_at(collection.len() / 2);
        let sorted_l = merge_sort(l);
        let sorted_r = merge_sort(r);
        let mut result: Vec<T> = collection.into();
        let (mut i, mut j) = (0, 0);
        let mut k = 0;
        while i < sorted_l.len() && j < sorted_r.len() {
            if sorted_l[i] <= sorted_r[j] {
                result[k] = sorted_l[i].clone();
                i += 1;
            } else {
                result[k] = sorted_r[j].clone();
                j += 1;
            }
            k += 1;
        }

        while i < sorted_l.len() {
            result[k] = sorted_l[i].clone();
            k += 1;
            i += 1;
        }

        while j < sorted_r.len() {
            result[k] = sorted_r[j].clone();
            k += 1;
            j += 1;
        }

        result
    } else {
        collection.to_vec()
    }
}
```

This behavior also pays off, creating a quasi-linear runtime complexity, as shown in the following plot:

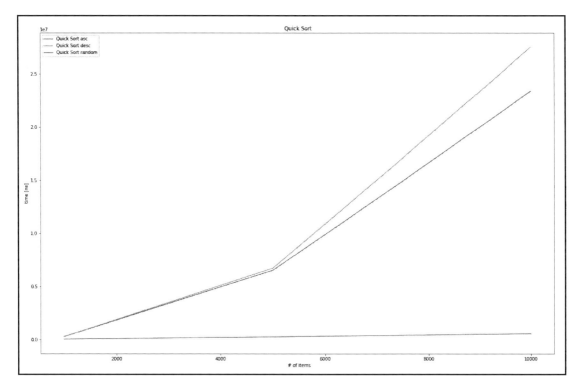

The output graph comparison between Quicksort asc. desc. and random

Another divide-and-conquer-type algorithm is Quicksort. It's a very interesting way to sort a list for a variety of reasons.

Quicksort

This algorithm significantly outperformed merge sort in best case scenarios and was quickly adopted as Unix's default sorting algorithm, as well as in Java's reference implementation. By using a similar strategy to merge sort, Quicksort achieves faster average and best case speeds. Unfortunately, the worst case complexity is just as bad as bubble sort: $O(n^2)$. How so? you might ask.

Quicksort operates, sometimes recursively, on parts of the full collection, and swaps elements around to establish an order. Hence, the critical question becomes: how do we choose these parts? This choosing bit is called the partitioning scheme and typically includes the swapping as well, not just choosing a split index. The choice is made by picking a pivot element, the value of which is what everything is compared with.

Everything less than the pivot value goes to one side, and everything greater goes to the other—by swapping. Once the algorithm detects a nice ascending (on the one side) and descending (from the other side) order, the split can be made where the two sequences intersect. Then, the entire process starts anew with each of the partitions.

The following illustration shows the picking and ordering of the elements based on the previous example collection. While the partitions in this example are only length one versus the rest, the same process would apply if these were longer sequences as well:

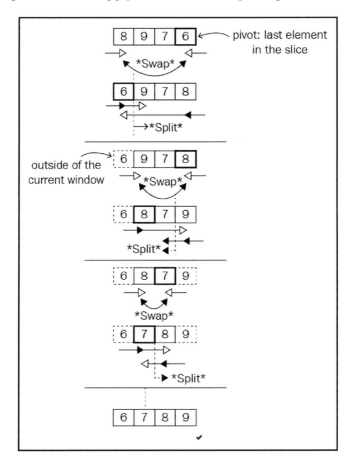

The partitioning scheme used here is called the Hoare scheme, named after the inventor of Quicksort, Sir Anthony Hoare, in 1959. There are other schemes (Lomuto seems to be the most popular alternative) that may provide better performance by trading off various other aspects, such as memory efficiency or the number of swaps. Whatever the partition scheme, picking a pivot value plays a major role in performance as well and the more equal parts it produces (like the median), the better the value is. Potential strategies include the following:

- Choosing the median
- Choosing the arithmetic mean
- Picking an element (random, first, or last, as chosen here)

In Rust code, Quicksort is implemented in three functions:

- The public API to provide a usable interface
- A wrapped recursive function that takes a low and high index to sort in-between
- The partition function implementing the Hoare partition scheme

This implementation can be considered in-place since it operates on the same vector that was provided in the beginning, swapping elements based on their indices. Here is the code:

```rust
fn partition<T: PartialOrd + Clone + Debug>(
    collection: &mut [T],
    low: usize,
    high: usize,
) -> usize {
    let pivot = collection[high].clone();
    let (mut i, mut j) = (low as i64 - 1, high as i64 + 1);

    loop {
        'lower: loop {
            i += 1;
            if i > j || collection[i as usize] >= pivot {
                break 'lower;
            }
        }

        'upper: loop {
            j -= 1;
            if i > j || collection[j as usize] <= pivot {
                break 'upper;
            }
        }

        if i > j {
```

```
                    return j as usize;
            }
            collection.swap(i as usize, j as usize);
        }
    }

    fn quick_sort_r<T: PartialOrd + Clone + Debug>(collection: &mut [T], low:
    usize, high: usize) {
        if low < high {
            let pivot = partition(collection, low, high);
            quick_sort_r(collection, low, pivot);
            quick_sort_r(collection, pivot + 1, high);
        }
    }

    pub fn quick_sort<T: PartialOrd + Clone + Debug>(collection: &[T]) ->
    Vec<T> {
        let mut result = collection.to_vec();
        quick_sort_r(&mut result, 0, collection.len() - 1);
        result
    }
```

Another new aspect in this implementation is the use of loop labels, which allow for better structure and readability. This is due to Hoare's use of a do-until type loop, a syntax that is not available in Rust, but that required the algorithm to avoid an infinite loop.

The break/continue instructions are relatives of the infamous go-to instruction, so they should only be used sparingly and with great care for the purpose of readability. Loop labels provide a tool to achieve that. They allow a reader to track exactly which loop is being exited or continued. The syntax leans slightly on that of the lifetimes: 'mylabel: loop { break 'mylabel; }.

Quicksort's performance characteristics are definitely interesting. The rare worst case behavior or $O(n^2)$ has triggered many optimizations over the decades since its invention, the latest of which is called Dual-Pivot Quicksort from 2009, which has been adopted in Oracle's library for Java 7. Refer to the *Further reading* section for a more detailed explanation.

Running the original Quicksort on the previous dataset, the worst case and best case behaviors are clearly visible. The performance on the descending and (curiously) the ascending datasets is clearly $O(n^2)$, while the randomized array is quickly processed:

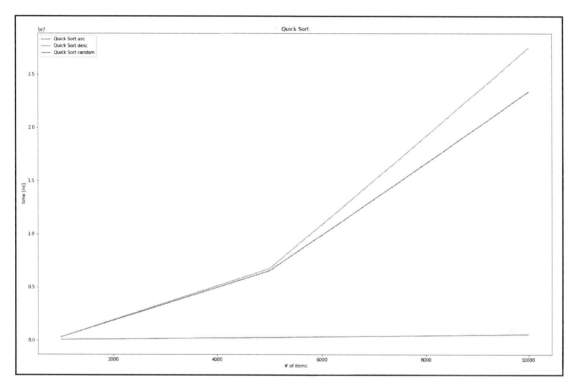

The output graph comparison between Quicksort ascensding, descending and randomly sorted arrays

This behavior speaks for the Quicksort's strong sides, which are more "real-world" type scenarios, where the worst case rarely appears. In current libraries around various programming languages though, sorting is done in a hybrid fashion, which means that these generic algorithms are used according to their strengths. This approach is called **Introsort** (from introspective sort) and, in C++'s `std::sort`, relies on Quicksort up to a certain point. Rust's standard library, however, uses Timsort.

Summary

Putting things in order is a very fundamental problem that has been solved in many different ways, varying in aspects such as worst-case runtime complexity, memory required, the relative order of equal elements (stability), as well as overall strategies. A few fundamental approaches were presented in this chapter.

Bubble sort is one of the simplest algorithms to implement, but it comes at a high runtime cost, with a worst-case behavior of $O(n^2)$. This is due to the fact that it simply swaps elements based on a nested loop, which makes elements "bubble up" to either end of the collection.

Shell sort can be seen as an improved version of bubble sort, with a major upside: it does not start off by swapping neighbors. Instead, there is a gap that elements are compared and swapped across, covering a greater distance. This gap size changes with every round that shows worst-case runtime complexities of $O(n^2)$ for the original scheme to $O(n \log n)$ in the fastest variant. In fact, the runtime complexity of some empirically derived gaps cannot even be measured reliably!

Heap sort makes use of a data structure's property to create a sorted collection. The heap, as presented earlier, retains the largest (or smallest) element at its root, returning it at every `pop()`. Heap sort therefore simply inserts the entire collection into a heap, only to retrieve it one by one in a sorted fashion. This leads to a runtime complexity of $O(n \log n)$.

Tree-based strategies are also found in **merge sort**, a divide-and-conquer approach. This algorithm recursively splits the collection in half to sort the subset before working on the entire collection. This work is done when returning from the recursive calls when the resulting sub-collections have to be merged, hence the name. Typically, this will exercise a runtime complexity of $O(n \log n)$.

Quicksort also uses a divide-and-conquer approach, but instead of simply breaking the collection in half every time, it works with a pivot value, where the other values are swapped before looking at each sub-collection. This results in a worst-case behavior of $O(n^2)$, but Quicksort is often used for its frequent average complexity of $O(n \log n)$.

Nowadays, standard libraries use hybrid approaches such as Timsort, Introsort, or pattern-defeating Quicksort to get the best absolute and relative runtime performance. Rust's standard library provides either a stable sorting function for slices (`slice::sort()` versus `slice::sort_unstable()`) based on merge sort, and an unstable sorting function based on the pattern-defeating Quicksort.

This chapter aimed to be the basis for the next chapter, which will cover how to find a specific element, something that typically requires a sorted collection!

Further reading

Here is some additional reference material that you may refer to regarding what has been covered in this chapter:

- *Dual-Pivot Quicksort* (`https://web.archive.org/web/20151002230717/http://iaroslavski.narod.ru/quicksort/DualPivotQuicksort.pdf`)
- C++ sorting explained (`https://medium.com/@lucianoalmeida1/exploring-some-standard-libraries-sorting-functions-dd633f838182`)
- Wikipedia on Introsort (`https://en.wikipedia.org/wiki/Introsort`)
- Wikipedia on Timsort (`https://en.wikipedia.org/wiki/Timsort`)
- Pattern defeating Quicksort (`https://github.com/orlp/pdqsort`)

20
Finding Stuff

The issue with searching for *something* is always directly related to the space in which you are searching. You will certainly have experienced looking for your keys in your house: the search space contains anything from jackets worn the previous day to the sock drawer into which the key might have slipped the last time you did the washing. Upon finding the item (and after a lot of wasted time spent running up and down stairs and searching in various rooms), you then swear to keep things tidier in the future....

We have encountered this issue more often than we are comfortable with admitting, but it illustrates a fundamental issue that we can solve algorithmically without any particular order to build on. In this chapter, we'll explore how to do the following:

- Finding items in an unordered array of chaos
- Making a trade-off between preparation and search

Finding the best

The search domain is present on various levels of abstraction: finding a word in a body of text is typically more complex than simply calling the `contains()` function, and if there are several results, which is the one that was searched for? This entire class of problem is summed up under the umbrella of **information retrieval**, where problems of ranking, indexing, understanding, storing, and searching are solved in order to retrieve the optimum result (for all definitions). This chapter focuses only on the latter part, where we actually look through a collection of items (for example, an index) in order to find a match.

This means that we will compare items directly ($a = b$) to determine closeness, rather than using something such as a distance - or locally-sensitive hashing function. These can be found in more specific domains such as a fuzzy search or matching bodies of text, which is a field of its own. To learn more about hashing, please check out Chapter 16, *Exploring Maps and Sets* or the *Further reading* section in this chapter.

Starting off with the most naive implementation, let's look at linear searches.

Linear searches

Linear searching is a fancy name for something that we do in almost every program and our everyday lives: going through a collection of items to find the first match. There is no need for any preprocessing or similar steps; the collection can be used as-is, which means that standard libraries commonly provide a generic implementation already. In Rust's case, the iterator trait offers this feature with functions called position() (or rposition()), find(), filter(), or even any(). fold() can also be used to find the thing you are looking for. The following is a diagram of the process:

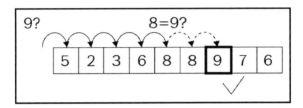

Fundamentally, however, it's a loop over each item that either exits or collects all items where a predicate (an evaluation function that takes in an item of a type to return a Boolean value) matches:

```
pub fn linear_search<T: Eq + Clone>(haystack: &[T], needle: &T) ->
Option<usize> {
    for (i, h) in haystack.iter().enumerate() {
        if h.eq(needle) {
            return Some(i);
        }
    }
    None
}
```

This algorithm obviously exhibits $O(n)$ runtime complexity, growing with the collection size. Iterating over 10,000 items will take a while, even if the predicate executes quickly, so how can this strategy be improved?

Jump search

Going linearly over a collection one-by-one is only efficient if you are already close to a potential match, but it is very hard to determine—what does *close to a match* mean? In unordered collections, this is indeed impossible to know this since any item can follow. Consequently, what about sorting the collection first? As discussed in Chapter 19, *Ordering Things*, sorting at quasi-linear runtime complexity can be significantly faster than going over each item of a long collection past a certain size.

A jump search makes use of knowing about the range it jumps over, not unlike a skip list:

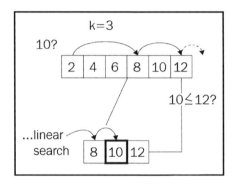

After sorting, a search can be significantly faster and a number of elements can be skipped in order to search in a linear fashion once the algorithm is close to a match. How many elements can be skipped at each jump? This is something to be tested, but first here is the code that does the work:

```
pub fn jump_search<T: Eq + PartialOrd + Clone>(
    haystack: &[T],
    needle: &T,
    jump_size: usize,
) -> Option<usize> {
    if jump_size < haystack.len() {
        let mut i = 0;
        while i < haystack.len() - 1 {
            if i + jump_size < haystack.len() {
                i += jump_size
            } else {
                i = haystack.len() - 1;
```

```
                        }
                        if &haystack[i] == needle {
                            return Some(i);
                        } else if &haystack[i] > needle {
                            return linear_search(&haystack[
                                        (i - jump_size)..i], needle);
                        }
                    }
                }
            None
        }
```

The API expects a pre-sorted slice, which means that sorting, strictly speaking, is not part of the algorithm's runtime. Without the sorting, the runtime complexity might be something around $O(n / k + k)$, with k being the step size, which can be reduced to $O(n)$ in a worst-case scenario.

Including the sorting mechanism, the sorting algorithm will trump the search's runtime complexity easily, raising it to $O(n \log n)$. While various choices for the jumps can improve the absolute runtime of this search algorithm by a significant amount, it will not perform as well as something like a tree structure. Binary searching as a strategy achieves that nicely, however.

Binary searching

Binary trees greatly reduce the number of comparison operations by creating branches from the collection, just like a binary tree would. This creates a tree on-the-fly, resulting in superior search performance. The significance is predictability, which allows us to build the tree and provides the options for what branch the algorithm can expect the result in.

A binary search, just like a jump search, requires the incoming slice to be ordered for it to work. Then the algorithm splits the array in half and chooses the side that will most likely contain the item. Once there are two collections, the behavior is very similar to that of a binary tree walk, as follows:

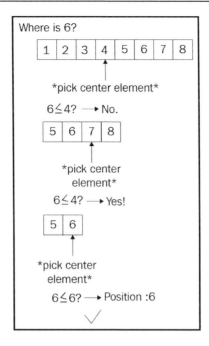

Again, given that the sorting effort trumps the algorithm's runtime complexity, it's that of the sorting algorithm that will be considered the outcome: *O(n log n)*. However, we should also be interested in the real performance, if the collection is already sorted; it's significantly lower! First, let's look at some code to make this easier to understand:

```
pub fn binary_search<T: Eq + PartialOrd>(
    haystack: &[T],
    needle: &T,
) -> Option<usize> {
    let (mut left, mut right) = (0, haystack.len() - 1);
    while left <= right {
        let pivot = left + (right - left) / 2;
        if needle < &haystack[pivot] {
            right = pivot - 1;
        } else if needle > &haystack[pivot] {
            left = pivot + 1;
        } else {
            return Some(pivot); // lucky find
        }
    }
    None
}
```

While the recursive implementation of the algorithm would have worked too, though it is not significantly shorter it harbors the risk of a stack overflow, hence the iterative approach.

After choosing a pivot (center) element, the algorithm has to determine the collection for the next iteration by one of the following three scenarios:

- The left part containing smaller values
- The right chunk with larger values
- Not at all; the pivot element is the result too

This tree-like behavior allows for a great runtime complexity of $O(log\ n)$, since the number of items searched keeps halving until the desired element has been found. However, how does all this compare?

Wrap up

The three approaches differ somewhat, with the binary search being the established state-of-the-art type algorithm. In fact, it can be used on any Rust slices (if they are sorted, of course) and used to find whatever is required.

Comparing these algorithms is tricky: a linear search works well on unordered datasets and is the only way to search those if sorting is not an option. If sorting is an option, then a binary search is faster by a large margin (asc is the sorting direction: ascending):

```
test tests::bench_binary_search_10k_asc ... bench:    80 ns/iter (+/-  32)
test tests::bench_binary_search_1k_asc ... bench:    63 ns/iter (+/-  17)
test tests::bench_binary_search_5k_asc ... bench:    86 ns/iter (+/-  28)
test tests::bench_jump_search_10k_asc ... bench:   707 ns/iter (+/- 160)
test tests::bench_jump_search_1k_asc ... bench:    92 ns/iter (+/-  10)
test tests::bench_jump_search_5k_asc ... bench:   355 ns/iter (+/-  46)
test tests::bench_linear_search_10k_asc ... bench: 2,046 ns/iter (+/- 352)
test tests::bench_linear_search_1k_asc ... bench:   218 ns/iter (+/-  22)
test tests::bench_linear_search_5k_asc ... bench: 1,076 ns/iter (+/- 527)
test tests::bench_std_binary_search_10k_asc ... bench:    93 ns/iter (+/-  10)
test tests::bench_std_binary_search_1k_asc ... bench:    62 ns/iter (+/-   7)
test tests::bench_std_binary_search_5k_asc ... bench:    89 ns/iter (+/-  27)
```

When plotted, the difference is clearly visible, with the linear search showing its linear characteristics. Taking the absolute runtime out of the game will show the runtime complexity as well, as demonstrated in the following chart:

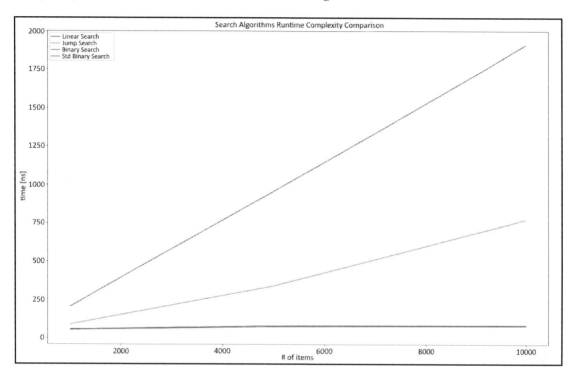

This chart shows the relative behavior of each algorithm in order to show its runtime complexities: a binary search with *O(log n)*, a linear search with *O(n)*, and a jump search, which is almost linear because of the parameter choice (the jump size is one-third of the length of the array):

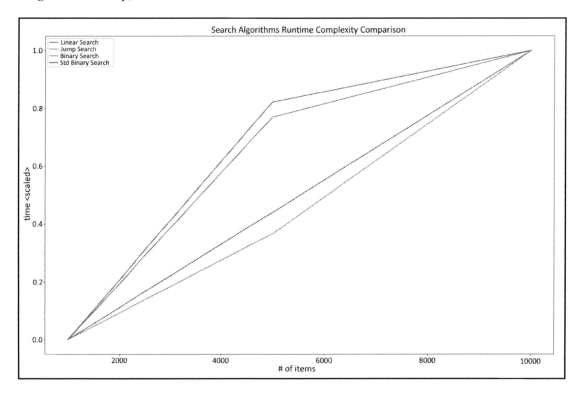

And that is it—a short introduction to search algorithms. Typically, it's more about the data, and having some way to sort beforehand creates a powerful opportunity to quickly find the item you are looking for.

Summary

Search, as a part of the information retrieval (among others) process, is an elementary way of finding something independently of the data structure being used. There are three popular types of algorithm: linear search, jump search, and binary search. Completely different approaches (such as locally-sensitive hashing) have been discussed in an earlier chapter about maps and sets, but they still need a mechanism to compare quickly.

A linear search is the least complex approach: iterate over a collection and compare the items with the element that is to be found. This has also been implemented in Rust's iterator and exhibits $O(n)$ runtime complexity.

Jump searches are superior. By operating on a sorted collection, they can use a step size that is greater than 1 (like a linear search) in order to skip to the required parts faster by checking whether the relevant section has already passed. While faster in absolute terms, the worst-case runtime complexity is still $O(n)$.

The (at the time of writing) fastest approach is a binary search, which also operates on a sorted collection and repeatedly splits the desired sections in half to work with a tree-like strategy. In fact, the runtime complexity of the algorithm itself is $O(\log n)$ as well.

In the next chapter, we will explore some more exotic algorithms: backtracking, random number generation, and more!

Further reading

Here is some additional reference material that you may refer to regarding what has been covered in this chapter: https://www.aaai.org/ocs/index.php/AAAI/AAAI14/paper/view/8357/8643.

21
Random and Combinatorial

While sorting and searching are two very fundamental problems in computer science, they are far from the only ones. In fact, those problems have been thoroughly solved by people who deeply specialize in such things. In today's world, it is more likely that a solution to a real-world problem involves generating random numbers, the best possible combination of several items (combinatorics) , "rolling up" several time periods into single numbers, and visualizing the results. Random number generation algorithms and solving combinatorial problems efficiently have become very important. Especially for the latter, the implementation will be specific to the solution, but there are fundamental approaches that remain. In this chapter, we will discuss a few of these fundamental approaches and learn about the following:

- Implementing backtracking algorithms
- Utilizing dynamic programming techniques
- How a pseudo-random number generator works

Pseudo-random numbers

In the last few years, random number generation has seen an interesting rise in popularity, yet many developers simply accept the generator provided by whatever technology they use. However, good random numbers are critical for many applications, such as encryption and security (or the lack thereof; see 2010's Sony PlayStation 3 security incident that prompted a famous XKCD—`https://xkcd.com/221/`), simulation, games, statistics, and biology.

As a basic principle: the more random a sequence is, the better. The reason for this is obvious. If any number in a sequence of random numbers is statistically dependent on one of the others, it becomes a pattern that can be predicted, and there is no such thing as predictable randomness. Thus, the numbers in a random sequence have to be statistically independent to qualify as good random numbers.

To get these random numbers, either a pseudo-random number generator or a true random number generator can be used (or you can buy a book—https://www.rand.org/pubs/monograph_reports/MR1418.html). Since computers are deterministic machines, the latter is impossible without an external influence, which is why there have actually been (unsuccessful) devices to try and achieve truly random numbers. **Pseudo-random number generators** (**PRNGs**), on the other hand, are deterministic, but start off using fairly random input (mouse pointer movements, network traffic, and so on) and periodically produce numbers based on that seed.

PRNGs also enjoy a speed advantage (since there is no physical interaction required, such as measuring atmospheric noise) and the output is often good enough for many applications. In fact, if the seed is very close to random, PRNGs do a great job, as can be seen in modern cryptography.

There are a range of institutions researching PRNGs and their effectiveness at producing cryptographically saved random numbers, for example, Germany's BSI provides an in-depth analysis paper (https://bit.ly/2AOIcB1). This is a fascinating topic with a close relationship to IT security. For non-security researchers, however, there is a simple way to appraise the quality of a random number generator at a glance: visual inspection. When randomly deciding whether to plot each single pixel in a scatter plot, there should not be any visible pattern.

The following graph is of Python's numpy.random random generator, which was created to provide the same number from the same seed:

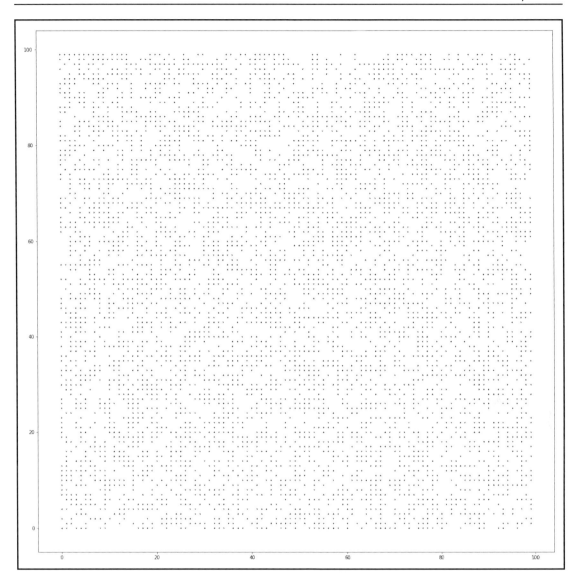

It fares well enough for statistical work and some simulations, but should not be relied upon for cryptographic work.

Regardless of the type of work, a bad random generator should never look like this:

As the pattern indicates, there are systemic errors that can be found in this random generator! Unfortunately, this is not unheard of, even in widely used technologies such as PHP on Windows (`https://boallen.com/random-numbers.html`).

Thanks to the seed, PRNGs can create reproducible as well as close-to-random numbers, which comes in handy for simulations or simply drawing a random sample for data science purposes. One very old and well researched method is the **linear congruential generator**, or **LCG**.

LCG

The LCG is one of the oldest ways of generating a pseudo-random number sequence. It follows a simple, recursive formula:

$$X_n = (a * X_{n-1} + c) \bmod m$$

X denotes the random number (or, more precisely, the nth random number in the sequence). It is based on its predecessor multiplied by a factor, a, and offset by a constant, c. The modulo operator makes sure that there is no overflow. What's the first X? The seed! So a random number sequence will start with the seed, providing determinism if needed.

These parameter settings are subject to significant testing; in fact, many library and compiler developers have different settings. The Wikipedia page provides an overview (https://en.wikipedia.org/wiki/Linear_congruential_generator):

```
pub struct LCG {
    xn: f32,
    m: f32,
    c: f32,
    a: f32,
}

impl LCG {
    fn seeded(seed: u32) -> LCG {
        LCG {
            xn: seed as f32,
            m: 2e31,
            a: 171f32,
            c: 8f32,
        }
    }

    fn new(seed: f32, m: f32, a: f32, c: f32) -> LCG {
        LCG {
            xn: seed,
            m: m,
            a: a,
            c: c,
```

```
        }
    }

    fn next_f32(&mut self) -> f32 {
        self.xn = (self.a * self.xn + self.c) % self.m;
        self.xn / self.m
    }
}
```

This parameter setting, while chosen at random, does not look terrible:

The bitmap that was generated as a bad example previously also used the LCG, but with another random parameter setting:

```
impl LCG {
    fn seeded(seed: u32) -> LCG {
        LCG {
            xn: seed as f32,
            m: 181f32,
            a: 167f32,
            c: 0f32,
        }
    }
    ...
}
```

Since the result is obviously bad, this goes to show how important the parameters are here. Typically, these are not settings you should adjust (or you'd know about them). Similarly, two scientists came up with a particular set of magic numbers that allow for a better random number generator: the Wichmann-Hill PRNG.

Wichmann-Hill

An extended approach to the LCG was taken by Brian Wichmann and David Hill when they invented their random number generator. It is based on the LCG, but uses three of them modified and combined by (magic) prime numbers.

These numbers, when added together, produce a sequence that is 6,953,607,871,644 (or 6.95 * 10^{12}) numbers long, which means that calling the PRNG after this number of calls will make it start over:

```
const S1_MOD: f32 = 30269f32;
const S2_MOD: f32 = 30307f32;
const S3_MOD: f32 = 30323f32;

pub struct WichmannHillRng {
    s1: f32,
    s2: f32,
    s3: f32,
}
```

```
impl WichmannHillRng {
    fn new(s1: f32, s2: f32, s3: f32) -> WichmannHillRng {
        WichmannHillRng {
            s1: s1,
            s2: s2,
            s3: s3,
        }
    }

    pub fn seeded(seed: u32) -> WichmannHillRng {
        let t = seed;
        let s1 = (t % 29999) as f32;
        let s2 = (t % 29347) as f32;
        let s3 = (t % 29097) as f32;
        WichmannHillRng::new(s1, s2, s3)
    }

    pub fn next_f32(&mut self) -> f32 {
        self.s1 = (171f32 * self.s1) % S1_MOD;
        self.s2 = (172f32 * self.s2) % S2_MOD;
        self.s3 = (170f32 * self.s3) % S3_MOD;
        (self.s1 / S1_MOD + self.s2 / S2_MOD + self.s3 / S3_MOD) % 1f32
    }
}
```

The generator does well, as the visual inspection shows. In fact, the Wichmann-Hill generator was used in various technologies and applications in the past, so this is not surprising.

Here is the visual analysis:

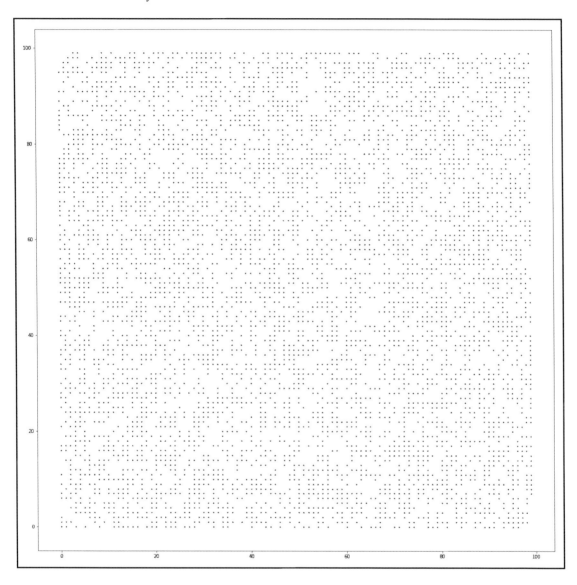

Clearly, implementing every variation of the random generator is not efficient for every project. Luckily, there is an excellent crate on `https://crates.io/` called `rand`.

The rand crate

When talking about random number generators, there is an excellent crate that cannot be skipped: `rand`. Since Rust's standard library does not include a random function, this crate provides that, and more.

In particular, there are several implementations that come with the `rand` crate, ranging from regular PRNGs, to an interface to the OS number generator (`/dev/random` on Unix-like systems), including a compatible interface for other targets, such as web assembly!

The features are impossible to describe in this chapter, so more information on these can be found in their own book (`https://rust-random.github.io/book/`).

Back to front

There are types of problems that humans can solve a lot easier than computers. These are typically somewhat spatial in nature (for example, a traveling salesman, knapsack problem) and rely on patterns, both of which are domains humans are great at. Another name for this class of problems is optimization problems, with solutions that minimize or maximize a particular aspect (for example, a minimum distance or maximum value). A subset of this class is constraint satisfaction problems, where a solution has to conform to a set of rules while minimizing or maximizing another attribute.

The brute force approach that's used to create these solutions is an algorithmic class called backtracking, in which many small choices are recursively added together to form a solution. Fundamentally, this search for the optimal solution can run to find all possible combinations (*exhaustive* search) or stop early. Why recursion? What makes it better suited than regular loops?

A typical constraint satisfaction problem requires incrementally adding items to a set of existing items and then evaluating their quality. A backtracking algorithm is such that it can backtrack once it encounters a bad solution early on so that it can skip at the best possible time. This is much clearer when talking about an example, so here are two famous problems that can be solved with regular backtracking algorithms: the 0-1 knapsack problem, and the N queens problem.

Packing bags or the 0-1 knapsack problem

The knapsack problem is very real: any time you fly with a cheap airline with cabin baggage only, things get complicated. Do I really need *this*? I could just leave my DSLR at home and use my phone for pictures, right?

These are statements that express the potential value of an item and the considerations regarding its weight (or volume on these flights), and we typically want to bring the most valuable (to us) items on a trip. While this smells like an algorithmic problem, it's far from simple. Let's start with the goal:

Given n items (with weights and values), find the subset of items providing the highest value without exceeding the knapsack's capacity, W.

Derived from this, the way to implement the solution can be constructed as follows: as an exhaustive search algorithm, every possible solution can be the best solution. However, this will only become clear once all solutions are evaluated. Thus, let's generate every possible solution first and then worry about the best one.

For any recursive scenario, it's important to worry about the exit condition first: when should the recursion stop and what will it return? In the case of the knapsack problem, the stopping condition is built around the current weight:

- The weight exceeds the capacity
- The current weight is at capacity
- There are no items left

If the capacity is already exceeded, the algorithm returns the data type's minimum value and "backtracks" on this execution branch. However, if the weight is exactly the same as the capacity, or there are no more items left, a neutral value is returned.

What does the return value indicate, then? It's the total value of the items and, since this is a search for maximum value, the return value of the two possibilities are compared:

- Including the item
- Excluding the item

Thus, we'll take the maximum of the return values of a recursive call either with or without the current item, thereby excluding any combination that exceeds the capacity provided:

```
pub trait Backtracking {
    fn fill(&self, items: Vec<&Item>) -> u64;
    fn fill_r(&self, remaining: &[&Item], current_weight: usize) -> i64;
}
```

A note on architecture: since this example is going to be improved using dynamic programming (refer to the following code), a nice way to structure this is to create and implement a trait for either technique:

```
#[derive(Debug, PartialEq)]
pub struct Item {
    pub weight: u32,
    pub value: u32,
}

pub struct Knapsack {
    capacity: usize,
}

impl Knapsack {
    pub fn new(capacity: usize) -> Knapsack {
        Knapsack { capacity: capacity }
    }
}

impl Backtracking for Knapsack {

    fn fill(&self, items: Vec<&Item>) -> u64 {
        let value = self.fill_r(&items, 0);
        if value < 0 {
            0
        } else {
            value as u64
        }
    }

    fn fill_r(&self, remaining: &[&Item], current_weight: usize)
      -> i64 {
        let w = current_weight;

        if w > self.capacity {
            return i64::min_value();
        }
```

```
if remaining.len() > 0 && w < self.capacity {
    let include = remaining[0].value as i64
        + self.fill_r(&remaining[1..], current_weight
        + remaining[0].weight as usize);
    let exclude = self.fill_r(&remaining[1..], current_weight);
    if include >= exclude {
        include
    } else {
        exclude
    }
} else {
    0
}
}

}
```

One question about the runtime complexity of this algorithm remains—and it's not very clear cut this time. Some people suggest that it's $O(2^n)$, but there are two main growth factors: the capacity, as well as the number of available items. In this book, the graphs will focus on the number of items to be added to the bag, which exercises (pseudo) polynomial complexity (greater than $O(n^2)$). Regardless, you should know that this is an expensive problem to solve using backtracking.

Another popular example in universities for backtracking is the 8 queens problem (or, in its general form, the N queens problem).

N queens

The N queens chess problem (the generalized version of the 8 queens problem/puzzle) is defined as follows:

On a chessboard with N by N squares, place N queens so that they cannot attack each other.

As a first step, it's important to understand the ways a queen can move in chess, which is luckily straightforward: they can move in a straight line up, down, left, right, and diagonally, as demonstrated in the following diagram:

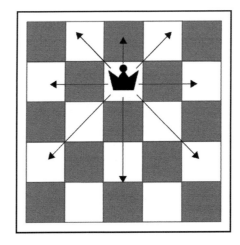

With this known, the rest is very similar to the preceding knapsack problem, but with a few more possibilities caused by various placement options. There are a number of strategies to tackle that:

- Each cell individually, which would result in a large number of recursive calls quickly
- Each row (or column) individually, and iterate over the cells within

The latter is clearly the preferred method, since a 10 by 10 board results in 100 recursive calls for each individual cell (including allocations, for example) and thereby quickly results in a stack overflow. Hence, the second option (by row) is the best trade-off, since each row/column has to have at least one queen placed and it rules out any other queen placements there:

```
pub struct ChessBoard {
    board: Vec<Vec<bool>>,
    n: usize,
}

impl ChessBoard {
    pub fn new(n: usize) -> ChessBoard {
        ChessBoard {
            n: n,
            board: vec![vec![false; n]; n],
        }
```

```
        }

pub fn place_queens(&mut self) -> bool {
    self.place_queens_r(0)
}

pub fn place_queens_r(&mut self, column: usize) -> bool {
    if column < self.n {
        for r in 0..self.n {
            if self.is_valid(r, column) {
                self.board[r][column] = true;
                if self.place_queens_r(column + 1) {
                    return true;
                }

                self.board[r][column] = false;
            }
        }
        false
    }
    else {
        true
    }
}

fn is_valid(&self, row: usize, col: usize) -> bool {
    for i in 0..self.n {
        if self.board[i][col] {
            return false;
        }
        if self.board[row][i] {
            return false;
        }
    }
    let mut i = 0;
    let (mut left_lower, mut left_upper, mut right_lower,
         mut right_upper) =
        (true, true, true, true);

    while left_lower || left_upper || right_lower || right_upper {
        if left_upper && self.board[row - i][col - i] {
            return false;
        }
        if left_lower && self.board[row + i][col - i] {
            return false;
        }
        if right_lower && self.board[row + i][col + i] {
            return false;
```

```
            }
            if right_upper && self.board[row - i][col + i] {
                return false;
            }
            i += 1;
            left_upper = row as i64 - i as i64 >= 0
                        && col as i64 - i as i64 >= 0;
            left_lower = row + i < self.n && col as i64 - i
                        as i64 >= 0;

            right_lower = row + i < self.n && col + i < self.n;
            right_upper = row as i64 - i as i64 >= 0
                        && col + i < self.n;
        }
        true
    }
// ...
}
```

The strategy is simple: for each cell in a row, check whether a valid queen can be placed under the current conditions. Then, descend deeper into the recursion and end it as soon as a valid setting has been found. The result looks as follows (*n* = 4):

However, the computational complexity of this algorithm grows exponentially ($O(2^n)$), which means that for large *n*, it will not finish in any reasonable amount of time:

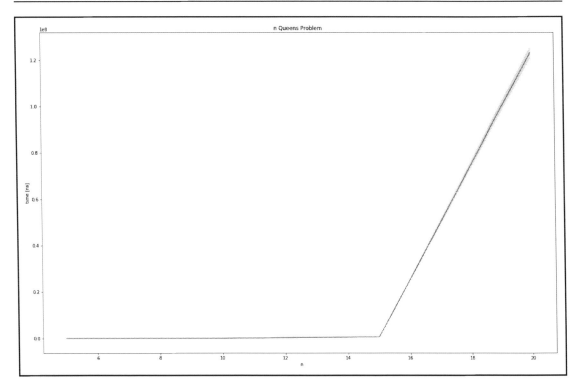

The output graph for N queens problems

While this particular problem is probably more like a teaching problem, this approach can certainly be applied to other (similar) use cases, especially in the spatial domain.

Advanced problem solving

Backtracking calculates and finds the best overall solution to a particular problem. However, as described in `Chapter 18`, *Algorithm Evaluation*, there are problems that have a really large computational complexity, which leads to a really long running time. Since this is unlikely to be solved by simply making computers faster, smarter approaches are required.

With several strategies and techniques available, the choice is yours to find an approach that best solves your problem. The position of Rust in this space can be critical, thanks to its great speed and memory efficiency, so keeping an eye on solutions for complex problems might pay off in the future (in the author's opinion).

First up is a surprising programming technique that is aimed at improving the complexities of backtracking algorithms: dynamic programming.

Dynamic programming

The concept of dynamic programming is one of these techniques that you thought had a different name: caching. The fundamental idea is to save relevant temporary results to a cache and use this precomputed result instead of recalculating something over and over again!

This means that a problem and a potential solution have to be examined to find relevant sub-problems, so any result can be cached. The main upside of this approach is that it finds the globally best solution possible, but at the price of a potentially high runtime complexity.

The knapsack problem improved

As an example, let's examine the recursive calls of the knapsack solver. For brevity, this knapsack is to be filled using a list of three items where the weight is uniformly one and has a capacity of two. Since the backtracking algorithm walks through the list of items in order (and tries either to include or exclude a particular item), the knapsack solver can be seen as a function K that maps any items that are remaining as well as capacity remaining to a particular value:

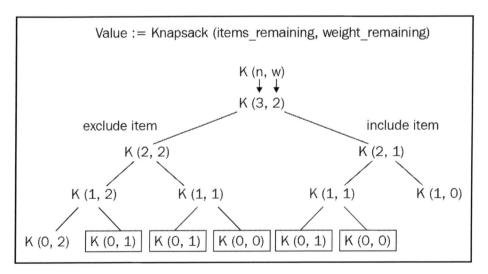

Therefore, at the same level, the same input parameter leads to the same value and this is easy to cache. In the preceding diagram, the nodes marked by the rectangle are calculated at least twice. This example was taken from the GeeksforGeeks' article (https://www. geeksforgeeks.org/0-1-knapsack-problem-dp-10/) regarding the 0-1 knapsack problem.

Before anything else, we can now implement a different trait to the backtracking:

```
pub trait DynamicProgramming {
    fn fill(&self, items: Vec<&Item>) -> u64;
}
```

Implementation then follows and, as a function with two input parameters, each combination of input parameters can be saved in a two-dimensional array, which reduces the runtime complexity to walking this matrix, leading to a *O(n * W)* runtime complexity:

```
impl DynamicProgramming for Knapsack {
    fn fill(&self, items: Vec<&Item>) -> u64 {
        let mut cache = vec![vec![0u64; self.capacity + 1];
                        items.len() + 1];
        for i in 1..items.len() + 1 {
            for w in 1..self.capacity + 1 {
                if items[i -1].weight as usize <= w {
                    let prev_weight =
                        w - (items[i - 1].weight as usize);
                    cache[i][w] = max(
                        items[i - 1].value as u64
                        + cache[i - 1][prev_weight],
                        cache[i - 1][w],
                    );
                } else {
                    cache[i][w] = cache[i - 1][w]
                }
            }
        }
        cache[items.len()][self.capacity]
    }
}
```

The code went from a recursive call chain to constructing a matrix where the maximum value for a particular combination is just a lookup, which seriously improves the absolute and relative runtime (20 items take 41,902 +/- 10,014 ns when using backtracking and 607 +/- 138 ns for dynamic programming):

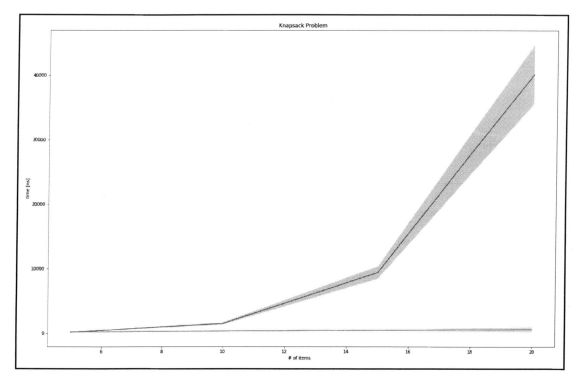

The output graph for Knapsack problems

In relative terms, the runtime complexity improved significantly:

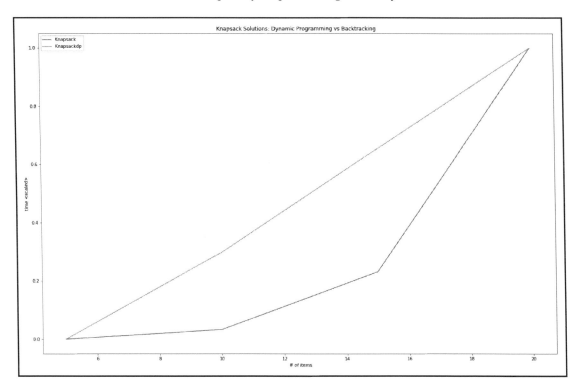

The runtime complexity graph comparison between dynamic programming and backtracking

Employing this strategy (or similar) to problems that allow for that kind of optimization permits far higher input parameters and therefore enable it to solve real-world problems! Imagine an airline trying to work out the most valuable cargo it can bring, but it's limited to 40 different items at once.

Since there are many harder problems (for example, a problem class called NP-hard problems), people came up with ways to find good solutions as well.

Metaheuristic approaches

Dynamic programming is great for constraint satisfaction problems. However, better solutions can be found using something akin to systematic guessing, or metaheuristics. These problem-agnostic solution generators can be classified in several ways, for instance, whether they are population-based, inspired by nature, and searching globally or locally.

Whichever optimization algorithm is chosen, it will treat the problem like a search problem, trying to find the best possible solution within the solutions provided. Absent of any guarantees to find the best solution possible, it will typically find a good enough solution. Thanks to the expensive runtimes of NP-hard problems, a wide variety of ways can lead to a better solution than a more specific solution.

Popular metaheuristics include the following:

- Simulated annealing
- Genetic algorithms
- Particle swarm optimization
- Ant colony optimization
- Tabu search

Rust's ecosystem features several crates that implement these metaheuristic strategies. The progress of some of these crates can be tracked on `http://www.arewelearningyet.com/metaheuristics/`.

Example metaheuristic – genetic algorithms

Examples include the traveling salesman problem, where a tour of the shortest path connecting *n* cities has to be found. With a *O(n!)* runtime complexity, only 20 cities prove to be computationally very expensive, but it can be solved well enough for a very large *n* by starting off with a random order of cities (tour), and then repeatedly recombining or randomly changing (mutating) several of these tours only to select the best ones and restarting the process with these.

Using the `rsgenetic` crate (`https://crates.io/crates/rsgenetic`), implementing the solution becomes a matter of implementing the `TspTour` trait, which requires a `fitness()` function to be supplied so that a solution can be evaluated, the `crossover()` function to recombine two parents into a new offspring tour, and the `mutate()` function to apply random changes to a tour:

```
impl Phenotype<TourFitness> for TspTour {
    ///
    /// The Euclidean distance of an entire tour.
    ///
    fn fitness(&self) -> TourFitness {
        let tour_cities: Vec<&City> = self.tour.iter().map(|t|
                                    &self.cities[*t]).collect();
        let mut fitness = 0f32;
        for i in 1..tour_cities.len() {
```

```
                fitness += distance(tour_cities[i], tour_cities[i - 1]);
        }
        -(fitness.round() as i32)
    }


    ///
    /// Implements the crossover for a TSP tour using PMX
    ///
    fn crossover(&self, other: &TspTour) -> TspTour {
        // ...

        TspTour {
            tour: offspring,
            cities: self.cities.clone(),
            rng_cell: self.rng_cell.clone(),
        }
    }


    ///
    /// Mutates the solution by swapping neighbors at a chance
    ///
    fn mutate(&self) -> TspTour {
        let mut rng = self.rng_cell.borrow_mut();
        if rng.gen::<f32>() < MUTPROB {
            let mut mutated: Tour = self.tour.clone();
            for i in 0..mutated.len() {
                if rng.gen::<f32>() < INDPB {
                    let mut swap_idx = rng.gen_range(0,
                                        mutated.len() - 2);
                    if swap_idx >= i {
                        swap_idx += 1;
                    }
                    let tmp = mutated[i];
                    mutated[i] = mutated[swap_idx];
                    mutated[swap_idx] = tmp;
                }
            }
            TspTour {
                tour: mutated,
                cities: self.cities.clone(),
                rng_cell: self.rng_cell.clone(),
            }
        } else {
            self.clone()
        }
    }
}
```

Once these are implemented, the framework allows you to set a selector to select the best *n* solutions in each generation to create the next generation's population. These steps are repeated until the fitness values stagnate (converge) and the highest fitness in the last generation can be considered a good solution for the problem.

Over several generations, a solution like this one can be found:

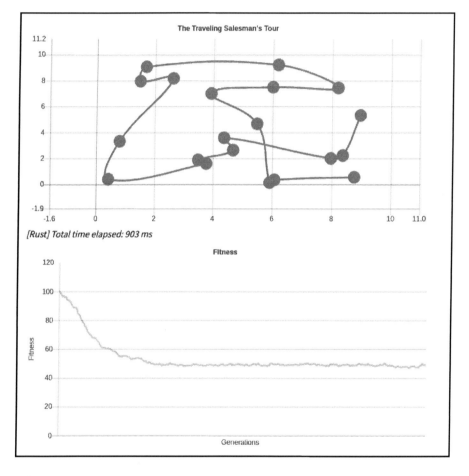

A more in-depth look at solving this problem in JavaScript, as well as in Rust (and Wasm), can be found on my blog at `https://blog.x5ff.xyz`. A similar approach can be taken to arrange a highly valuable combination of items in a knapsack, which is left for you to find out.

Summary

Other than regular data structures and sorting, as well as searching methods, there are several other problems that arise. This chapter talks about a small subset of those: generating random numbers and solving constraint satisfaction problems.

Random number generation is useful in lots of ways: encryption, gaming, gambling, simulations, data science—all require good random numbers. Good? There are two important types: pseudo-random numbers and "real" random numbers. While the latter has to be taken from the physical world (computers are deterministic), the former can be implemented with the LCG or the Wichmann-Hill generator (which combines LCGs using magic numbers).

Constraint satisfaction problems are problems that find the best combination that conform to a set of constraints. A technique called backtracking builds a state of the current permutation by using recursion to generate all combinations, but tracking back on those that do not satisfy the required constraints. Both the 8 queens (or N queens) problem and the 0-1 knapsack problem are examples of backtracking algorithms that exhibit expensive runtime behavior.

Advanced techniques such as dynamic programming or metaheuristics (that return good enough solutions) can lead to a significant improvement in solving these challenges quicker (or for larger sizes). Rust, as a fast and efficient language, can play a significant role in these techniques in the future.

In the next chapter, we will look into algorithms that the Rust standard library provides.

Further reading

Here is some additional reference material that you may refer to regarding what has been covered in this chapter:

- https://en.wikipedia.org/wiki/Random_number_generator_attack
- https://blog.x5ff.xyz
- https://en.wikipedia.org/wiki/Metaheuristic

22
Algorithms of the Standard Library

Rust's standard library provides a few fundamental data types that cover the basic needs of many projects and, typically, there is no need to implement your own algorithms if the appropriate data structure is available. If, for some reason, the data type is not perfectly suited to the task, the standard library has you covered as well. In this quick round-up, you can look forward to learning about the following:

- The `slice` primitive type
- The `Iterator` trait
- `binary_search()`
- `sort()`, stable, and unstable

Slicing and iteration

Similar to how interfaces standardize access to functionality in the libraries of other languages, Rust's standard library utilizes a type and a trait to provide fundamental implementations. The trait, `Iterator<T>`, has been looked at and used over the course of this book several times. The slice type, however, was not explicitly used a lot, especially since the Rust compiler automatically uses slices when `Vec<T>` is borrowed for a function call. How can you leverage this type, though? We have seen the `Iterator<T>` implementation in action, but does it provide more than that?

Iterator

To recap: an iterator is a pattern to traverse a collection, providing a pointer to each element in the process. This pattern is mentioned in the book *Design Patterns,* by Erich Gamma, Richard Helm, Ralph Johnson, and John Vlissides (the Gang of Four), in 1994 and can be found in basically every language one way or another.

In Rust, the term pointer to each element gets a new dimension: is it a borrowed or owned item? Can this be mutably borrowed as well?

Using the standard library's `Iterator<T>` trait makes a lot of sense, since it provides a serious amount of useful functions, which are all based around a single implementation of `next()`.

`next()` returns an `Option<Self::Item>`, which is the associated type that has to be declared when implementing the trait—and it can be anything you like!

Therefore, using `&MyType`, `&mut MyType`, and `MyType` can all be implemented separately to achieve the desired functionality. `IntoIter<T>` is a trait that is specifically designed to facilitate this workflow and to integrate it neatly with the `for` loop syntax. The following code is from the Rust standard library's source code:

```
impl<T> IntoIterator for Vec<T> {
    type Item = T;
    type IntoIter = IntoIter<T>;

    /// Creates a consuming iterator, that is,
    /// one that moves each value out of
    /// the vector (from start to end).
    /// The vector cannot be used after calling
    /// this.
    ///
    /// # Examples
    ///
    /// ```
    /// let v = vec!["a".to_string(), "b".to_string()];
    /// for s in v.into_iter() {
    /// // s has type String, not &String
    /// println!("{}", s);
    /// }
    /// ```
    #[inline]
    fn into_iter(mut self) -> IntoIter<T> {
        unsafe {
            let begin = self.as_mut_ptr();
            assume(!begin.is_null());
```

```
                let end = if mem::size_of::<T>() == 0 {
                    arith_offset(begin as *const i8, self.len()
                                    as isize) as *const T
                } else {
                    begin.add(self.len()) as *const T
                };
                let cap = self.buf.cap();
                mem::forget(self);
                IntoIter {
                    buf: NonNull::new_unchecked(begin),
                    phantom: PhantomData,
                    cap,
                    ptr: begin,
                    end,
                }
            }
        }
    }
```

Rust's Vec<T> implements precisely this pattern, but with a nice twist. The preceding code consumes the original data structure, potentially transforming the original into something that's easier to iterate, in the same way as trees can be expanded into a sorted Vec<T> or a stack. To return to the original theme, the Iterator<T> provides functions (implemented in further structures) that add many possible ways to search and filter through a collection.

Any Rust user will be aware of the iter() function of Vec<T>, however, which is actually provided by the slice type that Vec is implicitly converted into?

Slices

Slices are views into sequences to provide a more unified interface for accessing, iterating, or otherwise interacting with these memory areas. Consequently, they are available through Vec<T>, especially since they implement the Deref trait to implicitly treat Vec<T> as a [T]—a slice of T.

The Vec<T> implementation also hints at that for the IntoIterator implementation for immutable and mutable references:

```
    impl<'a, T> IntoIterator for &'a Vec<T> {
        type Item = &'a T;
        type IntoIter = slice::Iter<'a, T>;

        fn into_iter(self) -> slice::Iter<'a, T> {
            self.iter()
```

```
        }
    }

    impl<'a, T> IntoIterator for &'a mut Vec<T> {
        type Item = &'a mut T;
        type IntoIter = slice::IterMut<'a, T>;

        fn into_iter(self) -> slice::IterMut<'a, T> {
            self.iter_mut()
        }
    }
```

The slice itself is only a view, represented by a pointer to the memory part and its length. Since the compiler knows the nature of the data contained within, it can also figure out individual elements to provide type safety.

A more detailed explanation of slices and the way they work would warrant its own book, so it is recommended at least reading the documentation (or the source code) of the `slice` module (`https://doc.rust-lang.org/std/slice/index.html`).

Search

Finding things in a collection has been discussed throughout this book, and the Rust standard library provides a few ways by default. These functions are attached to the `Iterator<T>` trait or slice types and work regardless of the actual type, provided that a function to compare two elements is furnished.

This can either be the `Ord` trait or a custom comparator function, such as the `position()` function on the `Iterator<T>`.

Linear search

The classic linear search is provided via `position()` (or `rposition()`) on the `Iterator<T>` trait, and it even utilizes other iterator functions that are implemented on the trait itself:

```
fn position<P>(&mut self, mut predicate: P) -> Option<usize> where
    Self: Sized,
    P: FnMut(Self::Item) -> bool,
{
    // The addition might panic on overflow
    self.try_fold(0, move |i, x| {
```

```
        if predicate(x) { LoopState::Break(i) }
        else { LoopState::Continue(i + 1) }
    }).break_value()
}
```

`try_fold()` is a short-circuit variation on the `fold()` (or `reduce()`, following the map/reduce pattern) function that returns whenever `LoopState::Break` is returned. The call to `break_value()` transforms the result from the value returned in the `LoopState::Break` enumeration into `Option` and `None` if it ran through the entire collection.

This is the brute-force approach to searching and can be useful if the collection is unsorted and short. For anything longer, sorting and using the binary search function might pay off.

Binary search

A generic fast search function is provided through slices as well, called `binary_search()`. As discussed in `Chapter 20`, *Finding Stuff*, a binary search returns the index of an element after closing in on its position by repeatedly choosing a half.

To achieve that, there are two prerequisites that the input slice has to satisfy:

- It's sorted
- The element type implements the `Ord` trait

`binary_search()` cannot check whether the collection that's provided is sorted, which means that if an unordered collection returns the expected result, it can only be coincidental. Additionally, if there are multiple elements with the same value, any of those can be the result.

Other than using the implicitly provided comparison function (by implementing `Ord`), `binary_search()` also has a more flexible sibling—`binary_search_by()`, which requires a comparison function to be supplied.

Under the hood, this function is comparable to the naive implementation we created in `Chapter 20`, *Finding Stuff*; on occasion, it was even faster by a nanosecond or two. The code is just as simple, however:

```
pub fn binary_search_by<'a, F>(&'a self, mut f: F) -> Result<usize, usize>
    where F: FnMut(&'a T) -> Ordering
{
    let s = self;
    let mut size = s.len();
```

```
        if size == 0 {
            return Err(0);
        }
        let mut base = 0usize;
        while size > 1 {
            let half = size / 2;
            let mid = base + half;
            // mid is always in [0, size),
            // that means mid is >= 0 and < size.
            // mid >= 0: by definition
            // mid < size: mid = size / 2 + size / 4 + size / 8 ...
            let cmp = f(unsafe { s.get_unchecked(mid) });
            base = if cmp == Greater { base } else { mid };
            size -= half;
        }
        // base is always in [0, size) because base <= mid.
        let cmp = f(unsafe { s.get_unchecked(base) });
        if cmp == Equal { Ok(base) } else {
                Err(base + (cmp == Less) as usize) }
    }
```

Other variants of the function include searching by key or by the comparator function of the Ord trait (as mentioned previously). One major caveat can be the requirement to provide a sorted collection to the binary search function, but luckily, Rust provides sorting in its standard library.

Sorting

Sorting is an important feature in user interfaces, but also provides the predictability that's necessary for many algorithms. Whenever there is no way to use an appropriate data structure (such as a tree), a generic sorting algorithm can take care of creating that order. One important question arises regarding equal values: will they end up at the same exact spot every time? When using a stable sorting algorithm, the answer is *yes*.

Stable sorting

The key to stable sorting is not reordering equal elements, so in [1, 1, 2, 3, 4, 5], 1s never change their positions relative to each other. In Rust, this is actually used when sort() is called on Vec<T>.

The current (2018 edition) implementation of `Vec<T>` uses a merge sort variation based on Timsort. Here is the source code:

```
pub fn sort(&mut self)
    where T: Ord
{
    merge_sort(self, |a, b| a.lt(b));
}
```

The code is quite verbose, but can be split into smaller parts. The first step is to sort smaller (20 elements or less) slices by deleting and reinserting the elements in order (in other words, insertion sort):

```
fn merge_sort<T, F>(v: &mut [T], mut is_less: F)
    where F: FnMut(&T, &T) -> bool
{
    // Slices of up to this length get sorted using insertion sort.
    const MAX_INSERTION: usize = 20;
    // Very short runs are extended using insertion sort
    // to span at least this many elements.
    const MIN_RUN: usize = 10;

    // Sorting has no meaningful behavior on zero-sized types.
    if size_of::<T>() == 0 {
        return;
    }

    let len = v.len();

    // Short arrays get sorted in-place via insertion
    // sort to avoid allocations.
    if len <= MAX_INSERTION {
        if len >= 2 {
            for i in (0..len-1).rev() {
                insert_head(&mut v[i..], &mut is_less);
            }
        }
        return;
    }
```

If the collection is longer, the algorithm resorts to traversing the items back to front, identifying natural runs. The constant MIN_RUN (10 in the preceding code) defines a minimum length of such a run, so a shorter run (such as 5, 9, 10, 11, 13, 19, 31, 55, 56 in [5, 9, 10, 11, 13, 19, 31, 55, 56, 1, ...]) is expanded by doing an insertion sort on the 1 to get to 10 elements. The metadata of the resulting block (for [1, 5, 9, 10, 11, 13, 19, 31, 55, 56], it would start at 0, with a length of 10) is then pushed onto a stack for subsequent merging (note: we recommend reading the comments from the code authors):

```
// Allocate a buffer to use as scratch memory.
// We keep the length 0 so we can keep in it
// shallow copies of the contents of `v` without risking the dtors
// running on copies if `is_less` panics.
// When merging two sorted runs, this buffer holds a copy of the
// shorter run, which will always have length at most `len / 2`.
let mut buf = Vec::with_capacity(len / 2);

// In order to identify natural runs in `v`, we traverse it
// backwards. That might seem like a strange decision, but consider
// the fact that merges more often go in the opposite direction
// (forwards). According to benchmarks, merging forwards is
// slightly faster than merging backwards. To conclude, identifying
// runs by traversing backwards improves performance.
let mut runs = vec![];
let mut end = len;
while end > 0 {
    // Find the next natural run,
    // and reverse it if it's strictly descending.
    let mut start = end - 1;
    if start > 0 {
        start -= 1;
        unsafe {
            if is_less(v.get_unchecked(start + 1),
                    v.get_unchecked(start)) {
                while start > 0 && is_less(v.get_unchecked(start),
                        v.get_unchecked(start - 1)) {
                    start -= 1;
                }
                v[start..end].reverse();
            } else {
                while start > 0 && !is_less(v.get_unchecked(start),
                        v.get_unchecked(start - 1)) {
                    start -= 1;
                }
            }
        }
    }
```

```
// Insert some more elements into the run if it's too short.
// Insertion sort is faster than
// merge sort on short sequences,
// so this significantly improves performance.
while start > 0 && end - start < MIN_RUN {
    start -= 1;
    insert_head(&mut v[start..end], &mut is_less);
}

// Push this run onto the stack.
runs.push(Run {
    start,
    len: end - start,
});
end = start;
```

To conclude the iteration, some pairs on the stack are already merged, collapsing them in an insertion sort:

```
while let Some(r) = collapse(&runs) {
    let left = runs[r + 1];
    let right = runs[r];
    unsafe {
        merge(&mut v[left.start .. right.start + right.len],
            left.len, buf.as_mut_ptr(), &mut is_less);
    }
    runs[r] = Run {
        start: left.start,
        len: left.len + right.len,
    };
    runs.remove(r + 1);
}
}
```

This `collapse` loop ensures that there is only a single item left on the stack, which is the sorted sequence. Finding out which runs to collapse is the essential part of Timsort, since merging is simply done using insertion sort. The collapse function checks for two essential conditions:

- The lengths of the runs are in descending order (the top of the stack holds the longest run)
- The length of each generated run is greater than the sum of the next two runs

With this in mind, let's look at the collapse function:

```
// [...]
fn collapse(runs: &[Run]) -> Option<usize> {
    let n = runs.len();
    if n >= 2 && (runs[n - 1].start == 0 ||
                  runs[n - 2].len <= runs[n - 1].len ||
                  (n >= 3 && runs[n - 3].len <=
                   runs[n - 2].len + runs[n - 1].len) ||
                  (n >= 4 && runs[n - 4].len <=
                   runs[n - 3].len + runs[n - 2].len)) {
        if n >= 3 && runs[n - 3].len < runs[n - 1].len {
            Some(n - 3)
        } else {
            Some(n - 2)
        }
    } else {
        None
    }
}
// [...]
```

It returns the index of the run that is to be merged with its successor (r and r + 1; refer to the collapse loop for more information). The collapse function checks the top four runs to satisfy the aforementioned conditions if the topmost run (at the highest index) does not start at the beginning. If it does, the end is almost reached and a merge is necessary, regardless of any conditions that are violated, thereby ensuring the final sequence to be merged last.

Timsort's combination of insertion sort and merge sort make it a really fast and efficient sorting algorithm that is also stable and operates on "blocks" by building these naturally occurring runs. Unstable sorting, on the other hand, uses a familiar Quicksort.

Unstable sorting

Unstable sorting does not retain the relative position of equal values, and can therefore achieve better speeds thanks to the lack of additionally allocated memory that stable sorting requires. The slice's sort_unstable() function uses a Quicksort variation that is called a pattern-defeating Quicksort by Orson Peters, combining heap sort and Quicksort to achieve an excellent performance in most cases.

The slice implementation simply refers to it as Quicksort:

```
pub fn sort_unstable_by<F>(&mut self, mut compare: F)
    where F: FnMut(&T, &T) -> Ordering
{
    sort::quicksort(self, |a, b| compare(a, b) == Ordering::Less);
}
```

Looking at the Quicksort implementation, it spans the entire module—about 700 lines of code. Therefore, let's look at the highest level function to understand the basics; curious readers should dive into the source code (https://doc.rust-lang.org/src/core/slice/sort.rs.html) to find out more.

The Quicksort function performs a few preliminary checks to rule out invalid cases:

```
/// Sorts `v` using pattern-defeating quicksort, which is `O(n log n)`
worst-case.
pub fn quicksort<T, F>(v: &mut [T], mut is_less: F)
    where F: FnMut(&T, &T) -> bool
{
    // Sorting has no meaningful behavior on zero-sized types.
    if mem::size_of::<T>() == 0 {
        return;
    }
    // Limit the number of imbalanced
    // partitions to `floor(log2(len)) + 1`.
    let limit = mem::size_of::<usize>() * 8 - v.len()
                .leading_zeros() as usize;

    recurse(v, &mut is_less, None, limit);
}
```

The `recurse` function is at the heart of this implementation and is even a recursive function:

```
/// Sorts `v` recursively.
///
/// If the slice had a predecessor in the original array,
/// it is specified as `pred`.
///
/// `limit` is the number of allowed imbalanced partitions
///  before switching to `heapsort`. If zero,
/// this function will immediately switch to heapsort.
fn recurse<'a, T, F>(mut v: &'a mut [T], is_less: &mut F, mut pred:
Option<&'a T>, mut limit: usize)
    where F: FnMut(&T, &T) -> bool
{
```

```
// Slices of up to this length get sorted using insertion sort.
const MAX_INSERTION: usize = 20;

// True if the last partitioning was reasonably balanced.
let mut was_balanced = true;
// True if the last partitioning didn't shuffle elements
// (the slice was already partitioned).
let mut was_partitioned = true;

loop {
    let len = v.len();
    // Very short slices get sorted using insertion sort.
    if len <= MAX_INSERTION {
        insertion_sort(v, is_less);
        return;
    }
    // If too many bad pivot choices were made,
    // simply fall back to heapsort in order to
    // guarantee `O(n log n)` worst-case.
    if limit == 0 {
        heapsort(v, is_less);
        return;
    }
    // If the last partitioning was imbalanced,
    // try breaking patterns in the slice by shuffling
    // some elements around.
    // Hopefully we'll choose a better pivot this time.
    if !was_balanced {
        break_patterns(v);
        limit -= 1;
    }
    // Choose a pivot and try guessing
    // whether the slice is already sorted.
    let (pivot, likely_sorted) = choose_pivot(v, is_less);

    // If the last partitioning was decently balanced
    // and didn't shuffle elements, and if pivot
    // selection predicts the slice is likely already sorted...
    if was_balanced && was_partitioned && likely_sorted {
        // Try identifying several out-of-order elements
        // and shifting them to correct
        // positions. If the slice ends up being completely sorted,
        // we're done.
        if partial_insertion_sort(v, is_less) {
            return;
        }
    }
    // If the chosen pivot is equal to the predecessor,
```

```
    // then it's the smallest element in the
    // slice. Partition the slice into elements equal to and
    // elements greater than the pivot.
    // This case is usually hit when the slice contains many
    // duplicate elements.
    if let Some(p) = pred {
        if !is_less(p, &v[pivot]) {
            let mid = partition_equal(v, pivot, is_less);

            // Continue sorting elements greater than the pivot.
            v = &mut {v}[mid..];
            continue;
        }
    }
    // Partition the slice.
    let (mid, was_p) = partition(v, pivot, is_less);
    was_balanced = cmp::min(mid, len - mid) >= len / 8;
    was_partitioned = was_p;

    // Split the slice into `left`, `pivot`, and `right`.
    let (left, right) = {v}.split_at_mut(mid);
    let (pivot, right) = right.split_at_mut(1);
    let pivot = &pivot[0];

    // Recurse into the shorter side only in order to
    // minimize the total number of recursive
    // calls and consume less stack space.
    // Then just continue with the longer side (this is
    // akin to tail recursion).
    if left.len() < right.len() {
        recurse(left, is_less, pred, limit);
        v = right;
        pred = Some(pivot);
    } else {
        recurse(right, is_less, Some(pivot), limit);
        v = left;
    }
    }
}
}
```

Thankfully, the standard library's source has many helpful comments. Therefore, it's highly recommended to read through all the comments in the preceding snippet. In short, the algorithms make a lot of guesses to avoid making a bad choice for the pivot. If you recall, when Quicksort chooses a bad pivot element, it will split into uneven partitions, thereby creating very bad runtime behavior. Therefore, choosing a good pivot is critical, which is why so many heuristics around that process are employed and, if all else fails, the algorithm runs heap sort to at least have *O(n log n)* runtime complexity.

Summary

Rust's standard library includes several implementations for basic things such as sorting or searching on its primitive slice type and the Iterator<T> trait. The slice type in particular has many highly important functions to offer.

binary_search() is a generic implementation of the binary search concepts provided on the slice type. Vec<T> can be quickly and easily (and implicitly) converted into a slice, making this a universally available function. However, it requires a sorting order to be present in the slice to work (and it won't fail if it's not) and, if custom types are used, an implementation of the Ord trait.

In case the slice cannot be sorted beforehand, the Iterator<T> variable's implementation of position() (of find()) provides a basic linear search that returns the first position of the element.

Sorting is provided in a generic function, but comes in two flavors: stable and unstable. The regular sort() function uses a merge sort variation called Timsort to achieve an efficient and stable sorting performance.

sort_unstable() utilizes a pattern-defeating Quicksort to combine the efficiency of heap sort and Quicksort in a smart way, which typically leads to a better absolute runtime than sort().

This was the final chapter of this book. Keep exploring Rust!

Further reading

Here is some additional reference material that you may refer to regarding what has been covered in this chapter:

- *Design Patterns*, by Erich Gamma, Richard Helm, Ralph Johnson, and John Vlissides
- Iterator pattern on Wikipedia (`https://en.wikipedia.org/wiki/Iterator_pattern`)
- *OpenJDK's java.utils.Collection.sort() is broken: The good, the bad and the worst case*, by de Gow et al. (`http://envisage-project.eu/wp-content/uploads/2015/02/sorting.pdf`)
- Pattern-defeating Quicksort (`http://envisage-project.eu/wp-content/uploads/2015/02/sorting.pdf`)

Other Books You May Enjoy

If you enjoyed this book, you may be interested in these other books by Packt:

Hands-On Concurrency with Rust
Brian L. Troutwine

ISBN: 9781788399975

- Probe your programs for performance and accuracy issues
- Create your own threading and multi-processing environment in Rust
- Use coarse locks from Rust's Standard library
- Solve common synchronization problems or avoid synchronization using atomic programming
- Build lock-free/wait-free structures in Rust and understand their implementations in the crates ecosystem
- Leverage Rust's memory model and type system to build safety properties into your parallel programs
- Understand the new features of the Rust programming language to ease the writing of parallel programs

If you enjoyed this book, you may be interested in these other books by Packt:

Hands-On Functional Programming in RUST

Andrew Johnson

ISBN: 9781788839358

- How Rust supports the use of basic Functional Programming principles
- Use Functional Programming to handle concurrency with elegance
- Read and interpret complex type signatures for types and functions
- Implement powerful abstractions using meta programming in Rust
- Create quality code formulaically using Rust's functional design patterns
- Master Rust's complex ownership mechanisms particularly for mutability

Leave a review - let other readers know what you think

Please share your thoughts on this book with others by leaving a review on the site that you bought it from. If you purchased the book from Amazon, please leave us an honest review on this book's Amazon page. This is vital so that other potential readers can see and use your unbiased opinion to make purchasing decisions, we can understand what our customers think about our products, and our authors can see your feedback on the title that they have worked with Packt to create. It will only take a few minutes of your time, but is valuable to other potential customers, our authors, and Packt. Thank you!

Index

C

M

Made in the USA
Coppell, TX
18 November 2020